A DIPLOMATIC HISTORY OF
MODERN INDIA

A DIPLOMATIC HISTORY
OF MODERN INDIA

Charles H. Heimsath
Surjit Mansingh

ALLIED PUBLISHERS

BOMBAY   CALCUTTA   NEW DELHI
MADRAS   BANGALORE

First Published 1971

ALLIED PUBLISHERS PRIVATE LIMITED
15, Graham Road, Ballard Estate, Bombay 1
17, Chittaranjan Avenue, Calcutta 13
13/14, Asaf Ali Road, New Delhi 1
38-C, Mount Road, Madras 6
39/1, J. C. Road, Bangalore 2

© CHARLES H. HEIMSATH
SURJIT MANSINGH

PRINTED IN INDIA
BY DEBDAS NATH AT SADHANA PRESS PRIVATE LTD, 76 B. B. GANGULY
STREET, CALCUTTA 12 AND PUBLISHED BY R. N. SACHDEV FOR ALLIED
PUBLISHERS PRIVATE LTD, 17 CHITTARANJAN AVENUE, CALCUTTA 13

TO OUR PARENTS

PREFACE

India has the natural prerequisites of a great power. Although two decades after independence it has not achieved that status, its participation in global politics has sometimes been more in keeping with the potentialities of its size and geographic position than with the actualities of its economic underdevelopment and lack of internal cohesion. New Delhi's external moves for many years have attracted the attention of extra-regional and of neighbouring states, testifying to India's established place in contemporary international politics.

This historically novel phenomenon began while India was still a part of a global empire : British rule had terminated the interplay among states within the subcontinent and established an important position for the country as a whole in world affairs. India's dealings as a state with other parts of the British empire and with foreign countries were not altogether changed with the dissolution of the empire ; similarly, India's involvement with international organizations straddled the year of independence. One of our aims in this book is to show the threads of continuity which have run through Indian foreign relations since the First World War—threads often overlooked when considering India only in the post-independence era.

India's international dealings until 1947 were, properly speaking, British Indian foreign relations. The expansion of British India's influence over all of south Asia and beyond was initiated and engineered by the British, India being the major base for their political and military operations in Asia. India after independence, led by those who challenged the concept of imperialism, had more limited ambitions ; peace was preferred to a forced presence, free association to control. Yet the imperatives of national security had altered little from the British period. They sometimes created policy dilemmas for the new India, of whether to follow the precedents created under the British or the pronouncements of the Congress when it was in opposition to the government. The choices made did not fall uniformly on the side of consistency with the nationalist ideology or of the calculated requirements of national interest.

One of the striking developments of this century has been the change in India's attitude towards the world. From an inward-looking country, preoccupied with its own affairs, it tasted first the British version of Western culture and then became an increasingly committed participant in international life—cultural, intellectual, and economic. This unprecedented process was guided in the post-independence period by the ideas and policies of the most internationally conscious of all India's leaders, Jawaharlal Nehru.

Nehru also presided over the entrance of India onto the arena of world politics. Almost until his death Nehru's dominance in the formulation of his country's foreign policies prevailed without serious compromise or challenge. India in world perspective, even now, is largely the India moulded and projected by Nehru. This has been described and documented by many writers, and we have not presumed to examine the question further. The India of Nehru assumed an international posture that to Indians seemed comfortable and to foreigners appeared characteristic of Indian (at least Hindu) culture : nonalignment, etymologically negative as are many of the principal Indian concepts, an equilibrium position between two world-wide competing systems. Indian nonalignment as a concept and a posture is perhaps the most important theme appearing in this book.

In this first full-scale history of Indian foreign relations we have directed our angle of vision towards India as a state among other states. This is the classical approach to writing diplomatic history. It neglects the study of decision-making within the domestic body politic in order to produce a prominent silhouette of the state (as opposed to its different governments) in the world environment. Studies of policy-making necessarily portray foreign relations as a facet of internal politics and stress the latter. We have referred only to those internal developments which seemed to affect foreign relations decisively.

Our approach to the subject is reflected in the published sources on which this book is based. They are largely the official documents of the Indian government, fortunately a profuse body of material. Newspaper articles and similarly indirect and often misleading evidences of the affairs of state occupy virtually no place in the book, except in the occasional case where a document or direct quotation could be found in a newspaper and in no other convenient place. Documentation published by any government is apt to show

bias in the selecting and editing of material for public view; therefore, as often as possible we have examined the documents published
by other governments, notably by the Peoples' Republic of China,
Pakistan, and Portugal, before presenting our own conclusions on
controversial issues. We have benefited greatly from many inter-
pretative writings on Indian foreign relations and in a few places
depended heavily on the research done by others. Appropriate
acknowledgements are given in the Notes, and in the Bibliographies
pertaining to each chapter located at the end of the book we have
cited the books found most useful for the topics concerned.

We could provide a lengthy justification for the way in which
the book is organized, arguing that the existing plan is superior to,
let us say, a strictly chronological approach. This would be an
apologia post facto, because as we gathered material it almost fell
into a kind of order, within each of the three large sections, and
there was no reason to rearrange it drastically to suit another model
of organization. This almost automatic self-ordering of the documents on Indian foreign relations perhaps results from the fact
that Indian foreign policies responded to particular situations, varying from state to state and from problem to problem. Nehru's
policies were pragmatic and flexible, and at a given time a variety of
external relationships were proceeding, difficult for an historian to
recapture within a single coherent chapter. At the level of global
politics Nehru maintained the posture of nonalignment in a remarkably consistent fashion, and one could treat together India's relations with the US and the USSR and some of its policies in the UN.
But within the context of nonalignment one could not properly
discuss relations with Pakistan, China or the Union of South Africa.
We know that the present organization leads to some repetition of
ideas, and we hope that this will be tolerated.

We began work on this book shortly after Nehru's death in 1964,
and the bulk of it deals with foreign relations under Nehru. Our
coverage gets thinner after 1964, but we have tried to sketch in the
main developments even though full documentation has not always
been available for the most recent years.

Many good friends in the Indian Foreign Service and officials
from the US and other countries have talked with us frankly about
subjects in the book. We hereby acknowledge their help and respect
their desire for anonymity.

The American co-author received a grant from the Fulbright programme for research on this book in India in 1964-1965, for which he remains grateful. The Washington, D.C., *Evening Star* newspaper made available a handsome grant of funds to help complete this work. Equal to all other concrete assistance in writing this book has been the expert and unfailingly courteous attention given to us by the Indian Council of World Affairs Library at Sapru House, New Delhi; we wish to thank Mr Girja Kumar, the Librarian, and all of the staff, in particular, Mrs C. Andrade and Miss Shanta Sehgal.

Of the locations that could have been given for any document cited we have usually identified the most easily obtainable, for example, Nehru's published speeches rather than a parliamentary debate.

C. H. H.
S. M.

CONTENTS

PART ONE : LEGACY AND INNOVATION

PART TWO : THE SEARCH FOR ASIAN AND AFRICAN POLICIES

PART THREE : THE SUCCESSES AND FAILURES
OF NONALIGNMENT

ABBREVIATIONS

The abbreviations used in the Notes and References
are given below :

FAR   Foreign Affairs Record
GAOR   General Assembly Official Records
LSD   Lok Sabha Debates
RSD   Rajya Sabha Debates
SCOR   Security Council Official Records

PART ONE

LEGACY AND INNOVATION

CHAPTER I

INDIAN FOREIGN RELATIONS
IN THE INTER-WAR PERIOD

IN NO OTHER facet of independent India's political tradition has the impress of British ideas and institutions been stronger than in foreign relations. The unique characteristics of Indian foreign policy under Nehru, which resulted in an unusual and perhaps unexpected prominence for India in international politics, were special contributions of an erstwhile "opposition government" to a heritage of international dealings established under British rule. The fact that after independence the Indian government was free to overturn, within the limits of certain treaty obligations, the structure of external relationships built up over many decades by British rulers, but it chose not to do so, is the best evidence of the strength of the tradition of pre-1947 Indian international relations. In its administrative structure for conducting diplomacy, in some of its definitions of the national interest and formulations of policies on important subjects, and in its "style" of diplomacy, the Nehru government followed the precedents of the previous Indian government. Maintenance of the Commonwealth relationship illustrates that, and many other aspects of Indian foreign relations after 1947 could be viewed as an enlargement rather than a transformation of the relationships established before that date.

The continuity of certain of India's external relations from the First World War to the present, the absence of a point of major disengagement in August 1947, between an old imperial tradition and a new policy and practice freshly created by a nationalist government, is explained partly by the fact that India was a quasi-independent entity in international politics before 1947—indeed, since 1917. As in domestic political life following the First World War, so also in the sphere of international politics India became a partially self-directed entity, identified as separate from Britain—in foreign relations, though not in foreign policy. The fact that quasi-indepen-

3

dence in the international arena existed while India's sovereignty remained in the British Crown made it possible for the Nehru government, after the transfer of power, to reaffirm many of the foreign policies of the previous regime without denying the principles of Indian nationalism.

In fact, certain objectives of Indian nationalism were being pursued by the pre-independence government of India, and those objectives naturally became part of the determining principles of independent Indian foreign policy. As Ton That Thien summarized the case: "It is true that India's trade, defence and foreign policies were planned in Whitehall, and were designed primarily to serve British interests. But in their effects, they also, to no small extent, served Indian interests. Indeed, the British Indian Empire was more Indian than British . . . ."[1]

While the Indian government remained subordinate to the British parliament, Indian nationalist leaders lacked the capacity to contribute ideas of uniquely Indian origin to the international political community. Furthermore, certain important stated nationalist objectives in foreign policy were unrecognized in the government's policy formulations, and other officially accepted external interests of India were not pursued with adequate sincerity or vigour when they were not underwritten by larger imperial interests. Nevertheless, in the inter-war period India achieved a measure of autonomy in international affairs unprecedented for a non-self-governing dependency, its interests were influential in the councils of major states, and its fundamental objective of security was not neglected. Its status and prestige increased, as Indian representatives abroad became known for their statesmanship. The inter-war heritage of involvement in international affairs facilitated independent India's foreign relations and contributed to the effectiveness of its foreign policy.[2]

RELATIONS WITH THE EMPIRE

If India's national interests were fundamentally subordinate to the interests of the British empire and its spokesmen were not those of a fully sovereign state, such a status was shared by several more politically advanced states at the time of the First World War. The imperial government had committed the entire empire to war in 1914 without any formal consultation with the dominions, or India, nor was any such prior discussion regarded as necessary by the governments of the empire. During the war, which demonstrated the need and the reality of close collaboration and common loyalty among the component parts of the empire, the first steps were taken to establish formal political consultation between the imperial government and the dominions on matters of defence and foreign affairs. The Imperial War Cabinet provided the forum for the acknowledgement that the dominions and India should have an important influence in the foreign relations of the empire.

India was linked with the dominions in these important steps because of its significant military and economic contributions to the war effort, which in turn had elicited a momentous declaration from Britain on India's future. The 1917 statement by Secretary of State Montagu, that the British intention was to develop in India "self-governing institutions with a view to the progressive realization of responsible government in India as an integral part of the British Empire," placed India on a footing potentially equal to that of the self-governing dominions. In foreign relations the equality was more nearly actual than potential in the latter years of the war; thereafter, however, the dominions moved more rapidly toward fully autonomous foreign relations than did India.

In 1915 the Indian Legislative Council and Governor-General, Hardinge urged Britain to invite India to the next meeting of the major governments of the empire,[3] from which India had been excluded by a resolution of 1907. Lloyd George's government welcomed the request, Indian representatives attended the 1917 war conference and were assured a place in the imperial cabinet, whenever it met. The war conference of 1917 resolved that any constitutional readjustment among the component parts of the empire, should be postponed until the end of hostilities but at that time "should be based upon a full recognition of the dominions as autonomous nations of an Imperial Commonwealth, and of India as an important portion of the same, [and] should recognize the right of the dominions and India to an effective voice in foreign policy and in foreign relations . . . ."[4]

India's position in the empire, and hence in international political life, was transformed by the imperial war conferences of 1917 and 1918. The Government of India, responsible to the British parlia-

ment and not to the Indian legislature or people, was represented
at the conferences by the secretary of state for India, a member
of the British cabinet, accompanied by others, all of whom knew
how strongly the government in India felt that India should rise
to a position of major influence in the affairs of the post-war
world. Dominion delegates to the conference, some of whom were
expressing for the first time their governments' claims to autonomy
within the empire, understood and accepted the aspirations of
India, whose people were of a different race but whose government
was and would predictably remain within the imperial system.
India's new status in the empire made almost automatic the sending
of a separate delegation of India to the Paris peace conference and
its charter membership in the League of Nations. In 1920 a high
commissioner for India in London was appointed.[5] The war-time
and post-war emergence of India into the international arena was
thus premised on its association with the British empire.

India's influence expressed at the discussion stage of imperial
policy and in bilateral relations with dominion governments represented a quasi-independence vis-a-vis the other governments of the
empire, including the UK. Over a fully sovereign state no external
control is exercised to limit the interests that its government may
choose to pursue or the subjects of international concern on which its
representatives may express an opinion. But the Indian government
and its representatives promoted only those interests which the
British government had assigned to them for separate advocacy ;
here lay its quasi-independence. With the Balfour statement of
1926, which extended dominion sovereignty from the domestic
sphere into foreign relations, India's progress toward real independence in international affairs was outdistanced by those states
which, in Balfour's words, were "autonomous communities within
the British Empire."[6] India's position in the empire continued to
be defined by the 1919 act as one of constitutional subordination
to the British parliament. Nevertheless, certain of the Indian government's economic and political interests received a full hearing at
imperial conferences, and their influence on the policies of other
states within a circumscribed frame of reference was not unlike
that which a legally sovereign state could have exercised. India
lacked symbols of true sovereignty, but in a practical sense on
certain subjects, comparable to the "transferred subjects" of the

Indian Constitution, the authority had been delegated to its representatives to promote Indian interests in international affairs.

THE STATUS OF INDIANS OVERSEAS

The foremost concern of the Indian government with respect to imperial relations was the status of Indians in the dominions and colonies—a concern which stemmed, significantly, from the publicly expressed interests of Indians and was to be constantly reiterated by the independent Indian government.[7] In every British territory to which Indians had emigrated in large numbers, usually with the encouragement of the local authorities, certain regulations had been passed which discriminated against them, explicitly or implicitly on grounds of their race. Public political bodies in India constantly urged the government to intervene with dominion and Colonial Office authorities on behalf of the overseas Indians. As the nationalist movement in the 20th century stimulated fervent ideas of racial and cultural pride, the Indian government's anxiety grew, lest overseas mistreatment of Indians add to political resentments and troubles at home. On a loftier level of political concern, some imperial statesmen argued that the unity and smooth functioning of the empire could be destroyed unless its political ideals of equal treatment for all races were translated into legal reality. But the dominion governments, in varying degrees, continued to enforce regulations adversely affecting economic and political rights of so-called "Asiatics."

By the First World War, the problem of Indians overseas had taken on the chaacter of India against the rest of the empire. The British government, not yet beset by its own racial problems, was caught in the middle. Its proclamations often seemed to favour India's interests, but in concrete measures it followed a policy of drifting with the dominions and insinuating racial bars into the colonial statute books. An Indian memorandum on the emigration of Indians to self-governing dominions was presented to the 1917 imperial war conference.[8] Its main theme was that Indians should be able to move throughout the empire as freely as other British subjects ; any British subject could freely enter India, but even "Indians of good position" had to plead for a special permit to enter any dominion—even as tourists. The Indian government had drawn back from supporting freedom of Indian emigration to all parts of the empire as a feasible, or perhaps desirable, object ; it conceded each dominion's right to maintain the racial homogeneity of its population through restrictions on settlement and immigration.

But after making this major concession to the dominion position, India's representatives moved a resolution embodying the "principle of reciprocity of treatment" by the dominions and India of each other's nationals desiring to travel or settle temporarily within the empire.[9] The resolution created little enthusiasm, but it was vague enough to permit the conference to avoid discussing the specifically injurious regulations that Indians complained of in all the dominions.[10] The reciprocity principle could not be criticized, and India's resolution was unanimously accepted. At the 1918 conference a similar resolution also achieved unanimous consent. These resolutions left the basic issues of racial equality unaffected and were agreed to in an effort to appease Indian sentiment, rather than to establish principles which would henceforth determine racial policies of the empire.[11]

At the imperial conference of 1921, India's demands for more tangible progress toward racial equality, now more vocally made by nationalists at home and more vigorously promoted by Indians at the imperial gatherings, resulted in a resolution which recognized "that there is an incongruity between the position of India as an equal member of the British Empire and the existence of disabilities upon British Indians lawfully domiciled in some other parts of the Empire." Thus, the Indian government defined an objective broader than Indians' rights to travel and temporary settlement, namely the assurance of equal rights for Indians already settled abroad. As in the earlier resolutions, India gave up the claim that Indians should be free to emigrate to any dominion. The pressure at the imperial conference became too great for South Africa, and General Smuts refused to accept the resolution ; the unanimity rule was not applied, however, and the motion was given as the consensus of the conference, South Africa disagreeing.[12]

The pressure on the dominions increased again at the 1923 imperial conference when India tried to obtain concrete agreements to give substance to the 1921 resolution. For the Secretary of State, Lord Peel, and the Indian government the treatment of Indians in the dominions was "of very high Imperial importance" because it vitally influenced the political scene in India.[13] The cause of the problem, as he and most other British officials saw it, was the pride of Indians, constantly hurt by unwarranted assertion of their inferiority by dominion governments. Tej Bahadur Sapru, one of India's representatives, agreed that part of the problem was the question of "Izzat," as he put it, or honour and pride.[14] Sapru also put forward the more far-sighted ideal of the imperial statesman and loyal British subject[15] and warned that the empire would disintegrate unless coloured races were made equal parts of it. The conference debated the delicate matter for parts of three days with a rare frankness; there was no sentiment in favour of enunciating an imperial policy on race relations, and Sapru had to withdraw a resolution he had submitted. India had some support from Ireland and New Zealand; Canada, Australia, and South Africa reaffirmed and justified their varying discriminatory laws on grounds of political expediency.[16]

The 1923 conference provided some verbal satisfaction to Indian pride, and that was all. No substance was added then or later to the 1921 conference's resolution, which remained the high-water mark of good imperial intentions on the question of overseas Indians. Along with India's improved status within the empire went the burden of negotiating directly with the dominions on this matter ; the imperial government in London could no longer be relied upon to press the Indian case—nor could it have done so successfully after the Statute of Westminster of 1931.

Thus disappeared from prominent view and constructive debate at the imperial centre the vision of a truly multi-racial Commonwealth, a federation of dissimilar nations joined by their common adherence to general laws and political loyalties. One of the core institutions of such a Commonwealth had to be common citizenship or at least a common recognition of the basic rights of all individuals holding allegiance to the component states of the system. When the British Commonwealth failed to oppose the racially restrictive legislation of the dominions, and even of the colonial governments, it "turned its back on the ideal of the cosmopolis, which was the ideal of two great contemporary empires, the Union of Soviet Socialist Republics and the French Empire." It was acquiescing in a theory of multiple citizenships, or nationalities, based on race, which stood in "marked contrast with the theory generally adopted by other empires of the past and of the present."[17] By failing to meet squarely the problems of race conflict between communities and states within the empire at a time when its influence was great, the British government contributed to the contamination by racialism of mid-20th century international politics. The Commonwealth failed to provide the desired example of a harmonious multi-racial society of democratic states.

IMPERIAL ECONOMIC RELATIONS

By the early 1930's the world economic crisis had overshadowed all international political issues for India and the dominions. During the 1930's, the economics of the imperial relationship assumed greater importance than it had in the previous decade; the altered trade policies of the UK growing out of requirements of the global economic depression, called forth important changes in India's commercial relations with the empire.

In the immediate pre-First World War years, India's external trade experienced great increases, and while Britain remained its main trading partner, the US, Japan, and Germany for the first time became important in its trading relationships. After the war the tendencies in the Indian economy to shift buying and selling from British markets to those outside the empire were again apparent, and after 1924 they accelerated rapidly. During the same time an increasingly large percentage of the Indian economy's demand for manufactured goods, especially textiles, was being met by domestic production, whose growing capacity had been greatly stimulated by the hostilities. In percentage of total imports India's purchases from Britain, largely manufactured goods, declined from approximately 60 in the 1919-1924 period to approximately 40 in the 1929-1934 period. In percentage of total exports India's shipments to Britain rose slightly in a comparison of the same years. The share in India's trade held by the rest of the empire was comparatively slight for these years—about eight per cent for imports, about 17 per cent for exports, and was generally fairly stable.[18] Japan's increasing share in imports of textiles and cotton yarns was the most notable, and to Britain alarming, change in India's trading pattern in the 1920's. Whereas Britain was almost the sole supplier of imported cotton piece goods in 1913-1914, having 97 per cent of the market, by 1927-1928 Britain's share in the Indian market had fallen to 78 per cent, and Japan supplied 16 per cent. Whereas Lancashire supplied 80 per cent of India's imports of cotton yarn in 1913-1914 and Japan 2 per cent in 1925-1926 Lancashire supplied only 31 per cent and Japan 65.[19]

In the 1920's Britain tried to restore the conditions of pre-war "normalcy," but the effort was unavailing, and after the financial collapse of 1929 Britain was forced to abandon the gold standard and to disavow the practices of free trade and multilateralism in favour of controls, bilateral agreements and imperial preferences. In 1932 a system of preferential agreements among the states of the empire was established at Ottawa, whose purpose it was to divert trade into imperial channels by means of discriminatory tariffs and similar devices. India was pulled into the new system.

In no way could the quasi-independence of pre-1947 India in international affairs be more realistically appraised than by considering Indo-British economic relations. In 1919 the British government recommended that India be granted fiscal autonomy.[20] The recommendation led to the appointment of the Indian fiscal commission with authority to examine tariff policies ; the implication of this move was that the free trading policy which India had been following since the mid-19th century could no longer be defended against foreign economic or Indian nationalist challenges. The commission recommended, without much vigour, tariff protection for selected Indian industries and "conditional Imperial Preference"—preference only when it was reciprocated. In 1923 a tariff board was established with powers to recommend discriminatory duties to protect those Indian industries which met certain conditions for development.

In response to the board's favourable report on the steel industry's needs for protection, the legislature passed the steel industry protection act in 1924. Cautiously the tariff board considered requests of other industries for protective tariff walls, and within five years new duties had been set on cotton textiles, matches, certain wood products, and still later on sugar and paper. Thus the Indian economy had been launched on a course of economic independence from the UK similar to that undertaken by the dominions in the second half of the 19th century.

In the dominions economic nationalism had been as powerful

as political nationalism in loosening the imperial bond. To counter
the tendency toward economic independence certain British leaders
formulated schemes to enforce the empire's economic cohesion
by establishing a unitary imperial trading system. The dominions
responded with the idea of imperial preferences, but the free trade
interests in Britain were strong enough to squelch any proposal
for general preferential tariffs until the 1930's. The government of
India's interest in protection and in preferences differed from that
of the dominions because India's relationship to the world market
was not the same as the dominions'. Furthermore, having just
received the promise of fiscal autonomy, it could not lightly compromise its independence by adhering to a new set of imperial ties.

At the 1923 imperial economic conference, C. A. Innes representing India, voiced the view that India's economic interests might not
always coincide with those of the greater empire, and in case of
imperial preferences India distinctly opposed them for itself, as it
had done since the beginning of the century. Preferences, Innes
explained, normally benefited countries which exported manufactures, not those exporting raw materials, which usually entered
other countries free or with minimal duties. Furthermore, many
of India's exports went outside the empire—about two-thirds by
1930—, and hence there would be little imperial reciprocity deriving
from acceptance of preferences. The Indian government had a
traditional practice of imposing low tariffs for revenue purposes
alone; preferences might seriously injure the government's revenue.
Finally, Innes explained that his government was facing so much
criticism because of the racial policies of the dominions that concessions to dominion economic interests would not be politic.[21]

Ten years later, at another convening of the imperial economic
conference, at Ottawa, the Indian delegation was no longer able to
argue against preferences and in behalf of strictly Indian national
economic interests, because the empire had finally given up free
trade and adopted the preferences system. The UK dropped
the gold standard in 1931; in its place emerged the more limited,
and nationalistic, sterling area. In 1932 parliament passed the
protectionist import duties act ; imperial economies by receiving
preferences escaped part of the hardship of this act but were tied
more firmly thereby to the British economy. Atul Chatterjee signed
the Indo-British trade agreement at Ottawa in 1932.[22] The agreement

provided for preferences in tariff rates for Indian and British goods entering the other country's market ; it did not undermine Indian tariffs as a revenue source or alter India's domestic taxation policies.

The economic effects of the Indo-British agreement and India's adoption of imperial preferences are still a subject of controversy among economists. Indo-British trade increased temporarily, and India's trade within the empire also improved, but after 1935 when world markets became more active India's trade with non-preference countries rose more rapidly than with the empire. The Japanese depreciated the yen and continued to make gains in the Indian market after Ottawa, despite a temporary Indo-Japanese trade crisis and a special discriminatory tariff imposed by the Indian government. Probably the long-term effects of India's adoption of imperial preferences on its foreign trade were relatively slight.[23] However, the political allegation that they were forced on the country by British imperialist interests was of serious consequence for Indo-British relations. Indeed, India's fiscal autonomy was formally impaired by the new obligation to maintain preferences as well as by the provision in the 1935 India Act preventing certain forms of discrimination against British companies doing business in India.

An examination of the operation of the Indian tariff board also confirms the conclusion that the fiscal autonomy convention did not stand up when the pressure of British economic necessity was directed against Indian interests.[24] Indian criticism of the government's trade policies with the UK continued through the negotiations leading to a new agreement in 1939, and up to 1947. Yet the independent Indian government continued to adhere to imperial preferences, and up to the present writing Indo-British trade has been governed by the provisions of the 1939 agreement, modified to conform to the General Agreement on Tariffs and Trade (GATT).

REPRESENTATION IN INTERNATIONAL ORGANIZATIONS

The inner working of India's relations with the UK and the rest of the empire between the wars, as illustrated by the questions of overseas Indians and imperial trade preferences, could be overlooked by outsiders when the public international arena in which India acted was as broad as the League of Nations Assembly or the International Labour Organization (ILO). There India appeared to be independent. Nevertheless certain limitations on the actions of the only non-self-governing member of the League had to be understood by any government dealing with India at that time.

The impressive contribution of India to the allied cause in the world war[25] and the British commitment to the advancement of responsible government in India, as well as the important precedent of India's representation at imperial conferences, resulted in a separate Indian delegation to the Paris peace conference. India signed the treaty of Versailles and other peace treaties, except Lausanne, and became an original member of the League, along with the imperial dominions. That membership assured India of representation also in the ILO, the Permanent Court of International Justice, several other organizations affiliated with the League, and at most of the important international conferences of the inter-war period, such as the Washington conference on naval armaments of 1921-1922, the London naval conference in 1930, the Geneva economic conference of 1927, and The Hague reparations conferences of 1929 and 1930. While the peace conference admitted the representatives of India and the dominions as parts of the British empire delegation, the League Assembly seated the delegations from India and the dominions as members in their own right acting for their own governments. The validity of their separate status under international law was left undetermined; the "anomaly" of India's position, as an official study put it, was simply tolerated by the League and the governments concerned.

The ultimate power to control India's international relations was vested by law in the secretary of state, a member of the British government. But in order to give substance to the British claim of turning over real power to an Indian government the secretary functioned with the "deliberate object" of making "India's new status a reality for practical purposes within the widest limits. It was not open to him to relinquish his constitutional power of control ... but it has been his constant endeavour to restrict its exercise to a minimum ... and to allow the Indian government the greatest possible freedom of action under the influence of their Legislature and of public opinion." That statement of the official position[26] conformed to the facts. The Indian delegation to the League Assembly, consisting of three members, was always composed of a majority of Indians; it was led by a Britisher until 1928, after which Indians headed the group. Typically, India's delegation included a ruling prince and a high-ranking, usually knighted, Indian executive council member, judge, or person of great public repute. On the basis of their recorded speeches they appeared eminently loyal to Britain but at the same time anxious to promote the welfare of India.

The practical functioning of the Indian delegation at Geneva in the early years betrayed the absence of any precise definition of its relationship to the British government and delegation ; the British were no better able to conceptualize India's new international status than anyone else, and the matter had to "sort itself out" by trial and error.[27] As that definition emerged, through the cautious procedures by which the British self-consciously set about making precedents, the Indian delegation's independence of action in some areas appeared to be real—how else, indeed, could Britain justify its claim for separate representation of India and the dominions?[28]

In the early annual *Reports of the Delegates of India to the Assembly of the League of Nations* the independence of the Indian mission was a preoccupying subject. The first delegation reported that "the absolute independence of India, as of the dominions, in regard to her attitude and voting on questions coming before the Assembly and its Committees was fully recognized ; but, like the dominions, we felt that when our own interests were not directly or indirectly concerned we should endeavour to keep step with the mother country, and there were frequent informal meetings to this end . . . ."[29] The Maharaja of Patiala, a delegate to the 1925 Assembly, wrote candidly of the difficulty in determining what the Indian government's position was on certain issues. The delegation's briefs, therefore, "perhaps inevitably, were based rather upon the India Office view than upon the opinions of the government of India—which indeed, in some cases, could hardly be ascertained in time, and remained the subject of conjecture." Instructions to the delegations at the League, and at other international conferences, except international labour conferences, came from the India Office, which seemed to puzzle the Maharaja : "On several points, which I need not specify, it seemed to me that the opinion of the government of India and of the India Office was not necessarily completely coincident. Yet I had no means of discovering exactly what the government of India's views might be, and I was compelled to treat the suggestion put forward by the India Office as if they had been the one and only official guide to the proper course."[30]

The 1927 delegation grasped a clearer policy line : On the "big political questions," such as security and disarmament, all the empire delegations were expected to take a single stand. On matters of regional or non-political import the delegation had the liberty to follow an independent policy, as if India had been a dominion.[31] The delegates to the 1928 Assembly reported that they were explicitly informed at the India Office that: "While our authority and instructions emanated formally from the Secretary of State, they were, in fact, the result of discussion and agreement between the Secretary of State and the government of India. We were also told that it was intended that we should have the fullest amount of practical liberty and independence consistent with the existing constitutional position."[32] The restrictions constitutionally imposed on the delegation's ability to take independent stands or to raise issues on which India and the empire had opposing interests were occasionally irksome to delegates, and the official *Reports* of India's delegation to League Assemblies contain veiled references to the lack of independence of the delegation—whether from London or from New Delhi it is not always clear.

The reports of the delegations also reflect the large extent to which Indian participation was limited to social, economic and technical matters. The Indian delegations developed a speciality in League meetings for which they acquired an international reputation—that was their annual struggle for economies in League budgets. William Meyer, leader of the delegation to the first Assembly and the Indian High Commissioner in London, began the precedent of economy-mindedness and linked it to a demand for reduction in India's contributions to League budgets. The Indian delegation's continuing complaint about over-assessment was based partly on the allegedly slight benefits which India obtained from heavily financed League activities. India contributed more funds to the League than any state not a permanent member of the Council,[33] yet apart from the much appreciated work of the health organization in Singapore, Indians saw very little tangible return from what one delegate called the European-centred League projects.

In 1928 the Earl of Lytton, who led the delegation, pleaded for expansion of the League's activities to Asia in order to justify India's financial contribution, and the delegation went so far as to threaten not to vote for the budget, requiring unanimity for adoption, unless expenditures were reduced or the European bias in League activities was rectified. In the secretariat less than half a dozen Indians were employed, some only temporarily, and this increased India's dissatisfaction with the return on its contribution. As it happened, the League never overcame its preoccupation with European affairs ; few of its members or its secretariat officials regarded Asian countries as more than colonial appendages of Europe, insignificant in world affairs. India failed to obtain increased tangible benefits from the League ; instead its contributions, of 13 and 14 lakhs of rupees in the early 1930's, were reduced by 30 per cent in 1936.

WORK IN THE WORLD BODIES AND CRITICISMS
OF INDIA'S PARTICIPATION

Despite their severe but unavoidable disabilities in League Assemblies, Indian delegations for two decades contributed in a significant fashion to the social and economic work of the organization and the advancement of the institutions of international law. One success of the League was the establishment of international conventions on matters of social and economic concern. India's views on those League sponsored agreements were presented at the drafting stage and frequently affected the final terms in ways favourable to Indian interests.

The drafting of the Opium Convention involved India, as one of the important producers and exporters of that product. The Indian government gave support to a phased reduction of the opium trade and, after adhering to the convention, suppressed opium production and export from India almost completely, with a resulting heavy loss of government revenue—over seven million pounds sterling. India was able to subscribe to the convention on traffic in women and children after having it modified so as to conform to Indian laws on age of consent. The Slavery Convention, also adhered to by India, presented the tricky problem of the applicability of international agreements to the Indian states. Indian delegates at Geneva were anxious that a convention not to commit their government to suppressing social customs, especially in the princely states, which "might appear to the eye of an ignorant observer as akin to forced labour or to predial service"—in the words of the Maharaja of Patiala.[34] Their concern was overcome by drafting alterations and by the unprecedented reservation attached to India's adherence to the Slavery Convention in 1926, that it would not apply to certain areas under the government's "sovereignty, jurisdiction, protection, suzerainty or tutelage," i.e. the states, the Himalayan kingdoms, and certain unadministered tribal areas.[35] Conventions on transit and communications produced few problems for India, and the government adhered to those which were applicable, thus extending common international practices into the Indian Ocean region.

India followed the British lead in favouring new legal instruments for the peaceful settlement of international disputes. The government in India adhered to the Statute of the Permanent Court of International Justice in 1921 and in 1930 ratified the "optional clause" which it had signed the previous year. India also ratified the Protocol on Arbitration Clauses and the General Act for the Pacific Settlement of International Disputes. A large number of less important multilateral agreements were reached in the 1920's and 1930's, thus further obligating the government in India, rather than in London, to undertake international responsibilities directly.[36]

As economic affairs began to replace social questions as the main non-political concerns on the League Indian representatives became the major proponents of the interests of the industrially backward countries of the world. At the international economic conference at Geneva in 1927 Indian delegates explained that India's economic interests were not the same as Europe's, and therefore it could not be expected to follow recommendations of the conference made in the context of the industrialized economies. India's recently-achieved fiscal autonomy, a delegate said, would be guarded "jealously," and no changes were apt to be made in the policy of protective tariffs, despite moves to reduce trade duties by European states.[37] In League committee discussions and in international economic conferences for the next several years India's delegates pressed the case of the raw materials producing country whose weak control over export prices and heavy dependence on imported manufactures were being largely ignored by the Western delegations. In 1929 a representative of India stressed the inter-dependence of the economies of the West and India, the latter as a market for imported manufactures ; he flatly stated that until an economic conference was prepared to deal fairly with agriculture and raw material prices, India would not be interested.[38] But nothing was accomplished by the League to satisfy India's economic interests or assist in its industrial development ; after 1932 its quasi-independent economic status lost much of its substance and it no longer looked for economic benefits through international agencies.

Although seldom involved in the political discussions of the League, the Indian delegation assumed, fleetingly, an independent posture on the mandates issue. V. S. Srinivasa Sastri raised the question of race discrimination in the class "C" mandates of Tanganyika and South-West Africa when he addressed the League Assembly in 1921. Although there were no Indians residing in South-West Africa, Sastri warned against the extension of racial barriers by South Africa into its mandated territory. Tanganyika, ironically, had been conquered with the assistance of Indian troops and India was considered as a possible mandate holder for that territory in 1919. Yet Indian settlers, free from discrimination while under German rule, would probably suffer mistreatment when the British East African government took over direct administration.

If race laws were introduced into those two mandated territories, Sastri said, India would bring a formal complaint to the League. Sastri may have spoken out in the Assembly without prior discussions with his colleagues ; in any case, except for a milder speech by P. S. Sivaswamy Aiyer at the 1922 Assembly, India's complaint about racial discrimination in mandated territories, though supported by the Covenant, was not heard again.

India's participation in the League of Nations was ultimately subordinate to the interests of another state. Its rare contributions to political discussions and its overall reluctance to take initiatives, except in budgetary matters, were sufficient evidences of its position. Indian participation in the League from the outset was a bold defense of the progressive nature of British rule in India. Most of India's delegates were at pains to demonstrate that India's interests coincided with British interests and that the government in India was sincere in advancing the country's needs. When, on a few occasions, Indian and British interests formally diverged, the image

of an independent dependency was more satisfactorily conveyed
to foreign statesmen, who in many circumstances resented the
numerous votes that Britain seemed to control through its imperial ties. Within this framework of constitutional dependency
India's delegates defended admirably, sometimes brilliantly, the
interests which were placed in their custody.

Indian delegations to international bodies showed their greatest
devotion to India's own interests on subjects of a non-political
nature. Their record in the ILO, of which India was a founding member, was notable. At the Washington conference in
1919 India's representatives raised for the first time the claim
that India should be on the governing body of the ILO. William
Meyer brought the issue to the League Assembly in 1920 and threatened that India would reconsider its relations with the ILO if its
claim were not properly considered. After hearing strenuous arguments from British delegates about the size and importance of
India's industrial labour force, which included transport and maritime
workers, the League Council in 1922 decided that India should sit
on the governing body among the eight chief industrial states of the
world. The US was not then a member ; the aspirations of Poland
and Switzerland for status among the eight were judged less meri-
torious than India's.[39]

In 1927 Atul Chatterjee was elected chairman of the International
Labour Conference and in 1932 chairman of the governing body of
the organization. In the drafting stages of most of the conventions
originating in the ILO Indian delegates pressed amendments which
took account of Indian conditions, and in doing so, sometimes took
positions at odds with those of the UK. For example, in 1920
Indian and British delegates diverged on the question of the treatment of Indian seamen on British ships, and at the international
labour conferences in 1921 and 1924 they were at odds on the issue
of disinfecting wool entering international trade. In many cases of
Indian labour delegates' pressing for their own interests in the ILO
British labour representatives came to their support, and vice versa.
In 1919 for example, Indian labour delegates supported their British
counterparts' motion to restrict child labour in India. Labour delegates
functioned more cohesively than those from governments or employers ; the All-India Trade Union Congress's links with foreign labour
groups helped assure labour solidarity in the ILO meetings.

As they gained confidence and experience Indians used the ILO to publicize their grievances against economically more powerful states, including Britain, and their complaints against their own government. In 1939 an Indian labour delegate criticized the government's poor record in labour legislation and said: "I want to take this opportunity to protest, from this international platform, against the firing and baton charges in industrial disputes and against the suppression of workers' meetings and processions in India."[40] Employers' delegates spoke out too against any governmental weakness in protecting India's economic interests against threats from abroad, notably from Japan.

The Government of India did not ignore the activities of the ILO and submitted its conventions to the legislature for debate and possible ratification. By 1931 its record of adhering to international labour conventions ranked second only to the UK among the Commonwealth countries and bore witness to the close involvement between India and international organizations in the 1920's and 1930's. Conventions limiting night work of women and young persons (1919), limiting hours of work in industrial undertakings, (1919), dealing with unemployment (1919), and with minimum ages for certain types of employment (1921), and others gained ratification in the legislature and influenced, to a degree, domestic legislation in those fields.[41] Unlike its relationship with the League Assembly, which was always circumscribed by the formal or informal instructions of the India Office, India's participation in the ILO to a reasonable extent reflected the interests of its own government, labour unions, and businesses. Instructions to the delegations came directly from New Delhi.

For several reasons most nationalist political leaders in India ignored the League of Nations or were hostile toward it from the beginning. Indians could observe few benefits provided by the League, and there were no occasions when vital Indian interests received the attention of the League Council or Assembly. Even to India's delegates, the League appeared to be a European club with a few, ineffective non-European members, such as India, to provide an appearance of universality. In 1928 the Nawab of Palanpur, on India's delegation, exposed to the Assembly the doubts of an Asian that the League was "an association of equal peoples, with equal obligations and equal rights, affording equal

opportunities to all its members, irrespective of racial origin. . . ."
He observed that "in certain quarters in the East, there is a suspicion
that the League is intended for use as an instrument for perpetuating
the hegemony of the races which are of European origin over the
other races."[42] In the following year the Indian delegation was
headed for the first time by an Indian, Muhammad Habibullah,
and its report took full account of the unenthusiastic response in
India to the League's activities. The situation might be remedied,
the report suggested, if India were to occupy a non-permanent
seat on the Council. But despite India's size and the importance
of its financial contribution, its delegation was never authorized
to put India forward as a candidate for a Council seat, although it
became established League practice that one of the dominions
should occupy a non-permanent seat.

Criticism in India of the League began in the first years of its
operation ; the issue was mandates. Before the war had ended,
an Indian delegate at the imperial war conference had demanded
"the unrestricted opening to Indian business of any territory acquired
from the enemy in East Africa,"[43] and nationalists at home, such as
Gopal Krishna Gokhale, were publicly allowing their imagination
to focus on the possibilities of Indian colonies across the Arabian
Sea. The East African Indian Congress, based in Kenya, resolved
in 1919 to preserve Tanganyika for Indian immigration. The effort
of Sastri, noted above, to preclude racial laws from being introduced
into the mandates brought some home support to India's League
delegation ; when the issue was dropped at Geneva it arose in New
Delhi.

In one of its rare debates on the League, in July 1923, the Indian
Legislative assembly discussed a resolution questioning the government's support of the League in view of the latter's failure to protect
Indian interests in Tanganyika and also the ex-German islands of
the Pacific. "It is intolerable," one delegate held, "that the mandate
should be utilized in practice to keep out Asiatics, particularly
Indians. . . ."[44] Criticism in India of the League grew in the 1930's.
It became apparent that in personnel and in activities the League
would remain predominantly European. Beyond that, the League's
dramatic failures in the far east, in Abyssinia and later in Europe
itself denied it any grounds for recruiting new support. During the
sixteenth Assembly session Italy invaded Abyssinia, and the Aga

Khan, heading India's delegation, conveyed the distress that informed Indians felt because of the helplessness of the world body. In the following year, there was an adjournment motion in the legislative assembly to consider the failure of the Indian government to withdraw from the League because of the latter's failure over Abyssinia. Nothing came of it: the assembly was not normally able to discuss foreign relations,[45] although time had been allowed for discussion of League affairs, when they were non-political. The leader of India's League delegation in 1938 cited the feeling in India that the League neither served India's interests nor the requirements of world peace. He told the sixth committee that unless the League began to perform as its Covenant demanded India "might lose all interest in Article 16 and the other articles of the Covenant."[46]

By 1939 the legislative assembly could hold a full debate on the League, under Congress auspices, and at that time the nationalist resentment against the government's continued membership and disillusionment with great power politics in the West filled the chamber. The earlier criticisms of the League's preoccupation with Europe, the alleged over-assessment of India, and the small number of Indians in the secretariat gave way to broader condemnation of the League failures in disarmament and peace-keeping. The Congress leadership, especially Jawaharlal Nehru, was by then committed to the idea that British and French policies were leading the world toward war ; there was nothing that Indians could do but voice their contempt and perhaps adopt a pro-Soviet ideological position as an alternative to the discredited idealism of the League Charter. After bitter recitals of the history of League failures from Congress benches, the assembly passed a resolution recommending India's withdrawal from the League because of its failure to act against Covenant-breaking members and, by amendment, because of British policy in the Palestine mandate.[47]

At its Tripuri meeting in March 1939 the Congress recorded "its entire disapproval of British foreign policy culminating in the Munich Pact, the Anglo-Italian Agreement, and the recognition of rebel Spain. This policy has been one of deliberate betrayal of democracy, repeated breach of pledges, the evading of the system of collective security and co-operation with governments which are avowed enemies of democracy and freedom."[48] In the League itself India's delegates were passive spectators to the appeasement that resulted in war.

NATIONAL DEFENSE

An area of governmental concern between the wars which established important precedents for post-independence Indian foreign relations was that of defense policy. On that subject, as in relations within the Commonwealth, problems of overseas Indians, economic affairs, and on matters of representation in international organizations, the government and Indian nationalists often diverged. Yet when the nationalists assumed power in 1947, they chose to build upon the past, for the most part, rather than try to upset it. The security of any state is a notably consistent concern of all governments of that state, and although India's geopolitical situation changed with the creation of Pakistan, some fundamental interests remained along with the pre-independence approaches to their fulfilment.

British security policy in India developed from 19th century experiences of defense against possible overland invasion and from the more recent threat of sea attack. The defense system rested on the erection and control of a military barrier along the northwest land frontier and on the continued dominance by the British navy in the Indian Ocean and control over its three entrances, the Red Sea, the Cape, and the Malacca straits. The ultimate responsibility for Indian defense against external attack by a major power lay on the UK. After the First World War the British decided that India, if isolated from the rest of the empire in an emergency, should be prepared to bear more of the weight of its own defense and, as well, the defense of other segments of the empire in the Indian Ocean region. The specific revisions in military planning that followed led to the creation of the Indian navy with responsibilities for coastal defense. The need for economic self-sufficiency and the desirability of a major Indian military supply centre for imperial operations helped to foster British recognition of the need for Indian industrial development. But the Indian army remained, until the defense plan of 1938, essentially a continental defense force without permanently assigned overseas obligations.

During the inter-war period pressure was brought to bear on

India to take on a certain regional share of the burden of imperial defense.[49] The Indian legislature opposed that pressure, notably by a resolution in 1921, and the government hesitated to place Indian forces at the automatic disposal of the empire. Indian nationalist leaders until the outbreak of the Second World War, and some of them beyond that time, opposed using Indian forces for any purposes other than immediate national defense. Ultimately, the Indian government responded positively to a succession of special British requests in the 1920's and 1930's and agreed to make Indian troops available for service in Iraq, the Persian oil fields, Aden, Palestine, Somaliland, Egypt, Singapore, Burma, Malaya, and Hong Kong. By 1939 "India had become responsible not only for the defense of her frontiers, but also for the protection of Indian waters and the surrounding countries...."[50] During the Second World War, when India was threatened by land, sea, and air attacks from Japanese forces in southeast Asia, the Indian armed forces grew to over two and one-half million men and were committed to allied positions from the Mediterranean to the South China Sea.

The legacies of British Indian defense policy were apparent to anyone in contact with the post-independence Indian military forces. Pakistanis manned the Afghan frontier and dealt with the tribes of that region, and India and Pakistan found it necessary to construct military defenses along their new common, artificial boundary in the northwest and at the Kashmir cease-fire line : those were the major changes. For independent India the Himalayas and Tibet still stood as they had for the British, as majestic and impenetrable barriers which required little human effort to maintain. (That legacy proved to be a dangerous delusion.) Security from the sea for two centuries had been provided by British naval dominance, only briefly challenged by the Japanese in 1942. That security remained after 1947 because the British navy continued to provide it from the great bases at Singapore, Trincomalee, and in the Red Sea. Indians remained complacent about maritime dangers, despite the urgent writings of K. M. Panikkar, even into the 1960's. As an essentially continental state with leaders from the Gangetic plain possessing a continental mentality, India for almost two decades after independence failed to look purposefully toward the sea for defense preparations. The Indian navy, efficient for its size and under the command of British officers until 1954, was neglected. The imperial duties of the Indian army, of course, ended in 1947. The last of the overseas units, which had brought Indians into disfavour in southeast Asia, had returned home before the transfer of power; the legacy of overseas service was repudiated warmly by Indian leaders. The Anglicized character of the Indian officer corps, the great tradition and even mystique of some of the units, contributed to the effectiveness of India's fighting forces after 1947.

It is appropriate to end this introduction to the foreign relations of independent India on the subject of the individual Indians who carried forward their country's interests into the contemporary period. Their combined experience with foreign affairs formed an asset to the new government that compared favourably with the assets in personnel of many established states. Indians had been staffing some of their government's diplomatic posts since before the First World War. Not only in London but in the dominions and colonies Indian commissioners and agents-general were posted between the wars so that the Government of India could deal directly with those states and territories. Indian officials, usually under Foreign Office jurisdiction and usually under British chiefs of mission, handled India's and the empire's affairs in Persia, Afghanistan, and Nepal. Indian trade commissioners were appointed to such places as Hamburg, Alexandria, and Zanzibar. During the Second World War India's officers held posts in allied capitals, notably staffing the important purchasing mission in Washington. In international organizations India rightly complained of poor representation, but Indians did appear on international civil service rosters as well as on official delegations.

At home the expanding international ties after the First World War fell under the jurisdiction of the Foreign and Political Department, which was replaced by the External Affairs Department in 1937. A Department of Indians Overseas was created in 1941, which became the Department of Commonwealth Relations in 1944. In the Interim Government in 1946 Nehru held the portfolios of the External Relations and Commonwealth Relations Departments, which were merged in June 1947, resulting finally in the Ministry of External Affairs.

The training and personality of the Indians in government service before independence set the style and contributed in some measure to the ideas which characterized Indian foreign policy after 1947. A respect for international law and the conventions which underlie it ; an appreciation of the verbal approach to solving problems, which often leads to compromise ; moderation in personal behaviour and in ideas, coupled with a formality that often reflected class and caste status—those were some of the traits that Indians shared with their British colleagues as they undertook sovereign responsibilities. The British legacy, the continuity of tradition, had the advantage of providing "a ready model from which a quick copy could be made."[51] But the losses from the process of copying became obvious as the new service struggled to discover its own personality, and when the advocates of new initiatives in foreign policy clashed with those reared in the older tradition. There were, of course, new ideas, notably those of one of the greatest critics of the imperial tradition, Jawaharlal Nehru. He was the dominant personality, the major decision-maker on the Indian political scene. And it is largely his contributions that make up what appears in the following chapters.

NOTES AND REFERENCES

[1] Ton That Thien, *India and South East Asia 1947-1960*, Geneva 1963, p. 7.

[2] In the words of an Indian author : "It may well be said that the foundations of India's international status were firmly laid even while India was yet a dependency." S. R. Mehrotra, *India and the Commonwealth 1885-1929*, pp. 240-41.

[3] Lord Hardinge, speaking in his Council on a resolution of Khan Bahadur M.M. Shafi in behalf of India's representation at Imperial Conferences, said : "No conference can afford to debate great Imperial issues in which India is vitally concerned, and at the same time disregard her. To discuss questions affecting the defense of the Empire without taking India into account, would be to ignore the value and interests of the greatest Military asset of the Empire outside the United Kingdom." Quoted in P. Mukherji, *Indian Constitutional Documents, 1600-1918*, vol. I, Calcutta 1918, p. 611. See also discussion of this issue in S. R. Mehrotra, *op. cit.*, chapter II.

[4] The phrase referring to India was incorporated by an amendment proposed by S. P. Sinha of the Indian delegation. Prime Minister Robert Borden of Canada, the mover of the resolution, accepted Sinha's amendment, noting however, that "through the presence of the Secretary of State for India in the British

Cabinet, India already has had perhaps a greater voice in foreign relations than the Overseas Dominions." Imperial War Conference, 1917, *Extracts from Minutes of Proceedings and Papers Laid before the Conference*, pp. 5, 49-50.

[5] "The High Commissioner has taken over from the India Office such part of Indian official work as is of an agency character, and politics do not fall within his sphere." Gerald E. H. Palmer, *Consultation and Co-operation in the British Commonwealth*, London 1934, p. 68.

[6] See the Report of the Committee of Inter-Imperial Relations, in Imperial Conference, 1926, *Summary of Proceedings and Appendices*. The statement was confirmed by the Statute of Westminster, 1931.

[7] See chapter XII, ahead.

[8] India had also presented a memorandum to the 1911 conference, of which it was not a full member. Therein its representative, the Secretary of State for India, Lord Crewe, noted the "grave fact that a radically false conception of the real position of India is undoubtedly rife in many parts of the Empire" and regarded as ludicrous, if it had not been so grave, that "regulations framed with an eye to coolies should affect ruling princes who are in subordinate alliance with His Majesty, . . . members of the Privy Council of the Empire, or gentlemen who have the honour to be His Majesty's own Aides-de-Camp." Lord Crewe put forward the thesis that "each dominion owes responsibility to the rest of the Empire for ensuring that its domestic policy shall not unnecessarily create embarrassments in the administration of India." Quoted in Imperial War Conference, 1918, *Extracts from Minutes of Proceedings and Papers Laid before the Conference*, p. 196.

[9] Imperial War Conference, 1917, *Extracts from Minutes of Proceedings and Papers Laid before the Conference*, p. 7.

[10] Canadian rules, e.g. required an immigrant to arrive by steamer making a continuous voyage from the country of origin, which was then impossible for Indians using commercial vessels.

[11] The Indian Memorandum of 1917, prepared at the India Office, referred to Indians' grievances over racial discrimination as "in a great measure matters of sentiment. . . . If the dominions would make concessions which would meet feelings of this order, they would probably find that India would not be unreasonable on material points." Imperial War Conference, 1917, *op. cit.*, p. 161.

[12] The debate and lobbying on this resolution was keen, with General Smuts defending one position and V. S. Srinivasa Sastri, the Indian representative, supported by Secretary of State Montagu, the head of the delegation, promoting the other. See P. Kodanda Rao, *The Right Honourable V. S. Srinivasa Sastri ; A Political Biography*, p. 98f.

[13] Peel noted the intense concern on this issue among Indians and said : "The Viceroy, in his private letters, is constantly explaining and pressing upon me how strongly the feeling of soreness and bitterness is growing on this subject, and how, in many ways, the task of wisely governing India is made more difficult by this intensity of feeling." Imperial Conference, 1923, *Appendices to the Summary of Proceedings*, p. 67.

[14] "Any inequality of Indian nationals enters like iron into our souls," said

Sapru. "It permeates and sours our whole outlook in regard to Imperial relationship." *ibid.*, p. 74.

[15] Claiming that he was a fighter for King George he uttered his famous words, "I fight for a place in his household and not in his stables." *ibid.*, p. 72.

[16] Referring to Sapru's concern for "Izzat," General Smuts, the South African Prime Minister, said : "For South Africa, for White South Africa, it is not a question of dignity, but a question of existence, and no government could for a moment either tamper with this position or do anything to meet the Indian point of view." *ibid.*, p. 115.

[17] W. K. Hancock, *Survey of British Commonwealth Affairs*, vol. 1 : *Problems of Nationality*, p. 175.

[18] See the graphic illustration of these trends in Vera Anstey, *The Economic Development of India*, p. 334 ; also H. Venkatasubbiah, *Foreign Trade of India : 1900-1940 ; A Statistical Analysis*, Bombay 1946, pp. 48-49.

[19] See Anstey, *op. cit.*, p. 264. India was still heavily dependent in those years on imported yarn, but imports of piece goods were declining rapidly and accounted for about 35 per cent of the total supply in 1925-1926.

[20] No grant of fiscal autonomy could be made by statute without undermining the ultimate authority of parliament and the Crown, but the British government decided to allow a convention to grow up whereby the Secretary of State did not interfere with India's trading policies—unless they were out of line with general imperial interests. This was the origin of the fiscal autonomy convention, adopted in 1921. See Govt. of India, *Memorandum Submitted to the Indian Statutory Commission*, Calcutta 1930, vol. 2, pp. 1,334-35.

[21] Imperial Economic Conference, 1923, *Record of Proceedings and Documents*, pp. 51, 195-96.

[22] The Indian National Congress opposed the agreement and in 1936 registered its formal disapproval of the accord by rejecting a resolution in the legislative assembly supporting the supplementary Indo-British trade agreement of 1935. The agreement reached at Ottawa could be ratified by the Indian legislature in 1932 only because the Congress members had given up their seats.

[23] cf. Vera Anstey, *op. cit.*, p. 504f.

[24] See "Tariffs and Industry," a study by John Mathai, a member of the tariff board for nine years and its President from 1931 to 1934 ; Oxford Pamphlets on Indian Affairs, no. 20, 1944, pp. 6-7.

[25] About 1,200,000 Indian officers and men served in overseas operations during the war; the Indian legislature voted about £112 million to the war effort from the Indian budget.

[26] In *Memorandum submitted to the Indian Statutory Commission by the Government of India,* vol. 2, p. 1,632. In more concrete terms, in cases of a conflict between Indian and British interests in League debates, the Secretary of State acted as head of the Government of India rather than as a member of the British government and thus "he does not use his power to impose on the Indian delegation an artificial solidarity with the British delegates. . . . In matters which are not of first-class political importance it is not necessary that the seven British Empire Members of the League should preserve a united front." *ibid.*, p. 1,633.

[27] The "modus operandi" worked out in 1920 was : "(1) That a formal deci-sion to the effect that either the Secretary of State or the Government of India is the proper authority in Imperial and international questions should be avoided ; (2) that it should be tacitly recognized that the Secretary of State is, as a fact, responsible for the representation of India in those questions ; but (3) that the appointments and instructions should be subject to prior consultation and agree-ment between the Government in India and the Secretary of State ; and (4) that reports should be addressed according to circumstances." *Memorandum . . .,* *op. cit.,* p. 1,644.

[28] cf. A. B. Keith : "It was impossible to convince foreign opinion that the dominions were really autonomous, and indeed the doubt persisted for years after there had been seen the spectacle of the dominions freely disagreeing with the United Kingdom at meetings of the [League] Assembly." *Sovereignty of the British Dominions,* p. 386.

[29] *Report of the Delegates of India to the First Session of the Assembly of the League of Nations,* p. 43.

[30] Maharaja of Patiala, *Report on the League of Nations Assembly,* 1925, pp. 17, 19. V. S. Srinivasa Sastri, an Indian delegate in 1923, wrote, in contrast to the views of the maharaja, that India's delegation was not under instructions from London, but that a memorandum from the government of India was the basis of India's stands in the Assembly. If instructions had come from the India Office, wrote Sastri, : "We should have repudiatedi t with indignation. India Office has nothing to do with it. It is the Government of India which we represent." *Speeches and Writings of V. S. Srinivasa Sastri,* p. 414. From the other evidence now available it appears that Sastri was in essential error, although the memoran-dum he referred to may have indeed come from India.

[31] *Report of the Delegates of India to the Eighth Session of the Assembly of the League of Nations,* p. 4. From the fifth session the Indian delegation reported that : "As far as the principal questions before the Assembly, namely, that of reduction of armaments, security and arbitration, were concerned, the position of India, like that of the dominions, was necessarily one of subordinate co-operation with the British delegation. Such objections as the Delegation thought fit to urge against certain provisions in the drafts under consideration it was found more convenient to express in the informal meetings of the Empire Delega-tion than in open Committee or in the Assembly." *Report of the Delegates of India . . .1924,* p. 12.

[32] *Final Report of the Delegates of India to the Ninth Session . . .1928,* p. 1.

[33] *Ibid.,* p. 37.

[34] Patiala, *op. cit.,* pp. 58-59.

[35] The Indian government had sovereign power to bind the states on any matters which brought them into relations with foreign countries, but not to control their internal policies. Because the India which was a League member was the entire country, not just British India, the government had to make a special case to have the states exempted from certain international commitments. A ruling maharaja's presence on the Indian delegation signified nothing about

princely India's commitment to the work of the League. His presence there was largely "ornamental."

[36] A discussion of India's international obligations stemming from its League membership appears in Lanka Sundaram, *India in World Politics*, p. 39f.

[37] *Report of the Delegates of India. . .1927*, p. 100.

[38] *Report of the Delegates of India . . .1929*, p. 78.

[39] A good discussion of India and the ILO appears in Lanka Sundaram, *op. cit.*

[40] Quoted in N. N. Kaul, *India and the International Labour Organization*, p. 64.

[41] See *ibid.*

[42] League of Nations, *Official Journal : Records of the 9th Ordinary Session of the Assembly*, Geneva 1928, pp. 50-51.

[43] Quoted in W. K. Hancock, *Survey of British Commonwealth Affairs*, vol. 1 : *Problems of Nationality*, p. 211.

[44] *Indian Legislative Assembly Debates, Official Report*, vol. 3, 1923, parts VI and VII, p. 4,568.

[45] *Memorandum submitted to the Indian Statutory Commission, op. cit.*, p. 1,637. An effort to adjourn the assembly in 1937 to consider China's appeal to the League against Japanese aggression was disallowed on grounds that it was detrimental to the national interest. See *Indian Legislative Assembly Debates, Official Report*, vol. V, 1937, pp. 1,888-89, and 1902. At the imperial conference of 1937, the Indian government's incapacity to express its views on the impending world political crisis was frankly admitted by Muhammad Zafrullah Khan of the Indian delegation. Defense and foreign affairs were the main topics of the conference ; "both these," said Zafrullah Khan, "are subjects respecting which the Government of India is responsible, and even under the Federal Constitution will continue to be responsible, not to the people of India but to the United Kingdom Parliament." Imperial Conference, 1937, *Summary of Proceedings*, p. 70.

[46] *Report of the Delegates of India . . .1928*, p. 32.

[47] See *Indian Legislative Assembly Debates, Official Report*, vol. I, 1939, pp. 170-200.

[48] *Indian Annual Register*, 1939, vol. I, pp. 341-42.

[49] An appreciation of British strategic planning for India is available in B. Prasad, *Defense of India : Policy and Plans*, chapters I and II in particular.

[50] *ibid.*, p. 58.

[51] Nair, N. Parameswaran, "The Administration of Foreign Affairs in India with Comparative Reference to Britain," unpublished Ph. D. dissertation, Indian School of International Studies, 1963, p. 644.

CHAPTER II

THE COMMONWEALTH ATTACHMENT
AND RELATIONS WITH THE
UNITED KINGDOM

ONE DOES NOT need to partake of the Commonwealth mystique
to recognize the fact that Prime Minister Nehru did so, and that
the Commonwealth attachment embodied many of the continuities
of Indian foreign relations in the 20th century. The areas of official
Indian involvement dealt with in the previous chapter remained
important after independence, as did the Commonwealth context
in which they originated. For some years after 1947 the Commonwealth also continued to be the vehicle for India's contacts with a
wider international arena. India's decision not to leave the Commonwealth, taken in 1947 and reaffirmed in 1949 (after Eire and
Burma had opted out) equalled a decision not to break with the past.
A great deal had to be added on to past policies in order to meet
the needs of a sovereign democracy, but the process adopted by the
Indian government was one of building on established foundations
of domestic and international law and custom, not of ripping them
away. The Commonwealth, in nomenclature as well as in content
transmuted from the British empire and the British Commonwealth
of Nations, was one of the initial cornerstones upon which India's
foreign relations were built.

The Commonwealth relationship for India had to be understood
as something different from relations with the UK, although Indian
critics of the tie were loth to accept that interpretation and tended
to react to every dispute between India and Britain with renewed
demands to sever Commonwealth connections. But the associations
built up in the Commonwealth had a merit of their own, and the
benefits of India's membership were frequently cited by supporters
of the association. Economic relations with the UK remained
strong long after independence ; and later, in Africa, were more
easily established with members of the Commonwealth than with

32

the other newly independent states. In the post-war era of closed borders and travel restrictions Indians enjoyed a relatively greater freedom of movement within the Commonwealth and empire than outside of it. India's defense after 1947 was no longer the responsibility of Britain, but a tacit understanding remained that London would not be indifferent to the security of India as a member of the Commonwealth. In a broader context, Indian and other Commonwealth governments reinforced each other in some international conferences and important capitals, the English speaking officials exchanging information and providing helpful contact on a closer basis than took place with "foreign" delegations and missions. In domestic life the Commonwealth tie nurtured the academic, cultural, and professional links on which modern Indians had depended for over a century; to break those links before others were established, for example with the US, would have been self-defeating. In defending his decision not to repudiate Commonwealth membership, Nehru told the Indian parliament, "if we dissociate ourselves from the Commonwealth, then for a moment we are completely isolated."[1]

The intangible assets of Commonwealth membership were more important than the tangible ones in the 1940's and remained so even after India had emerged from its chrysalis of dominion status and developed its own arrangements for the conduct of foreign relations. "India's close association with a worldwide group of nations," wrote K. M. Panikkar, "gives her a prestige and influence which she would not otherwise possess."[2] Membership in the Commonwealth signified a state's attachment to certain values and modes of behaviour in political affairs which were originally sponsored by Britain and generally praised by other countries. The attachment was not only self-proclaimed but—and here was the source of the prestige—was acknowledged by other states. Moreover, voluntary membership of the Commonwealth, as distinct from being part of the British empire, implied equality of status and full independence —an important consideration for newly independent states.

The Commonwealth functioned like a club, in the British meaning of that term.[3] Its exclusiveness gave it some immediate measure of importance, and its prestige carried over to all its members. At unprescribed intervals of approximately two years, the prime ministers of the member states met in conference, as if in a well-

3

appointed lounge ; there were no rules save those of good manners, no agenda, no minutes, and only the most general statement was issued at the conclusion. The chief ceremonial embellishment of these meetings continued to be a well photographed joint audience with the reigning British monarch : symbol and head of the Commonwealth, focus of the pomp and heraldry to which even ardent republicans were seldom averse. The club image did not adequately convey all the meanings that the Commonwealth held for Nehru. For him that loose association was the epitome of "civilized" political behaviour, the repository of a certain "content of democracy," and the provider of a "temper of peaceful discussion." As he told the Commonwealth parliamentary conference in December 1957, "restraint in behaviour and restraint and consideration shown towards one's neighbours are a badge of civilization. . . . Democracy, in other words, is peaceful co-existence, not only between those who are like each other but also between those who are unlike each other. . . . What strikes me about the Commonwealth is not so much the points of likeness, . . . but rather the points of difference which have not been allowed to come in the way of our meeting."[4]

India itself made a major contribution to diversity within the Commonwealth when it created the precedent of retaining its membership after becoming a republic. Nehru won Congress party approval for his course of action in December 1948 and overcame strenuous opposition from those—such as the Socialist and Communist parties—who wished for a complete break with the immediate past, by stressing the genuine freedom of action permitted within the new Commonwealth. He denied that Indian independence in foreign policies was compromised in any way by membership in the Commonwealth.[5] The Labour government in the UK on its side, consulted all the members and prepared the way for the historic change in the Commonwealth's constitutional structure ;[6] the sole purpose of the prime ministers' conference in April 1949 was to consider the problem posed by India's request to continue membership as a republic. A suitable solution was found in India's "acceptance of The King as the symbol of the free association of its independent member nations, and as such the Head of the Commonwealth."[7] Thereby, the Crown, common allegiance to which had been the binding tie of the Commonwealth since its inception, was transformed for India's sake into a symbol of a free connection and divested of all authority or function as constitutional head of state for the new republic. (The British monarch was honoured in her personal capacity, but, unlike the dominions, India issued no proclamation of title on the occasion of Queen Elizabeth II's coronation in 1953.) The Indian Constituent Assembly confirmed Nehru's decision in May 1949 and in October of that year abolished Indian juridical appeals to the Privy Council, thereby severing the last legal link with the UK.

The 1949 decision on India's membership prevented the Commonwealth from dwindling to a small group of white dominions bound to Britain by ties of kinship and culture, and made it instead a bridge between races and continents. Not only did Pakistan and Ceylon choose to follow the example of India rather than Burma, but Ghana in 1957 and other African states later found it advantageous to embrace the Commonwealth tie while discarding their legal dependence on the UK. Until 1958 all members shared a commitment to a representative parliamentary form of government ; the authoritarian systems subsequently adopted in some member states introduced a new, and not entirely welcome element of diversity into the growing group. The club lost its former harmony of likemindedness and greater effort was needed to preserve the illusion of unstructured and agreeable discussion on divisive issues.

The Commonwealth demonstrated its flexibility by surviving these changes, but it was not unaffected by them. A strain between the older white members and the newer non-white members became especially evident in the 1960 and 1961 discussions on South Africa's continued membership after it would become a republic. The Commonwealth was faced with the implicit choice of losing one or several of its members ; it chose the former. South Africa was virtually compelled to withdraw "in the light of the views expressed on behalf of other member Governments and indications of their future intentions regarding the racial policy of the Union Government. ..."[8] Discussions by the prime ministers at the conferences of 1964 and 1966 on Rhodesia revealed a split of opinion on what policy the UK and the Commonwealth as a whole should adopt towards the Ian Smith regime. The lively debates also revealed that the now huge Commonwealth[9] was functioning more like the UN than like the formerly intimate club, which had relied heavily on a consensus of opinion.

CONSULTATION AND COOPERATION

The main functions of the Commonwealth were consultation and cooperation. Members were expected to exchange full information and engage in prior consultation on matters of common concern. This convention afforded India an opportunity of influencing the policies of other member states, especially on the changing situation in Asia after the war—a matter of vital concern to India. The UK, Australia, and New Zealand were invited to the conference held in New Delhi in January 1949 on Indonesia as well as to a smaller informal conference in February to discuss the disrupted conditions in Burma. Nothing concrete emerged from the latter meeting, but renewed discussions at the prime ministers' conference later that year led to offers of assistance to the new Burmese government. Asian affairs dominated the talks at the Commonwealth foreign ministers' conference held in Colombo in January 1950. The communique showed the impress of Nehru's thought : progress and security would most likely come about through the improvement of economic conditions ; "progressive policies" in southeast Asia could contribute to world peace.[10] The conference welcomed recent Indonesian independence and discussed recognition of the Peoples Republic of China ; it was there that the initial planning for the Colombo Plan began.

The revolution in China required revised policies by democratic states with interests in Asia, and Nehru was anxious that his proposition of drawing China into the ranks of peaceful, "civilized" states through friendship gain Commonwealth acceptance. For some years it did, especially in the UK and Canada, which were keen to have ties with both India and China and willing to accept Nehru as the spokesman for the aspirations of a new Asia. During the Korean war, when US policy tended toward a vigorous military response to China's moves, some Commonwealth governments supported India's efforts to mediate the conflict and limit UN military objectives. At the Geneva conference of 1954 Anthony Eden, British foreign minister, wanted to obtain at least the benevolent approval of India, Pakistan and Ceylon, as well as other Commonwealth states, to the settlement being worked out over Indo-China; to this end he tried to keep their governments abreast of the course of the negotiations and was "encouraged by the close accord maintained throughout the conference" by Commonwealth governments, including India.[11] British colonial policy was also influenced, to some extent, by the existence of an anti-colonial sentiment, as in India, within the Commonwealth.

Indian policy, too, was not unaffected by intra-Commonwealth discussions, and Nehru informed parliament in 1950 that "we do hardly anything without consulting the countries of the Commonwealth."[12] Almost forgotten a decade later was the moral support which Nehru gave to British and hence to Western interests at the early prime ministers' conferences. In October 1948 India subscribed to the communique which stressed the community of outlook among Commonwealth members on economic and defense problems as well as their resolve to work together with other governments "to establish world peace on a democratic basis."[13] The public release of the 1951 conference, after emphasizing the need for negotiated settlement between the two sides of the "cold war," restated the members' resolve, as long as the threat of aggression existed, to strengthen their defenses "with all speed and diligence."[14] Again in 1953 the Commonwealth prime ministers agreed that "no opportunity should be lost of composing . . . the differences which at present divide the world. But they recognized that the democracies must maintain their strength and exercise unceasing vigilance to preserve their rights and liberties."[15] That same year Nehru told the Lok Sabha that the nations of the North Atlantic Treaty Organization (NATO) "have every right to defend themselves. They have every right to fight against any aggression that may come to them"—provided that they did not use their power in defense of colonialism.[16] Nevertheless, Nehru continued to assert that India's manoeuvrability was not hampered by its Commonwealth membership.

The early Commonwealth conferences illustrated the link between consultation and hope of conversion, as well as the assumption that there would be no clash of vital interests between member states. But by the mid-1950's the assumption was no longer valid ; India's regional security interests collided with those of Commonwealth countries which had joined the US in extending military alliances into west and southeast Asia. India's sympathy diminished sharply for Western defense policies, and Western support for India's nonalignment was yet to be born—despite sympathy in

Canada and efforts made by the British to reconcile the views of Nehru and America's John Foster Dulles.[17] There were tentative consultations in connection with a southeast Asian security arrangement, but India drew away from such involvements. With the divergence of policy on vital security matters the value of Commonwealth consultations declined.

The obligation of Commonwealth members to "inform or consult, as may be appropriate, all other members on any projected action which might affect their interests, especially in relation to foreign affairs,"[18] was seldom completely fulfilled. When the UK devalued the pound sterling without prior warning in 1949, India's finance minister opined that "in a matter which so vitally affects the whole economy of every country in the sterling area," the Commonwealth finance ministers should have been called to secret conference "before this decision was sprung upon them."[19] India itself tried to avoid all discussions on Kashmir, thereby upholding the custom that intra-Commonwealth disputes should not be allowed to disturb the equanimity of the conferences. But in 1948 and 1951 the Pakistani prime minister managed to introduce informal talks on the subject in London. In 1964 the Commonwealth prime ministers in their communique referred to differences between the Indian and Pakistani governments and expressed "their hopes that the problem between their countries will be solved in the same friendly spirit"[20] that characterized the recent statements made by Prime Minister Sastri and President Ayub Khan. On another issue of intense national feeling, Goa, India made its decision to take over the Portuguese colony without conferring with Commonwealth governments.

The Suez crisis of 1956 caused the most serious breach of the convention of consultation. The negotiations following the nationalization of the canal revealed the vast differences of approach among Commonwealth members. Governments adhering to the British line, such as Australia, received more candid and confidential treatment in London than governments, such as India attempting to mediate between the UK and Egypt. For the UK as for India the Suez Canal was a matter of vital economic and security interest. Britain's course of action leading to the attack on Egypt was worked out with France ; Commonwealth countries were merely informed of the decision. India's shock at the UK's apparent reversion to the procedures of imperialism and repudiation of all that the new Commonwealth stood for produced a vociferous public debate on breaking or retaining the Commonwealth tie. The opening question was posed by C. Rajagopalachari : "Must we retain what remains as but an evil-smelling shell?"[21] All the advantages and disadvantages were aired precisely, and Nehru continued to urge the critics to examine the Commonwealth without emotion and value it as an example of consultation among governments holding diametrically opposing views. The vehement disapproval of the Anglo-French action by the Labour minority party and an articulate public within the UK may have saved the Commonwealth.[22] In the UN it was largely the cooperation of India and Canada that produced a formula for a cease-fire and peace-keeping, which received the support of all Commonwealth states.

The Suez episode was glossed over and within a few years the Commonwealth appeared almost as lively as before, though with reaffirmed leeway for each member to pursue its separate foreign policies. Conferences took place not only between the prime ministers, but also between foreign ministers, finance ministers, and representatives of functional Commonwealth organizations. Nehru's concern for the issue of nuclear arms was shared by others, and in March 1961 the Commonwealth came out with a joint appeal for general disarmament and the creation of a global authority for inspection and control. That was "the first occasion on which members of the Commonwealth have sought, on a public issue, to exercise a collective influence in international affairs."[23] In the years following, as American policy in southeast Asia greatly increased the risks of war in that region, India, Britain, and Canada urged caution on Washington and tried to discover a means of reaching peaceful settlements. In June 1965 the prime ministers' conference pleaded for new US efforts to reach a non-military solution in Vietnam. The conference set up a mission, headed by the British prime minister, to urge suspension of US bombing of North Vietnam, to gain North Vietnamese agreement to end its infiltrations into the south, and to assist in convening a peace conference leading to neutralizing of the country, the establishment there of an international peace force, and ultimate reunification.[24]

Another example of constructive consultation among Commonwealth members took place when the UK sought approval—

not a veto, or mere confirmation of a fait accompli—for its decision to seek entry into the European Economic Community (EEC). Every country likely to be affected, including India, discussed internally the hurtful implications of this move. Britain faced severe criticism at the prime ministers' conference of 1962, which finally agreed that when negotiations between the UK and the EEC were resumed "British Ministers would take full account of the views, both general and particular, which had been expressed on behalf of other Commonwealth Governments at this Meeting and would continue their efforts to safeguard essential Commonwealth interests."[25]

Though Britain's entry into the EEC was blocked by France, its decision to apply for membership was of great significance for the rest of the Commonwealth. To an important extent Commonwealth countries had come to rely on the system of imperial preferences described in the previous chapter and had neglected to search for non-Commonwealth markets. The revelation of Britain's weakness without either the empire or Europe to support it was a blow to the Commonwealth, which had been aptly compared to a wheel with the UK at the hub and the other members on the circumference.[26] The diminution in the UK's status of leadership was reflected in the suggestions made to rotate the venues for conferences and otherwise modify the British monopoly on important functions of the Commonwealth. At the same time attempts were made to formalize the consultative and cooperative associations, which no state was willing to destroy. One expression was the revival in 1964 of a twenty-year-old idea of a Commonwealth secretariat.[27] India agreed to its formation only reluctantly (as did the UK) perhaps because it mistrusted the tightening of an institution whose value was seen as lying partly in its lack of rigidity. India also opposed the idea of a Commonwealth court of appeals voiced in 1966.

The Commonwealth provided means of cooperation among member states greater than opportunities for consultation ; the form of cooperation most useful to India was economic assistance from developed to underdeveloped members. The benefits were not entirely one-sided because India also provided assistance to less developed Commonwealth states within the Colombo Plan,[28] and its nationals, notably technical personnel, added skills to certain Commonwealth nations and imperial territories.

Chapter XIV outlines the main trends in India's economic relations after 1947 and discusses the external assistance programmes. To anticipate, the Commonwealth share in India's trade fell during the 1950's ; the US and, later, West Germany and the USSR were the major national sources of economic aid, but British private investors remained far ahead of all others in the amount and diversity of their holdings in India. Commonwealth economic and technical assistance was overshadowed by the massive American programmes, but in crucial areas, such as steel production and nuclear technology, British and Canadian help left major marks. In December 1959 a consortium of British steel interests brought into production India's third public sector steel mill, at Durgapur, West Bengal ; the British government underwrote the investment with a loan equivalent to $42 million. At Trombay, near Bombay, the Canadians joined with the Indian government to construct and supply the world's largest international project in peaceful uses of atomic energy, a radio-isotope reactor, which began operation in July 1960.

While it functioned, the sterling area, of which India remained a member, provided another form of Commonwealth cooperation. It maintained a central clearing house for international transactions, especially useful when dollar exchanges had to be controlled and dollar reserves pooled. The fact that the UK owned India substantial sums after the war—even after deducting India's previous debts to the UK—obliged India to remain within the sterling area and abide by its rules of currency withdrawal. In the 1950's the sterling area ceased to have much usefulness. India depleted its sterling reserves, developed its own central banking system, and engaged in trading and financial relationships outside the sterling area. London's position as international banker weakened, and crises recurred for the pound sterling. By the 1960's, the Commonwealth no longer acted as a unit in an international financial crisis, because the problems of each member state were different.

During the two world wars the Empire-Commonwealth had coordinated its defense strategy ; cooperation within the Commonwealth traditionally implied a continual reinforcement of defense policies among member states. But India's posture of nonalignment after independence was achieved partly by its refusing to associate in any formal manner with Commonwealth defense policies. Neither

Nehru himself nor his Cabinet officials participated in discussions on military strategy and planning, frequently held in conjunction with prime ministers' conferences.[29] In view of the divergent security policies of India and later Ceylon, on the one hand, and the rest of the Commonwealth including Pakistan, on the other hand, the most that could be expected was that Commonwealth states would not undermine each other's defenses. But the Indo-Pakistani hostility created an example of enmity—the first of its kind—between independent states of the Commonwealth.

If the conditions of the new Commonwealth lacked the "high instincts and instantaneous cohesion"[30] of the old association, Britain at least remained true to the principle that "it would be impossible for Her Majesty's Government to engage in hostilities against any member of the Commonwealth."[31] Except for Ceylon and Pakistan all Commonwealth states supported India verbally when the Chinese attacked in 1962, and Britain immediately supplied equipment to Indian forces.

SPECIAL PROBLEMS

Issues of recurring importance in the empire and Commonwealth were freedom of movement and settlement by the natives of one country in another member country and common citizenship rights. At a conference of Commonwealth countries held in 1947 recommendations were made to consider Commonwealth citizens on a more favourable basis than other aliens in matters of travel and naturalization. That principle was generally accepted, and Indians benefited from the resulting privileges afforded them. Reciprocally, India extended similar special rights to the nationals of other Commonwealth countries, except South Africa and Pakistan ; those included exemption from the elaborate rules for issuing visas and controlling aliens contained in the Foreigners Act of 1946 and the Foreigners Order of 1948. No common nationality was implied, however, by the term, Commonwealth citizen, which remained, in its ideal formulation, unrealized. "A Commonwealth citizen simply means that an individual possesses the citizenship of some Commonwealth country and nothing more."[32] Each independent Commonwealth country had its own citizenship laws; India's was the Citizenship Act of 1955.

The citizenship laws of the dominions did not materially assist Indians wishing to settle permanently there, or guarantee them equality of treatment if they did so. Only the UK permitted free entry by Commonwealth citizens and British subjects ; it held steadfastly to the idea in domestic policy that a multi-racial Commonwealth should stand also for racial equality. But the British adherence to this principle finally weakened under the impact of an unprecedented influx of nonwhite immigrants from the Indian subcontinent and the West Indies.

In 1958 for the first time on a large scale, English cities experienced racial incidents, in which Indians, among others, were involved. The British government sent an aide memoire to the Indian and other governments asking for help in restricting the flow of their emigrants. India tried to do so. But pressures in the UK from the native Whites for an end to the policy of open immigration rose with the increase in the coloured immigrant population. The resulting Immigration and Deportation, Commonwealth Citizens Act, of 1962 placed restrictions on the free entry of Indians and other Commonwealth citizens into Great Britain. Clearly aimed at coloured immigration, the act nevertheless did not cut out the movement of qualified persons of any race. In the first year of the working of the act, for example, a net Indian immigration of 10,450 headed the list of Commonwealth migrants into Britain ; Pakistanis numbering 3,481 followed and then West Indians and Africans.[33] The Indian government took the position that it had formulated years earlier, that fair treatment of Indians already settled abroad was of greater concern than continued unrestricted migration.

New Delhi's seemingly unshakeable aplomb when dealing with questions of British racial policies finally dissolved in early 1968, when the British parliament passed emergency legislation to restrict the inflow into the UK of persons of Indian and Pakistani origins (so-called Asians) living in Kenya and holding British passports. Faced with a step-up in Africanization of jobs and businesses in Kenya and rumours of impending withdrawal of the right of free entry into the UK for nonwhite subjects, many Kenyan Asians had scrambled to reach the UK fearing that their opportunity to do so might soon be curtailed. The panic which affected the Asians influenced the British labour government to act in equal haste to introduce a measure which was explicitly discriminatory on grounds of race.

Effective on March 3, the law introduced the novel doctrine that a British passport holder could be excluded from entering the UK ; previous restrictions had applied only to nationals of Commonwealth countries. Spokesmen of the Indian government in parliament held that the UK had a moral and legal responsibility for its citizens of whatever race, and before the bill was passed warned of the "serious repercussions on Indo-British friendly relations and on the concept of the Commonwealth"[34] that would follow its enactment. Indeed, in India and elsewhere the new law undermined, possibly irreparably, the considerable confidence in British sense of fair play, in what Nehru would have called "civilized behaviour." Within the UK, however, legal equality among races still prevailed, and for domestic racial discrimination backed by law India reserved its harshest condemnation.

For several decades South Africa was the target of Indian criticism because it placed Indian settlers, along with Africans and coloureds, in a permanent position of inferiority within the country. India had raised the issue of South African racial policies in the imperial conferences, had threatened to take it to the League of Nations, and in 1946 initiated the discussion of it before the UN General Assembly. For many years, however, India refused to lay it before the Commonwealth prime ministers' conferences ; Nehru considered that the introduction of intra-Commonwealth disputes relating to domestic matters would threaten the integrity of the association.[35] On the delicate matter of race relations India preferred to deal bilaterally with countries such as Britain and Kenya ; took no action in cases such as Fiji and British Guiana, where Indians had migrated in substantial numbers ; did not officially condemn the "White Australia" policy—blatantly racial in purpose —because it upheld the right of every country to restrict immigration of foreigners ; and in the case of South Africa followed various policies, as later chapters describe.

The issues of South African racial policies and Rhodesian independence, under a minority white government, nearly destroyed the Commonwealth in the 1960's. Though the prime ministers' meetings did not end in open ruptures, they had lost their former harmony born of like-mindedness. Disillusionment spread within the membership, even in the UK, about the Commonwealth's contemporary purpose, despite new ideas for its rejuvenation.

For India the Commonwealth had been a point of contact with other countries which could be richly cultivated, as with Canada, or not, as with Australia and New Zealand. But on the whole, the Indian government failed to use the association as an instrument for attaining national goals ; it justified continued membership on the basis of lack of harm rather than of positive good derived from it. After the death of Nehru Indian leaders appeared to be indifferent to the Commonwealth's fate. From being a cornerstone in the structure of India's foreign relations, the place of the Commonwealth diminished to that of an embellishment.

BILATERAL RELATIONS WITH THE UNITED KINGDOM

India's relations with Britain became closer after independence than they were in the years just preceding 1947. These relations included official and personal contacts, intellectual and cultural bonds, and even connections through such voluntary agencies as missionary bodies. In most areas of modern Indian life, and to the apparent satisfaction of everyone concerned, there was a post-independence Indo-British rapprochement. One reason for this remarkable amity after the British Labour government granted independence to India was that "the so-called conflict between Britain and India was really a conflict between the Conservative Party and the Indian National Congress. . . . There was no conflict between Britain as such and India as such."[36] Another reason was that many Indians, above all Nehru, had developed admiration and affection for Britain, which they saw no reason to conceal. The deep friendship struck between Nehru and Lord and Lady Mountbatten was one example of a companionableness that many educated Indians enjoyed with their English counterparts. Indians looked up to English culture and often affected it ; they admired the style of British diplomacy and tried to emulate it. The self-assurance, the concern for correct procedure, the under-statement in the propaganda field, the seeming open-mindedness in the British approach appealed to Indians. Having won its independence with comparative ease, at least without a violent revolution, from the greatest modern empire, India was prepared to judge its former rulers magnanimously.[37]

Nehru was particularly impressed by the dignity with which the

UK divested itself of the empire and sympathized with its exhaustion and loss of power after the Second World War. To those Indians who were unreconciled to the idea of friendship with Britain Nehru tried to convey his belief that imperialism was a dying force : "If you talk of British imperialism and the rest of it, I would say that there is no capacity left for imperialism even if the will were there. ...."[38] Towards the remaining British dominion over foreign territories after 1947 the Indian government adopted a distinctly more tolerant attitude than towards any other colonial system. India's criticism of British security policies, closely tied to those of the US though they were, appeared almost friendly in contrast to the vigorous repudiation of similar American policies. In turn, British officials tolerated and even encouraged India's nonalignment as early as 1950. Many Britishers retained pleasant memories of India and a sense of involvement with the subcontinent.

Serious disputes stemming from a divergence of national interests, however, did arise between India and the UK. The over-sensitivity which either country sometimes displayed towards the policies of the other indicated that a consideration of Indo-British relations after independence could not ignore the emotional attitudes crystallized in the years before 1947. Some Britishers reacted to events on the Indian subcontinent with a vigour born of identification with events of their own shaping. Others recalled "the way in which [their] Indian friends would criticize British policy, not as citizens of a foreign country, but as if they belonged to the British opposition."[39] On the other hand, the efforts of both governments provided an unusual example of the way in which careful diplomacy and restraint in political dialogue could reduce conflicts to bearable proportions. When Anthony Eden visited New Delhi in 1955, at a time when Indian and Western policies in Asia were diverging markedly, Nehru spoke of Indo-British disagreement, which, however, "does not make a difference to our mutual regard for each other and our mutual respect for each other's bona fides...."[40] Such compliments were always mutual and reached their height in the ceremonies connected with the visits to India of Prime Minister Harold Macmillan in 1958, Prince Phillip in 1959, and Queen Elizabeth in January 1961.

While Britain ruled India it was sometimes accused of encouraging the demands of the Muslim League over the National Congress.

Similarly, a persistent Indian complaint about post-partition British policy arose from the UK's alleged partiality towards Pakistan, as expressed in UN debates on Kashmir and within the framework of the Baghdad Pact and SEATO. Various British governments in fact tried to maintain formal impartiality on the Indo-Pakistan conflict, and some measure of their success were the Pakistani complaints that India was being favoured. In 1957, however, the UK openly supported Pakistan's case on Kashmir in the UN, thereby giving rise to another of the periodic suggestions by some Indians that the Commonwealth tie should be broken, and another of Nehru's defenses of the association. More serious evidence that some British officials held an unconcealed bias towards Pakistan appeared during the 1965 Indo-Pakistan war. After consultations with other ministers about the seriousness of the fighting Prime Minister Harold Wilson issued a statement on September 6 which expressed distress at India's "attack" on Pakistani territory, without referring to the earlier Pakistani invasion into Kashmir.[41] The Indian protest was predictably vehement, and the British government's efforts to re-camouflage the views of some of its highest representatives left New Delhi unconvinced.

This lapse of good form was one indication that the ruling groups in both countries in the 1960's were less aware of the other's problems, less enthusiastic for the other's causes, than the previous generation had been. Though the imprint left on their cultures by two centuries of close association seemed indelible—especially in India—there was a contemporary absence in each country of deep knowledge about the issues facing the other, for example, British membership in the EEC.

The most tangible ties between India and Britain were those of trade and investment. In the period 1958-1961 the UK took an average of 27 per cent of India's exports while supplying an average of over 19 per cent of all Indian imports. Of the exports an estimated 80 to 90 per cent entered British markets under preferential tariffs.[42] By accepting the tariff and import restrictions of the EEC Britain would have reduced its demand for certain major Indian products, both primary and manufactured : coffee, tobacco, wool carpets, jute goods, leather goods, oils and nuts, and cotton textiles. In negotiating for admission to the Community Britain managed to gain continental countries' concessions to only a few Indian goods, notably tea and cricket equipment. The higher EEC tariffs, mostly on processed and manufactured goods, and its quota system had helped to create grossly unbalanced Indo-EEC trade patterns by the 1960's ; India's imports from the EEC countries were four times as great as its exports during the second five-year plan, ending in 1961. Indo-British trade came closer to being balanced.

Apart from the direct effects of tariffs, the prospect of India's having to compete on equal terms in the UK's market with producers of manufactured goods such as Japan and primary product producers such as the African countries of the French economic community caused a certain degree of panic in Indian commercial and governmental circles. In short, India had geared much of its trade to Commonwealth preferences and feared the consequences of their removal, whether suddenly or by stages as the EEC was willing to grant for certain commodities. As Nehru put it at the Commonwealth prime ministers' conference in London in September 1962, "It is true that we did not like the Ottawa Agreements, because when they were concluded most of the gains accrued to the United Kingdom. It is only lately that duty-free imports into the United Kingdom and preferential arrangements over the Commonwealth as a whole have helped us to build up a sizeable trade in our manufactures. . . ."[43] He was more than customarily blunt in criticizing the British desire to join the EEC and suggested that the future of the Commonwealth could be affected by such a move.

The shock to India of the end of preferences in the British market was not administered at the time because of the French veto on the UK's entry into the EEC. But contemplation of its possible effects produced some constructive thought and policy for the future of India's trade with the European economies. India established a mission at the EEC headquarters in Brussels in November 1961 ; in May 1962 the Indian position was put forward in the form of a memorandum on UK-EEC negotiations. The EEC negotiators indicated that they would prefer to deal directly with India alone than as a part of a Commonwealth "deal" possibly accompanying the admission of Britain. Thus began the bilateral discussions that continued over several years on India's specific requests for liberalization of EEC import policies and on the more basic issue of the EEC's providing nondiscriminatory preferences for the exports of all the developing countries, a subject to be discussed in the final chapter.

A NOTE ON DEFENSE POLICY

While avoiding all formal Commonwealth military commitments the Indian government relied heavily on Britain in defense matters for some years after independence. Until 1949 the Commander-in-Chief of the Indian Army was British ; until 1953 and 1954, respectively, the commanders of the Air Force and Navy were British. Most of India's military equipment was purchased in the UK ; Indian officers received training at the Imperial Defense College and the Joint Services Staff College ; Indians participated in military exercises with British forces and in conferences such as the Commonwealth Advisory Committee on Defense Science. But those arrangements called for no special political or military agreements. India obtained the equipment by purchase, and the training exercises were convenient, not essential. After the Chinese attack in 1962 Indo-British military relations took a different turn as formal aid agreements replaced purchase arrangements, and the Anglo-American commitment to India's defense build-up temporarily emerged. Subsequently, India took out major loans for military supplies, the UK specializing in the provision of naval material.

For nearly two decades after independence India's oceanic defense was underwritten by the British navy, whose obligation to protect the imperial life-line required its continued presence in the Indian Ocean. The Indian defense ministry was not navy-oriented, and even if it had been so, the cost of building a naval force adequate to defend the coastline and achieve dominance in the Indian Ocean would have been prohibitive. When, in the 1960's, Indians began to realize that Indonesian, Pakistani, or in time Chinese naval forces might be able to inflict damage on Indian shipping or coastal installations, the government began a naval improvement programme. Simultaneously, for economic and political reasons, the UK was cutting back its naval forces in the Indian Ocean area. The great naval base at Trincomalee and air stations in Ceylon were evacuated on Ceylonese request in 1958, and the independence of British colonies—on both sides of the ocean portended further withdrawals from the mainland bases of Aden and Singapore.

But the British presence was not yet at an end ; the UK revised its Indian Ocean strategy and in co-operation with the US made

4

plans for the construction of new island airfields, naval supply bases, and communication centres. The new sites were in the Maldive islands southwest of Ceylon, the Chagos archipelago (including Diego Garcia) still further south, the Aldabra, Farquhar, and Desroches islands off Madagascar, and the Cocos islands five hundred miles south of Sumatra. Arrangements to purchase or lease some islands for new bases or transit facilities were made with Mauritius and the Seychelles. Several islands were joined into a new entity, the British Indian Ocean Territory, in November 1965.

The Indian government opposed the planned establishment of the new bases, despite its apparent reliance on Anglo-American emergency assistance in case of a full-scale Chinese attack. At first the protests were half-hearted. But by 1968, after the UK had announced that it would withdraw its naval presence in the Indian Ocean by 1971 and the question of filling a vacuum had to be faced, New Delhi said it was planning to exert itself fully to preclude a new kind of Western dominance in the Indian Ocean. It argued for self-sufficiency in the region and refused to consider any alternative to the British presence that would entail military collaboration with another state, even with a small regional power. The American interest in establishing island bases as communication and transit facilities, and for emergency use if a state in the Indian Ocean area should be endangered by external attack, began during the John F. Kennedy administration. Units of the seventh fleet visited the Indian Ocean, and henceforth the US regarded the area as part of its global military responsibilities.[44]

India's opposition to the Anglo-American military planning for the Indian Ocean region in the mid-1960's and its own statements of intention to fill the naval vacuum may have been partly aimed at avoiding a Western-Soviet confrontation of power in the region. Or, an equally plausible case could be made that the government was reserving its right to assume the dominant role of defender of its own sea coast and even some of the strategic places in the Indian Ocean region, such as Ceylon and the mid-sea islands, in the future, when Indian naval and air forces had competence to do the job. But in keeping with previous practice the government issued no public policy directives that indicated its thinking on matters of regional defense. Indeed, even on matters of territorial defense no broad planning, such as the British had drawn up in the inter-war period, was made public, much less debated in public.

In contrast to the many apparent advantages to India in maintaining the continuity of its 20th century ties with the Commonwealth and the UK, a singular disadvantage revealed itself in the government's views on security policy. In the first place, the prolonged experience of having India's security interests included in those of a global empire with powerful defense forces gave Indians a false feeling of national security, even when the UK was withdrawing from the Asian and middle eastern regions. Nehru candidly told a conference of state information ministers in New Delhi on October 25, 1962, that the strategic thinking of Indians had been conditioned by British rule. As he explained it : "Under British rule, it was the job of the British to fight, with the Indian army no doubt. There were two great wars in our recollection, and the Indian army took part in them. Nevertheless, it was not in India, may be in a little corner of Assam, that the Japanese came in last time, but it did not affect India very much. We were not conscious of war, emotionally conscious, just like countries in Europe were."[45]

The absence of "military-mindedness," in Nehru's words, among officials in the government eliminated an important stimulation for private individuals and institutions to indulge in strategic studies. Neglect of those studies, illustrated by the paucity of published works on defense policy,[46] contributed to the general public's ignorance of security matters for two decades after independence, during which India fought two wars over Kashmir and a major engagement in the Himalayas. This volume, which treats of the end-results of foreign policy rather than the processes of policy-making, deals with defense policies in the chapters following in connection with India's relations with specific countries and its responses to regional and global military affairs.

Another result of British rule, contrary to the complacency that it engendered on defense matters, could be witnessed in the actively hostile attitudes of Indian nationalists toward the military establishment, which extended beyond the days when the Indian army defended Britain's imperial interests. In particular, Nehru and Congress leaders had a psychological aversion to overseas military commitments and involvements in strategic considerations beyond the boundaries of the subcontinent. They regarded India's pre-1947 external military involvements as entirely the impositions of imperial interests and, therefore, not legitimate. Because the Indian army had regarded its responsibilities as including imperial defense and because the attitudes of army officers were heavily influenced by the British, the nationalists tended to discount the army's think-ing on overall defense policies. The strategic isolationism of the post-independence Indian government was, therefore, rooted in pre-war and war-time opposition by Congress to external commit-ments, which had been largely the result of the British connection.

NOTES AND REFERENCES

1 Speech to the Constituent Assembly, May 16, 1949 ; *Speeches 1946-49*, p. 286.

2 Panikkar in the *New Commonwealth* of April 29, 1954 ; quoted in Taya Zinkin, "India's Foreign Policy," *World Politics*, vol. VII, 2.

3 Other images of the Commonwealth existed, as one proposed by Mrs. Vera Anstey : "The Commonwealth is becoming more and more like a family whose children are gradually coming of age. . . ." Anstey, "The Intangible Com-monwealth," in *Indian Year Book of International Affairs*, vol. V, 1956, p. 272. The metaphor here did not accurately suggest the egalitarian spirit of the new Commonwealth outside of Britain.

4 Nehru to the 5th Commonwealth parliamentary conference, held in New Delhi—for the first time in Asia—in Dec. 1957, *India's Foreign Policy*, p. 160.

5 Nehru answering a critic in parliament on June 12, 1952, said : "I do not think our membership of the Commonwealth has affected our policy in the sligh-test." *Speeches 1949-53*, p. 224.

6 The British Prime Minister, Clement Atlee, sent out personal envoys for preliminary talks with Commonwealth prime ministers. Patrick Gordon Walker, later Commonwealth Secretary, was sent as one of these envoys to Delhi, Karachi, and Colombo in January 1949. See his book, *The Commonwealth*, London 1962, p. 182.

7 Communique of the Commonwealth Prime Ministers' Conference, 1949 ; quoted in Mansergh, *Commonwealth Perspectives*, Durham 1958, p. 30.

8 From the communique on South Africa issued March 15, 1961 by the Com-monwealth Prime Ministers meeting in London, March 8-17, 1961. Mansergh, *Documents and Speeches on Commonwealth Affairs 1952-1962*, p. 365.

9 The Commonwealth expanded from 5 members in 1946, to 10 members in 1961, to 23 members in 1966.

10 See the final communique issued on Jan. 14, 1950 in Mansergh, *Documents . . . 1931-1952*, vol. II, pp. 1186-88.

11 Anthony Eden, *Full Circle*, London 1960, p. 128.

12 Speech in parliament Dec. 7, 1950 ; *Speeches 1949-53*, p. 189.

[13] See the final communique issued Oct. 22, 1948 in Mansergh, *Documents ...1931-1952*, vol. II, pp. 1137-38.

[14] See Mansergh, *Survey of British Commonwealth Affairs 1939-1952*, London 1958, p. 352.

[15] Quoted in Mansergh, *Documents ...1952-1962*, p. 407.

[16] Quoted in Mansergh, *ibid.*, p. 459.

[17] See Eden, *op. cit.*, pp. 94, 97.

[18] *Commonwealth Relations Office List*, London 1957, p. 65.

[19] John Matthai, speech to the Constituent Assembly, Oct. 5, 1949 ; quoted in Mansergh, *Documents ...1931-1952*, vol. II, p. 1034.

[20] Final communique July 15, 1964 ; *Keesing's Contemporary Archives 1963-1964*, p. 20196.

[21] A full statement of his views appeared in *Jana*, Colombo, Dec. 1, 1956, and later in *Swarajya*, Madras.

[22] Aneurin Bevan, Labour Party leader, stated to a large anti-Suez rally in Trafalgar Square : "I want to say to Mr. Nehru. . . . Do not turn your back on the Commonwealth because of Sir Anthony Eden. He does not represent us or the Commonwealth." *Statesman* (Calcutta), Nov. 6, 1956.

[23] Duncan Sandys, "The Modern Commonwealth" ; issued by the Commonwealth Relations Office in January 1962; text of Commonwealth proposals in *FAR*, vol. VII, 3 (March 1961).

[24] *FAR*, vol. XI, 6 (June 1965), p. 124.

[25] See final communique, September 1962 ; Mansergh, *Documents ... 1952-1962*, p. 660.

[26] This metaphor was most often used in the UK. It was given substance by the fact that the cooperatively administered institutions of the Commonwealth were almost all in Britain, and that the UK was the only member state which had a separate Office of Commonwealth Relations headed by a minister of cabinet rank.

[27] The secretariat was meant to be a clearing house for ideas and information, an aid in the preparation of conferences, and a "visible symbol of the spirit of cooperation which animates the Commonwealth." *Keesing's op. cit.*, p. 20198.

[28] See ahead, chapter IX.

[29] Nehru told parliament on June 12, 1952 : "We have never discussed defense policies in the Commonwealth, either jointly or separately." *Speeches 1949-1953*, p. 225.

[30] Australian Prime Minister Robert G. Menzies' phrase ; quoted in Mansergh, *Documents ... 1931-1952*, vol. II, p. 1212.

[31] Foreign Secretary Lord Home's statement made to the Portuguese government at the time of India's take-over of Goa, when Portugal sought to activate its defense treaty of 1642 with the UK.

[32] A. N. Sinha, *Law of Citizenship and Aliens in India*, Bombay 1962, p. 140.

[33] R. B. Davison, *Commonwealth Immigrants*, London 1964, p. 4.

[34] Minister of State for External Affairs B. R. Bhagat's statement in the Rajya Sabha, Feb. 29 ; quoted in the *Indian Express*, March 1, 1968.

[35] See for example Nehru's speech to the Constituent Assembly, May, 16, 1949 ; *Speeches 1946-1949*, p. 280.

[36] Ivor Jennings, *Problems of the New Commonwealth*, p. 13.

[37] For example, Panikkar wrote in the *New Commonwealth, op. cit.* : "It is not correct to say that the like-mindedness which exists today between India and England is a superficial one. It is based on a common experience of 150 years of history. The inheritance from Britain is of even greater importance than the Hindu traditions of the past."

[38] Nehru's speech to the Constituent Assembly, May 17, 1949 ; *Speeches 1946-1949*, p. 296.

[39] Maurice and Taya Zinkin, *Britain and India : Requiem for Empire*, p. 171.

[40] FAR, vol. I, 3 (March 1955), p. 44.

[41] *The Times*, Sept. 7, 1965.

[42] D. K. Rangnekar, *India, Britain and the European Common Market*, pp. 131-32.

[43] Speech on Sept. 11, 1962 ; *Speeches 1957-1963*, p. 399.

[44] See speech by the US Secretary of the Navy, Paul H. Nitse, on Jan. 9, 1964 ; in *Vital Speeches*, vol. XXX (Feb. 1, 1964), p. 242. The British point of view was expressed by P. C. Gordon Walker in "The Labour Party's Defense and Foreign Policy," *Foreign Affairs*, vol. XLII (April 1964), p. 396.

[45] Ministry of External Affairs, "Prime Minister on Chinese Aggression," New Delhi 1963, pp. 16-17.

[46] Some of the best written works on defense policy were hidden in the files of the major English language newspapers, in editorials or articles by sometimes anonymous defense correspondents. Several of K.M. Panikkar's books contained analyses far in advance of the thinking of his colleagues in government ; e.g. his *Problems of Indian Defense*, Bombay 1960. Major-General P. S. Bhagat's *Forging the Shield*, Calcutta 1965, demonstrated the fact that the army kept abreast of modern strategic concepts but added little to public comprehension of India's defense needs. The Indian Council of World Affairs' *Defense and Security in the Indian Ocean Area*, Bombay 1958, was an illustration of the mediocre level of non-professional analyses of military affairs in the mid-1950's. The somewhat greater public controversy and awareness of the 1960's was revealed in A. B. Shah, ed., *India's Defense and Foreign Policies*, Bombay 1966. The best foreign work on India's defense policies was Lorne J. Kavic, *India's Quest for Security ; Defense Policies 1947-1965*, Berkeley 1967, thoroughly documented and providing an historical background, and almost devoid of policy alternatives.

CHAPTER III

NONALIGNMENT AND ITS PRACTICE

IF INDIA SOUGHT strategic isolation for many years after independence, its major spokesman, Jawaharlal Nehru, also yearned for international political involvement. Both were made possible by means of the posture of nonalignment, which "reflects at once a desire to avoid commitment—an understandable attitude for any people of meagre resources—and a wish to be among those who count in world affairs."[1] While India's relations with the UK and its post-independence membership in the Commonwealth carried forward legacies of an earlier era, nonalignment was the Nehru government's major innovation in foreign relations. A posture more than a policy, made significant by the unique configuration of post-Second World War politics, nonalignment provided India with the influence, even power, to pursue its major national objectives in the international arena. In a wider sense, that peculiarly Indian contribution to world politics almost literally added a new dimension to the world political scene : with the spreading of nonalignment through most of the newly independent states the world became tri-polar, rather than bi-polar.[2]

The literature dealing with nonalignment (and all the semantic variations that the idea elicited in the minds of scholars and politicians) proliferated as the phenomenon spread and evidenced a staying power.[3] Much of that writing failed to stress that the idea of nonalignment for India did not emerge with independence, or even with recognition of a bi-polar world, but grew naturally out of the movement for independence, as enunciated by the main foreign policy spokesman of the Indian National Congress, Nehru. As such a development, it should be placed in context with the foreign policy platform of the Congress in the decades preceding independence and described very briefly ahead.[4]

Many of the Congress foreign policy proclamations came forth in reaction to British Indian foreign policies. But the tenor of the

55

statements could not be termed purely negative. For nationalist leaders, stimulated and influenced by Nehru's personal involvement in non-official international relations as delegate to international bodies and periodic traveller abroad, developed a world view into which they fitted India as a future independent state. Thus, Congress resolutions on foreign policy matters in the 1920's and 1930's not only criticized failures of the government to support Indian interests in the League of Nations and to press more strongly for the rights of Indians overseas, and condemned the use of Indian troops in China and the middle east, but also identified India's political struggle with world movements against imperialism and all forms of oppression. India, according to Mohandas K. Gandhi and Nehru, could act as an example for all subjugated peoples who desired freedom, a leader in a general human revolt against a political system based on economic exploitation, racial discrimination, and warfare. In the early 1920's the Congress began sending its greetings and verbal support to nationalist movements in other countries, many of which looked to India as their leader and example. China, by the mid-1930's, became a favourite subject of sympathetic Congress resolutions because of its travail under Japanese attack. Nehru's vision of an eventual Indian-Chinese collaboration for the resurgence of Asia began then. On that basis Nehru also conceived of an Asian federation dominated by India and China, which would help to rectify the balance of global power heavily weighted toward the Western states.

Gandhi's thoughts had for many years tended towards a messianic vision of India's spiritual purpose. As independence approached, Nehru's writings and speeches increasingly emphasized the importance of India's "voice" in world affairs. Nehru wrote in 1944 that when it gained independence India would have a large role to play in international affairs—its "very bigness and potential strength and resources" made one think in big terms. "India could not be a mere hanger-on of any country or group of nations ; her freedom and growth would make a vital difference to Asia and therefore the world."[5] Refusal to align India's policies with those of other states appeared even then to be a prerequisite to the assumption of its natural position of prominence in the world. The preoccupation of Gandhi, Nehru, and other leaders before independence with India's mission of peace and its avoidance of all entanglements in power political arrangements stimulated "a tendency to conceive of India's role in the world in terms of a preacher of moral principles and to rely more on the declaration of such principles than on the skilful practice of diplomacy and military preparedness for safeguarding vital national interests."[6]

Many Indian leaders, while not pacifists as Gandhi was, sincerely believed in world disarmament ; a weakly armed state, they observed, does not threaten other states, and therefore it is less likely to be attacked itself—fear, not spontaneously aggressive motivations, promotes war, they argued.[7] The historical experience of India for at least one century, when Britain had effectively guaranteed Indian security, had left the bulk of informed Indians complacent about possible foreign attack. Congress resolutions urging disarmament were passed while Indians saw no clear menace of foreign attack. The Japanese advance toward their territory in 1942 failed to alter Indians' thinking about national security both because it was successfully repelled and because the Japanese attack could be regarded as anti-British, not anti-Indian. Nehru fully accepted Gandhi's psychological analysis that fear was the cause of most wars. Through the 1940's and 1950's his pronouncements on global crises and his predilections about India's overall defense preparedness stemmed from that analysis. (Indo-Pakistani hostility could not be viewed in that framework, and as in the case of some other disputes directly involving India Nehru departed from his general prescriptions and acted through expediency.) Naturally, if India feared no overpowering assault on its own territory it could afford to abjure military alignments which, equally importantly, increased the chances of war.

Nehru and Congress leaders before independence often stated India's domestic needs for economic development and social progress in international contexts, notably world movements for socialism and against imperialism. Largely due to Nehru's influence many, though by no means all, Congress leaders expressed solicitude for the socialist experiments in the Soviet Union and were not quick to criticize Soviet foreign policy. Nehru himself, however, tried not to allow his ideological proclivities to blind him to political realities. He anticipated the power rivalries of the post-war era and prepared himself to judge issues without ideological bias, although his disposition to view long-range political changes as determined by economic drives did not diminish, and he continued to believe that a socialist economy was apt to be the least aggressive. Nehru held considerable hope that a new international organization, the United Nations, could redress the imbalance between the economically weak and the powerful states, but he also foresaw the possibility that any world body might be another arena in which the great powers would vie for hegemony. Apart from such a general world view, Nehru and other Congress leaders identified specific national interests which an independent India would pursue, such as diplomatic support for Indians abroad and for the independence movements in other Asian countries, notably Indonesia.

All of those ideas formed one of the tributaries leading into the main stream of India's foreign policy, the direction of whose flow had already been established by the time of independence. The other important source of that stream were the actual precedents in foreign relations established by the British Indian government and described in chapter I. The merging of those two contributing sources produced some counter-currents in the shape of mutually-conflicting policies, but pragmatism and the absence of doctrinal rigidity on Nehru's part brought them together into a remarkably well-integrated course.

The proof of India's independence for Nehru was the posture of nonalignment in foreign relations. That was as much the culmination of the nationalist struggle as was the physical withdrawal of British rule. To the Constituent Assembly on March 8, 1949, Nehru said : "What does independence consist of ? It consists fundamentally and basically of foreign relations. That is the test of independence. All else is local autonomy. Once foreign relations go out of your hand, into the charge of somebody else, to that extent and in that measure you are not independent."[8] Nehru had prepared his colleagues and followers for India's cutting loose from all restricting entanglements of the past and for an assertive avoidance of new external bonds. Almost one year before the transfer of power in a speech broadcast to the nation he defined the posture of nonalignment that he hoped to achieve : "We propose, as far as possible, to keep away from the power politics of groups, aligned against one another, which have led in the past to world wars and which may again lead to disasters on an even vaster scale."[9]

At the Asian Relations Conference convened in New Delhi five

months before independence Nehru told his fellow nationalist
leaders that : "Far too long have we of Asia been petitioners in
western courts and chancellories. That story must now belong to
the past. We propose to stand on our own feet. . . . We do not
intend to be the playthings of others."[10] It would be India's task
after independence to provide leadership, even to chart a new course
in world politics, for all states which wished to join in breaking
with political alignments centering on the established great powers.
Such a course would not demand withdrawal from all international
involvement ; indeed Nehru recognized the advantages of retaining
links with the Commonwealth and the duty of intervening when
desirable on behalf of the goals of peace and national independence.
Nonalignment was not to mean political or economic isolation,
though for India it certainly would demand military self-sufficiency.
That posture would be the result of a truly "independent foreign
policy," a phrase that Nehru later said was the proper way to
describe India's behaviour.[11]

As it happened, the unique configuration of world politics after
the Second World War admirably suited the establishment of
India's nonalignment and gave it greater significance than it would
have had in other circumstances. The great power rivalry, which
Nehru had almost prophetically anticipated before the war ended,
tended to attract most states into one or the other of the antagonistic
coalitions, each putting forward its ideological system to achieve
global adherence. India would have pursued nonalignment vis-a-vis
any greater powers as an assertion of its true independence, but
when that posture was proclaimed, and later achieved, with respect
to the two coalitions dominating the global arena India's uniqueness
gained for it a special kind of influence, or power.[12]

During the early years of independence India had few opportunities to establish and exert power internationally. Its position
in world politics, as an independent, nonaligned state, had not
yet created a forceful enough impression on the major foreign
offices to cause them to adopt special policies toward New Delhi.
The rapidly emerging alignment of states into a bi-polar system
preoccupied the attention of the major governments and nonalignment seemed to have no place in the evolving scheme. Both the
Soviet and the Western coalitions tended to view nonalignment
as merely a verbal exercise, not a posture that by itself could alter

India's basic commitment to the West—a commitment rooted in economic necessity and the need for political support from those countries whose constitutional systems India was endeavouring to emulate.

The US failed to recognize that a government's commitment to democracy did not always result in a pro-American foreign policy and initially looked upon India as a candidate for the Western alliance. After the defeat of the Chinese Nationalists, India appeared to some American officials as the strongest potentially anti-communist force in Asia. Simultaneously, Soviet leaders rivalled their Western counterparts in disbelieving Indian nonalignment and also acted on the assumption that Nehru's government, all verbal protestations notwithstanding, was linked to Western interests. Therefore, they failed to foster the close ties with New Delhi that Nehru might have expected, gave support to the revolutionary Communist Party of India, and apparently awaited the 'inevitable' transfer of power into truly "popular" Indian hands. Under these conditions, wherein neither of the great coalitions was prepared to recognize nonalignment as a significant factor in world politics, India's power remained weak, in global terms.

As discussed ahead, the Korean War transformed Indian nonalignment from a verbal assertion into a global posture which served as an effective instrument of power. As a result of Korean War diplomacy, the essentially negative and passive character of nonalignment was altered. India proved its ability to assume the role of mediator and impartial arbitrator, and no further demonstrations of its unique posture were needed to establish in fact what Nehru had been proclaiming in theory. The Soviet Union at the same time began to revise its assessment of India's foreign policy and even before the death of Stalin in 1953 recognized India's nonalignment as a fact of international politics.

THE NATURE OF NONALIGNMENT

India's posture of nonalignment, which achieved its greatest effectiveness in the 1950's, was not designed with the physical security of the country chiefly in mind. The most that could be said for it as a defense policy was that an India which refused to take sides might hope to escape involvement in a major war—a very doubtful proposition and never very strongly put forth by the Indian government. Nonalignment was aimed at achieving two cardinal national objectives : full national independence, which meant recognition by all states of India's freedom to define its own interests and policies ; and a stature of great significance in world affairs, whose acknowledgement by established states would assist in the downfall of colonialism and racialism, strengthen the "resurgence of Asia," in Nehru's words, and lend support for India's modernization. A third objective, whose relationship to national interest in the minds of Indian policy-makers was never clear, was the maintenance and extension of a "third area" which could act on behalf of world peace by offering mediation and providing a kind of buffer between the conflicting power groups. All those objectives were substantially realized in the brief span of a single decade and might not have been, to such a degree, had India committed itself to one or the other coalitions.

Although nonalignment was not a posture requiring vigorous assertion of national capabilities, as a predominantly military posture would have been, it was not at all a passive, inactive retreat from political involvement ; hence, the misunderstandings engendered by the word, neutral, applied to India. Nonalignment, as India pursued it, was incessantly active in the political sense of constant and rapid manoeuvring. The fox-like alertness, the diplomatic aggressiveness, and the temerity to engage in novel political procedures which characterized the Indian statesman, V. K. Krishna Menon, at his best, set the standard, which few other nonaligned states could match. In contrast, the international political behaviour of those states which associated themselves with a great power, often for well-considered reasons, could be described as passive, or at least highly predictable.

India's nonalignment was the main source of its power in international political relations. The power derived from nonalignment existed only in relation to those states whose peculiar interests were affected when that posture was assumed by another state. That came to be the case with the US and the USSR. But nonalignment was powerless against such states as Pakistan and China whose interests vis-a-vis India would have been constant regardless of New Delhi's diplomatic stance. The governments of the US and the USSR, as the leaders of powerful coalitions seeking adherents

to their respective causes, recognized by the early 1950's India's important position. Neither side was able to obtain any sort of commitment
from New Delhi to provide support, and therein lay India's power.
Nehru recognized his position, and in 1950 put it this way : "At
the present moment, what many people want us to do is to say
that we stand by this group or alignment of nations or that. Now,
just look at it. What does that mean? It means simply that we
cease to count for the moment. We have no views left. We are
just taken for granted."[13] Because India's policy on many issues
could not be predicted, and in a larger sense because India's ultimate
attachment to one or to the other of the competing ideologies was
uncertain, both the US and the USSR were induced to modify
their policies in certain instances so as better to attract Indian support.
In regard to issues such as colonialism and racialism, on which India's
policies were generally consistent and reflective of Asian-African opinion as a whole, the policies of the great powers were also affected
by India's stand, because to offend Indian interests in one situation
might lessen the chances of gaining Indian support in the next.

This is not to suggest that India was ever capable of altering
decisions of the major states involving the latters' important interests;
in fact, on numerous occasions India's interests, as in disarmament negotiations, were blatantly ignored or repudiated by those
states. What seemed clear was that the US and the USSR recognized
the importance of Indian support for, or opposition to, many of
their respective policies. When those states understood that the
chances of such support grew or diminished partly in response to
their efforts to satisfy Indian interests, and when they acted in
order to produce a favourable Indian response, the power of India
was an established fact. In short, India's power rested on the acknowledgement by other states that India had something to offer
and could be induced to supply it. The achievement of that acknowledgement, which occurred in the early 1950's, was the outstanding
success of the Nehru government in foreign relations.

By the mid-1950's, India's nonalignment had passed through
the period of rebellious, sometimes irresponsible, youth into the
confidence of middle age, and its posture was regarded as a stable
and relatively permanent feature of international politics. Both
power coalitions came to regard that posture as a tolerable or even
a beneficial state of affairs, and henceforth their respective policies

toward India were directed toward the preservation of its special relationship to both sides.

A comparison of India's nonalignment with the classical posture of a buffer state might clarify further the reasons why the great powers first tolerated, then respected, and finally supported India's international stance. As a buffer state traditionally acts to maintain between opposing states, and by their consent, a zone where contending interests are kept from open conflict, so the nonaligned states maintained an area free from direct great power conflicts. This was Nehru's "no-war zone," which he hoped to extend to all of south Asia, and if possible beyond, until Pakistan's military agreement with the US made that ambition impossible. At first, this zone existed at the sufferance of the great powers as a possibly temporary feature of world politics. But as India proved itself agile and occasionally fearless in respect to great power controversies, such as in Korea and Indo-China, tolerance merged into respect for India's ability to sustain its posture in the face of definite risks. (India's fearlessness may have been largely verbal and was certainly enunciated with the confidence that the powerful states had no intention at that time of militarily coercing India into positions of alignment. But economic assistance from the US—for example, the $190,000,000 grain loan negotiated in early 1951—and later from the Soviet Union might have been withdrawn in retaliation against certain Indian policies ; the Indian government recognized those risks and pressed its own independent policies despite them.) Governments of smaller states gained the courage to become or remain nonaligned on the Indian model, which appeared eminently workable and profitable. After 1958, the emerging African states, one after the other, made debuts in world politics with Indian-sounding pronouncements about nonalignment, and the global buffer zone was extended, though no longer under India's leadership.

In a manner analogous to a buffer against military and political conflict between more powerful states, India acted as an ideological buffer by refusing to commit its nearly 500 million people to either of the two great global causes. From the point of view of the great powers, that meant that the lines of ultimate confrontation between Western and Soviet values could not be drawn : India had not yet made its choice. From India's standpoint, its refusal to align itself with either the US or the USSR seemed to contribute vitally to the avoidance of world war. As Nehru saw the situation : "If all the world were to be divided up between these two big power blocs what would be the result? The inevitable result would be war. Therefore every step that takes place in reducing that area in the world which may be called the 'unaligned area' is a dangerous step and leads to war. It reduces that objectivity, that balance, that outlook which other countries without military might can perhaps exercise."[14] India benefited, as did the world, from the maintenance of an area free from direct great power conflict. It gained the additional advantage of receiving economic support for its development programmes from the contenders in what came to be called "competitive coexistence." Both sides were engaged in exporting assistance for basically the same reason, to try to influence the course of India's future development in the direction of a certain structure of values.

To the extent that the long-range goals of the US and the USSR were understood by both sides to be primarily ideological—a doubtful premise, but one which probably underlay many foreign policy decisions of the great powers, especially towards nonaligned countries—India, in a buffer status, also assumed certain of the characteristics of holder of the balance of power. When India became the object of great power competition for ideological or moral support, it was not merely a passive spectator in a great power struggle endeavouring to stay clear of the conflict or dampen it. It knew it had the capacity to influence the outcome of that struggle by leaning to one side or the other. While India's economic and military support could not have been crucial to either side immediately, its potential was immense. The West and the communists thought that they competed for the ideological future of the world. Therefore, the Indian government gained the capability of influencing the policies of those great powers from the possibility of commiting its people to one system or the other.

To contrast India's posture vis-a-vis the great powers with its relations with the important states in Asia is to juxtapose ideological interests against the realities of tangible power. Because of its military, economic, and geographic inferiority in regard to India, Pakistan formulated its Indian policies on the narrow, and the logical assumption of permanent geopolitical insecurity. China, on the other hand, sought dominance in Asia and regarded India as a rival which had to be subdued. India's capabilities to influence those states lay in their recognition of the ways in which India could affect their respective interests. Almost all of those ways could be equated with India's economic and military capabilities, although Indian political decisions at certain times, as in negotiations with Pakistan on Kashmir, carried some weight. Much the same analysis could be applied to India's relations with other states in Asia. Thus, India's foreign policies must be understood in the context of at least two international systems, the global system dominated by the US and the Soviet Union and the regional Asian system.[15]

The nature of India's effective power differed according to the system of states in which India operated. Its power in the global system was greater than in the regional system during the 1950's, because India chose not to stress military and economic capabilities, but rather to rely on the diplomacy of nonalignment to support its objectives—except occasionally in relation to Pakistan when direct military and economic policies were adopted. Such reliance resulted from a conscious decision to allocate the maximum of available resources, internal and external, to economic development and to avoid as far as practicable displays of tangible coercive power, which many Indians regarded as unworthy of their nation's image as a peacemaker. Also, the Indian government was directed by men who had participated in the demise of British rule, brought about primarily through the psychological power of the nationalist movement. The Congress believed moral persuasion to be a perfectly adequate substitute for physical might, and indeed superior to it. The same leadership of independent India placed great reliance on a similar kind of power in international politics. In settling international disputes, said Nehru, "the basic thing is the psychological approach and not purely the political approach, the approach of trying to win over the other party, trying to be friends with the other party. . . ."[16] The posture of nonalignment provided a base from which to exert psychological power on a global political configuration susceptible to that influence.

THE ACHIEVEMENT AND THE PRACTICE OF NONALIGNMENT

Ironically, the global power struggle that Nehru condemned created the conditions in which Indian nonalignment could become a signi-

5

ficant force in world affairs. Nonalignment succeeded, as one witness pointed out, for the "wrong" reasons—not because of situations which India itself brought about.[17] In the diplomacy of the Korean War India achieved its desired place in international political relations and established for itself and for other states the political viability and the advantages of nonalignment.[18]

As a non-permanent member of the UN Security Council at the time of the North Korean attack in June 1950, India was drawn into the diplomacy of the early stages of the war. Partly because of its earlier active involvement in the Korean question and its commitment to the UN sponsored integrity of the Republic of South Korea, and partly because of the unmistakable fact of aggression southward, witnessed by an Indian delegate on the United Nations Commission on Korea, India voted for the resolution of June 25 which identified the aggressor and called upon North Korean forces to withdraw from below the 38th parallel, the de facto boundary between the two states. Two days later, after the US had ordered its air and sea forces to assist South Korea, had taken steps to defend Formosa, and had accelerated its military aid to the French in Indo-China, the Council passed a second resolution calling for collective action against the aggressor. The Indian government hesitated, not wishing to endorse US preparations for an expanding area of conflict, but finally accepted the June 27 resolution in its purely Korean implications. Nehru explained, thinking in the historic context of the League of Nations : "If aggression were allowed to proceed and to succeed, then the structure of the United Nations would inevitably collapse and a large-scale war would result."[19]

But he found considerable parliamentary opposition to his Korean policy during the debates in August. Strongly isolationist legislators argued that India's policy did not appear sufficiently neutral, and Nehru found it as difficult to educate them as it was to convince foreign critics of the meaning of India's nonalignment. India, he said, was not "permanently neutral." That would mean "a permanent retirement from public affairs, a kind of national Sanyasa. No country can do that and certainly we have no desire to retire from the world. . . . I should like to make this point clear to this House and country about our neutrality, because there is so much confusion and vagueness about it and it surprises me when

I am told that you have left your policy of neutrality. I have never had it, much less have I left it."[20]

By supporting the West in the Security Council India did not commit itself to Western policy, as subsequent moves demonstrated. Even above an obligation to the UN, Nehru held that India had an obligation to the re-establishment of peace in Asia, and once aggression had been forcibly met he could then turn his attention to mediation, if that seemed necessary for peace. By early July, when India abstained on a Council resolution to establish a unified command in Korea, Nehru's thoughts were not far from possible mediation attempts. His explanation for the abstention was that India offered no troops for Korea, but the refusal to commit troops had resulted in some measure from India's desire not to offend China or Russia. The delicacy of India's position was apparent, and the government realized that it had to move gradually into its new role.

The first public step came on July 13. Nehru sent identical messages to Premier Stalin and Secretary of State, Dean Acheson, proposing steps to a peaceful settlement which included seating of the Peoples Republic of China's representative in the Security Council and direct dealings among China, Russia, and the US to solve the Korean problem. The reactions were predictable— Stalin's support for and Acheson's opposition to the proposal. The US and India consistently disagreed on China's UN representation, and therefore Nehru's messages tended further to accentuate the gap between US and Indian far eastern policies. In Security Council debates, after the Soviet delegate returned in August, India's representative, B. N. Rau, avoided any suggestion of hostility toward Soviet policy and began earnest efforts to mediate between the hostile parties.

At the beginning of October, when the UN forces had taken the offensive and threatened to push the North Korean army back into its own territory, a UN debate formed which plainly removed India from the US side for the remainder of the war. The question was whether or not the UN forces should cross the 38th parallel in pursuit of the retreating enemy and thereby totally destroy North Korean military potential and politically unify the two Koreas. A Western resolution that sanctioned such strategy brought an unexpected amount of argument. India's vigorous criticism of the proposal on grounds that a precipitous crossing at that time would prolong the war and place the UN in the role of agressor against the northern regime set a high standard for verbal opposition to Western policy. It was based on sincere fear that a crossing of the parallel would bring China into the conflict.

The Indian government did not rely on conjecture to arouse that fear. Its envoy in Peking, K. M. Panikkar, relayed the precise warning to the West on October 2 that Chou En-lai had informed him in an emergency interview that if American forces crossed the parallel—South Koreans made no difference—China would intervene.[21] Despite India's warning and its other diplomatic manoeuvres to delay precipitous American action the General Assembly's First Committee approved the Western resolution on October 4. President Truman thought the Indian reports probably concealed a Chinese bluff, and in any case Panikkar "had in the past played the game of the Chinese Communists fairly regularly."[22] Had the US accepted the Chinese threat as a genuine intention to intervene it might have provoked the move anyway, in order to force the North Koreans to negotiate a peace settlement, which they had not yet been willing to do. Also, the military need to preclude a fresh attack launched from within a privileged sanctuary entered into the decision to continue the advance, which in places reached up to the Yalu river border of China.

Nehru and many others who wanted to avoid any provocation of China suspected that US policy in Korea aimed at enlarging the war so as to inflict a military defeat on China as well as on North Korea. The removal of General Douglas MacArthur in April 1951 indicated that concern about the Supreme UN Commander's personal military objectives had spread beyond New Delhi. However, Washington did not conclude from the fact of Chinese intervention that India possessed special insights into future Chinese behaviour ; Peking's threats to intervene had come through various sources, and India then had the reputation in the West of discounting Chinese aggressiveness. After Chinese involvement established itself and an "entirely new war," in MacArthur's words, was underway, Indian diplomats often defended Chinese action in Korea and elsewhere, explaining it as defensive and the result of misunderstandings generated by China's non-representation in world councils. They opposed American policy in Asia because of its militantly anti-Chinese character and led the non-communist criticism of US moves in the UN, including in particular the "uniting for peace" resolution, which Nehru said "seemed like converting the UN into a larger edition of the Atlantic Pact and making it a war organization more than one devoted to international peace."[23]

India kept up its proposals to have the Peking government represented in the UN. By the winter of 1950-51, India had established its middle position in the developing far eastern crisis and had, by leaning sharply away from the Western stand, converted itself into a political neutral. (By not repudiating its earlier support for the UN's resolutions of June and by maintaining an ambulance unit with UN forces in Korea it was not a legal neutral.) Part of the reason for adopting that position lay in India's concern for its good relations with China.

The complex diplomatic and military proceedings in the winter of 1950-51, when a Peking representative sat briefly in the Security Council and Chinese forces were driving southward toward the 38th parallel—India urged them not to cross it—left Indian diplomats struggling for a position from which to undertake the mediation that Nehru wanted. The Asian and Arab representatives at the UN were drawn into joint action by B. N. Rau so as to give their appeals to the opponents more weight than separate moves could bear. The group sought to mediate by constituting small committees to investigate issues and propose solutions, while the US prepared its diplomatic forces to pass a General Assembly resolution condemning Chinese "aggression." Just before the resolution was to come to a vote, in late January, India, which had been energetically probing governments on three continents in hopes of finding an opening for peace talks and believed that a resolution of condemnation could lead to a wider war against China, announced that Peking was willing to negotiate.

Again, it was a message from Panikkar that purported to convey Chinese intentions. Though it shook the unity of the Western position, the resolution of condemnation received the Assembly's approval over Rau's vehement objections. The momentum of the Asian-Arab states' peace efforts disappeared by February 1951, because of consistent failures, and the political attention of major governments swung back to Korea itself, where by late spring a kind of military equilibrium was reached at about the 38th parallel. The Soviet Union proposed peace talks in June, and in July they began, at Panmunjom. India's diplomatic intervention was temporarily withdrawn while the two sides tried to reach a settlement. Up to that point the only gain for India resulting from its risky efforts to mediate were the strengthening of its position as a nonaligned or independent state. On the other hand the losses to India's prestige in the US were considerable as a result of statements on China, and it also lost standing in Peking and Moscow by appearing at times to side with the West. It could not convince both sides at once of its impartial intentions.

After one year and a half of truce negotiations the circumstances seemed auspicious, in the autumn of 1952, for India's resumption of its diplomatic intervention into the diplomacy of the war. The critical issue, which had held up agreement since the previous May, and on which talks broke down in October, was the disposition of the prisoners of war (pows) held by UN forces. The Western position that prisoners should only be returned voluntarily to communist control could not easily be accepted by the other side because of the fact that most prisoners apparently desired to stay in South Korea or Formosa, depending upon their nationality. The UN's negotiator at Panmunjom, an American admiral, gave the main reasons for the Western stand : "It must be admitted that besides humanitarian considerations, the major objective of the Washington decision to insist on voluntary repatriation was to inflict upon the Communists a propaganda defeat which might deter them from further aggression ... if any substantial portion of the ex-communist soldiers refused to return to Communism, a huge set-back to communist subversive activities would ensue."[24] The Chinese-North Korean side repudiated the Western position and charged that the pows were being detained against their will. At the UN the Asian and Arab states took hold of the pow problem in early November 1952, when the failure of the principals to solve it seemed complete. Soon the intricate charting of a verbal course between Western and communist positions fell to V. K. Krishna Menon, who had just joined the Indian delegation, while Mrs. Vijayalakshmi Pandit remained its head. Menon's capabilities for conceiving and drafting a document of face-saving compromise were matched by his painstaking work of interviewing delegations and testing possible solutions, all of which went into the Indian draft resolution on pows submitted on November 17.

United States and Soviet officials had encouraged the resumption of India's active mediation, but when its results appeared, both sides criticized it. To reach a verbal centre point between the conflicting demands for voluntary and for forcible repatriation of pows Menon devised a formula for "non-forcible" repatriation to be carried out by an impartial body of "neutral" states. It was a detailed proposal which tried to avoid total acceptance of the announced position of either side ; in fact, it stretched the communists' reluctance to demand forced return of the pows into a harmony with the Western insistence that pows should be given a chance not to return to the army of which they were members. Despite the obvious support given to the Western position the US government unofficially rejected the Indian draft, possibly to avoid committing the incoming Republican administration on existing Korean policy. The Soviet Union also turned it down later in November, in an official statement which treated Indian mediatory efforts roughly. After the Soviet's rejection the American delegation altered its stand and officially supported the draft, and non-communist support for the Indian move developed a considerable momentum of enthusiam. The Indian resolution was passed on December 3. Menon's purpose, however, was not overwhelming support from only one side, and the failure to obtain Russian and Chinese acceptance of a plan that the communists regarded as "a slightly camouflaged American draft" meant the temporary failure of his work.

But four months later, on March 31, 1953, after the death of Premier Stalin, Chou En-lai cabled the President of the General Assembly virtually accepting the terms of the Indian resolution, and the North Korean regime quickly followed suit. Negotiations resumed at Panmunjom, and various proposals moved back and forth ; ultimately the two sides came to agreement along the lines of the December 3 resolution, on June 8. The most important differences between the UN resolution and the final pow settlement lay in India's specifically stated function according to the latter, as chairman and "umpire" of the Neutral Nations Repatriation Commission (NNRC) and as supplier of the custodian force which would control the prisoners. Apart from the Indian chairman the NNRC was composed of representatives from Czechoslovakia and Poland, Sweden and Switzerland, whose votes on crucial issues taken together could be expected to result in deadlocks. India's decisions therefore were to be decisions of the Commission.

The reason for India's undertaking the prisoner exchange operation was that its diplomatic activities had demonstrated its impartiality on the question of the disposition of the pows. It was a tribute to Indian diplomacy that neither side could escape recognizing the fact that India's main aim was to promote an acceptable peace settlement and that it had assumed a truly neutral attitude on the repatriation issue. By taking on the assignment in Korea the Indian government undertook one of the most delicate and complex tasks ever assigned to a neutral state. Facing the open hostility of the South Korean government under President Syngman Rhee and the militantly-indoctrinated prisoners, by then numbering about 22,000 Koreans and Chinese, camped on a narrow demilitarized zone between two hostile armies, Indian officials and lightly-armed troops took up their positions in early September under conditions of considerable adversity. Lieutenant General K. S. Thimayya, chairman of the NNRC, and Major General S. P. P. Thorat, in charge of the Custodian Force India, headed the operations of interviewing the prisoners and of holding them in their assigned camps. Somewhat less than 6,000 Indian troops and administrative personnel made up the custodian force, which was separate from the small Indian delegation on the NNRC.

The conduct of India's military and civilian representatives in Korea demonstrated a mixture of firm control and willingness to compromise in order to maintain the truce and ultimately dispose of the pows in one way or another. The Indians' main task, to assure that the pows had a chance to choose freely whether or not to return to their original commands, was almost impossible to carry out because of the manner in which the prisoner organizations operated to inhibit freedom of choice. The interviews could only be conducted for ten days out of the ninety days which the armistice agreement provided for that purpose. India refused to try to break up the prisoner organizations and compel the pows to undergo interviews in a free environment because to do so would have required use of excessive force and might have led to mass outbreaks from the camps and an intervention by South Korean troops south of the zone. As a result, General Thimayya had to report at the end of his mission that "I cannot really say it (the work of the

Commission) has been a success because the Commission's main task of explanations to the prisoners could not be completed, owing to conditions beyond our control."[25]

India faced a delicate and even dangerous task in determining what to do with the bulk of the pows who had undergone no interviews at the end of the assigned period. Their disposition should have been dealt with by a political conference attended by both sides, but it was not held in time to relieve the Indians of their responsibilities. The communists demanded that the period for prisoner interviews be extended, which might entail an indefinite extension of the prisoner custodianship ; the UN side insisted that the prisoners be freed, in effect to join the South Korean or Formosan Chinese armies. Caught again between two opposing pressures India followed an ingenious course : the pows were released to their former detaining sides *as prisoners*, rather than as civilians, thus disposing of them but not permitting the UN side to claim that the prisoners had freely chosen non-communist sanctuary. To satisfy the communists, the pows were not released as civilians, as the Terms of Reference required, and thus India agreed with the communists that the Terms had not been fulfilled. But to satisfy the US and its allies the pows were not repatriated. India expected the equally vigorous criticism that both sides administered to General Thimayya's final disposition of the prisoners. But it was gratified later when principal spokesmen from the governments on both sides gave fulsome praise to the impartial and courageous manner in which the Indians performed their functions in Korea.

While the Korean war diplomacy and the disposition of pows substantiated India's claims to being truly nonaligned in global politics, that achievement did not qualify India for participation in the political conference which ultimately tried to solve the Korean problem. Despite its intimate connection with the Korean armistice, India was excluded from the conference which met in Geneva from April 1954, because of US and South Korean opposition to its presence there. The Commonwealth states and many others urged that India be included, but the US refused to relent, partly because it anticipated difficulty in reaching agreements with the communists while nonaligned representatives participated. American officials often expressed dislike for the round-table, multi-sided discussions which Nehru believed encouraged a meeting of minds, and they would agree only to a two-sided direct confrontation at Geneva. The Korean part of the conference reached no conclusions, and the negotiators proceeded to discuss Indo-China on which, partly through Indian informal mediation, they finally reached an agreement.

NONALIGNMENT AS A GROUPING OF STATES

If the Korean war brought India into prominence it also focused global attention on the nonaligned grouping of states. It now appears historically significant that three of the non-permanent members of the Security Council, when the Korean crisis arose, were India, Egypt and Yugoslavia : those three states became the pillars of the nonaligned edifice as it was constructed during the Korean war debates and afterwards. The edifice of nonalignment gave shelter at various times to a large majority of newly independent states and because of its location vis-a-vis the two great power coalitions gave rise to tri-polarity in international politics. But though the third, nonaligned pole had several fairly consistent supporters, it could not be counted upon to act as a bloc. Except on colonial issues, those states which were technically nonaligned in the sense of having no military commitments to either great power coalition did not always act in concert, in the UN or outside its chambers.[26] When it moved as a body on colonial issues it was always reinforced by the communist coalition and hence presented an appearance at those times of being aligned with the communists or being "nonaligned versus the West."[27]

Nonalignment in global politics was a pervasive feature of the 1950's, luring adherents, but not forming them into a coherent alliance or bloc. India urged states to become nonaligned, specifically to abjure foreign military entanglements, but avoided trying to organize them into fixed opposition to the coalitions led by great powers. To so organize them, Nehru felt, would have created a bloc undermining the independence of its members almost as the coalitions did. He encouraged states in Asia to form a "peace area," neutralized from great power conflicts, but hesitated to exert pressure to that end lest nonalignment appear to be alignment with India and hence unacceptable to smaller states. As the originator of nonalignment India was credited by other states with a leadership which did not have a predictable following, but from the Korean war onward, predictably, had a following. The initial support came from Asian and Arab states, and hence the confusion of nonalignment with a geographic area began.

The most dramatic reason that nonalignment could not properly be designated as an Asian-African phenomenon centred on its adoption by an important European state, Yugoslavia, in the years following President Josip Broz Tito's break with Stalin in 1948. The peculiar situation of Yugoslavia geographically and to some extent ideologically demanded the assumption of a nonaligned posture as a condition of national independence. Finding his state isolated from other communist regimes, yet not desiring a merger with the Western bloc, Tito sought support from India and Egypt. In December 1954, when he visited India, he and Nehru discovered a substantial basis for Indo-Yugoslav collaboration in diplomatic affairs—their equally fervent desire to inhibit the outbreak of a major war. Their joint statement at that time repudiated the "erroneous conception" of a third bloc or third force but expressed their desire to "widen the area of peace," or nonalignment, which they explained was "not 'neutrality' or 'neutralism' and, therefore, passivity, as sometimes alleged, but (was) a positive, active and constructive policy seeking to lead to constructive peace, on which alone collective security can really rest."[28] The statement embodied the doctrine advocated by Nehru, based on his psychological insight, that peace did not derive from security, but security from peace.

Nehru returned the visit to Yugoslavia in July 1955, and the two leaders referred to the "identical concepts and principles in their international activities" which underlay their policies and reiterated the need for great power agreement on the control of atomic weapons and for solution of the problems of Germany and Formosa. They also agreed on the desirability of representing mainland China in the UN.[29] Meanwhile Nehru was cultivating relations with the new head of the Egyptian government, Gamal Abdel Nasser, and at their first meeting, in Cairo in February 1955, a similarity of their positions on military pacts was publicized. At another meeting, again in Cairo in July 1955, a more precise agreement was reached (in the face of a spreading alliance system) that "involvement in military pacts or alignment with great powers does not serve the cause of peace. . . ."[30] Finally, at Brioni island in Yugoslavia, in

July 1956, the three leaders held a joint conference which, if nothing else, demonstrated the vigour and geographical spread of the principle they advanced for the amelioration of international crises. Their general prescriptions for a more peaceful world seemed to be directed specifically at the forthcoming "summit" meeting in Geneva of the great powers ; on more specific problems, such as the Algerian crisis, and the dispute over Cyprus, jointly proposed solutions were more difficult to arrive at. The Brioni conference linked states in three continents and more clearly than other international gatherings of the mid-1950's marked those years as the high point of Indian nonalignment diplomacy.

Events in the decade following the Brioni conference of 1956 reinforced the tripartite accord established at that time. The growing threat of nuclear war, the attack on Suez, American inter- vention in the middle east and later in Cuba, the Berlin crisis, and the hostility of China towards India and Yugoslavia brought reaffir- mations of the validity of nonalignment and the common interest of the three states in staving off menacing moves by the great powers. President Tito made another mid-winter visit to India in January 1959, when both Yugoslavia and India were experiencing a hostile shift in Chinese policy towards them. But China did not appear in their public pronouncements, which dealt mainly with the threat of nuclear war and the necessity for peaceful coexistence. By that time Indo-Yugoslav economic links had developed, and that bilateral interest also appeared on the public record.

The desire of some established nonaligned states to bring together the increasing number of governments professing nonalignment, so as to enhance the prestige of the group as a whole, produced the dramatic Belgrade conference of September 1961. The preceding June a preparatory meeting called by Tito and Nasser brought forward the most widely accepted definition of nonalignment, a version of the original Indian idea amended and broadened to receive acceptance from states with diverse interests, such as Ghana, Cuba, Algeria (represented by the Provisional Government), Ethio- pia, and Afghanistan. The criteria of nonalignment were held to be : following of an independent policy or evidence of a trend in that direction, consistent support of movements for national indepen- dence, abjuring of multilateral military alliances concluded in the context of great power conflicts, the refusal to permit the establishment of foreign military bases for purposes related to great power conflicts. Those stipulations both added to and detracted from the concept of nonalignment as enunciated by Nehru. Anticipating distortions of the concept from the efforts of an indeterminate group of states to mould it to suit their needs India had hesitated to attend the preparatory conference in Cairo. Not satisfied with the choices of the twenty-five states invited to Belgrade, India hesitated also to attend the main gathering. But in the end Nehru agreed to go to Yugoslavia, if only to avoid offending the host government and Egypt.

For India, nonalignment in 1961 was no longer a burning issue ; the great powers and particularly in recent months the new American president, John F. Kennedy, supported India's noncommitment and therefore the posture was no longer a goal for which to strive, but an established fact. The tumbling of the newer states into self-proclaimed nonalignment may have gratified Nehru, but it also detracted from India's uniqueness and from its leadership of the rapidly enlarging group. Like a man bored and jaded after attending too many professional conferences all of which seemed to result in redundant expositions of theory and methodology, Nehru appeared in Belgrade with a message that no longer struck the familiar note of anti-colonialism or even peaceful coexistence. He wanted the conference, he said, "to get out of the rut of meeting together, passing long resolutions and making brave declarations, and then going home and allowing the world to drift to disaster."[31] He implored the assembled leaders to make a special pronouncement on the most urgent task facing the governments of the world, "at this particular crisis in human destiny," that of avoiding a global war. "First things must come first, and nothing is more important or has more priority than this world situation of war and peace. Everything else, however, vital to us . . . has a secondary place."

Nehru's words were a blunt retort to those speakers coming before him and those to follow who still struck out against "imperialism, colonialism, racialism and the rest. . . ." He was demonstrating his broader, global vision of mankind's problems, and he knew that his words would not be popular. He would have to force his lessons upon an audience of politicians reluctant to abandon the parochial nationalist appeals that had brought most of them into power. He had said it before to Indians in the narrower context of the debates on the Commonwealth, and he chose Belgrade to announce his convictions among governments which had less than one year earlier moved the General Assembly to pass a resolution on the necessity of ending colonialism : "The era of classic colonialism," he said, "is gone and is dead. . . ." If there should be a major war, he reminded the conference, nothing else really mattered. He advised against specific recommendations to the major powers on the pressing crises of Berlin and escalation of nuclear weaponry because he understood the impossibility of mediating when the vital interests of the great powers were at stake : "When big countries feel that their national honour is involved they risk war, whatever the consequences." But the countries at Belgrade, representing a large portion of mankind, should assert their combined moral weight for peace—"our voice counts to some extent."

The idea of a special, forceful plea for peace was not only Nehru's ; Tito and Nasser before him had voiced identical fears. But Nehru's voice was the strongest, and many people in the world had become accustomed to listening to him. His staff, headed by Krishna Menon, managed to obtain a special section in the conference declaration devoted solely to the need for peace.

A certain annoyance by Western states sprung from the Belgrade states' refusal to condemn the resumption of Russian nuclear testing on the eve of the conference's convening after a long moratorium by both sides. Nehru, however, accused the Russians of enhancing the danger of war by resuming the tests. He 'deeply regretted' the move. The US hoped for ringing condemnation of Russian testing from Belgrade. Nehru probably asked himself, for what constructive purpose benefiting the countries assembled should the conference condemn Russia. But in perspective[32] the Belgrade conference could not be easily judged as a set-back for the US position. No bloc of nonaligned states emerged, and individually many of the governments represented at Belgrade, including India, respected the policies of the new American President.

Nehru's and Menon's participation in the Belgrade conference gained nothing for India and lost it some friends and admirers. Menon's presence, incidentally, may have further undermined India's popularity among many African and Asian delegations ; according to one observer, he was "at his most acerbic throughout the conference."[33] Nehru seemed to have used the conference not to strengthen nonalignment, much less anti-colonialism, but to add force to his dialogue with the great powers. He left Belgrade to keep a prior appointment in Moscow, and in November he was in Washington. The year, 1961, marked a weakening of Nehru's and India's influence on world politics. At the Belgrade conference India relinquished much of what remained of its leadership in Asia and Africa. The invasion of Goa in December undermined some of Nehru's prestige in the West. The Chinese attack in 1962 revealed India's military weakness, its reliance in a crisis on the West and on the Soviet Union, as well as the failure of its policy of peaceful coexistence towards China.

India's disenchantment with conferences of a nonaligned or Afro-Asian character increased when such meetings yielded almost no public support for India at the time of the Chinese attack in 1962. But other states, notably Indonesia and Yugoslavia, were still pursuing the gains in national prestige that they felt derived from ad hoc international gatherings and sought Indian agreement to a "second Belgrade" or "second Bandung." A great deal of discussion finally resulted in plans for a second nonaligned conference, at Cairo in October 1964. India supported it partly to postpone or avoid an Afro-Asian meeting which would have China and other aligned states in attendance ; nevertheless nonaligned groupings always had the appearance of being Afro-Asian, despite the presence of Yugoslavs and a few latin Americans. From twenty-eight members at Belgrade the nonaligned or quasi-nonaligned grouping grew to forty-seven at Cairo, and the debates and resolutions were accordingly more diffuse and characterless. Lal Bahadur Sastri had succeeded Nehru as Indian Prime Minister in June 1964 and made his international conference debut at Cairo.

Chief among Sastri's objectives was the gaining of support at Cairo for India's stand against China. In pursuit of that goal Sastri introduced, without warning, a proposal to send a mission to China to try to persuade it to desist from developing nuclear weapons ; he thereby applied still another test to determine what supporters India had among the nonaligned. Only President Makarios of Cyprus gave him public support. Others ignored the proposal or thought it was inappropriate. (China exploded its first nuclear device less than a week after the conference ended.) Further, the nonaligned conference might have added its influence to the proposals for an Indian-Chinese Himalayan border truce made two years. before at Colombo and not yet fully carried out. But no state at Cairo wished to offend China : India's international problems were its own, as its lonely position at Cairo demonstrated. The states did pledge themselves "to respect frontiers as they existed when the States gained independence," in deference to India's wishes, and the conference declaration reflected Indians' drafting skills. But those were the meagre benefits derived from the second conference of the nonaligned by the founder and one-time leader of that grouping.

The government of Mrs. Indira Gandhi, which succeeded Sastri's in January 1966, recaptured some of the benefits from association with the nonaligned when Tito and Nasser came to New Delhi in October 1966 for a meeting of the three original Brioni conference states. Away from the confusion and conflicting interests of a large conference the three states managed to identify again the nonaligned posture at the very time when communists were holding a world conference in Moscow and the US was convening a Vietnamese strategy meeting with six allies in Manila. For India at least it was a posture considerably removed from the original stance of the early 1950's, when the "cold war" was at an apex, but on the surface it still provided the benefit of highest value to India, relative independence in what was then a polycentric global political system. Nonalignment as a doctrine, not a political posture, by 1966 had developed into a powerful expression of opposition to the uses of military power by great states. In specific reference to the current military escalation in Vietnam the New Delhi conference took a stand for an unconditional end to American bombing of North Vietnam and a settlement in accordance with the Geneva accord. The doctrine of nonalignment also had by then extended its terms to include the protest of economically underdeveloped countries against the insufficient transfer of resources to them from the advanced economies and against the barriers inhibiting their exports of processed and finished products.

Conferences of the nonaligned had not proved, on balance, of much value to India, which had independently and by practical example achieved what some other states hoped to gain through joint declarations. Nonalignment in practice was India's singular contribution to post-Second World War international politics.

If newly independent states endeavoured to achieve that posture it was because India had demonstrated the power that nonalignment could provide. If the great powers learned to respect that posture it was because Indian diplomacy had proved a valuable instrument for the settlement of disputes and the maintenance of peace.

NOTES AND REFERENCES

[1] Charles Burton Marshall's observation, in Martin, ed., *Neutralism and Nonalignment*, p. 28.

[2] See George Liska's analysis of "tripartism," in *ibid.*, p. 211f.

[3] Some major works on the subject were Martin's, *op. cit.* ; Peter Lyon, *Neutralism* ; Cecil V. Crabb, Jr., *The Elephants and the Grass*, perhaps the best of them ; and the *Annals*, Nov. 1965. In this book we are less interested in explaining why India adopted the posture of nonalignment than in understanding what were the results in foreign relations of its adoption. Further, we excuse ourselves from the game that searches for the distinctions among nonalignment, neutrality, non-commitment, neutralism, et cetera, which is either too obvious or to devious to play honestly.

[4] The foremost study on the foreign policy ideas of the Congress is Bimla Prasad, *The Origins of Indian Foreign Policy* ; see especially pp. 275-77. Most of the information in these paragraphs derives from that book.

[5] Nehru, *Discovery of India*, N. Y., 1946, p. 426.

[6] Prasad, *op. cit.*, pp. 276-77.

[7] Nehru told the Lok Sabha on March 31, 1955 : "What is the trouble with the world today? Not perhaps so much the aggressive intentions of any country, though individuals may have them, but the terrible fear of each country that the other has aggressive intentions. In order to prevent the other from being the aggressor you become the aggressor yourself." *FAR*, vol. I, 3 (March 1955), p. 53.

[8] Nehru, *Independence and After*, p. 237.

[9] *ibid.*, p. 340

[10] *ibid.*, p. 298.

[11] A sensitive appreciation of the attitudes of newly independent states toward entangling alliances with great powers was written by John Spanier in his *World Politics in an Age of Revolution*, N. Y., 1967, chap. VII. The author draws on early American diplomatic history to explain the reasons for nonalignment among states in the mid-20th century.

[12] We use the term, power, when referring to international politics, to mean influence on the policies of other states. See Harold D. Lasswell and Abraham Kaplan, *Power and Society*, New Haven, 1950, p. 74f. R. H. Tawney's use of the term, quoted therein, is : "Power may be defined as the capacity of an individual or group of individuals, to modify the conduct of other individuals or groups of individuals in the manner which he desires. . . ." From his *Equality*, N. Y., 1931, p. 230.

[13] Press Conference, July 7, 1950 ; Nehru, *Press Conferences, 1950*, p. 127.

[14] Nehru's speech at the Bandung Conference in 1955 ; in *Asian African*

6

Conference ; Speeches of the Prime Minister of India in the Closed Sessions, New Delhi (Ministry of External Affairs), 1955, p. 14.

[15] cf. Michael Brecher's analysis in his *The New States of Asia*, London, 1963, chap. III.

[16] *FAR*, vol. IV, II (Nov. 1958), p. 258. See the commentary on Nehru's reliance on that approach in Willard Range, *Jawaharlal Nehru's World View*, pp. 26-27, 89.

[17] Werner Levi, "Necrology on Indian Neutralism," *Eastern World*, Feb. 1963, p. 9.

[18] In the following treatment of India's diplomacy in the Korean war an unpublished Ph. D. dissertation, Yale, 1957, guides the narrative : C. H. Heimsath, "India's Role in the Korean War." See also Shiv Dayal, *India's Role in the Korean Question*, Delhi, 1959.

[19] Press conference, July 7, 1950 ; Nehru, *Press Conferences, 1950*, p. 105.

[20] *LSD*, vol. V, pt. II, Aug. 4, 1950, cols. 382-83.

[21] Panikkar, *In Two Chinas ; Memoirs of a Diplomat*, London, 1955, pp. 104-10.

[22] Harry S. Truman, *Memoirs*, vol. II, N. Y., 1956, p. 362.

[23] Press conference, Oct. 16 ; Nehru, *Press Conferences, 1950*, p. 209.

[24] Turner Joy, *How Communists Negotiate*, N. Y., 1955, pp. 150-52.

[25] Quoted in *Indiagram*, Indian Embassy, Washington, March 3, 1954.

[26] Francis O. Wilcox analyzed the nonaligned voting record in the UN in chap. VII of Martin, *Neutralism and Nonalignment*. G. H. Jansen, *Nonalignment and the Afro-Asian States*, tried to disabuse anyone of the idea that there was any real unity in either nonalignment or Afro-Asia.

[27] "It is often asked why India and other Asian countries are so loud in their protests against European colonialism, while they are silent about the colonialism of the Soviets. The answer is clear. The Soviets have never claimed that they represent the free world and have never asked India or any other country to join forces with them. Their ideology is different, and so long as they do not force their views on us, we do not force our views on them. But the case of the free world is different. It is claimed that by refusing to line up with the free world we are doing something morally reprehensible and politically bad. It therefore becomes important for us to know what the free world represents. Such a question does not arise with regard to the Soviet Union, as we know what Communism means and have been fighting it even while others were fraternizing with Moscow." "P" (Narayana Raghavan Pillai), "Middle Ground Between America and Russia : An Indian View," *Foreign Affairs*, January, 1954, p. 266.

[28] *Foreign Policy of India ; Texts of Documents, 1947-1959*, pp. 145-47.

[29] *ibid.*, pp. 195-97.

[30] *ibid.*, pp. 157, 201-02.

[31] *The Conference of Heads of State or Government of Nonaligned Countries*, published by Yugoslavia, provided texts of all the speeches ; this and other quotations are taken from that document. In this case, as in others, the collected speeches of Nehru published by the Indian govt. do not present the entire text.

[32] Such as that of Arthur M. Schlesinger, Jr. in *A Thousand Days*, Boston 1965, pp. 520-21.

[33] Jansen, *op. cit.*, p. 302.

CHAPTER IV

THE EMERGENCE OF INDIAN FOREIGN POLICY IN THE UNITED NATIONS

SECOND ONLY TO the statements of Jawaharlal Nehru the voluminous records of the UN provide the clearest exposition of India's interests and objectives in international affairs. They reveal India's unique style of diplomacy premised on nonalignment and heavily dependent on the power of the spoken and written word to alter or amend the policies of other states. For India, no less than for other recently independent states, the UN served as a stage on which a nation's role in world affairs could be enacted, a setting in which the audience as well as the fellow players were the governments (and public opinions) that wielded power in the world. Previously a member of the League of Nations and continuously represented in the major world organizations from 1919, independent India saw the UN as its primary vehicle for innovation in foreign policies. The most radical changes in Indian international objectives and diplomatic methods which followed the transfer of power were translated at once into positions in the UN and its specialized agencies.

Like other political movements with liberal heritages the Indian National Congress viewed the new world organization after the Second World War with a mixture of scepticism and idealism. In terms of power, the UN offered India an obvious and facile means of exerting influence not available on a global level through any other political mechanism. To be able to conduct verbal interchanges with representatives of the great and middle ranking states on an apparent basis of equality, both privately and publicly, brought unparalleled benefits to an Indian government whose purpose was to proclaim its independent identity and plead for an international recognition of its interests. Indian representatives, who excelled in the use of language and many of whom were keen in law and cosmopolitan in manner, contributed in a major way to the accumulation of their nation's intangible power, based, as just described, on nonalignment. Nonalignment, in fact, though conceived earlier, was given birth in UN chambers in the late 1940's and early 1950's. It was there, in the debates and voting records, that India established the pattern of independence of action that reached its climax during the Korean War diplomacy. It was there, too, that India and other Asian and African states approached, on occasions, that unity of purpose and action which they desired in order to bring about some redistribution of the tangible power factors in the world.

The Indian government under Nehru's leadership should not have been characterized as idealistic on the basis of its policies in the UN, which persistently·and sometimes dogmatically aimed at fulfilling India's own national interests. Nevertheless, Nehru and most knowledgeable Indians spoke and acted with a genuine conviction that the ideals of the Charter could be realized. The Indian delegation at San Francisco in 1945, functioning without any authoritative nationalist mandate under the chairmanship of A. Ramaswami Mudaliar, made no major contributions to the drafting of the Charter.[1] Instead, it found itself embarrassed by the presence in San Francisco of a non-official "delegation," whose most vociferous member was Mrs. Vijayalakshmi Pandit, sister of Nehru ; the official delegation was forced occasionally to uphold publicly its position against the widely publicized attacks upon it by Mrs. Pandit.[2] But after independence the Charter became Nehru's most consistent criterion for judging international conduct and a compendium of ideals to which his government could subscribe. He felt that if there was hope in the world for a new dispensation that might lessen conflict and promote international justice it might lie in the reconstructive efforts that the UN could undertake ; if a new age was indeed at hand, of greater human welfare and equality, and of peace and cultural development, then the foundations and first evidences of that epoch would most readily be apparent within the framework of the new organization.

Indian leaders hoped, chiefly because of the vastly altered status of India by 1947 but also because of an informed appraisal of the trends in world affairs, that major transformations in human affairs would follow the Second World War and would benefit particularly those peoples who had hitherto reaped few returns from the advances of the modern age. The domination of the world by white Europeans seemed to be giving way and the possibilities for the advancement of all peoples were thereby opening up. The UN with its provision for universal membership and its promises of world-wide progress was the most likely agency through which those transformations could take place. These ideals and hopes were the long-range and philosophical expressions that appeared in Indians' discussions of the UN in its early years of operation.

In the pursuit of its global ideals as also in the narrower defense of its own interests and establishment of its unique kind of influence, India participated, broadly, in two types of UN proceedings : settlement of disputes involving global powers and advancement of special Indian interests.

ATTEMPTS TO SETTLE GLOBAL DISPUTES

Nehru recognized that the major purpose for which the UN was established was to lessen the chances of war, and if the peace of the world could be kept through the UN nothing more was needed to justify its existence. The Charter made effective peace-keeping by the UN dependent upon the cooperation between the great powers, but this cooperation had given way to the "cold war" even before the world organization had begun fully to function. In a message broadcast from UN headquarters on May 5, 1950, Nehru already understood that the "high hopes with which the United Nations Organization was started have not been fulfilled". He deplored the growth of "two hostile camps" in the world, which threatened the peace-keeping functions of the organization, but he acknowledged that the UN was "the only hope of finding a way for peaceful co-operation among nations. If the United Nations ceases to be or if it radically changes its position and nature, then there is nothing left which would inspire hope for the future. We shall have to go through terrible experiences and face disasters again. . . ."[3] Under such conditions the UN's major task, scarcely recognized in the language of the Charter, lay in reconciling the conflicting interests of the two great power coalitions. Without that reconciliation peace was impossible.

Following the lead of their prime minister Indian diplomats in UN bodies appeared deeply troubled by the great power conflict and quickly became involved in issues raised by the "cold war." The quality of the Indian endeavours to create a "climate of peace," to mediate constructively in critical disputes, and to strengthen the UN's peace-keeping functions sprang from a conviction inspired by Nehru and Mahatma Gandhi and many other modern Indian leaders that India had a peculiar mission of encouraging peace in the world. Such a conviction, and the public recognition that derived from upholding it, stimulated many Indian representatives at the UN to hard and creative work, more satisfying perhaps, and evoking more sensitive political skills than justifying their government's special interests.

If the UN was to fulfill its proclaimed purpose of promoting peace, Indians argued, the Security Council and the General Assembly would have to function as bodies seeking harmonization and compromises among competing interests, not as vehicles for the advancement of the special interests of states. The UN, in short, should be used as an instrument of negotiation and compromise. (That view seemed to conflict with India's approach to issues in which its own special interests were at stake, but in proper perspective the discrepancy was not as severe as it sometimes appeared to be : the subduing of the great power struggle required more hard-wrought compromises and greater efforts to reduce conflicts—for the sake of world peace, perhaps for the continued existence of civilization itself—than were necessary in disputes between a great and a small power or among small powers.) Indian delegates could therefore almost always be found leading the opposition to any great power—most often the US—whose proposed resolutions condemned the other great power or offended against its interests.

While the Western coalition controlled the majority of votes in the Security Council and General Assembly India frequently voted against or abstained on majority resolutions which accomplished nothing more than to proclaim the faults of communist policies and thereby win propaganda victories for the West. Such was the explanation for Indian voting abstentions during the 1956 Hungarian crisis and during earlier debates on Soviet denials of human rights in eastern Europe. India achieved a reputation in its UN diplomacy of subordinating its principled advocacy of democracy and human rights to its desire not to partake in what it believed was a Western effort to chastize communist regimes. Likewise, but less frequently, it refused to support communist efforts to embarrass the Western democracies.

To inhibit any domination of the UN by one great power India favoured retention of the veto power in the Security Council. Indians argued during the late 1940's and early 1950's that a veto-free UN would become a Western-dominated UN, although it might also become a stronger instrument in the process. To avoid distorting the functions of the General Assembly by permitting it to discharge responsibilities for maintaining peace and security, the primary concern of the Security Council, India voted against the "uniting for peace" resolution sponsored by the US in 1950. Furthermore, India was doubtful of the wisdom of forming a UN police force on a permanent basis, because in the absence of great power accord such a force would probably function in the interests of only one of the "cold war" rivals. For the same reason it refused to support the work of the Collective Measures Committee in the early 1950's, a Western supported body whose declared aim it was to strengthen the ability of the UN to maintain peace and security. On the other hand, temporary or ad hoc UN peace-keeping operations, such as in Gaza and in the Congo, prompted strong Indian support and contributions of personnel ; chapters XI and XIX include considerations of those Indian involvements.

In short, India's diplomacy aimed, almost instinctively, at securing a balance of power in the world organization as a partial political guarantee against the resort to force by one or the other of the major coalitions. That balance, best secured by the Security Council's voting procedure, permitted a measure of flexibility in world politics, a healthy inconclusiveness of "cold war" disputes that improved the chances of peace. The great power deadlock in the UN on the global issues provided, in addition, a broader platform on which the smaller, and particularly the uncommitted, states could act than would have been possible under conditions of a UN dominated by one global coalition—or, for that matter, by both global coalitions.[4]

Consistent with its desire to promote the UN's mechanisms for peaceful settlement of international disputes the Indian government favoured the representation of all states in the world organization. The membership issue was most fervently joined over the question of the admission to the UN of representatives of the People's Republic of China ; apart from the Soviet Union India expended more effort in trying to have Peking's delegates seated than did any other state. Some of India's enthusiasm for that annually publicized cause derived from its calculated policy of friendliness toward China. But the main argument that Indians used in support of their case was that the representation of mainland China in the UN would facilitate negotiations with the Peking regime, notably during the Korean War, and possibly also encourage that government to rely more heavily on diplomacy than on force to achieve its ends.

India's commitment to the UN as a vehicle for peaceful settlement of disputes did not imply its willingness to adhere uncompromisingly to international legal mechanisms to achieve the same end. "In reviewing the history of relevant United Nations projects and business, it is quickly observable that, apart from a lawyer's professional interest in his subject, the Indian delegations have studiously avoided the temptation to build international controls in terms of legal maxims."[5] The practical results of a line of action, not its formal adherence to legal precedents, captured the interest of most Indian UN delegates. The spirit rather than the precise wording of a resolution bore its main meanings. V. K. Krishna Menon's legal facility often received commendation from his non-Indian colleagues, but their greatest praise was reserved for his skill not in defining words but in stretching their meanings to allow for compromises.

India's representatives often sensed that a rigidly legalistic approach to solving a problem inhibited the free flow of ideas and the political manoeuvring that often ended in compromises. As might have been expected, they failed conspicuously to apply that understanding in their own dispute with Pakistan over Kashmir ; Indians held rigidly to the legal fact of Kashmir's accession to India and made subordinate to that the more flexible facets of the situation where compromises might have entered in. In attempting to mediate in the disputes of other states Nehru led his colleagues in appreciating the fact that international affairs did not conform to legal norms and that the dealings of any state and any international organization were at base political.

India's emphasis on political rather than legal mechanisms to solve international disputes partly explained its reluctance to refer its own disputes to the International Court of Justice or to any ad hoc tribunal. Although the contending parties to several disputes with India, such as the Kashmir dispute and the treatment of Indians in South Africa, offered to submit their cases to international legal bodies for decisions or advisory opinions, India usually refused to become a party to such procedures. New Delhi submitted the case of the demarcation of the Indo-Pakistani boundary in the desolate and uninhabited Rann of Kutch to an ad hoc tribunal for adjudication, and two agreements with Pakistan, a 1959 boundary accord and the 1960 Indus waters agreement, had arbitration provisions. But those were exceptions not involving national interests of primary status. Generally, India held to the position that legal decisions—if such ever emerged from international courts and tribunals—could not resolve the fundamental political problem underlying disputes, namely that of reconciling conflicts of national interests.

Despite India's legal approach to international conflicts and its hesitancy to submit its own disputes for arbitration or adjudication, it was, among non-European states, an early adherent to the "optional clause" of the statute of the International Court of Justice, which gave the Court automatic jurisdiction, when applied for, in disputes both of whose parties were committed under the clause. In 1929 and again in 1940 India declared its willingness to be bound by the clause except in regard to disputes "which by international law" fell exclusively within its domestic jurisdiction. In late 1955 Portugal, within three days of its own adherence to the "optional clause," invoked it against India in a dispute over the Portuguese enclaves in Indian territory. India was thereby forced to submit that dispute to the World Court, but it did so under protest and then promptly withdrew the 1940 declaration of acceptance of the clause. In a new declaration made in January 1956 India's definition of domestic jurisdiction was considerably tightened. And in September 1959 it deposited with the Court another statement of the exceptions to its commitment to compulsory jurisdiction, which included disputes in which it was involved with members of the Commonwealth (attention here directed towards Pakistan), with a state having no diplomatic relations with India, and with a state whose acceptance of the "optional clause" was deposited less than one year before the dispute was filed.[6]

India's reluctance to submit its own international disputes to juridical bodies whose judgments had to conform to the established tenets of international law illustrated an attitude toward the substance and procedures of that formalized code of international conduct shared by most newly independent states.[7] The proportion of the Asian and African states which had subscribed to the "optional clause" of the World Court's statute in 1960 was much lower than the proportion of European and American states which were parties to that instrument.[8] All newly independent states manifested a disliking similar to India's for settlements of disputes through legal mechanisms, and the reasons for that state of affairs were not difficult to ascertain. The division of the material wealth and power of the world resulted in a gross disequilibrium among states which traditional international law upheld by protecting the economic and political status quo. Private investments in foreign countries gained protection from traditional international legal arrangements ; the international creditor-debtor relationship was similarly underwritten by law ; and, above all, imperialist control over large sections of the earth's surface had several centuries of legal norms to support it.

In other words, wealth and political power in great disproportion to population lay in the grasp of the established states, whose general adherence to international law demonstrated the fact that the law served their interests. Existing law governing (and reflecting) international behaviour thus was a product of a state system which imposed great disabilities on Asian and African nations. Newly independent states could not accept that law in toto and at the same time succeed in redressing the imbalances under which they suffered disadvantages. They openly repudiated the law governing sovereignty in all cases where it could be invoked in order to defend a colonial regime. India's blatant and successful challenge to established legal sovereignty in Goa was one of the more remarkable examples of that repudiation.[9]

India and similarly situated states recognized that international law had never been a single fabric which had been woven or could be unwoven at one time. Those states had no complete alternative to offer in place of existing international law, and they knew that their interests, for example in economic development, would suffer from any breakdown in the established pattern of inter-state relations. India was committed, to a degree, by article 51 of its Constitution, which declared the state's willingness to "foster respect for international law and treaty obligations," and Indian courts followed the pre-independence pattern upholding the binding effect of inter-national law on municipal law. India fully accepted the high place of law in peaceful dealings among states. But it demanded that the law move with the political realities of the times in order to achieve as nearly as possible general adherence from old and new states alike.

On the foregoing general matters of the UN's political structure and the procedures for peaceful settlement of disputes India's views and its diplomatic endeavours could be regarded as significant but not as exceptional. A fuller measure of the quality of its UN diplomacy could be revealed by examining the efforts of its repre-sentatives to apply the "climate of peace" approach to political conflicts. Their persistent efforts to encourage constructive com-munication between the contending parties during most of the Korean War crisis and their fruitful search for a compromise formula for settling the prisoner of war issue were unique contributions, the second of which was essential to the signing of the truce. Other Indian efforts to mediate and to promote the conditions for settle-ments achieved less public notice, except as they dramatized the Indian posture of nonalignment. On many of the great issues of the "cold war," such as Soviet policies in eastern Europe, the division of Germany and Berlin, American involvements in the far east, and disarmament, Indians searched with greater skill and persistence than many other delegates for possibilities of great power agreement. Most of those issues will be discussed in later sections of this volume.

Indian efforts to encourage solutions to particular problems in the UN were an inseparable part of Nehru's global peace-making objective. Nehru put faith in the UN as a mechanism for peace for the same reasons that he often called for round-table talks and "summit" meetings, namely, that face-to-face encounters among principal policy-makers or their immediate spokesmen could elicit that essential rationality, even humaneness, that political relations conducted at a distance always managed to obscure. UN resolu-tions that would receive Indian support, therefore, were likely to be those which pointed the way to talks between contending parties (and sometimes included nonaligned buffers and potential mediators) rather than those specifying particular solutions offered by one side.

THE UN ARMS DEBATE

One UN question consistently illustrative of the Indian diplomatic peace-making work arose annually on the issue of arms control and disarmament. At the time of Indian independence the UN debate on that issue centreed on contending US and Soviet proposals for the control of atomic energy, the one side suggesting international—which under the current circumstances meant Western—control, the other urging immediate outlawing and destruction of atomic weapons. The position assumed by India during the acrimonious and fruitless debates on those proposals and on the related ones of international inspection and conventional arms reduction was to support the work of any agency, such as the Disarmament Commission, seeking a solution to the problem of the arms race, and to avoid taking sides.

Although disarmament negotiations were conducted under the aegis of the UN, in fact only states with nuclear arms capacity had any direct influence on the discussions, which for the most part provided little more than a propaganda forum for the "cold war" contestants.[10] On an issue vital to the security of both great powers the mediating efforts of no third state were welcomed by the principals. India's UN delegation had no choice during the 1950's but to assert from the sidelines what was obvious—no agreement could be reached on the specific terms of any arms measure until the great powers were prepared to end their political confrontation. As a pious hope the Indian delegation always favoured the diversion of atomic energy and military expenditures to the cause of economic development and general welfare.

Because the Soviet Union frequently offered to its major rival and to the world vague proposals for complete disarmament, and because in more concrete terms its suggestions aimed at inhibiting nuclear weapons capacity and eradicating foreign military bases as first steps, Indian spokesmen, including Nehru, appeared biased in favour of the communist stands on arms questions. The US, whose nuclear capability, some of it located in overseas bases, acted as a rough balance against Russian manpower superiority, was vulnerable in its global public relations on the nuclear disarmament issue. It found India's persistent criticisms of nuclear stockpiling a painful confirmation of the view that nonaligned states usually wavered in the direction of pro-Soviet stands. Washington evidenced little receptivity to Indian statements on disarmament and criticized Indian UN delegations for seeming to want international arms agreements even of a purely verbal sort, with no pragmatic effects, rather than no agreements at all. Indeed, Indian proposals tended to be couched in terms of wide generalizations, or amounted to little more than the "sum of the opposing positions divided by two," as an Indian diplomat once admitted to the authors. This type of mediation, which sought to cover controversy with words of conciliation, was called "semantic diplomacy ;"[11] and in the hard bargaining atmosphere of the arms negotiations there would have been little scope for verbal conciliation even if the great powers had wanted it.

During the 1950's India's diplomacy concentrated on two aspects of the arms debate, nuclear weapons testing and the mechanisms for negotiations on disarmament. Among the non-nuclear armed states India was the foremost exponent of the dangers of nuclear testing, and Nehru was the first head of government formally to propose a test ban. On April 2, 1954, after contamination from American tests had injured Japanese fishermen, he issued an appeal in parliament to the great powers to reach an understanding to cease testing nuclear weapons "even if arrangements about the discontinuance of production and stockpiling must await more substantial agreement."[12] Nehru's words, spoken at the time when India's influence on critical international disputes was at its peak, defined the major short-term goal of Indian diplomacy on arms control during the 1950's, and Indian representatives followed the lead by relentlessly publicizing the hazards to public health and genetic normality of continued explosions of nuclear devices in the atmosphere.

In December 1955 the Indian UN delegation presented a draft resolution in the General Assembly on a cessation of testing, which was not pressed to a vote ; in the years following the Indians pursued the goal of test cessation and sometimes managed to have their ideas approved by the Assembly, but usually in an amended form and incorporated into Western sponsored resolutions urging further consideration by the Disarmament Commission. While the Indian press and eminent national leaders, such as C. Rajagopalachari, appealed to a global audience to arouse popular sentiment against testing, V. K. Krishna Menon tried to get a hearing in the Disarmament Commission for his government's views. In July 1956 Menon was permitted to present to the Commission India's opinion that nuclear explosions violated international law and morality and that they should be stopped, at least as a confidence-building measure. His speech, later incorporated into a note verbale to the Commission, argued that testing could be suspended without attendant guarantees and checks because of the advanced stage of detecting mechanisms. It was a masterful enunciation, typical of Menon, of the proposition that some degree of faith and a "climate of peace" were the only ways to reduce the tension which seemed to threaten the world with disaster.

India's campaign against weapons testing displayed an intensity of conviction and a persistence of endeavour probably unequalled by any other Indian international crusade. From 1954 onward Indian representatives and Nehru introduced the subject into nearly every bilateral and multilateral general discussion of which they were a part, and the catalogue of joint statements, communiques, and conference resolutions that Indians helped to draft witnessed the success of their campaign.[13] The conferences of the so-called Colombo powers, the 1955 Commonwealth prime ministers conference, the Afro-Asian meeting at Bandung, Nehru's meetings with Bulganin and Khrushchev and with Tito and Nasser, his bilateral talks with leaders from Asian and middle eastern countries, and even the working committee meetings of the League of Red Cross Societies all issued public statements conforming in varying degrees to India's position on nuclear testing. American representatives sometimes gave their assent in principle to the Indian stand but steadily maintained that inspection methods had to be built into any test ban—it would not take the leap of faith than Menon and Nehru promised would cleanse the psychological atmosphere of its fear and mistrust. Furthermore, as President Eisenhower wrote to Nehru, the US was "at a stage when testing is required particularly for the development of important defensive uses of these weapons."[14]

Because the existence and threatened use of weapons of mass destruction and the testing of nuclear devices presented real dangers to small as well as great powers India and other relatively weak states sought the right of participation in negotiations dealing with arms control and disarmament. Their claim to a voice in those matters constituted, in effect, the claim of an innocent humanity witnessing the preparations of a few powerful nations for a war that was likely to mean global annihilation. In 1956 India began a campaign to achieve nonaligned participation in arms talks, partly on grounds that states outside the "cold war" might introduce a buffering element into the stalemated proceedings. The Disarmament Commission was enlarged by an Assembly resolution in November 1957, which demonstrated the growing importance of a powerful movement among non-nuclear states to force the nuclear powers to attend more seriously to general world opinion in arms questions.

Until 1958 the most that could be claimed for India's influence on the arms debate was that as a prominent member of the General Assembly, which nominally sponsored the various arms control conferences, and as a major component of the public international audience witnessing and judging that debate, its reaction helped to convince the American and Russian governments that non-nuclear powers would not relax their criticisms of the arms race until meaningful agreements emerged.

A voluntary moratorium on nuclear testing by the US, the UK, and the USSR began operation in 1958, but it was not observed by France. And a series of political ruptures in American-Russian relations during the succeeding years eroded the hopes placed in the moratorium and assured that one side or the other would eventually break the accord. That indeed happened in September 1961, when the Soviet Union resumed testing. The next phase of disarmament negotiations will be dealt with ahead, in chapter XIX.

The "cold war" decade of the 1950's might be said to have ended with the unsuccessful Paris meeting in May 1960 of the three Western heads of government and the Soviet premier, an ending symbolic at once of the failure of the great coalitions to come to any stated accord on arms control and the other great issues between them and yet also of their desire not to precipitate a world crisis that would lead automatically to war. No confidence or trust, of the kind that Nehru had long pleaded for, existed between the US and the USSR ; yet neither side wanted a conflict with the other. In short, it was a stalemated balance maintained by the terror of nuclear weapons. The Paris meeting broke down after Khruschev's attack on Eisenhower for authorizing U-2 reconnaisance flights over Russia.

The unprecedentedly boisterous General Assembly session beginning in September, equally, marked the culmination of a post-war era of mutual suspicions and threats among the great powers, but it also signalled the beginning of a new era of what was later called polycentrism, the breaking up of the two coalitions into disunified components and the emergence of new power centres in global politics. The UN session attracted the leaders of most of the influential, or would-be influential, member states, including Khrushchev, Eisenhower, Macmillan, Tito, Nasser, Castro, Sukarno, and Nehru, each of whom sought to advance his government's special purposes in a confused and dramatic setting of portentous futility. The outcome of public meetings and private conferences between many of the most responsible and talented political leaders in the world was a triumph of national interests over the hopes of internationalism in a pattern that had become predictable in the 1950's..

Nehru's original scepticism about the UN's chances of success as well as his personal brand of pessimism about the nature of world politics immunized him from the disillusionment that the fifteenth UN session could have easily inspired. His assessment of one and one-half decades of the UN's functioning consisted in saying "definitely ... the United Nations has amply justified its existence and repeatedly prevented the recurrent crises from developing into war. It has played a great role, and it is a little difficult now to think of this troubled world without the UN. If it had defects, they lay in the world situation itself which inevitably it mirrored."[15] Nehru reviewed the structural disabilities that India deplored : the imbalance between Europe and the Americas on the one hand and the Afro-Asian world on the other, which however was soon to disappear with the flood of new African member states ; the absence of representation for communist China ; a new threat to the smooth working of the office of the secretary-general embodied in the Soviet "troika" proposal for a three-man executive head of the secretariat, which India strongly opposed. He mentioned the urgency demanded by the specific crises in Algeria and the Congo and the long-lasting problems of colonialism and racialism.

But Nehru's speech in the politically overheated setting of the

General Assembly lay its major weight on the UN's failure to check the arms race. All other swift and slow moving crises had been at least partially relieved by UN action ; yet the growth of nuclear arms stockpiles implied the possibility that international progress in other areas might be negated, and the world's creeping efforts toward general progress reversed suddenly and perhaps irrevocably by the actions of a handful of people. The influence of Nehru and of his state, which had extended widely over diversified UN questions since 1946, in 1960 began to focus narrowly on the single issue of disarmament, which for Nehru overrode all other issues. He offered no panacea, no formula for an overall arms reduction. He addressed himself, as he had before, to the US and the USSR to serve mankind in the highest way possible, by removing the threat to its existence. The tapering off of the "cold war" during the years following could not be explained in simple terms, but the diplomatic pressures of India and other weaker states effectively applied in the public forums of UN bodies made their mark on the minds of the most influential men in world politics.

THE ADVANCEMENT OF SPECIAL INTERESTS : HUMAN RIGHTS

Nehru made his formal debut in the world political arena on November 3, 1948, when he addressed the General Assembly meeting in Paris. Following an admonition on the futility of trying to build a peaceful world within an atmosphere of "hatred and violence" the Indian leader proceeded to "present the views and wishes of the Indian people," which appeared as an interlinked set of values and objectives. Desire for peace was paramount ; peace in turn had to rest on the foundation of political, racial, and economic equality among the world's nations.[16] Political inequality manifested itself chiefly as colonialism, and "Great countries like India who have passed out of that colonial state do not conceive it possible that other countries should remain under the yolk of colonial rule." Racial inequality, Nehru asserted, was "a menace to world peace." Economic inequality he noted in passing ; it was many years before Indian delegates took up that problem with the energy that they devoted to the first two issues. Nehru's address touched only on the main themes. His government's representatives were left to defend India's narrower interests in the sessions that followed.

An international inequality persistently felt by Indian nationalists was the treatment given to their countrymen overseas, a subject that the British government was pleased to see avoided in League of Nations discussions, because most overseas Indians resided in British territories and dominions. Frustrated by the failures of a half century of protestations about discrimination against Indians abroad the Indian government brought the problem to the UN in 1946, under articles ten and fourteen singling out the Union of South Africa as a violator of international law and the Charter because of its many disabling ordinances aimed against residents of Indian background.[17] Further discussion of Indo-South African relations appears in chapter XII, ahead, where it is suggested that the Pretoria regime, among those governments with which India sought to negotiate settlements of the problems of overseas Indians, was the least willing to compromise and certainly the most vigorously attached to doctrines of racial inequality. The immediate reason for India's bringing the dispute to the UN was the Union government's enactment of the Asiatic Land Tenure and Indian Representation Act of 1946, following which India recalled its high commissioner and banned trade with South Africa.

The Indian move in the General Assembly aimed at bringing changes in South African policies through moral or psychological pressures from outside ; no tangible UN sanctions were suggested in the early years of the dispute. The move failed to bring results in South Africa, possibly for the same reasons that similar manoeuvres within the Commonwealth had failed in the 1920's : the states which could have influenced South African policies—the UK in the 1920's, the US and possibly the UK in the post-war years—were not sufficiently sympathetic with India's case to risk alienating the Union government.

Nevertheless, because of the astute presentation of its case against South Africa from 1946 onward and equally because of the liberal temper of thought in the world on racial issues India managed to achieve an excellent record of support on UN resolutions critical of South African politics. In the early years when those resolutions were severely worded the voting was sometimes close, but by the mid-1950's overwhelming Assembly support was consistently given to the more mildly worded motions asking the Union to negotiate a settlement of the issue with India and Pakistan. The issue for debate in the often repeated UN consideration of the South African question was not the merits of racialism : the controversy lay in the procedural question of whether or not South Africa's racial policies were solely matters of domestic jurisdiction. Anticipating that problem India tried to show that South African racial measures contravened the Capetown agreement of 1927 and the Indo-South African joint communique reaffirming it in 1932.

But India's main argument rested on the human rights provisions of the Charter, and it was on that basis that the Assembly majority appeared to accept the proposition that South African policies merited international attention. In addition, the Assembly judged that racial discrimination in the Union could be a threat to international peace. In a resolution sponsored by France and Mexico the Assembly recorded its views in December 1946 favouring the Indian case ; it defeated a South African amendment, supported by the US and the UK, which would have referred the matter to the World Court.

At that time India's diplomatic success could not be pressed in the direction of stronger language of condemnation or of sanctions. The US, with its important following in the Assembly, urged "conciliation, not recrimination," and lent support to those measures which merely recognized that the UN had a legitimate function in trying to arrange friendly negotiations among the states directly concerned.

The Assembly did not face the domestic jurisdiction question squarely in the South African case during the 1950's. India opposed submitting that question to the World Court for an advisory opinion, despite its stated conviction that there was sufficient legal backing for its case, arguing that consideration by the Court would serve only to postpone any action that the UN might wish to take. The UK and several other Western states denied the competence of the UN to deal with the allegedly internal affairs of South Africa, while the US, though equivocal on such measures as the Assembly's request that South Africa suspend the Group Areas Act, affirmed the legality of UN resolutions dealing with the question and voted in favour of many of them. The communist and Afro-Asian groupings firmly backed India's position. As a result of the inconclusive debates on the domestic jurisdiction question the Assembly resolutions on South Africa in the 1950's seemed to be worded with studied vagueness. Solely because the body insisted on considering the issue regularly and its resolutions referred to dangers to friendly relations between states, international obligations in general, and Charter provisions in particular, was India able to assume that it had won its procedural battle. In 1960, following the disturbances at Sharpeville, the domestic jurisdiction argument was finally put aside firmly by the Security Council's resolution recognizing that South African race policies—no longer only the complaint of discrimination against Indians—"might endanger international peace and security."

India's stress on the Charter's human rights clauses followed from its view that the moral and political aspects of any problem took precedence over the legal ones. The Assembly appeared to accept the Indian set of priorities, and its resolutions emphasized the offense against human rights implied by the South African measures. It overruled, in effect, the Union government's pleas that the human rights provisions of the Charter were too vague to create legal obligations on sovereign states and that in any case no violations of human rights were taking place in South Africa.

But the South African case on the human rights issue in fact probed to the shaky foundations of the international human rights movement, of which the Indian government was a part. Human dignity, the South African representatives argued, in rebuttal to the Indian case, could not be regarded as a fundamental right because it had never been concretely defined. It did not necessarily depend on legislative representation or racial integration. The Union's racial measures, misunderstood elsewhere, were explained by South African representatives as essential in order to promote simultaneously the rights and freedoms of several major communities with widely disparate cultural backgrounds and current capabilities. Segregation aimed at protecting while nurturing and advancing the interests of the South African negroes, threatened by Whites and Indians alike.

Even governments, such as the UK, which voted against the majority resolutions critical of South African policies could not publicly accept the arguments on the human rights question put forward by South Africa, however skillfully argued. (The UK's negative votes stemmed from the domestic jurisdiction principle.) Racial ideologies had so recently fostered international conflict that a fresh enunciation of them in a great world forum had to be repudiated as offensive to informed minds. The US government, while sensitive to its own failings in domestic racial relations, instructed its representatives to draw a distinction "between the haphazard, vestigal, unsanctioned violations of human rights, which continued to occur in all countries, and a government policy which ran counter to the whole current of modern philosophy and scientific knowledge and to the line of social and humanitarian conduct recommended in the Charter. . . . "[18]

The convincing Assembly majorities on the question of the treatment of Indian settlers encouraged New Delhi and twelve other governments to enlarge the UN's consideration of the race issue in 1952. Again relying on the human rights clauses of the Charter as well as on its peace and security provisions India argued that an international crisis loomed in Africa largely because of the Union's refusal to abandon racial discrimination and persecution. The new question on the Assembly's agenda dealt with apartheid and soon attracted more debate than the limited matter of the treatment of Indians. With the increasing importance of African opinion in the later 1950's India and other states pressed the wider question of equal rights for black and white races in the whole of Africa. The Assembly passed an average of more than three resolutions on racial questions each year from 1954 to 1962, and in the latter year thirty-four states sponsored a successful motion recommending sanctions against South Africa for the first time. The steps suggested for member states to impose were the breaking off of diplomatic relations with South Africa, closing ports to its vessels, prohibiting ships of national registry to visit South Africa, boycotting South African goods and banning exports to that state, and refusing landing rights to South African aircraft. India found those new measures unburdensome because it had already introduced virtually all of them. Few other states, however, followed India's lead. Indeed, by the mid-1960's many independent African states continued trade with the Union and a few established diplomatic relations with Pretoria for the first time.

India's purpose in persisting in the South African case extended beyond the aim of supporting the grievances of settlers of Indian origin or of supporting the interests of Africans in the Union's territories. South African policy, which "imposed a permanent stigma of inferiority on almost half the human race,"[19] was taken up as the most notorious example of a world-wide inequity under which Indians as a whole society had suffered during foreign rule and which continued to contaminate international relations in many parts of the world. Other widely acknowledged abstract human rights, political and socio-economic, were more difficult to define or implement in an international context. Tangible concessions to the principle of racial equality appeared to be an achievable goal, and India's endeavours in the UN helped to make it so.

One of the best examples of the difficulties that India and other states faced in trying to achieve meaningful gains in the field of human rights emerged from discussions of political equality. For India it meant recognition of the right of national self-determination, and in debates on the drafting of human rights covenants India's efforts concentrated on achieving priority for that principle. All rights of a social and economic nature, Indians argued, though no less important, had to derive from the prior condition of political freedom. The Western states, with their "responsibilities" for dependent colonial peoples high on any list of national interests, found themselves opposing or at least seeking to amend that proposition, on the well known grounds that political freedom could be constructively enjoyed only by peoples who were prepared for it in other areas of national life. Thus, when political questions arose in connection with human rights debates India's liberal position tended to put it in opposition to the Western states—a hint that the human rights movement, begun in the Western democracies was becoming a weapon for Afro-Asians to use against the West.

The most telling tactics used by certain Western states to weaken the Afro-Asian formulation of the right of self-determination found expression in what became known as the Belgian thesis, which extended the idea of self-determination to include scores of ethnically identifiable groups throughout the world which allegedly did not fully participate in the governing of the states of which they were parts. The Naga tribes of India, the Dyaks in Borneo, and the aboriginal Indians in the US were some of the "non-self-governing" people that the Belgian delegate identified.[20] Indian representatives felt that the Belgian thesis distorted the problem, which for them was essentially colonialism. Western governments put the Belgian argument to little use in drafting resolutions, but they nevertheless agreed for many years with Belgium that the right of self-determination had been vaguely explained in the Charter, and that "non-self-governing" might be taken to refer to many categories of people and territories. The Indian government formulated its definition of non-self-governing territories as early as 1946, when it advanced the view that such territories could "be defined to mean and to include Territories where the rights of the inhabitants, their economic status and social privileges are regulated by another State . . . ," i.e. colonial territories.[21]

The dispute over a definition, reflecting diverse national interests, continued in discussions both on human rights and on trusteeship and colonial matters—mainly in the latter, however, because the human rights movement, aimed at gaining international legal sanction for a set of fundamental directive principles, had lost much of its momentum by the 1960's. The general agreement to separate political from all other rights for the purposes of drafting a covenant on human rights, which India strongly favoured, did not make easier the reconciliation of opposing points of view. Furthermore, the problem of consistency for a single state often presented itself. India, for example, refused to support US sponsored resolutions condemning forced labour practices by the Soviet Union and China, by labyrinthine arguments rather than by openly acknowledging that it subordinated even human rights issues to the requirements of nonalignment.

THE ADVANCEMENT OF SPECIAL INTERESTS : ANTI-COLONIALISM

Certainly the most highly publicized Indian advocacy of its special interests in the UN appeared during the debates on colonial questions. Like institutionalized racial discrimination, the maintenance of the colonial system anywhere offended Indians and was apt to arouse the protests of their government. Nehru argued that colonialism had to disappear in order for the world to achieve peace and a "friendly relationship" between Asia and Europe.[22] But beyond that self-evident proposition lay Nehru's more speculative recognition of "an inevitable change and transition from an era of colonialism to another era which has yet to be given a shape . . . ," and the conviction that "colonialism is obsolete in the modern world."[23] India under Nehru's leadership decided to hasten an historical process which by the very fact of India's independence was known to be well under way. His vision naively conjured up glories of the post-colonial world which reinforced his determination to encourage its coming. Nehru believed that "The end of colonialism and imperialism will not mean the splitting up of the world into a host of additional nation states intent on their isolated independence. It will lead to [a] new grouping together of all nations ; a new outlook, to cooperation gradually replacing competition and conflict, to the utilization of the wonders of modern technique and the vast resources of energy at the disposal of man for the advancement of the human race as a whole. It will lead to that One World of which wise statesmen have dreamed and which seems to be the inevitable and only outcome of our present troubles, if we survive disaster."[24] With such a prospect perhaps only vaguely present in their minds Indian representatives in UN bodies advocated freedom for colonial nations.

But even in the early years of its UN membership after independence India demonstrated a selectivity in championing the causes of dependent peoples. Only those political movements for independence which had a mass base and which claimed to desire democratic, free societies received India's full, official support in international discussions on colonialism. Negatively, only those metropolitan governments which flatly refused concessions to nationalist movements in their territories or which refused to accept the ultimate goal of self-government became the objects of India's uncompromising verbal attacks.

The first direct political campaign against colonialism that India sponsored in the UN was aimed at forcing the Netherlands government to withdraw its control over Indonesia. India and Australia called the Security Council's attention under articles 34 and 39, respectively, to the fighting which had broken out in July 1947 between Dutch and Indonesian nationalist forces. Against the wishes of the Netherlands representatives, who argued that the UN had no competence to intervene in the internal affairs of his state, the Council took up the question, called for an end to hostilities, and asked the parties to settle their dispute by arbitration or other peaceful means. The US and the USSR together voted for the resolution, while the UK, France, and Belgium abstained. While not on the Council India as well as Australia and the Philippines were allowed representation during the Council's debates and added the weight of words to the Indonesian side in an almost evenly divided body. In particular, the Indian representative was able to make a convincing case for the de facto status of Indonesia as a state and not a colonial dependency, thus undermining the main defense of the Netherlands' position in the Council.

The Indian delegate brought into the debate a theme which the newly independent states were beginning to develop in the late 1940's, namely the inapplicability of existing international law to the postwar relationship between metropolitan powers and their dependent territories. Colonialism could be upheld by a narrow interpretation of international law ; the Indian government held that the law would have to bend to reflect the realistic situation in such territories as Indonesia. As one Indian delegate put the matter, "These issues of racial, national, and colonial conflicts affect the very foundations of modern society, and surely cannot be dealt with in terms of hair-splitting legalism."[25]

Pressure from the UN Security Council through its good offices committee, which included an American member, brought about a truce in January 1948. However, by the end of that year fighting had again broken out in Java and Sumatra, and India called a conference in New Delhi in January 1949 to support the Indonesians at what seemed a crucial period in their struggle. Nehru forwarded the conference's resolution to the Security Council, and the specific nature of its terms at once appealed to several members. The UN representatives of the states present in New Delhi were able to work together in New York on a single, concrete proposal, which, as it turned out, could be combined with a resolution already before the Council into a forceful resolution calling for a cease-fire and resumed negotiations. The lengthy resolution gained overwhelming Council support on January 28, 1949.

India and Australia pursued the Indonesian question and brought it to the General Assembly in March 1949. That new diplomatic move, adding to the pressure building up against the Dutch, had no direct result but probably increased the tempo of the conciliation efforts which motivated a Dutch-Indonesian conference at The Hague from August to December. By the end of the year Indonesia gained full sovereignty.

The nice timing of the multilateral diplomatic work organized by India outside the UN and the persuasive manner of Indian delegates concerned with the matter in New York produced a remarkable success for those opposing colonialism. The victory, in fact, may have been too easily won. For in the more complex colonial questions that later emerged, no New Delhi conference and no nearly unanimous UN resolutions materialized. The first UN battle against a colonial regime, in which India took a commanding lead, turned out to be the easiest to win. On the closely related question of West Irian (West New Guinea) Indonesia had to wait eight years from the time it raised the issue in the UN, in 1954, before a settlement took place. Possibly struck by the unsuitability of the usual anti-colonialist argument in that case—Indonesians are ethnically different from the population of West Irian—and certainly having become more temperate in their stand on colonialism, Indian representatives mixed their advocacy of the Indonesian case with an encouragement of conciliation between the disputing parties.

Apart from Indonesia, the major issues for India and the anti-colonialist grouping in the UN in the 1950's formed around French policies in north Africa. India's handling of the Tunisian, Moroccan and Algerian questions revealed nothing new about its adherence to the principle of national self-determination, but it illustrated the selectivity and discrimination in supporting anti-colonial struggles, already noted. The north African freedom struggles were not of a single pattern. In the Algerian dispute, which first appeared on the General Assembly's agenda in 1955, there were "special factors and complexities," according to Nehru,[26] namely the existence of one million resident Europeans, whose interests could not be ignored in any constitutional reform, and the special relationship of Algeria to France. India's policy on the Algerian struggle, therefore, was not to recommend a specific solution to the problem, as it had done in the case of Indonesia, but to support in the UN an "approach of reconciliation." "I use the word 'reconciliation'," said Nehru, "and I do feel that that should be the governing approach to this issue."[27]

The issues were simpler in the Tunisian and Moroccan disputes, which reached the UN in 1952, and India's participation in the debates, though minor, showed an unqualified support for the immediate independence of the two protectorates. But in the three north African territories India's diplomacy in the UN was neither as uncompromising nor as demanding as it had been in the

Indonesian case. Perhaps in recognition of the greater interest in those disputes on the part of the Arab states India remained somewhat in the background, while west Asian states took an obvious lead. Moreover, during the UN debates on the north African territories India discovered that strong, unbending anti-colonial pressure appeared to harden the French attitude rather than induce new compromises, as it had done with the Netherlands. India's diplomatic strategy was framed accordingly.

The Cyprus question, a UN concern from the year 1954, revealed India's caution in specifying solutions based on a simplistic interpretation of nationalism. India recognized the cruel problem of a colony divided into two major communities, Greek and Turkish, which was reminiscent of the communal division facing the pre-partition subcontinent. It appreciated the dilemmas facing the British in formulating a policy for the transfer of power and indicated that it would support whatever plan assured that the process would be peaceful. In the final analysis India gave support to the major nationalist figure in Cyprus, Archbishop Makarios. After Cyprus became independent, in 1960, the communal antagonism on the island remained, despite constitutional arrangements for a representative balance between Greek and Turkish communities. Fighting broke out at the end of 1963, and the UN intervened by sending a military force for peace-keeping operations. The contingent, composed of Canadian, Swedish, and Irish troops as well as some remaining British forces was headed by the Indian general, K. S. Thimayya, who had earlier directed the Korean prisoner of war exchange. Under Makarios the Cyprus government strongly supported India—notably at the time of the Chinese invasion of 1962.

Perceptive observers of India's strategies in the UN could note a shift away from a hard, threatening posture toward colonial powers in the direction of a more cautious, conciliatory approach during the years when the north African and Cypriot disputes were under discussion.[28] That long-term trend culminated in Nehru's rejection of colonialism as the world's most urgent problem at the Belgrade conference of nonaligned states in 1961. The trend could be most successfully accounted for not as a shift in basic policy but as a manifestation of the selective approach to anti-colonialism apparent in Nehru's thinking from the time of independence and a discrimination in the choice of methods to conduct anti-colonial campaigns. By 1961 the great anti-colonial struggles had been won, and those that remained, mostly in Africa, called for flexible approaches by the UN.

The diplomatic work of Indian delegates in behalf of national self-determination in the General Assembly debates culminated on December 14, 1960, in the overwhelming vote in favour of an Afro-Asian resolution, 1514 (XV), instructing member states to recognize the sovereign rights of all non-self-governing peoples. The UN made unconditional its opposition to colonialism : the resolution declared that "all peoples have an inalienable right to complete freedom, the exercise of their sovereignty and the integrity of their national territory."[29]

India's work on the Trusteeship Council and on the Committee on Information from Non-Self-Governing Territories probably exceeded in output, though not in the publicity attached to it, the endeavours in the other UN bodies in behalf of self-determination. The Indian government believed that the main function of the UN in advancing self-determination lay not in settling open disputes between dependent people and their colonial rulers but in providing a mechanism for the orderly, peaceful transfer of power to all colonial peoples. The UN, according to India's view, should thus acquire from the ruling powers as much control or influence as it could and act as the intermediary for the ultimate legal transfer of government.

The Charter created a distinction between non-self-governing territories, for which in chapter XI the administering authorities declared their intention—it was not a firm pledge—to promote self-government and general welfare and to submit information to the secretary-general ; and trust territories, for which under chapters XII and XIII, as in the case of the League mandates, more definite requirements were demanded of the executors of the trusts. In keeping with that distinction the Charter established no UN body to oversee the implementing of chapter XI, whereas the Trusteeship Council had full powers to supervise the working of chapters XII and XIII. Clearly the most influential framers of the Charter were unprepared to turn over to the UN any real authority on the major colonial matters. Chapter XI was not only a vaguely worded state-ment, but it was not self-implementing ; the only concrete obliga-tion that it placed on member states was to transmit information, but not specifically political information, which might touch on the subject of self-determination. India, along with other states, assumed for itself as soon as it could the task of breaking down the distinction in practice between chapters XI and chapters XII and XIII of the Charter, to tighten the meanings of the declared intentions in the former and infuse some UN body with an authority to enforce its provisions.

During the early sessions of the General Assembly India joined a large number of states which urged that permanent machinery should be created to encourage the enforcement of all of chapter XI's provisions. Over the objections of France, the UK, Belgium and other administering states, the anti-colonialist members managed to press through a resolution that set up a special committee in 1947 to receive information on dependent territories. After initial doubts about the legality of such a committee, whose functions, as everyone realized, would predictably lead it into discussions and recommendations on colonial administrations, it became a quasi-permanent instrument of the UN, until it was superseded in 1963 by the Committee of Twenty-Four with a more powerful mandate.[30] India became a member of the Committee on Information and retained membership in almost every successive reconstitution of that body.

The very existence of the committee constituted an important step towards strengthening the Charter's provisions on colonialism, and in its functioning it came to have an influence similar to that of the Trusteeship Council, though not as determining. By several resolutions in the early 1950's the General Assembly registered the majority's view that administering states should submit information on the political development of non-self-governing territories, but the obligation to do so was not made mandatory. In India's opinion, the political status of colonial peoples could not reasonably be excluded from the overall "well being of the inhabitants" stipulated in article 73. India held not only that the committee was competent to receive political information but that the General Assembly could judge when a territory had been properly promoted out of the category of non-self-governing. The latter issue arose on several occasions, including the American refusal in 1953 to continue supplying information on the newly formed Commonwealth of Puerto Rico.

In its diplomacy connected with the Committee on Information India abjured the radical position on colonialism taken by the communist states, chiefly because such a position could not lead to fruitful results ; the US, at the same time, dissociated itself from the extreme views of some of its European allies. Accordingly, the Indian and the American approaches to the UN's role in supervising the orderly and peaceful transfers of power to dependent peoples often coincided.[31] However, in crisis situations, when the comparatively bureaucratic procedures of the Committee on Information were overshadowed by great debates in the Assembly or Security Council, the US and India more frequently found themselves in opposition.

Because certain UN members, the last of which was Portugal, admitted in 1955, refused to submit reports on their colonial territories on grounds that the overseas regions were not constitutionally set apart from the metropolitan centre, the General Assembly tried to lay to rest persistent questions concerning article 73. In 1959 it appointed a six-member committee with the purpose of determining the extent of obligation on member states to report under part (e) of the article. C. S. Jha, India's permanent UN representative, was made chairman, and the group unanimously concluded that an obligation did indeed exist "to transmit information in respect of a territory which is geographically separated and is distinct ethnically and/or culturally from the country administering it,"[32] a definition of a colony with which India could conveniently concur. The Jha committee's report received the General Assembly's approval in its resolution 1542 (XV), passed on December 15, 1960.

THE ADVANCEMENT OF SPECIAL INTERESTS : ECONOMIC AID

India's policies on racial and political equality were sharply focused in the UN. Less definitively revealed in UN proceedings were India's policies on the knotty problem of how to achieve greater economic equality among the countries of the world. India's professed desire for greater multilateral economic assistance to underdeveloped countries had to be measured against its pragmatic experience that bilateral negotiations were more advantageous.

To India, one of the most attractive prospects held forth by the

UN organization lay in the economic benefits proclaimed as objectives in the Charter and written into the functional goals of various specialized agencies. India participated fully from the outset in all UN bodies having competence in economic affairs—as well as those dealing with social matters, which for lack of space will have to be omitted from the scope of this chapter.[33] India was one of the main recipients of the economic and humanitarian benefits derived from participating in the Food and Agricultural Organization, the World Health Organization, the UN Educational, Scientific and Cultural Organization (UNESCO), the International Labour Organization, the International Bank for Reconstruction and Development (IBRD, or World Bank), and other UN sponsored organizations with less significant budgets.[34] The annual reports of all those bodies and even a cursory inspection of the work accomplished in economic and social advancement in India—e.g. the virtual eradication of malaria with the assistance of the World Health Organization—testified to the impressive mark made by the UN's specialized agencies on the record of India's progress. India was the recipient of the largest amount of funds and personnel emanating from UN economic assistance programmes during the period, 1951 to 1967.[35] It also contributed personnel and funds to UN programmes : about 2,000 experts sent to other countries up to 1967 and an annual rupee contribution to UN economic programmes which rose to the equivalent of $3 million (almost one and one-half crores rupees) by 1966.

In the first decade following the Second World War, while India's foreign exchange balances were strong and the government still counted on traditional sources to finance its modest development efforts, the UN programmes in India appeared specially advantageous, and most Indian representatives merely called for more of the same thing. During that same period India placed considerable reliance on the IBRD, which was then the only UN sponsored institution capable of making direct contributions towards major development projects. A charter member of the Bank with a permanent representative on its executive board, India succeeded in obtaining major loans from that source but criticized the Bank's conservative lending policies and urged the creation of other multilateral lending institutions to supplement the Bank's work. When India's development efforts began to stretch far beyond its economic resources, in the later 1950's, UN technical agencies could not fill the gap ; the World Bank held some of the financial resources that India needed to meet its sudden foreign exchange crisis, but the Bank's policies prevented any significant increases in loans. Therefore, India had to rely on bilateral assistance, which began to flow in rapidly increased quantities after 1956.

That sudden and unexpected need for massive external capital supplies, described more fully in chapter XIV, began to undermine India's earlier preference for multilateral aid programmes. The country continued to seek and receive loans from the IBRD, but the Bank's most useful function in meeting the new economic crisis was to organize the flows of Western capital through its Aid India Consortium, formed in 1958. By the 1960's few Indian representatives could have advocated a reliance on UN economic assistance programmes in place of the bilateral ones. India was not an exceptional case among states receiving heavy foreign economic assistance : "Although some recipients show a marked preference for multilateral aid because it is untied and is considered to be less political, other factors can modify this leaning. Some recipients, who through skillful and energetic efforts have received relatively high inflows of aid, fear that a strengthened multilateral agency focusing on worldwide priorities might reduce their relative share of the total. In addition, the centralization of the sources of aid would limit the recipients who maximize their assistance by playing donors off against each other. Also the centralization of aid through a single source might put too much power in the hands of a few aid administrators. Another disadvantage of multilateral aid is that most of it is in the form of loans. . . ."[36]

With those practical considerations and the record of bilateral aid receipts before it the Indian government nevertheless did not give up the vision of a world agency whose purpose was to bring into some closer balance the economic condition of the "haves" and "have-nots". That vision was expressed by Indian representatives in the Economic and Social Council (ECOSOC) in the late 1940's and was repeatedly brought forward through Indian arguments in favour of a UN economic development fund, SUNFED, during the 1950's. Indeed, one Indian representative, V. K. R. V. Rao, deserved credit for introducing the idea of SUNFED, during UN sessions in 1949 and 1950.

For many years the developed countries opposed the idea of a multilateral agency to make loans or undertake projects for development on a basis more liberal than the criteria used by the IBRD. They opposed it on financial grounds and because such UN sponsored development programmes would probably be controlled by the aid recipients, acting through the General Assembly or the ECOSOC, not the donors. India's support for a UN development programme continued even during the years of greatest increases in bilateral aid receipts. India favoured the establishment in 1960 of the International Development Association (IDA), the soft loan subsidiary of the World Bank, which began to respond to the need for more easily obtainable development loans ; India received IDA commitments amounting to $585 million (about 280 crores rupees) by the end of 1965. More akin to the proposed SUNFED was the UN Special Fund, founded, again with Indian backing, in 1959 for the purpose of improving investment opportunities in under-developed countries through research, educational and survey projects. As certain limitations on bilateral aid became obvious— by the mid-1960's Indians realized that greater economic equality in the world would not emerge through bilateral transfers of goods and technology, and most of the bilateral programmes were no longer growing in annual commitments—the Indian government intensified its activities in behalf of multilateral efforts both for development directly and for improved trading conditions for developing countries. Chapter XIX will carry this discussion further.

Beyond the great issues of special concern to India, the UN took up certain questions of narrower focus in which Indian interests were very much involved. Most of these will be dealt with elsewhere in this volume—the Kashmir dispute, the Suez crisis, the invasion of Goa, Chinese repression in Tibet. Only one requires cursory notice here, the question of India's forcible annexation of Hyderabad. That southern Indian princely state, whose ruler was a Muslim Nizam, tried briefly to establish its independence following the transfer of power to India in 1947, rather than to accede to the state of which it was an integral geographic and cultural part. In a manner somewhat analogous to Pakistan's efforts to coerce Kashmir into acceding to Pakistan, India brought pressure on the Nizam and finally moved troops into Hyderabad to assure that the state would in fact become part of the new India. The

8

government of Hyderabad brought a complaint to the Security Council on August 21, 1948, of the forcible measures being employed by India to destroy the state's "independence", and in September it informed the secretary-general of the movement of Indian troops into the state.

The Hyderabadi play for international support for its local quarrel with New Delhi received scant attention at the UN, despite the Security Council's willingness to allow a Hyderabadi representative to present his government's case. The Indian delegate, in reply, questioned the competence of the UN to deal with the question on grounds that Hyderabad was not an independent state and that the issue fell within the domestic jurisdiction of India. Whatever the legal aspects of the case might have been,[37] the Council was soon faced with the fact of India's assumption of sovereignty in Hyderabad, followed immediately by the Nizam's withdrawal of the complaint. The Council did not at once remove the item from its agenda but allowed it to lapse, following the refusal of India in 1949 to participate in any further discussions of the issue. Pakistan's endeavours to promote further interest in the topic could not elicit support from other states.

Though not strictly an international question the Indian government's actions in Hyderabad manifested the blend of state necessity and verbal self-righteousness which became a hallmark of the foreign policy of India—as of most modern states. Nehru told the nation, "I have repeatedly said, we are men of peace, hating war and the last thing we desire is to come into armed conflict with anyone. Nevertheless, circumstances, which you know well, compelled us to take this action in Hyderabad. Fortunately, it was brief and we return with relief to the paths of peace again." Nehru promised, after the military occupation was complete, "that the future of Hyderabad will be determined in accordance with the wishes of her people," but he supplemented that declaration with his own view that that future "lies in the closest association with India."[38]

The emergence of India's foreign policies and the defining of its relationships with other states were simplified by its UN membership and the intense concern with global problems that accompanied it. The various forums of the world organization served to amplify India's voice in international affairs, and the nature of certain disputes which were taken to the UN provided admirable opportunities for a nonaligned delegation to intervene and sometimes offer mediation. Involvement in global diplomacy plus the opportunity to further its special interests made up the substantial advantages that India gained from UN membership.

In nondiplomatic ways, too, India benefited by the spreading of its influence within the organs of the UN.[39] Indian international civil servants composed the largest and most influential non-Western contingent among the executive-level staffs of the secretariat and major specialized agencies.[40] Although by their contracts loyal to the UN and not representatives of their own government, their personal preferences as Indians, their methods of work, and their social relations generally contributed to the advancement of India's reputation. The availability of superior Indian administrative personnel "for export" and their achievements as officers led to India's consistently overfilling its informal quota of jobs in the secretariat which were subject to geographic distribution. Following the secretary-general's calculation in 1962 of what would be "desirable ranges" of numbers of employees by nationality it could be seen that Indians were about 300 per cent overrepresented: their "desirable range" was twenty-seven to twenty-two whereas there were already sixty-six short-term and career Indians on the staff of the secretariat.[41]

NOTES AND REFERENCES

[1] B. V. Govinda Raj, *India and Disputes in the United Nations 1946-54*, pp. 33-37. See also M. C. Setalvad, "India and the United Nations," *India Quarterly*, vol. VI, 2 (April-June, 1950), pp. 107-29. Few states other than the US, the UK, and the USSR had any major part in drafting the Charter.

[2] The California legislature adjourned to hear her nationalist case against Britain and against the Indian government's representatives at the conference, *The Hindu*, May 16, 1945. See also *ibid.*, April 7, 9, 27 ; May 2, 6, 1945. From an unpublished paper by Kathryn Martin, American Univ., 1965.

[3] Nehru, *Speeches 1949-1953*, p. 131.

[4] The preceding chapter gave brief notice to the fact that India's nonaligned posture and hence its independence and power were enhanced by the "cold war" struggle. This anomaly appeared often in the proceedings of UN bodies.

[5] Berkes and Bedi, *The Diplomacy of India*, p. 12.

[6] *FAR*, vol. V, 12 (Dec. 1959). India's policies on the compulsory jurisdiction of the court are discussed by R. P. Anand in "India and the World Court," *International Studies*, vol. II, 1 (July 1660) and in his *Compulsory Jurisdiction of the International Court of Justice*, Bombay 1961, pp. 253-57.

[7] See the discussion of this point in R. P. Anand, "Attitude of the 'New' Asian-African Countries Toward the International Court of Justice," *International Studies*, vol. IV, 1 (July 1962), pp. 119-32. See also Jorge Castaneda, "The Underdeveloped Nations and the Development of International Law," *International Organization*, vol. XV, 1 (winter 1961), pp. 38-48.

[8] Quincy Wright, "Asian Experience and International Law," *International Studies*, vol. I, 1 (July 1959).

[9] See ahead, chap. XII.

[10] The analysis of disarmament talks in John W. Spanier and Joseph L. Nogee, *The Politics of Disarmament*, N. Y. 1962, provides a realistic background for understanding this subject.

[11] By Joseph L. Nogee, "The Neutralist World and Disarmament Negotiations," *The Annals*, Nov. 1965, p. 76.

[12] Nehru, *Speeches 1953-1957*, p. 249.

[13] See *Foreign Policy of India : Texts of Documents 1947-64*.

[14] Quoted in Spanier and Nogee, *op. cit.*, p. 37.

[15] Speech at the General Assembly, Oct. 3, 1960, *India's Foreign Policy*, p. 217.

[16] Nehru's address appeared in his *Speeches 1946-1949* (a rearranged edition of *Independence and After*), New Delhi 1958, pp. 317-23.

[17] The text of the Indian memorandum to the UN, August 26, 1946 (UN Doc. A/68) provided part of the legal background for its case against South Africa. A second memorandum in September 1947 explained further developments in the Union which affected non-Whites. See India, Dept. of Commonwealth Relations, *Question of Treatment of Indians in the Union of South Africa Before the United Nations*, 1947 and 1948 ; excerpts from these documents were included in S. L. Poplai, *India 1947-50*, vol. II, *External Affairs*, which also provided excerpts from appropriate UN resolutions and from the key speeches of Indian and South African delegates. South Africa's case was presented historically in UN Docs. A/167, Oct. 31, 1946 ; and A/167/Add. 1, Nov. 15, 1946.

[18] Cited in M. S. Rajan, *United Nations and Domestic Jurisdiction*, p. 236.

[19] The words of Mrs. Pandit, India's chief UN representative in 1950 ; quoted in Govinda Raj, *op. cit.*, p. 179.

[20] See discussion of this thesis in Usha Sud, *United Nations and the Non-Self-Governing Territories*, pp. 117-121.

[21] UN Doc. A/C. 4/52 ; quoted in *GAOR*, 4th Cmttee., mtgs. 1-27, p. 274.

[22] In a speech at the Indian Council of World Affairs, New Delhi, March 22, 1949, *Speeches 1946-1949*, p. 266.

[23] *New York Times Magazine*, March 3, 1946 ; cited in Dorothy Norman, *Nehru, the First Sixty Years*, vol. II, p. 208.

[24] *ibid.*, p. 213.

[25] P. P. Pilai, *SCOR*, Aug. 26, 1947, p. 2220.

[26] Statement in the Lok Sabha, May 22, 1956, *India's Foreign Policy*, p. 506.

[27] Statement in Rajya Sabha, Dec. 13, 1957, *ibid.*, p. 508.

[28] e.g. Berkes and Bedi, *op. cit.*, p. 160f. See also chapter XI, ahead, for further discussion on India's relations with the north African states.

[29] For a useful discussion of the international legal implications of this possibly precedent-setting resolution see M. K. Nawaz's paper presented to the 57th annual meeting of the American Society of International Law, Washington, April 27, 1963, entitled "International Law in the Contemporary Practice of India : Some Perspectives."

[30] A helpful description of the committee's formation and functions is to be found in Usha Sud, *op. cit.*, chapter III.

[31] See *ibid.*, p. 179.

[32] The Jha Committee report, Sept. 19, 1960, UN Doc. A/AC. 100/L. 1, p. 11.

[33] Some idea of India's efforts in the field of international social betterment, which reflected interests continuing from the League days, may be gained by checking the index of Robert E. Asher, et al, *The United Nations and Promotion of the General Welfare*, Brookings Institution, Washington 1957. A summary of certain aspects of India's relations with UN technical agencies through the mid-1950's appeared in Indian Council of World Affairs, *India and the United Nations*, chapter VIII.

[34] The Lok Sabha Secretariat published a series of pamphlets in the years 1959 and 1960 on India's relations with each of these bodies. A more complete discussion of the ILO appeared in N. N. Kaul, *India and the International Labour Organization*, Delhi 1956.

[35] The cost figures of the combined UN economic assistance programmes in India were $30 million for equipment (to 1966) and almost $40 million in foreign exchange (to 1967) for forty-one projects under the UN Special Fund. Eighteen hundred foreign experts worked in India, while 1,700 Indians went abroad for training, all under UN auspices. From UN Development Programme, New Delhi, "The United Nations Development Programme, India 1967," Delhi 1967, p. 14.

[36] Wolfgang G. Friedmann, George Kalmanoff and Robert F. Meagher, *International Financial Aid*, N. Y. 1966, p. 432.

[37] Those aspects were dealt with by Govinda Raj, *op. cit.*, chapter III.

[38] Nehru's broadcast from New Delhi, Sept. 18, 1948, *Speeches 1946-1949*, pp. 154, 156.

[39] And paid, too, for its UN membership : 3.41 per cent of the total UN budget in 1956, which placed India seventh in line of contributors, after the US, UK, USSR, France, West Germany, Canada.

[40] See the chart in Sydney D. Bailey, *The Secretariat of the United Nations*, London 1964, pp. 86-88. It refers to the staff by nationality in 1963, but the Indian component was no less significant in the 1950's.

[41] *idem.*

PART TWO

THE SEARCH FOR
ASIAN AND AFRICAN POLICIES

CHAPTER V

THE BURDEN OF PAKISTAN AND THE EFFORTS TO RELIEVE IT

THE TERMINATION OF British rule in 1947 had an immediate and weighty effect on India's foreign relations, because it was accompanied by the partition of the subcontinent and the creation of Pakistan. A mutual antagonism inherited by the new neighbours from the events leading up to partition made the existence of Pakistan India's most vexing international burden. The formation of a sovereign state from provinces and districts subtracted from the northwestern and northeastern parts of the country undermined India's economy and external trade ; and, because the new state was hostile, led to acute embarrassment and continuous rivalry for external support, as well as to a transformation in India's defense deployment.

Relations with Pakistan could not initially be conceived as truly international ; there was no modern precedent for international dealings with another segment of the subcontinent as there was for relations with foreign countries overseas. Diplomatic formalities slowly developed—although many strictly international procedures were arranged by local Indian and Pakistani officials who had previously been colleagues in the same administration. Much more slowly, and with greater difficulty, grew the mental assumption in India that Pakistan was a separate, independent entity and would remain so.[1] Many Indians could not accept the reasoning which made Pakistan a nation different from their own multi-religious society and rejected the oft-repeated phrases of "Hindu India" and "Muslim Pakistan." The pre-independence ideological rift between those Indians who argued that the Muslims constituted a separate nation with a right to self-determination and statehood, and those who claimed that Indian nationalism embraced all religious groups and all regions of the subcontinent, was never resolved, because neither post-independence government accepted the position of the other on the two-nation theory.

The close cultural, linguistic, and racial identification of Indians and Pakistanis did not lead to an ability to harmonize national differences ; but, instead, to doubts in India that the secessionist state had national interests of its own other than those artificially whipped up by communal passions, and in Pakistan to a more vigorous assertion of its different interests and culture. Mutual suspicions, which sometimes reached fratricidal proportions, produced a diplomacy from which emotion and personal grievance could scarcely be eliminated.

As a larger, more powerful state wishing to have peaceful relations with an inferiorly placed neighbour, India's responsibility, ideally, was to help Pakistan achieve what it needed most—a sense of security in its new identity. But the Congress government could not do that without acknowledging the Muslim League's argument for the separate nationhood of the Indian Muslims, and by so doing deny its own premise of a unified Indian nationalism. Pakistan's sense of insecurity was heightened by the vast distance between its dominant western wing and the almost indefensible East Bengal, as well as by its inability to gain control of Kashmir. Pakistanis often conceived of themselves as struggling for survival against Hindu domination ; and of their state as striving for recognition, with no asset other than its sovereignty, in a world where India's status was already assured.[2] Having gained its real independence in 1947 from India, not from Britain, Pakistan sought to enhance its right to exist by postulating Indian hostility ; Pakistani politicians used the spectre of an aggressive Hindu India to revive the nationalistic fervour of their followers. Substance was lent to those fears by India's refusal to relinquish control over the better part of Kashmir—a Muslim-majority area which escaped automatic incorporation into Pakistan because of its status as a princely state. The Indian government, whose sobriety and unaggressive intentions were periodically put to the test, gave little credence to Pakistani fears and tended to interpret Pakistan's behaviour as reflecting its self-image of a minority community in the subcontinent rather than of a sovereign state.

With such a psychological background, the foreign policies pursued by successive Pakistani governments were not surprising. In essence, they sought external support to redress the permanent geopolitical inequality of their bifurcated country vis-a-vis India, and to obtain a favourable settlement on Kashmir. For a few years after independence Pakistan's policies on global problems were similar to those of India.[3] But Pakistan disliked the image that such similarity projected to the world, of following Indian leadership, and altered its posture so as to gain greater status, as well as foreign assistance for its special problems. Disappointed in Britain's unwillingness to assure support in disputes against India, and in the lack of Arab interest in a proposed Islamic front, Karachi turned for aid to the great powers. Simultaneously the US was extending the policy of military alliances into Asia, and Pakistan's bid for alignment found an interested response in Washington. The US-Pakistani mutual defense agreement and Pakistan's membership in regional alliances improved its military capability but intensified, rather than relieved, Indo-Pakistani tensions. New Delhi resented the introduction of Western military interests into the subcontinent and increased its own defense spending, thus giving rise to additional Pakistani fears. The circle of animosity could not be broken by either government and, having no single cause and simple effect, was etched into apparent permanence during the 1950's.

Though unable to eradicate the deep-seated distrust of the other country which existed both in India and in Pakistan, the two governments, from time to time, sought solutions to their similar difficulties arising from the hurried division of 1947. On their various disputes, except Kashmir, both governments sought settlements based on compromises and were careful not to allow public pressures to subvert the working of reasonable accords. The issues on which partial or complete agreements were reached are dealt with in this chapter : refugees of the minority communities, their settlement and compensation ; division of pre-partition assets ; and allocation of the waters of the Indus river basin. However, the basic political rift between the two states has remained unsolved until the mid-1960's. The symbol of that rift, and a major contributory cause of it, was Kashmir, about which the next chapter is concerned.

SOLVING THE IMMEDIATE PROBLEMS OF PARTITION : REFUGEES AND THEIR PROPERTIES

All the disputes between India and Pakistan emerged from the separation of the two states. One of the most tragic and serious was the movement of populations under conditions of great stress. Beginning months before August 1947 the migration was the largest in modern history, involving perhaps 12 million persons flowing both ways. Even so, the religious minority problem was not solved in either state : about 40 million Muslims remained in India and ten million Hindus in East Pakistan. The "fever" of religious communalism,[4] which Nehru once remarked was mistakenly thought to have been cured by the "surgical operation" of partition,[5] was heightened, if anything, by the happenings of 1947. It has continued to the present day in both countries with Hindus and Muslims still seeking refuge, during outbreaks of communal violence, in the country where their community predominates. If there was justification for the view, held by many Indians and adopted by Nehru in 1961,[6] that Pakistan's hostility to India was innate and precluded harmonious relations even with a settlement of the Kashmir dispute, it could be found in the chronic domestic unrest in both countries caused by communalism.

While India sought to solve its minority problems by establishing a secular state, Pakistan's incorporation of Islamic ideas into its various constitutions preserved the communal issue among its own people and kept it alive in India as well. Reports of mistreatment of minorities in either country presented a sure hazard to good relations ; the exodus of minority groups, especially between East Bengal and India, could have led to a renewal of the partition fighting and even to an Indo-Pakistani war. In 1956, during one of the upsurges in the flow of Hindus into West Bengal, Nehru told an agitated parliament that the refugee movement was "more important" than the Kashmir dispute.[7]

Figures on migratory movements are always approximations, and Indo-Pakistani transfers were clouded by the exaggerations born of propaganda warfare. India did not attempt to keep accurate count until 1952, when passport and visa schemes were introduced by both states to control the traffic.[8] The number of Hindus leaving East Pakistan for India varied from a few thousands to tens of thousands per month throughout the 1950's and was probably higher than the number of Muslims crossing into Pakistan.

In the early years after independence both governments faced strong public demands for direct action in behalf of minorities across the borders—notably Hindus in East Bengal and Muslims in Indian-held Kashmir. Nehru frequently took pains to explain to parliament that Pakistan was a sovereign state and thus ameliora- tion of the minority's position there was a matter for international negotiation, not unilateral measures. The Pakistani government under Liaquat Ali Khan shared Nehru's desire for a peaceful solution of the minorities problem, and days after independence both govern- ments issued statements and arranged joint tours of enflamed areas to demonstrate their genuine concern for the human suffering and the political stakes involved. Inter-dominion conferences were held on this and other problems, [9] and the prime ministers met and corresponded in order to dispel the fears of the minorities and admonish majority communities against threats of violence. Temporary successes were followed by renewed tragedies, however. Early in 1950 the flood of Hindu refugees into Indian Bengal began to resemble the Punjabi migrations of 1947. Against strong and influential pressures for retaliatory action Nehru held firm for an international approach, and Liaquat Ali responded with equal desire to achieve a reasoned solution. The agreement of April 1950 negotiated between the two prime ministers again gave state guaran- tees for minorities, promised return or transfer of properties belong- ing to refugees and recovery of abducted women, assured freedom of movement and protection in travel to migrants, and set up minority commissions in East and West Bengal so that the arrangements could be carried out. [10] Refugee movements from both sides abruptly dropped off following the accord between the governments but erupted again in mid-1951, though on a lesser scale than before. [11]

The comparative lull in refugee movements in 1952-1953, coinci- dent with a general reduction of tensions, ended in 1954, when Indo-Pakistani relations reached another crisis over Pakistan's acceptance of US military aid. From the end of 1954 through early 1956 the influx of Hindus into West Bengal increased month by month as the Indian and Pakistani governments took opposite positions on most global political issues. Both governments intro- duced measures at a high level to check and regulate the flow, in accord with earlier agreements ; Indian and Pakistani ministers for minority affairs made joint tours of parts of East Pakistan, and the Pakistani government made statements to try to aleviate Hindu fears. Finally Pakistan suggested ministerial talks in Dacca, and they were held in May 1956. The Indian government indicated satisfaction with the new efforts that Pakistan made to reduce refugee movements, and by the end of the year the migration slowed down. But 1956 had become the record year for refugee flows since the counting began. In July of that year a conference in Karachi specially held to deal with women and children abducted during migratory movements came to a successful conclusion ; thousands of such persons were recovered by both sides from 1947 onward.

From the latter half of 1956 through the early 1960's refugee numbers dwindled to tolerable levels, a few hundreds rather than thousands each month. But in 1961 communal riots, first in India (at Jabalpore and elsewhere) and later in Pakistan, aroused minority fears. Outbreaks again in December 1963 caused another resumption of the refugee flows in early 1964, in both directions in the Bengal-Assam region. At the highest levels in both governments strenuous efforts were required to control domestic violence, and joint talks were held in Delhi to try to alleviate the misery. Months passed, however, before harrassed migrants ceased to appear on the Indo-Pakistani frontiers.

The treatment of minorities in both countries and their periodic migrations were affected by, and frequently the cause of, Indo-Pakistani tensions. Specific incidents, however, were usually the result of factors beyond the control of the governments. The pacification or the inflammation of communal rioting was dependent on local conditions as well as on the ability of the various state administrations to restore order. Therefore, no international agreements between India and Pakistan could entirely solve the problem. New Delhi and Karachi did make efforts to improve the situation and to obviate further transfers of populations. Every successful Indo-Pakistani meeting alleviated communal fears but, correspondingly, every hostile confrontation stimulated disturbances. (The 1965 Indo-Pakistani war proved exceptional in India by providing a platform of patriotism overriding communal feeling.) These facts indicated that the communal atmosphere which produced partition could, under favourable conditions, prove amenable to control by the joint political efforts of the two states in the subcontinent.

Related to population movements was the complex problem of the recovery of or compensation for abandoned properties in India and Pakistan. Never allowed to become a major issue of dispute, this problem was largely brought under control either by coordinated or by unilateral measures.

Vast assets in farming lands, buildings, and moveable property, such as bank deposits, jewellery, manufacturing equipment, and household goods, were left behind in both countries by minorities moving in haste to the other state. Both governments were beseiged by demands from refugees within their borders that they take action to make these tremendous losses less painful ; neither government could ignore the demands. But no complete cataloguing of so-called evacuee properties, no fair assessment of their value, and no certain determination of legal ownership in all cases could be made. The work of reconstructing ownership records alone was beyond the capacities of both governments ; the problems of judging claims and transferring assets so taxed the administrations that it is remarkable that any satisfaction of claims resulted. The work of gathering information, processing claims, and negotiating on compensation began shortly after the partition and continued through numberless meetings of Indian and Pakistani administrators at all levels during the decade of the 1950's.[12]

Moveable property claims proved easier to settle than claims to immoveable holdings. The two governments reached an agreement with respect to the western sector in December 1947, that the refugee owner had title to his property in the other state and that in most cases he could retrieve it himself or through an agent ; after a certain period an official custodian of evacuee property could take charge of certain goods and sell them, crediting the owner with the proceeds. Following the eastern sector migrations of 1950 Bengali refugees were included in a moveable evacuee property agreement, which after a few years of negotiating refinements appeared to work satisfactorily in the bulk of cases. The Moveable Evacuee Property Agreement of 1950 remained the basic document for discussions during the decade ; by 1961 the Indian Ministry for Rehabilitation reported that the only remaining issue was the ownership and transfer of capital assets held in banks and shares of stock in businesses.[13] Agreement was reached on these matters in July 1961.

On the two categories of immoveable evacuee property, agricultural land and urban buildings, collaborative efforts proved impossible because of the great disparity between the assets left by Hindus and Sikhs in Pakistan and those abandoned by Muslims leaving India. Some of the best irrigated land in the subcontinent was owned by non-Muslims in West Punjab, and much urban property in both wings of Pakistan was in legal possession of those who had migrated to India. The great bulk of Muslims leaving India, on the other hand, were poor agriculturists, many of whom had scarcely any property. Both governments faced gigantic tasks in settling refugee farmers, but for India the problem in the Punjab was made worse because the homes and lands evacuated by Muslims could not equal those left behind in Pakistan by Hindus and Sikhs. Although both governments agreed in September 1947 that no property should be alienated, the West Punjab government at the same time ordained that refugees from India could settle temporarily on abandoned lands in order to raise crops. At an inter-dominion conference in December 1947 such a temporary settlement programme found support also from India, and henceforth the locating of refugees on abandoned lands was the normal procedure. Compensating refugees for assets left behind, however, was never settled by an agreement, but by unilateral action on each side.

The Indian government proposed in 1947 that all abandoned immoveable properties in both states be taken over by the respective governments, assessed, and distributed to refugees in amounts comparable and in ratio to their lost properties in the other state. The difference in value between abandoned properties in India and in Pakistan, which was highly favourable to Pakistan, would be made up by international payments to compensate the state whose refugee claims were higher. In July 1948 Pakistan objected to India's proposal and suggested instead that immoveable property be sold or transferred freely on an individual basis. A government-to-government compensation scheme would obviously place Pakistan in a debtor position ; some officials in Pakistan also held that its net gains in the assets of evacuees were negated by its losses from India's refusal to pay fully its obligations under agreements for division of state assets at partition. Discussions and partial or temporary arrangements on refugee lands and buildings continued for several years without bringing the problem much closer to resolution. A tense stalemate developed, broken only by correspondence between Nehru and Liaquat Ali in 1950.

When formal contacts on these matters again began in 1952 India informed Pakistan of its intention to acquire outright all urban evacuee properties for distribution to refugees within its borders, whose immediate needs overshadowed the government's desire to reach an ultimate settlement with Pakistan. India proceeded with its new policy through an interim measure in November 1953 to compensate urban dwellers, followed by a general displaced persons act passed in October 1954 covering all evacuee properties. The act gave the government the right to acquire legal rights over all evacuee properties and thereby compensate refugees for their losses in Pakistan. By this means plus large governmental contributions India completed the settlement, albeit partial, of its refugees' claims. In February 1955 the Pakistani government introduced a similar programme of giving permanent ownership of evacuee property to refugees. The immoveable property problem was thus settled in probably the most expeditious manner.

ANOTHER IMMEDIATE PROBLEM OF PARTITION :
DIVISION OF STATE ASSETS

An inescapable dispute arose between India and Pakistan over the division of the material and financial assets of British India. Both new states acknowledged the need for fair settlements along rational lines and were prepared to compromise on unrealistic claims, although rising tensions in other areas of their relations precluded prompt agreements.

Once it was obvious that a common army could not serve both dominions, a joint defense council under Field-Marshall Claude Auchinleck, the Supreme Commander of both Indian and Pakistani armed forces from the date of independence, was given the task of dividing the forces and reconstituting separate armed services. A comparatively simple formula was used for the operation, of assigning Muslim units and military personnel to Pakistan and non-Muslims to India. As an exception, a temporary Punjab boundary force, made up of all communities, was established to maintain order during the migrations in the Punjab. The force proved unreliable and unable to cope with the chaos ; it was disbanded at the end of August 1947.[14]

The bulk of the military stores and all of the military ordinance establishments remained in Indian territory at partition, while

9

Pakistan inherited most of the training institutions and the only air force maintenance workshop, near Karachi. The defense council arranged for transfer to Pakistan of one-third of the military stores of undivided India, but this did not take place as planned because of military operations in Kashmir and Hyderadad. India turned down Pakistan's demand for the transfer of military stores on grounds that they might be used in Kashmir ; for more than a decade Pakistan charged India with violating the agreement, which New Delhi could not deny.

In June 1947 the viceroy's partition council, with a steering and various expert committees, began its assigned task of dividing the vital civilian services and other assets of the subcontinent. Disturbances and rising tension hampered its work. On December 12, 1947, an inter-dominion financial agreement was reached allotting to Pakistan shares of the combined assets. The share varied according to the nature of the asset—whether revenue-producing, as the railroads, or not ; whether moveable, as office supplies, or immoveable, as government factories ; and so on for an almost incalculable range of items. Most of the physical property transfers of civilian assets ultimately came about. A nearly disastrous delay occurred at the beginning of 1948 when Sardar Patel decided to withhold from Pakistan the unpaid share of the cash balances due under the partition agreements, amounting to 550 million rupees. Patel held that the cash should be transferred only after the Kashmir war ended. Mahatma Gandhi, then fasting in behalf of communal harmony, announced that he would continue his fast unless India turned over the funds. Patel had to alter his stand, and India fulfilled its obligations at once. Division of civilian supplies, from typewriters to railroad equipment, led to disputes over evaluations of assets and their condition at transfer which occupied years of negotiations. Thousands of transactions were involved, the last of them, on the assets of the pre-partition railways and the post and telegraph department, taking place in the 1960's.

More controversial than the division of assets was the division of pre-partition debts. The financial agreement of 1947 provided that India would assume liability for all public obligations of the undivided country subject to recovery of an appropriate contribution from Pakistan. The Pakistani share of these obligations, calculated after subtracting India's dues to Pakistan and estimated by

India at rupees 300 crores, was to be paid to India beginning in 1952 in yearly installments over a period of fifty years.[15] Disagreements over the interpretation of the financial agreement, the values of assets, the extent of liabilities, and the means of payment arose almost at once. For example, how were the provincial shares—especially in the partitioned provinces—of income tax returns gathered before August 1947 to be determined ; what was Pakistan's rightful reimbursement for the construction of ordinance factories and mints ; what was Pakistan's portion of the payments due to the International Civil Aviation Organization? The finance ministers of the two countries discussed those issues in May 1951 and then, after a long interval, in August 1959, but no agreements were reached and no payments were made. Pakistan put up claims against India which cancelled out all Indian claims on Pakistan, and neither government found any purpose in pursuing the matter further.

INDO-PAKISTANI TRADE

Few issues emerging from the partition stimulated as much discussion and constructive negotiation as the one over trade relations between the two new states. At first India and Pakistan assumed that their economies would remain interlocked and agreed just prior to the transfer of power to maintain free flow of goods until a formal pact could be negotiated. This so-called standstill agreement was to guarantee continued movement of grain, tobacco, leather, raw jute, cotton and wool from Pakistan and coal, textiles, rubber and jute manufactures, iron and steel, sugar, and consumer items from India. But in the unjustifiable haste of the transfer of power, trade problems, which could have been anticipated, were overlooked. One of the most disruptive occurred almost at once. India refused to transfer to Pakistan a share of the excise duties collected on Pakistan's raw jute exported from Calcutta ; the latter imposed a duty on jute shipped into India ; a trade war began. Retaliations came from both sides in an atmosphere of suspicion aroused by the many less manageable conflicts then emerging. Nevertheless, each country's dependence on the other conduced to reasoned discussion early in 1948 and to fresh agreements based on each country's right to control and tax traded goods.

An unforeseen crisis struck in September 1949 when India, but not Pakistan, devalued its currency in line with the British devaluation of sterling. Shipments of the major traded commodities, jute and coal, stopped, and, except for a flourishing contraband trade, inter-dominion commerce halted. The resulting disastrous economic effects in Bengal were a main cause of the severe communal outbreaks and attendant migrations of that period. These crises in addition to the Kashmir fighting appeared capable of inducing a war. But the governments were unprepared for that. The Liaquat-Nehru pact of April 1950 calmed minority tensions and also led to a temporary barter trade agreement for certain goods.

In February 1951 a new accord set an exchange ratio between India and Pakistani rupees. The trade war had ended. But rail transportation between the two neighbours remained cut until late 1954, and no general agreement on coal and jute shipments was reached until March 1953, when India revoked its surcharge on coal exports to Pakistan, and Pakistan abolished its duties on jute sent to India. In July 1955 Pakistan also devalued its currency, thus restoring parity with the Indian rupee. Further Indo-Pakistani trade agreements were reached with few difficulties, and in March 1960 an accord was signed providing for most-favoured-nation treatment and a substantial increase in jute and cotton supplied to India, and iron, steel, cement, and coal supplied to Pakistan.

Reasonable approaches of both governments to the trade relations of the subcontinent during the 1950's overcame the economic hostilities of the immediate post-independence period, but they could not negate the disruption caused by drawing international boundaries within an integrated economic region. Both countries sought greater self-sufficiency in resources once available to the entire region—India in raw jute and cotton, Pakistan in jute and cotton mills, power resources, and oil seeds.[16] A pattern of export competition emerged between them ; each country tried to expand its trade relations with third states at the expense of the other's trade. By 1960 the economic division of the subcontinent appeared so permanently established that Ayub Khan's suggestion that India and Pakistan could form a common market once their political conflicts were resolved induced no public discussion.

Recorded Indo-Pakistani trade fluctuated according to the following valuations :

| | *(in lakhs of rupees)* | |
Indian Imports from Pakistan		*Indian Exports to Pakistan*
1952	2,914	4,735
1954	1,782	994
1956	2,093	809
1958	628	712
1960	1,518	943
1962-63	1,665	938
1965-66	565	488

DIVIDING THE WATERS OF THE INDUS BASIN

Most Indo-Pakistani disputes drew the attention and often active intervention of other states and international organizations. The dispute over the division of the water supplies of the Indus valley resulted in a renowned settlement by the International Bank for Reconstruction and Development. Although the two states alone could never have come to such a settlement, the involvement by an international agency would have produced no results without the need and desire for agreement evident on both sides. Twelve years of complex negotiations, temporary agreements, recriminations, unilateral water schemes, and conflicting engineering assessments preceded the accord. For both countries the economic stakes in the dispute over the Indus basin waters—irrigating before partition over thirty million acres—were greater than those of all other disputes between them taken together. The very fact that the conflict could be resolved by economic and technological means alone made the IBRD's settlement possible.

The problem of the canal waters could be simply stated : East Punjab in India was relatively underdeveloped in irrigation works, while West Punjab in Pakistan included most of the canal systems of the pre-partition Indus basin ; but most of the Pakistani canals originated in rivers and head-works located in and controlled by India. The initial approach to the problem by both India and Pakistan centered on maintaining the status quo ante partition, with Pakistan's agreeing to pay India for the continued flow of water from the Sutlej and Ravi rivers, which flow through India ; a standstill agreement was signed in December 1947. On Pakistan's refusal to sign a further accord following the expiry of the standstill agreement, the East Punjab government cut off water supplies to Pakistan, causing immediate panic among West Punjabi farmers and great alarm in their government. Ministerial negotiations in April resulted in an agreement of May 4, 1948. This important pact appeared to establish the principle that India would resume supplies of water, but that Pakistan would construct new irrigation works so that India could progressively diminish the flow of water as it brought new lands in East Punjab and Rajasthan under irrigation.[17]

The May 4 agreement implied the need for new engineering works in both countries to be built under fresh implementing accords. No such accords could be reached, chiefly because of the continuing quarrel over Kashmir. Pakistan argued that Indian control over Kashmir, particularly over the upper Chenab valley, endangered the sources of existing Pakistani irrigation works. After discussions with Indian representatives in 1949 and 1950 the Pakistani government concluded that diversionary schemes to replace the waters supplied by India were of doubtful feasibility and beyond its financial means. Therefore it repudiated the May 4 agreement as a basis for future settlement ; Liaquat Ali denounced it as having been reached "under duress."

Pakistan continued to claim an uninterrupted flow of waters from dams and canals located in India and challenged India's right to divert those waters to newly planned irrigation schemes. As the chief beneficiary of the pre-partition irrigation system, Pakistan clung to the status quo. India's main objective was to irrigate its own dry lands in East Punjab and Rajasthan and for that purpose to alter the water usage pattern of the Indus basin. India postulated an expansion of existing irrigation and storage resources to the benefit of both states as the best solution of a problem which was primarily one of economic development. New Delhi, therefore, refused Pakistan's urgings to take the dispute to the International Court of Justice, because it could see no benefits from a judicial decision on the basis of static legal rights.

In the absence of general precepts of international law governing utilization of waters from rivers flowing through more than one state, the rights of India and Pakistan would not have been easy to determine.[18] In their negotiations with the IBRD the two countries advanced various legal arguments to bolster their respective cases.[19] Pakistan's case, very briefly, was based on the following arguments :

India was bound by the pre-partition obligations of British India to deliver water to West Punjab ; West Punjab had, by usage, established a "servitude" on East Punjab;[20] a state should exercise its sovereign control over a river within its boundaries with "due consideration for its effects upon other riparian states ;"[21] a state proposing new utilization of waters must consult the other concerned states and, in the absence of agreement being reached, resort to arbitration.[22] India's case, on the other hand, did not rest on the theoretically attractive principle of territorial sovereignty over waters[23] but on the principle which had been established in British India for the equitable apportionment of the Indus waters for the greatest good of the greatest number irrespective of state boundaries.[24] India asserted that "riparian states should join with each other to make full utilization of the waters of a river, both from the viewpoint of the widest variety of uses of water, so as to assure the greatest benefit to all ;"[25] in the absence of accord, however, India did not accept arbitration as a suitable solution. In short, India refused to permit Pakistan a veto over its vital programme of agricultural development, and proceeded with the construction of a gigantic multi-purpose water control project on the Sutlej at Bhakra-Nangal.

Because "water disputes are generally agreed to constitute a classical example of disputes which cannot be satisfactorily solved by judicial decision,"[26] the Indus basin controversy was more amenable to the diplomacy of compromise than to arbitration. That approach governed the activities of the World Bank, which maintained a decade-long interest in the dispute.

In 1951 David E. Lilienthal, formerly chairman of the American Tennessee Valley Authority, published a proposal for joint Indo-Pakistani development of the Indus basin with financial help from the IBRD.[27] Lilienthal recognized Pakistan's case against any unilateral Indian diversion of waters but suggested fuller use of the Indus basin for the benefit of both sides. Eugene Black, president of the World Bank, saw the possibilities of Lilienthal's scheme for an international Indus development authority, similar to the TVA. The Bank's proposal for mediating between the two sides followed.[28] Both India and Pakistan accepted the mediation of the Bank in March 1952, India agreeing not to diminish water supplies to Pakistan while the cooperative efforts continued. Engineers from both sides met with the chief Bank negotiator, General Raymond

Wheeler, in 1952 and 1953, but neither side appeared to have sufficient confidence in the other to establish a joint authority. The
Bank then dropped consideration of a joint authority and issued
its own proposal in February 1954.

The Bank's plan suggested that the three eastern rivers (Ravi,
Beas, and Sutlej) should be used for Indian irrigation, that the
three western rivers (Indus, Jhelum, and Chenab) should be used
by Pakistan, and that India should pay the cost of Pakistani construction of new replacement canals. More specifically, the Bank
proposed that Pakistan build new canals to transfer water from
the Indus and the Jhelum into the Chenab and Ravi to compensate
for losses due to India's new dams and works on the upper Ravi,
Beas, and Sutlej. India accepted the Bank's proposal, which was
close to its own suggested solution, but Pakistan hesitated and
asked for a re-examination. In June 1954 India interpreted Pakistan's hesitation as its rejection of the Bank's plan. In July India
opened the first of the Bhakra canals on the Sutlej, justifying the
action on the old May 1948 accord.

The Bank, nevertheless, arranged for resumed negotiations
in December 1954 in Washington. The pace was slow, and the
mediation of the IBRD essential just to keep the two sides in contact. It arranged for meetings, prepared engineering studies, assisted
the governments in reaching ad hoc transitional arrangements,[29]
and sent its officers to the subcontinent for personal talks with
the two parties. Much of its effort appeared directed toward assuring Pakistan that Bank proposals allowing India to go ahead with
its massive schemes would not lead to dust bowl conditions in
West Punjab. The Pakistani government hesitated to reach agreement because of conflicting advice from its experts, uncertainty
as to the feasibility of the Bank's plan, and fear that India would
not abide by any agreement which relieved it of the obligation of
supplying water to Pakistan.[30]

India's interest in the Bank's proposals lay in their granting to
India full use of the eastern rivers, unencumbered by the quasi-
legal obligation to continue supplying water to Pakistan. An
important step toward settlement resulted from a Bank mission
to the subcontinent in June 1957, after which both sides made
clear their views—Pakistan for the first time—on general principles set forth by the Bank as the basis for an Indus treaty. In

July 1958 Pakistan put forward a plan for a replacement canal system from the western rivers and a storage facility on the Jhelum river, where it forms the boundary between Pakistan and Pakistani occupied Kashmir. The Indians studied the plan and gave their reactions in December 1958. In the spring of 1959 the main issues of disagreement were settled in talks between the Bank's president and vice-president, Nehru, and Ayub Khan, the new president of Pakistan ; a draft treaty was ready in August. The remaining task before the Bank was to obtain international financing for the immense canal and storage facilities to be built in Pakistan : India could not be expected to finance projects which were far more elaborate than the diversionary canals originally conceived in 1948.

The Indus Waters Treaty of 1960, signed in Karachi, September 19, was made possible by financing through the IBRD of the largest programme of construction ever to be undertaken anywhere. The treaty followed in general the division of the eastern and western rivers between the two countries envisaged by the Bank in 1954 but included two new features, the establishment of a Permanent Indus Commission and the Indus Basin Development Fund. The latter was the key to both countries' agreeing to a ten-year construction programme to replace for Pakistan water which India used to supply from the Ravi, Beas, and Sutlej rivers. The fund agreed to pay most of the cost of building 400 miles of canals in Pakistan to bring water from the Indus and Jhelum eastward into the existing canal colonies and two large storage dams on the same rivers.[31] India simultaneously obtained financing from the Bank and the US government for a large dam on the Beas river chiefly to irrigate tracts in Rajasthan.[32] The Indus Commission, composed of one Indian and one Pakistani, had the responsibility for carrying out the treaty and reconciling any disagreements ; in the absence of agreement between the commissioners a neutral expert or a court of arbitration should decide an issue.

The cost of the construction programme was estimated at $1,070,-000,000, of which approximately 80 per cent was to be spent on works in Pakistan. The new Pakistani canals were expected to transfer annually fourteen million acre feet of water, or an amount equal to the entire annual flow of the Colorado river. The fund was to be administered by the Bank and financed by half-yearly contributions from India (totalling rupees 83.3 crores), a World Bank loan to Pakistan ($80,000,000), a US loan to Pakistan ($70,000,000 repayable in Pakistani rupees), a contribution by Pakistan itself (£440,000), and grants from Australia, Canada, Germany, New Zealand, the UK and the US. The largest grant commitment came from the US in the form of 177,000,000 in dollars, and in addition the US agreed to contribute the equivalent in Pakistani rupees of $235,000,000. Pakistan also agreed to contribute the rupee equivalent of £9,850,000. The total cost of the project was expected to rise much above these initial commitments, because the original estimate of costs prepared by the Bank was made without detailed hydrological and engineering data. Additional international funds were committed to the Pakistani project in 1964 by an Indus Basin Development Fund (Supplemental) Agreement.

The signing of the treaty and the establishment of the fund gained for India the right fully to exploit the multiple potentials of the three eastern rivers ; for this benefit its government considered its financial cost reasonable. Pakistani gain derived from the great increases it could expect in total irrigation of the Indus region and comparative independence from India in the matter of water supply ; in return Pakistan withdrew its claim to any water from the Ravi, Beas, and Sutlej rivers. The settlement of the dispute rested on India's and Pakistan's recognition that greater economic advantages could be obtained through the Bank's compromise proposal than by unilateral irrigation programmes threatened by conflict between the two states. The Bank's solution, in turn, depended on the commitments to economic development in the subcontinent already established by the industrialized Western states. A fine concurrence of interests was achieved by skillful diplomacy transcending regional politics.

A strenuous test of the strength of the Indus agreement was passed in late 1965, when India turned over to Pakistan its stipulated payment to the fund, despite the recently fought war between them. Further disputes over water resources, however, could be anticipated. An Indian scheme to improve the water flow of the Hooghly river, serving Calcutta port, by damming the Ganges at Farakka raised Pakistani concern over the effect of this scheme on the lower Ganges,. which flows into East Pakistan. The matter was under bilateral discussion at the time of writing.

RATIONALIZING THE BORDERS

The years 1959 and 1960 marked the highest point in Indo-Pakistani cooperation. Not only was the Indus basin dispute settled, but other problems melted under the hopeful rays produced by meetings of Nehru and Ayub Khan. In October 1959, following such a meeting at Palam airport, New Delhi, an amicable solution was found to the India-East Pakistan border problems, and in January 1960 an India-West Pakistan border agreement was reached. Like the Indus dispute the border conflicts were subject to rational compromises because neither side had staked important ideological objectives on the outcome. The areas whose boundaries had remained unsettled between the two countries were intrinsically unimportant and, except for the Rann of Kutch over which major fighting took place in 1965, never became serious threats to subcontinental peace. Armed clashes frequently occurred, but the issues were local and could be at least temporarily settled by joint action of the central governments. The long delays in reaching permanent boundary agreements derived from the extraordinary intricacy of the problems involved for both states. Most of the territorial disputes arose from conflicting interpretations of the boundaries as laid down by Cyril Radcliffe at the time of partition, and of the further awards of Justice Bagge, given three years later referring to disputes in the eastern (Bengal) region. Two disputes, over the Rann of Kutch and the Cooch Behar enclaves, had other origins.

During the 1950's the most troublesome boundary problems lay along the 2,480 miles of India-East Pakistan frontier, of which distance about one-half had been demarcated by 1958.[33] The press and some officials in both India and Pakistan exaggerated the importance of the many violent incidents associated with that novel and often undefined frontier. The two governments, on the other hand, tried to settle most of the border problems quietly through on the spot administrative arrangements, and at higher levels only when necessary. Most of the disputes were settled in this way, by compromises or by one side's withdrawing its claims.

By 1956 certain stubborn boundary disputes began to arouse national attention in both states. Parts of the frontier between Assam and East Pakistan where refugee movements into India reached serious proportions, the enclaves created by the accession to India of the old state of Cooch-Behar, and the Berubari Union No. 12 were the major areas of local incidents. It was the character of the border regions rather than the malintentions of the two governments which caused the incidents.[34] Existence of 123 enclaves of Indian territory in Pakistan and 74 Pakistani enclaves similarly surrounded by Indian territory amounted to a chaotic state of affairs, which defied description.[35] After a decade of unsuccessful administrative efforts to solve the eastern frontier disputes Nehru and Prime Minister Firoz Khan Noon met, in September 1958, and in three days decided policies on ten disputed areas.

The Nehru-Noon Agreement, as it was called, reaffirmed at the Nehru-Ayub Khan meeting in September 1959, embodied territorial compromises along the frontier between the two Bengals. Nehru agreed to an equal division of the Berubari Union No. 12 between India and Pakistan and an exchange of all the Indian Cooch-Behar enclaves in Pakistan for those of Pakistan in India. (The latter agreement had been reached in principle during negotiations in 1953.) He soon encountered an obstacle in carrying out Indian responsibilities, which had still not been overcome by the mid-1960's : The West Bengal government challenged the constitutionality of New Delhi's ceding territory to another state. The issue, raised to critical proportions in the West Bengal legislature, went through the local courts and to the Supreme Court on two occasions, while boundary demarcation and final transfer was held up by the Indian side. There was little doubt that India would ultimately be able to fulfill its part of the territorial exchange, but the lengthy delays and the rising of political tempers in West Bengal demonstrated again how intimately Indo-Pakistani relations were determined by domestic interests and popular passions.

It proved easier to settle disputes arising from the Radcliffe Award on the India-West Pakistan frontier. Between October 1959 and January 1960 agreements were reached whereby India dropped its claim to the villages of Theh Sarja Marja, Rakh Hardit Singh and Pathanke, Pakistan dropped its claim to Chak Ladheke, and local compromises were made on the Hussainiwala and Suleimanke irrigation headworks. The demarcation of the East Punjab-Pakistan boundary was completed in June 1960 and the Rajasthan-Pakistan boundary by 1963.

In a separate category from the frontier disputes arising from the

1947 drawing of partition lines was the Kutch-Sind boundary question. This dated back at least to a 1908 dispute between the province of Sind and the Maharao of Kutch. India declared that the Government of Bombay's resolution No. 1192 of February 1914 had settled the matter finally. Pakistan asserted that the issue was still in dispute because the Kutch-Sind boundary had never been demarcated. Pakistan contended that the boundary should run through the middle of the Rann of Kutch—an area which is sometimes swamp and sometimes desert—and not at its northern edge, as India claimed it did. India repudiated persistent Pakistani claims through the 1950's, and in 1956 Indian forces drove out Pakistani troops encountered in the Rann. Negotiations on the Kutch boundary were postponed in 1960, pending the familiar "collection of further data;" India, however, was unwilling to agree that a dispute in fact existed.[36]

Into that area, with the longest doubtful boundary of the Indo-Pakistani frontier, Pakistani troops moved in force in April 1965. The Indian army met the attacks, but New Delhi decided not to mount a full-scale operation in the desolate Rann but to threaten retaliation elsewhere if the fighting continued. As military action on the frontier tapered off in late April the British prime minister, Harold Wilson, made proposals for a cease-fire and a final settlement. Both India and Pakistan accepted them after Prime Minister Sastri and President Ayub Khan met in London in July at the Commonwealth Prime Ministers Conference.

The military clashes in the Rann of Kutch were indecisive and, when all of the evidence becomes available, will probably be determined as a part of the broader confrontation for which both sides began to prepare. The Indian government explained the Pakistani challenge in April as an effort to divert Indian forces from the Kashmir-Punjab front prior to the major attempts in August and September to wrest Kashmir from Indian control.

The Indo-Pakistani agreement of June 30, 1965, on the Rann of Kutch dispute contained a provision for arbitration in case the two governments could not reach a boundary accord by themselves within two months. This was a mode of international settlement rarely agreed to by New Delhi and suggesting in this instance that the territory involved was not regarded as vital. When no efforts at bilateral agreement followed, a three-judge international tribunal was set up with a Yugoslav member appointed by India, an Iranian member by Pakistan, and a Swedish chairman named by the UN secretary-general. After meeting in Geneva for two and one-half years the tribunal in February 1968 decided against the Pakistani case that the international boundary of the Rann passed through its middle but nevertheless awarded to Pakistan some 350 square miles (about ten per cent) of the disputed area, which the tribunal's chairman stated had been under Pakistani control. Indians and their prime minister, Mrs. Gandhi, took the decision as a defeat, and parliamentary protests against giving up any Indian claimed land embarrassed the Congress government. But Mrs. Gandhi's ministry held fast to the terms of the 1965 agreement and accepted the award unconditionally.

Thus, despite difficulties presented by the Indo-Pakistani disputes arising from the partition, all of them save Kashmir were totally or partially solved by negotiated compromises and, in one case, by arbitration. The achievements thereby recorded leave an impression of constructive diplomatic endeavour less often publicized than the unhappy dealings over Kashmir.

NOTES AND REFERENCES

[1] Deputy Prime Minister Vallabhbhai Patel and other powerful Congress leaders openly expressed their view that Pakistan would collapse in the early years after independence. Nehru, too, doubted that Pakistan was viable. "India cannot and will not remain divided," said Nehru on November 28, 1947. "This is my conviction no matter how much I am criticized for having accepted the partition." Govt. of India Information Services, Washington, D. C., issuance of Dec. 4, 1947 (no. 3590). See also Brecher, *Nehru : A Political Biography*, pp. 377-78.

[2] The partition did not change the international status of India, which continued to possess all the treaty rights, the obligations, and the prestige, inherited from British India. India's continued membership in the UN was not questioned ; Pakistan had to apply for UN membership as a new state. See the relevant UN document in K. Sarwar Hasan and Zubeida Hasan, *Documents on the Foreign Relations of Pakistan : The Kashmir Question*, pp. 393-95.

[3] See B. C. Rastogi, "Alignment and Nonalignment in Pakistan's Foreign Policy," *International Studies*, vol. III, 2 (Oct. 1962), p. 165f. Also G. W. Choudhury and Parvez Hasan, "Pakistan's External Relations," Pakistan Institute of International Affairs, Karachi 1958.

[4] "Communalism" in the context of modern Indian history always refers to religious communalism and in this book to Hindu-Muslim antagonism.

[5] Nehru's speech in parliament, Aug. 7, 1950, *Speeches 1949-1953*, p. 294.

[6] See his speech in the Lok Sabha, Aug. 16, 1961, *Speeches 1957-1963*, p. 294.

[7] *RSD*, vol. XV, Dec. 3, 1956. col. 1,325. In that same year Nehru acknowledged that the Pakistani government at the higher levels had not encouraged nor was directly responsible for the exodus. Lok Sabha, Mar. 29, *Speeches 1953-1957*, p. 357.

[8] Nehru acknowledged the unreliability of his government's figures and offered the following estimate of population transfers in 1955 : migration of Hindus from East Pakistan to India : 3,500,000 ; migration of Muslims from India to East Pakistan : 1,500,000 ; migration of Hindus from West Pakistan to India : 4,700,000 ; migration of Muslims from India to West Pakistan : 6,100,000. There were also movements of refugees returning to the country from which their original exodus had occurred, Lok Sabha, Sept. 26, 1955 ; *FAR*, vol. I, 9 (Sept, 1955), p. 194.

[9] Texts of various Indo-Pakistani agreements on minorities and other matters appear in S. L. Poplai, *India 1947-50 : External Affairs*.

[10] Text of the Nehru-Liaquat minorities agreement, April 8, can be found in *Middle East Journal*, vol. IV, 1950, pp. 344-46. Two of Nehru's cabinet ministers, S. P. Mookerjee and K. C. Neogy, resigned over the agreement, calling for sterner measures against Pakistan.

[11] Frequently the real causes of such movements were unknown, and often they were the result of a mass sense of insecurity rather than direct communal threats. The fear of an Indo-Pakistani war, which might bring terrible suffering to minorities in both states, was a major cause of the insecurity.

[12] Extracts from the proposals and agreements issuing from early meetings are in S. L. Poplai, *op. cit.*, p. 128f.

[13] *FAR*, vol. VII, 3 (March 1961), pp. 77-79.

[14] A controversial account of the partition which holds British officials responsible for much of the Punjab tragedy is Leonard Mosley, *The Last Days of the British Raj*, N. Y. 1962.

[15] See C. N. Vakil, *Economic Consequences of Divided India*, p. 493f.

[16] Pakistan with almost no textile industry in 1947 became after 1959, the world's largest exporter of cotton yarn. With regard to raw jute trading, Indian imports from Pakistan were at a level of rupees 7,124 lakhs in 1948-1949, fell to rupees 143 lakhs in 1959, after which they rose slightly to rupees 718 lakhs in 1961, and by 1962-1963 had fallen again, to rupees 335 lakhs. Trade figures in this book, unless otherwise attributed, have been taken from the annual publication of the Indian Ministry for Information and Broadcasting, *India 19 - -*.

[17] The agreement technically applied only to the current dispute over the supply of water to the Central Bari Doab and the Depalpur canals in West Pakistan. However, the Indian government inferred the broader principle of progressive diminishing of all water supplies to Pakistan from this accord. See *Foreign Policy of India : Texts of Documents 1947-64*, pp. 219-20.

[18] Only in recent years did an interest develop in the law governing the uses of international rivers. The studies undertaken for the meetings of the International Law Association at Dubrovnik in 1956 and New York in 1958 on this subject and the resolutions there adopted helped to clarify the legal principles and practices which could be accepted by a majority of states.

[19] The Indian and Pakistani governments employed F. J. Berber and John

G. Laylin, respectively, as their legal advisors in the IBRD negotiations. See their opposing points of view on the uses of waters from international rivers in Berber, *Rivers in International Law*, London 1959, and in Laylin's paper at the 51st Annual Meeting of the American Society of International Law : *Proceedings*, April 25-27, 1957, p. 36.

[20] These two arguments were probably invalid under international law. They appeared nevertheless in the Royal Institute of International Affairs publication, *The World Today*, Dec. 1957, in an article by Frederick Honig.

[21] Principle III of the resolution on the uses of international waters unanimously adopted at the International Law Association conference in Dubrovnik, 1956. The resolution was seconded both by M. C. Setalvad, Attorney General for India, and by Manzur Qadir, Senior Advocate, Supreme Court of Pakistan.

[22] Principle VI of the same.

[23] See Barber, *op. cit.*, p. 13 for a statement of alternative principles governing uses of international rivers. See also *The World Today*, June 1958, for a statement of the Indian view by K. Krishna Rao, legal advisor to the Ministry of External Affairs.

[24] See *Proceedings* of the International Law Assoc., N. Y. 1958, appendix B, pp. 79-83 and appendix D, pp. 97-99.

[25] Principle VIII of the resolution passed at Dubrovnik, *op. cit.*

[26] According to Berber, *op. cit.*, p. 263.

[27] See Lilienthal, "Another Korea in the Making?," *Colliers*, Aug. 4, 1951.

[28] An account of the Bank's intervention and solution of the Indus basin dispute is found in Aftab Ahmed, "The Indus Basin Project and the World Bank : A Case Study of Diplomacy and Administration in Economic Development," unpubl. Ph. D. dissertation, George Washington University, Washington 1965. See also Eugene Black, *The Diplomacy of Economic Development*, Cambridge, Mass. 1960.

[29] Three successive agreements were made for India's continued supply of water to Pakistan up to 1957, and from 1959 to 1960. From 1957 to 1959 India continued to supply water in accordance with the May 1948 agreement, despite Pakistan's repudiation of it. Three new link canals were built by Pakistan while negotiations for a final settlement took place. Transitional agreements provided India with increasingly larger amounts of water from the eastern rivers.

[30] For Pakistani accounts of the dispute and negotiations see Chaudhri Muhammad Ali, *The Emergence of Pakistan*, chapter 15, and Ayub Khan, *Friends Not Masters*, pp. 107-13.

[31] The Mangla dam on the upper Jhelum inundates land and over 100 villages in a part of Kashmir under Pakistani occupation. India's agreement to the Indus basin settlement appeared to give Pakistan a legal right to this region and precluded further protests over Pakistani construction of the dam. India formally congratulated Pakistan on the completion of the Mangla dam in early 1968, thereby eliciting protests from some members of parliament in New Delhi.

[32] India also obtained from Pakistan final payment on "undisputed" charges for water supplied since 1948 and partial, but final, payment of "disputed charges."

[33] See *FAR*, Vol. IV, 3 (March 1958), p. 52.

[34] See "Ground Rules for Border Guards," on the Indo-Pakistan frontier,

in *FAR*, vol. V, 10 (Oct. 1959), pp. 339-40. Attempts by farmers from both sides to cultivate new "char" lands along rivers after floods receded, lifting of cattle across shallow streams, suspected smuggling, and movements of unidentified local people caused many serious firings.

[35] Many pre-partition princely states, such as Cooch-Behar, held villages and lands which were non-adjacent, separated by the territories of other states or British India.

[36] A lengthy document presented an elaborate brief for the Indian position no the Rann of Kutch dispute : *The Kutch-Sind Border Question*, prepared by K. Krishna Rao under the auspices of the Indian Society of International Law, New Delhi 1965.

CHAPTER VI

THE BURDEN OF PAKISTAN AND THE UNSOLVED KASHMIR DISPUTE

BY 1960 ALL of the most irritating Indo-Pakistani disputes arising from the partition had been largely disposed of, except Kashmir. On that one remaining guaranteed source of Indo-Pakistani hostility were concentrated the psychological frustrations and nationalist irredentisms which inevitably followed the partition on both sides. Indeed, the agony of 1947 stretched on into the second decade after the event in the shape of a crucial state whose final disposition remained in doubt.

When Westerners turned their minds to the Kashmir dispute in the 1950's and early 1960's the first idea which was apt to merge was "plebiscite." To Indians the same dispute always brought forth the thought of "Pakistani aggression." Without trying to identify the automatic response to Kashmir of a Pakistani or a Russian, the essence of a serious international misunderstanding already was established in the Western versus the Indian conception of the problem. The problem of Kashmir drew the attention of the great powers to Indo-Pakistani relations initially because the dispute appeared on the Security Council agenda, on the initiative of India ; but, like the explosive situations accompanying partitions of nations in other parts of the world, the Kashmir situation would probably have attracted great power involvement even without the intervention of the UN. Jammu and Kashmir, despite its deep poverty, relative inaccessibility, and small population (about 4,250,000 in 1947), was regarded by major powers as a kind of "cockpit" of Asia, a geographical epicentre almost the tri-junction of the three largest countries of the continent. For India and for Pakistan the incorporation of Kashmir—the shortened form of the administratively con-joined Jammu and Kashmir—became, a few months after independence, a national objective of paramount importance.

For Pakistan, Kashmir embodied that which it later became for India : the fulfilment of its national destiny. A state whose population in 1947 was about three-fourths Muslim, adjoining West Pakistan and geographically and economically linked to it, Kashmir should have become part of Pakistan according to the logic of partition. But the legalities of partition, by which Muslim majority provinces and districts adjacent to one another were incorporated into Pakistan, applied only to British India, not to the semi-autonomous Indian princely states. By the Indian Independence Act of 1947 the princes were given the option to accede to one or the other of the new dominions. The Kashmir maharaja's failure to do so, until he was virtually compelled by circumstances, partly set the stage for the conflict.

Mohammad Ali Jinnah, leader of the Muslim League and rightly called the founder of Pakistan, encouraged the princes to exercise their personal discretion in deciding to which dominion they should accede. He recognized them as constitutionally independent if they had not acceded when British paramountcy lapsed on August 15, 1947. (The Indian government, in contrast, refused to attribute sovereign status to any princely state. The British stand on the question was never made clear.)[1] By adopting that approach Jinnah hoped that certain princely domains geographically a part of India might become independent, thus weakening India ; or at least that their ambitions for independence would be a source of embarrassment to India. The first test of Jinnah's policy, and a partial precedent for the Kashmir imbroglio, appeared when the Muslim ruler of Junagadh opted for Pakistan in August 1947. Although Junagadh in the Kathiawar peninsula had a Hindu majority and did not adjoin Pakistan Jinnah accepted the accession. When civil order broke down in the state India took control of its small area and administered a plebiscite whose result confirmed Junagadh's de facto merger with India. Pakistan, however, held that the ruler's original act of acceding to Pakistan remained valid, and official maps a decade later showed a green Pakistani enclave in Kathiawar.

It was inconceivable to Pakistanis that Kashmir should not become part of the new Muslim state. For Kashmiri Muslims to be incorporated in an Islamic state only a stroke of the Hindu maharaja's pen was necessary. Pakistan would then be complete. And the maharaja's accession to Pakistan in 1947 would probably not have stirred up any official Indian action to counter the move. But Maharaja Hari Singh appeared to want Kashmir's incorporation neither into Pakistan nor into India : some form of autonomy or independence might result from an indefinite postponement of the act of accession. The indecisiveness of Kashmir could not be tolerated for long by either dominion, but Pakistan took the initiative in trying to force the issue. In control of the traditional routes into Kashmir, the Pakistani government placed a ban on trade into and out of the state, knowing that India could not immediately compensate for the sudden economic boycott. Shortly thereafter, in late October, Pakistan permitted and encouraged bellicose tribesmen from the northern areas of Hazara and Peshawar to invade the valley with the object of scattering the maharaja's civil and military forces. If that tactic had succeeded, the Pakistani army and administrators could have (as India had done in Junagadh) entered the state with the declared purpose of reestablishing law and order and putting an end to persecutions of Muslims, for which Hari Singh's administration was noted. There could follow an ascertainment of the people's will (as in Junagadh) and a de facto accession to Pakistan. Failure of this strategy, the interpretation of which appears to us sound though undocumented, by no means weakened the will of the Pakistani government to complete the construction of an Islamic state by any means at hand. The years following bore witness to the persistence of the Pakistani effort.

　Unlike Pakistan, India had no pre-established, publicly-expressed policy on Kashmir ; the purposes behind statements and actions of Indian leaders concerning Kashmir may remain unclear for decades to come.[2] However, Indian interest in the state was certain, if only because of the close affiliations which existed between the Jammu and Kashmir National Conference headed by Sheikh Mohammad Abdullah and the liberal wing of the Indian National Congress under Nehru's leadership. Indian communications with Kashmir were rudimentary, but at least one fair weather road existed as a result of the Radcliffe Commission's award to India of Gurdaspur district in the Punjab.[3]

　When the Pakistani policy of trying to force the maharaja's hand and the communal disorders in the state itself led to a tribal onslaught which the Kashmir army could not contain the maharaja appealed to India for protection, and the Indian government offered support on condition of Kashmir's accession to India. The maharaja complied—he scarcely had a choice and was in flight himself at the time—, and on October 27 Kashmir became a legal part of India, technically in the same manner as had hundreds of other princely states. Units of the Indian army flew into Srinagar, the capital of the state located in the strategic valley of Kashmir, in an extraordinary last-moment manoeuvre which barely saved the airfield from capture. They were launched on a successful offensive to throw out the tribesmen.

The case of Kashmir was different from that of most other states acceding to either dominion. The Muslim majority in Kashmir had been brought into India by the decision of a Hindu ruler. Further, an invasion was in progress, which led Pakistan to charge that the maharaja's decision was made "under duress." It was a Pakistani-inspired duress, however, and if it had forced the issue the other way it might have been depicted as "liberation." Some Indian officials recognized the accidental appearance that Kashmiri accession to India assumed. The government gave official sanction to its private doubts about the procedures followed in obtaining the accession, and in accordance with the precedent established in Junagadh and the preferences expressed by Congress leaders for Kashmiri self-determination[4] offered to hold a plebiscite in Kashmir. The plebiscite after accession was probably first suggested by Lord Mountbatten, who had earlier advised the maharaja to ascertain his people's wish before acceding to either dominion.[5] Nehru immediately accepted the idea and permitted Mountbatten in accepting the accession to add the proviso that "as soon as law and order have been restored in Kashmir and its soil cleared of the invaders, the question of the State's accession should be settled by a reference to the people." Nehru later made it clear that the "reference" intended was to be a plebiscite held under international supervision.[6]

The offer of a plebiscite, which Nehru later explained was a "pledge to the people of Kashmir—if you like, to the people of the world,"[7] proved disastrous to India's position on Kashmir. It raised doubts over the legality of the accession and the wishes of the Kashmiri people, and it directed international attention away from India's complaint against Pakistan. But the offer was not unsoundly based. The Union government did not control Kashmiri politics ; rather the National Conference did, under the leadership of Sheikh Abdullah, who had been released from prison by the maharaja and asked to form a government in Srinagar. Abdullah's interests had to be respected, and before partition he had called for a popular determination of whether to accede to India or Pakistan.[8] He could not be expected to base a democratic government on a determination of the state's status dictated by the maharaja. Nehru also, because of his democratic ideals, rebelled at the thought of obtaining control over Kashmir as a concession from a disreputed prince. With Abdullah firmly committed, as he was then, to the accession to India and the memories of the barbarous invasion from Pakistan fresh in the minds of the people, a fairly-conducted plebiscite would probably have favoured India. Furthermore, the plebiscite offer was designed to assure Pakistan, and other states as well, that India was not seeking territorial acquisitions. Nehru and Mountbatten hoped that the Indian army's action would not be taken as a challenge to Pakistan, which in the enflamed post-partition atmosphere could lead to general war ; India was seeking Pakistan's cooperation in a peaceful settlement.[9]

For a time the plebiscite offer seemed capable of producing a negotiated settlement, although not until Jinnah had been disuaded by the acting Pakistani commander-in-chief, General Gracey, from ordering the army into Kashmir to complete the take-over that the tribals had tried to initiate. Forceful measures failing, Jinnah sought to negotiate, and he presented Pakistan's terms to Mountbatten when the latter visited Lahore in early November.[10] In subsequent exchanges between Nehru and Liaquat Ali Khan both sides agreed that a plebiscite should be held, probably under UN auspices. An unbridgeable disagreement, however, appeared in their opposing ideas on the appropriate conditions in the state prior to a vote—a disagreement that became the predominant feature of the Kashmir dispute. Pakistan insisted then on a simul-taneous withdrawal of forces and some kind of "impartial" adminis-tration of the state, which would neutralize the vote-getting power of the Sheikh. India could not regard its military presence in Kashmir as equivalent to the raiders' and insisted that no plebiscite could occur until the invaders were driven out ; Abdullah was, in fact, the most representative Kashmiri leader, and his administration had to prevail, in the popular interest, during a plebiscite.

While the Nehru-Liaquat correspondence continued, Indian troops made limited advances against the invaders. Reports from the front made Nehru harden his views and favour a complete defeat of the aggressing forces, after which UN observers could "advise us as to the proposed plebiscite."[11] In Pakistan too the mood was for increased military commitment rather than for diplomatic concessions. A general Indo-Pakistani war was a distinct possibility, and Mountbatten urged both sides to submit their dispute to the UN. His suggestion received support, especially from Liaquat Ali, at a meeting he held with both prime ministers and their advisers in Lahore on December 8. On December 20 the Indian cabinet decided to take its case to the Security Council ; on January 1, 1948, India's request was formally submitted.

THE UN EFFORTS TO MEDIATE

Years later, Indians criticized their government for not invoking chapter VII of the UN Charter dealing with breaches of the peace and acts of aggression, but rather chapter VI (article 35), dealing with pacific settlement of disputes, in its complaint against Pakistan. India's move may have been a tactical error. But more likely it reflected the fact that India sought the assistance of the UN in reaching a settlement which both sides were striving for bilaterally almost up to the week that the dispute came to New York. United Nations condemnation of one side or collective action against an aggressor was not the response needed, but rather mediation by a third party. India's message to the chairman of the Security Council claimed that Pakistan's support of the attacking forces in Kashmir "constitutes active aggression against India," but India's delegates avoided direct mention, in these early debates, of Pakistani aggression. A harder Indian line against Pakistan at that time could have given substance to charges from Karachi of unmitigated Indian hostility. India merely requested the Council to prevent Pakistan from further aiding the attackers, so that peace and order could be restored in the state.

During that first UN debate on Kashmir Indian delegates spelled out terms for a final settlement which did not substantially change

during the years to follow : Pakistan must use its influence to secure
withdrawal of all invading tribesmen and Pakistani nationals from
Kashmir ; India would withdraw the "bulk" of its forces leaving a
number "adequate" to guarantee security ; the administration of
the entire state must be controlled by a popularly formed government ; and UN representatives should oversee a plebiscite conducted
under the state administration. The case had strength on the surface,
but as years of debate wore on an essential inconsistency protruded
more clearly : the premise of the legality (and later the finality) of
the accession, which underlay every Indian policy on Kashmir,
conflicted with the offer of a plebiscite and even with the acceptance of any UN mediation. That inconsistency weakened India's
position.

   The Pakistani case was far more involved than India's and was
presented with great conviction and at unprecedented length by
the brilliant Pakistani foreign minister, Muhammad Zafrullah Khan.
It centreed on the theme that the Kashmir dispute was merely a
tragic facet of the deep conflicts between Muslims and Hindus in
the subcontinent which could only be resolved by a peaceful separation of the two communities (Kashmir becoming part of Pakistan).
With lengthy reference to the recent migrations, rioting, and attacks
on minorities in the Punjab, Kashmir, and Bengal, Zafrullah Khan
sought to place the dispute at hand in the context of Hindu and
Sikh hatred of Muslims and India's aim of destroying Pakistan.
Specifically, he alleged that India had engineered the accession of
Kashmir by fraud and by a policy of "genocide" planned to transform
the state into a Hindu-majority region. He denied Pakistan's
complicity in the tribal invasion. For a solution he reiterated Jinnah's
earlier proposals to Mountbatten : an impartial Kashmiri administration, withdrawal of all armed forces, the return of residents who
were forced to flee the state, and a UN plebiscite. Compared with
the brief and frequently inconclusive recitation of the Indian case
by Gopalaswami Ayyengar, Zafrullah Khan's exhaustive history of
Muslim-non-Muslim and Pakistani-Indian relations scored a diplomatic advance from which Pakistan benefited for years to come.
The Council accepted the new terms of reference for the dispute and,
ultimately without Indian objection, changed its title from the
Jammu-Kashmir Question to the India-Pakistan Question. Henceforth India's identification of the main cause of the conflict as

aggression from Pakistan and its effort to gain recognition of the legal accession to India were submerged under the mixed account of communal outbursts and military and political manoeuvres on both sides.

In presenting its case on Kashmir India suffered in the early years from the unfortunate disadvantage of mediocre diplomacy at the UN[12] and clumsy public relations. India's missions in almost every country were notably weak in the arts of persuasion. The Indian government was confident of the justice of its case on Kashmir and was openly bewildered when the world audience, especially in the West, failed to understand or appreciate it. When the UN members turned their attention to the sources of Indo-Pakistani hostilities and found therein many causes for grievance on both sides their natural response became one of recommending compromise solutions, of balancing grievances and demands, in short of acting in the role of a mediating third party, which was the role assigned to the UN commission dealing with the dispute. Finding itself an equal party to a complicated dispute rather than a party with a justified complaint requiring immediate and specific action, India returned constantly to the charge that the trouble was initially caused by Pakistan. But the Security Council was by then seized of the question by the terms in which *it* wished to deal with it, and India's rising protests of unfair treatment were interpreted as efforts to divert the Council from its self-chosen search for an equitable solution. "The fundamental issue has been slurred over and by-passed and passed over," Nehru said in 1948,[13] and for more than a decade to follow Indian resentment over the UN's handling of the question increased the difficulties of reaching a settlement. (Chastened by the experience of being a party to a dispute in the UN, India avoided in the future bringing to the attention of the world body questions in which its national interests were directly involved.)

The Security Council delayed action through the spring of 1948 as the local fighting flared up again. The United Nations Commission for India and Pakistan (UNCIP) finally began its sessions in June in Geneva. When it reached the subcontinent in July the Pakistani foreign minister informed it that two months earlier his government had sent regular troops into the state to face the increasing Indian military commitment. The UNCIP's resolution of

August 14, 1948, drew attention to the "material change" in the situation caused by the presence of Pakistani forces and specified terms for a cease-fire, troop withdrawal, and an administration during a plebiscite, which met most of India's conditions. India therefore accepted it ; Pakistan did also, after an initial rejection and with enough provisos to constitute rejection. The UNCIP completed its work in India and Pakistan, returned to Geneva and New York, where, on December 11, it issued further plebiscite proposals which reflected its decidedly favourable regard for India's position. The proposals were accepted by both sides as the basis of a cease-fire, effected January 1, 1949. They were then embodied in a resolution of the UNCIP on January 5, which remained the only firm commitment to agreement between the parties in the years to follow.[14]

Both sides found it impossible to translate the formal agreements of the January 5 resolution into action, or to accept the Commission's plebiscite proposals. Pakistan reverted to its demand for synchronized withdrawal of troops, and India insisted on demilitarization of the one-third of the state under the control of the Pakistani supported Azad Kashmir government as conditions preceding a plebiscite. The UNCIP failed to discover a set of arrangements acceptable to both sides and suggested, in August 1949, that points of difference be submitted to arbitration. President Truman and Prime Minister Atlee publicly asked the parties to accept arbitration ; Pakistan accepted, and India refused. (Then and on several occasions in years to follow India refused arbitration on any matters connected with Kashmir, probably because a tribunal or court would judge any given narrow issue on its own merits, without taking account of what India considered the original cause of the dispute.) The UNCIP's efforts to mediate the dispute had failed. Its only achievement had been the cease-fire. Its final report of December 9, 1949, suggested the appointment of a single mediator to replace the Commission.

By this time the Security Council members had begun to incline toward support of Pakistan's case—except for the Soviet bloc states, which began to support India.[15] In the majority view it mattered little which side had initiated the struggle or what were the historic rights and wrongs of the case. The object was to reach a settlement. Because a plebiscite appeared to be an equitable solution

—especially to countries long attached to the doctrine of self-determination—and because both sides had agreed to it in principle, it was this formula that the Security Council continued to explore. In March 1950 a Western sponsored resolution based on the proposals of General McNaughton, the Canadian representative, provided for appointment of a single mediator to resolve the problems of demilitarization ; the man chosen was the Australian jurist, Owen Dixon. Pakistan accepted it. India objected that it ignored its demand that the Pakistani occupied northern regions of Kashmir be administered by the Srinagar government, and it placed the Azad Kashmir authorities on an equal footing with Sheikh Abdullah's legal administration. India felt that it had to accept the resolution but did so with burdening qualifications.

As the Council sessions focused public attention on the plebiscite proposal, Pakistan's case had the convenient advantage of displaying Indian objections as the main obstacle to holding a vote. Pakistan at the same time benefited from the UN's unwillingness to stipulate a disbanding of Azad Kashmiri forces as a prior condition. By 1950 Pakistan had acquired a status of equality with India in the Council's handling of the dispute chiefly because of the Council's preoccupation with the plebiscite question. In contrast, India's position appeared weak and ambiguous throughout the decade of the 1950's. It clung to its offer of a plebiscite so as not to appear inconsistent, and it continued to treat with UN mediators on the subject out of deference to the world organization. But the plebiscite conditions under discussion and embodied in UN proposals after 1949 did not fit the facts as India understood them.

First, according to India, the UN and its Commission and mediators did not differentiate sufficiently between India and the aggressive state, Pakistan, in stipulating conditions for a plebiscite. Despite the UNCIP's noting, in its third interim report in December 1949, the unanticipated consolidation of Pakistani military power in the Azad Kashmir region and the changed situation thereby created, it recognized the occupation of this area by Pakistan as equivalent to India's presence in the remainder of the state. As V. K. Krishna Menon said much later of the Security Council's informal mediator, General McNaughton, he "approached this problem as though this territory really did not belong to anyone, as though two parties were fighting over it ; he tried to place us both on an equal status."[16]

Second, the UN's proposals ignored the fact of Kashmir's legal accession to India, which gave the Srinagar government a locus standi in any final settlement especially by a plebiscite. In essence, then, whereas India's continuing commitment to a plebiscite created in the UN the expectation of an early solution to the dispute, India's real position and the UN's assumptions about it diverged markedly. Under suitable conditions India might have sanctioned the holding of a plebiscite—the conditions of the January 5, 1949, resolution and the attendant elucidations of the UNCIP chairman, Lozano—, but when the UN mediator proposed plebiscite terms which struck a balance between India and Pakistan, India could not agree.

Furthermore, the Indian government could scarcely agree to plebiscite conditions in opposition to Sheikh Abdullah, whose support for accession to India was a sine qua non of a favourable plebiscite outcome. And the Sheikh refused to agree to any change in the Kashmiri administration during a plebiscite. If New Delhi had agreed to replace or supersede Abdullah's administration with a neutral regime during a plebiscite it would have broken faith with the Kashmiri leader and would probably have been denied his support for accession to India. Nehru regarded Kashmir's incorporation into India as a vindication of the secular state principle which the Congress upheld, but which had been badly tarnished by Pakistan's creation and the attendant communal disorders. The longer that a settlement was postponed the stronger grew Nehru's stake in retaining Kashmir, under its own Muslim government, to prove the secularism of independent India. His friendship for Abdullah and his deep emotional ties with Kashmir, his ancestral home, lent an intensity to Nehru's Kashmir policies commensurate with the strong feelings about that state held by officials in Pakistan. By 1950 the public positions of both governments on the suitable conditions for a plebiscite had become incorporated into their respective definitions of the national interest to such an extent that outside mediation was used only as a resonating chamber to amplify their opposing assertions.

In the summer of 1950 the UN's first individual mediator, Owen Dixon, forwarded proposals for a plebiscite. Most of them ran afoul of India's interests, as just noted. Two of his suggestions could not be accepted by Pakistan : that plebiscites be held by regions (including the valley) some of which might opt for Pakistan and others for India ; that the state be partitioned, except for the valley, where a plebiscite should be held. In order to explore every conceivable avenue Dixon even suggested a partition of the state without a plebiscite. At that time, and on many occasions to follow, each government indicated an acceptance of the idea of partition, provided it was allocated the valley of Kashmir.

Dixon's abrupt but thorough mediation efforts which ended in August 1950 were heatedly criticized by both sides. Particularly harmful to Pakistan's case was the fact that Dixon had been the first UN representative to state categorically that the troop movements into Kashmir from Pakistan were violations of international law. But Dixon further held that whether Pakistan had or had not been an aggressor should have nothing to do with a proposal to partition the state and hold a partial plebiscite. Most Western opinion shared Dixon's pragmatic view but did not agree with him in ruling out a full plebiscite on political grounds. Dixon suggested that the Security Council return the dispute to the parties for negotiation. But the Council appointed another mediator, Frank P. Graham, an American. Meanwhile, in January 1951 at Liaquat Ali's insistence the Commonwealth prime ministers' conference in London permitted a discussion of the Kashmir dispute, from which emerged the suggestion to use a Commonwealth police force to guard the security and order of the state during a vote. Pakistan favoured the plan, but India laid down a policy that has not altered to date— no outside troops would be allowed to enter Kashmir.

The Graham mission, lasting two years, coincided with such unsettling events in the subcontinent as a movement of Indian troops to the Pakistani border in July 1951, the assassination of the Pakistani prime minister, Liaquat Ali Khan, in October 1951, and the convening of a Kashmiri constituent assembly in the same month. Nevertheless, with almost phenomenal patience Graham succeeded in reducing the areas of important disagreement. Avoiding questions of high principle he sought agreements on separate issues and thus avoided antagonizing the two governments by his methods. But his five reports and the Security Council's two resolutions during that period did not meet all the vital demands of either side. Those demands, particularly India's, had been substantially cut down under Graham's persistent skill—to the point, however, that the immediate unsettled issue, the numbers and character of the troops on each side, had to bear all the weight of the basic disagreements still unresolved.

The UN's active mediation ended in February 1953 when the Graham mission was finally recognized as a failure. The Dixon and Graham missions could only have succeeded if both parties had desired settlement and needed an intermediary to improve communications and provide leeway for compromises. The fact was that neither side truly wanted settlement along the lines of the UN resolutions, Dixon's and Graham's terms of reference. Those resolutions were themselves mediatory and did not seek definitions of legal rights or political prescriptions for a settlement. The UN's efforts to find a compromise solution were unsuccessful because of the opposing stands on matters of high principle, on which the Security Council refused to express its opinion. The Council never took stands on the legality of the accession, on the question of Pakistan's aggression, on the legal right of Abdullah's government to administer the entire state, or on the status of the Azad Kashmir government.[17] The Council's representatives suffered from the prevailing ambiguity on these issues of which both governments took advantage, while trying to persuade a yet unconvinced Council of their basic positions.

The UNCIP in its third interim report observed that the entrance of Pakistani troops into the fighting and the greatly increased forces of Azad Kashmir had made its two earlier resolutions inappropriate. It therefore suggested that a new plan for demilitarization was called for. But the Security Council resolutions that followed continued to refer to the August 13, 1948, resolution of the UNCIP as if it were still applicable. Although India did not bring the Kashmir issue to the UN under Charter provisions covering aggression, and although it accepted resolutions which contained no condemnation of Pakistan, the Security Council could have shifted its terms of reference to take account of Pakistan's officially acknowledged action. By thus satisfying India its influence on that state to hold a plebiscite would have been more effective.

BILATERAL NEGOTIATIONS AND NEW FACTORS IN THE DISPUTE

In the summer of 1953 the Kashmir dispute reverted to the arena of bilateral negotiations. The effort to gain international recognition for its case was not a primary objective of either government during the private talks, and a solution might have emerged had not new factors of Kashmiri politics and great power policies intervened. Each government wanted to reach a settlement if only to reduce the tensions in its public life. Subcontinental war remained a possibility. Nehru's periodic offer of a "no-war" declaration was a proposal which Pakistan could scarcely accept unconditionally because its ultimate recourse in the absence of political agreement was renewed warfare.[18] Bilateral talks, first held at the Queen's coronation in June 1953 continued in Karachi and Delhi in July and August between Nehru and the new Pakistani prime minister, Mohammed Ali. The atmosphere was unusually good at first, and general understandings emerged at the Karachi meeting on the questions of evacuee property, trade and travel, and an exchange of the Cooch-Behar enclaves, noted earlier. But an abrupt change in mood and in Indian policy occurred on August 9, when the Kashmiri government overthrew its popular leader, Sheikh Abdullah. Abdullah's dismissal precluded any agreement at that time.

Kashmir's peculiar status in the Indian Union had led to the development just mentioned. In 1950 Abdullah's National Conference party decided to convene a Kashmiri constituent assembly. Despite the protests of Pakistan, reinforced by a Security Council resolution of March 30, 1951, the assembly was formed after a general election by universal secret ballot. There was virtually no opposition permitted to the National Conference, which controlled all the assembly seats. A new constitution was drafted reaffirming Kashmir's accession to India and its autonomy in areas other than foreign affairs, defense, and communications. The next year, in July, Nehru and Sheikh Abdullah signed an agreement at Delhi which confirmed Kashmir's unique status, as stipulated in article 370 of the Indian Constitution. Criticisms of the agreement by non-Muslim Kashmiris and some members of the Indian parliament who wanted closer Kashmiri links with India were overridden by the combined influence of Nehru and Abdullah, the latter being interested in maintaining as much autonomy for his state as possible.

But by 1953 the Nehru-Abdullah tie was weakening. Postponing the assembly's ratification of the agreement with India, the Sheikh put forth the idea of an independent Kashmir. He may have looked for support for it from outside powers, such as the US. Nehru

was "greatly distressed," as he later put it, by Abdullah's statements. Following a series of unpublicized manoeuvres the Kashmiri
deputy prime minister, Bakshi Ghulam Mohammad, arranged for
the removal of his chief on August 9 and himself took power.
Following these events the Pakistani Prime Minister left in haste for
Delhi, apparently to judge how recent Kashmiri affairs might affect
the prospects for future understanding. The correspondence between
the two prime ministers which followed their three-day meeting
indicated that some new issues, such as the nationality of the plebiscite administrator, had come up to replace certain old ones, and
the two sides were as far from agreement as ever.[19]

India's apparent interest in an early settlement through bilateral
negotiations leading to a plebiscite ended when Abdullah publicly
advocated some form of independence for the state and when the
Kashmiri government could no longer be regarded as popularly
supported.[20] The Indian government did not then repudiate its
pledge to hold a plebiscite, but from 1953 it drew attention to altered
conditions militating against carrying out that pledge. Since any
pledge or statement of national intentions had to serve immediate
national objectives in the context of prevailing affairs, it could not
remain indefinitely applicable.

If the dismissal of Sheikh Abdullah was not enough to preclude
or at least delay any agreement in mid-1953, the drastic shift in
Pakistani foreign policy later in that year would have achieved the
same end. Pakistan badly needed external support to balance the
tangible power of India and if possible exert pressure on its larger
neighbour to make concessions on Kashmir. It therefore gave up
its uncommitted position in the "cold war" and sought military
assistance from the US.[21] Nehru deplored any Pakistani effort to
seek outside military support because it would create a breach in
the nonaligned area which India had done much to foster and would
introduce into southern Asia the military presence of a great power.
He warned Mohammed Ali of the classic dangers of the loss of
independence which followed any military alliance with a more
powerful state and predicted that a Pakistani alliance with the US
would raise a new obstacle to any Indo-Pakistani settlement on
Kashmir. In particular, Nehru identified the problem of demilitarization in Kashmir as one which would become insoluble once
Pakistan acquired American weapons.

India's "peace area" based on the isolation from great power conflicts was no asset to Pakistan, whose main preoccupation was with India, not with the great powers. In February 1954 the US-Pakistani pact was announced amid tremendous official and popular protests in India. In statements to parliament and in letters to Mohammed Ali, Nehru affirmed that the US-Pakistani agreement had "changed the whole context of the Kashmir issue" by making an Indian troop withdrawal from the state impossible.[22] The Nehru-Mohammed Ali contacts lost their value, and they were terminated in September. Without demilitarization no plebiscite could be held in Kashmir, and India adopted the position that US aid to Pakistan forced India to remain fully prepared against any renewed Pakistani attack in Kashmir. While Pakistan formed tighter military links with the West, India consolidated its hold on Kashmir through the new government of Bakshi Ghulam Mohammad. In February 1954 Kashmir's constitutent assembly, with several of its members under detention, unanimously ratified the accession to India, an action which spokesmen for India later claimed was equivalent to a plebiscite. In the following year Kashmir's autonomy was gradually eroded as various articles of the Indian Constitution previously inapplicable to Kashmir became operative in the state.

In the global context Pakistan's alignment with the West appeared to be balanced by Indian efforts to consolidate its beneficial relations with Russia and China ; Nehru's apprehension that US military assistance would inject the "cold war" into southern Asia was justified.[23] Yet India's nonalignment was unwavering : its government sought no military assistance to match that of Pakistan. The result of the US-Pakistani alignment most harmful to any agreement on Kashmir was the altered military strength of Pakistan, which India could rightly regard as a factor changing the circumstances that existed when India originally offered a plebiscite.

Despite the set-backs in Indo-Pakistani relations during 1953 and 1954, the Pakistani governor-general, Ghulam Mohammad, who exerted a dominant influence on the government of Mohammed Ali, refused to give up all hopes for successful bilateral negotiations. His government postponed resubmitting the dispute to the Security Council and instead made a dramatic gesture to try to convince Nehru and Indian public opinion of Pakistan's desire for a peaceful

11

solution. Ghulam Mohammad appeared in Delhi with three cabinet ministers on India's Republic Day (January 26) celebrations in 1955 and induced an aura of goodwill which opened the minds of officials in both countries to the idea of further talks. They took place in Delhi in May 1955 in a cordial public atmosphere.[24] Apart from a substanceless communique the content of the discussions remained secret, to avoid the press and public clamour which would have greeted a revelation of what went on.[25]

Nehru and Mohammed Ali discussed a Kashmir settlement based on partition, not plebiscite, as the subsequent statements of both of them clearly suggested. One possibility was a modification of the cease-fire line to bring the districts of Punch and Mirpur, inhabited by a majority of Muslims before 1947, under Pakistani control and the transformation of the line into an international boundary. The disposition of the valley alone would be determined by plebiscite—a suggestion made in 1950 by Owen Dixon. A high official closely associated with the discussions informed the authors that Mohammed Ali was considering relenting on the valley plebiscite in order to reach a settlement if Nehru would agree to ascertain the wishes of the people there within ten years—a prestige-saving promise for Pakistan which neither side would regard as a means of transferring the valley out of Indian control. But no agreement could be reached : important factions in Pakistan and Nehru and his home minister, G. B. Pant, did not accept the compromises urged by the Pakistani governor-general and his prime minister.

The 1955 talks brought nothing but a revival of press hostilities, begun in Pakistan on the return of the prime minister; Mohammed Ali was forced publicly to withdraw his compromising stands. His government was out of office in August, and the ailing Ghulam Mohammad left the country for Europe without achieving the settlement for which he had worked. In September Pakistan acceded to the Baghdad Pact. The Indian government, probably less willing to compromise than the Pakistani in mid-1955, announced the inviolability of the Kashmir accession as Nehru prepared for the state visit of the leaders of the Soviet Union, the only major power willing to support India on Kashmir.

In 1956 the breach between India and Pakistan opened further, as a new Pakistani government under Chaudhri Muhammad Ali, supported by the Baghdad Pact states, prepared to resume the struggle in the UN, and Nehru himself made public for the first time his opposition to a plebiscite.[26] In November 1956 the constitution of Kashmir was finally adopted. Article III stated that the "State of Jammu and Kashmir is and shall be an integral part of the Union of India." Indeed, by then the state had already become almost fully integrated, economically and constitutionally with India, and no knowledgeable person in the subcontinent continued to believe that a plebiscite would be likely ever to take place.

The years 1952 to 1955 had witnessed changes of political scenery in the Indo-Pakistani relationship and in Kashmiri politics startling enough to suggest new ways of solving the Kashmir problem. There were many opportunities to settle the dispute without either side's losing international prestige, and, domestically, quid pro quos and rationales might have convinced public opinions that compromises on Kashmir were desirable. At the end of that period of flux, however, as the great powers began to align themselves to different states in the subcontinent, the positions of the two principals hardened along much the same lines as in 1949, reinforced by then with new factors born of expediency and frustration. When Pakistan was able to persuade its great power supporters to revive the UN's consideration of the dispute in January 1957, just after Nehru's visit to the US, the permanent members of the Security Council seemed aware that the occasion called for proofs of support for India's or for Pakistan's general posture in world politics rather than for novel plans for breaking the old empasse. In particular, Pakistan looked to a UN debate as a fitting occasion for the US to cease its balancing of diplomatic support to both countries and stand forth with firm support for Pakistan—as the USSR had done for India during the 1955 visit of Premier Bulganin and Nikita Khrushchev. India's handling of the Egyptian and Hungarian crises had created enough Western ill will toward Delhi so that Pakistan's expectations were high.

RENEWED UN ATTENTION AND MORE POLITICAL COMPLICATIONS

The Security Council debate on Kashmir in January 1957 provided both Indian and Pakistani governments with opportunities to publicize their uncompromising positions, to test the responses of the great powers, and to dramatize to their own peoples their skill and persistence in furthering national interests. Nothing more was expected, or accomplished. The Pakistani foreign minister, Firoz Khan Noon, gave a tight summary of the history of the dispute and concentrated his arguments on the weakest points in India's case, the internal conditions in Kashmir and the delay in holding a plebiscite. His delegation's effort, then as often before and after, focused on recalling early agreements which India and even UN representatives later viewed as inapplicable. Noon's forthright and relatively brief presentation concluded by asking the Council to request India to refrain from accepting the new Kashmiri constitution and spell out the obligations of both parties under earlier UN resolutions. He also suggested the introduction of a UN force into Kashmir.

India's response to the debate came as a numbing rebuttal of every point in the Pakistani case, which lasted for four sittings of the Council on January 23 and 24 and wore down the patience of most delegates. This nerve-racking performance, which included the near physical collapse of the main figure himself, was staged by V. K. Krishna Menon, India's chief delegate since 1953. Outlasting the previous record-holder for length of speaking, Zafrullah Khan, but failing to persuade the Council as the Pakistani had done, Menon achieved a minor hero's image among Indians, whose interests he valiantly upheld. On the defensive against Western delegates, Menon searched their words for each criticism of India's case and gave lengthy retorts. He denied that Pakistan had fulfilled the stipulated conditions prior to a plebiscite and reiterated India's protest that the Council failed to recognize Pakistani aggression. He saw the actions of the constituent assembly in Srinagar as internal matters which in any case could have no effect on the status of Kashmir, which had been part of India since 1947.

His words on the plebiscite commitment gave the UN its first exposure to India's altered position on the matter. India's offer, Menon explained, was a policy suited to the political conditions of its day and would have been fulfilled had Pakistan not sent its troops into Kashmir, built up the Azad forces, and then refused to carry out agreements on demilitarization. He implied that as conditions affecting Kashmir changed so India's policy had to change—it had never been an international legal commitment. (Nehru's statements in earlier years that the plebiscite offer was a pledge "to the people of the world" was downgraded by Menon to "an expression of a wish," which could no longer be carried out.) Menon was unable to reconcile the plebiscite offer with the "indissoluble bond," in the current phraseology, which had been created between India and Kashmir. At that point he was faced with the overriding illogic of India's position : why all the negotiation, if there was no chance of a settlement? He could not put this confusion aright, but spoke of the impossibility of permitting regions to secede from unified states by expressions of popular will.[27]

As the debate dragged without constructive purpose into the month of February Western delegates tried to end the desultory proceedings by moving a resolution which called for the Council's president, Gunnar V. Jarring, to visit the subcontinent to mediate again, and they suggested the possibility of using a UN force in Kashmir during a plebiscite. India's delegate vigorously condemned the resolution as an affront to Indian sovereignty, and the Soviet Union vetoed it. Another resolution omitting the UN force suggestion was adopted, the Soviet Union abstaining. The Council debates had partially accomplished Pakistan's purpose of aligning great powers to a side of the dispute, but the Russian alignment to India's position was firmer than the US to Pakistan's.

Mr. Jarring's brief mission in March and April 1957 resulted in a nicely balanced report, whose chief political impact was in support of the status quo ; such indeed was Jarring's purpose. Pakistan's cause was credited by noting the unfulfilled plebiscite agreement, but India's interests were upheld by noting the "grave problems that might arise in connection with and as a result of a plebiscite." Jarring's report showed sensitivity to a major Indian contention : "I could not fail to take note of the concern expressed in connection with the changing political, economic and strategic factors surrounding the whole of the Kashmir question, together with the changing pattern of power relations in West and South Asia. The Council will, furthermore, be aware of the fact that the implementation of international agreements of an *ad hoc* character, which has not been achieved fairly speedily, may become progressively more difficult because the situation with which they were to cope has tended to change."[28] Despite such plain acknowledgement that the earlier UNCIP resolutions could not meet current conditions, Jarring proposed arbitration to determine whether the two sides had met the terms of the first resolution, which specified preliminary steps to a truce and plebiscite. India immediately refused to submit its case to arbitration : a legal determination that Pakistan had not fulfilled its agreements would not suit Indian interests, if it also opened the way for the holding of a plebiscite.

Pressed by Pakistan for greater support for its position than Gunnar Jarring's report provided, the Western members proposed to the Security Council in September 1957 that Frank Graham try to rekindle the spirit of hope and accommodation that his earlier missions had done. By a resolution of December 2, after modifications necessitated by a threatened Soviet veto, the Council sent Graham on his last official mission to the subcontinent to explore any new ways to work with the UNCIP proposals of August 1948 and January 1949. Krishna Menon advised the Council of India's current mood of adamancy and annoyance that the Kashmir dispute should be used by Pakistan to try to undermine India's increasingly favourable international position, especially in respect to the US. His government was unable to accept the resolution. Nevertheless, Graham held discussions with both governments and submitted his report in March 1958. The UN took no action on it, and in fact did not deal with Kashmir again until 1962. Graham's "beaming goodwill and good intentions" (in Nehru's words) confronted a total Indian unreceptiveness but a Pakistani willingness to agree to any proposal, even the novel one of stationing UN troops on the Pakistani side of the Kashmiri border (not the cease-fire line) to eliminate Indian fears for the security of a demilitarized state. Graham's proposals could not have been turned down by India ten years earlier, and they would not have been acceptable then to Pakistan, but by 1958 the scope of the dispute and the interests of the two states had been transformed.

The responses to Graham's proposals demonstrated how closely the Kashmir dispute had become a factor affecting India's and Pakistan's relations with the great powers : each state presented a posture suited to its relations with third states and almost irrelevant to the cause of a Kashmir settlement. India's determination not to yield to increased pressure from Pakistan—the latter reinforced by messages to India from middle eastern members of the Baghdad Pact—increased as the Kashmiri government finally brought its

case against Sheikh Abdullah into court in October 1958 and anticipated unfavourable publicity abroad.

The apparent weakness of India's case on Kashmir in the international arena was unexpectedly overshadowed by the events in
Pakistan following the coup d'etat by President Iskander Mirza
on October 7, 1958, and the subsequent transfer of power to General
Ayub Khan under a regime of martial law. The termination of parliamentary democracy in Pakistan gave new meaning to India's
argument that Kashmir should not be turned over to the control
of an "unprogressive", unstable state. Distrusting the "military
mind," and especially Ayub Khan, who had pursued American
military aid, Nehru formed the immediate opinion that the new
regime would be a hindrance to good relations and that it might
even initiate a war against India. Ayub Khan's early years in power
justified neither of these views, and in fact opportunities to
settle major problems improved as Pakistani politics became
muted.

The chief factors complicating Indo-Pakistani relations during
Ayub Khan's first five years in power, apart from the weary stubborn-
ness over Kashmir which Nehru displayed after ten years of international misunderstanding of his position, were Pakistan's receipt
of advanced US military equipment and both countries' changing
relations with China. Nehru justified his initial reluctance to use
the bloodless revolution in Pakistan as an opportunity to improve
the depressed state of Indo-Pakistani relations by the fact that the
US and Pakistan were strengthening their military ties and Pakistan
was not amenable to compromise as a result. A US-Pakistan bilateral pact was signed in March 1959 reaffirming American military
support for Pakistan after the disruption of the Baghdad Pact
caused by the Iraqi revolution of the previous July. Although the
US assured India, as in 1954, that the agreement could not be used
against India and was no more than an extension of the Eisenhower
Doctrine for meeting communist aggression, its signature came
at a time of shooting incidents on the East Bengal border and on
the Kashmir cease-fire line and preceded an increase in US arms
deliveries to Pakistan which included F-104 jet fighters and ground-
to-air missiles. Whether or not the possibility of an Indo-Pakistani
war increased after Ayub Khan's accession to power, the public
statements of V. K. Krishna Menon, Indian defense minister from

April 1957, continued to remind his country that Pakistani power had to be met by substantial growth of India's strength and that no compromises should be made on Kashmir.

But by mid-1959 the active hostility from China appeared to take precedence, in the public expression of Nehru's thought, over the possible danger from Pakistan. Ayub Khan's government hoped to grasp a lever of persuasion, namely the Chinese military threat to India, to affect India's stand on Kashmir ; the loose coordination of Pakistani and Chinese policies toward India began. In April 1959 Ayub Khan suggested that India and Pakistan should together defend the subcontinent in case of external aggression ; he emphasized that a settlement on Kashmir and other major issues would be a prerequisite to an understanding on joint defense.[29] The proposal was well timed because it coincided with the spreading revolt in Tibet, the escape to India of the Dalai Lama, and the growing crisis of conflicting Himalayan border claims.

But Nehru refused to admit publicly the possibility or even the desirability of a common defense policy with Pakistan and raised objection to India's being drawn into any military alliance. In early 1959 the Indian government was not disposed to seek a general detente with the new Pakistani regime, but negotiations on the important issues of border demarcation and the Indus waters were already in progress. Ayub Khan and Nehru met on September 1 at New Delhi airport and agreed to attempt settlement on outstanding issues ; an Indus waters treaty was already nearing its final drafting stages. If joint defense was impossible for India to consider, a less hostile Pakistan was a worthy objective in view of the alarming developments on the Himalayan border.

Recently concluded agreements on border issues, on distribution of pre-partition assets and liabilities, and on the vast Indus basin irrigation scheme created a short-lived optimism when Nehru and Ayub Khan met for the second time in September 1960. The occasion of the signing of the Indus waters treaty in Karachi provided the two leaders with four days of discussions on outstanding issues, almost all of which were found amenable to rapid solution. Opening the broadest vista for future collaboration was Ayub's proposal to discuss an expansion of trade relations and a common market between India and Pakistan. All the advantages of cooperative relations spelled out in the joint communique and the constructive approaches of both leaders, however, stuck and held fast against the formidable obstacle of Kashmir. The seemingly rational approach to that problem adopted by both leaders merely clothed two irreconcilable national interests in fresh garb. The words of optimism disappeared in both countries within weeks of the Nehru-Ayub meeting : the Indian government indicated its continuing satisfaction with the status quo, while Pakistani frustrations were building up. By the end of 1960 the Pakistani government had lost hope of reaching a favourable Kashmiri settlement merely by offering positive incentives to India in other areas of their relationship ; communal rioting in India and anti-Indian riots in Karachi in February 1961 established the background for a rising level of militancy on both sides.

FURTHER INTRODUCTION OF OUTSIDE INTERESTS

Powerful states outside the subcontinent were by then so deeply involved or committed in the Indo-Pakistani antagonism that a truly bilateral dialogue, such as that between Mohammed Ali and Nehru in 1953, could no longer have reflected the existing political and military configuration. Furthermore, alignments in the south Asian region were shifting. India became preoccupied with China's hostile policy, and the new American administration of President Kennedy indicated greater awareness of India's importance. Pakistan, therefore, sought to utilize its own strategic position and secure new sources of external support in addition to the US alliance. China, and to a lesser extent the USSR, were the best possibilities ; in January 1961 the Pakistan government announced that it was discussing with China the demarcation of a border between Pakistani held Kashmir and China. But Pakistan also hoped to impress the Kennedy administration with the continued vitality of the US-Pakistan military link and also to persuade it to exert pressure on India to make concessions on Kashmir. To this end Ayub Khan visited Washington in July 1961. A resounding social success, his visit failed to elicit American assurances that Ayub had hoped to get on Kashmir. (Kennedy was unwilling to jeopardize US relations with India by attempting a task of unlikely success ; in November 1961 Nehru also visited the US.)

Perhaps in order to strain Indo-US friendship—already under stress because of the Indian takeover of Goa—, or perhaps to test the strength of Soviet support for India, and to once again publicize its case on Kashmir, Pakistan had the issue revived in the Security Council in January 1962. The American government wished to avoid another distasteful public debate on Kashmir, and Kennedy suggested that Eugene R. Black, president of the World Bank, assist the two states to a settlement outside the UN, as he had succeeded in doing on the Indus waters accord.[30] India refused the offer. In the Security Council debates on Kashmir in April, May, and June the arguments presented were familiar, and the responses of the great powers did not deviate from the norm. V. K. Krishna Menon concluded India's case at the 104th Council meeting on Kashmir by asserting again : "We regard the accession of ... Kashmir to the Union of India as full, complete and final, irrevocable and what is more, perpetual. . . ."[31] No Council resolution could possibly improve chances for a solution, but the US had to arrange for one for the sake of the trembling Pakistani alliance. It came forward in June under the sole sponsorship of Ireland, calling for renewed bilateral talks, and was vetoed by the Soviet Union, as expected.

Hostility between states at some stage develops its own momentum and creates its own causes. Indian-Pakistani hostility, nourished by the Kashmir dispute, reached a self-sustaining point by the 1960's. One government's trust of the other's intentions, at least on the great issues, was almost totally absent, and the highest officials on both sides publicly warned their people of possible war in the subcontinent. Under those conditions the Kashmir dispute itself became a symbol of the enmity for which it was in a major way responsible, and the two states could not overcome the distrust and fear of each other long enough to make use of opportunities for solving the underlying problem. Nehru revealed his government's state of mind when he observed that even if "the Kashmir question was removed from the scene, even then the Pakistan authorities . . . would fiercely attack India because their whole policy is anti-Indian, based on dislike of India and envy of India making progress."[32] The Pakistani government viewed the relationship in a like manner. If the leaders of the two states themselves showed any willingness to compromise, powerful critics of rapprochement and press opinion in both countries were able to reverse those tendencies.[33]

An opportunity for a peaceful settlement had appeared in Ayub Khan's initiatives of 1959-1960, but it was allowed to pass. Another opportunity arose when Chinese troops invaded India in October and November 1962, but the Pakistani government used that critical moment to try to enhance its power vis-a-vis its neighbour. On the assumption that India's troubles were Pakistan's advantages, Ayub Khan's government gave no public evidence that it deplored the movement of Chinese troops into the subcontinent. Some high Pakistani officials so welcomed the "tiger come to get the bear off our back" that they could disregard what the "tiger" would do if it succeeded with the "bear".

At the time of the Chinese attacks in NEFA and Ladakh in late October 1962 the Indian army faced the possibility of a two-front war and was maintaining substantially more than one-half of its force on the front facing Pakistani troops. Of particular concern was the possibility of a simultaneous Chinese and Pakistani push into northern Kashmir. An attack on the western front would have seriously aggravated India's military problems ; a Pakistani gesture of support against China would have simplified them and probably softened the Indian attitude towards Pakistan. No such gesture was made, but no hostile military action was taken by Pakistan at that time.[34] Denunciations of India issued from the Pakistani press and from officials of the government, and when the US and Britain agreed to ship emergency supplies to the Indian forces Ayub Khan and Pakistani ambassadors in Washington and London conveyed the vigorous protest that military equipment for India "may have the effect of enlarging and prolonging the conflict between China and India and, secondly, add to the serious concern already existing in the minds of our people that these weapons may well be used against them in the absence of an overall settlement with India."[35] The Pakistani leaders calculated that Chinese military intentions were limited ; then and subsequently they argued that India exaggerated its military threat from China so as to acquire Western arms which could be used against Pakistan. Pakistan maintained a constant and potent complaint against Anglo-American military aid to India, which had the effect of blocking the shipment of at least certain types of arms, notably jet fighters, under the assistance programme.

Western military support for India was premised on the conviction that the only successful long-term regional defense against China would be through joint Indo-Pakistani endeavours. British and American special emissaries to the subcontinent, Duncan Sandys and Averell Harriman, had instructions to use their good offices to arrange for bilateral discussions on the Kashmir dispute, whose settlement they regarded as a prerequisite to a joint subcontinental defense system.[36] The Harriman-Sandys initiative, reinforced by communications to Ayub and Nehru from President Kennedy and Prime Minister Macmillan, secured an agreement from the two governments on November 29 to hold ministerial level meetings "at an early date." But Western pressure, made possible by the needs of both countries for military and economic aid, could not be a substitute for a new recognition of mutual interests. The Pakistani government interpreted the forthcoming discussions as an opportunity to gain concessions from an India anxious to avoid a future two-front war ; it urged the US to make a Kashmiri settlement a condition for military aid to India. The Indian government, on the other hand, could not expect to retain popular support if it conceded to Pakistan's terms just after a humiliation inflicted by China. Nehru did not encourage the Western hope that India might relax certain of its "basic principles" on Kashmir.[37]

The Indo-Pakistani talks on Kashmir began in the new Pakistani capital near Rawalpindi on December 27 with more finely drawn bargaining positions on each side than in previous negotiations. Recently defined interests, such as India's requirement for defending Ladakh and Pakistan's desire to control the upper Jhelum and Chenab rivers, added to the burden of demands that had already been publicly recorded. Admitting good faith by both parties, any reconciliation had to rest on retraction of vital claims ; the disposition of the valley of Kashmir remained the major point of contention. But the question of good faith arose as the first issue at the meetings when the Pakistani government announced that it had signed a joint communique with China on the alignment of the border between Sinkiang and Pakistani-controlled Kashmir.[38] That Pakistani-Chinese negotiations going on for almost two years should have concluded in agreement at the precise moment of the Islamabad talks suggested to the Indians not only a Chinese effort to affect adversely the proceedings but Pakistan's interest in cooperating with India's major foe. The chief representatives in the talks, Swaran Singh of India and Zulfikar Ali Bhutto of Pakistan, dealt with no specific proposals and announced only that further meetings would ensue.

The Pakistani-Chinese boundary agreement had been expected in India[39] and was objectionable to the government for two reasons. First, although the agreement was provisional and left the final boundary to be determined by the sovereign states concerned when the Kashmir dispute should be settled, it compromised India's sovereignty over Kashmir by formalizing under international agreement Pakistan's de facto control over part of Kashmir. Second, the terms of the agreement were unfavourable to any subcontinental state and gave China a locus standi in Kashmir. When the actual agreement was signed on March 2, 1963, the Indian government vigorously protested to both states, asserted that it was not bound by the accord, and claimed that Pakistan had transferred legal control of some 2,000 square miles of Kashmiri territory to China. Above all, however, Pakistan's policy of collaborating with the Chinese, whose own interest was to keep the subcontinent divided, forewarned India of critical events to come if either country decided to move again across Indian borders. In January 1963 Pakistan signed a trade treaty with China and announced that its foreign minister would shortly visit Peking ; Ayub Khan declined an invitation to visit India for the continuing Kashmir talks.

The New Delhi discussions on Kashmir in January and the Karachi discussions in February brought the parties no closer to agreement. Three more Indo-Pakistani ministerial meetings took place, following Bhutto's visit to Peking in March, the last one in May 1963. The secrecy of the sessions did not conceal the rapid deterioration in the hopes of the participants and the attentive Western diplomats. The only positive achievement of the meetings was the forum they provided for exposing a variety of ways by which the Kashmir dispute might some day be settled : by partitions of several kinds, by partition and a plebiscite in the valley, by a condominium, by internationalization. In contrast to previous adamancy on both sides—that a plebiscite must be held, that nothing but "minor adjustments" of the status quo should occur—the governments, even under adverse domestic and international conditions, did exchange new thoughts of these kinds, and the exchanges focused more on tangible national interests (rivers, roads, strategic boundaries, people) than on ideologies. Enough suggestions of compromises were made, in fact, that both governments, after the discussions ended, decided to announce formally that they were no longer bound by the suggestions that they had made. The chief sticking point, as always, was the disposition of the valley of Kashmir, but on other issues as well both governments calculated that compromises could be postponed in expectation of achieving better negotiating postures in the future. The main factor in the calculations of both governments was the Chinese military presence, which brought about the 1962-63 negotiations but which also made any agreement difficult to achieve at that time.

In 1962-1963, as in 1954, the introduction of military power into the subcontinent from the outside altered both India's and Pakistan's assessments of their future opportunities to achieve their interests in Kashmir. Pakistan, continuing its search for security and equality in the face of what some of its spokesmen regarded as the "militant Hinduism" of India,[40] swept its anti-Indian interests into conjunction with those of China. Pakistan entered a period of very active diplomacy, guided by Foreign Minister Bhutto, whose purpose was to create international embarrassments for India.[41] An Indo-Pakistani negotiated settlement at that time was receiving only secondary priority in Islamabad. India, conscious of its military unpreparedness, became more closely associated with US and simultaneously received Russian support on both of its defensive fronts, against Pakistan and China. The Kashmir dispute, rather than subsiding into a tacit, de facto stalemate, as India desired, broadened into a general struggle between the two countries for regional power and external support.

The major responsibility for linking the Kashmir dispute to the international power structure lay on the Pakistani policy of improving its negotiating position vis-a-vis India. The Indian government failed to anticipate the implications of that development, even after 1954. Indeed, India did not define its objectives toward Pakistan and therefore was pursuing no systematic policies on its major disputes with that state. Its preoccupation with the issues of UN recognition of Pakistan's aggression in 1948 and of India's sovereign status in Kashmir precluded fruitful thought and debate about ways of ending the Indo-Pakistani conflict. Apart from the desire to "live in peace" with its neighbours, which every state wants, the Indian government stated no general prescriptions for international relations among the states of the subcontinent. It often seemed genuinely to believe that the Kashmir issue could be treated solely as a domestic problem, as Krishna Menon told the Security Council that it should be.

Nehru himself presented a confusing posture on Kashmir by announcing and permitting others to proclaim that Kashmir was an integral part of India and would always remain so, but then entering negotiations over the state—in 1963, "without preconditions." The domestic political costs of compromising its stand on Kashmir for India, as equally. for Pakistan, increased every year that the dispute was permitted to continue. Both governments recognized that the ideological bases of their existence as well as their immediate control over domestic politics and religious communalism could be threatened by an unfavourable settlement. Nehru saw this practical concern in the context of an ideological principle : "Kashmir is symbolic as it illustrates that we are a secular state, that Kashmir, with its large majority of Muslims, has nevertheless of its own free will, wished to be associated . with India."[42] And. there lay the problem.

Not only had the dispute been elevated to a testing ground of competing national ideologies and identities ; not only had policy toward Kashmir become a domestic political issue capable of over-throwing a government—those conditions applied for both India and Pakistan. But also, for India, the Kashmiri people had been offered the power, through some expression of their wishes, to affect the destiny of the union.

THE SECOND KASHMIR WAR

Towards the end of Nehru's life he may have realized that his greatest failure in managing India's external relations had been the continuation of Indo-Pakistani hostility. The Kashmir dispute, the major reason for that hostility, had become a seemingly perma-nent, unhealing wound infecting the affairs of a great part of Asia. It began to take on characteristics not unlike those of the Franco-German dispute over Alsace-Lorraine. Perhaps in order to change radically the direction of Indo-Pakistani relations Nehru unexpectedly decided to release Sheikh Abdullah from confinement in April 1964, after his almost continuous detention since 1953. Nehru's decision might have been a manoeuvre to assuage communal fears in India and Pakistan, which had produced the bloodiest riots in many years. Whatever the purposes were for his release Abdullah immediately plunged into active negotiations on the future of his state, first with Nehru and then with Ayub Khan. Many people hopefully awaited the results of this novel approach to a possible settlement and tried to gauge the real intentions of Nehru. Before Abdullah could promote a serious exchange of ideas between the two leaders, Nehru died. Apart from futile contacts with foreign states Abdullah could do no more. A meeting with Chou En-lai in Algeria and statements harmful to India's interests led to his re-arrest.

Pakistan surely foresaw no further opportunities for a satisfactory settlement on Kashmir, and the opportunities for peripheral gains in the UN by raising the dispute had proved worthless, in the spring of 1962 and in early 1964. Ayub Khan's government prepared for war. The conditions seemed as favourable as they would ever be for Pakistan. A decade of heavy American military aid gave the army and air force the confidence it needed to challenge India. If the attack should be long postponed, increasing American military aid to India might give the latter sufficient strength to inflict serious damage on Pakistan. Whether there was or was not consultation with China, the latter's proven hostility to India would add to the advantages that Pakistan reckoned on. Ayub Khan's visit to Peking in March 1965 made certain of that, and of China's full diplomatic support for Pakistan's case on Kashmir.

These words and the brief interpretation of events that follows must be offered tentatively. The second Kashmir war does not yet provide the material for even a valid contemporary history.

A military probing operation, which might have been a dress rehearsal for later events, began in March and April in the Rann of Kutch, as mentioned in the previous chapter. The international reactions suggested that the great powers were not interested in taking sides in an Indo-Pakistani war : it could be an entirely local test of strength. India decided that it would be disadvantageous to meet fully the Pakistani challenge in Kutch, which might well have been a diversionary action to draw Indian forces away from the real prize, Kashmir. When military force failed to settle the issue, therefore, both sides agreed to submit the territorial dispute in Kutch to an international tribunal, after direct British mediation had been only temporarily useful.

The Indian army did not search long for a means of restoring some of the prestige that it had lost in the Kutch engagements. In May Indian troops occupied Pakistani posts in the Kargil area, across the cease-fire line in Kashmir, in order to halt Pakistani interference with traffic on the Leh road. The UN intervened, and India drew back its forces. Meanwhile on the Azad Kashmir side of the cease-fire line popular excitement developed, as it had often in the past, over the possibility of a *jehad*, or holy war, to liberate Indian-held Kashmir. "Freedom fighters" on the Algerian model appeared ready to join their Muslim brethren in Indian-held Kashmir for a final struggle. By August infiltration began, as a UN report put it, "in the form of armed men, generally not in uniform, crossing the CFL [cease-fire line] from the Pakistan side for the purpose of armed action on the Indian side."[43] Attacks across the line grew in number and size by both Indian and Pakistani armies in August. Claiming the need to cut off a route for Pakistani infiltrators, who were said to be inflicting damage to civilian installations and trying to arouse the populace, the Indian army captured Pakistani positions in the Kargil and Tithwal areas and at the crucial Haji Pir pass on the Uri-Punch road.

Then, on September 1, Pakistan launched an attack across the international frontier in the Chhamb section of south-western Kashmir toward Akhnur in an obvious drive to cut the main Indian road supplying Srinagar. The UN observer group in Kashmir and Secretary-General U Thant regarded Pakistan as mainly responsible for the growing hostilities. They understood that Pakistan regarded the cease-fire, in effect since 1949, as a benefit to India and was not therefore anxious to disengage.[44] Indian forces met the attack on Akhnur but saw that the best and only certain way to relieve the Akhnur front was to launch an attack elsewhere to divert the Pakistani assault. On September 6 Indian forces moved with armoured strength across the international frontier into Pakistan aiming at Lahore, West Pakistan's second city. Two days later another attack was launched against Sialkot, to the north. The Pakistani forces had to reduce their activities in Kashmir and rush to the de-

12

fense of their own territory. India's main purpose was thereby achieved.

A secondary Indian objective quickly supplemented that of defending Kashmir, namely to prove its ability to acquit itself favourably in an outright campaign against Pakistani military forces equipped and to some degree trained by the US. This objective was achieved within the context of the limited war that both sides fought. (In an all-out war India could have successfully attacked East Pakistan, and both sides could have committed double the amounts of men and equipment over a much larger area in the northwest.) Pakistan's apparent superiority in modern tanks and aircraft and the often-alleged superior fighting qualities of Pakistani soldiers did not result in defeat of the Indian army, and the Pakistanis themselves were seriously thrown back in the largest armoured vehicle engagements since the Second World War.[45] In an unmeasurable manner the Indian army regained the self-confidence and the prestige that it had lost in the engagements in NEFA against the Chinese three years before. Because Pakistan lost the strategic advantage on the Kashmir front and failed to gain the initiative in the much larger battles in the Lahore and Sialkot sectors its military efforts in August and September must be judged as failures.

Outside powers and the UN brought the war to an end. The US, the UK, and the USSR all realized that continued fighting in the subcontinent was to their disadvantage, if only because it opened up the possibility of China's gaining some advantage from it. Chinese threats on the Indian border, which aimed at diverting Indian troops from the Pakistani front, turned out to be bluffs, but continued warfare would reduce Indian strength, as the Chinese desired. The Security Council unanimously called for an immediate cease-fire, and although the resolution itself had no effect, U Thant's attendant emergency visits to Islamabad and New Delhi eventually provided a means for achieving a truce. U Thant's mediation was reinforced by an immediate stoppage of arms shipments to both sides by the UK and the US. The American move, despite the fact that it affected Pakistan far more critically than India, seemed to be a minimal adherence to its several public commitments that Pakistan would not be permitted to misuse American weapons. Short of enlarging the struggle, both sides had no feasible alternative to accepting the Security Council's demand for a cease-fire. The fighting fronts were quiet by September 23.

While the brief Indo-Pakistani war achieved nothing in terms of the Kashmir dispute and scarcely altered the balance of power in the subcontinent it did bring about a major change in the international setting of the Indo-Pakistani dispute. The Soviet Union entered the arena with greater forcefulness and constructive purpose than it had before. During the fighting Chairman Kosygin offered to mediate, and finally, after the truce, both sides accepted his invitation to meet at Tashkent for talks. For reasons not yet entirely clear the tripartite conference, held in January 1966, was a remarkable success. Both India and Pakistan did not wish to lose an opportunity to reach closer relations with Russia—India because it needed Russian support against China, Pakistan because it hoped that a tie with the USSR could compensate for its deteriorating alliance with the US. The US and Britain, furthermore, backed the Russian effort and added privately to the pressure for an Indo-Pakistani accord. The Tashkent Declaration, as it was called, signed by President Ayub Khan and Prime Minister Sastri on January 10, committed the states to a brief set of actions which in effect restored the status quo and opened the possibility of future negotiations on major disputes, including Kashmir. Largely, the accord was adhered to by both sides, but three years later relations appeared to be no better than they had been before the war. Prime Minister Sastri's death of a heart attack at Tashkent shortly after the agreement was signed certified with tragedy the work that the statesmen had done.

The USSR's novel role at Tashkent created conditions crucial to achieving the accord. But the courage of both Sastri and Ayub Khan in facing powerful forces in their respective countries which urged no compromises and even a renewal of warfare remained the most significant feature of Tashkent.

NOTES AND REFERENCES

[1] Most authorities agree with the Pakistani position that princely states after August 15, 1947 reverted to a status of independent sovereignties. Such was the view of V. P. Menon in his *Integration of the Indian States*, N. Y. 1956, p. 476 ; and J. S. Bains in *India's International Disputes*, Bombay 1962, p. 66.

[2] Many of the moves made by Indian officials and by Gandhi, which raised more questions than they solved, have been described in Sisir Gupta, *Kashmir*,

A Study in India-Pakistan Relations, p. 90f ; and Alastair Lamb, *Crisis in Kashmir*, pp. 41-42.

³ This Muslim-majority district was awarded to India, rather than Pakistan, apparently because it contained the headworks of the Upper Bari Doab Canal, which supplied water to Amritsar, the centre of the Sikh community, and because its transfer to Pakistan could have cut off Amritsar District from surrounding Indian territory. Radcliffe was authorized to consider factors other than religion in awarding districts to one state or the other, and in the case of Gurdaspur economic considerations seemed determining. But the district's main city is Pathankot, a rail head from which a motor road leads to Jammu, from which place India was able to supply its forces in Kashmir during the fighting. Without Gurdaspur India could not have maintained a defensive position in Kashmir. Many Pakistanis believe that Radcliffe's award in this case showed bias towards India. See the illuminating accounts of this controversial issue in Birdwood, *Two Nations and Kashmir*, p. 74f ; Brecher, *Nehru*, p. 359f ; and Chaudhri Muhammad Ali, *The Emergence of Pakistan*, pp. 215-19.

⁴ See Sisir Gupta, *op. cit.*, p. 92.

⁵ Authoritative accounts of Mountbatten's role and other details of the Kashmir affair can be found in Alan Campbell-Johnson, *Mission with Mountbatten*, esp. p. 225 ; also V. P. Menon, *The Integration of the Indian States*, esp. p. 399.

⁶ Speeches of Nov. 2, 1947 and Nov. 25, 1947 ; in *Independence and After*, pp. 59, 65.

⁷ On Aug. 7, 1952 ; *Speeches 1949-1953*, p. 353.

⁸ Early in October 1947, also, Abdullah was reported to have stated that Kashmiris should be given self-government so that they could decide for themselves to which dominion to accede. India, *White Paper on Jammu and Kashmir*, 1948, pp. 13-14.

⁹ See Menon, *op. cit.*, p. 403 ; and Campbell-Johnson, *op. cit.*, p. 225.

¹⁰ Jinnah was quoted by Mountbatten as saying that if India accepted his terms, he "will call the whole thing off." Campbell-Johnson, *op. cit.*, p. 229.

¹¹ Telegram to Liaquat Ali, Dec. 12, 1947 ; *White Paper*, *op. cit.*, p. 73. The proposed relegation of the UN to an advisory capacity was not missed by the Pakistanis.

¹² Mountbatten's press attache confirmed what is obvious from reading the debates, that India's case was "abominably presented," that the delegation was "awkward and angular" and failed "to make its mark." Campbell-Johnson, *op. cit.*, pp. 290, 287.

¹³ On September 7 ; *Independence and After*, p. 97. When the UN Commission interviewed Girja Shankar Bajpai, secretary-general of the Indian External Affairs Ministry in July 1948 Bajpai told them that until the UN decided on Pakistan's "guilt" it was inappropriate to discuss details of a plebiscite. Korbel, *Danger in Kashmir*, p. 124. This remained India's position.

¹⁴ The pertinent Security Council and UNCIP resolutions are conveniently included as appendices to Josef Korbel's *Danger in Kashmir*.

¹⁵ The Chinese delegate gave assistance to India in the initial stages of the deba-

tes, but his support waned after New Delhi offered recognition to the revolutionary communist regime in China.

[16] *SCOR*, 769th meeting, Feb. 15, 1957, p. 21.

[17] A participant in the UNCIP, Josef Korbel, noted the disadvantages that the Security Council faced in dealing with a dispute without first making a determination on the legal merits of either party's case. If the Council had got an advisory opinion from the International Court of Justice on the legality of Kashmir's accession to India, "the handling of the dispute would have been easier," according to Korbel. "One of the parties would then have been in the wrong, and the Security Council would in turn have had a stronger moral and political position for the recommendation of appropriate measures." *Danger in Kashmir*, p. 114.

[18] In December 1949, Nehru first offered to exchange "no-war" declarations, and Liaquat Ali's response was favourable provided all outstanding disputes, notably on canal waters, evacuee property and Kashmir, were made subject to international arbitration. Nehru would not agree to arbitration over Kashmir, because it was a matter of sovereign rights, and the proposal for a "no-war" declaration remained henceforth an insubstantial propaganda theme used by India. See also Ayub Khan, *Friends Not Masters*, pp. 121-22.

[19] See India, *White Paper : Kashmir: Meetings and Correspondence between the Prime Ministers of India and Pakistan* (*July 1953, Oct. 1954*).

[20] A frank statement of conditions in Kashmir in 1953 appeared in Nehru's speech to the Lok Sabha, Sept. 17, 1953 ; in *Speeches 1953-1957*, p. 210 f.

[21] For details see Selig Harrison's articles in the *New Republic*, August-September 1959 ; and James W. Spain, "Military Assistance for Pakistan," *Amer. Pol. Sci. Rev.*, vol. XLVIII, 3 (Sept. 1954).

[22] "We can take no risks now, as we were prepared to take previously," wrote Nehru, "and we must retain full liberty to keep such forces and military equipment in the Kashmir State as we may consider necessary in view of this new threat to us." *White Paper : Kashmir, op. cit.*, p. 72.

[23] Nehru made his point dramatically by insisting on the removal of all Americans from the UN cease-fire observation corps in Kashmir. After months of discussion of the issue in the UN secretariat—the question of denationalization for purposes of UN service was at stake—and India's refusal to issue visas to American replacements on the corps, the last American left General Nimmo's force in Kashmir in December 1954.

[24] Earlier in that month Pakistani troops violated the Kashmiri cease-fire line at Nekowal and killed twelve Indians. The UN observers judged the action premeditated, and the Pakistani government publicly apologized for it and paid compensation. This gravest cease-fire violation to date may have originated among Pakistani officers who sought to preclude any political compromises by their government during the negotiations in Delhi.

[25] All of the aforementioned bilateral negotiations had been carried on within reach, so to speak, of the press of both countries, sensitive to minute shifts in the stands of the opposing party and eager to publicize any waver from publicly committed positions of the domestic government. In the efforts to find a solution

away from the arena of world politics the two governments had discovered that their own political environments were as unconducive to compromises as were the UN chambers.

²⁶ At a press conference in Delhi, April 2. See also his speech in the Lok Sabha, March 29, 1956, *LSD*, vol. III, pt. II, cols. 3, 740-52.

²⁷ The Indian government had discovered that a democratically based union must restrict the implementing or even the free expression of popular will in situations which threatened to break up the union. Whenever it became clear to the government that such a situation had emerged in connection with Kashmir, and it did, India could no longer permit a plebiscite : the integrity of the union took precedence over all other policy commitments.

²⁸ The Jarring report, UN doc. S/3821, is included in *SCOR*, 12th yr., Supplement for April, May, June 1957, pp. 13-16.

²⁹ See Ayub Khan, *Friends Not Masters*, pp. 126-27. Ayub asserts that his proposal did not involve any formal defense arrangement that would have violated India's nonalignment policy, and that Nehru deliberately misunderstood him : "The crux of the proposal, I stated in unequivocal terms, was that, once differences between the two nations were resolved, the Indian and Pakistani forces then facing each other could be released to defend their respective territories." Of obvious merit, the idea of joint defense was successfully propagated in Washington by the Pakistani ambassador, thereby increasing American sympathies for the Pakistani position on Kashmir.

³⁰ American Vice-President Lyndon Johnson, during his visit to the subcontinent in May 1961 reinforced American neutrality on the Kashmir issue, which was not even mentioned in the communique from his Karachi talks.

³¹ Text taken from Special Supplement of *FAR*, vol. VIII, 5 (May 1962), p. 58.

³² Speech in Lok Sabha, Aug. 16, 1961, *Speeches 1957-1963*, p. 294.

³³ From discussions with Indian and Pakistani officials concerned with the relations between their countries and from reading the speeches and correspondence of Nehru and Pakistani leaders we conclude that press opinion and reporting has strongly affected the relations between the two states, so much so that on several occasions special bilateral agreements were in effect to reduce the levels of press irritation and antagonism while administrators sought to reach and carry out agreements in a calm public atmosphere. Neither government was ever free from the fear that public animosity would impede mutually advantageous accords. Even the Indus waters treaty was criticized warmly by the press of both countries. The fact that both governments could exert certain press controls led to suspicion of malafides by each of them whenever the other's press began a hostile campaign.

³⁴ President Kennedy wrote to Ayub Khan suggesting that the latter assure Nehru privately of his concern about the Chinese attack and that Pakistan should take no action to alarm India. Ayub Khan rejected Kennedy's suggestion in a letter of Nov. 5, 1962, in which he summed up Pakistan's assessment of the situation on the subcontinent. Text in *Friends Not Masters*, pp. 141-43.

³⁵ Ayub Khan statement, Nov. 5, 1962 ; press release no. 51 of the Embassy of Pakistan, Washington. See also Ayub's letters to Kennedy and Macmillan of Jan. 2, 1963, after they had intimated to him the extent of the arms that

THE BURDEN OF PAKISTAN

183

Britain and the US agreed to supply to India at their Nassau meeting, *Friends Not Masters*, pp. 150-52.

[36] See Duncan Sandys' report to the House of Commons, Nov. 27, 1962, on his visit to Delhi and Rawalpindi ; in N. Mansergh, ed., *Documents and Speeches on Commonwealth Affairs 1952-1962*, London 1963, pp. 625-28.

[37] See Nehru's speech in Lok Sabha, Nov. 30, 1962, *Speeches 1957-1963*, p. 302 ; also his unexplained statement that India would enter discussions without "any preconditions or restrictions on the scope of the talks." *New York Times*, Dec. 2, 1962.

[38] The Indian analysis that the Pakistani-Chinese boundary alignment favoured Chinese interests, that Pakistan had given up good claims over territory previously under Kashmiri control, in order to obtain political advantages from China has been verified by outside estimate ; see W. M. Dobell, "Ramifications of the China-Pakistan Border Treaty," *Pacific Affairs*, fall, 1964. The Pakistani government regarded the alignment as a fair compromise, desirable if only to commit China to a firm boundary.

[39] Nehru had protested in May 1962, that the Pakistani-Chinese negotiations interfered with India's legal rights as the sovereign power, though not in full occupation, in one of the areas concerned.

[40] An American scholar has recorded that in the year 1963, 307 daily issues of the Pakistani semi-official newspaper, *Dawn,* each carried at least one front-page story on the aggressive designs of India. Karl Von Vorys, *Political Development in Pakistan*, Princeton 1965, p. 167.

[41] The Chinese boundary agreement was followed, in August 1963, by a pact on air transport which gave China access to Africa and the West through Karachi and Pakistan a route to Peking. Pakistan made diplomatic and economic overtures to the regional powers—Nepal, Burma, Ceylon and Indonesia—as well as certain African states in an effort to undermine and if possible replace India as the most influential south Asian state.

[42] Speech in Lok Sabha, Sept. 17, 1953, in *Speeches 1953-1957*, p. 213. In the same speech Nehru acknowledged his fear that a plebiscite might be made the cause of a "fratricidal war [which] ... will spread to other parts of India and upset the delicate balances that have been established."

[43] Report by Secretary-General U Thant, based on information from General Nimmo, the head of the UN military observer group in Kashmir. S/6651, Sept. 3, 1965.

[44] *ibid.*, paragraph 10.

[45] See an assessment of the war in Leo Heiman, "Lessons from the War in Kashmir," *Military Review*, XLVI, 2, February 1966. From the Indian side several published accounts of the war are available, two of which are P. S. Bhagat, *The Shield and the Sword*, Calcutta 1967, and D. R. Mankekar, *Twenty Two Fateful Days*, Bombay 1966. Useful Pakistani articles appeared in *Pakistan Horizon*, vol. 18 (1965), 4.

CHAPTER VII

AN EXPERIMENT IN FRIENDSHIP WITH CHINA

THE TWO GREATEST Asian states, India and China, experienced only tenuous, partial relations with each other until the 1950's. Visits between the two lands by travellers, often on religious missions,[1] and traders were recorded in ancient and medieval texts, but exchanges of cultural influences and commercial products resulting from those contacts were few—except for the one-way movement of the gospel of Buddhism eastward from India in the period before and contemporaneous with the beginnings of the Christian era. During European dominance in Asia Indian-Chinese contacts took place under the auspices of the British, who used Indian troops and policemen in dealings with China and stimulated Indian-Chinese trade in such commodities as opium. The almost totally separate development of Indian and Chinese civilizations and the remarkably few instances of their interaction even on a small scale can best be explained by noting the enormous physical barrier between the two countries. The vast, desolate Tibetan plateau and its mountainous boundaries made contact overland formidable and hazardous. The Himalayas created a special problem in communications but were never impassable, and without the Tibetan wilderness they would not have constituted an insuperable hindrance to Indian-Chinese communications.

The British-Indian government regarded Russia and, to a much lesser degree, China as potential threats to Indian-based dominance in the Himalayas. Therefore, in the 19th and 20th centuries, when Russian power was moving into central Asia and the Chinese state showed some interest in extending its influence westward, Britian endeavoured to establish the Tibetan area—under the weak suzerainty of Peking—as part of a vast buffer zone, or sanitary cordon, between India and the politically unpredictable Russian and Chinese empires. Of the various treaties in the late 19th and early 20th centuries by which Britain sought to make the buffer zone viable the Simla convention of 1913 became the most famous and controversial. The convention was the culmination of a decade-long British effort to limit Chinese and Russian influence in Tibet by building up the status of the Lhasa government as an autonomous regime sufficiently under British-Indian influence to preclude any dangers from that quarter to India and the Indian sphere of influence south of the Himalayan watershed. Because of the weakness of the central government of China following the revolution in 1912 the British in India were able to become the major outside influence in Lhasa, and the Simla convention appeared to give the Tibetan government a de facto independence by the very fact that the Tibetan representative signed the accord on his own.

But the convention recognized that "Tibet is under the suzerainty of China" (article II), and therefore the legality of the Tibetan government's separate signing of the treaty was itself open to question. More important, China refused to sign the Simla convention and in years following repudiated it verbally while awaiting the time when it could reassert its legal power in Tibet. The most beneficial result for India from the Simla negotiations was the defining of the eastern extreme of the Indo-Tibetan boundary in the sector between Burma and Bhutan. Even though not always regarded as a legally binding definition, the so-called McMahon line did add to the legal precedents and customs underwriting a natural geographic.

Indian nationalists in the 1930's and 1940's looked to China with the sympathetic and hopeful vision of a future Indian-Chinese friendship and collaboration after the defeat of Japan and the withdrawal of Western power from Asia. In 1939 the Indian National Congress sent Nehru to Chungking to bring greetings and encouragement to the Chinese government and people, then besieged by Japanese forces. In 1942 Chiang Kai-shek visited India and publicly urged Britain to transfer more power to the Indians during the war ; he expressed the same idea in communications with the American government. After the war Indian-Chinese relations became direct and official, under the interim Indian government, and the tentative beginnings of political collaboration appeared in similar stands in the early UN debates and at the Asian Relations Conference in New Delhi in 1947.

Nehru viewed Indian-Chinese collaboration as an essential foundation on which to construct a "new Asia" independent of

external rule and forceful in pursuit of its interests in the world.
He set out to build that structure—with any Chinese government
having the support of its people. India exchanged diplomatic relations with the government of Nationalist China in 1948, and K. M.
Panikkar was sent as the first Indian ambassador to China, whose
capital was then at Nanking. His first public act was to attend the
installation of Chiang Kai-shek as the president of the Chinese
Republic. In Panikkar's assessment, "The Kuomintang attitude
toward India, while genuinely friendly, was inclined to be a little
patronizing. It was the attitude of an elder brother who was considerably older and well established in the world, prepared to give
his advice to a younger brother struggling to make his way. Independence of India was welcome, but of course it was understood
that China as the recognized Great Power of the East after the war
expected India to know her place."[2] When similar attitudes were
later apparent in the communist Chinese government they resulted
in a predictable conflict with the Indian government's self-assumed
role as the spokesman for "resurgent Asia."

Toward the end of 1949 the communists gained military supremacy
in China and on October 1 inaugurated the People's Republic,
under Mao Tse-tung's leadership, with Chou En-lai as prime minister
and foreign minister. India recognized the new government on
December 30, 1949, and Panikkar returned to China as ambassador
with a mission, as he saw it, to prove to Mao that a "neutral," or
nonaligned posture was possible in international affairs.[3] Such a
view was not easy to get across to the Chinese communists, whose
official party line on India could be judged by the following message
from Mao to the Indian Communist Party : "I firmly believe,"
Mao wrote on October 19, 1949, "that relying on the brave Communist Party of India and the unity and struggle of all Indian
patriots India will certainly not remain long under the yoke of
imperialism and its collaborators. Like free China, free India
will one day emerge in the socialist and People's Democratic
family ; that day will end the imperialist reactionary era in the
history of mankind."[4] Nehru managed to ignore such doctrinaire sentiments as those and proceeded to meet and temporarily overcome two acute problems in Indian-Chinese relations
which occurred within one year of the establishment of formal
relations.

THE EARLY DIFFICULTIES

The first arose from the North Korean aggression, which elicited India's condemnation and its support of the UN stand in Korea. Although India tried to dissociate itself from American policy in the far east in the summer of 1950 its diplomatic support for the UN military effort in Korea must have confirmed its identity with Western interests in the minds of the communist governments. As described in an earlier chapter,[5] India gradually managed to assume the position of a mediator in the diplomacy of the Korean war, a role which in New Delhi appeared to be the only appropriate one, especially after Chinese forces were involved in the conflict. Even before then, however, Ambassador Panikkar had begun his strenuous efforts to localize the war and eventually help bridge the diplomatic gap between China and the West. His *Memoirs* told the fascinating story[6] and revealed also his sympathy toward the Chinese position during the war, which helped largely to cause American suspicions about the Indian moves. By explaining the Chinese intervention in Korea as a defensive measure, by vociferously urging the representation of the Peking government in international bodies, by advocating the return of Formosa to mainland control, and above all by its vigorous refusal by late 1950 to support American policies in Asia, India gradually succeeded in convincing China of its nonalignment. By late 1952 China had accepted India's good offices and mediation efforts and seemed more anxious to conclude a cease-fire under terms suggested by India than did the Soviet Union. At the end of India's prisoner custodianship, which followed the truce in Korea, the Peking government had ended its vilifying of India's international posture and may in fact have decided on a policy of sincere friendship with New Delhi.

The second crisis that faced India in its relations with China coincided with the first hints that China might intervene in the Korean war. Its "liberation" of Tibet began in October 1950. Preceding that move Peking's known intentions to reassert its authority in Tibet had resulted in Indian offers to assist the Chinese in reaching a peaceful settlement with the Tibetan government. Tibetan representatives and the Chinese ambassador in New Delhi had held brief talks ; they were broken off, however, shortly before the Chinese liberation was launched. The Indian government at first reacted to the Chinese military moves with almost instinctive annoyance and despair, openly expressed in a series of notes to Peking. Somewhat more carefully planned responses followed China's assertion that it sent troops into Tibet to "defend the frontiers of China" and its allegation that India's viewpoint on Tibet was "affected by foreign influences hostile to China."[7] India's position and traditional rights in Tibet thus came under immediate attack and formed part of the doctrine of "liberation."

India's traditional rights derived mainly from the Simla convention of 1914 which gave Britain a position in Tibet which resembled the extraterritorial privileges granted to Europeans in China itself. Under the convention the British established trade marts at important trading centres in southern Tibet and attached them to Indian territory by telegraph and postal links maintained by the government of India. British subjects had virtual freedom to conduct their business in Tibet in any manner they chose, and if they were charged with crimes within the jurisdiction of the trade marts or on the routes to the marts their cases would be heard by a British trade agent in Tibet, to be tried and punished according to the laws of India. Beyond those trading rights there grew up considerable British political influence in Tibet, and by the late 1930's there was a permanent British resident in Lhasa. The Simla convention provided for British export of military stores to Tibet (article VIII), and arms were sent openly from India, with the apparent object of helping maintain Tibet's autonomy.[8] It is likely that the Tibetan government imported arms through India until 1950.

The result of British-Tibetan relations between the world wars was at the very least that the Tibetan government looked to British India as a balance against undue Chinese influence and as a window opening into the world at large ; at the most, that the British government through India had a protectorate-like influence on Tibet's foreign relations while exerting considerable control over its commerce. Communist China was determined to bring to an end the influences and controls exerted on Tibet from India and, additionally, cut off the attraction that many Tibetans saw in the Indian connection. A dilemma therefore faced the Indian government and lingered unresolved for a decade. If India clung to the inheritance of British-Indian rights in Tibet it would antagonize China, offend against the concept of Chinese suzerainty in Tibet (which the very existence of those rights denied), and open itself to being charged with defend-ing the gains in Tibet made under imperialist auspices. On the other hand, if India abandoned all rights in Tibet and withdrew into a position of isolation from Tibetan affairs it would leave open the way for Chinese power to extend to the very edge of the Himala-yan barrier, and it would make India an accomplice in any future subjugation that China might impose on the Tibetan people, a kind of neo-imperialism in the minds of some Indians. Urging opposite courses of action on Nehru were chiefly Panikkar, on the one hand, and certain officials in the External Affairs Ministry with experience in Tibet, on the other hand. The ambassador urged on the prime minister a conciliatory policy toward China ; some offi-cials argued for measures to protect Tibet from outright Chinese domination. Indian newspaper opinion generally supported the latter approach partly on humanitarian and partly on strategic grounds.

Nehru's course of action in the delicate and dangerous dealings with China over Tibet appeared to be a rough compromise between the two extreme recommendations made to him and hence between the two sides of the dilemma that faced his government. Groping for a middle position on the legal status of Tibet, Nehru reaffirmed Chinese suzerainty but argued that Tibet's autonomy, which had been established factually for forty years, should remain unble-mished.[9] Such a status for Tibet would have lessened the chances of any Chinese military threat along the Himalayas. Stung by Chinese claims that they were going to "liberate" Tibet—apparently from Indian influences—Nehru informed the Peking government in a note of October 31, 1950, that India had "no political or terri-torial ambitions as to Tibet and [does] not seek any novel privileged position" therein, but that the traditional Indian trading rights in Tibet, including a small Indian military force stationed at Gyantse, "should continue."[10]

Adding still further confusion to its policy the Indian government agreed to transmit—indeed, one of its officials privately drafted—a Tibetan appeal to the UN in November, which claimed Chinese aggression against Tibet. The Tibetan case was based on the "com-plete independence" of the country achieved by 1912 and which thereafter "depended entirely on her isolation, her faith in the wisdom of the Lord Buddha, and occasionally on the support of the British in India for her protection."[11] El Salvador requested that the Tibetan item be placed on the agenda. But towards the end of November India decided not to press the case against the Chinese in Tibet, and its UN representative withdrew whatever support he might have previously given to the Tibetan appeal. He stated that his government believed that a peaceful settlement between China and Tibet was still possible, one which would maintain the autonomy of the latter.[12] The Tibetan issue was abandoned at that time in the UN.

Above all, India wanted to avoid further Chinese military action against the Tibetans, which among other undesirable consequences would introduce Chinese forces more deeply into the country than they had already proceeded. Nehru was certain that India was incapable of putting an army into Tibet to defend its independence. "A hungry army cannot fight," he explained to those in parliament who urged a more aggressive policy line in Tibet and elsewhere. "Hungry people behind an army are bad material. It is difficult to fight both on the home front and on the battle front. The food problem, therefore, comes first of all, whatever the issue. The problem of industrial development and growth becomes equally important in order to build up the resources necessary for defense."[13] Following this list of priorities defining national interest, which Nehru always appeared to have in mind when determining his China policy, a logical course of action for India was to try diplomatically to stall the Chinese advance into Tibet and seek the best terms possible for the Tibetans without the use of force. Any vigorous international defense of Tibetan rights could have been calculated to challenge China to move more rapidly towards destroying all opposition to its policies in Tibet.

With India's support, a Sino-Tibetan agreement ended the first phase of China's policy of reasserting physical control. On May 23, 1951, Tibetan delegates signed the agreement in Peking, which recognized Chinese control of Tibet's army and its external affairs, trade, and communications but which guaranteed the continuation of the existing political and social system in Tibet.[14] That agreement was a partial support for India's interests ; it appeared at the least to postpone further building up of Chinese power in Tibet, if the Korean war was not then accomplishing the same end.

India and China then began direct negotiations on Indian relations with Tibet, while Nehru continued his search for a settlement in the far east which would satisfy the Chinese government, as well as the US. Hints of improved Indian-Chinese relations, such as a shipment of 100,000 tons of rice from China to help relieve Indian shortages in April 1951 and an exchange of cultural missions in late 1951 and in 1952, provided an atmosphere conducive to compromises on both sides. In June 1952 Nehru appeared sanguine about India's retaining certain rights in Tibet within the context of effective Chinese suzerainty. He spoke of withdrawing Indian guards from the trade mart at Gyantse and from the Tibetan trade routes—about 300 troops in all, including garrisons at Yatung and Gartok—once Chinese forces could provide security, but he indicated hope that the Indian trading rights might be respected and the Indian mission might remain in Lhasa.[15]

Nehru's policy on Tibet in the early 1950's was fitted into the context of an overall assessment that China, as well as India, wished to pursue policies of peace in Asia, because only thereby could progress for both countries be assured. The events in Tibet, however, at that time and for a decade to follow, were the major source of Nehru's doubts about Chinese intentions and constituted an unspoken proviso in his efforts to construct an Indian-Chinese entente.

THE EXPERIMENT IN FRIENDSHIP WITH CHINA

India in the 1950's had no well coordinated military defense policy towards China, as it did towards Pakistan, the only other state which presented a security problem. Instead, India adopted a psychological approach to relations with China. Lacking convincing physical power, India used instruments of diplomatic persuasiveness which had proved beneficial in relations with other states—states, however, which were either weaker than India or not interested in threatening Indian security. In pursuit of the short-term objective of containing Chinese power or limiting its effectiveness in Tibet, and at the same time attempting to reach broader understanding with its influential neighbour, India negotiated an agreement for eight years on Tibet, which was signed on April 29, 1954.[16] It had two parts, one, a preamble that set forth the five principles of peaceful coexistence, known as the *panchasheel* doctrine ; the other, specific articles relating to Indo-Tibetan relations. As a doctrine defining a fundamental concept of Indian foreign policy the preamble had the greater significance.[17] The five principles were : (1) mutual respect for each other's territorial integrity and sovereignty, (2) mutual non-aggression, (3) mutual non-interference in each other's internal affairs, (4) equality and mutual benefit, and (5) peaceful coexistence.

In reaching the *panchasheel* accord with China Nehru reasoned that India was establishing proof of its own intentions and allaying any Chinese fears about India's pursuit of interests in Tibet. "So far as Tibet is concerned," Nehru told the Lok Sabha, the 1954 agreement "is a recognition of the existing situation there. . . ."[18] He further reasoned that China, for its part, would restrain its expansionist drives in the Himalayas and in southeast Asia in deference to the accord, or, at least, that the accord would provide an obvious test of Chinese intentions. The *panchasheel*, in short, was not merely proclamatory of a "climate of peace" but was intended to be inhibiting as well. In a remarkably candid recital of his thoughts about the psychology that lay behind *panchasheel* Nehru told the Lok Sabha : "I suppose in the final analysis, no country can trust another country. . . . Therefore, it is not a question of my trusting any of these big or small countries ; but it is a question of our following a policy which . . . makes it more and more difficult progressively for the other country to break trust. We need not live in a fairy world where nothing wrong happens. . . . But we can create an environment wherein it becomes a little more dangerous to the other party to break away from the pledges given."[19] For Nehru and most of the members of his government a policy of deliberately pressing friendship on China, of nurturing the habits of coexistence, constituted the best guarantee of security in the Himalayas.

It was easy for critics of the Government of India's China policy in the mid-1950's to allege that Nehru and certain of his advisors displayed naivety in promoting the *panchasheel* doctrine. To prove that the contrary was the case would require a deeper probing into the documents than can presently be accomplished. One hint above all others suggested the calculated, conditional character of India's reliance on the adherence of the People's Republic to the five principles. To the Pradesh Congress committees Nehru addressed a circular on foreign policy which gave this partial defense of the

Indian-Chinese accord : "It is said : how can we put faith in such declarations? In international affairs, one can never be dead certain and the friends of today might be enemies of tomorrow. That may be so. Are we then to begin with enmity and suspicion and not give any other approach a chance? Surely it is better, with nations as with individuals, to hope for and expect the best, but at the same time to be prepared for any eventuality. . . ."[20]

The specific terms of the 1954 Indian-Chinese treaty dealt with trade between India and the "Tibet region of China." To avoid the appearance of inequality the agreement provided China with three trade agencies in India to match India's three main commercial centres in Tibet, which were to remain. Pilgrim travel was also defined as a mutual privilege ; provisions were made for customary movements of local people. Six passes were cited as the routes for intercourse between India and Tibet. In an exchange of notes accompanying the treaty India agreed to withdraw its military forces in Tibet, to turn over to China its post, telegraph, and telephone facilities, and to transfer its twelve rest houses. India retained its physical installations only at Yatung and Gyantse. Other terms were of lesser importance. The sense of the treaty and the notes was to create equality between India and China, replacing the extraterritoriality of the earlier period. India was of course bowing to the inevitable : Nehru explained in parliament that if Indians tried to maintain the rights in Tibet that the British imperialists had forced upon the country, they would be compelled to give them up.[21]

The essence of the 1954 agreement was its spirit, not its specific provisions. For the crucial matter of where Indian and Chinese administrative jurisdictions met in the Himalayas was omitted ; even the specific reference to six passes through which trade was allowed did not include mention of whether the passes were Indian, Chinese, or were situated on the boundary line. The Indian government saw no reason to enter discussions with Peking in 1954 on the question of the boundary, because no dispute had yet arisen. Indeed, the Chinese government continued to assure New Delhi up to 1959 that "there was no territorial dispute or controversy between India and China."[22] Adhering to the spirit of the 1954 agreement, and the Bandung accords in 1955, which elaborated on the *panchasheel* ideals, became the theme of Indian diplomacy toward China from 1954 to 1959. Like the repetition of *mantras* (which should have psychological effect on both the spokesman and the listener), the reaffirmation of the peaceful coexistence phraseology constituted the chief instrument of India's China policy in pursuit of the short-term objective of containing Chinese expansion. While certain External Affairs Ministry officials grew doubtful that the public image of Indian-Chinese friendship— "Hindi-Chini bhai-bhai"—could be sustained, the prime minister insisted, publicly and within the Ministry, that China's intentions were essentially peaceful so far as India was concerned.

Superficial evidence during that period existed to support Nehru's view. The Chinese foreign minister, Chou En-lai's visits to India reinforced the image of China as a state reluctant to use force and willing to settle all its disputes (except those with the US) peacefully. Chou and Nehru appeared to be exchanging advices on such matters as a settlement in Indo-China and control of nuclear weapons, and their joint communiques suggested a common approach to many world problems. In October 1954 Nehru visited China and returned impressed by the efficiency of the Peking regime, the hard working character of the Chinese people, and the similarities between India's and China's problems. Delegations moved between the two countries and a trade agreement took effect, which rapidly increased Indian-Chinese commerce. In diplomatic circles Nehru and Indian representatives argued the Chinese case for incorporation of Formosa and the immediate off-shore islands into the mainland.[23]

Above all other evidences of India's adherence to the spirit of the 1954 agreement in its relations with China were the periodic pleas by Indian UN representatives and by Nehru for the Peking government's admission to the world organization. UN delegates in late 1956, weary of speeches condemning governments which had violated the terms of the Charter, did not find much relief in listening to Krishna Menon's eulogy of Peking's adherence to UN principles. Menon spoke of "the depth of sincerity of the Chinese government in its attachment to the Charter" and asserted that Peking had never denied its acceptance of the Charter. Referring to his experience at Bandung he told the Assembly, "There were no greater adherents to the Charter of the United Nations in the Conference of Asian and African Nations than the People's Government of China and its Prime Minister." The Indian *mantra* on China was again recorded by Menon when he said, ". . . so far as we

Asian people are concerned, we have no reason to think that these people [Chinese] are expansionist or belligerent or imperialistic in any way. It is their desire to live in peace with their neighbours."[24]

IMPLEMENTING THE CHINA POLICY

Major reliance on the psychological diplomacy of frequently announcing that China was a peace loving state and was adhering to the *panchasheel* did not preclude India's taking certain further diplomatic precautions to assure the security of the frontier with China. During Chou En-lai's visits to India Nehru brought to his attention Chinese maps showing large areas claimed by India as parts of China. Chou amiably assured the Indian leader that those maps were "out of date" and that China had not yet got around to publishing new editions.[25] The Chinese government was shown on several occasions the newest Indian maps of the Himalayan border in order to elicit any Chinese challenge to the delineation as made by India. China made no protests on such maps.

In practice, however, small border incidents began to occur less than three months after the signing of the April 1954 agreement. The scene of the first Indian encounter with Chinese or Tibetan officials encroaching on what was allegedly Indian territory was near a 16,000 foot high, two square mile plain known as Bara Hoti in the Garhwal district of the United Provinces. Bara Hoti was traditionally a seasonal Indian border outpost in the Hoti plain, and when the border security force sought to re-establish itself in the summer of 1954 it encountered Tibetan officials already present in the area—a region the Chinese called Wu-Je. A tedious series of notes and memoranda on Bara Hoti, or Wu-Je, followed. In August 1955 India requested China to order a Tibetan official, supported by Chinese troops, to cease collecting grazing taxes from Indian herdsmen at Hoti. In November Chinese troops were camped there alongside Indian troops, and these or other troops tried to stop an Indian patrol near Damzan in the same area. After four seasons of Indian-Chinese military and civilian encounters around Hoti, in April 1958, diplomatic talks began in New Delhi concerning that region. The talks broke down.

Although news reports of frontier clashes concentrated for years on Bara Hoti, the first Indian white paper on China[26] showed that other areas were actively disputed since 1956. At Nilang, below the Tsang Chokla pass, Chinese soldiers armed with tommy and sten guns were encountered in the spring of 1956, and in the fall a clash took place near the Shipki pass leading into Himachal Pradesh. An Indian patrol met a Chinese force on the south side of Shipki, and the Chinese threw stones and threatened to use grenades against the Indians. Noting that Shipki was mentioned as a border pass in the agreement of 1954, the Indian government stated in an aide memoire that it would "consider any crossing of this border pass by armed personnel as aggression."[27]

The details of those border incidents and scores of others that were rapidly filling white papers by the end of the 1950's suggested little more than the predictable frictions on any long, undemarcated frontier between two states which for the first time were both aware of the needs of frontier security and capable of exerting control. The early clashes were in the so-called middle sector of the Indo-Tibetan border, which the British and the Indians had neglected, generally allowing Tibetans "to raise taxes, impose duties, and graze flocks at a number of points south of the British boundary."[28] Those disputes alone, which the Indian government did not publicize until more serious conflicts appeared, in 1959, would not have been likely causes for a major confrontation.

The outstanding problem in Indian-Chinese relations until 1959 was not the border but the happenings in Tibet. India's acquiescence in Chinese policies in Tibet was not equivalent to isolating itself totally from developments there. As a democratic state, which permitted freedom of expression and movement, even to those working against Chinese interests in Tibet, India could not—nor was it willing to—do its part in completing the erection of an iron curtain around Tibet in order to assure its Sinofication. There was, thus, a duality in India's China policy so far as Tibet was concerned : it agreed not to interfere with what went on in Tibet, and yet it was deeply concerned with the affairs of its Himalayan neighbour. In the absence of any active policy so far as Tibet was concerned the Indian government in the 1950's hoped that China would respect the traditions of the Tibetans and introduce changes gradually and without excessive use of force. For the Chinese government, however, committed to a revolutionary doctrine of socio-economic change in all areas under its control, the status quo in Tibet had to be overturned rapidly, if necessary by the use of force and without regard for India's interests in the matter.

Peking was far more aware than New Delhi seemed to be of opportunities open to India to subvert the Chinese regime in Tibet—in the extreme case, by introducing military equipment for use by anti-Chinese forces and permitting Indian territory to be used by counter-revolutionary elements ; but, more modestly and without any overtly anti-Chinese motive, by keeping open the channels of communication between Tibet and the non-communist world. China, therefore, despite Chou En-lai's reiteration of the *panchasheel* doctrine, looked upon Indian and Chinese interests in the Himalayan region as hostile, even before the issue of territorial jurisdiction arose in an acute form. In contradiction of the explicit terms of the 1954 agreement Chinese officials in Tibet, within months after its signing, began harassing the remaining Indian trade agents and other Indian nationals, and gradually they placed such obstacles in the way of India's legitimate interests in Tibet that their exercise was reduced to almost nothing.

After the establishment of the preparatory committee for the Tibet Autonomous Region in 1956 the Chinese intensified their measures to bring Tibet more fully into the new order. The subsequent movement of communist political cadres, Chinese military personnel and settlers into Tibet produced fierce resistance, as the "religious beliefs, customs, and habits of the Tibetan people," protected by the 1951 agreement between Tibet and China, were substantially undermined. Khampas and several lesser tribal peoples in eastern Tibet and the adjoining regions of China maintained a state of military revolt against Chinese efforts to occupy their territories and reorganize their societies. In response to the increasing rebelliousness in Tibet, and as an aspect of its generally more aggressive policy in all domestic and international spheres, China intensified its repression of Tibetan rebels in 1957 and charged that foreign agencies were engaged in trying to overthrow the new order. Allegations of foreign assistance to the Tibetan rebellion necessarily implicated India.

In 1958 the revolt in eastern Tibet, which had continued for over two years without open assistance from the Lhasa government, began to spread into the area of the capital. More refugees fled across the border into India, and Tibetan exile leaders in Kalimpong sent an appeal to the UN to take cognizance of Chinese aggression, as it had in the case of Russian intervention in Hungary. In August 1958 and September 1959 the Tibetans appealed for UN help. In the latter year Ireland and Malaya moved to put the issue on the agenda of the General Assembly, and a debate was held, with India adopting an uncommitted position. An Assembly resolution deploring the repression taking place in Tibet was passed on October 21, 1959, with India abstaining.[29]

This abbreviated sketch of happenings in Tibet may fail to suggest the significance that they had for India. Even ignoring other issues on which Indian and Chinese interests were in conflict, the Tibetan revolt and its repression alone caused open hostility between the two states and aroused mutual distrust in New Delhi and Peking. The Indian government, which looked upon the mutual non-interference clause of the *panchasheel* as a binding promise, apparently avoided all official entanglements in Tibetan affairs and tried to control the activities of exiled Tibetans who were seeking help from India (and elsewhere) to combat the Chinese. By the terms of the 1954 agreement, however, the Indo-Tibetan border was to remain open, and nothing short of sealing it for a considerable part of its length would have eliminated the movement of political agents and arms from India into Tibet.[30]

Prime Minister Nehru and his government repeatedly discouraged and even contradicted reports about Chinese repression against the Tibetans and insisted that Tibet was an internal affair of China. When the Dalai Lama visited India in 1956, on the 2,500th anniversary of the Buddha's *parinirvana*, Nehru sought to reassure him about Chinese guarantees of Tibetan autonomy ; on the basis of Nehru's discussions with Chou En-lai, then in New Delhi, the Dalai Lama agreed to return to his country and not seek Indian asylum. In response to the 1958 appeal to the UN and to many governments from Tibetan exile leaders, India did nothing, except to impose further restrictions on the exiles, operating in Kalimpong and Darjeeling. India's unwillingness to support UN resolutions against Chinese activities in Tibet was based on several considerations : (1) UN resolutions could do nothing to improve the conditions of the Tibetan people and might even add to the burden of Chinese oppression. (2) Such resolutions would be used by certain governments for their own purposes, as propaganda against the Peking regime, which the Indian government could not at that time condone. (3) Most important, India could not support any resolution stating or even implying the right of Tibetans to independence ; partly because of possibly embarrassing precedents applying to Kashmir or other Indian regions the government could not defend internationally the principle of self-determination for peoples already a part of an independent state.

Nevertheless, unofficially and officially India continued to be involved in the happenings in Tibet, just as it had been for at least the previous one-half century. In 1959, after nearly a decade of postponement by both sides, the terms of that involvement were made plain, and they extended far beyond the international politics of the Tibetan revolution, as a later chapter explains.

Until 1958 or 1959 the Indian government's experiment with a policy of peaceful coexistence towards China did not appear unworkable. It met the short-term interests of avoiding any major conflict of interests in the Himalayas. The longer that such a conflict could be postponed—assuming that it was inevitable—the better prepared India would be, industrially and therefore militarily, to meet it.

The long-range goal of the Nehru government was to reach a stage of collaboration with China for common purposes—mutually reinforcing economic policies, common fronts on specifically Asian issues in world politics. Though recognizing the difficulties in dealing with a communist regime in Peking Nehru believed that nationalism, not communism, was the stronger force in China. He therefore treated China and Russia as separate, not joined irrevocably in an international communist bloc. He tried to appeal to China's Asian heritage to woo its government away from dependency upon or support of the USSR so that India and China might form a bi-polar Asian link, an entente, capable of asserting a powerful non-European voice in world affairs. Such was Nehru's purpose at the Bandung conference (described elsewhere), and it lay behind his efforts to have Peking represented in world organizations.

Nehru recognized the areas of conflict with China, first in Korea, then in Tibet, and later in southeast Asia. But he also saw the possibilities of substantial collaboration between India and China. To bring them about was the aim of his experiment of *panchasheel*.

NOTES AND REFERENCES

[1] See Prabodh Chandra Bagchi, *India and China : A Thousand Years of Cultural Relations*, Bombay 1944.

[2] Panikkar, *In Two Chinas*, pp. 26-27.

[3] *ibid.*, p. 73. Although there were in India, as in the US, a good many public expressions of sympathy for the Chinese communists in the period from 1945 to 1949, there was no reluctance, except possibly from Indian communists, to support the Nationalist government as long as it was in power. See "Indian Views of China Before the Revolution," Centre for International Studies, M. I. T., Cambridge 1955.

[4] New China News Agency, Nov. 21, 1949.

[5] Chapter III.

[6] See Panikkar, *op. cit.*, chapter IX, on Korea.

[7] Cited in Indian Press Digests, "Indian Views of Sino-Indian Relations," (Berkeley), pp. i-vii. Chinese communist propaganda since Sept. 1949 had been accusing India of "colluding" with American "imperialists" in a "plot to annex Tibet." From *People's Daily*, Peking, Sept. 13, 1949 ; cited in C. N. Satyapalan, "The Sino-Indian Border Conflict," *Orbis*, vol. VIII, 2, p. 375. An excellent summary of the Chinese propaganda line against Nehru—the "loyal slave of imperialism," the "Chiang Kai-shek of India"—appeared in Girilal Jain, *Panchasheela and After*, pp. 8-14.

[8] Such is the judgment of Alastair Lamb, *The McMahon Line*, vol. II, p. 522.

[9] Speech in parliament, Dec. 6, 1950 ; *Speeches 1949-1953*, p. 174.

[10] Quoted in "Indian Views of Sino-Indian Relations," pp. vi.

[11] Texts of Tibetan appeals to the UN are in appendix II of Dalai Lama, *My Land and My People*.

[12] See "Indian Views of Sino-Indian Relations," p. 11.

[13] Speech in parliament, Dec. 7, 1950 ; *Speeches 1949-1953*, pp. 180-81.

[14] Text of the Sino-Tibetan agreement is in *Foreign Affairs Reports*, Indian Council of World Affairs, New Delhi, vol. VIII, 6 (June 1959).

[15] Press conference, June 21, 1952 ; Nehru, *Press Conferences 1952*, pp. 50-51.

[16] Text in *Foreign Policy of India : Texts of Documents 1947-59*, pp. 103-109.

[17] Nehru confirmed in parliament that "The real importance . . . of this agreement is . . . its wider implications in regard to non-aggression, recognition of each other's territorial integrity. ..." *LSD*, vol. V, pt. II, May 15, 1954, col. 7497.

[18] *ibid.*, col. 7496.

[19] *LSD*, vol. VII, pt. II, Sept. 29, 1954, col. 3683.

[20] *Congress Bulletin*, no. 5, June-July 1954, pp. 245-51, quoted in "Indian Views of Sino-Indian Relations," pp. 26-27n.

[21] *LSD*, vol. V, pt. II, May 18, 1954, col. 7666 (in Hindi).

[22] Speech in Lok Sabha, Nov. 25, 1959 ; *India's Foreign Policy*, p. 360.

[23] V. K. Krishna Menon was in Peking in May 1955 following the Bandung conference and tried there and later in Western capitals to find a solution in the Formosa crisis. Given Menon's views that China was not an expansionist state, it is doubtful that he calculated the possible effects on India's northern frontier of the release of major concentrations of Chinese troops from their positions in

the coastal provinces facing the Formosa Straits, which would have been made possible by the termination of Formosan independence, or even of US support of the island's defenses. A summary of Indian-Chinese relations during the years immediately following the 1954 agreement appears in P. C. Chakravarti, *India's China Policy*, chap. 5, as well as in other widely published places.

[24] *GAOR*, 580th Plenary Meeting, Nov. 16, 1956, pp. 78-79.

[25] Certain External Affairs Ministry officials during those years doubted that the communist regime in China would repudiate, in new maps, any territorial claims made by a previous regime during which the "out of date" maps were printed ; it could not afford to renege on such obvious nationalist objectives.

[26] *Notes, Memoranda and Letters Exchanged and Agreements Signed Between the Governments of India and China, 1954-1959* (White Paper), the beginning of a lengthy series.

[27] *ibid.*, p. 19.

[28] Alastair Lamb, *The China-India Border*, p. 171.

[29] In 1959 the International Commission of Jurists, a non-governmental organization with consultative status with UNESCO, issued a statement charging the Chinese with genocide in Tibet. A report supporting the charge was prepared by the Indian member of the Commission, Purshottam Trikamdas ; it did not, of course, express the official views of the Indian government. See International Commission of Jurists, *The Question of Tibet and the Rule of Law*, Geneva 1959.

[30] For a very personal and revealing account of trans-border activities see George N. Patterson, *Tragic Destiny*.

CHAPTER VIII

THE STRUGGLE TO MAINTAIN AN HIMALAYAN BUFFER ZONE

THE INDIAN-CHINESE power struggle in the Himalayas transformed that region from a tranquil buffer zone into an arena of unprecedented confrontation between Asia's largest states. Many years before Indian officials publicly recognized that confrontation the government, almost instinctively, was preparing itself to meet the challenge. The instinct for maintaining a power balance and, if possible, a buffer zone was a response built into administrative and military procedures by the British, whose early concern for Himalayan security seemed in the 1950's farsighted.

Just as India's policy towards Tibet displayed mutually contradictory facets, its official statements and its official and unofficial actions towards Nepal, Sikkim, and Bhutan were self-contradictory and sometimes self-defeating. As with Tibetan policy, the problem for Indian political leaders lay in their attachment to ideals of anti-imperialism and representative government simultaneously with their recognition of the inherited and seemingly unchanged requirements of territorial security. That basic, inner conflict pervaded Indian policy toward the three border states, but was particularly evident in relations with Nepal, where national political participation emerged in the 1950's, and advanced further than in the other two states. India's relations with Nepal, and to some degree Sikkim and Bhutan, embodied many of the dilemmas and contradictions of US relations with certain states in central America during the 19th and 20th centuries. Nehru's definition of a security zone wherein India would not tolerate foreign interference corresponded to the American Monroe Doctrine, and Indians often drew that analogy. Indian policies toward the three states fluctuated among virtual military occupation, assertion of a dominant influence on foreign relations, and an effort to be a "good neighbour." For the small states of the Himalayas India was the "colossus of the south."

Unlike the Latin Americans, for whom there loomed only one colossus, however, the Himalayan states began to discover in the 1950's that for them there was also a "colossus of the north."

THE FLUCTUATING POLICIES TOWARD NEPAL

India's future relations with its largest cis-Himalayan neighbour had elicited almost no public comment from Indian leaders by the time of independence. When the new Indian government began to enunciate a policy toward Nepal, in 1950, it turned out to be premised on the same regard for territorial security that had motivated the previous government in New Delhi.[1] The British had treated Nepal as constitutionally independent without the overshadowing paramountcy that circumscribed the freedom of Indian princely states. But Britain had predominant influence over Nepal's foreign relations and, because of geographic circumstances, controlled virtually all of its external trade. Nepal and Tibet taken together constituted a buffer system between British India, on the one side, and Russia and possibly China on the other. British-Nepali treaties, the last one made at Sagauli in 1923, and the presence of a British resident at Kathmandu set the relationship under which the ruling Rana ministers of Nepal thrived for a century. The Nepali government permitted the British to recruit Gurkha soldiers for the imperial army, whose salaries remitted to Nepal provided the largest source of non-rupee foreign exchange. (Rupees were legal tender in Nepal.)

In July 1950 India signed with the government of the Ranas a new treaty which cancelled all previous agreements but in effect restated the Nepali-British treaty of 1923 with the addition of the words "complete sovereignty" applied to Nepal's status.[2] By the treaty the two governments promised to inform one another of "any serious friction or misunderstanding with any neighbouring state," which could only be China. For many years informed persons suggested that even stronger mutual security terms had been agreed upon, and in December 1959, when China's full intentions in the Himalayas were finally revealed, Nehru made public "an essential, operative part" of the 1950 accord. An exchange of letters with Nepal, he said, contained the stronger stipulation, that "Neither Government shall tolerate any threat to the security of the other by a foreign aggressor.

To deal with any such threat, the two Governments shall consult with each other and devise counter-measures."[3] In 1950 an Indo-Nepali trade treaty was also signed, which gave Nepal the right to import goods through India free of customs duties and in 1953 an agreement covering extradition was reached.

Nehru's statements on Nepal even in 1950 had the virtue of being candid to a degree seldom reached in modern diplomacy, and over one decade later they were still being cited by Nepalis who resented their implications of Indian dominance. Nehru pointed out that India's security along the Himalayas must include the defense of Nepal, because the Himalayas lie on the northern border of Nepal. Nepal is a kind of political enclave within India's well-defined geographic boundaries. Nehru asserted that "in so far as certain developments in Asia were concerned, the interests of Nepal and India were identical. For instance, to mention one point, it is not possible for the Indian Government to tolerate an invasion of Nepal from anywhere, even though there is no military alliance between the two countries."[4] And again, several months later, he explained that "much as we appreciate the independence of Nepal, we cannot allow anything to go wrong in Nepal or permit that barrier (the Himalayas) to be crossed or weakened, because that would be a risk to our own security."[5]

India's intentions toward Nepal did not rest with verbal proclamations. India dispatched units of its army to Nepal, trained Nepal's security forces, posted intelligence personnel on the Nepali-Tibetan border, and for many years bore the main responsibility for building roads and airfields linking Nepal to India. The word, sovereignty, appeared in statements regarding Nepal, but those who constructed the Indo-Nepali relationship knew that there existed an overriding Indian influence in Nepal's affairs of a stronger character than even the British had usually exerted over that country.[6]

Nepal had scarcely any foreign relations other than with India in the 1940's and early 1950's, and therefore India's influence in Nepal was felt strongly in domestic politics. Nepali liberals for many years looked to the Indian National Congress for sympathy and ultimately for support in their efforts to create democratic institutions in their own country. In 1950 they openly defied the Rana rulers and tried to launch from Indian territory a liberation of Nepal. Simultaneously Nepal's titular monarch, Tribhuvan Bir

Bikram Shah, took refuge in the Indian Embassy in Kathmandu and later was flown out to asylum in India. Fully supporting democratic reforms in Nepal, Nehru managed to mediate between the insurgents and the Ranas, having got the parties to New Delhi in January 1951. With Indian backing King Tribhuvan was restored to power in February, ruling under a new form of parliamentary democracy. For ten months in 1951 the Ranas continued to struggle for power along with other factions, including the Indian supported Nepali Congress. Indian officials and the Indian army had to intervene on several occasions to try to avoid a complete collapse of administration in the strategically located state, and no Nepali politician could survive long without some support from India. By the end of 1951 the Ranas had been eliminated as a contender for power, which seemed, however, to open the way for further splits among the democratic forces. Because of the instability of democratic politics the King was forced to use his full powers regularly just to keep the bureaucracy functioning. "The nation drifted ; politicians squabbled ; unrest flared up periodically in the countryside, and, as the government printed money to finance its directionless operations, inflation became rampant."[7]

The Indian government could scarcely avoid continual involvement in the affairs of a country whose effective lines of communication from east to west lay through India. In addition, the liberalism of many Indians made them active sympathizers with the struggles of Nepal toward democracy, and of course China's increasingly apparent presence on the other side of the mountains required constant precautions. The New Delhi government worked primarily through the king to try to establish political stability, military security, and some economic advancement, all of which aimed at strengthening Nepal's ties to India without however making the weak neighbour a satellite. It was a tricky operation, worked out on an ad hoc basis from crisis to crisis, and characterized by the classic dilemma of democratic foreign policy—the attachment to freedom versus the need for security.

King Tribhuvan's secretary was an official of the Indian civil service ;[8] the Nepali bureaucracy included Indians in advisory positions ; Nepal's army was reorganized and trained through an Indian mission set up in 1952 ; and in May 1954, less than a week after the Indian-Chinese agreement on Tibet (which included the *pancha-*

sheel), Nepal announced that Indian communications units would henceforth be stationed on the Tibetan border as a precaution against border violations. The growing Indian influence within Nepal stimulated a new spirit of nationalism in the country based on anti-Indian sentiments.[9] Alleged Indian economic exploitation reinforced other charges against Indians and resulted in violent demonstrations in Kathmandu and elsewhere. But the Nepali government knew then as it still did years later, that unless it could isolate itself from international politics—and that was no longer physically possible—its relations with India had to remain good and its collaboration had to be close.

India's policy of strengthening its influence in Nepal after the overthrow of the Ranas was carried out through attempts to infuse the country with economic assistance. The Indian aid, most of which fell nominally under the Colombo Plan, almost coincided with a very early American technical assistance programme in Nepal. (In fact the American development project, for community develop- ment, got underway, in July 1952, before the Indian operation did.)[10] Both the Indian and the American aid to Nepal aimed at keeping the country free from Chinese influence. Unfortunately, but not surprisingly in view of the failures of India and the US to cooperate in other international arenas, the two aid programmes did not supple- ment each others's political objectives in any planned way, until perhaps the mid-1960's. The failure of India and the US to colla- borate was partly due to differences in the philosophies of their economic aid and partly due to mutual suspicion of each other's influence. India apparently judged that economic progress combined with its own close ties with Nepal would be sufficient protection against China, and communism ; the US could not agree and was anxious to make its own contribution to preclude communist subversion.

The importance that India attached to constructing close physi- cal links with Nepal through economic assistance was revealed in its choice of projects and the efficiency with which they were carried to completion. Probably the most satisfactory Indian development efforts in the 1950's were building communications between Nepal and India, which the Nepalis as much as the Indians desired. Indian engineers completed construction by 1954 of the first airport serving the Kathmandu valley, the centre of the country's economic and political life. By 1955 the Tribhuvan Rajpath, a road from Kathmandu to the Indian border town of Raxaul, was in use, built in record time for such difficult terrain by the Indian army engineers. In 1954 an Indian aid mission in Kathmandu began searching for assistance projects to win for India the goodwill of the Nepali government. The latter, however, was so in the throes of competing interests and so lacking in administrative skills that it could not take full advantage of Indian (or American) willingness to undertake development projects. Irrigation and drinking water projects were launched and ultimately benefited limited numbers of people, but long delays in construction and the absence of any overall development plan disillusioned administrators and politicians on both sides.

Meanwhile King Mahendra had succeeded his father to the throne in 1955, and with the help of Prime Minister Tanka Prasad Acharya began to cultivate ties with China. Nepal's interest in "regularizing" its relations with China could have been interpreted as a move in harmony with current Indian policy. India had not objected the year before when Nepal discussed with China the opening of formal diplomatic relations on a regular basis for the first time. In 1955 ambassadors were exchanged. By 1956 King Mahendra's government appeared to be moving toward a posture of balancing its relations with India by its new ties with China, a classic posture for a state in Nepal's circumstances and one with which historically-minded Nepalis must have been familiar. A Nepali-Chinese treaty amending Nepal's traditional rights in Tibet was signed in 1956,[11] and in the same year Tanka Prasad negotiated an economic aid agreement in Peking. India became concerned ; President Rajendra Prasad made a state visit to Kathmandu, and the Nepali prime minister was persuaded to visit India. After 1956 the Nepali government applied the doctrine of nonalignment explicitly to its relations with India and China, drawing support for its policy partly from the international prestige already attached to the doctrine, and partly from the domestic appeal of an anti-Indian move.

If Nepal often appeared to be "nonaligned in favour of China" it was because its new posture required somewhat of a break with India and a special effort to cultivate China. Of course Nepal could not sensibly break its economic and cultural bonds with India, just as India could not deny itself the benefits of close Western attachments. But both states could gain, in their respective spheres, by adopting political nonalignment vis-a-vis the great powers which immediately confronted them. The analogy between India's dealings with Nepal and the West's dealings with India could be carried further by noting that both India and the West believed that they were protecting their own security and defending a weaker state against the inroads of communism when they dispensed economic and military assistance. The responses of weaker states in those circumstances were apt to be similar.

In January 1957 the Chinese prime minister, Chou En-lai, took advantage of Nepal's interest in a more independent foreign policy by visiting Kathmandu. He cemented the new trans-Himalayan ties and tried to diminish Nepali fears of Chinese intentions along the Tibetan border, which had not then been demarcated. The global powers, too, increased their overtures to Nepal, once the doors, so to speak, had been opened. Many small American undertakings began in the mid-1950's. The US involvement in the actual administration of the country in those years must have rivalled the involvement by Indians in the early 1950's[12] and naturally resulted in spasms of anti-American outbursts by politicians. Perhaps to balance US aid to his country the king visited Moscow in 1958 and returned with a promise of substantial assistance ; the following year the American programmes received a sudden increase in appropriations to meet the Soviet challenge, and in 1960 the King visited the US.

Indian and American aid efforts increasingly faced competition from the two communist states, but they could not be coordinated. Instead there was open competition and sometimes hostility between the Indian and American aid missions over such issues as the controlling interest in village development. Indo-US friction emerged again from an arrangement whereby India and the US together with Nepal undertook to build a road network—which, largely because Nepalis were unable to coordinate such a complex project, ended in near failure.[13] From the Nepali point of view, the competitive proliferation of aid projects from major and minor states such as Israel and from international agencies had the advantage of precluding dominant influence by a single foreign power. It also satisfied the aspirations of a growing middle class for an open door policy toward the outside world.

India's economic aid to Nepal increased markedly in 1956 after

China made its initial grant of rupees six crores in cash and goods. India offered rupees 10 crores for Nepal's loosely constructed first five-year plan (1956-1960) ; the US promised the equivalent of rupees eight crores. Indian aid projects included irrigation and power (the Trisuli project), health, education, village development, and road, rail, and airfield buildings. The number of Nepalis receiving training in India increased under Indian government technical training programmes. The largest item of Indian expenditure by 1962, after the Tribhuvan Rajpath, went for an aerial survey and mapping of Nepal, which along with the expanding transport network with connections into India could be considered part of the cost of India's own defense. Nepalis charged that the speed with which Indians completed the quasi-strategic projects in Nepal as compared with those having only developmental value revealed New Delhi's main interest in giving aid.

Nevertheless, and despite difficulties with the Nepali bureaucracy, India's purely developmental assistance made some headway and was expanded during the second plan (1961-1965) to include forestry and mineral projects and the completion of major multi-purpose dams on the Kosi and Gandak rivers. The projects to control the Kosi and Gandak admittedly served primarily India's long recognized need to avoid the periodic destruction that those flooding streams caused in Bihar. Some irrigation and power benefits of the two dams, located in Nepal, would remain with the Nepalis, who could not have built the dams, canals, and hydroelectric facilities themselves. But most of the controlled water supply went to India, a fact that Nepali critics of India frequently used to demonstrate their alleged exploitation by Indians. Whether or not Indian or any other aid projects in Nepal would ultimately serve to strengthen the democratic fabric of the society or keep the country free of Chinese domination was a question that the Nepalis themselves could best answer.

With or without Indian aid Nepal's foreign trade could not deviate much from its Indian orientation. India's policies on Nepali trade relations were traditionally liberal : Nepal was allowed freely to import goods across India, to tax goods entering the country from India, and to export to India without paying tariffs. Much commerce between the two countries was unrecorded because of the long, loosely guarded frontier. The 1950 trade treaty was suited to the

14

circumstances of Nepal's close dependence on India, but as Nepalis gained self-assurance in foreign policy matters they increasingly criticized certain of its terms—the requirement that Nepali and Indian tariffs be the same towards third countries, the lack of foreign exchange control separate from India's, the awkwardness of the procedures for transit of goods across India. As a result Nepal and India signed a new treaty in 1960 which permitted Nepal to construct a tariff policy independent of India's, created a Nepali foreign exchange reserve and aimed at improving transit facilities.[14]

Though Nepal's trade patterns broadened slightly beyond the traditional links with India, mostly as a result of foreign aid schemes, an estimated 95 per cent of the country's foreign commerce was still with India in the 1960's.[15] Once imports were liberalized after the overthrow of the Ranas, Nepal experienced continued trade deficits with India, only partially balanced by payments received from Gurkha soldiers in the Indian army. Contrary to popular opinion Nepal's main exports were not Gurkha troops but rice sent to India, along with tobacco, timber, hides and skins, jute goods, and some manufactures. The total values of those exports was rupees 70 million in 1957-58, 116 million in 1958-59 and 129 million in 1959-60. For the same years Nepal's imports from India were rupees 157 million, 218 million, and 269 million, consisting mainly of cotton cloth, cigarettes, hardware, kerosene and gasoline, machinery, cement, and edibles. The great value of Gurkha remittance lay in the pounds sterling earned by those serving under British colours.[16] The Nepali government refused to permit the recruitment of Gurkhas by any foreign armies other than the Indian and the British.

Political events in Nepal at the end of the 1950's revealed the continuing interest of foreign powers in the future of the most important Himalayan state. King Mahendra's personal power by then held the balance between contending political parties. After dismissing K. I. Singh, who had followed Tanka Prasad as prime minister, the king announced a general election, to be held in 1959. The Nepali Congress and the communist parties could count on some foreign support and accused each other of receiving such. The Indian government was relieved when the Nepali Congress won the elections and was allowed to form a government under B. P. Koirala, whose sympathies toward India and the West were well known. Less than a month later, in June 1959, Nehru paid his second visit to Nepal, and a joint communique proclaimed an identity of views on subjects including "the recent developments in Tibet," which had profoundly worried New Delhi.[17]

Koirala's government, however, dared not antagonize China by appearing to move towards India, especially at a time when an Indian-Chinese confrontation was clearly emerging. The very popular prime minister therefore continued the policy of balancing Chinese against Indian influence. His visit to India in January 1960 resulted in the new trade treaty, noted above, and a promise of rupees 18 crores for Nepal's new development programme. Three months later he was in Peking negotiating a border agreement and accepting a Chinese offer of rupees 10 crores of economic aid. B. P. Koirala's success in balancing Chinese and Indian external pressures was not equalled by success in overcoming domestic opposition and carrying out a programme of reform. His government grew weaker, central authority was flouted in certain districts, and finally in December 1960 King Mahendra dismissed the ministry and resumed direct, personal rule.[18]

The king's move had an immediate effect on Nepali-Indian relations, not because Mahendra wanted to alter the advantageous posture of nonalignment, but because Nehru expressed distaste for the king's abrogation of democratic forms. Nehru's words in parliament did not carry a message of animosity towards King Mahendra, just a tone of scorn.[19] They and comments appearing in the Indian press remained for several years thereafter fixed points in Nepali-Indian relations against which tides of Nepali resentment struck again and again. One year earlier, in November 1959, Nehru had restated the strategic postulate that aggression against Nepal would be considered an attack on India. Such statements were taken even by friends of India in Nepal as arrogant assertions of India's supervisory role in Nepali affairs.

Another great spurt of Nepali diplomatic effort to free the country from alleged Indian domination followed King Mahendra's seizure of the government in 1960. Unlike the earlier assertions of nonalignment, which India did not oppose, however, the king's bold international manoeuvres from 1961 to the end of 1962 elicited unofficial but strong Indian reactions, which were nearly disastrous in their effects on Nepali-Indian relations and failed to alter Nepali policies. Of greatest significance was New Delhi's tolerance of anti-Mahendra forces, chiefly the Nepali Congress, operating against the regime from the sanctuary of Indian territory. Propaganda, subversion, and outright raids against the Nepali government were launched or appeared to come from India by dissident Nepali factions, while the Indian government seemed to be unaware that flagrant breaches of international law were thereby being perpetrated.

Uncontestable facts on those activities may never be collected by unbiased historians. Even Nepalis in official positions at the time issued statements which differed on the extent of Indian involvement in efforts to shake Mahendra's rule.[20] But the fact that India became a base for certain anti-governmental moves was certain, and Nehru acknowledged it. After stating that India did not create the opposition in Nepal, he said that Nepali politicians who fled to India had been allowed to carry on peaceful propaganda against their government. "But we do object," he continued, "to India being made the base of any kind of operations against Nepal by these people. We have a long border with Nepal. There have been free entry and communications through Nepal and India and there are no check posts. It is very difficult to protect that long border. Our attitude is that we do not encourage gun-running between India and Nepal but they say we have encouraged or acquiesced in it. We have not consciously done it, and in fact we have tried to arrest it. But it is very difficult to prevent individuals from coming and going across a long and unprotected border."[21]

The king's efforts to reinforce Nepal's independence internationally naturally took the form of acquiring more outside support for his policies. Pakistan was a logical source, and although diplomatic talks on an exchange of representatives had started in early 1960, useful political relations began only when King Mahendra visited Pakistan after the Belgrade conference in September 1961 ; a trade and a transit agreement were signed in 1962 and 1963. Mahendra and Ayub Khan encouraged each other's experiments with non-parliamentary forms of government and put up a well-worded defense against Nehru's vocal criticisms of them both.[22] Mahendra continued extending Nepal's contacts with distant lands, such as Israel, New Zealand, and Argentina, often journeyed abroad—to China and Mongolia in October 1961—, and cultivated relations with regional states, such as Afghanistan and Burma.

Relations with China were of paramount concern to Nepal,

especially because Chinese troops had violated Nepali territory in June 1960 and killed a border guard. Nepal needed a firm boundary with Tibet, and China seemed prepared to reach a compromise border agreement. Chou En-lai's visit to Kathmandu in April 1961 hastened the negotiations already underway, and in October King Mahendra was able to sign a treaty defining the border when he visited Peking. Shortly thereafter China's plan to build a road from Kodari on the Nepali-Tibetan frontier to Kathmandu was finally accepted by Nepal. Although Tibet and China could not be expected to compete with India as trading partners of Nepal, the road would offer some help in opening up sections of the country and in expanding trade. But the political effects might be more startling, especially to India. Once the route from Kathmandu to Lhasa was in full service, in May 1967, China's physical contacts with the centre of Nepali political life would begin to rival India's. China's economic aid to Nepal, never as effectively used as aid from other countries, and subject to delays and cancellations, nevertheless stood as a political balancer to Indian aid. China promised another rupees 10 crores of assistance in 1960, most of which could not be immediately used, but the offer brought some political gain to both countries.

By 1962 the Indian government was trying to patch up its relations with King Mahendra, China's attack on India late in the year accelerated the process of Nepali-Indian rapprochement. New Delhi probably used its full powers to stop the anti-governmental movement operating from India ; at least the voice and activities of the latter ceased. Nepal, too, must have understood what dangers there were in a Chinese military presence on the southern side of the Himalayas and reciprocated India's moves. Large and small irritations were faced and mostly settled in the following year or two. For example, India abolished its awkward system of bonding of Nepali goods in transit across India, opened new transit points, and agreed to permit Nepal's trade with Pakistan through Indian territory. During the many official visits exchanged from 1963 onwards Nepal's main interest, in economic development, rather than India's main interest, security, gained the prominent position in the communiques. A great building project which combined the interests of both parties, the Sanauli-Pokhra highway, was revived in 1964 and opened to traffic in April 1968.

Nepal remained firmly nonaligned and took neither side in the Indian-Chinese border conflict. For its military security and its external economic relations Nepal had to rely on India and would indefinitely remain in that position. But by the mid-1960's it had achieved a remarkable political independence and international standing by adopting a posture that had brought India similar rewards.

THE MORE PREDICTABLE RELATIONS WITH SIKKIM AND BHUTAN

India's relations with Sikkim and Bhutan were an almost classic example of the pattern established between great and small states. For Sikkim at least there was scarcely an alternative, poised as it is on the edge of the most accessible route from the Indian plains into Tibet, through the Chumbi valley. For Bhutan, less accessible from the Indian side and with long standing family and religious links with Tibet, there might have been a choice once British rule in India ended, but Chinese actions in Tibet persuaded the Bhutanese government against losing Indian protection.

The characteristics of Indian dominance over the two small, weak, undeveloped Himalayan states were those of a country anxious about its physical security ; they were not those of a state seeking economic domination or ideological conformity from dependent neighbouring peoples. Furthermore, India gave evidence of being desirous to improve the well-being of the Sikkimese and Bhutanese people and to encourage their fuller participation in national life. Inevitably, successful efforts in these directions eroded the simplicity of relations as they had previously existed and created new points of contact and of friction. Because of India's often patronizing approaches, and the increasing presence of Indians in their territories, the governments of Sikkim and Bhutan felt compelled on occasions to assert their independence in order to safeguard their pride and avoid losing their identity—or, perhaps, to strike a better bargain in an economic transaction with India.

Sikkim's status when Britain ruled India was that of a protectorate, slightly superior in a legal sense to the position of the Indian princely states. But in fact, because Britain's interest in Tibet after 1890 made Sikkim's geographic position of critical importance, the British maintained stronger authority through their resident political officer in Gangtok than they held in some of the larger Indian states. By treaties between Britain and China in 1890 and 1893 the latter recognized the protecting political position of Britain in Sikkim and agreed to a delineation of the border between Sikkim and Tibet along the crest of the watershed, in return for a waiver of Sikkim's claim on the Chumbi valley.

Independent India inherited the British rights in Sikkim, but the new government entered into deliberations with the ruling family and representatives of political parties in order to define India's future relationship with that state. During the deliberations opinions on both sides which favoured either accession to India or greater autonomy for Sikkim gave way to what was essentially a reaffirmation of the British-Indian Sikkimese relationship. The treaty of December 5, 1950[23] declared that "Sikkim shall continue to be a Protectorate of India," that it "shall enjoy full autonomy in regard to its internal affairs," and that it would receive an Indian subsidy of rupees three lakhs a year. It used the strongest terms imaginable to state India's obligation and right to defend Sikkim by any means necessary and to manage the state's foreign affairs, adding that "the Government of Sikkim shall have no dealings with any foreign power." The accord also stipulated India's "exclusive right of constructing, maintaining and regulating the use of railways, aerodromes and landing grounds and air navigation facilities, posts, telegraphs, telephones and wireless installations in Sikkim," as well as the "right to construct and maintain in Sikkim roads for strategic purposes and for the purpose of improving communications with India." Sikkim was obligated to render all assistance necessary for the above. Sikkimese subjects were treated as Indian protected persons while travelling abroad and had the same rights of movement, property holding, and employment—including government service—within India as did Indian citizens. Extradition clauses were included in the treaty.

The Maharaja of Sikkim, Tashi Namgyal, relied heavily on India for advisers and administrative officials, who could also assist him in overcoming the disorders created by the unsettling demands of certain groups within the state, such as the majority Nepali community and the state Congress party. In 1949 an Indian was appointed *dewan*, chief officer of the government. The maharaja did not delegate his powers, however, and took a vigorous interest in the state's affairs. This pattern continued under his successor, the more cosmopolitan Palden Thondup Namgyal, or the Chogyal, who attained power in December 1963. Both rulers took initiatives in inaugurating schemes for economic development and social welfare and made considerable concessions towards a greater degree of representative government. In their foreign travels and articulation of views, particularly the younger man's, they sought to strengthen the image of Sikkim as an entity separate from India, and they succeeded. But they acted in the knowledge that the power of the hereditary royal house depended upon continued Indian support, and the prosperity of Sikkim was the result, at least partly, of Indian assistance. Few Sikkimese of any group desired closer relations with Tibet, especially after witnessing about 7,000 refugees from Chinese repression moving through their state in 1959. Thereafter, with the closing of the traditional trade routes into Tibet, the importance of Sikkim's new links with India increased.

From India's point of view Sikkim had to be incorporated into the forward defense structure more tightly than it was before 1950, when the buffer zone of Tibet still lay beyond. As in Nepal and elsewhere along the Himalayas supreme priority was given to communications, which could provide effective administrative control within the state and could assure immediate contact with any foreign invaders. Indian engineers succeeded in adding about 500 miles of motorable roads to the state's single road in 1951, from Rangpo to Gangtok. The strategic highways to Nathu pass and Jelep pass overlooking Yatung in the Tibetan Chumbi valley and the northern road to Lachung and connections to Patra pass reaching above Yatung provided the Indian army with excellent support for the major outposts on the Tibetan border. Sikkim gained convenient access routes to Bagdogra, the nearest civilian airport, and Siliguri, the railhead, both in West Bengal. These roads and the improved trails served Sikkim's economic development plans, which were almost entirely financed by India. Hydroelectric projects, experimental agricultural centres specializing in fruit growing, and explorations of timber and mineral resources did not equal the investments in strategic enterprises, but they demonstrated India's consideration for the progress of the local population, numbering about 750,000.

Because Sikkim was a protectorate India had no embarrassment in announcing its intention to defend the state from any Chinese attack. India used its own troops for Sikkim's external defense instead of entrusting that to a locally recruited militia. Though the Sikkim-Tibetan border was clearly delimited, and no dispute arose on its location,[24] it was the frontier most often chosen by China for its psychological show-downs with India, beginning in 1959; one example was China's threat of action during the Indo-Pakistani war in 1965.[25] Both India and China charged violations of the Sikkim-Tibetan boundary on several occasions. With India and Chinese troops literally eyeing other across the Nathu pass, and clashing there in the summer of 1967, Sikkim's position resembled a trip-wire for any major Chinese attack.

India had to accustom itself to shifting Chinese policies towards Sikkim, which often appeared as measures of China's overall intentions towards India. At one time, in early 1960, Chou-En-Lai acknowledged India's "special relationship with Sikkim,"[26] but at another, later that same year, his government refused to recognize the borders of Sikkim and Bhutan as parts of the Sino-Indian border question.[27] China progressively demonstrated its wish to deal with those two states directly. While India protested any formal communication from Peking to Gangtok not channelled through New Delhi, it was unable to counteract China's innovation in 1968 of directing messages to Sikkim through open press and radio media. China's policy added one element of unpredictability to India's relationship with Sikkim. Other factors which could affect the smooth working of the 1950 treaty were the resentment created within the formerly isolated state by the sheer numbers of Indian personnel stationed there, and the political advancement of the Sikkimese people. The conduct of India's changing relations with Sikkim was likely to benefit from its experience in dealing with Nepal.

Bhutan's position was different, and certainly was less well defined than that of Sikkim. A sparsely populated state of possibly 850,000 people with "no towns, no banks, no shops worthy of the name."[28] Bhutan's relations with India were variable and the subject of occasional misunderstandings, some of which grew out of the previous British treatment of the state. In 1910 the treaty of Punakha maintained British control of Bhutanese foreign relations within a relationship that British officials came to regard as implying suzerainty over Bhutan.[29] The treaty also provided that Britain would not intervene in Bhutanese internal affairs, and Bhutan consequently remained in almost complete isolation from outside influence until the 1950's. Not even a motorable road extended inward from its frontiers. The vagueness of the treaty, which carried over into Bhutanese-Indian relations after 1947, stemmed from the fact that Bhutan was an independent state, and therefore it could argue that its submission to Britain on foreign policy matters was merely a matter of convenience and could be withdrawn at any time. In short, Bhutan's status was not that of an internationally recognized protectorate as was Sikkim's. India's relations with the state were limited ones conducted through the political officer resident in Sikkim.

After independence India and Bhutan negotiated a new treaty, signed in August 1949, which virtually repeated the provisions of the treaty of Punakha : "The Government of India undertakes to exercise no interference in the internal administration of Bhutan. On its part the Government of Bhutan agrees to be guided by the advice of the Government of India in regard to its external relations."[30] The possibly intentional vagueness in the phrase "agrees to be guided," should be read with the treaty's provision that a disagreement over its terms had to be settled either by negotiation or by reference to a three-man tribunal made up of nominees of the two governments and an Indian federal or high court judge chosen by Bhutan. In an effort to erase some of the harsher memories of the British era, India returned to Bhutan 32 square miles of territory in the Dewangiri district of Bengal and raised the annual subsidy to rupees five lakhs a year.

Nothing in the treaty gave India the specific right or obligation to defend Bhutan. Indian officials claimed that India had that duty,[31] but on at least one occasion the unofficial prime minister of Bhutan, Jigme Polden Dorji, denied that the treaty implied such an obligation. The Bhutanese ruling families appeared anxious at once to have Indian support so as to avoid the fate of Tibet, yet not to lose their freedom of manoeuvre or be attached to India as closely as Sikkim came to be. In 1954 one of the authors met members of the Dorji family who expressed fear of possible Chinese encroachments and an almost fervent reliance on India for protection, but Bhutan refused to have Indian troops guard the Tibetan border and had stationed its own there in 1953. Jealous of its independence and unawakened from its backwardness, Bhutan sought at that time to retain its barrier of physical isolation and hesitated to allow even foreign technical specialists into the country. A decade later they were there in considerable numbers, from India.

China's aims in Bhutan, as in Sikkim and Nepal, were by no means clear, and any simple assertion of Chinese expansionist desires towards the area could not be validated. Communist Chinese atlases and maps published after 1949 listed Bhutan as an independent country, and Mao Tse-tung's written works generally avoided stating revisionist intentions toward the Himalayan states.[32] In exchanges with the Indian government on border issues China repudiated any aggressive designs on Nepal, Sikkim and Bhutan. With regard to the latter two states a Chinese note on December 26, 1959, stated that it had "no other intentions than that of living with them in friendship without committing aggression against each other. Concerning the boundary between China and Bhutan, there is only a certain discrepancy between the delineation on the maps of the two sides...."[33] Still, reports from within Tibet attributed to lesser officials for many years suggested Chinese ambitions of reasserting a control or influence over all the Himalayan regions, which were allegedly taken forcibly from China by the British imperialists. And the "discrepancies" in the Chinese note could be seen on small-scale maps of the region. A reasonable judgment was that China wanted to loosen India's influence in Bhutan, as in Nepal and probably Sikkim, either as a defensive measure or to lay foundations for a future extension of Chinese political influence southward. The first step was to deal directly with Bhutan instead of through the government of India, and Chinese efforts to do so were a recurrent cause of protest from India.

The years 1958 and 1959 put an end to Bhutan's voluntary isolation, when Chinese-Indian hostility and Chinese repression emerged into the open. Without publicly announcing a choice between the obvious alternatives of increased reliance on India or accommodation with China the Bhutanese rulers responded more favourably to Indian overtures. In September 1958 Nehru paid a unique visit to Bhutan (and Sikkim), assuring it of its independence and freedom, and also promising that India would defend Bhutan against any act of aggression. He renewed for the third time India's offer of economic aid which Bhutan's maharaja, or Druk Gyalpo, continued to refuse. The Druk Gyalpo did, however, accept Nehru's offer of Indian assistance in building roads to link the two countries and in mapping the Bhutan-Tibetan frontier. For the first time, in the 1960's, Bhutan's physical obscurity was broken, by Indian surveying parties and road builders ; in 1962 the first motor vehicles appeared in Paro, the state's temporary capital. Bhutan began its journey into the present century and the wider world.

The first and most significant Indo-Bhutanese project was the building of the lateral Phutsholing-Thimphu highway connecting three or four new roads between India and Bhutan. These new roads were meant to replace the traditional route from India via Sikkim and the Chumbi valley, which required Chinese permission to cross. They were also meant to facilitate the redirection of Bhutan's rice and other exports, an economic necessity once the Chinese sealed the Bhutan-Tibetan border and Bhutan withdrew its representative from Lhasa. In 1960 the Bhutanese government decided to reverse its earlier decision to accept some Indian economic aid. India granted rupees 10.5 crores for the first five-year plan and deputed technicians to train the Bhutanese and assist in the establishment of an infrastructure for a modern economy.

In the late 1950's India had made few preparations to meet any threat to Bhutan from the north. But in 1961 and 1962 the Indian army was able to make preliminary plans with the Bhutanese for improvement of the state's defenses, including arrangements for air as well as road transport of forces in case of emergency. (No operations took place in Bhutan's territory during the 1962 conflict with China.) The period of vastly increased Indo-Bhutanese collaboration initiated in 1959 reached its climax when the Druk Gyalpo, Jigme Dorji Wangchuk, and his chief advisor, Jigme Dorji, toured India in January and February 1961. On that occasion the two governments reportedly reached agreements on India's defense responsibilities in Bhutan, trade relations, an Indian military training mission, increased economic aid, Bhutan's entry into international organizations and its agreement not to deal with the Chinese except through India.[34] The public's vagueness about those proceedings resulted, in some measure, from Bhutan's anxiety about provoking any counter-measures from China against the unprecedented relations with India. High level exchanges of visits continued to be made on both sides, and Prime Minister Sastri and the Druk Gyalpo met at Calcutta in 1965.

Having begun to open itself to alien, i.e. Indian, influence on a large scale Bhutan became more interested in having contacts with other countries as well. Without being anti-Indian, this desire was allied to a doubt about the wisdom of total reliance on India. China's overtures of friendship and its demonstrated military superiority in 1962 fanned the doubts and intensified Bhutan's insistence on its right to establish direct relations with other states—subject to the general guidance on foreign affairs by India. Nehru's government was against the idea of having foreign missions in sensitive areas of the northeast. But India was obliged to respect Bhutan's wishes, if only to avoid antagonism, and could not confuse "guidance" with "control." Accordingly, in 1961 India sponsored Bhutan's membership in the Colombo Plan and in 1966 agreed to do so for the Universal Postal Union. Bhutan's postage stamps alone assured it international recognition, and the trend was unlikely to turn back toward isolationism.

The leadership of Jigme Dorji, who constructed Bhutan's more open door policy towards India, ended abruptly on April 5, 1964, when he was assassinated in a vaguely identified plot against the government. The event did not succeed, however, in dislodging the ruling family from its position of power. Jigme Dorji's younger brother, Lhendup Dorji, assumed charge of the government, temporarily as it developed, until the Druk Gyalpo himself took charge as chief executive in November. Bhutan continued its close reliance on India and its adherence to the 1949 treaty. But as his brother had done so Lhendup Dorji insisted that his country was not an Indian protectorate and retained its full sovereignty.[35]

India's interests in the three Himalayan states continued to rest, after independence, on considerations of security. Political and economic relations acquired far more substance, but for India and often for the states themselves, those important links had to reinforce the inescapable mutual security interests of all states bordering on Tibet. India's only permanent sphere of influence existed in the Himalayas, unashamedly inherited from Britain. India had to proclaim its intention to defend that area against any foreign threat, and that constituted the only external defense commitment made by the government after 1947.

India learned to tread softly when national or princely pride and desire for freedom of action among the leaders of the three states seemed to threaten its position of influence, and New Delhi had gained considerable skill by the 1960's in tailoring its policies to the unique needs, sensitivities, and physical condition of each state. After blundering for over a decade in dealings with Nepal India finally adjusted to the latter's nonalignment posture and recognized Nepali determination to use it to maintain independence. If a case should have developed in which Nepal might have lost that independence, India would certainly have intervened. In a more patronizing and assured manner it dealt with Sikkim and Bhutan within the terms of the treaties made respectively with those states, which gave India virtually all the influence that it needed.

NOTES AND REFERENCES

[1] An isolated reference to Nepal made by Nehru in October 1946 hinted at the attitude that soon became apparent in official policy : |"Nepal is an independent country so far as we are concerned. If, in future, Nepal chooses to have some kind of closer union with India, we shall welcome it." Cited in D. Norman, *Nehru : The First Sixty Years*, N. Y. 1965, vol. II, p. 269.

[2] The 1923 treaty referred only to Nepal's "independence, both internal and external." Texts of both treaties are in Girilal Jain, *India Meets China in Nepal*, appendices D and E. The 1950 text is in *Foreign Policy of India : Texts of Documents 1947-59*, p. 31f.

[3] Nehru's statement in the Rajya Sabha, Dec. 8, 1959, Nehru, *India's Foreign Policy*, p. 374.

[4] Speech in parliament, March 17, 1950, *Speeches 1949-1953*, p. 146.

[5] Speech in parliament, Dec. 6, 1950, *ibid.*, p. 177.

[6] The close Indo-Nepali ties, particularly in defense matters, were discussed by the Nepali statesman, Rishikesh Shah, in his *Nepal and the World*, published by the Nepali Congress, Kathmandu, in 1955, with an introduction by the eminent politician, B. P. Koirala. See, esp., p. 45.

[7] Mihaly, *Foreign Aid and Politics in Nepal*, p. 24.

[8] *ibid.*, p. 25.

[9] See Anirudha Gupta, *Politics in Nepal 1950-60*, p. 55f.

[10] A full and critical discussion of all foreign economic aid efforts in Nepal may be found in Mihaly's book, *op. cit.*

[11] Text in Jain, *op. cit.*, appendix F.

[12] See Mihaly, *op. cit.*, pp. 75-76.

[13] *ibid.*, p. 128

[14] See *FAR*, vol. VI, 9 (Sept. 1960), p. 204f.

[15] Y. P. Pant, *Economic Development of Nepal*, p. 103.

[16] *ibid.*, pp. 98-104.

[17] Text of communique in *Foreign Policy of India : Texts of Documents 1947-59*, pp. 375-76.

[18] The complex reasons for the move were dealt with in Gupta, *op. cit.*, p. 157f. and Joshi and Rose, *Democratic Innovations in Nepal*, p. 384f.

[19] Statement in Rajya Sabha, Dec. 20, 1960, *Speeches 1957-63*, p. 274.

[20] Tulsi Giri and Rishikesh Shah, both members of the council of ministers, took opposite sides on the nature of alleged Indian involvement and how to deal with it. See Joshi and Rose, *op. cit.*, pp. 426-28. An official statement of the case against India appeared in Prakash Bahadur, K. C., *Hostile Expeditions and International Law*, Kathmandu : Department of Publicity and Broadcasting, April 1962.

[21] Press conference, London, Sept. 20, 1962, *Speeches 1957-1963*, pp. 274-75.

[22] cf. Girilal Jain in the *Times of India*, Nov. 14 and 23, 1961.

[23] Full text in *Foreign Policy of India : Texts of Documents 1947-59*, pp. 37-40.

[24] Govt. of India, *Notes, Memoranda and Letters Exchanged Between the Governments of India and China* (White Paper), no. III, p. 79 ; and *ibid.*, no. XIV. Included in the latter citation was a Chinese note of April 1967, which stated that "The boundary between China and Sikkim has long been formally delimited, and there is neither any discrepancy between the maps nor any dispute in practice." p. 14.

[25] See China's notes of Sept. 8 and 16, 1965, in *ibid.*, no. XII, pp. 39, 43.

[26] At a news conference on April 25, 1960 ; discussed in the *Asian Recorder*, 1965, p. 6753 ; noted by the Indian government in *Report of the Officials . . . on the Boundary Question*, New Delhi 1961, p. 270.

[27] At the boundary officials' talks ; see *ibid.*, pp. 270-71.

[28] Karan and Jenkins, *The Himalayan Kingdoms*, p. 37.

[29] See Charles Bell, *Tibet, Past and Present*, London 1924, p. 203 ; and Benegal Rau, *India's Constitution in the Making*, rev. edn., Bombay 1963, p. 395f.

[30] *Foreign Policy of India : Texts of Documents 1947-59*, p. 17.

[31] *RSD*, vol. XXVI, Aug. 25, 1959, cols. 1703-04 ; and *RSD*, vol. XXVII, Dec. 8, 1959, cols. 1716-17, provided Nehru's statements on Bhutan's defense.

[32] See Mao Tse-tung, *Selected Works*, vol. 2, Bombay 1954, p. 196 ; vol. 3, p. 72.

[33] White Paper no. III, p. 79.

[34] Those and other reported terms agreed upon were not officially publicized ; they were collected from published sources and reproduced in an unpublished paper written by a US State Department official which cannot be directly cited.

[35] See *The Statesman*, Calcutta, Aug. 11 and Nov. 30, 1964.

CHAPTER IX

RELATIONS WITH NONALIGNED
STATES IN SOUTHEAST ASIA

THE HISTORY OF India's external relations with certain countries before 1947 provides a basis for understanding post-independence Indian foreign policies. But this background was so nearly absent with regard to southeast Asia that a discussion of India's relations with that region can easily appear to be an afterthought, a superficial digression from the main themes. Many writers have discussed at length the substantial cultural influences of India on southeast Asia, and contemporary statesmen have suggested that those ancient ties could bear the loads of modern diplomatic interchanges. Nehru and other leaders stressed the importance of traditional ties, which had been broken by several centuries of foreign domination. But when that foreign domination withdrew, and succession states had to initiate new relations with each other, the traditional unformulated cultural and economic contacts could scarcely be revived as a basis for modern diplomacy.

Geographic propinquity meant much less in Asia than it did in Europe—international transportation was rudimentary, and distances seemed vast. The economies of south and southeast Asian states were largely competitive, defense arrangements for both regions in modern times were based on Western imperial considerations instead of regional needs, and the cultures and languages of India and of southeast Asia (whether native or Western) provided few links of modern significance.[1] Indian leaders recognized the lack of many unifying elements between their country and their Asian neighbours, particularly to the southeast. Scarcely any of them had visited southeast Asia, nor did they show much interest in travelling in that direction after independence ; their important foreign political and economic interests were in the West, and the inspiration for India's modern economic and cultural development was also there.[2] If India was to have any but the most perfunctory relations with southeast Asia the government would have to become alert to possibilities for new bonds of common interest with some or all of the states of that region, and if possibilities were not apparent it would have to invent them.

Nehru and many other Asian leaders expected that once the "artificial" isolation imposed by Western colonialism on the states of Asia was removed Asian peoples would coalesce into mutually beneficial association. A "resumption of old ties" would somehow take place, and possibly those ties would spread to include other nations whose political destinies seemed more closely aligned with Asia than with Europe. Nehru's conceptions of regional unity in Asia were known before independence. They appeared in his writings,[3] and he restated his views publicly. In August 1946 Nehru spoke of "federations" of Asian countries which would include India and lands to the west or to the southeast,[4] and in parliamentary debates after independence he struck the same theme with suitable variations. Indian diplomats initiated the Afro-Asian bloc in the UN, and the Indian government led others in the region in calling international conferences.

However, by the early 1950's Nehru had lost interest in promoting the unity of Asia in any organized fashion : several regional conferences and diplomatic experiences in the UN had revealed as many conflicts among Asian states themselves as between Western and Asian states. The Asian Relations Conference of 1947 brought out the fears of small states of possible domination by China or India.[5] China's new and militant adherence to a communist system precluded any general Asian collaboration, if only because of the reluctance of a communist state to align itself with the interests of non-communists. Furthermore, while pursuing a policy of friendship with China India could not justifiably seek political arrangements with non-communist south and southeast Asian states, because such associations could not avoid the appearance of being anti-communist, thus anti-Chinese.

India's main objective in southeast Asia was to assist the creation and support the maintenance of independent states in the region. In pursuing that objective India had to face the dilemma that doing anything concrete to that end would also tend to defeat it, because India could be regarded as a powerful alien influence in the area. The Indian government discovered that the isolation of India from

15

southeast Asia which had taken place during the colonial period was not as artificial as it had appeared. To break down that isolation would have required an assumption of active leadership by India of a kind that smaller states might have found objectionable and that Nehru's own philosophy of international relations would have condemned. Nehru felt genuine repugnance against power alignments based on military agreements. The other possibilities for creating bonds of common interest between India and southeast Asia were economic and cultural arrangements ; but in those also India could easily be accused of dominating the associations. In the mid-1940's Nehru had spoken and written of an "inevitable" Indian leadership in Asia,[6] so openly in fact that smaller countries in the Indian Ocean region suspected that an independent India might inherit the British concept of Indian Ocean hegemony.[7] The fact that Indian troops were used to re-establish alien control in parts of southeast Asia after the war could not easily be forgotten.[8] After independence spokesmen for India showed great caution in suggesting that India was destined for leadership in any part of Asia, and the government exerted no specific pressures in behalf of Indian influence in Asia.

As a result of caution, Nehru's dislike of any power-wielding tactics, and the absence of close traditional political ties among Asian states, India's diplomacy in Asia was very largely a diplomacy by proclamation, which brought an immediate, post-independence sense of psychological unity to south and southeast Asia and created for it influence in other parts of the world, but which produced few tangible long-term benefits for India. India's diplomacy by proclamation was intended to encourage nationalism and result in a unified political front among the states of Asia, based on common interests defined, varyingly, as anti-colonialism, nonalignment, peaceful coexistence, and *panchasheel*. Sometimes added to these notions were anti-racialism, the economic development effort, and the commonly-expressed "resurgence of Asia." Each of these ideas developed a rich literature of its own, and each of them reflected some real interest of Asian states. Indian diplomacy endeavoured to create and extend an "area of peace," as Nehru termed it, the nonaligned "third bloc" in the terminology of others, particularly in south and southeast Asia. Nehru eschewed direct approaches to build up a cohesive regional arrangement, because, he said, to do so "frightens people, especially those we wish to approach."[9] India relied, therefore, on the psychological approach of proclaiming common purposes and trusting perhaps that real unity would thereby emerge.

As described in chapter III, Nehru's "peace area," wherein military alignments had no place, served as a kind of buffer between conflicting spheres of influence of the great power coalitions, and it might also have gradually nurtured regional unity and tangible collaboration. However, the countries of southeast Asia interpreted Indian policy as one of weakness and formulated their own policies according to the actual power available to themselves, and sometimes through alliances with others, for the pursuit of their own objectives. Southeast Asia rapidly melted into a fluid political instability reminiscent of the 19th century, when European states and China vied amongst themselves for power in that region. Proclamations by Indian and regional spokesmen about nonalignment could not erect a meaningful barrier against pressure of foreign governments and of domestic contenders for power, none of whom were deterred from their objectives by the intangible influence of ideas.

Nonalignment described a common posture vis-a-vis the major military blocs ; it did not create mutually beneficial links between the nonaligned states themselves. Similarly, other proclamations of common interest, for example, anti-colonialism, made by India and the states of southeast Asia aligned and nonaligned were more often doctrines applicable to relations between Asian states and the great powers than to relations among the regional states themselves. Though unproductive of the support from southeast Asian states that India needed, its diplomacy by proclamation had the substance of a national purpose behind it. Nehru and some Indian leaders believed that the new international order envisioned in the UN Charter could most easily be realized among states which had not participated in the modern European heritage of power politics, broken treaties and wars. Newly independent states could build their relations with each other on new basis and provide an example to other states beset by the fears and rivalries of the past. Contrary to the interpretations placed on it by Western statesmen, the concept of "resurgent Asia" did not mean that a new and rapidly growing power centre had entered global politics—Nehru was sincere when he denied wanting to promote a third bloc of non-aligned states. It meant that many newly independent states insisted that their interests in peace and in international cooperation should weigh heavily in the policy decisions of the established powers. With the breakdown of imperialism a new era had begun ; its rightful spokesmen, it was argued, were non-Europeans and others who could comprehend the aspirations of long subjugated peoples.

The paramount requirement for the emergence of a state system in south and southeast Asia based on the Indian conception of international peace and cooperation was the elimination of all Western power from the region. It was trite to demonstrate that the main, or only, interest held in common among most of the states of Asia and Africa was the negative one of anti-colonialism. There was nothing artificially contrived in India's efforts to encourage a united diplomatic front against the remaining imperial regimes in southeast Asia (Malaya excepted) : European governments still dominated large portions of the region and were reluctant to withdraw. The promotion of anti-colonialism in the wider context of west Asia and Africa was an Indian foreign policy because of the moral and psychological inclination to conceive of any remaining colonial regime as a standing threat and challenge to nationalism and human freedom everywhere.

Nehru's government did not subscribe to the view, common in American thinking, that the withdrawal of Western power from southeast Asia would leave a "vacuum," into which the power of other states would automatically be drawn.[10] From the Indian standpoint such a view was put forward to justify the continuation of Western imperialism in some form and disregarded the character and strength of Asian nationalism. Indians accepted the premise that the presence of alien governments in the region had originally introduced the politics of military power, because of the need to hold nations in subjugation and defend one imperial regime against another. It therefore seemed to them to follow that Western withdrawal would leave southeast Asian nations free to pursue their own peaceful, non-aggressive ways—as the US cut itself off from the entanglements of European politics in the 19th century. The Indian government made no arrangements to replace Western military power with its own, and until the 1960's it did not agree with Western states that force was required to inhibit an expansion of Chinese power into southeast Asia.

The main difficulty experienced by India and other Asian states in repudiating Western imperialism and its heritage of power politics resided in the continued and necessary involvement of the West in Asian affairs. Some Asian states welcomed that involvement, others could not escape it. India, while proclaiming against it, worked more closely on regional matters with Western than with Asian states. India's persistent efforts to assist in the withdrawal of Western power from southeast Asia began with the declarations of the Asian Relations Conference in New Delhi in 1947, and publicity in behalf of anti-colonialism continued through conferences passing resolutions on Indonesia (New Delhi 1949) and Indo-China (Colombo 1954) and dealing with colonialism in general (Bandung 1955). But Indian diplomacy was more effective in the UN (on Indonesian-Dutch relations), at Geneva (on an Indo-Chinese truce and a Loatian settlement), and in private Commonwealth consultations (to meet crises in Burma and Malaya). A regional economic conference was held in Simla in 1955, but it failed to produce agreement among southern Asian governments on regional collaboration in the allocation and use of foreign aid. The Colombo Plan, however, with largely Western financing, succeeded. In the collection of data and the analysis of economic conditions the United Nations ECAFE was the only source for south and southeast Asia as a whole.

India's apparently excessive reliance on Western collaboration in diplomatic and technical arrangements for southern Asia was mitigated by certain direct relationships that it established with the countries of the region. There were technical and military assistance schemes between India and the countries to the south. Southeast Asia's surplus food production and certain of its raw materials went to Indian markets, and Indian textiles and consumer goods competed with imports from Japan and later China throughout the region. The problems of Indians settled in Malaya, Burma, and Ceylon brought these states into direct negotiations with India.

But in none of these direct relationships with southeast Asia were India's crucial political or economic interests directly at stake. Southeast Asia, from the vantage point of New Delhi, was peripheral to the geographic and political centres of major concern to it.

The secondary status of southeast Asian states in India's political perspective was reinforced in the conduct of diplomatic relations by conscious feelings of cultural superiority on the part of some Indian officials assigned to dealings with those countries. Furthermore, the disintegration of democratic political institutions in southeast Asia discouraged the Indian government from viewing the area as susceptible to close political collaboration.

In the early 1960's India began to shift the priorities of its objectives in southeast Asia. Whereas the creation of regional unity through encouragement of nonalignment and anti-colonialism appeared to be a prime Indian objective in the region in the 1940's and 1950's, the physical security of the region against overt communist attacks became a major concern in the 1960's. Awareness of the dangers of communist subversion within southeast Asian states and the support they received from Peking and Moscow was a recognizable aspect of India's foreign policy since 1947.[11] Nehru supported the Burmese and Malayan governments' anti-communist campaigns. But he believed that communism was chiefly a social and economic movement, which could best be checked by reform and advancement. He rejected the propositions that the main threat of communism was its militancy, which could be defeated by force alone, and that all communist movements formed parts of a grand strategy of expansionism based on a monolithic Moscow-Peking axis. Specifically, he doubted China's interest or capability of "extension toward southeast Asia or in any other direction."[12]

Without publicly altering those general views, in the 1960's Nehru recognized the imminent danger to the independence of southeast Asian states from the expansion of Chinese power through the agency of local communist movements. A belated Indian desire to achieve collaboration with regional states, notably during the brief tenure of Prime Minister Sastri in 1965, faced the formidable fact that there had been little close contact on matters of concrete mutual interests over the previous two decades. Without political leverage in the area India could by then do little more than witness the struggle for power conducted by China and the US and their respective allies.

A closer examination of India's diplomatic dealings with southeast Asian states may illustrate the various objectives that India sought in that region and explain why its diplomacy in Asia was one of its least effective efforts.

THE IMPORTANCE OF ANTI-COLONIALISM :
RELATIONS WITH INDONESIA

For Nehru, hopes of Asian unity were linked to expectations of Indian influence in an Asia where nationalism would overcome imperialism. "We have become," said Nehru to the constituent assembly, "—let us recognize it—leaders of the freedom movement of Asia. . . ."[13] China, racked by civil war, could not challenge such a view. In March-April 1947 thirty-one Asian governments, including Egypt and Turkey and "autonomous" Soviet provinces attended an Asian Relations Conference in New Delhi. The only inspiring and influential part of the proceedings, held in a ruined Moghul fort, was that they took place at all. The Conference record, with its visionary and imprecise semantics, stands as a testament to the non-political, non-pragmatic approach of democratic Asian leaders at that time : "spiritual" and "cultural" values, most delegates said, should govern their newly-resumed relations and reveal the beneficent influences of Asia on the world's problems.[14]

Far more effective was a second Indian sponsored meeting, in January 1949, whose specific purpose was to provide diplomatic support for the Indonesian independence movement. Western governments, notably the US, expressed their apprehension privately to India that the meeting might inaugurate a regional bloc of anti-Western states. Official Indian statements linking the American and Dutch policies in Europe supported that concern.[15] The timing and the issue were right for an initiative toward a regional union ; tentative discussions took place in New Delhi, and on March 8 Nehru said in parliament that his government was continuing its exploration of possible methods of "close cooperation." No discernible results, however, came from those moves. Nehru did not wish to antagonize the West or the Soviet Union, and the Indian government issued statements to assuage foreign fears about a non-White bloc of states.

More determining still of the future of Asian unity in 1949 was the rise of the communist regime in China : "It was impossible to think of accepting China in any regional arrangement for Asia without making it a hotbed for communist intrigues ; likewise, any association formed to counter the Chinese situation would mean a definite lining up of Asia with the West and behind some of the regimes of the continent which felt threatened by China. . . ."[16] Later efforts at unity, no longer sponsored by India, foundered on the same rocks of communism and "cold war" alignments ; no regional identities could move safely over those obstacles.

The conference on Indonesia in 1949 succeeded in binding closer together the interests and policies of India and Indonesia. India had recognized the Indonesian republican government in March 1947, just after the signing of the Indonesian-Dutch Linggadjati agreement. When the Dutch resumed their "police action" later that year India ended all Dutch flying rights over India and in concert with Australia brought the issue to the Security Council, which censured the Dutch move. During the next two years of debate on the first great colonial issue to come before the UN India led the diplomatic action. The 1949 regional conference added weight to the pro-Indonesian forces in UN, which ultimately with American pressure on the Netherlands, resulted in the permanent withdrawal of the Dutch.

The enthusiasm for Indonesia's nationalism in India matched the importance of the new nation in Indian external relations. The largest southeast Asian state is also the one, with the exception of Burma, most strategically placed from the standpoint of Indian security. The defense of the Indian Ocean and its narrow exists and entrances on the east are equally the concern of Indonesia and India. The island of Sumatra reaches so close to the Indian Nicobar Islands—about 100 miles distance—that Indonesia's friendship meant much to India's defense planners. As the world's most populous Muslim state a friendly Indonesia struck Indian political leaders as a great asset exposing the Pakistani contention that Muslim states should support each other against such threats as "Hindu India." The trade between India and Indonesia, governed by a treaty of 1951 and periodic extensions which identified commodities to be traded, increased during the 1950's, and Indonesia was one of the few countries in southeast Asia with which India did not have an unfavourable balance of payments. The bilateral trade, however, was of marginal significance to both countries ;

India's main export, textiles, had to meet tough competition from Japan in the 1960's.

Beyond the tangible Indo-Indonesian involvements in the 1940's and 1950's lay more fundamental reasons for the political collaboration between the two states. Like Nehru's government, the government led by Sukarno and Hatta was anti-totalitarian, inclined toward socialist goals, and vigorously nonaligned. The similarity of Indian and Indonesian responses to political crises, such as in Korea, Indo-China, and Suez, seemed almost instinctive, but the numerous meetings between Nehru and President Sukarno and other officials suggested carefully planned joint political strategies. In the UN the two states supported each other's resolutions, and in regional conferences they acted in powerful concert. Even in military affairs India and Indonesia discovered the advantages of some lightly publicized cooperation. In 1951 Indonesian officers began training at Indian bases ; in 1953 the practice began of exchanging air force personnel, and over 3,000 Indonesian air force pilots were trained by Indians ; in 1958 mutual assistance in naval development was agreed to, which led to exchanges of officers and India's first non-Commonwealth joint naval exercises, in 1960 ; and a general agreement on collaborative relations between the two armies was signed in 1960, to continue for five years. India gave Indonesia the benefit of its UN diplomatic skills in pressing for negotiations between the Netherlands and Indonesia on the transfer of West Irian (West New Guinea) ; Sukarno provided strong statements supporting India on Goa. Both governments sought to make the *panchasheel* doctrine a viable alternative to the introduction of military forces from outside the region ; if proclamations could have settled the civil wars of the area and produced the local strength necessary to preclude outside interferences those of India and Indonesia would have amply sufficed.

The supreme product of proclamation diplomacy and Indian-Indonesian collaboration was the Asian-African Conference at Bandung in April 1955. Ali Sastroamidjojo, prime minister of Indonesia, was the main initiator of the unprecedented Bandung meeting, where 29 states in Asia, Africa, and the middle east were represented for a six-day period of getting acquainted and drafting resolutions. Sastroamidjojo had been doubtful of Nehru's and U Nu's approval of the conference idea when he had raised the subject at the top level meetings in April 1954 of the leaders of Indonesia, India, Ceylon, Pakistan and Burma. Later Nehru agreed to the plan, and at Bogor, Indonesia, in December 1954 the five states reached agreement on the subjects to be discussed and coun- tries to be invited. On Nehru's initiative the Peking government received an invitation, and China's anticipated participation became the major attraction that the conference could offer and a major reason for holding the affair.[17]

To bring China into peaceful involvement with the other parti- cipants and thereby to help to break through China's diplomatic isolation, to gain reassurance from China about its reported support of subversive movements in the region and the political use it was making of Chinese residents in various southeast Asian states, and to establish an Asian rather than an international communist identification for Chinese policies were the main thrusts of Indian diplomacy at Bandung. The conference's sponsors conceived of the meeting "as an educational device which would serve to enlighten the Chinese as to the realities of their international environment and to educate leaders of those non-Communist Asian and African states which had little or no contacts with Communist China as to the actual attitudes of Peking's leaders. . . ."[18] Of less importance to India was the appearance of unity among Afro-Asian states that the conference might give and the possibility of spreading more widely the doctrines of *panchasheel*, or peaceful coexistence, and nonalignment.

The Bandung conference was a dramatic affair from the time that an Air India plane carrying Chinese and North Korean delega- tes from Hong Kong crashed, possibly due to sabotage, to the occasion of Chou En-lai's offer to reach accommodation with the US possibly through the mediation of some conference participants. The gathering drew attention to the strengths of will of many non- European statesmen and the potential of their states in tangible power. The political talents represented at Bandung produced a formidable array by any international standards, and the compara- tive smoothness of the proceedings and the high level of the discus- sions gave an impressive surface manifestation of the "resurgence of Asia."

Viewed in perspective, the Asian-African Conference was the greatest exploration of the possibility of Asian regionalism in our times. But no changes in the political configuration of Asia resulted from the six days of discussions and debates, because the three groupings of states, communist, nonaligned, and pro-Western, had reached a certain degree of rigidity. Despite great differences the states found their way to agreement on broad principles, such as human rights and colonialism, and a few specifics, such as West Irian and Palestine. But "their discussions were conspicuous for their concern with matters over which they had little direct control, as in case of nuclear weapons, or which represented grievances against nations not in attendance. . . . the less the assembled nations could do about a given problem, the louder they talked about it."[19] Apart from the Chinese gestures of conciliation towards their southeast Asian neighbours, the most noted and influential stand taken at the conference issued from governments which had announced their opposition to communism and had aligned themselves with the West. The conference halls resounded on many occasions and with unexpected eloquence with explanations of the Western alignments of nearly one-half of the states present.

India's diplomacy and Nehru's personal stature suffered in the Bandung atmosphere which the prime minister himself had helped to create. Ironically, the loss of influence experienced by India at Bandung, and after, derived from the vigorous repudiation there by many states of Nehru's foreign policy pronouncements, while they acknowledged with gratification many of the same doctrines being enunciated by Chou En-lai. Not the pronouncement but the power of the state behind it, it might appear, carried the greater weight. Chou En-lai gave offense to no one ; his moderation and graciousness escaped no one's attention. Nehru on several occasions appeared in sharp contrast, demanding that certain procedures be followed and subjects discussed, peevishly acting as one used to being the centre of attention but then passed over. One witness reported that "both the Indonesian and Ceylonese delegations were antagonized by what they regarded as overbearing and patronizing attitudes on the parts of Nehru and V. K. Krishna Menon."[20] Nehru's attacks on states which had aligned themselves, either way, seemed to militate against his stated aim of avoiding disputes and stressing unity ; by accepting alignments with great powers, said Nehru, African and Asian states "degrade themselves . . . humiliate themselves."[21]

In addition to the failure of Nehru's personal diplomacy, India's example of nonalignment no longer attracted many Asian leaders, who faced concrete problems that appeared to require immediate solutions from positive policies. The Iraqi representative, for instance, challenged India to propose an international arrangement, a third bloc united in mutual defense, that would preclude the necessity of small states' depending on a great power for security. The Filipino delegate, answering Nehru's criticism of military arrangements, observed that India was spending about one-half of its national budget (sic) on military preparations against Pakistan. Thus, the conference defined, at last, the limitations of India's influence in Asia through sponsorship of the doctrines of peaceful coexistence and nonalignment ; it was a watershed in India's political use of those doctrines. China's verbal adherence to the *panchasheel* and downplaying of its own aligned posture, on the other hand, threw a novel and reassuring light on its foreign objectives, and Chou En-lai grew accordingly in personal stature and influence. Nehru's aim of conducting China onto an arena of predictable diplomatic dealings succeeded at Bandung, and simultaneously India's own influence suffered an eclipse in southeast Asia.

India's difficulty at Bandung could be summed up in this way : among states which were rapidly settling into fairly predictable patterns of diplomatic behaviour in keeping with contemporary assessments of their respective interests, India offered little more than verbal support—or criticism. Except with respect to Pakistan and perhaps China, India appeared unable or unwilling to exert tangible power, at a time when other states, notably China and the US, brought their power into play. As it happened in other contexts, India's posture of nonalignment suited its relations with the great powers but not with the regional ones.

At Bandung and elsewhere Nehru pointed out the way for improved relations between southeast Asian states and China. Indonesia, for one, decided to pursue that course and within a few years thereby jeopardized its relations with India. The increasing radicalism of the Indonesian government in the later 1950's notably in its relations with Western states, contrasted sharply with India's growing economic dependence on the West and moderation on colonial issues. Indonesia's intemperance was met by apparent sympathy and tangible support from Peking and Moscow, but by apprehension in New Delhi. In response to Indonesia's uncompromising anti-colonialism and its plea for support in demanding that the Dutch give up West Irian, India provided the expected favourable pronouncements but refused to admit the propriety of Indonesia's threat to use force to take the territory ; Nehru publicly cautioned Indonesia on any resort to force.[22]

In 1961, at the Belgrade conference, Sukarno discovered that Nehru had lost much of his old anti-colonialist bite and had to accept a conference declaration that did not mention West Irian. The divergent manners in which India and Indonesia dealt with Western cultural influences and businesses in their territories, the great contrast in the relative strengths of the communist movements in the two countries, and the disparity between Indian constitutionalism and President Sukarno's "guided democracy" reinforced the alienation between the two states that foreign policy differences were bringing about.

The main difference appeared when the Indian-Chinese conflict in the Himalayas erupted into public view. Although in 1958 Indonesia had a grievance against Peking's support of the Chinese minorities in its territories, it nevertheless failed to criticize the Chinese repression in Tibet and its military policy on the Indian frontier. At the time of the Indian-Chinese war in 1962 Indonesia assumed impartiality and with other regional states tried to mediate in the dispute, an open acknowledgement of how slender the old tie with India had become. Even earlier, at the Fourth Asian Games in Djakarta in September 1962 a public turning point in Indian-Indonesian relations had arrived. Indonesian mobs had shown their disrespect for India and Indians by raiding the Indian embassy, and the crowd at the games had jeered the winning Indian soccer team. Those incidents resulted from a statement by the Indian vice-president of the Asian Games Federation criticizing Indonesian refusal to issue visas to athletes from Israel and Nationalist China, charter members of the federation.

In 1963 Indonesian foreign policy moved into greater conformity with Chinese policies, not only in the vigour of its anti-Western propaganda but more concretely in the drive against the newly formed state of Malaysia. Whereas India welcomed the formation of Malaysia in September 1963 Indonesia sought to destroy the new union and launched a military "confrontation" against the state. Nehru and later Foreign Minister Swaran Singh sympathized with Malaysia's efforts to protect itself against Indonesian attacks.[23] They invoked the *panchasheel*, which Sukarno had earlier supplanted by his contrary proposition that peaceful coexistence was impossible so long as "old established forces" held sway.

What brought India's relations with Indonesia to a state of such disrepair in the early 1960's, however, was not so much the divergence of policies toward Malaysia and China, as the growing gap between the two leaders, Nehru and Sukarno, and their styles of political behaviour.[24] Sukarno's ambitions stretched beyond Indonesia and ran against the already established reputation of Nehru in world affairs and the prestige of India, which surpassed that of Indonesia. Proclaiming his intentions of downgrading India, Sukarno renamed the Indian Ocean the Indonesian Ocean in July 1963. He travelled widely canvassing support for a bloc of "New Emerging Forces" and cultivating relations with states with which India had difficulties. In June 1963 he was in Pakistan pointing out the mutual interest of the two countries in checking the power of India. On that occasion Sukarno hesitated to announce publicly his sympathy for Pakistan's stand on Kashmir, but he did so when Pakistani Foreign Minister Bhutto visited Djakarta in April 1964. When Sukarno again visited Pakistan, in September 1964, even clearer backing was offered to Pakistani policy on Kashmir.[25]

Sukarno's rivalry with the Indian prime minister and his flagrant personal demeanour offended Nehru and other Indians, and Indonesia's military potential worried them. When Indonesia broke its ties to the UN, in January 1965, the Indian government's assessment of Sukarno's foreign policy as irresponsible and dangerously pro-Chinese was confirmed. In September of the same year the Indian embassy in Djakarta and consulate in Medan were sacked by mobs of young Indonesians with the obvious approval of their government. At the Second Nonaligned Conference in Cairo the following month Indian and Indonesian delegates clashed repeatedly, as they did in the preparatory meetings of the abortive second Afro-Asian conference, over the appropriateness of peaceful coexistence and the seating of Malaysia.

During the many years of deteriorating Indian-Indonesian relations the New Delhi government, stifled in foreign relations by what the British used to call masterly inactivity, merely watched and waited. No moves were made publicly to antagonize Indonesia or to check its growing political collaboration with China or Pakistan ; some unpublicized strengthening of the Andaman and Nicobar island bases was the only concrete step known to have been taken. Such a policy can occasionally reap benefits : when Sukarno was overthrown in 1966 nothing from the Indian side stood in the way of the new government's offering to establish friendlier relations with New Delhi, and that was one of the first foreign policy changes undertaken from Djakarta.

THE ABSENCE OF A SECURITY POLICY : RELATIONS WITH BURMA

Of great strategic importance to India is Burma, the only adjacent southeast Asian state and administratively linked to India under British rule. Any hostile government or occupying power in Burma would be rightly regarded as a direct threat to India, because of the land connection and also because Burma helps control the Bay of Bengal. K. M. Panikkar once wrote that "the defense of Burma is in fact the defense of India,"[26] and the experience of Japanese troops penetrating into India through Burma in 1942 bore out that assertion. The emergence on India's northeastern frontier of two hostile states (Pakistan and China) by the 1950's and the possibility of alien supported uprisings among the northeastern Indian hill tribes were further reasons for seeking the friendliness of the Burmese government.

Despite its obvious defense interests the Indian government did not reach any security agreements with Burma and made no statements of intent about defending Burma as it did with regard to Nepal. Consultations were frequently held with the Rangoon government on defense problems, for example, on the Burmese border dispute with China, but New Delhi went to great lengths to recognize that Burma's foreign policy was independent of India's and had to remain so for the sake of Burmese national feeling. The Burmese were quick to note, as one did at the Asian Relations Conference in 1947, that they feared pressures from both their great neighbours, India and China. The large Indian population in Burma increased Burmese sensitivity toward any suggestion of Indian governmental control over Burmese policies ; already individual

Indians were in control over a distressingly large share of the Burmese economy. The Indian government's forbearance toward Burma, despite the Rangoon government's harsh measures against the Indian settlers, suggested a conscientious policy in New Delhi of avoiding any cause for Burma to resent the intentions of its enormous neighbour.

The Indian and Burmese leaders within a few years after British withdrawal from their countries found an identity of basic views on world problems, which, to the credit of their larger visions, overshadowed the unresolved problem of the Indian minority in Burma. On specific policies India and Burma occasionally diverged, as was appropriate for states making separate efforts to judge issues on the criteria of national interests. For example, Burma after independence decided to withdraw from the Commonwealth ; Burmese statesmen voiced keener awareness of the aggressiveness of Soviet policies than Indians did at the 1954 Colombo and the 1955 Bandung conferences and during the Hungarian crisis ; Burma nurtured closer relations with Israel than India chose to do and risked offending Arab states in the process ; Burma decided against accepting US aid in 1953, and though some aid programmes were resumed later, Burma never availed itself as India did of American economic assistance. Nevertheless, by 1950, Burma constituted one of the pillars of nonalignment, and despite constant warfare within its own territory its government supported the proclamations of *panchasheel* and peaceful coexistence. At international gatherings Burmese spokesmen, particularly Premier U Nu himself, could be relied on to reinforce the Indian prescriptions for international peace and prosperity. That similarity of outlook on the parts of Nehru and U Nu did more to encourage close ties than even the treaty of friendship signed by the two governments in July 1951. Nehru once observed that "we are much more intimately connected with Burma—. . . I mean informally—than with the Commonwealth countries."[27]

But Burma reached its nonaligned posture only after failing to make any arrangements for "good and powerful" allies, in U Nu's words, preferably the US and Great Britain.[28] A three-year military agreement was in fact made with Britain at the time of the negotiations for transfer of power, without, however, any binding provisions for mutual defense ; it was a training and supply arrangement,

At an early stage in the development of Burma's foreign policy its foreign minister, U Tin Tut, reportedly hoped for a defense arrangement with India : "Together we should be able," he said in December 1947 after a visit to New Delhi, "to form the nucleus round which could be created an alliance of Southeast Asian countries united in a desire for world peace and impregnable against external aggression."[29] As a possible second best foreign policy Burma turned to nonalignment at the end of the 1940's.

Burma's vulnerability to internal and external attacks made national security a primary objective of Burmese foreign policy. The Indian government, however vocal in behalf of peaceful settlement of international disputes, evidenced support for Burma when combatting internal rebellions from communists and tribal separatists. At the beginning of 1949 the Burmese government had almost lost control of the country, and Rangoon was threatened by attack. Indian, Pakistani, and British ambassadors intervened in the crisis to try to secure some compromise with the Karen rebels—there was much at stake for all of their governments. Failing in that effort, Nehru at a Commonwealth conference in New Delhi in early 1949 persuaded the delegates to try to assist the Burma government. The result was a shipment of arms from Britain and a Commonwealth loan, the latter never used. Of more immediate importance, India sent arms and ammunition to Burma and aircraft to Air Burma Ltd., and made advances and loans to cover some of the losses suffered as a result of the insurrection.[30] From 1951 India provided training to Burmese military personnel. A large percentage of Burma's main export, rice, traditionally went to India. In the desperate early years of its independent existence, when the rice production was disorganized and world markets uncertain, Burma found that only India could be relied upon to purchase large quantities of the commodity at reasonable prices. The practice continued through the mid-1950's, although the total Indian rice imports from Burma declined during this period. In addition, the Indian government reduced and finally wrote off in 1954 a substantial Burmese government debt arising out of the 1937 separation agreement and wartime advances to the Burmese government in exile, and in 1957 India extended a substantial loan of rupees 200 million to Burma for its development programme.

The urgency of New Delhi's concern over the security of Burma

16

could be felt during the many official consultations between Indians and Burmese, especially Nehru and U Nu, on the problem of Chinese Nationalist (KMT) troops in Burma. India assisted Burma in its complaint to the UN in 1953 on the matter and guided a UN resolution, without itself introducing it, condemning the presence of KMT troops in Burmese territory. Only about one-half of the troops was withdrawn with belated help from the US, and from Thailand. Chinese communist forces moved into Burma to engage the remaining KMT forces, a territorial violation publicized in 1956. U Nu appealed to Nehru for assistance in dealing with the Peking government, with which India was then on good terms.[31] Though India shared many of Burma's problems with border tribes and boundary delimitation, India's moves on behalf of Burma were discreet enough to avoid any suggestion of a common front against China.

Burma also desired no anti-Chinese coalition. By the 1960's the Peking government indicated its willingness to settle outstanding problems with Burma, perhaps to preclude the coalescing of a common front against itself, and perhaps to isolate India on the Himalayan border question by appearing conciliatory towards its smaller neighbours. (China later followed a similar course of action with respect to Nepal and Pakistan.) By 1960 Burma had moved away from any reliance on India and toward a rapprochement with its more threatening, more effectively powerful northern neighbour. In October of that year a border agreement was signed between the two countries along with a ten-year treaty of friendship and non-aggression. On the whole, the border demarcation followed the watershed principle advocated by New Delhi for the India-China border, but India disputed the delineation on the map showing the tri-junction of India-Burma-China, because it had a "prejudicial effect on 75 square miles of Indian territory."[32]

It was from this area and further south along the Indo-Burmese border that India's worries increased over the years. Hilly, thickly vegetated, and sparsely populated by tribes which had moved freely between India and Burma and enjoyed a high degree of administrative autonomy during British rule, the region proved resistant to India's attempts to integrate it more fully into the nation. From 1953, when Nehru and U Nu had toured their countries' common border, Indian and Burmese officials frequently collaborated to prevent illegal border crossings and the smuggling of goods and arms. Uniquely for south and southeast Asia neither country feared the other's intentions in the keeping of border peace, although both governments found it difficult to control the tribal peoples in their territories. During the 1960's the problem was exacerbated for India by the activities of China and Pakistan, geographically well placed for interference, in assisting the struggle of those alienated from India. Once again India turned to Burma for cooperation in preventing or controlling the egress and entry of armed tribesmen in eastern India.

In 1962, following the military takeover of the state by General Ne Win, Burma seemed to turn its attention inward for a period of profound social and political reorganization. Although Ne Win continued to proclaim his state's adherence to nonalignment, Burma cut most of its remaining ties with the West and was cautious not to offend any major national objective of China. The Indian government knew that it had a critical stake in the continued independence and friendship of Burma but decided that it could not defend Burma against a possible Chinese intervention. The collaboration built by U Nu and Nehru, which had given substance to the ideas of a nonaligned "peace area" in Asia, diminished in face of India's failure to support vigorously the physical security of Burma, although it had tried to make some contributions to that end in the early years after independence. The Burmese were not in a position to resist Chinese pressures. It could not have surprised any knowledgeable Indian when Burma applied the nonalignment principle to the India-China hostilities of 1962. Ne Win joined the other nonaligned statesmen at Colombo in December to try and mediate in the dispute and also tried personal mediation when Chou En-lai visited Rangoon for five days in February 1964.

Recognizing the ineffectiveness of Nehru's diplomacy in south and southeast Asia, and having paid the price for it, the Indian government under Prime Minister Sastri took cautious measures to improve relations with Burma and other neighbouring countries. Official visits were exchanged, Ne Win going to Delhi in February and Sastri to Rangoon in December of 1965. Three years later, Ne Win seemed to be re-establishing the links of Indo-Burmese collaboration with the same deliberate caution ; he also reopened a dialogue with the US. But neither India nor Burma appeared to have begun a reconciliation of their divergent relations with China.

Whereas the Indian and Burmese economies for many years had functioned as complimentary, that relationship was no longer apparent by the 1960's. Indo-Burmese trade, in the 1930's, had formed significant parts of both countries' external economic relations. Next to Britain Burma became the largest source of India's imports (chiefly rice) by the late 1930's, when Burma was India's third best customer. After the war trade between the two states failed to reach former levels, but Burma remained for a time an important rice supplier to India. Burma's imports from India were textiles, jute goods, coal, betel nuts, tobacco, and a great variety of small manufactured articles. In 1951 a trade agreement was concluded, supplemented by further accords in 1956 and 1962. The latter provided for most-favoured-nation treatment and specified goods to be traded, India agreeing to purchase 150,000 tons of grain yearly from Burma for three years. But trade, nevertheless, continued to decline, partly because Burma abolished Commonwealth preference arrangements in 1953, thus forcing Indian textiles to compete with Japanese and others in the Burmese market. India's rice imports at about the same time declined, leaving Burma to find other markets, among them European communist states and China. A few years later American rice began to enter south Asian markets, as parts of economic aid programmes, thus interfering with the traditional rice trade between Burma and India.[33] The following conveys its own meaning :

INDIA'S TRADE WITH BURMA (in lakhs of rupees)

Years	Exports	Imports
1952	2349	3108
1954	1644	4405
1956	1018	571
1958	748	4554
1960	681	2045
1961-62	526	1124
1962-63	508	909
1963-64	637	845
1964-65	641	876

For India the fall-off in textile exports to Burma was particularly distressing ; India's share in Burmese textile imports declined from a postwar high of 68 per cent to 15 per cent in 1955. In an economic sense Burma's relationships with Japan and later with China replaced that which it previously had with India. Japan's share in the Burmese textile market rose from 14 per cent in 1953 to 60 per cent in 1955, almost entirely at the expense of Indian products, and Japan could also receive payment by importing rice.

If the break-down of complimentary Indo-Burmese economic ties seemed shortsighted—the result of uncoordinated phasings in and out of demands and supplies—, it could be explained by the unwillingness of the two governments and, for that matter, all the regional governments to work out economic collaborations for the general benefit of the area.

When Burma was drifting away from Indian influence in the early 1960's New Delhi reinforced its attitude of avoiding any provocations or disputes that might widen the policy gap between the two states. The 1963-1964 nationalization programme in Burma affected Indian settlers severely, but the Indian embassy's over-burdened staff could do no more than give receipts for unexportable valuables as they assisted the sudden evacuation. Though avoiding the xenophobic public demonstrations that accompanied the forced withdrawal of Dutch businessmen from Indonesia years before, the Burmese did not give the impression that they were following the non-discriminatory policy toward nationalization that their leaders proclaimed. Nevertheless, India's official reaction to Burma's new policy, which led to the first mass exodus of overseas Indian settlers and might have set a disturbing precedent for other countries to follow, could scarcely have been milder. Faced with arranging transport home at New Delhi's expense of tens of thousands of people, India's foreign minister signed a joint communique in Rangoon in September 1964 in which he "noted with satisfaction that the various measures introduced by the Government of the Union of Burma towards achieving a socialist society are not discriminatory against foreigners as such and equally apply to Burmese nationals and foreigners alike."[34] The episode proved what Frank N. Trager subsequently wrote : "Relations between Indians and Burmese as individuals are not as good as they are between the two governments."[35]

NOTES AND REFERENCES

[1] A very helpful analysis of the politics among the south and southeast Asian states, which discusses the low intensity of their mutual interactions, and which sets up a scheme for relating them to the general international arena can be found in Michael Brecher, "International Relations and Asian Studies : The Subordinate State System of Southern Asia," *World Politics*, vol.XV, 2(Jan. 1963).

[2] At the Asian History Congress meeting in Delhi, Nehru remarked, on December 6, 1961, that he was sceptical of the use of the term, Asian history ; he could not conceive of Asia as an organic entity and felt that in some cases, such as India's, a country might have more in common with a European society than with a fellow Asian. *Cultural News From India*, vol. 3, 1 (Jan. 1962).

[3] See *Toward Freedom*, N. Y. 1941, p. 367, *The Unity of India*, London 1941, p. 327 ; *Discovery of India*, N. Y. 1946, p. 547f.

[4] Address to Bombay branch of the Indian Council of World Affairs, in *India Quarterly*, vol. II, 4 (Oct.-Dec. 1946), p. 327.

[5] See G. H. Jansen, *Nonalignment and the Afro-Asian States*, pp. 68-72.

[6] "So it seems that in the modern world it is inevitable for India to be the centre of things in Asia. (In that term I would include Australia and New Zealand too, being in the Indian Ocean region. East Africa comes into it also.)" Bombay Indian Council of World Affairs speech, *op. cit.* In 1944 he wrote that "India will also develop as the centre of economic and political activity in the Indian Ocean area, in South-East Asia and right up to Middle East." *The Discovery of India*, pp. 547-48. See also the discussion of Nehru's view of India's role in Asia in Ton That Thien, *India and South East Asia 1947-1960*, p. 57f.

[7] K. M. Panikkar's writings on the requirements of Indian defense, e.g. *India and the Indian Ocean : An Essay on the Influence of Sea Power on Indian History*, London 1945 ; and his position of influence in the Indian government must have reinforced such suspicions.

[8] In 1946 the disposition of Indian troops in south-east Asia stood as follows : in Burma, 22,500 ; in Indonesia, 32,500 ; in Malaya, 5,000 plus 15,000 Gurkhas ; as compiled by V. Siddhartha Charry, in "The East Asian Countries and India," Asian Relations Conf., New Delhi 1947.

[9] Speech in parliament, Feb. 17, 1953, *Speeches, 1949-1953*, p. 237.

[10] The American "vacuum" theory and its relevance to India was enunciated by former President Dwight D. Eisenhower in an interview with David Schoenbrun in August 1964. Speaking about his relations with French President de Gaulle, Eisenhower said : "We Americans had to move into a vacuum there (in Vietnam) after the French pulled out in 1954. What bothers me most about de Gaulle's policy is that he does not give enough weight to the vital importance of this whole Southeast Asia struggle and what would happen if we let the thing go. What is India going to do then? India would become totally isolated. I think that really the defense of Southeast Asia today, in my opinion, is the defense of India, and if that whole subcontinent of some 400 million people and more falls to the Communists or breaks with the West, well, I'll tell you, then we become more and more isolated in this world." Schoenbrun, *The Three Lives of Charles de Gaulle*, New York 1966, p. 337,

[11] See, for example, Nehru's speech in the Lok Sabha, Sept. 29, 1954, in *Speeches, 1953-57*, pp. 272-73.

[12] See *Talks with Nehru : A Discussion Between Jawaharlal Nehru and Norman Cousins*, N. Y. 1951, p. 53.

[13] Quoted in Nicholas Mansergh, *The Commonwealth and the Nations*, London 1948, p. 100.

[14] See *Asian Relations, being the Report of the Proceedings and Documentation of the First Asian Relations Conference*, New Delhi, March-April, 1947.

[15] See, e.g. Nehru's speech at the Indian Council of World Affairs, March 22, 1949, *Independence and After*, pp. 252-53. A discussion of the conference on Indonesia appears in Jansen, *op. cit.*, pp. 83-98.

[16] Sisir Gupta, *India and Regional Integration in Asia*, p. 44.

[17] For these and other details of the Conference, see George McTurnan Kahin, *The Asian-African Conference.*

[18] *ibid.*, pp. 6-7.

[19] Amry Vandenbosch and Richard Butwell, *The Changing Face of Southeast Asia*, Lexington 1966, p. 356.

[20] Kahin, *op, cit.*, p. 36.

[21] *Asian African Conference : Speeches of the Prime Minister of India in the Closed Sessions*, p. 16.

[22] e.g. in *RSD*, vol. XIX, Dec. 12, 1957, col. 2347.

[23] e.g. Swaran Singh's statement in Rajya Sabha, Sept. 24, 1964, *FAR*, vol. X, 9 (Sept. 1964), p. 206.

[24] For a discussion of the effects on Indonesian foreign relations, though not specifically with India, of Sukarno's personality, see Bernard K. Gordon, *The Dimensions of Conflict in Southeast Asia*, Englewood Cliffs, N. J., 1966, chapter IV. In dealing with this and other subjects in this section the authors relied on Jeffery R. D. Crockett, "Indian Relations with Indonesia," an unpublished paper at American University, 1965.

[25] See *Asian Recorder*, 1964, pp. 5839, 6128.

[26] Panikkar, *The Future of South East Asia*, p. 46.

[27] *LSD*, vol. II, pt. II, March 17, 1953, col. 2246.

[28] A detailed discussion of Burmese efforts to reach security alliances can be found in Frank Trager, *Burma : From Kingdom to Republic*, N.Y. 1966, pp. 216-27.

[29] *New Times of Burma*, Dec. 16, 1947 ; quoted in Richard J. Kozicki, "India and Burma 1937-1957 : A Study in International Relations", pp. 277-78.

[30] Ton That Thien, *op. cit.*, pp. 170-71 ; also Kozicki, *op. cit.*, pp. 311, 337n.

[31] Trager, *op. cit.*, p. 242.

[32] *FAR*, vol. VII, 2 (Feb. 1961), p. 13.

[33] Trager, *op. cit.*, p. 330f.

[34] *FAR*, vol. X, 9 (Sept. 1964), p. 197. See ahead, Chapter XII, for further discussion of the Indians in Burma.

[35] Trager, *op. cit.*, p. 258.

CHAPTER X

RELATIONS WITH ALIGNED STATES IN SOUTHEAST ASIA

SECURITY CONSIDERATIONS : RELATIONS WITH MALAYA

WITH NO COUNTRY in southeast Asia did India develop a consistent pattern of coincident interests and good relations. Nonalignment did not provide an adequate base for partnership, as relations with Indonesia and Burma demonstrated. The possibilities of cooperative friendship between India and those Asian states which accepted alignment with a great power were even less apparent ; criticism of their actions often blunted Indian sensitivity to their needs. But Indo-Malayan relations formed an exception to this latter generalization and in fact were strongly influenced for many years by security considerations appreciated by both governments. India's relations with Malaya also refuted the proposition that New Delhi gave the highest priority to anti-colonialism in its policies on Asia and Africa.

India exhibited varying degrees of opposition to colonialism depending on the administering power and on the nature of the local nationalist movement. In the case of Malaya, anti-British activities after the Second World War were confined mainly to communist led revolutionaries, almost entirely ethnic Chinese. India found no nationalist organization to which it desired to give support and officially opposed the revolutionaries, sympathizing instead with the British programme of giving security needs precedence over a transfer of power to local politicians.

"I believe all of us here are in favour of Malayan independence," Nehru said in a Lok Sabha debate.[1] "But remember that the problem in Malaya is not an easy one. It is difficult because, oddly enough, in Malaya the people of Malaya are in a minority. . . . No single group is in a majority. The indigenous people of Malaya are not at all keen on something happening which might give power to non-Malayans there." Nehru had visited Malaya in 1946,

1950, and 1954 and was aware of the local fears of domination by overseas Chinese, who composed 45 per cent of the population of Malaya-Singapore in 1947. He welcomed the British policy of preparing the Malays—44 per cent of the population in 1947—for self-government so that British withdrawal could lead to a democratic, independent government and a truly multi-racial nation. The Indians in Malaya, about 11 per cent of the population in 1947, mostly underprivileged rubber estate workers, elicited a more sensitive concern on India's part than that showed in behalf of the larger, more prosperous Indian community in Burma. The insurgency hurt the Indians in Malaya, and the prospect of a Chinese dominated Malayan government was equally distressing. Nehru refrained from questioning British good faith in eventually turning over power smoothly, and from criticizing the length of the nurturing process.[2]

Malaya was of special interest to India because it controlled the eastern route through the Indian Ocean, which passed through the Malacca Straits. Control of the important naval base at Singapore should not be allowed to fall into hostile control as it had been from 1942 to 1945. Politically India backed the British effort to gain control of the Malayan countryside and suppress the communist insurgency in the interests of law and order and, incidentally, to preclude the introduction of Chinese influence in that strategic peninsula. Nehru did not regard the rebels in Malaya as nationalists, as he did the insurgents in Indonesia or Indo-China ; he pointed out in 1950 that "recent communist activities in southeast Asia . . . had, firstly, by their extreme violence and terroristic methods and, secondly, by their going against one of the dominant urges of these countries, that is nationalism, performed a counter-revolutionary act."[3] To be fighting a colonial government was not sufficient to elicit India's support.

In contrast to its frequent criticisms of SEATO and its statements at the Bandung conference India refrained from criticizing Malaya's defensive alignments, especially its mutual assistance treaty contracted with Britain at independence in August 1957. Nehru was reported to have justified Malaya's "wish to conclude a defensive alliance "[4] which permitted the stationing of Commonwealth troops—mainly from Britain, Australia and New Zealand—within Malaya. He saw the need for external buttressing of Malaya's tenuous unity and security,

The official contacts between India and Malaya produced a good, if somewhat sparse record of mutual support and cooperation. In July 1947 India sent a representative to Kuala Lumpur, whose status was raised to high commissioner when Malaya gained independence. High officials on both sides visited the others' countries and exchanged the usual diplomatic felicitations. Some part of the official cordiality was due to Indians' respect for Malaya's prime minister, Tungku Abdul Rahman, a former student at Cambridge, like Nehru, and an admirer of parliamentary democracy and the Gandhian methods of political action. India contributed technical aid to Malaya through the Colombo Plan, and in 1959 India's Major-General E. Habibullah was assigned to the post of deputy general officer, commanding, Malayan Federation Army to assist in its training and personnel work. Malayan army officers attended advanced instruction courses in India. Further, official Indo-Malayan relations after Malayan independence suffered no strain over Indian settlers, a problem affecting Indian dealings with Ceylon and to a lesser extent Burma. As a community inferior to the Chinese in size and wealth the Indians did not face threats of persecution or expulsion, at least until the mid-1960's, but were regarded as vital to Malaya's economic and political progress by a government which was itself drawn from a political party bridging the three ethnic groups.

Indo-Malayan trade relations in the 1950's produced a balance favourable to Indian exports, which were traditionally cotton textiles, tobacco, coal, sugar, and semi-processed goods. Malaya sent India rubber, tin, mineral and vegetable oils, and betel nuts. But by the early 1960's Malaya became an area of vigorous competition among the major Asian exporters of manufactured goods—Japan, China, India, Pakistan, and Hong Kong. India increased its exports of petroleum products, and its prospects of selling consumer goods appeared to improve, but Indian goods on the whole were not maintaining their accustomed share of the market.[5] Trade between the two countries became more nearly balanced.

The policies of India and Malaya had diverged on issues related to China and on Vietnam in the 1950's but came together in late 1962 on the basis of common fear of China. In October 1962 Abdul Rahman, then on his first official visit to India, announced his government's support for India against the Chinese invasion. On his return to Kuala Lumpur he created a "Save Democracy Fund" and collected a substantial sum to help India. Malaya was the only state in southern Asia, except for Thailand and the Philippines, that declared its support for India, and the gesture was reciprocated by India the next year, when Malaya itself faced invasion from Indonesia.

When the federated state of Malaysia entered upon its experimental and Western supported existence in September 1963 it found Indonesia prepared for a policy of "confrontation" in order to destroy the new entity. Among the first regional governments to welcome the formation of Malaysia was India. Indian officials criticized Indonesian attacks on Malaysia and did not respond favourably to Philippine claims to Sabah (North Borneo), part of the new state. Diplomatically, India persistently pressed for Malaysia's inclusion (along with the USSR) in a second Afro-Asian conference. Singapore separated from Malaysia in 1965, and India maintained good relations with both states, but at a lower level of practical cooperation than they seemed to desire. The leaders of both Malaysia and Singapore were aware of the need to balance the power of China in their area with a greater involvement of India, especially in the face of British withdrawal of forces. For example, Lee Kuan Yew, prime minister of Singapore, said in New Delhi in September 1966 that his state would like to "share some of the security" which India's size and historical integrity provided,[6] and he put out inquiries subsequently to the same end. But India was unable to respond positively to his suggestions.

Something may be learned about India's foreign policies by seeking an answer to the question, why was India willing to support Malaya's staunch anti-communist and pro-Western policies when similar stands by Thailand, for example, were condemned and ridiculed? Malaya's anti-communist stance emerged from the threat of an internal communist movement, and India could appreciate and support the Malayan reaction to such a situation, which had its parallels in India. Internal communists were utterly condemned by Nehru, whereas fears of external communist aggression, such as expressed by the Thai government, found little Indian sympathy until the 1960's. Malaya's openly stated apprehensions about Chinese policy could be traced to the predominance of the Chinese community in Malaya and Singapore and the allegiance of some of its members to Peking ; often Nehru showed that he understood the undermining potentialities of overseas Chinese, and he therefore refrained from advising Malayan leaders on their China policies. Finally, Malaya and Singapore were Commonwealth states and found their external support in a British, not an American, alignment. Commonwealth ties, even military ones, in Asia and Africa received India's sympathy and support ; Britain's dying empire could be tolerated a bit longer because of its stabilizing character. But America's burgeoning power in Asia looked to many Indians like a new Western onslaught into their region, which had to be condemned. Malaya, later Malaysia, did not join SEATO, perhaps partly because of Indian urging.

SELF-CONTRADICTING POLICY : RELATIONS WITH THE INDO-CHINESE STATES

Some observers of the vagaries of India's southeast Asian policies have explained that India recognized a division of the mainland area into spheres of influence between itself and China, drawn along a line of historical cultural influence.[7] By this argument India would have consented to a Chinese presence in all of Vietnam and consolidated its own influence in Burma, Thailand, Laos and Cambodia. Although such a thesis may in the long run be proved, in the 1950's and 1960's no one could find much evidence to support it, apart from Nehru's occasional expressions of special interest in Indian cultural remains in the latter countries. Instead, the two consistent factors in India's self-contradicting policy towards the Indo-Chinese states were, first, New Delhi's opposition to communist domination of any of the Indo-Chinese states and, second, its unwillingness to extend India's power, or even to exert its influence to the full, in order to inhibit any undesirable political development in that region. For the successor states of former French Indo-China, India desired unity and independence from all outside entanglements ; but this policy goal was supported chiefly by proclamations.

India in 1950 could be regarded as a very interested observer in the Indo-Chinese war between the French and the Viet Minh. India was a very cautious observer, however, in a struggle with no clear-cut beginning or end, and the reason for that caution and hesitation was a common topic of Indian discussion and debate. Nehru never gave a full explanation of why India urgently supported Dutch withdrawal from Indonesia but temporized on the withdrawal of French influence from Indo-China, or why India recognized and aided Indonesian nationalists but refused to do the same for Ho Chi Minh's movement, although Indians regarded it as an authentic nationalist cause. Yet his actions and statements presented a pattern suggesting that Nehru was reluctant to support Ho Chi Minh because of Ho's communist affiliations and in addition wished to avoid taking sides in a struggle which by 1950 had become an offshoot of the global great power confrontation.[8] Nehru refused to recognize the Ho Chi Minh regime, to cut off French logistic flights over India, and to raise the Vietnam question in the UN ; yet he had no kind words for French imperialism—except as it peacefully withdrew from Pondicherry and other enclaves in India.

By the end of the Korean war Nehru, while still avoiding any direct intervention between the two contestants in Indo-China, tried to use India's considerable experience with compromise settlements to produce a negotiated peace. After appealing for a cease-fire in February 1954 he issued in April a six-point proposal, which reflected his view that negotiations should take place between "the parties immediately and principally concerned."[9] Nehru expressed anxiety over the accelerated deliveries of American and Chinese supplies into Vietnam and the threats from both sides of greater military commitments. Then, while the major world powers met at Geneva to seek an Indo-Chinese settlement, the prime ministers of five governments of southern Asia agreed at Colombo on a peace proposal, largely a redraft of Nehru's six points.[10] Its reception at Geneva seemed mixed. India's absence from Geneva, where a Korean political settlement was also discussed, resulted from the US government's view that India's "neutralist" influence would tend to undermine the Western negotiating posture, as it was alleged to have done in some of the previous negotiations on a Korean settlement. But at Geneva the formally uninvited Indian representative, V. K. Krishna Menon, maintained close contacts with all the parties and received official and unofficial praise for his constructive mediatory role.[11]

The final Geneva accords on Indo-China established three International Commissions of Supervision and Control (ICSC) for

Vietnam, Cambodia, and Laos, each composed of an Indian chairman and Polish and Canadian members, a pattern for overseeing
settlements which had succeeded in Korea and accurately reflected
the tri-polar structure of world politics. Other features of the settlement, the cease-fire, a transfer of sovereignty to the three states by
France, provisions by outside states to end the bulk of their military
ties with the states of former French Indo-China, and understandings
about the neutrality of Laos and Cambodia, closely resembled
Nehru's earlier proposals. Indeed, the Indian formula for regional
peace—independence and nonalignment—for once appeared to
have been acceptable to all the states involved in southeast Asia,
except possibly the US.[12]

India's nonalignment globally and its carefully nurtured neutrality
toward the conflict in Vietnam made it eligible for the chairman-
ships of the ICSCs.[13] Those demanding positions were filled by
many of India's most experienced and resourceful diplomats,
whose roles on the commissions were expected to include sensitive
mediation between several contenders for power. Nehru prized the
position that his government had achieved and rigorously avoided
any semblance of deviation from the posture that had made it
possible. As the politics of southern Asia gradually congealed
into patterns of alignment and counter-alignment, and as major
states, after a pause, resumed and expanded their military programmes in the Indo-Chinese area, India clung to its nonaligned
and neutral policies. The result was that the possibilities for India
to influence the courses of local events in the former Indo-Chinese
states were few and infrequent. The Indo-Chinese conflict had begun
as an anti-colonial movement, developed into an internal struggle
between local factions, and later became an aspect, like the Korean
war from its outset, of great power rivalry. Indian policy was not
designed to cope with all those features of the struggle.

In relations with Cambodia, however, Indian policies were
comparatively more successful than with the other two Indo-Chinese
states.

The basis for friendly Indo-Cambodian relations was the fact
that both states were nonaligned. After Prime Minister Nehru's
visit to Phnom Penh in November 1954 and an exchange of permanent representatives, a large number of high level visitations on
both sides paid tribute to the proclaimed similarity of Cambodian

and Indian views on international questions. In fact, however, neither state provided the other with tangible support of its basic national objectives. Cambodia's decision to adopt nonalignment appeared after it had failed to obtain firm Western guarantees backing its disputes with South Vietnam and Thailand over border issues. Even then, Cambodia managed for a time to combine proclamations of nonalignment with heavy dependence on the US for military and economic assistance. Independence for the Cambodian government, unlike India's situation in the 1950's, meant physical capability of controlling and defending territory from communist revolutionaries or neighbouring states, both of which ridiculed nonalignment. Cambodian nonalignment was not a global posture, like India's, and had familiar roots in southeast Asian politics. The balancing of regional impingements was a technique of Thailand's diplomacy in the 19th century.[14]

Beyond the Indo-Cambodian proclamations on nonalignment and *panchasheel* the Indian government possessed some political leverage in Phnom Penh through its position on the ICSC. For the most part the commission functioned smoothly in Cambodia and was able to act in concert with the government on most matters of interest to both. In comparison to other control commissions its role was not exacting, but it assumed the important task of advising the government on procedures for holding the national elections of 1955 (and in a somewhat baffling move unanimously sanctioned Cambodia's military aid agreement with the US). The outstanding issues on which members of the ICSC disagreed were the cases of intrusion into Cambodia of troops from South Vietnam, which the commission investigated in 1957 over the objections of its Canadian member, and the matter of concluding the commission's work. On both of those issues India and Poland voted against Canada, the chairman acting in a manner designed to support the interests of the Cambodian government. In general through the work of the commission the Indian government was able to establish some understanding with Phnom Penh. By that means also India was able to strengthen the authority of the Cambodian government and encourage its adoption of a nonaligned international posture, harmonizing with the Geneva accords as well as with India's interests.

Yet Prince Sihanouk's flexible foreign policy, formulated in conformity with India's proclamations, failed to result in close

Indo-Cambodian collaboration ; Cambodia could rely on no concrete Indian support for its immediate interests. Specifically, on his trip to New Delhi in August 1958 Prince Sihanouk found Nehru unwilling even to join in verbal criticism of the Thai and South Vietnamese policies toward Cambodia ; the ebullience of his 1955 visit had disappeared as Sihanouk realized the incapacity of India to assist him. More directly than ever before, therefore, Cambodia began to cultivate its political and economic ties with China, losing some American assistance in the process. At the same time Sihanouk tried to avoid losing touch with India. In January-February 1963 the Cambodian leader again visited India and expressed his "real sadness and growing alarm" over "the events which India has had to face up to in the course of the past months."[15] India, in turn, continued to exert a moderate amount of pressure in support of Cambodia's desire for a guaranteed neutral status. In 1964 New Delhi revived an earlier request to the British government as a co-chairman of the Geneva conference of 1954, to convene with the Soviet Union a new conference to formalize Cambodia's neutrality ; but India did not press the issue with the vigour that it urged Laotian neutrality ; a conference on Cambodia was not immediately held.

India's direct relations with Laos were less significant than those with Cambodia, but through international diplomacy New Delhi exerted an important influence on Laotian affairs.

The communist led intervention and revolution in that country, before and after the Geneva settlement, threatened the independence of a state which India was supporting. More vigorously than was necessary in Cambodia or possible in Vietnam India tried to give substance to the prescriptions of *panchasheel* in Laos.[16] The Royal Laotian government had expressed its desire for neutrality at Geneva and identified itself with India's *panchasheel* proclamations.[17] But India's efforts were ultimately thwarted, not only by the communist Pathet Lao, the North Vietnamese government, and China, but increasingly after 1957 by the US.

The problem of the Pathet Lao dominated the activities of the ICSC in Laos and presented the Indian chairman with difficult problems. The commission was nearly always divided over questions on the Pathet Lao, and India therefore was in a position to arbitrate in much the same way that its representative on the NNRC had done in Korea. But whereas a balancing of decisions for and against each contender in Korea had helped maintain the equilibrium of the cease-fire, in Laos neither side was satisfied with the status quo, and any clear Indian decision appeared to give advantage to the Royal government or the Pathet Lao. For a time, in 1956 and 1957, it appeared that Indian efforts through the ICSC to bring the Pathet Lao and Royal elements together had been helpful, but in March 1958 the new government of Prince Souvanna Phouma requested the commission to terminate its activities. Without its leverage through the ICSC India lost direct touch with the shapeless events that followed in the war-torn country.[18]

During the next three years, while the American government's operations in Laos failed to bring stability, peace, or a reduction in the strength of the communists, India persistently sought the re-establishment of the ICSC in the country. In May 1959 Nehru proposed to Britain and the USSR, co-chairmen of the Geneva conference, that they support a resumption of the commission's activities. The presence of the ICSC, he believed, would assist the neutralization of Laos and "would exercise a soothing influence."[19] More specifically, "The trouble with Laos . . . has been the attempt of parties outside Laos to influence and to help with arms. . . . So long as the International Commission was there . . . there was some check and it was not easy to do this publicly. . . ."[20] Britain declined to sponsor such a move, while the Soviet Union announced support of India's suggestion.

In the winter of 1960-1961 the matter of reviving the ICSC again created international debate. In December India again asked Britain and Russia to reactivate the commission ; this time Britain accepted the Indian request. The early months of 1961 brought intensified fighting in the country and world-wide alarm that increasing great power involvement might result in more widespread conflict. The newly installed American president, John F. Kennedy, decided that military intervention rated a distinctly lower priority than a negotiated settlement and offered American support to the plan of neutralization. The US and the Indian policies had finally coalesced in one region of southeast Asia. US ambassador-at-large, W. Averell Harriman, brought word to Nehru of Kennedy's desire for a Laotian cease-fire and neutralization, which would require the reinstallation of the ICSC to oversee any new agreement. Britain

17

and Cambodia had proposed a new conference to discuss a settlement ; Kennedy endorsed the plan and asked Nehru to help in obtaining Soviet agreement.[21] The secretary of state, Dean Rusk, followed Harriman to New Delhi to try to coordinate US and Indian moves on both the Laotian and the Congolese crises.[22] On April 1 the Soviet Union agreed to holding a conference, and on the 24th the UK and the USSR issued invitations to the meeting and simultaneously asked India to reconvene the ICSC in New Delhi.

At the 14-power Geneva conference on Laos, which began on May 16, 1961, and ended on July 23, 1962, India's views on the general problem of neutralization and its specific recommendations, as chairman of the revived ICSC, on how to assure the success of the plan received close attention from all the participants. Of the states meeting at Geneva India, a full participant in the conference and "by now an essential part of any Laotian settlement,"[23] often found itself holding crucial keys to success or even continuation of the negotiations. Before the conference had begun in Geneva the ICSC had been reconvened in New Delhi. In less than two weeks after its opening session the commission had managed to re-establish itself in Laos and thereby had nominally met American stipulations that a cease-fire had to be certified before the Geneva conference started. At Geneva the principal Indian representative, V. K. Krishna Menon, and his deputy, Arthur S. Lall, fashioned their proposals with experienced Indian skill in mediation in addition to knowledge "from the field" in Laos. Their objective, as Menon put it, was to create a guarantee of Laos' neutrality without using outside military forces to support that guarantee[24]—by then a predictable Indian formula for solving any southeast Asian crisis. After unsuccessful discussion had continued for two months, the Indian delegation submitted a draft statement on neutralization, which marked the start of detailed negotiations. India's approach lay in partially satisfying each side—the US, which wanted enforceable guarantees that a cease-fire would last and that the non-communist Vientiane government would continue in power ; the communist governments, which desired firm assurances that Laos would be free from external, i.e. American, influences.

With Lall participating, the drafting committee ultimately turned out the declaration on the neutrality of Laos and its protocol in

July 1962. India's contributions during the Laos talks were constructive, but not unique, partly because India's views on the peace of southeast Asia were by then fairly widely accepted and partly also because the Soviet Union upheld with more authority than India could muster the objective of a genuinely neutral state.

In Laos the ICSC's activities during the second Geneva conference, and after, were curtailed by the Pathet Lao's refusal to provide easy access to its territory, through which men and supplies moved from North to South Vietnam. The Laotian communists, like the Chinese, were suspicious of India's intentions, and, indeed, Indian members of the ICSC team seemed determined to place observers in contested areas, such as the Plain of Jars, in order to inhibit resumption of communist offensives. India opposed the communist suggestion that each member of the commission have a veto over decisions, because such a procedure would have negated hopes for a strengthened peace-keeping body, and on occasions the Indian and Canadian members proceeded with an inspection and made reports without the cooperation of the Polish member. India's anxiety about the weakness of central authority in Laos grew as the war in Vietnam escalated after 1964 ; but its position as ICSC chairman and therefore a nominally neutral observer of events conflicted with its desire to inhibit communist advances in southeast Asia.[25] From 1962 through June 1965 the ICSC's reports were not made public, contrary to established practice ; but its influence on local affairs seemed minimal.

Under the circumstances of not wishing to identify itself with American policies in Vietnam or Laos but realizing its own incapacity to exert power in the region, India had to content itself with friendly gestures toward the neutralist prime minister, Souvanna Phouma, and a subdued diplomatic commentary on the disrupting situation. The Laotian king and his prime minister visited the Indian capital in March 1963 and Souvanna Phouma arrived again in July 1965 on both occasions receiving India's strong backing. But diplomatic gestures were at a substantial discount as the attention of all states was increasingly directed towards events in Vietnam.

If Indian influences in Cambodia and Laos were often minimal, they were usually nonexistent in the two Vietnams, where no prominent political faction recommended nonalignment as a solution to Vietnamese problems.

India's policy of official neutrality in the French-Viet-Minh struggle continued, following the 1954 conference, as impartiality between the North and South Vietnamese governments, befitting the chairman of the ICSC. Sympathy in India toward Ho Chi Minh's regime could not be concealed, however, and events tended to reinforce it even at the official level for several years after the Geneva settlement. India's impartiality required that Nehru's stop-over in Hanoi en route to China in October 1954 be balanced by a visit to Saigon on the return flight. But the meeting in North Vietnam brought results—Ho Chi Minh's assurance not to interfere in Laos and Cambodia—,whereas the visit to the south produced nothing. In April 1955 the North Vietnamese deputy prime minister and foreign minister visited India, reaffirmed *panchasheel*, and joined India in adherence to the Geneva agreement and especially its terms for a unified state through elections, to be held by July 1956.

While India and the Democratic Republic of Vietnam (North Vietnam) advocated broadly similar policies based on nominal adherence to the Geneva accords, the Republic of Vietnam (South Vietnam) had not signed the accords and was receiving encouragement from the US, also a non-signatory, to avoid elections and to help build an anti-communist front in southeast Asia. For two years Saigon attacked India's general and specific prescriptions for the region. But the Indian government's publicly expressed anxiety over the delay in holding all-Vietnamese elections diminished considerably after the Geneva conference co-chairmen jointly agreed, in May 1956, that the status quo in Vietnam should continue, with an election date unspecified. Reluctantly, India had to accede to the existing state of affairs. Simultaneously the South Vietnamese government decided to cooperate with the ICSC and tempered its criticisms of Indian policies. India gave de facto recognition to both Vietnams in October 1956. Official visits between India and South Vietnam took place in 1956 and 1957, symbolizing a rapprochement ; in 1958 the ICSC headquarters made a long-delayed move from Hanoi to Saigon. Thus, with Vietnamese elections no longer a feasible policy objective for India, the alternative appeared to be a return to genuine impartiality toward the contenders for power. When Ho Chi Minh visited New Delhi in February 1958 the warmth of his welcome betrayed Indians' special interest in the most venerable of Vietnamese nationalists, but his presence did nothing to alter the new Indian relationship with the Saigon regime of Ngo Dinh Diem.

That relationship improved with New Delhi's increasing awareness of China's power and therefore the common interests of India and the avowedly anti-communist governments of southeast Asia. Furthermore, the regime in the north did not appeal to Indian liberals as much as had the vaguer revolutionary mystique surrounding Ho Chi Minh's proclamations in earlier years, and the Hanoi regime's support for the Pathet Lao helped undermine the Indian supported neutrality of the Laotian government. On the ICSC the Indian and Canadian members joined in 1959 for the first time in recognizing South Vietnam's charge of North Vietnam's subversive activities below the 17th parallel. During the next three years the ICSC on balance increased its criticisms of North Vietnam, and in June 1962 its special report laid the responsibility for the enlarging conflict in the south to the "armed and unarmed personnel, arms, munitions and other supplies . . . sent from the Zone in the North to the Zone in the South with the object of supporting, organizing and carrying out hostile activities, including armed attacks, directed against the Armed Forces and Administration of the Zone in the South."[26] In the same report appeared a milder note complaining that the Saigon regime had failed to inform the ICSC about the arrival of fresh American military supplies and its de facto alliance with the US. Apart from the latter observation, the Indian representative refused to take cognizance of the obvious increases in US military deliveries and the numbers of American military advisers in the south as violations of the Geneva accords. Chinese criticism of the Indian-Canadian policy on the ICSC rose accordingly.

In the 1960's and notably after the extension of the US air attacks to North Vietnam in February 1965 the weak voice of the ICSC could scarcely be heard, and the Indian government's policy, like that of most other governments, showed signs of unclear formulation around wavering principles. The current official New Delhi line, which criticized the American build-up in South Vietnam, diverged from the majority opinion of the ICSC, despite the fact that the chairman had submitted the special report noted above to his government for clearance.[27] The Indian government criticized the American use of non-lethal gas and the bombings of the north, though not of locations in the south ; it was careful to call for "immediate suspension of all provocative action in South Vietnam as well as in North Vietnam by all sides involved in the Vietnam situation"[28] not merely for suspension of American involvement. The well publicized and increasing brutality of the war elicited less fervent public protest, official and non-official, among Indians than among Americans. India could certainly not condone American intervention, but on the other hand New Delhi had withdrawn its one-sided sympathy for North Vietnam, and in fact the American and South Vietnamese anti-communist stands found much quiet support among informed Indians.

The absence of Nehru's imaginative, if outspoken, suggestions for international peace-making could be felt by anyone surveying the perplexity and impotence of the Indian government and the ICSC chairman in the mid 1960's. From the sometimes conflicting statements and omissions from statements made in New Delhi the following policy toward the Vietnamese war could be constructed : there should be a cease-fire, for which a prior condition was an end to American air attacks on the north followed by a "Geneva-type conference" on Vietnam without further "preconditions ;" a political settlement should be substituted for a military one ; a cease-fire could be supervised by an Afro-Asian force ; because free elections had become an impossible condition for a political settle-ment, and pending another peaceful means of creating unity, both North and South Vietnam should remain sovereign states ; finally, the US should not withdraw its forces from Vietnam or southeast Asia until compensating non-communist influences could develop in the area.[29] But if those elements constituted an Indian policy or a proposal, they received neither the publicity nor the energetic support by the government to make them a forceful alternative to continued war. Fearful perhaps of American displeasure at a time of critical dependence on imported food grains, Indian leaders subdued most of their criticisms of the US conduct of the war. Regarding themselves still as potential mediators in any ultimate settlement they avoided antagonizing the communist forces in Vietnam. India, for the first time since independence and largely because of Nehru's absence from the scene, laid low. And yet, that was not a major change from the position in the mid-1940's : there never was a clearcut policy towards Indo-China.

CHALLENGES TO NONALIGNMENT : RELATIONS WITH THAILAND
AND THE PHILIPPINES AND INDIA'S REACTION TO SEATO

The only southeast Asian country without any evidence of significant Indian influence dating from pre-modern times is the Philippines. On the other hand, Thailand's past is replete with references to cultural contributions emanating from India. Whereas to many informed Indians after independence the Philippines seemed to be an Asian country only because of its geography and appeared irrevocably linked with the US in a position of only nominal independence, Thailand, Indians knew, was an Asian neighbour with which India had economic and other ties and which had cherished and defended its independence. Following the Second World War the Philippines and Thailand indicated their interest in alignment and alliance with the US, and thereby they eliminated themselves from the Indian sponsored "peace area" that Nehru was contemplating for south and southeast Asia.

Perhaps because of the traditionally good relations between India and Thailand ; because of the steady, though small, export surplus that India enjoyed in trading with the Thais ; because of the ten or twenty thousand Indians living in Thailand ; and because of Thailand's strategic location on the Indian Ocean Nehru's government avoided antagonizing the Bangkok regime. Thailand did not seek to press obtrusively against the nonaligned grouping in the region, except when compelled to defend its position, as at Bandung in 1955, and it frequently identified itself with the Afro-Asian voting bloc in the UN. The Indian government reasoned that Thailand represented a not intolerably critical absentee from the area of nonalignment and no threat to India's position. Even after Thailand concluded a military assistance agreement with the US in October 1950 and joined SEATO in 1954 official Indian comments on Thai foreign policies did not reach the point of offensiveness that they did on Pakistani or Philippine policies. On the other hand, Nehru failed to respond to overtures from Thai leaders for warmer relations between the two countries.

The Philippines' dependence on the US created a scarcely veiled disrespect for the new republic among Asian nationalists.[30] The Philippine leaders and government, a few notable exceptions apart, neglected the cultivation of Asian links and took only a nominal

interest in the affairs of south and southeast Asia ; the isolation of
the Philippines from Asia after its independence in 1946 was real
and only slowly overcome.

An exceptional effort to establish closer contacts between the
Philippines and other Asian states, however, was initiated in 1950
by the Manila government, which envisioned at that time an Asian
union against communism, to include and possibly be led by India.
Nehru himself had called for broad Asian collaboration at the
conference on Indonesia, and a resolution of the conference had
been passed to that effect. The following year the Philippines proposed a conference of democratic states at Baguio with political
and perhaps military arrangements as main topics for discussion.
The Filipino president, Elpidio Quirino, and his chief foreign
affairs advisor, General Carlos P. Romulo, interpreted the invitation
to Baguio as a logically concrete step following the bold proclamations at Delhi in 1947 and 1949. But the Indian government at
once dissociated itself from the enterprise because of Nehru's generally unfavourable views on military arrangements, especially those
hostile to the new regime in China. Thus slipped away an opportunity for regional political and perhaps military cooperation in
Asia which would not have relied on outside sponsorship and
support by Western states.

But the Philippines persisted and made concessions to Nehru's
sensitivities on regional alignments : the conference at Baguio
would discuss neither political nor military matters but merely
common economic and cultural interests. On that understanding
India agreed to attend, and the meetings convened in May 1950.
The conference chairman, Romulo, accepted the restricted agenda
but perhaps believed that once in Baguio the Indian delegation would
not fail to give some encouragement to regional governments which
recognized the menace to new democracies of communist movements internationally as well as internally. India's delegate, Ramaswami Mudaliar, while giving no possible offense candidly told the
delegates that any political or military alliance was "utterly foreign
to our conception of how we can bring about peace in the world."[31]
The final recommendations of the conference merely underlined
the need for consultation, economic and social progress, and joint
action in the UN, ideas scarcely worth the effort at drafting. Almost
everyone soon forgot Baguio, except the Philippine government,

which had been badly rebuffed and waited a decade before again broaching the subject of a regional union—the Association of Southeast Asia (ASA), established in 1961.

India and the Philippines signed a treaty of friendship and consular privileges in July 1952 with the unusual provision that disputes between the two states not otherwise peacefully settled shall be referred to the International Court of Justice for final adjudication. (But Indo-Philippine contacts were too few to require invoking this clause.) Verbal political controversy between the two states flared up on several occasions, the most notable being the famous Nehru-Romulo exchange at Bandung on the subject of military alliances. It was Nehru's public ridiculing of the Asian SEATO states as well as his manner at the conference that stimulated perhaps the severest assessment of the Indian leader to be published by an official of any government. Romulo wrote of Nehru : "His pronounced propensity to be dogmatic, impatient, irascible, and unyielding, especially in the face of opposition, alienated the goodwill of many delegates. Here was a conference which everybody thought would be dominated by him.... But he typified the affectation of cultural superiority induced by a conscious identification with an ancient civilization which has come to be the hallmark of Indian representatives to international conferences."[32] General Romulo took special pains to lobby at Bandung for the exclusion of the phrase, "peaceful coexistence," from the final communique, and his efforts succeeded.

By the end of the 1950's India and the Philippines had given up their debate ; Nehru by then appeared to regard SEATO as somewhat innocuous,[33] and the Philippines was engaging itself in a rediscovery of its Asian heritage. Vice-President Diosdado Macapagal spent eleven days in India in 1960 and suggested, as in 1950, that the Philippines would welcome collaboration at any level with India. But that transparently friendly message failed again to penetrate very deeply into the mind of Nehru, whose preoccupation with China in the 1960's led his government to the chancelleries of the great powers, not to the similarly situated Asian states, for military support.

Many years before India saw the need for military containment of China, the US and its allies worked out a loose arrangement for dealing with various kinds of communist sponsored threats to stability in the region of southeast Asia. At the outset of the Geneva conference on Indo-China British-US open disagreements over policy toward southeast Asia had included the question of trying to coordinate Western and Indian interests in the area, the British urging that India be consulted about any arrangements and brought in, if possible, to help guarantee the stability of the region.[34] Not only was Secretary of State Dulles unsympathetic toward the British suggestion, but the Indian government as well failed to encourage them. Thus, the Southeast Asian Treaty Organization was created in 1954 ; it drew its main inspiration as well as its military capabilities from the US and used its Asian members, the Philippines, Thailand, and Pakistan, mainly as bases of operation conveniently situated along the southern flank of communist power centres. Regarding Indian nonalignment and the *panchasheel* doctrine as a definite encouragement to communists, whose advances, it was held, could best be halted by forceful means, the American government, through SEATO, tried to check Indian influence in southeast Asia as well as build up domestic anti-communist strength.

Simultaneously, India was engaged in the most important diplomatic enterprise relating to southeast Asia that originated in New Delhi in the two decades after independence. Suspicious of the intentions of both China and the Western coalition, but convinced that each side acted in southeast Asia mainly from fear of the other's policies, Nehru's government put forth its proposals for neutralization—specifically, in the case of Indo-China, at Colombo and Geneva. China, not wishing to join an all-out war in the region but needing assurances that the West would not move into southeast Asia in greater force, accepted India's solution at Geneva, which could most effectively be carried out with the help of Indian chairmen on the three ICSCs.[35] The spurt of Indian diplomatic activity in connection with Indo-China had its counterpart in the Nehru-Chou En-lai negotiations over Tibet, which took place at the same time and aimed at inhibiting further Chinese aggressiveness.

Nehru felt that regional peace would be adversely affected by SEATO because the organization would constitute a persistent provocation to China and possibly Russia, whose governments could not afford to allow Western powers to remain in dominant positions just at the periphery of the communist world. Probably of even greater importance to India, SEATO appeared to curtail the independence of its small Asian members and also threatened the freedom of action of non-members in the area. India's most clearly defined and consistent policy toward southeast Asia for half a decade was its promotion of the *panchasheel* and neutralization in opposition to SEATO. The shortcoming of the Indian endeavour, in 1954 and later, was its failure to satisfy American requirements for a satisfactory southeast Asian settlement.[36] Partly for that reason the US was reluctant to see Indian involvement in any Asian settlements and was entering an alliance with Pakistan, as a more reliable Asian partner. Unable to stop American collective security programmes from taking place, with many of the characteristics of traditional European imperialism, Nehru concentrated on reassuring the Chinese, bringing them into fuller normal contacts with their southeast Asian neighbours. *Panchasheel* was not as hollow as it appeared, because the neutralization that it implied for the former Indo-Chinese states suited certain governments with interests in the area. But it did not suit the US, and possibly not North Vietnam.

India's preoccupation with its relations with China, the drawbacks in its diplomatic style, and its own economic and military shortcomings were disadvantages secondary to the tendency of New Delhi to deny the existence of external military threats to the states of the region and to overestimate their chances to survive or prosper individually in the context of "cold war" politics. In his pre-1949 writings and speeches Nehru expressed India's obligations and almost natural drives to stand forth as a major regional leader, and he advocated unity as the best basis for Asia to make its influence felt and preserve its independence. But soon after 1947 he feared the reaction from smaller states—and later from China—to any Indian efforts to organize and lead the area. His views on national independence, on the inherent inequality of political and military alignments between strong and weak states, and on the need for Asian states to abjure power politics also precluded India's making its influence felt forcefully and thereby purposefully.

The possibilities of economic arrangements among the states of south and southeast Asia also failed to stimulate strong Indian leadership in behalf of regional unity and collective advancement. Apart from UN sponsored organizations and projects, such as the Economic Commission for Asia and the Far East (ECAFE), the United Nations Technical Assistance Board (UNTAB), and the

World Health Organization (WHO), the only organization of economic significance operating in southern Asia was the Colombo Plan, founded in 1950 as a Commonwealth enterprise but spreading within a decade to most of the non-communist states in the area and including also the US and Japan. Its unique function was to enlist mutual aid among the states of southern Asia mostly of a technical variety. Its results were hard to judge, but it provided a meeting place for exchanging information on needs and capabilities of member states and produced more intra-regional aid than would have grown up on a strictly bilateral basis. India used the plan as a channel for its export of technical assistance to south and southeast Asian countries. By 1963 India had trained over 2,000 persons from member states and sent out to them over 550 experts.[37] The largest recipient of Indian technical aid was Nepal, which might have received the bulk of it without the coordinating and book-keeping intermediary of the plan. The looseness and informality of the Colombo Plan and its avoidance of any supranational character was partly its appeal to India. The steps it might have taken toward regional economic unity or even collaboration in the highly competitive areas of trade and capital assistance from developed states were never initiated.

In 1955 India invited thirteen states of the Colombo Plan consultative committee to send delegates to a conference at Simla chiefly for the purpose of exploring a common approach to the requesting and using of US economic aid. The outcome of the Simla conference demonstrated clearly the hollowness of Indian and other regional proclamations of Asian unity. On matters of tangible national interest—in contrast to such intangibles as voting behaviour in international bodies—the states of south and southeast Asia were not interested in collaboration and often vigorous in their mutual competition : they unanimously agreed at Simla that they wished to retain their bilateral aid relationships with the US.

In September 1961 a conference of Asian economic planners convened in Delhi, this time under the sponsorship of ECAFE, which then advocated wide regional cooperation with a possible ultimate goal of economic union. Again caution prevailed among the governments represented and no collaboration ensued, except an agreement to exchange information on planning. The percentage of India's trade conducted with the ECAFE region declined steadily during the 1950's, which could explain some of New Delhi's reservations about closer cooperation.[38] In addition, India realized that its power in negotiating for foreign aid was stronger when it did so bilaterally than as a member of a group of recipient states.

In the 1960's, as political and military crises affecting the major powers began to recur in Asia, particularly southeast Asia, India's increasingly weak regional posture militated against an effective voice in global diplomacy concerned with the area. The Western states, China, and the Soviet Union all possessed more influence than did India in a region adjacent to its borders. New Delhi's policies toward the southeast Asian region gained no lasting advantages for India and, in fact, left the area exposed to the external penetration that most adversely affected India's interests.

NOTES AND REFERENCES

[1] Sept. 29, 1954, Nehru, *Speeches 1953-1957*. p. 271.

[2] See Nehru's comments on the end of British imperialism in a speech in the Lok Sabha, June 12, 1952, *India's Foreign Policy*, p. 57.

[3] Press conference. July 7, 1950, *Nehru's Press Conferences 1950*, p. 122.

[4] In an interview for the *Straits Times* appearing April 20, 1956 ; quoted in Ton That Thien, *India and South East Asia 1947-1960*, p. 245.

[5] See, e.g., "India's Poor Salesmanship in Malaysia," *Hindu Weekly Review*, Aug. 16, 1965.

[6] *FAR*, vol. XII, 9 (Sept. 1966), p. 237.

[7] See, e.g., the report of Nehru's trip to Laos and Cambodia in Oct. 1954 in the *New York Times*, Nov. 6, 1954.

[8] cf. Ton That Thien, *op. cit.*, p. 126f. Another student of the question, D. R. Sar Desai, expressed "no doubt" that the Indo-French negotiations on the transfer of enclaves to New Delhi restrained the Indian government's criticism of French policy in southeast Asia, but he cited no evidence to support that assertion. See Sar Desai, "India's Relations with Vietnam, Laos, and Cambodia : 1954-1961," unpublished Ph. D. dissertation, U. C. L. A. 1965, p. 89.

[9] Speech in the Lok Sabha, April 24, 1954, *India's Foreign Policy*, p. 399.

[10] The Colombo conference, so-called, was initiated in order to discuss US aid to Pakistan, but the latter's representative refused to attend a meeting with that purpose. Therefore, that subject was omitted from the agenda, Pakistan attended, and the "compulsion of events" ultimately determined that the meeting should make recommendations on an Indo-Chinese settlement. See S. L. Poplai, "The Colombo Conference of South-East Asian Prime Ministers," *Foreign Affairs Reports* (Indian Council of World Affairs), vol. III, 7(July 1954).

[11] For a collection of comments on Menon's role, see M. S. Rajan, *India in World Affairs 1954-56*, p. 129 ; and Bhansali, K. G., "India's Role in the Settle-

ment of the Indo-Chinese Conflict," Ph. D. dissertation, American University, 1962, p. 96.

[12] Technically, the Geneva accords did not impose neutrality on Cambodia and Laos, but Nehru and other statesmen interpreted the "spirit of the accords" as requiring outside powers to avoid future military involvements in any of the former Indo-Chinese states. See Sar Desai, *op. cit.*, pp. 214-15, 223.

[13] India's share of the expenses of the ICSC was limited to reimbursements to its national delegations, fixed and mobile. *FAR*, vol. I, 3 (March 1955), p. 49. In 1955, 1,086, Indians were assigned to the various ICSCs ; Sar Desai, *op. cit.*, p. 195.

[14] Prince Sihanouk explained in his article, "Cambodia Neutral : The Dictate of Necessity" (*Foreign Affairs*, 36, 4, July 1958), that his state was "neutral in the same way Switzerland and Sweden are neutral—not neutralist like Egypt or Indonesia"—or India.

[15] Sihanouk's farewell message broadcast over All-India Radio, Feb. 8, 1963 ; *FAR*, vol. IX, 2 (Feb. 1963), p. 51.

[16] In Hanoi in October 1954 Nehru and President Ho Chi Minh issued a statement in which the Vietnamese leader said that he "wished to apply" the *panchasheel* "in the relations of Viet-Nam with Laos and Cambodia as well as with other countries." Again, in New Delhi in February 1958 President Ho proclaimed his dedication to *panchasheel. Foreign Policy of India :Texts of Documents 1947-59*, pp. 131, 327-28.

[17] Crown Prince Savang Vathana and the Laotian prime minister, Kathay Don Sasorith, agreed with Nehru on the five principles in New Delhi, Sept. 21, 1955, *Foreign Policy of India*: *Texts of Documents 1947-59*, p. 205.

[18] For a recital of those events see Arthur J. Dommen, *Conflict in Laos : The Politics of Neutralization*, N. Y. 1964.

[19] News conference comments, *New York Times*, June 11, 1959.

[20] *RSD*, vol. XXXI, Dec. 20, 1960, col. 2703.

[21] The Indian ambassador in Moscow, K. P. S. Menon, delivered Nehru's message to Khrushchev ; Menon, *The Flying Troika*, London 1963, pp. 293-96.

[22] See chapter XI.

[23] George Modelski, "International Conference on the Settlement of the Laotian Question 1961-62"; working paper no. 2 in the Dept. of International Relations Research School of Pacific Studies, Australian National University, Canberra 1962, p. 13.

[24] See Menon's statement at the Geneva conference, May 18, 1961, Modelski, *op. cit.*, p. 48.

[25] When the heads of mission of Western alliance governments in Vientiane convened in June 1964 to judge what moves could be taken to meet Pathet Lao attacks, the Indian ambassador to Laos participated in the consultations. But he surrounded his involvement by disclaimers of any intention to take an official position on the fighting because India's ICSC role would not permit that. India at the time was urging a reconvening of the 14-power conference to try to reach a fresh agreement. *FAR*, vol. X, 6, pp. 166-67.

[26] Her Majesty's Stationery Office, Cmd. 1755, London 1962, p. 7.

[27] *RSD*, vol. XL, Aug. 24, 1962, cols. 3051-56.

[28] Statement of the Govt. of India, Feb. 8, 1965, *FAR*, vol. XI, 2 (Feb. 1965), p. 39.

[29] The authors are indebted to Thomas W. Wilson and Philip I. Estermann for their illuminating analyses of Indian policy in Vietnam presented in unpublished papers at American University, 1965, 1966.

[30] Because of American insistence on continuing economic privileges and military base rights in the islands the new state could scarcely be regarded by anyone as fully independent. See George E. Taylor, *The Philippines and the United States*, N. Y. 1964, chapter 6.

[31] "Final Act and Proceedings of the Baguio Conference of 1950," published by the secretariat of the conference, n.d., p. 44.

[32] Romulo, *The Meaning of Bandung*, Chapel Hill 1956, pp. 11-12.

[33] *LSD*, vol. XXVII, March 17, 1959, col. 6686.

[34] See Anthony Eden, *Full Circle*, London 1960, pp. 87, 123-24 ; and *Collective Defense in South East Asia*, Chatham House : Royal Institute of International Affairs, London 1956, p. 4.

[35] For a tracing of these developments read the analysis by Rosemary Brissenden in George Modelski, ed., *SEATO : Six Studies*, Canberra 1962, pp. 206-10 ; and Brissenden, "India's Opposition to SEATO : A Case Study in Neutralist Diplomacy," *Australian Journal of Politics and History*, vol. 6, 2 (Nov. 1960).

[36] J. C. Kundra showed that US views on SEATO as well as those of the Philippines and Thailand were "almost completely missing from Indian newspapers." The Indian press had few reliable channels of information on Indo-China or any southeast Asian country. See Kundra, "SEATO Seen Through Indian Eyes : A Study of Differential Perception in News Reporting," *Indian Council of World Affairs Study*, New Delhi, n.d.

[37] "The Colombo Plan," Central Office of Information Reference Pamphlet no. 58, London 1964, p. 79.

[38] An admirable summary of the need for and possibilities of regional economic cooperation appeared in the *Ceylon Journal of Historical and Social Studies*, vol. 5, nos. 1 & 2 (1962).

CHAPTER XI

INDIA, WEST ASIA AND AFRICA

EVEN AS THE Indian Ocean provided a connection between India and southeast Asia since the time of the earliest navigators, so the deep western bay of that ocean, the Arabian Sea and its two prongs, the Red Sea and the Persian Gulf, loosely linked all the countries bordering on it. The trade carried across those waters through history was important in every period from prehistoric times to the present. Furthermore, the security of western India was seldom divorced from the conditions prevailing in the Arabian Sea. But in contrast to the intimacy of India's connections with the middle east—or west Asia, the term presently preferred in India—its relations with Africa south of the Sahara were fragmentary and of recent rather than traditional importance. The geographical configuration of the African continent partly explained this : it has its back, so to speak, turned on the Indian Ocean. Partly, also, there was an absence of high contemporaneous civilizations (other than in the Nile basin) towards which Indians might have been drawn. But most important, there was no land bridge between India and Africa. It was the land, more than the sea, that produced a firm bond between northern India and the peoples and lands to the north and west.

The Pamir Knot and the Hindu Kush mountains form the natural north and north-western boundaries of the Indian subcontinent and have been, historically, the keys to control of northern India. From the time of the Aryan incursions onward, migrating tribes and ambitious armies have traversed the passes of the Hindu Kush, usually into India. The resulting inter-mixture of races in northern India, the common religious teachings—pre-Buddhist, Buddhist, and, much later, Islamic—, and the continuous flow of peaceful travellers, combined with geography to make a cultural unity of the area west of the Indus and east of the Tigris and Euphrates rivers—a unity, however, which was almost never able to transcend

272

the political divisions that the land had known in historic times. It was possible for the leaders of modern India and their counterparts in Afghanistan, Iran, and Iraq to refer to the cultural contacts between their countries "which go back thousands of years,"[1] and to talk of renewing ancient ties before discussing their present-day problems.

The establishment of British power in India created an attendant British control over all the major routes to India by sea or by land.[2] Because the most important of those routes passed through west Asia India's pre-independence defense policy was more preoccupied with that region than with any other outside the subcontinent. The British fear of Russian penetration into Iran and Afghanistan was a dominant theme of its 19th century diplomacy, and two German efforts in the 20th century to control the region south and east of the Mediterranean were directly aimed at India. Garrisons of British-Indian troops in west Asia and commitments of Indian armed forces in the area in two world wars built up legacies that post-independence subcontinental states could not ignore. Events in Africa south of the Sahara did not affect India's security, and Western expansion into Africa was unconnected with British rule in India. The late 19th century partition of Africa between the European powers could be fairly isolated from the European empires in Asia.

India's commercial contacts with west Asia and Africa before the Second World War brought export profits from sales of cotton textiles, jute goods, and tea, and also encouraged the settlement of Indians in great and small trading centres throughout the Arabian Sea region. Imports into India from west Asia consisted primarily of raw materials, notably long-staple cotton and petroleum products.

Post-independence Indian policy towards the countries of west Asia and Arab world, on the one hand, and sub-Saharan Africa on the other revealed the same basic objective of ridding the two regions of European colonialism. The theme of anti-colonialism, pervading most Indian pronouncements on Africa and west Asia, provided a platform on which the independent countries of the two regions could stand together and temporarily ignore their differences. Since, perchance, European colonialism had meant the rule of white people over non-white people and since, deliberately, such rule had almost always been accompanied by racial

18

discrimination, anti-colonialism was inescapably bound up with anti-racialism. The question of race relations was never explicit in west Asian problems, though perhaps implied in the exclusion of "European" Israel from the coloured Afro-Asian world, but it was central to all African problems. Almost by accident India became the first international champion of racial equality in Africa by virtue of Gandhi's early efforts to improve the lot of the people of Indian origin in South Africa. India raised the same issue in the UN in 1946 and annually thereafter, until in 1952 it widened into discussions on the general question of the race conflict and the apartheid policy in South Africa. The bond of a common grievance between India and sub-Saharan African countries did not weaken after the African countries won the right to speak for themselves in the councils of the world. When confronted by racist policies, as followed by white minority governments in southern Africa, or by colonialism, the ranks of the non-white nations of Asia and Africa tended to close behind a common front of oratorical splendour.

Beyond oratory and conference proclamations and conjoint diplomatic efforts in the UN, however, the mutual objectives of anti-colonialism and anti-racialism fostered little tangible collaboration between India and west Asia or Africa. In fact, despite the geographic and historic relationships that west Asia had with India, the modern Arab-Islamic world, struggling for its own self-identity, did not regard India as a part of its own natural grouping—or scarcely Pakistan, whose culture was subcontinental. Sub-Saharan African states were comparatively isolated not only from India but from the rest of the world, except where the influence of the Commonwealth, the French Community, or newer organizations helped to bridge the immense cultural and economic gap that stood between African and all other modern civilizations.

Regional organizations in Africa and west Asia had no significance for India's relations with the countries involved in them. The Arab League, formed in 1945, neither unified the Arabs nor strengthened their relations with non-Arab states. The Afro-Asian Solidarity Committee, an outgrowth of the Afro-Asian Peoples' Solidarity movement, which started in India in 1955, never enjoyed the support of the Indian government, because of its communist sympathies ; although Cairo was prepared to use the movement to further its aims in Africa, New Delhi was not. One of the most significant organizational strides within Afro-Asia was made in Africa in 1963, when the two almost hostile camps of the Casablanca and the Monrovia groupings joined together at Addis Ababa in the first summit meeting of heads of African states or governments. But as the pan-African movement grew in strength, and as the African members of the UN grew in number and formed their own caucusing group, the concept of Afro-Asia lost its cementing quality. Meanwhile, India was finding increasing difficulty in subscribing to the more radical nationalist doctrines associated with some African and west Asian states. As a result, it gave only lukewarm agreement to participate in the abortive second Conference of Asian and African States, which was to have taken place at Algiers in 1965.

India's efforts to build up good will for itself in west Asia and Africa were hampered by two circumstances of recent Indian history. One was the immigration of Indian nationals as representatives of the British Empire and as traders and settlers into British spheres of influence. The other was the internal conflict between the National Congress and the Muslim League, which culminated in the creation of Pakistan as an Islamic state on the subcontinent. The first circumstance created problems for India's relations with certain of the new states of Africa which had Indian minorities identifying themselves as separate from both the Africans and the Europeans.[3] The second was even more serious because it undercut the most obvious basis for unity between post-independence India and the Muslim states of west Asia : a continuous land bridge and a common religion. Pakistan inherited the advantages of both and used them for its own benefit. (In the case of Afghanistan, however, Pakistan also inherited the problems of a common frontier and a divided Pathan people.) In order to counteract the threat of being completely isolated from the Islamic world India opposed the mixture of religion with politics, publicized its secular state doctrine, and deplored international ties based on religion alone. But at the same time it tried to project the image of India as the third most populous Muslim country, thereby courting the approval of traditional Islamic leaders.

Within the general context of India's search for the maximum number of friends and well-wishers in west Asia and Africa, relying on the concepts of anti-colonialism and nonalignment to provide community of interest, India's policies toward certain critical developments can be understood.

THE DILEMMA POSED BY ISRAEL

The creation of Israel out of three-quarters of the British mandated territory of Palestine in 1948 brought about a festering political sore which taxed the ingenuity of all interested states. India's official response to the formation of the new state was determined by the fact of an implacable, unmitigated hostility manifested towards Israel by the Arab states. India's policy was conscientiously low-keyed. Most informed Indians had sympathy for the Jewish victims of Nazi persecution. But they failed to understand the fervour with which the Zionists looked to Palestine as the "promised land," and they were suspicious of the British complicity in the displacement of a relatively backward native Arab community by European Jewish settlers. After the UK requested the General Assembly, in 1947, to consider the question of Palestine, India was named a member of the special eleven-member committee set up to make recommendations on the future of the area following British withdrawal in August 1948. Along with Yugoslavia and Iran, India presented a minority plan for a federated state with local autonomy for the Jewish and Arab units, and a limitation on Jewish immigration after three years ; India voted against the majority plan providing for partition into two states and an internationalized Jerusalem. On November 29, 1947, the Assembly adopted the latter plan and thus gave international sanction to the creation of Israel. In the war that followed, the Arab League and its national armies were discredited, Israel emerged victorious with de facto boundaries extended, and 940,000 Arabs were displaced from their homes in Palestine. The Indian government supported and contributed to the UN Relief and Works Agency for Palestinian refugees, on which devolved the task of assisting those homeless Arabs not absorbed by Jordan. In the years following, India persistently upheld the view, usually in communiques with Arab states, that the Palestinian refugees should be allowed to return to their homes.

In September 1950 India formally recognized Israel as a legal entity in the international community[4] but was reluctant to enter into close relations with the Jewish state. India acknowledged

Israel's right to exist, accepted an Israeli consul at Bombay, and recognized the desirability of solving the Arab-Israeli dispute without resort to threats of annihilation and provocations by the Arabs. But India also expressed its disapproval of Israeli military retaliations and Israel's appropriation of additional territory and its alteration of the flow of the river Jordan's waters.

Israel was eager, indeed anxious, to exchange ambassadors with Asia's second largest and at the time most influential state and win approval for the Asia-oriented neutralist policy that it followed until 1952.[5] India had to decide between, on the one hand, the logic and principle of establishing diplomatic relations with a state which was clearly in existence and whose energy, rate of economic development, and general European character evoked increasing admiration from a section of the informed Indian public ; and, on the other hand, the indisputable fact that friendship with, or at least lack of animosity from, the Arab states was desirable for India's security and general policy objectives. The longer New Delhi deferred its decision on exchanging diplomatic envoys the more difficult it became to do so without giving the impression of conscious approval and friendship for Israel and of deliberate offense to the Arabs. Time exacerbated rather than eased the Arab-Israeli rift, and thus India's dilemma remained. Nehru could not resolve it. In August 1959 he explained that : "This attitude was adopted after a careful consideration of the balance of factors. It is not a matter of high principle, but it is based on how we could best serve and be helpful in that area. . . . After careful thought, we felt that while recognizing Israel as an entity, we need not at this stage exchange diplomatic personnel."[6]

Although Nehru did not wish his policy to be interpreted as one of hostility toward Israel and regretted the circumstances that prevented normal relations between the two states, the consequence of India's ambivalent policy was first the disappointment, then the anger and even hostility of the Israeli government. Israeli pique with India often coloured its diplomacy in other Afro-Asian countries. Israeli premier, Ben-Gurion, frequently criticized India's west Asian policies and sometimes expressed his disappointment with Nehru. In March 1959 he told the Israeli parliament : "Mr. Nehru, the illustrious leader of a great country who claims to believe in neutrality, has behaved in an unneutral fashion towards Israel all along. In all his visits to the Middle East and neighbouring countries he stayed away from Israel, and, in spite of his promises to the representatives of our Foreign Ministry, he did not establish normal diplomatic relations with Israel."[7] A change in the Congress government's attitude would probably not come about without a general settlement in west Asia following the 1967 war, or a significant increase in the Indian public's demand for a change.

NATIONALISM AND FOREIGN INTERVENTION IN WEST ASIA

The countries of north Africa, geographically part of Africa, were most closely identified in culture and religion with the Arab lands to the east. But a strong link with Europe was established through the French conquest of Algeria in 1848 and its protectorates over Tunisia and Morocco established in 1881 and 1912, respectively. After the Second World War France recognized that the protectorate arrangements could not survive nationalist challenges. But it was slow to find a solution that would meet Tunisian and Moroccan demands and yet not upset its position in Algeria, regarded as part of metropolitan France.

The debates in the UN on the Moroccan and Tunisian situations from the early 1950's were guided from the anticolonialist side by Arab delegations, with India in a supporting position. Partly through UN efforts the two north African territories gained their independence in 1956.

In Algeria the incipient nationalist movement erupted into an armed uprising in November 1954 and consolidated itself behind the Front of National Liberation (FLN) and an army which waged a long and bitter struggle against the French. The FLN set up a provisional government in Cairo (GPRA) and gained recognition from several members of the Arab League. Indian policy toward the Algerian dispute had three aspects : sympathy and support for the FLN was the first, expressed directly as well as in the UN ; second, New Delhi attempted to understand the special interests of the French in Algeria, which led to suggestions on a basis for negotiations, a moderate approach aimed at not antagonizing France ; third, India's concern for the legalities of the Algerian situation persuaded it to deny formal recognition to the provisional government. Indian backing for the cause of Algerian freedom was predictable and axiomatic. As in the case of other anticolonial struggles, India avoided sending arms or men to Algeria, but its tangible support was demonstrated by shipping medical supplies and receiving with cordiality a permanent FLN representative in India. Nehru voiced his government's admiration for the struggle of the Algerian people in a contest "in which basically all the urges, passions, hopes, aspirations, and that mass upsurge of peoples which go to make the great movements of rising nationalism are engaged."[8] Indian UN delegates were associated with resolutions calling for a recognition of the right of the Algerian people for self-determination and criticizing French repression. Like other Afro-Asian states India was particularly disturbed by the indirect support that France received from NATO countries for its Algerian policies, by its withdrawals of French contingents from NATO for Algerian service and use of NATO arms against the FLN.

But Nehru saw the peculiar difficulty caused by the one million people of European origin settled in Algeria, who represented about one-tenth of the population and gave their allegiance to France. Nevertheless, as the war dragged brutally on it was to Nehru "perfectly clear that the Algerian question cannot be solved except on the basis of independence.... We have realized always that in considering the Algerian problems the fact of a million or more people of European descent living there is an important one. We cannot ignore this aspect, but important as it is, the fact of ten times that number wanting independence is more important still."[9] Indians placed their greatest stress, in the UN debates on Algeria, on the need for French-Algerian negotiations and tried to keep open the lines of communications between the warring parties. Their public statements on the war in Algeria expressed their dismay, rather than their condemnation of French policies. In 1955, on the first occasion that Algeria was debated in the General Assembly, the French foreign minister warned of the possible repercussions of the discussion on France's relations with the UN and led his delegation out of the meeting. Realizing the futility of UN debates without France present, V. K. Krishna Menon, India's delegate, led a move to mollify Paris by proposing a resolution, which was passed unanimously, that precluded further consideration of Algeria during the tenth session of the Assembly. UN competence was uncompromised, and the French delegation returned, appeased. Nehru met the

French foreign minister, Christian Pineau, in New Delhi and the
Algerian provisional government's leader, Ferhat Abbas, in London
in 1956, and on May 22 of that year he presented to parliament
five points as a possible basis for an Algerian settlement. Nehru's
proposals envisioned a free Algeria with equality for all persons,
implied special arrangements to be made for the Europeans, and
called for a renunciation of violence on both sides.[10] France rejected
the Indian suggestions.

While India urged France to negotiate directly with the Algerian
provisional government as representative of all elements of Algerian
nationalism, it did not itself recognize that government.[11] From
1954 the GPRA tried to secure Indian recognition, and its New
Delhi representative was sufficiently persuasive that questions in
parliament recurred on the reasons for non-recognition. The government explained that its reasons for not doing so were legalistic,
in that the provisional government did not fulfill the normal criteria
for recognition—functioning in the territory it was supposed to
govern—and that it was not customary in international law to
recognize a government in exile except in wartime cases of occupied
countries. Underlying the Indian hesitancy was the knowledge that
any premature recognition would be justifiably looked upon by
France as an unfriendly act. Moreover, although the de facto transfer of power in the erstwhile French enclaves in India was complete
by 1956, the passing of the de jure transfer was held up by the French
Assembly, and the Paris governments pleaded with India not to
endanger its passage by taking an antagonistic position on Algeria.
Finally, Nehru retained a belief that India might be called upon
to act as a mediator between France and Algeria, in which case the
gesture of recognition would not be worth the forfeiture of French
confidence. Nevertheless, India did not oppose the representation
of the provisional government at the Belgrade conference in 1961,
and Nehru explained that same year that : "In fact . . . although de
jure recognition was not given [to the provisional government] de
facto recognition to some extent has taken place."[12] India issued
de jure recognition immediately after Algeria's independence in June
1962, and friendly relations soon developed between the two states.

Once having achieved their independence, new states were not
thereby freed from the continuing threats of foreign intervention,
either by former colonial powers or by great powers with interests

in the area. The apparent withdrawal of the bulk of Russian forces and all of the Western military presence from Iran at the conclusion of the Second World War, for example, did not guarantee that country's freedom from further outside influence. Russian efforts to incorporate the northern Iranian province of Azerbaijan brought on the first great power confrontation at the UN, before India gained independence ; it ended in a Russian withdrawal. United Kingdom economic control in Iran was exercised through the Anglo-Iranian Oil Company, which the Teheran government nationalized in 1951. In the ensuing dispute India adopted no public stand, perhaps because of its mixed interests in the matter—on the one hand, sympathies toward Iran's desire for greater economic independence, but on the other hand, dependence on the continuing supply of oil from the Persian Gulf. The Anglo-Iranian oil dispute was resolved in 1954 when an international consortium of oil companies was set up to manage Iran's oil resources. India continued to purchase crude petroleum from Iran and in 1965 became the first country to which the newly established National Iranian Oil Company made large scale foreign sales independently. India and Iran also initiated collaboration in petroleum extracting and processing in that year.

Of all the traditional Indian interests in west Asia the Suez canal held by far the greatest significance. India could not avoid the expression of its vital concern for the continued functioning of the canal, which for a century had provided the major route for its access to foreign markets and in the mid-1950's accommodated the passage of 76 per cent of its imports and 70 per cent of its exports. The canal was operated by a foreign owned company and until the early 1950's was defended by British forces based in the Suez Canal zone. The canal's location within Egyptian territory would by itself have required New Delhi's cultivation of good relations with Cairo. But beyond that, Egypt was the largest and perhaps the most influential state in west Asia and parts of Africa.

The revolt of military officers against King Farouk in 1952 increased the tempo of Egyptian activities to force or persuade the British to withdraw from the area of the canal. India and Pakistan, both anxious for a permanent Anglo-Egyptian settlement which would protect their interests in the canal, offered to mediate in the dispute, which Egypt declined on grounds that a British agreement to withdraw had to precede negotiations on any final disposition of the problem. In October 1954 Cairo and London reached an accord, which among other provisions committed Egypt to maintain free navigation in the canal and gave the UK the right to re-enter the area in case of an attack on Arab states or Turkey by a power other than Israel. Nehru sent his congratulations to both sides. The state of crisis in the strategic Suez region, however, had not ended.

On July 26, 1956, the fourth anniversary of the Egyptian revolution, President Nasser announced the nationalization of the Suez canal company "to compensate for the past and build up new edifices for pride and dignity," asserting also that the canal "is a part of Egypt and belongs to Egypt."[13] His action was a reply to a US decision followed by the UK and the World Bank to cancel assistance that they had proposed to give for the building of a new high dam at Aswan. But the canal belonged not only to Egypt, but also to the world, in the sense that a substantial portion of the world's trade passed through it, and that its operator, the Universal Maritime Canal Company, had been pledged to freedom of access since the Constantinople Convention of 1888. The crisis of 1956 lay in the apparent irreconcilability of Egyptian sovereignty over the canal and the principle of free access to it by all states. In the first period of the crisis Britain, France, and their allies tried unsuccessfully to impose their solution of international control over the canal. The second period was precipitated by the Anglo-French invasion coordinated with an Israeli attack on Egypt. The international repercussions of the military action were grave, and the status quo had to be re-established before any other problem could be taken up, by which time Egypt's right and ability to operate the canal was no longer seriously questioned.

India's dominant interest lay in keeping the canal open. It regarded an armed conflict over Suez as a major threat to its economic interests, apart from the threat to regional and world peace. But scarcely secondary in importance was India's support of Egypt, as a friendly state and as another example of a relatively weak country's subjection to immense pressures from greater powers. India's position during the first period of the crisis was not enviable, because although it acknowledged Egypt's right to nationalize the canal company, it could not approve of the way it had been carried out. As Krishna Menon later put it : "We would like to have seen that nationalization carried out in the normal way of international expropriation, where there is adequate notice, and the way of taking over is less dramatic. . . ."[14] Nehru, too, may have thought that on such a portentous issue Nasser could have prepared his diplomatic support in advance, for example, by discussing Suez with Tito and himself at their Brioni conference in mid-July.

British and French reactions to Egypt's move brought on immediate economic sanctions and preparations for military intervention against Egypt,[15] whose earlier challenges to Western policy in the middle east and northern Africa had already created antipathy toward Nasser's regime.[16] (The American position, even at the time of nationalization, diverged in the direction of moderation away from that of its European allies.) The British-French confrontation with Egypt temporarily turned into diplomatic channels at two conferences of the principal users of the canal held in London in August and September. There India's dual interests, the canal's normal functioning and support of Egypt, placed it in a unique position to attempt mediation.

No Egyptian representative attended the London conferences ; so India's main delegate, Krishna Menon, assumed the role of an informal negotiator and mediator between the conference members and the Cairo government. His frequent trips between London and Cairo symbolized India's self-appointed function and its intense desire to achieve a peaceful solution. Menon acknowledged the weight of prior agreements which internationalized the operation of the canal so as to protect its many users, and he saw the need to obtain from Egypt certain assurances that would satisfy the major Western users. On the other hand, he pointed out that the Suez canal company fell under Egyptian law and that nationalization was not illegal in itself. As a practical matter, furthermore, only Egypt could guarantee freedom of navigation in the canal, and therefore Egypt's interests would have to be satisfied in any regular, peaceful canal operation. India, of course, rejected vigorously the implied British and French purposes of bringing about a defeat for Nasser, or his removal from power, as a precondition or by-product of any Suez settlement.

From the London conferences emerged a majority Western proposal for a Suez canal board to operate the canal in accordance with the 1888 convention ; Egypt's sovereignty would be nominally recognized along with its rights to fair returns from the canal's operation. This plan was conveyed to Cairo by the Menzies mission in early September and, as could have been expected, was rejected by Nasser. More in tune with Egypt's interests was the five-point plan presented by Menon on August 20, which was supported also by the USSR, Indonesia, and Ceylon. Its key provision would have set up a "consultative body of user interests"—a replacement for the Western scheme of canel control—"charged with advisory, consultative, and liaison functions."[17] India's suggestions on a revision of the 1888 convention included giving Egypt the responsibility for maintaining and further developing the canal, a provision for arbitration in cases of dispute between Egypt and the canal users on alleged discrimination, and an association of the UN with these arrangements.

The Indian compromise plan could not achieve majority approval in London, but its general approach, elaborated in other Indian proposals, continued to be a viable alternative to the impasse that developed. By September Egypt's position appeared somewhat more flexible than that of Britain and France, largely as a result of Indian advice.[18] Cairo offered to convene a conference for review of the Constantinople Convention, to respect the principle of freedom of navigation, and to fix toll rates with international agreement. (The issue of Israel's right to use the canal was avoided, but no change in the existing boycott could have been expected.)

Britain and France took the dispute to the Security Council on September 23 where it was the subject of intensive lobbying and personal interest by the secretary-general. On October 13 the foreign ministers of Egypt, Britain, and France announced agreement on a six-point plan as a basis for future negotiations, which embodied the essence of the Indian proposals offered at the time.[19] Hopes of a peaceful resolution rose but were doomed, because Egypt's enemies were determined to strike harder than was necessary merely to keep open the canal. Israel invaded Egypt on October 29, and the next day a British and French ultimatum was delivered to Cairo, and rejected. On the 31st, the Anglo-French intervention, in the style of a 19th century punitive expedition, was under way.

In India, as in the rest of the Afro-Asian world, the Anglo-French attack—justified by Britain and France as a police action in behalf of the international community—produced immediate and unmitigated condemnation. India gave complete diplomatic support to Egypt, which was reinforced, after the cease-fire, by a joint statement of the prime ministers of the Colombo powers (minus the prime minister of Pakistan).[20] Although the possibility of Israeli collusion with the British and the French was a hypothesis too tempting to be ignored, India refused to associate the problem of the Western invasion with the more complex relations between the Arab states and Israel. The earlier Israeli attack was taken up by the Security Council on October 29 at the initiative of the US, whose representative also submitted a draft resolution calling for Israeli withdrawal from Egypt, but the Council could take no action because of British and French vetoes. The later Anglo-French invasion was also criticized by the US, and when the General Assembly emergency session took cognizance of the crisis, on November 1, the US and the USSR acted together, along with India and the great majority of the membership, to stop the fighting.

The Assembly debates brought about a confusing display of accusations and counter-accusations and shifting voting alignments because the question of Russian intervention in the Hungarian revolution arose simultaneously.[21] India's policy in the Suez crisis was clearer than on the situation in Hungary because the issue was more straightforward, as India saw it, and the facts far better known. The General Assembly passed several resolutions on the Suez crisis in early November, which, since they were backed by American and Soviet power, brought into effect the cease-fire of November 5. India participated in the negotiations that ensued on the implementation of the cease-fire and the withdrawal of occupying troops from Egypt, but it was Canada which played the part of the main mediator. The roles of both countries were vital in the setting up and manning of the United Nations Emergency Force sent to maintain the peace in the middle east.[22]

The resort to force in Suez brought an abrupt end to India's attempts to achieve a canal settlement ; it also obviated the need for further such efforts, because the canal's management and operation were henceforth undisputably Egyptian and soon accepted as such by the maritime world. The sudden crisis matured the Indo-Egyptian relationship, which was already rooted not only in common stands on anti-colonialism and on nonalignment, but in the consistent opposition of both states to the Western sponsored defense system in west Asia.

British and American efforts lasting several years to set up a middle eastern defense organization as a military and political barrier against a feared southward spread of Soviet influence eventually resulted in the formation of the Baghdad Pact with Iran, Iraq, Pakistan, and Turkey as original members. Pakistan's adherence to this grouping in 1955 alone was enough to assure India's disapproval of the organization. Taken together with Pakistan's membership in SEATO the new alliances "tend to encircle us," Nehru pointed out with a degree of understatement.[23] But Nehru's abhorrence of military alliances, especially those between great and weak states, and his desire to extend nonalignment into as wide an area as possible would also have guaranteed his opposition. Egypt's hostility toward the pact and its strained relations with certain of its regional members were equal to or surpassed India's.

The interventions and conflicts of the great powers in west Asia were frequent and intense throughout the 20th century. However fervently Nehru, or Nasser, proclaimed the capabilities of the regional states to defend their own independence, it was not easy to demonstrate the truth of their convictions. Nehru tried to dispute the Western theory that following the British and French withdrawals from west Asia a political and military "vacuum" was left behind. "That, I feel, is a dangerous approach," he said in 1957, because a "power vacuum" would provoke renewed intervention—"if someone else comes in, it is a repetition of the old story, perhaps in a different form." But he concluded his argument by admitting that in reality there was such a "vacuum" in west Asia, which "can only be filled by the people of that country [or region] growing and developing themselves economically, politically and otherwise."[24] The Baghdad Pact, Nehru felt, retarded the emergence of individually strong west Asian states and exacerbated the conflicts between states of the area, thereby postponing any true regional strength. Furthermore, applying the "climate of war" thesis, Nehru saw the West's method of anticipating hostile communist movements in west Asia as a provocation for Soviet intervention.

Events of the summer of 1958 demonstrated again how extra-regional intervention into the internal conflicts of the middle east could precipitate an international crisis. The pro-Western governments in Lebanon and Jordan feared the effects on their peoples of Nasser's rising prestige and Egypt's possible expansion ; in February

1958 Syria and Egypt had joined together to form the United Arab Republic, with which Yemen was also associated. Lebanon's President Camille Chamoun complained of Egyptian intervention to the Security Council in June ; he was not satisfied when the UN Observer Group despatched to Lebanon, which included India's Rajeshwar Dayal, reported no evidence of it.[25] When the coup d'état of July 14 destroyed the Hashemite dynasty of Iraq, Lebanon and Jordan requested and received, respectively, American and British troops. The West feared possible repercussions of the Iraqi revolt. The Anglo-American moves cast a harsh image in post-colonial Asia and evoked immediate criticism. The Soviet government was quick to announce its special interest in the region, and Khrushchev wrote to Nehru suggesting a summit meeting with the three Western leaders to discuss the issue. Nehru agreed to attend, if invited,[26] but he also praised the newly announced Eisenhower plan for economic development in the middle east. He urged American and British leaders to withdraw their troops, and this was effected under the face-saving device of a unanimous General Assembly resolution of August 24.

The new leader of Iraq, Brigadier Abdul Karim Kassim, opted his country out of the Baghdad Pact and developed friendly relations with India. These were momentarily marred when India refused to support Iraq's claim to the oil-rich island of Kuwait, which gained its independence from the UK in 1961. Kuwait and the other sheikh-doms of the Persian Gulf enjoyed a special relationship with India and until recently used the rupee as their unit of currency. India and Kuwait exchanged ambassadors in 1963 and developed bilateral relations, which enabled Kuwait to profit from India's exportable trained personnel and India to benefit from Kuwait's capital and petroleum products. India made no objection to the defence arrangements of the UK in this area.

NATIONALISM AND FOREIGN INTERVENTION BELOW THE SAHARA

India's commitment to the permanent withdrawal of European colonial rule from Africa produced verbal expressions of emotion from Indian leaders. Nehru told the Asian Relations Conference and the Bandung Conference that the people of Asia had a special responsibility towards helping the people of Africa find their freedom, and he was eloquent on the "agony of the African continent throughout history."[27] Indian delegations at international conferences and the UN generally espoused the African causes, although their reluctance to be identified with the more radical group among the Afro-Asians was also manifest.

But the bases for India's relations with the newly independent countries between the Sahara and South Africa were tenuous, and seldom warranted even the exchange of resident diplomatic missions. Apart from the links established early with Ethiopia and the Sudan, it was membership in the Commonwealth, with the common language and similarity with British patterns of education and public life that it implied, which provided the best means of understanding among Indian and African officials. This advantage was lacking with states belonging to the French Community, whose close economic and political ties with the former metropole precluded their interest in nonaligned India. Though Nehru welcomed the emergence of an "African personality"[28] in the late 1950's the Indian people found it difficult to modify their feelings to take account of such an unfamiliar phenomenon, even in respect to African students who were being trained in Indian institutions on Government of India fellowships.[29]

The Indian reaction to colonialism and anti-colonialism in Africa differed according to the character of the rule. On British Africa India could hope to have some influence, exerted in London, and in any case had confidence in British promises to withdraw their administrators as quickly as possible. The independence of the Gold Coast, as Ghana, in 1957 started the process of decolonization, which for most British territories followed a course not unlike that of India : the Commonwealth attachment remained as did British economic and professional connections with new states. India's example of an orderly legal transfer of power and Nehru's post-independence foreign policies inspired emulation by such nationalists as Kwame Nkrumah, who acknowledged this on his visit to India in December 1958.

India's closer connections with east Africa brought it into touch with the struggle there against British rule and white settler dominance. Ignoring the community of interests between the British and some Indian entrepreneurs in Kenya, New Delhi backed the nationalist leader, Jomo Kenyatta, deputed a lawyer to assist his defense against government prosecution, and gave him an official welcome in India. The Indian high commissioner in Nairobi in the early 1950's, Appa Pant, gave financial support in his individual capacity to Kenyatta's movement,[30] although his government declined endorsement of any violent means to upset the British Kenyan government. New Delhi backed independence in principle and Kenyatta in practice, but it refused to criticize British policy on the pace of constitutional reform. The dualism resulted from India's dislike of the Mau Mau's violent methods ;[31] Kenyatta's hand in directing the Mau Mau was not always obvious. In Tanganyika and Uganda the process of political transition was less dramatic than in Kenya and offered less scope for Indian participation at any level. New Delhi calculated that good relations with the three east African states should not be jeopardized by exerting any pressure upon them in behalf of the Indian settlers there, as the following chapter explains.

With regard to sub-Saharan French territories, India had no contacts and enunciated no special policies. The same silence applied in the cases of the Belgian territories, until the Congo crisis erupted in 1960 and evoked India's criticisms of the character of Belgian rule as a totally inadequate prelude to independence—British constitutional procedures having been accepted as an implied standard. The Portuguese unwillingness to contemplate African rule in Angola and Mozambique and the evidence of political repression there raised a crescendo of Indian criticism, which found its most powerful expression in UN resolutions on the subject. Finally, in those territories, particularly Southern Rhodesia, where independence implied the continuation of white minority rule, India added its weight to the international pressure directed towards persuading the sovereign power, the UK, to use every method necessary to assure that a transfer of power would benefit the African majority.

India's relations with the Congo developed within the unique framework of the UN military intervention. Within a month of achieving independence on June 30, 1960, an army rebellion ; secession on the part of the richest province, Katanga ; intervention by Belgian troops ; and challenges to the authority of the prime minister, Patrice Lumumba, threw the whole state into chaos. The possibility of further external involvement especially by the great powers was grave, and India supported the secretary-general's moves to despatch

19

a UN peace-keeping force to the Congo as a preventive measure. As chapter XIX describes, India was one of the countries which argued the need for a maximal role for the UN force, after the assassination of Lumumba had demonstrated the inefficacy of a strictly non-interfering position ; Indian troops became the backbone of the operations undertaken to end Katanga's secession and avert civil war. Throughout the tortured political conflicts within the Congo the Indian government urged adherence to the legalities of a parliamentary government and a unitary state rather than support for particular personalities angling for power.[32] India gave full support to the Adoula government, and despite its earlier stringent criticisms of Moise Tshombe and Joseph Mobutu maintained relations with each of them during their prime ministerships. Though India opened an embassy in Leopoldville, or Kinshasa, in 1960 it had no special interest in that country beyond a concern for its insulation from foreign interference and a desire to extend, if possible, the zone of nonalignment. It was the Indian military and technical involvement through the UN that led to the Indian presence in the Congo, and not the other way around.

SPECIAL RELATIONSHIPS

Because of special circumstances and deliberate effort, India's relations with certain states in west Asia and Africa grew very close, in contrast to the fairly low level of contacts maintained with the region as a whole. Earlier pages have described the similarity of views between Cairo and New Delhi. A structure of tangible co-operation was built by the two countries during and after the Suez crisis in a way that no conference proclamations could possibly have accomplished. India's skilful presentation of the Egyptian case at the London meetings along with its energetic efforts to reach a negotiated settlement, and then its unstinting support during the three-power attack were recognized in Cairo. Nasser's government turned to India to handle its relations with Britain and France when diplomatic ties with those two states were broken off ; they were resumed in 1958 and 1961, respectively. Egypt was one of the first countries with which India established a practice of balancing trade payments in domestic currencies and during the 1960's became the second largest purchaser of Indian tea. The first excavating team ever sent abroad by the Indian archaeological department was to a prehistoric Nubian site near Aswan.

More significantly, India assisted in the training of Egyptian air force personnel, and in 1964 the two countries agreed to collaborate on the production of supersonic combat aircraft.[33] New Delhi supported Egypt's position that the Gulf of Aqaba and the Strait of Tiran were territorial waters of Egypt and Saudi Arabia, and that therefore the consent of those states was necessary to all navigation in those waters ; that support was publicly reiterated during the crisis of 1967.[34] Through a succession of state visits beginning in 1955 and at tripartite conferences with President Tito, Nehru and Nasser cultivated a personal understanding and regard that brought equal benefits to both sides. Egypt, lacking Western support and cautious of a too deep involvement with the communist states, relied on India's prestige and support for its own independent foreign policy and its standing in world affairs. It courted India's pro-Arab stance on the Palestine issue. India gained the goodwill of the largest Arab state and thereby undermined any Pakistani plans to promote a pan-Islamic bloc hostile to India. At the time of the Chinese invasion of 1962 Egypt demonstrated a more active concern for the withdrawal of Chinese forces than any other state in Africa or west Asia. It remained neutral in the Indo-Pakistani war of 1965 and on the Kashmir issue in general.

Though the close tie with Cairo seemed to hamper New Delhi's interest in cultivating other west Asian states more actively, it did not prevent an early and continued sympathy for the Sudan. Controlled by an Anglo-Egyptian condominium from 1899, the Sudan was given the option of independence under an Anglo-Egyptian agreement of 1953. The elections held that November were supervised by an international commission chaired by an Indian, Sukumar Sen. After declaring its independence in 1955, in an atmosphere of deteriorating relations with its northern neighbour, the Sudan turned to India for technical and professional personnel to assist in its development. Relations developed along mutually beneficial lines with Nehru praising the Sudan's efforts at bridging the Arab and African worlds during his visit in 1957, and President Ibrahim Abboud supporting India's secular approach to the Kashmir problem when he toured India in 1964. The Sudan was India's largest supplier of long staple cotton.

Perhaps the most intimate relations that India enjoyed with a state in continental Africa were with Ethiopia, where Indian troops had assisted in the defeat of the Italian occupying forces in the Second World War. Because of Ethiopia's long history of independence and because of the high prestige of Emperor Haile Salassie, a relationship of psychological equality and mutual respect was possible. When Ethiopia adopted the use of English in 1948, it applied to India, as an English-speaking but non-Western, nonaligned country, for much needed technicians and teachers. Indian officers were also asked to organize and staff the Ethiopian military academy at Harrar, but the importance of India's military mission diminished sharply after the US was invited to assist Ethiopia's defenses in 1958. Unlike many African leaders, but in concert with Nehru, the Emperor followed a moderate line on anti-colonialism and an unvitriolic nonalignment. In the 1960's India became the third largest source of Ethiopian imports but purchased little in return. The Emperor firmly supported India's case against China in 1962 as well as the Indian stand on Kashmir. By careful diplomacy India's friendship with Ethiopia was not allowed to mar, or be marred by, a developing relationship with the Somali Republic, to which deputations of Indian medical and technical personnel were being sent by the mid-1960's.

Nigeria in west Africa, because of its size and potential, was singled out by many foreign offices, including India's, as the country which could exercise the most profound and moderate influence on sub-Saharan Africa. Though Ghana's position was also appreciated in New Delhi, the mercurial temperament of Kwame Nkrumah prevented a fruition of relations between the two governments.[35] Nigeria was the only tropical African country visited by Nehru (in September 1962), but he failed to establish a rapport with Prime Minister Abubakar Tafawa Balewa. In the absence of any traditional ties, other than the Commonwealth, and in the face of serious internal problems faced by Nigeria, the two countries remained in an exploratory stage of their relationship through the mid-1960's, though they took similar positions in the UN on such matters as the Congo and disarmament. Indian economic, professional, and military advisers were sent to Nigeria, on request. The vast distances and heavy freight charges, combined with the fact that India needed almost nothing that Nigeria produced, except palm oil, frustrated their mutual desire to extend trade relations. A heavy balance favouring India's exports of cotton textiles and jute goods remained.

A return to a consideration of that great Islamic bloc from Afghanistan to Morocco suggests that India sought to secure goodwill even where contacts were low-keyed and maintained a studied detachment from the intra-regional rivalries, of which Egypt was often a protagonist. In north Africa India, as expected, supported Tunisian complaints against France over the Bizerte incident of 1958. Indo-Tunisian trade increased after the conclusion of a bilateral trading agreement in 1960. To Morocco's claim on neighbouring Mauretania India lent tacit support by refraining from recognition of Mauretanian independence until after that country was accepted as a member of the UN. Closer to home, Turkey and Iran remained members of the Central Treaty Organization (so renamed after Iraq, to Nehru's gratification, withdrew from the Baghdad pact), and India objected to the assistance they extended to their fellow pact member, Pakistan. Nevertheless, efforts were made by India as well as by Turkey and Iran to maintain good relations, to which various exchanges of visits attested. Indian dependence on Iran as a channel of air and telecommunications and as a major source of petroleum, as well as the traditional link between Iran and the Indian Muslims, were important interests underlying New Delhi's diplomacy. India imported oil from Saudi Arabia, sent ship loads of Muslim pilgrims annually to Mecca and Medina, and saw in that fast changing land an expanding market for its goods. India's concern for the troubled situations preceding independence in Aden and the south Arabian sheikhdoms was restricted to statements in the UN.

Afghanistan's location as a neighbour of Pakistan and the frequent tensions between those two states, chiefly over the issues of Pakhtoonistan[36] and transit rights, suggested possibilities of an Indo-Afghan entente that might have benefited both states strategically. The Pathan leader, Khan Abdul Ghaffar Khan, a former supporter of Gandhi and the Congress, sought Indian support for the Pathan cause, but to no avail. Support for Pakhtoonistan or an entente with Kabul remained a power-political move abjured by Nehru, if only because of his real desire not to give Pakistan concrete cause for suspicion of India's military intentions. Furthermore, any Indian support for a revision of the 1893 Durand Line boundary between Afghanistan and Pakistan would have compromised New Delhi's stand on the integrity of the pre-independence frontiers of India. During the 1961 Pakistan-Afghan crisis Nehru refused to comment on the relations between those states, noting that Pakistan inherited the interest that undivided India had in the Durand Line—a remark interpreted in Karachi as an affirmation of Pakistan's legal position.[37] Thus, India avoided involvement in Pakistan-Afghan disputes, and, similarly, Kabul eschewed entanglement in disagreements between India and Pakistan. Afghan caution was illustrated during the negotiations to demarcate its 30-mile border with China—an incongruous left-over of Britain's efforts to maintain Afghanistan as a buffer against Russia. The Kabul negotiators refused the Chinese request to designate a point on the boundary as adjacent to territory defended by Pakistan, thus maintaining its perfect neutrality on the Kashmir controversy.

India and Afghanistan signed a treaty of friendship in 1950, and the two states engaged in periodic exchanges of visits by various dignitaries, all of which signified their common adherence to non-alignment and a mutual goodwill that had blossomed after Pakistan inherited the tension of the subcontinent's northern frontier. India furnished some technical help to Afghanistan, and the two states tried to overcome the occasional serious interference in their trade caused by Pakistan. The subcontinent remained the prime market for Afghanistan's staple export of fresh and dried fruit, the overland route being especially important for northern Indian fruit lovers : about one hundred trucks each day brought Afghan fruit into the Amritsar markets during the peak season of August and September. Indo-Afghan relations were perhaps best summarized by Nehru when welcoming Afghan prime minister Mohammad Daud to India in 1959. "As between Afghanistan and India," he said, "I cannot remember any point of real difference, and it is odd that when two countries have no particular point of difference, they take each other for granted. There is not much to argue, because we agree more or less. And that has been the case with India and Afghanistan in these ten or twelve years."[38]

The major emphasis of Indian diplomacy in west Asia and Africa in the later 1960's lay in the cultivation of economic relationships. Both west Asia and Africa are natural trading areas for India but were long divided into separate regions of European market control.

The continuing Western monopoly over the infrastructure of trade—shipping lines, banking and insurance, trade routes, and patterns of trade—hampered the emergence of new economic relationships once European political rule had been rmoved. However, the intention to expand trade and enter into economic cooperation was expressed in every joint communique issued by the leaders of India and the countries of west Asia and Africa. Tangible steps lagged behind intentions, but Indian trade agreements charted a course of future expansion of commerce, and Indian business delegations explored possibilities for industrial collaboration,[39] such as in the sugar industry of Uganda. New Delhi realized that any growth of trade would have to go beyond the mere commercial exchange of goods and involve a participation in economic development, particularly in Africa. But India's own low level of economic performance made its aid programmes a disappointing trifle in comparison even to the Chinese effort, not to speak of Western assistance.

Despite strong competition from more developed countries, India's trade with the middle east and Africa showed an upward trend in the 1960's. The former region provided India with three of its most vital raw materials, petroleum from Iran, Saudi Arabia, Kuwait and Bahrein ; raw cotton from Egypt and the Sudan ; and rock phosphate from Tunisia, Morocco, and Jordan. India's exports remained, as in earlier periods, the traditional cotton textiles, jute goods, and spices. India's best hope for increasing its exports rested on increased shipments of engineering goods, such as bicycles, fans, and sewing machines, and agricultural implements, such as diesel pumps, for all of which the demand was growing. Sales of those items steadily rose in Iraq, Iran, Kuwait, Aden, and Saudi Arabia.

Trade with Africa below the Sahara was more limited and tended to be restricted to the English-speaking areas, where Indian settlers had formed a bridgehead—Kenya, Uganda, and Tanganyika—and to a much smaller extent Nigeria. India's offtake of African commodities was negligible and comprised wattle bark, sisal, asbestos, and cloves from east Africa—Zanzibar was India's only source of the latter—and non-ferrous metals from the Congo, Malawi, and Zambia. The export trade was once again dominated by tea, jute manufactures, and cotton piece goods, all facing new competition ; but the sale of spices and of engineering goods showed potentials for growth. India's trade with individual countries in Africa tended to be unbalanced, either favourably or adversely, and the position was unlikely to change without an acceleration of industrial development and an improvement in Indian export techniques, and a diversification of the largely single-commodity African economies. The Indian government became aware that India's economic development was connected with that of the rest of Asia and Africa as logically as the struggle for Indian independence had spawned anti-colonialist struggles elsewhere. India, therefore, was an important partner in the effort of the underdeveloped countries of the world to make the UN responsive to their economic needs through the creation of new institutions, notably the United Nations Conference on Trade and Development (UNCTAD). As discussed in chapter XIX, India's interest lay both in raising the level of economic cooperation between itself and other developing countries and in winning better terms of trade and aid for all of them from the developed nations.

Any general comment on India's relations with west Asia and Africa must emphasize the modest and undramatic role assumed there by India. Having renounced the British-Indian imperial mentality, and suffering the loss of its northern Muslim majority areas, India had neither the ambition nor the means to play the role of an aggressive leader in the African and Arab worlds. In any joint actions proposed by the states of the two regions for the realization of specific objectives India had little or no place ; this was in contrast to southeast Asia, where India's refusal to exercise its potential influence left some states with no alternative but to align with the US or turn towards China. As in the case of southeast Asia, few Indian officials welcomed assignments to the countries of west Asia or Africa or maintained as high a standard of diplomatic effort in those capitals as they did in the lobbies of the UN, where Afro-Asian solidarity was a frequent objective. Cultural contacts with Africa and even with west Asia were few. The Indian public was poorly informed about both regions and disappointed in the response, or lack of it, by the countries of west Asia and Africa to the Sino-Indian conflict of 1962.[40]

But on the whole, India succeeded in furthering its major objectives in west Asia and Africa. These were to maintain the goodwill of as many of those states as possible, in the face of active rivalry from Pakistan in the middle east and from China in Africa, as well as some opposition from Western states ; and to increase substantially its economic connections. When occasions arose which affected concrete Indian interests, such as the Suez crisis of 1956, India acted promptly and with constructive effects.

NOTES AND REFERENCES

[1] Nehru's speech in Kabul, Sept. 14, 1959, Nehru, *India's Foreign Policy*, p. 291.

[2] See Halford Hoskins, *British Routes to India*, for a discussion on how this was accomplished.

[3] See the following chapter for a discussion of the Indians in Africa.

[4] Among the reasons given by the official spokesman for the decision to recognize Israel was the assessment that "continuing non-recognition is not only inconsistent with the overall relationship but even limits the effectiveness of the Government of India's role as a possible intermediary between Israel and the Arab states." From a communique of Sept. 17, 1950, quoted and discussed in K. P. Misra, *India's Policy of Recognition of States and Governments*, p. 58.

[5] Michael Brecher, *The New States of Asia*, London 1963, pp. 123-52.

[6] Nehru's statement at a press conference, New Delhi, August 7, 1958, *India's Foreign Policy*, pp. 414-15.

[7] *Asian Recorder*, 1959, April 4-10, p. 2594.

[8] Nehru's statement in the Lok Sabha, May 22, 1956, *India's Foreign Policy*, p. 505.

[9] Nehru's speech in the Rajya Sabha, Dec. 15, 1958, *India's Foreign Policy*, p. 510.

[10] Nehru's statement in the Lok Sabha, May 22, 1956, *India's Foreign Policy*, p. 506.

[11] See K. P. Misra, *op. cit.*, pp. 117-45, for a complete discussion of this subject.

[12] *LSD*, vol. LVI, Aug. 16, 1961, col. 2413.

[13] Nasser's speech, Cairo, July 26, 1956, in Fisher and Krinsky, *The Middle East in Crisis*, p. 140.

[14] Menon's speech to the London conference, Aug. 20, 1956, "The Suez Crisis and India," p. 10.

[15] See A. J. Barker, *Suez : the Seven Day War*, London 1964, for a description of the early preparations and the conduct of the operation.

[16] See Anthony Eden, *Full Circle*, Boston 1960, book three, "Suez," esp. pp. 419-41.

[17] See "The Suez Crisis and India" for texts of Menon's speeches and proposals at the London meetings.

[18] See Robert Mathews, "The Suez Canal Dispute : A Case Study in Peaceful Settlement," *International Organization*, vol. XXI, 1 (winter 1967).

[19] See text of Indian proposal of Oct. 24, in *FAR*, vol. II, 10 (Oct. 1956), pp. 158-59.

[20] Text in *Foreign Policy of India : Texts of Documents* 1947-64, pp. 275-79.

[21] See chapter XVI, ahead, for a discussion of India's policy on the situation in Hungary.

[22] See chapter XIX, ahead, for India's role in this peace-keeping operation.

[23] Speech in the Lok Sabha, March 29, 1956, *Speeches 1953-1957*, p. 319.

[24] Speech in Lok Sabha, March 25, 1957, *ibid*, p. 343.

[25] See M. S. Agwani, "The Lebanese Crisis in Retrospect," *International Studies*, vol. IV, 4 (April 1963), pp. 329-49, for an interpretation of that crisis.

[26] Text of Nehru's letter in *FAR*, vol. IV, 7 (Aug. 1958), p. 127.

[27] Nehru's speech to a seminar on the problems of Portuguese colonies, New Delhi, Oct. 1961, in *Nehru and Africa*.

[28] Speech in the Rajya Sabha, Sept. 15, 1958, *India's Foreign Policy*, p. 502.

[29] The difficulties of adjustment by African students to conditions in India often deprived India of the goodwill it expected to generate through assisting in the education of the African people.

[30] See F. D. Corfield, *Kenya : The Origin and Growth of Mau Mau : An Historical Survey*, Kenya Govt. Sessional paper no. 5 of 1959/60, Nairobi 1960, pp. 222-23 : "As the political situation deteriorated in the months prior to the declaration of the Emergency, the continued support given to the overt political activities of Jomo Kenyatta by the office of the Indian Commissioner encouraged him in his course of subversion, and so was an embarrassment to the Kenya Government and to the more liberal element in the Indian community."

[31] See Congress resolutions on Africa in 1953, "The Evolution of an Indian Policy Toward Africa," *A.I.C.C. Economic Review*, Feb. 15, 1963, p. 5. Also Nehru's enunciation of policy on east Africa in *RSD*, vol. VII, Sept. 15, 1954, col. 2217.

[32] While India's sympathies lay with Prime Minister Lumumba rather than with his rivals, India did not support the "Lumumbaist" group which set itself up at Stanleyville after his assassination and challenged the authority of the central government at Leopoldville, with some external assistance.

[33] See *The Statesman*, New Delhi, Sept. 18, 1964.

[34] Menon in the General Assembly on March 1, 1957, and Chagla in the Lok Sabha, May 25, 1967. Quoted in "India and Palestine," pp. 45 and 59.

[35] India was disturbed at Nkrumah's attitude toward the Chinese aggression in 1962 which led him, for example, to oppose Britain's military assistance to India. See Nkrumah's messages to Prime Minister Macmillan on Oct. 31, and Nov. 1, 1962, in Nicholas Mansergh, ed., *Documents and Speeches on Commonwealth Affairs 1952-1962*, London 1963, p. 621.

[36] The concept of a Pathan state or integrated nation, encouraged by Afghanistan and opposed by Pakistan ; the Pathans inhabited both sides of the legal boundary between Afghanistan and Pakistan.

[37] See *Asian Recorder*, Nov. 5-11, 1961, p. 4250.

[38] Text of speech in *FAR*, vol. V, 2, (Feb. 1959), pp. 13-14.

[39] See "Report of Indian Industrialists Goodwill Delegation to Some African Countries" (Sept.-Oct. 1964).

[40] See M. S. Agwani, "The Reactions of West Asia and the UAR" and S. N. Sharma, "India and Africa," in *International Studies*, vol. V, nos. 1-2 (July-Dec. 1963), pp. 75-79, 188-97.

CHAPTER XII

MINOR PROBLEMS WITH FAR-REACHING ASPECTS

I. Overseas Indians

A LITERATURE[1] WITH a world-wide audience grew up after the Second World War dealing with the problems of peoples of Indian origin settled abroad (overseas Indians) and with the bits of foreign held territory that remained within the geographic confines of independent India. The politically coloured human drama present in the first and the curiosity evoked by the symbolism of the second problem caused international interest ; but for India those two matters defined national values central to its objectives in international affairs.

THE TURMOIL SURROUNDING OVERSEAS INDIANS

Apart from the British themselves, Indians (including those Muslims who gave their allegiance to Pakistan after 1947) were the largest group of colonizers in the British empire. Of the many estimates of the numbers of Indians settled overseas a figure of four to five million appeared reasonable for the mid-1960's.[2] Indians left their homeland in the 19th and 20th centuries under a variety of circumstances, almost all of which included opportunities for economic betterment outside the country. No region or country of the world which was open to Indian settlement lacked some Indian immigrants by the mid-20th century. Like other wandering nationalities—the Greeks, the Chinese, the Armenians—certain communities of Indians seemed to adapt themselves to environments as diverse as Shanghai and British Columbia, Fiji and east Africa, once labour conditions or commercial and professional opportunities had beckoned to them there. But compensating for their voluntary exile they retained their Indian traditions, including endogamous marriages and religious and linguistic identifications : adaptation

299

did not lead to assimilation with local people, except perhaps in north America.[3] In the great bulk of cases those Indians who settled abroad found themselves "economically and socially better off than the corresponding categories of people in India ; immigration had justified itself. Few Indians who were settled overseas by the middle of the 20th century wished to return to India."[4]

Most emigrating Indians headed for territories under British control : those were in fact the areas from which requests were made throughout the 19th and part of the 20th centuries for unskilled labourers from the poorer classes of Indian peasants. Responses came mostly from south India. Later Indian merchant and professional classes, from Gujarat and Punjab as well as south India, moved abroad to serve the already settled Indians and also the indigenous people. The problems that first arose in connection with this movement and settlement overseas resulted from the inhumane treatment of indentured labourers, sent to sugar plantations in Mauritius, British Guiana, Trinidad, and Jamaica in the 1830's and 1840's and Natal in the 1860's. The Indian government in 1856 adopted rules governing the conditions of indentured labour which if not followed by recruiters and the overseas authorities could result in selective prohibition of emigration. Further regulations were laid down in 1883 and in the 20th century.

Somewhat later to appear were difficulties which could not easily be affected by the Government of India's policies, namely the unwillingness of white settlers in the temperate territories to concede equality to Indians whose indentures had lapsed or who had immigrated freely and who expected to be treated on a par with other British subjects. In the crown colony of Natal by the 1870's the white controlled government was imposing discriminatory restrictions on so-called coolie labourers (Indians), and matters grew much worse by the end of the century, when Indians outnumbered Europeans in the colony. "Natal clearly wanted the best of both worlds. Indian labour was considered essential for the welfare of the colony, at least by the planters, but the white settlers were not willing to tolerate a permanent Indian population and Indian business competition in return."[5] A similar confrontation of European and Indian interests emerged elsewhere and with especially hostile overtones in east African British territories in the 20th century.

A third type of problem, often neglected by Indian writers who associated most of the troubles of overseas Indians with white racial discrimination, arose after the First World War as a result of antagonisms between Indian settlers and indigenous colonial people. Prime examples appeared in Burma and Ceylon in the 1930's and in east Africa, Fiji, and British Guiana following the Second World War.

All of the major difficulties experienced by Indians emigrating and settling abroad received some sort of attention from the British Indian government. Most of the strenuous efforts to ameliorate the conditions of overseas Indians were undertaken in the 20th century under pressure from domestic Indian opinion ; the outstanding example, relating to race discrimination in African territories, were the Government of India's appeals in the imperial conferences for equality of treatment for all British subjects, as described in chapter I. Indian nationalists spared no criticisms of the indenture system, which created as much misery as it brought economic benefits. In 1917 the Viceroy, Lord Hardinge, terminated the system as a war-time measure, after he and Secretary of State Montagu read reports from two of their countrymen, C.F. Andrews and W. W. Pearson, on the deplorable conditions of indentured Indian workers. After the war the reformed central Indian legislature passed the Emigration Act (1922), which gave the government authority to define the conditions under which the exodus of unskilled labourers could be resumed, in the absence of which India could prohibit further departures to specified countries. Agents of the Indian government were assigned abroad where necessary to oversee the working of the act. Their endeavours were reinforced by tours of special emissaries who visited imperial domains under government sponsorship.

At the time of independence the new Indian government inherited the administrative and diplomatic proceedings of the previous regime relating to overseas Indians. To carry forward the work already in progress, such as negotiations with the Ceylonese and South African governments, would be increasingly difficult because of the loss of whatever influence London had been able to exert. (One reason for India's continuing the Commonwealth attachment was that the Commonwealth tie was expected to be beneficial in negotiations on the rights of Indians abroad.) In addition, the New Delhi government seemed committed to the active championing of the interests of overseas Indians because of previous resolutions of the Congress. At almost every annual meeting since the 1890's Congress had deplored the conditions under which overseas Indians were forced to live and urged stronger governmental action to bring about improvement. Publications of the Congress commended the cultural and psychological bonds between Indian settlers and their homeland;[6] the organization appeared to encourage emigration under beneficial conditions but at the same time hoped, or assumed, that Indians anywhere would remain loyal to India, just as India was not to forget her departed countrymen. Delegations, sponsored by Congress and other organizations, frequently toured the empire to investigate the complaints of their overseas brethren and widely publicized their findings at home, thereby tightening the links between Indian society and its overseas members.

After 1947 the Congress had to enunciate a more responsible policy on overseas Indians than that of the pre-independence days. Protests about their treatment became matters of international relations, no longer directed in part at British imperial policy but at sovereign or potentially sovereign states with interests that had to be reconciled with India's. Following independence, except in dealings with South Africa, the tone of Indian communications concerning the settlers was usually mild and reasoning.

But Indian policy was self-contradictory. With respect to those overseas Indians who were foreign nationals—the bulk of them were in that category—it acknowledged the legal jurisdiction of foreign states and their responsibility for the settlers. But it simultaneously intervened diplomatically in order to improve their legal status. Nehru candidly acknowledged the contradiction in 1957. There were Indians, he said, "who have been in countries like Ceylon for 30, 40, 50 or 60 years, whatever the period may be, whom we do not consider our nationals. . . . So far as we are concerned, strictly, legally and constitutionally, it is none of our problem. . . . But we do not take up that particular attitude, although it is the correct attitude. For, we are interested in their welfare and we are interested in finding a solution because there is a history behind this."[7] That history included the emotional attachment of Indians toward their kinsmen abroad, expressed with particularly strong political force in the states, such as Madras, from which emigrants had departed in large numbers. Reflecting that bond was a clause in the Indian

Constitution (part II, article 8) which provided that any person living abroad one of whose parents or grandparents was born in India could be granted Indian citizenship, by registration.

When the complications attendant on India's wavering approach to the overseas settlers grew increasingly obvious Nehru's pleas grew stronger for them to "associate themselves as closely as possible with the interests of the people of the country they have adopted."[8] This line, in fact, became part of the official response to continuing pressures on the government from home and abroad to intervene whenever any country's policies adversely affected the position of Indians. Nehru tried to make it clear that he wanted no special privileges or advantages for the settlers (which they had gained in some territories by collaborating with the British in administering the areas and exploiting their natural resources). At the same time, and when the cases merited it, New Delhi was prepared to exert considerable diplomatic pressure on other states to gain what it considered equitable treatment under non-discriminatory laws for overseas Indians.

The effects on India's foreign relations of the difficulties encountered by overseas Indians varied in accordance with the local circumstances and the overall requirements of Indian foreign policy. India's relations with South Africa, east Africa, Burma, and Ceylon can provide brief illustrations of this proposition. A fuller survey, describing the less significant effects of the Indian communities in Malaya, in the Pacific and Indian Oceans, and in the Caribbean region, does not seem appropriate to the present undertaking.[9]

INDIANS IN SOUTH AFRICA

The dispute between India and South Africa over the treatment of Indian settlers was a veteran problem, and before independence it involved equally the New Delhi government and the National Congress. The dispute arose from the treatment by white South Africans of Indians who had left the plantations on the expiry of their indentures or had immigrated on their own from India in order to enter the economy as free labourers and businessmen. They competed with Europeans, often to the disadvantage of the latter, and their numbers and manner of life appeared to threaten the integrity of the South African outpost of European civilization.

Indians settled mainly in Natal, where by 1894 there were already 43,000 of them and 40,000 Europeans. The discriminatory laws and regulations and social inequalities that affected all Indians persuaded Mohandas K. Gandhi to organize and lead the Indian community in a novel form of agitation, which he termed *satyagraha*, in order to focus local and imperial attention sympathetically on the plight of the Indian population. Gandhi's efforts, begun in 1893 and lasting for twenty-one years, by no means reversed the trend towards white dominance and inequality for Indians in South Africa ; he was able only to mitigate its harsh effects. By organizing local movements, such as the Natal Congress, he offered Indians hope that in the future they could exert some influence on the government.[10] The hope-inspiring climax of Gandhi's movement was his compromise agreement with Jan Christian Smuts, a Union minister, in 1914 which led to an Indian Relief Act cancelling some of the more detrimental anti-Indian regulations. In exchange Gandhi agreed on virtual stoppage of free Indian immigration into South Africa, accepted a plan for voluntary repatriation, and acknowledged that South Africa was to remain white dominated, politically and culturally.

During the years of Gandhi's campaign the Indian government maintained pressure on the local South African regimes and the home authorities in London. The government's chief instrument of political leverage had been its power to cut off the supply of labourers which the plantation owners (in contrast to other Europeans) wanted to maintain. That threat was no longer of use after indentured labour emigration to South Africa was cut off by India in 1911, and the Gandhi-Smuts agreement terminated the free labour supply. The National Congress, of course, annually condemned anti-Indian policies in South Africa while also criticizing the British for not taking a more forceful stand against the Union's racial measures. Its emissaries frequently visited South Africa.[11]

In the 1920's India entered negotiations with South Africa in order to avert legislation that would tighten restrictions already imposed on Indians' rights of residence, ownership of land, and conduct of businesses. The two states managed to conclude the Capetown Agreement in 1926, distinctly favourable to Indian interests, by which the Union agreed not to proceed with segregation measures in exchange for a government sponsored repatriation scheme for Indians.[12] But repatriation proved an illusory solution to the increasingly acrimonious race relationships in the Union : most Indians, like the Europeans, regarded South Africa as their permanent home, and those who returned to India (with free passage and a £200 bonus from the Union government) discovered living conditions there inferior to those in South Africa and advised their compatriots to stay out of India.[13] By the end of the 1930's, when there appeared to be no chance that the Indian population would decrease through emigration to India or elsewhere, white South Africans were demanding an enactment setting up separate areas in which the different races could live and work. During the Second World War a temporary measure, the Trading and Occupation of Land Act, which "pegged" the existing position in Indian ownership and occupancy of property, was passed. New Delhi's formal protests, supplementing more vigorous opposition by the local Indian settlers, had a mitigating effect on the operation of the act. The Indian legislature passed the Reciprocity Act, which placed equivalent disabilities on the few non-Indian South Africans domiciled in India.

After the war, in 1946, the Union, while not ignoring the continuing protests from India and the settlers, passed the Asiatic Land Tenure and Indian Representation Act, which confirmed and extended the segregation programme of the "pegging act" but also gave Indians representation—by Europeans, however—for the first time in the Union parliament. Despite the intention of Prime Minister Smuts that the new act should convey some benefits to both Europeans and Indians, it was taken as a challenge by the Indian government. The latter had sought a round table conference with South Africa but had been told by Smuts that the segregation policy was entirely a domestic concern. On the verge of independence India appeared to be losing even the slim influence that it had been able to exert on the Union's racial policies.

The Interim Indian government decided to meet South Africa's challenge by following precisely the course of action recommended to it by the South African Indian Congress : it terminated the Indo-South African trade agreement and announced a trade boycott, it withdrew its high commissioner from Pretoria (though diplomatic relations were not formally broken until July 1954), and it filed a complaint with the UN. Simultaneously the South African Congress

20

began passive resistance against the new act. Those diversified measures brought to bear against the Union were calculated to produce a positive effect but in fact probably worked against the interests of South African Indians. Indo-South African trade, which had increased during the war so that India was South Africa's third most important source of imports, turned out to be less vital to the Union than expected. The main commodity imported from India was jute manufactures, and after an initial dislocation the Union arranged to obtain them indirectly through Australia and directly from Pakistan, which did not follow India's boycott policy.[14]

The criticism of the Union's policies by South African Indians and white liberals and by the UN General Assembly contributed to the South African nationalists' sense of zeal born out of feelings of martyrdom and international persecution. Nehru asked the Union prime minister for bilateral negotiations on the basis of the UN resolution of December 8, 1946. Smuts declined the offer on the grounds that talks premised on the critical resolution would offend and prejudice his country's position.

Indo-South African direct relations then seemed to have come to a halt, after more than one-half century of negotiations on South Africa's Indian population, which numbered 282,407 in 1946.[15] But another opportunity arose for a resumed discussion when Nehru and the new Union prime minister from the Nationalist party, Daniel F. Malan, met at the Commonwealth Prime Ministers conference in London in April 1949. They agreed there to hold a conference in 1950. Before it could take place, however, Malan's government proceeded with the Group Areas Act, legislation aimed at the goal of apartheid, and when Nehru asked Malan to postpone the action until a conference discussed the matter, the Union premier refused. India then cancelled its participation in the conference. Although Pakistan did not do so, then or in 1954, when a similar conference was proposed, a meeting of the three states never materialized.

Nehru's government had severed all of its relations with the Union of South Africa by the mid-1950's, a step which was later regretted in the External Affairs Ministry and certainly looked inconsistent with Nehru's ideal of creating positive psychological settings for settling international disputes. The public demands for a hard line toward the Union could not alone account for India's stand, which was more adamant than that adopted toward any other state, Pakistan and Portugal included. Nehru's policy arose as a manifestation of the most precious intangible value that any society possesses, its pride. In 1947 Mrs. Pandit defined the "real issue involved" in the General Assembly's debates on the South African question as an issue "which affects not only the Indians in the Union of South Africa, but all the peoples of Asia and Africa. For us," she said, "it is not the mere assertion of certain rights and privileges. We look upon it primarily as a challenge to our dignity and self-respect."[16] On such an issue no democratic government could afford to compromise. The Union government, though not a democracy by modern standards, had equally basic reasons for not altering its policies : the alleged integrity of European civilization in South Africa.

In the 1940's Nehru believed that UN action provided the most feasible means of moving South Africa in the direction of an equitable settlement with its citizens of Indian origin. The Commonwealth had failed to support India with enthusiasm, and unilateral measures proved unavailing soon after India introduced them. But the apartheid policy, which was defined and put into practice in the 1950's, was immune from effective UN action. India's reliance on the world organization in that dispute was not so naive as it was necessary : there were simply no other steps that it could take.[17]

THE EAST AFRICAN INDIANS

The problems associated with Indians settling in British east African territories resulted first from discriminatory regulations of the colonial administrations, particularly in Kenya, imposed upon non-whites for many of the same reasons that South Africa introduced its racial policies. East African Indians formed associations to protect their interests and sent delegations to London and New Delhi. The British government temporized, the Indian government protested, and finally the issues were decided by turning them over to representatives of the native African communities, which eventually won independence and dealt with both white and Indian settlers as they saw fit. When Indians' future in east Africa became a matter for Africans, not Europeans, to decide, a second problem came to the fore, that of antagonism between Africans and Indians, the latter sometimes backed by nationalists in India. Fortunately, both of the problems in east Africa could be approached with some expectations of solutions because the demands of the contending parties were more flexible and the influence of the UK and Indian governments more beneficial than was the case in South Africa.

East Africa was "opened"—that suggestively imperialistic term! —to European and modern Indian settlement only in the 1890's, and the Indians made a heavy contribution to the effort by building, in the absence of willing African labour, the Kenya-Uganda railway. Some of the Indian railway labourers, who were mostly from northern India, took advantage of a British offer to remain in east Africa after the completion of the line in 1901. Their successes in business and the increasing numbers of their countrymen who followed them into the comparatively underdeveloped territory brought the relations of Indian and white settlers to a crisis after the First World War.

Conflict grew out of the British policies of excluding non-European settlers from the Kenya highlands[18] and of gross overrepresentation of Europeans in the increasingly influential legislative councils in all the east African territories. Indian settlers, some of whose ancestors in east Africa antedated any white colonists and many of whom were filling crucial roles in the development of the region, thought of east Africa as a permanent home and even as an area for increased Indian colonization in the future. They had the backing, at that time, of prominent nationalists in India, who envisioned a permanent Indian colony across the Arabian Sea. Some notable Indians, among whom was Gopal Krishna Gokhale, asked for an Indian protectorate over Tanganyika, captured from Germany during the war.[19] Mrs. Sarojini Naidu exposed a broader vision in her presidential address to the Congress in 1924 : ". . . it does not take a very learned student to realize that naturally and inevitably East Africa is one of the earliest legitimate territories of the Indian Nation going so far back as the first century of the Christian era. . . . East Africa is, therefore, the legitimate colony of the surplus of the Great Indian Nation, whether they went forth to colonize these unknown lands from an economic point of view or to satisfy their desire for venture. . . ."[20] The Indian government failed to support the nationalists' claims in east Africa, but it did remonstrate with the Colonial Office against measures discriminatory to Indians, particularly the land and franchise policies in Kenya, where the race question assumed greater importance, because of the larger number of Indians and Europeans, than in Uganda or Tanganyika.

In the early 1920's, when the British government was conducting a major review of racial policies in Kenya, New Delhi despatched representatives to London to plead the Indians' case for equality of political representation, access to the highlands, and freedom from urban segregation. At that time there were about 23,000 Indians and about 10,000 Europeans in the colony and an estimated two and one-half million Africans. Indian businessmen dominated the economic life of the capital, Nairobi, as they did four decades later. After many shifts and compromises Britain, typically caught in the middle of a serious intra-imperial quarrel, introduced into the increasingly threatening political air the novel doctrine that in Kenya "the interests of the African natives must be paramount, and that if, and when, those interests and the interests of the immigrant races should conflict, the former should prevail."[21] In carrying out that doctrine neither the Europeans' nor the Indians' demands were fully met. The chief exponent of India's position in London, Srinivasa Sastri, felt that his cause had been betrayed,[22] but he nevertheless had to acknowledge the justice of Britain's giving primary consideration to Africans in their native land. (He might have recognized also that the British advocacy of native paramountcy appeared to justify the continuation of White political dominance in east Africa for an indefinite period of time.) Thus, inadvertently, the Indian settlers and the New Delhi government achieved for the Africans an advantage which they were unable at the time to obtain for themselves. East Africa, partly thereby, escaped the fate of South Africa.

The Indian National Congress during the inter-war period paid no attention to the interests of Africans in its anxiety to promote nondiscriminatory treatment for the overseas Indian communities, whose numbers in east Africa grew to 184,000 by the end of the Second World War, about one-half of them in Kenya. The transfer of power in India did not at once alter the Congress attitude : in 1949 India protested against east African legislation which greatly restricted the immigration of Asians—the term used after 1947 to refer to both Indians and Pakistanis.

But early in the 1950's Nehru's government realized that it could no longer ignore the desires of the bulk of the east African population and began to acknowledge the fact that African and Asian settler interests seldom coincided. On the question of entry for new settlers those interests were clearly in opposition, and the Indian government decided to give up its defense of open immigration into east Africa. On another matter of conflicting interests, namely the uninhibited pursuit of business gains, independent India adopted the policy of ignoring economic regulations introduced by east African governments aimed at enhancing the position of Africans, usually at the expense of the Asians. Nehru saw the justice of the Africans' charges that Indian tradesmen, industrialists, and landowners often wanted the best of three worlds (African, British, and Indian) and exploited Africans as much as the British had done. He recognized no need for India to defend an overseas community which had the economic power of Asians in east Africa.[23] Enunciating what became the new policy toward east Africa, Nehru said in 1950 : "Naturally, we in India have sympathy with the Africans and have repeatedly, not only as a government but before we became a government, assured them that we do not want Indian vested interests to grow in Africa at the expense of the African people."[24] (Nehru's reference to pre-independence Congress policy on the overseas Indians seemed to be reading his own later views into the party's official stands.) In 1952 and 1953 Congress finally passed resolutions which subordinated Indian interests to those of Africans wherever they conflicted.

Thus, India's new policy on Asians in east Africa, even before the area achieved independence in the 1960's began with the proposition that Africans should be masters in their own lands and that the economic interests of Asians there did not justify any attempted intervention by foreign governments. Indians and Europeans had together developed the economy of east Africa, and if Africans later considered themselves exploited, proceeded with Africanization of the economies, and invoked discriminatory regulations against non-Africans, New Delhi was not going to criticize those developments. By the 1960's, when many Indian businessmen were leaving the area for the UK or India, the Indian government's interests centreed on recruiting African political support in the UN, and elsewhere, and on increasing Indian exports across the Arabian Sea. The settlers had to fend for themselves.

Their future depended largely on their ability to assimilate, which meant giving up characteristically deep sentiments of racial exclusiveness. If assimilation through intermarriage could not have been tolerated by most Indians, [25] then a genuine political and business integration with the African peoples in the countries of their birth or adoption might have protected the Indian position. As a separate community the Asians suffered from the threats of racial riots (such as occurred in Durban, South Africa, between Africans and Indians in 1949) and near forced exodus (such as from Zanzibar in 1964). Despite, or because of this, by the mid-1960's most Asians had not yet accepted the citizenship of their east African homelands.[26] Tension and uncertainty were likely to continue, while New Delhi tried to prevent this problem from contaminating its good relations with the east African governments.

THE INDIAN COMMUNITY IN BURMA

For an Indian labourer or businessman to emigrate to Burma before the Second World War was almost as easy as to move to a distant province in India in search of economic betterment. Burma was a part of India until 1937, and no restrictions existed on the thousands of Indians who continuously traversed the Bay of Bengal to settle temporarily or permanently in Burma. Induced into Burma in the 19th century in the wake of the conquering British-Indian armies, Indians developed the country's rice-growing and lumber potential, built and ran the railways and ports, and administered the expanding governmental services. Rangoon was largely constructed and heavily populated by Indians, some of whom invested their rapidly expanding earnings in real estate and business firms ; a preponderant share of the immovable wealth of the capital city was in Indian hands by the time of the First World War.

With free immigration—Burma was excluded from the 1922 immigration act—the number of Indians grew from one-half million at the turn of the century to over one million in 1931, or about seven per cent of the total population of Burma.[27] Fifty-three per cent of Rangoon's population in 1931 was Indian. As elsewhere abroad Indians in Burma formed a distinct and unassimilated community, which differed, however, from African-Indian groups because most of its members, in the 1930's, were not born in Burma. Indians came and went like "birds of passage," according to Burmese nationalists. The latter resented the alleged exploitation by Indians, particularly of one business group, the Chettiars, whose money-lending resulted in their owning about one-fourth of Burma's best rice lands in the 1930's.

Burmese political agitation against both the Indian government (which refused to restrict emigration) and local Indian interests began during the First World War and reached a crescendo in the 1930's, when two serious anti-Indian riots occurred, in 1931 and 1938. They separately established Burmese government managed to obtain Indian agreement to restrict emigration to Burma just before the Second World War in exchange for Burmese assurance that Indians born and raised in Burma would have rights of domicile. Debates in the Indian legislature during the inter-war period revealed the nationalists in apparent support of the colonial system in Burma ; they demanded the government's intervention in support of the established economic interests, which were both Indian and British, and in 1941 criticized the efforts being made to limit free movement of persons between the two countries.[28]

The Burmese Indian community "poorly led, divided among themselves in a foreign country . . . never realized that its greatest safeguard was the goodwill of Burmans and not isolation or alignment with the ruling power. Separate schools for Indian children, separate Indian business houses in which Burmans had no share, exclusive Indian clubs, banks, co-operative stores, all gave the impression of Indian non-participation in Burmese national life. Aloof from Burmans, Indians had one eye fixed on India and the other on Britain for protection. They were never prepared to sink or swim with Burmans."[29] Predictably, when the Japanese threatened Burma in 1942, nearly one-half million Indians fled the country, mostly on foot across the border to their homeland. Although after the war many of them were helped to return by the British military administration, the Japanese occupation permanently lifted the burden of Chettiar landlords off the backs of Burmese peasants. The new Burmese interim government in 1946 began imposing immigration barriers to limit the number of returning Indians and adopted a policy of Burmanization of the civil service. According to an Indian in Burma at the time, "the elimination of Indian interests in the administration, the army, commerce, banking, trade, agriculture, and labour was nothing less than a second revolution" following the achievement of independence from Britain.[30] In the face of an independent Burmese policy of favouring native elements of the population at the expense of Indian interests, while simultaneously offering citizenship to anyone who had resided in Burma for eight years or more, the New Delhi government at first continued the old policy of defending the economic stakes of Indians in Burma. Moved by vehement claims from repatriated Chettiars, Nehru's government sent a high level deputation to Rangoon in 1950 to seek more compensation for dispossessed ex-landlords than Burma was willing to grant under the 1948 legislation which nationalized agricultural properties. The Burmese leadership resented the Indian attempts to influence its policies, and that may have partially explained Burma's initial unwillingness to follow Nehru's formula for nonaligned south Asian solidarity in foreign relations.[31] But India soon abandoned the posture of a large state ruffled by a small state's unorthodox economic measures and insistent on recompense for its aggrieved foreign investors. Its desire for cordial relations with Burma led to the tolerant attitude that several other states learned to assume when their nationals lost property abroad.[32] Nehru did not dispute the Burmese allegation that the new laws were nondiscriminatory : there was indeed no official policy directed against Indians, as Indians ; the reforms aimed at democratizing land holdings and a gradual replacement of foreign by Burmese business interests.

In Burma, as obviously as in any other country, most people of Indian origin were unable to follow Nehru's advice to identify with the land they had chosen for residence. Many were in Burma only temporarily, but even permanent residents refused to apply for citizenship. The Rangoon government, therefore, found it comparatively simple in the 1960's to force tens of thousands of Indians to leave Burma merely by decreeing that certain businesses and professions were no longer open to foreigners. The nationalization programme, which began in 1962 and reached effective proportions by 1964, robbed the Indian business community and many workers of their means of support in Burma. Most of them had to leave, and only a few survived the mass exodus with much more than their personal clothing, so thorough were the Burmese in preventing any large outflow of transferable wealth. Many impoverished Indians were evacuated by their own government in ships chartered for the purpose, while wealthy businessmen saw their financial domains crumble overnight before choosing their own means of departure. In June 1964 the Indian government announced that it expected "a lakh or so" of refugees from Burma by the end of the year ;[33] they would have to be brought back home and somehow accommodated into the Indian economy of scarcity. Perhaps 300,000 altogether would leave Burma, leaving about 200,000 people of Indian origin in Burma, mostly in lowly occupations and not debarred from applying for citizenship, but of course more fearful than before of discrimination and even persecution.

Burma's action against its Indian settlers was unprecedented, and the Indian government hoped it would remain the sole case of virtually forced large-scale exodus. Nothing could be salvaged by India from the experience except the example of how to tolerate a humiliating adversity with forbearance and even grace in the interests of good foreign relations. The fate of Indians in Burma probably accelerated New Delhi's reaching an agreement with Ceylon to preclude a similar occurrence in that country.

INDO-CEYLONESE RELATIONS

For almost two decades following the British withdrawal from south Asia, India and Ceylon, which had been economically and strategically inseparable under the imperial umbrella, bickered over the future of about one million Indian residents on the island. It was their only important quarrel, and fortunately for both states it did not lead to a breach in relations or to desperate, xenophobic measures against an alien community such as Burma indulged in.

Ceylon's population during most of the 20th century contained the largest number of Indian residents outside of India. The ancestors of many of them began to migrate there, legally or illegally, across the narrow Palk Straits, in the early 19th century to work in British tea, coffee, and rubber plantations. The labourers moved back and forth between the two British domains in unrecorded numbers according to the economic needs of Ceylon's planters ;

many of them regarded themselves as permanently settled in Ceylon while at the same time free to visit India, remit savings to India, and retain their separate identity in an alien (but not truly foreign) land. In addition to plantation workers some Indian merchants and professionals entered Ceylon ; they usually obtained visas, often worked under specific contracts, and seldom had the intention of remaining permanently abroad.[34]

The interdependence of the Indian and Ceylonese labour economies was challenged after the First World War by Indian nationalists who agitated for controls on emigration to Ceylon in order to force improved conditions for those already on the island, and by Ceylonese politicians who feared the political power of the increasing numbers of resident Indians. The steps toward national self-expression in both countries, in short, encouraged the breaking down of the imperialist-capitalist economic system with its basis in labour mobility across national boundaries. The Ceylonese government met the stipulations on equal treatment imposed by the Indian legislature : Indians were granted representation and qualified franchise. An Indian agent was stationed in Colombo, and his annual reports constituted the best account of Indo-Ceylonese relations available up to 1948.[35]

In the 1930's anti-Indian agitation began in Ceylon partly as a result of the greatly increased numbers of Indian voters under the constitution of 1931. By 1939 nearly one-quarter million of them met voting qualifications, based on proof of residence and intention to remain in the country. In addition, the economic depression in Ceylon focused attention on the substantial number of well paying jobs held by Indians. Though under pressure from India to continue the policy of equal treatment, Ceylon's government introduced ordinances to reduce the Indian labour force, particularly in government offices. Jawaharlal Nehru visited Ceylon in 1939 as the representative of Congress to help in finding a solution to the intensifying dispute, and in 1940 Indo-Ceylonese negotiations opened in New Delhi. The chief representatives of the two governments, G. S. Bajpai and D. S. Senanayake, guided the New Delhi discussions quickly to what were then, as well as a generation later, the main issues in the controversy : control of Indian immigration into Ceylon, Indian domicile (later linked to citizenship) and franchise, and miscellaneous restrictions on rights of Indians.

From the outset the conference took a hard tone. The Ceylonese spokesmen clearly rejected the idea of granting full rights to the bulk of Indian labourers and acknowledged that their proposals for future legislation on citizenship would aim at substantial reductions in the numbers of resident Indians. Senanayake remarked that : "If it is a question of Indians becoming Ceylonese, well then, it is only a small number that can be absorbed in our country."[36] In a more impassioned style S. W. R. D. Bandaranaike, a member of Ceylon's delegation who, sixteen years later, became prime minister, spoke of the "complete political and economic extermination of the Ceylonese, primarily the Sinhalese," should Indians in large numbers continue to reside (and multiply) in Ceylon. "It is really becoming now a stark question of survival," he said.[37] The further argument advanced by the Ceylonese claimed that most Indian labourers were unassimilable ; their cultural, linguistic, and economic ties remained in India, despite long residence in Ceylon. Bandaranaike's case took on a familiar political tone when he replied to Bajpai's doubts that one million Indians in fact threatened to dominate five million Ceylonese : "This five million is divided into a number of minorities," said Bandaranaike. "One-sixth of the population (including urban as well as plantation workers), with the economic predominance which they now have, can very easily and quickly convert that position into one of political dominance," if they were given full rights.[38]

Bajpai's response stressed his government's desire that Indians in all parts of the Commonwealth should have the right to acquire full citizenship, just as immigrants to other countries did, provided that they had in a practical sense made their homes there. The assumption he made was that Indians wished to participate fully in the economic and political—it was difficult to argue social life—of the territories in which they had chosen to live. Bajpai foresaw the difficulties of any Indian government's agreeing to second-class status for Ceylon's Indians : "Once we concede any qualifications in the matter of citizenship, we open the door to similar claims all over the British Commonwealth of Nations." His colleague, Ramaswami Mudaliar, focused on the disabilities imposed by South Africa against Indians, who could not claim cultural affinity with the dominant community, as did Indians in Ceylon : What could be the Indian government's reply "if General Hertzog or General Smuts were to tell us, 'we find that even Ceylon does not give you certain rights, but you expect us to give you those rights' ?"[39] A frank examination of the issues disclosed no possibility of reaching a solution, and the talks failed. One year later another Indo-Ceylonese conference was convened in Colombo ; this time results were reached, which, however, proved unacceptable to the Indian legislature and were not ratified in Delhi.

During the war sporadic negotiations continued, unsuccessfully, while in 1943 the countries exchanged fully accredited permanent representatives. As Ceylon approached independence Nehru urged Ceylonese leaders to accept as citizens all Indians who had resided in the island for five (later amended to seven) years and grant them voting rights. At the same time he urged Indians to make a choice between Ceylonese and Indian nationality and not expect special minority treatment if they were granted voting rights. Nehru's talks and correspondence with D. S. Senanayake[40] when they both had become prime ministers in 1948 produced no agreement, and in early 1949 Ceylon promulgated the Indian and Pakistani Residents (Citizenship) Act, which laid out stringent requirements for citizenship by registration, i.e. uninterrupted residence for at least seven years—Indians often returned for extended periods to the subcontinent—, an assured income, and the intention of settling permanently in Ceylon. The ultimate purpose of the act was to exclude, not include, as many Indians as possible in the newly independent political life of the country ; by a subsequent revision of franchise rules only citizens were allowed to vote.

Tainted by the unsolved problem of Indian residents in Ceylon the relations between the independent neighbouring states nevertheless remained normal. Neither government ignored the fact that its nation's security was ineradicably linked to that of the other and, therefore, an issue capable of producing passionate public outcries was systematically deflated in official statements from both sides. But the governments seemed equally cautious in discussing the security interests common to both. On India's side the reticence resulted from Nehru's efforts to minimize matters of military power and perhaps his complacency about the security of the Indian Ocean so long as Britain retained its great base there, at Trincomalee. Furthermore, Nehru could not have been unaware of Ceylonese speculation that India ultimately might assume dominance in the region ; historic memories persisted of Tamil invasions of the island from the tenth to the fourteenth centuries. The vision of a mighty country almost abutting the frontiers of a tiny state ; the uncertainties about the future ambitions of that huge nation with swelling population, oppressive economic problems, and a yet undefined long-range defense posture ; the recognition of Ceylon's inability to protect itself from any Indian pressure backed by force— all produced fears which the reiteration of soothing Indian assurances could not entirely dispel.

Nehru was therefore exceedingly reluctant to broach the subject of regional security, which could easily suggest relegating Ceylon to an Indian sphere of influence. He had to repudiate—even if he agreed with it—the idea of K. M. Panikkar, who had viewed Ceylon as "an integral part of India" for defense purposes. Ceylon, as well as Burma, wrote Panikkar, was in no position "to follow an independent policy, and the safety and security of both are interdependent with those of India."[41] Nehru also had to obliterate a notion which he himself had expressed on his visit to Ceylon in 1939, that "ultimately Ceylon is bound to become a part of the Federation of India."[42] Nehru's personal stature and his respect for the integrity of other nations overcame the suspicions of most Ceylonese about India's possible intentions ; indeed Nehru, a political hero in Ceylon, stood as the best guarantee of cordial Indo-Ceylonese relations.

The Ceylonese leadership until 1956 did not rely solely on Nehru's reputation or his government's commitment to peaceful coexistence to assure Ceylon's freedom of international action. It cultivated the lingering tie with the UK (symbolized by the British base rights) as a counterbalance to Indian influence and refused to subscribe to India's nonalignment posture.[43] Ceylon and India followed almost identical policies on colonial and racial issues, and Ceylon was easily identified as a participant in the Afro-Asian grouping, heavily influenced by India. But during the United National Party ministries of the Senanayakes and John Kotelawala, and particularly of the latter, Ceylon searched for a unique international personality to be jealously guarded against India's overarching ascendancy in southern Asia.

It was during that period that Ceylon and the People's Republic of China built up a close relationship of economic reciprocity based on a 1952 agreement to exchange rubber for rice. However, that development could not justly be interpreted as mainly a political move, from Ceylon's standpoint. Heavily dependent on foreign exchange earnings from exports of tea, rubber, and coconut products, which India also produced and therefore did not purchase from Ceylon, the Colombo government needed guaranteed markets, unaffected by world price fluctuations, and a guaranteed source of imported rice. China helped to fill both needs. Ceylon's persistent and large adverse balance of trade with India after independence could not be rectified by increasing exports to India. So Ceylon gradually reduced its dependence on Indian goods, in favour of Chinese and later Japanese products, which could more successfully be exchanged for Ceylon's raw materials.

During Kotelawala's ministry the simmering problem of the Indian estate workers reached a climax. Prime Ministers Nehru and Senanayake had almost reached a compromise formula in 1953, when definite numbers were discussed of Indians who would be absorbed into the Ceylonese nation, those who would be repatriated, and those who could make up their minds over a ten-year period. But those discussions never ripened into a concrete accord. Nehru took up the matter again with Kotelawala in January 1954, and this time an agreement was signed. It set up a time-limit of two years for registration of Indians in Ceylon under the Indian and Pakistani Residents Act of 1949 ; those wishing it could apply for Indian nationality at the Indian high commission.[44]

Within ten months the agreement proved unworkable, and subsequent talks held in October of that year brought the dilemmas into such clear focus that misunderstanding and distrust increased rather than diminished. Because registration of Indians was to be voluntary, and no one knew the numbers who could qualify for either Indian or Ceylonese citizenship, the 1954 agreement failed to meet the main issue, namely how many Indian workers would Ceylon be willing to absorb, and how many would India be prepared to repatriate. Realizing Ceylon's great need for Indian estate labourers—its main export industry, tea, depended upon them—and perhaps suspecting that economic necessity alone would lead most Indians to express their desire to remain in Ceylon, Indian negotiators anticipated relatively few persons opting for India. Ceylon's representatives, on the other hand, knew that their government could not tolerate the bulk of Indian labourers' becoming citizens and planned to use the 1949 act to keep the numbers down. They

hoped that Indians who failed to meet Ceylon's citizenship requirements would automatically be accepted as Indians. Given such intentions on both sides the failure of the agreement was almost inevitable.

No fresh effort was made to settle the matter during the ministry
of S.W.R.D. Bandaranaike, which succeeded Kotelawala's in
1956. As a result, by the 1960's the majority of the over 900,000
estate workers could be regarded as neither Ceylonese nor Indians.[45]
The Indian high commissioner and Nehru himself referred to those
people as "stateless" : they neither wished to be registered as
Indians—some were rejected by the high commission as not meeting
citizenship requirements—nor could they obtain Ceylonese citizenship. Many applications lay inactive for lack of full supporting
documentation and the reluctance of officials to grant citizenship
even to those who could qualify.

Although the Bandaranaike government moved sharply away
from the pro-Western outlook of the earlier ministries, closed the
British naval base, and associated itself with India's nonaligned
grouping, it could not restrain the increasingly intemperate public
protestations against Indians in Ceylon. Indeed the victory of the
People's United Front led by Bandaranaike's Sri Lanka Freedom
Party in 1956 resulted from its Sinhalese nationalist appeal, which
rejected a pluralistic society, in which an Indian minority might
be accommodated, in favour of a Ceylonese nation rooted in Buddhist
culture and the Sinhalese language. Very slim chances remained
for the largely Hindi- and Tamil-speaking Indian estate workers
to gain equal status with the older population of the island.[46] Mrs.
Sirimavo Bandaranaike, who succeeded her husband as prime
minister after the latter's assassination in 1959, made no attempt
for several years to tackle the dilemma of the estate workers. Many
other Indians, mostly urban dwellers, were meanwhile leaving Ceylon
for good as a result of Ceylonization in government and business
firms—between 120,000 and 150,000 left Ceylon between 1947
and 1964.[47]

On the political level Indo-Ceylonese relations prospered under
the Bandaranaikes.[48] Ceylon's UN delegation produced a telling
defense of India's take-over in Goa in 1961, and the next year
the Colombo government convened a conference of six states to
urge a Chinese withdrawal from its conquered territories in northern India and to seek an arrangement for avoiding future Himala-

yan fighting. Minor irritants, such as a dispute over Kachcha Thivu island and conflicting views on Ceylon's commercial radio broadcasts, could not affect the two state's nearly identical political stands in world affairs.[49] Economic relations continued to deteriorate slowly as Ceylon located manufactured goods sold on more favourable terms than India offered. Still, in the first half of the 1960's, Ceylon ranked eighth among buyers of Indian goods and first among the underdeveloped country buyers.

At the end of a decade of postponement, during which the political conflict and human tragedy surrounding the problem of "stateless" plantation workers in Ceylon were being publicly debated, the new Indian prime minister, Sastri, and Sirimavo Bandaranaike met in New Delhi to search again for a compromise. After tense bargaining for six days in October 1964 they achieved a settlement,[50] which specified the numbers of "stateless" persons which would be absorbed as citizens by each state. For the first time in a formal pact India and Ceylon committed themselves to an exact formula : India would repatriate 525,000 persons, and Ceylon would register 300,000 as citizens under a fifteen-year phased programme. The ultimate status of 150,000 others would be decided later. Sastri's acceptance of a definite number of repatriates implied some degree of non-voluntary repatriation, a procedure which Nehru had refused to accept because it might form a precedent for other countries with Indian minorities to follow.

Ceylon's responsibilities under the accord included enacting a new citizenship law to accommodate its allocation of persons of Indian origin. The fall of Mrs. Bandaranaike's government and the return to power of the United National Party in 1965 partly explained Ceylon's delay in implementing the so-called Sirima-Sastri agreement, but the new regime introduced the requisite legislation in 1966. Its final passage came shortly before a state visit to Ceylon by Prime Minister Indira Gandhi in September 1967, at which time generous statements about interests in common permeated the political atmosphere. A phased granting of citizenship simultaneously in a ratio of seven processed Indian applications to four Ceylonese was by then the administrative formula that should govern the final disposition of the largest concentration of overseas Indians.

21

II. FRENCH AND PORTUGUESE ENCLAVES

Britain tolerated the existence, within the body of its Indian empire, of almost one dozen European enclaves, holdovers from the decades of Portuguese and French dominance in parts of India. Located chiefly on the eastern and western coasts, they were political anachronisms but nevertheless created pride for sentimental European colonialists and lent a certain dying grandeur to the West's days of imperial glory in Asia. The administrative capitals and most important centres for the French and Portuguese holdings, respectively, were Pondicherry and Goa, each of which gracefully combined the architecture, religion, music, and language of Mediterranean Europe with the basically Hindu culture of the Coromandel and Konkani coasts. Latin Catholicism spread from those centres into south India, and the religious and to a small extent the racial mingling of two great traditions made a unique and colourful contribution to a modern India which otherwise knew the West almost entirely through its contacts with Anglo-Saxon culture.

It was axiomatic that independent India should insist on the complete incorporation of the French and Portuguese territories into the Indian Union. Anything less than that would have compromised in an intolerably intimate way the stand on colonialism to which Nehru had committed his government. One could scarcely have predicted in the 1940's, however, that the absorption of French India would be so uneventful that the local populations themselves scarcely knew what changes had taken place, and that the long drawn-out struggle over Goa would eventually culminate in a forceful Indian take-over that precipitated a UN debate and shook the image of Nehru's government in many parts of the world.

THE TRANSFER OF FRENCH INDIA

Indian-French negotiations on "the problems of French Establishments in India" began auspiciously within a few days of the transfer of British power with the joint acknowledgement that the desires of the colonial French populations would be recognized, and that French cultural connections with the territories could be harmonized with the political "evolution" of India.[51] Chandernagore, a small inland French possession in Bengal, initiated the process of orderly integration with India by holding a public referendum in June 1949, in which a great majority of the 6,387 polled voters expressed their desire to join India. A de facto transfer of administration took place in May 1950, and a treaty turning over sovereignty followed in February 1951.[52] The much larger southern territories of Karikal, Mahé, Yanam (or Yanaon), and Pondicherry presented more difficult problems of integration, but the principle that a peaceful transfer of sovereignty would in fact take place was hardly doubted in either New Delhi or Paris.

France saw no reasonable benefits from refusing to transfer the enclaves to India. The comparatively free political life in the territories had resulted in a marked expression of pro-Indian popular sentiment, and public demonstrations within and outside the enclaves indicated future difficulties for the French merely in maintaining law and order. Indeed in Yanam volunteer liberators raised the Indian flag in June 1954, and there and in Mahé French administration was in virtual abeyance by the mid-1950's.[53] The economic dependence of the enclaves on India and their vulnerability to blockade and to military attack suggested to the French authorities the real possibilities of a humiliating and unconditional withdrawal from their Indian holdings. A diplomatic settlement would preclude local disaster and might prove to be a political investment with beneficial returns for French interests elsewhere.

The main difficulty in reaching a settlement arose from the provision in the French constitution that the sovereignty of no territory of the French Union could be transferred without direct approval of the population concerned. In 1950, local French authorities began making arrangements at Pondicherry to hold a referendum, which everyone expected would result in overwhelming sanction for union with India. New Delhi, however, raised various objections to the method of holding a vote, thus delaying the proceedings. And in October 1952 India signified that it wanted no plebiscite in French India, but rather a simple cession of the territories : India had by then decided that in view of possible precedents for dealing with the Kashmir impasse it would oppose plebiscites anywhere, even if their results would certainly favour its immediate interests. Although the Indian position reversed its commitment made in June 1949 to referrenda in French enclaves, France accepted the shift in India's views and arranged for a simulated democratic expression of popular will.

By an Indo-French agreement reached in October 1954 the elected representatives from Karikal, Mahé, Yanam, and Pondicherry voted together by a great majority in favour of cession to India. France held that, somehow, constitutional requirements had been met, and of course India avoided a plebiscite. Three days later in New Delhi the Indo-French agreement was signed, which provided for India's assumption of de facto authority while maintaining the separate administrations of the territories. About 320,000 people and 196 square miles were thereby added to the Indian Union. India agreed to preserve scientific, cultural, and religious institutions of a French character in the territories, a commitment which appeared to be France's major objective in the drafting of the accord. On May 28, 1956, India and France signed a treaty embodying the provisions of the agreement.[54] Six years elapsed before the French Assembly ratified the document, while New Delhi persistently requested final action. The ratification, on July 12, 1962, followed events in the Portuguese enclaves which may have suggested to France that India's patience was not unlimited.

INACTION AND ACTION ON THE PORTUGUESE ENCLAVES

Portugal's domestic political life and its international position and purpose contrasted sharply with those of France in the postwar decades, but for many years the Indian government failed to deal differently with the two states. While France demonstrated willingness to alter its imperial structure, and ultimately to dispense with it altogether, Portugal was determined to retain its colonies, which after 1951 were elevated to "provinces" within the Portuguese nation.[55] For over one decade Nehru's government sought to treat Portugal as it had France and by diplomatic pressure reinforced by mild local harassment persuade Lisbon to transfer power peacefully.[56] It opened a legation in Portugal in 1949 mainly to conduct negotiations on Goa, the main enclave of 1,394 square miles and over 600,000 people, and the minor holdings of Daman (or Damao) and Diu, 148 and 20 square miles, respectively. But the government of Antonio Salazar held that there was nothing to negotiate on the sovereignty of Portuguese India :

it was an integral part of his state and would remain so.[57] Failing
in its diplomatic purpose India closed the Lisbon legation in June
1953 and turned to other means to move out the Portuguese administration.

In July and August 1954, Goan nationalists operating within
India—there were over 80,000 Goans in the Bombay region, some
of whom joined the Indian nationalist opposition to Portuguese
rule—led an attack on two Portuguese enclaves, Dadra and Nagar
Haveli and "liberated" them by methods which escaped impartial
observation. The two enclaves were administered from Daman
at the entrance to the Gulf of Cambay, but were situated inland
and completely surrounded by Indian territory. Following the
"liberation" the Indian government ceased issuing visas for Portuguese officials to visit the territories and appeared to regard European rule as having lapsed there—Nehru termed Dadra and Nagar
Haveli as "now more or less independent" in 1957.[58] India's de
facto termination of Portuguese control in two small areas constituted its first and an almost symbolic defiance of international
legal norms in the name of anti-colonialism. The Portuguese enclaves were parts of India, Nehru never tired of saying, and India's
freedom movement would not have been complete without their
incorporation into the "motherland." But in the 1950's Nehru
and his government drew back from a more precise assertion of
the superior claim of national independence over international
law, somehow seeking a reconciliation of the two. Such was the
Indian response to Portugal's complaint to the International Court
of Justice about India's denial of passage to Dadra and Nagar Haveli.

Portugal's case, presented in late 1955, claimed a right of passage
to the enclaves, charged India with violating its legal obligation
to allow Portuguese access, and asked the Court to request India
to restore the situation that had existed for over one century. India
raised six preliminary objections of a technical and jurisdictional
nature to the Court's hearing the case. The usual delays in preparing pleadings postponed the oral hearings on those objections
until late 1957, and 1959 drew to a close before the merits of the
case were discussed. India's procedural objections were overruled.
But on the substance of the dispute it had greater success.

When the Court gave its decision, on April 12, 1960, it upheld
India's contention that denial of access to the enclaves was justified.

India had held that once the "liberation" movement had succeeded any attempt to restore European control "would encounter desperate resistance,... [which] could not fail to extend to surrounding Indian territory...[and] result in an undoubted threat to the internal order and external peace of the Indian Union."[59] The Court accepted the validity of that argument. It therefore did not demand the restoration of Portuguese control of Dadra and Nagar Haveli, but neither did it recognize the legality of India's control. It held that Portugal had a right of passage to the enclaves for private persons, civil officials, and goods, but not for armed persons, and always subject to the power of regulation and control exercized by the Indian authorities in the intervening territory. India's action in prohibiting movement of Portuguese personnel during the events of 1954 was judged to be legitimate. The court added that the pre-1954 rights of passage were unenforceable in 1960 and by implication must therefore be considered extinguished.

Although the Portuguese government could take some satisfaction in the Court's upholding of its right of passage for civilians and argue that India had terminated that right by force, the decision sensitively reflected the new political realities of the anti-colonialist epoch, which were embodied in the UN's recent resolutions. One resolution, 1542 (XV), passed on December 15, 1960, cited Portuguese Goa and its dependencies as non-self-governing territories, i.e. as colonies, not a province of Portugal, for which Portugal had to submit information under article 73 (e). Another, 1514 (XV) passed on December 14, could be construed, and was interpreted by India, as a declaration which substantially undermined international legal norms upholding a metropolitan state's sovereignty over its colonies. The same resolutions also provided India with an alleged legal basis for its eventual disposition of Goa, Daman, and Diu.

In the mid-1950's the Goa issue became one of the paramount preoccupations of Indian public life, with the help of Nehru's statements and vigorous campaigns by all sections of the press, which highlighted the evidences of Portuguese security measures in its Indian territories. Stimulated by the successful and largely peaceful occupation of Dadra and Nagar Haveli a movement to "liberate" Goa by non-violent means attracted wide support, and the sympathy of the government. The date for the crossing of the international boundary was set for August 15, 1954, Indian independence day, and several teams were selected for the assault. The crisis passed when less than fifty border violators were unceremoniously arrested.

The next year grander preparations were made for *satyagrahis* (non-violent protestors) to cross the borders of Goa and Daman and Diu, and all Indian political parties aroused mass opinion for what some enthusiasts hoped would be a final show-down with Portugal. Demonstrators urged the government to impose sanctions against Goa, and Nehru responded by asking Portugal to close its legation in New Delhi and by suspending rail service into Goa. On August 15 about two thousand volunteers crossed the Goan borders at various points, witnessed by a corps of foreign correspondents invited by Portugal to view the illegal spectacle. About twenty demonstrators were killed by the Goan police, and the sufferings of scores of others were pictured and reported throughout the country. Facing a regime that refused to respect the lives of peaceful, though illegal, *satyagrahis*, the "liberation" movement failed, and there was no evidence of a popular revolt within the enclave in response to calls to rise up at the time of the border crossings.[60] In Bombay riotous mobs had to be controlled by police firings ; other cities experienced hartals (closing of business and public activities).

The Goan crisis of 1955 was a domestic one for the Indian government : with the possible exception of its relations with Pakistan no issue of foreign policy had hitherto aroused as much public interest. Nehru had encouraged the attempts at "peaceful liberation" and abjured the threat of war against the Portuguese, but that approach had failed, with a sacrifice of lives and a sense of national impotence. His grip on Indian politics at that point was firm and assured : he prohibited further assaults on Portuguese territory and in parliament explained that no state could use *satyagraha* against another state. The government would no longer permit illegal entries into Portuguese territories. "We have taken into consideration," Nehru announced, "not only what happened in Goa but what happened subsequently in the city of Bombay and elsewhere. . . ."[61] The government wanted to discourage the domestic tradition of *satyagraha*, which had become a potentially disruptive political force. It also could not afford to sanction international *satyagraha*, which could conceivably be used against Indian interests, for instance in Kashmir. Nehru offered no alternative means of attaining his announced objective. He broke all remaining diplomatic ties with Portugal in protest against the killing of the *satyagrahis* at Goa.

Answering critics who suggested methods to coerce Portugal into evacuating its holdings Nehru repeated his pledge not to use force against the remaining foreign enclaves. Acknowledging that India was not committed to non-violence he said, "Nevertheless, we have made it perfectly clear that we shall use force only in defense and that we shall not provoke a war or start a war or adopt any aggressive tactics in regard to a war."[62]

The Goa issue could not be forgotten, but some of the frustrations that it engendered could be vented into a wider, international arena. Official Western reaction to the conflict over Goa always appeared to Indians as insufficiently sensitive to the nationalist principles that were involved there. Furthermore, Portugal's membership in NATO, its centuries old relationship with the UK, and the American use of its strategic air base in the Azores raised the suggestion that the Western alliance might support the Portuguese in Goa. Western disclaimers that the NATO alliance covered Portuguese possessions in Asia satisfied Nehru on the matter : "I think it has been made fairly clear by responsible people," he said, "that the NATO alliance has little relevance to this question. . . . We may, therefore, set aside the NATO alliance."[63] But the prime minister still held foreign governments accountable for their views on Goa as "a symbol of decadent colonialism trying to hold on." The Goa dispute, he announced in September 1955 "has become an acid test by which we can judge the policies of other countries."[64]

At the end of that year the Russian leaders, Nikolai Bulganin and Nikita Khrushchev, who were touring India, took easy advantage of the "acid test" that Nehru had proffered and enthusiastically proclaimed Soviet support for India's incorporation of the Portuguese enclaves. The warmth of Indians' reaction to that pronouncement, as sincere as it was naive, prompted the American secretary of state, John Foster Dulles, to perpetrate one of the most egregious diplomatic blunders of his illustrious career. He joined Paulo Cunha, the foreign minister of Portugal visiting the US in December, in a statement deploring the inflammatory effect of "various statements attributed to the Soviet rulers now visiting Asia," including "allegations concerning the Portuguese provinces in the Far East."[65] The joint statement, which Dulles said was "not lightly issued,"[66] touched on the pulse of the sensitive Goa issue by using the word, province, rather than colony. The US later denied that it had veered from its neutrality on the question, but in the propaganda arena echoes of Dulles' words reverberated for years to come. Nehru sought more from the US and other states than neutrality on a matter crucial to India's domestic and international interests. He referred to Dulles' statement in June 1956 and ridiculed Western neutrality on colonial questions. Revealing the priorities of his government in assessing the wishes of the population of Goa he said, "I know they are eager to come in and I want them to come in. But that is not the point now. India's national interest demands the removal of the Portuguese from Goa."[67]

Without taking the explicit issue of Portugal's Indian territories to the UN, India finally won the kind of international support that it had been seeking when the General Assembly during its fifteenth session passed the resolutions noted earlier. Those resolutions, whose main purpose was supported by the US, signified to Nehru that "the general opinion in favour of Portugal has now almost disappeared ;"[68] therefore the years of passive waiting had not been wasted. In August 1961 the prime minister demonstrated the effects on his government's thinking of the changed international atmosphere : "If I am asked," he said on August 17, "to give any kind of assurance that we shall not use armed forces in regard to Goa, I am not in a position to give it."[69] In case Nehru's statement was meant to be a signal to Portugal that the time for a diplomatic settlement had almost passed, Lisbon reacted with no more reasoned calculation than to urge courage on its 3,500 Goan troops. On the eve of India's invasion in December Portugal discovered that the UK would not recognize its security treaty with Portugal in any struggle against a Commonwealth member and that the US would offer only diplomatic support to its European ally if India invaded.[70]

V. K. Krishna Menon had become India's defense minister in 1957, and his influence on India's foreign relations was at its height up to the Chinese invasion in late 1962. Menon used the Goan issue as part of his repertoire of domestic political assets and was reviving interest in its "liberation" among his Bombay constituents in mid-1961. He might have considered that the reputation of

India's defence forces needed a fillip in the face of steady Chinese encroachments in the Himalayas. Of equal importance appeared the possibility of opposition parties leading new demonstrations on the Goa issue and so gaining public support on the eve of the general elections. The accurate details accounting for the decision to invade Portuguese territories may not be made available for many years,[71] but no knowledgeable person questioned Menon's crucial part in formulating the new policy. The decision was probably not reached by the cabinet as a whole. Arguments in favour of military action must have included the pressure on India from African and Asian states to prove its anti-colonialist bona fides, which had been questioned after Nehru's address to the Belgrade conference.[72] After the Goan invasion, in a lengthy, tortured explanation for his decision, Nehru stressed the connection between Goa and Portuguese colonialism in Africa : how could India, he asked, sincerely disapprove of the Portuguese presence in Africa while passively tolerating it in India?[73]

But Menon's arguments for an early attack on Goa, which Nehru in fact anticipated in his own thinking, may have been less persuasive than the actual preparations for the operation, about which Nehru possibly knew very little until the last moment. Menon and his supporters in the defense ministry mobilized the manpower, got it into position, and put the Goa operation in motion before the prime minister had fully decided on the desirability of military action.[74] Nehru told the press on December 28, "to be perfectly frank with you, the decision crept up so gradually that the circumstances forced the decision on us. Step by step we were compelled to do it, till there was no choice left. . . . It was not like sitting down and clearly deciding that we will do this and that. . . . "[75]

India made little effort to plead a defensive war against Portugal, a patently untenable proposition. In explaining the reasons for the attack of December 18 the government accused Portugal of various provocatory acts, including firings on Indian shipping, but none of them was confirmed by impartial witnesses. India's action was an unashamed and thrilling liberation of ethnically Indian people living in geographically Indian territory, most of whose ancestors had acknowledged Portuguese sovereignty for about 450 years. It was the last, anticlimactic, act in the drama of India's freedom movement, and it needed no more historic justification than any of the moves taken to oust foreigners from their positions of political dominance. When the Indian invaders were poised in overwhelming numbers for the invasion the US government and the UN secretary-general requested postponement or abandonment of military measures in order to allow negotiations to begin. The American ambassador in New Delhi persuaded Nehru to postpone the attack for one day on the basis of extremely tenuous hopes that Portugal would relent and agree to mediation. But Salazar never deviated from his refusal to discuss the issue of Goa's sovereignty, and in any case to reverse the military momentum of India's army would have brought incalculable domestic protests. Once underway the Indian armed forces overran Goa, Daman, and Diu in three days, causing seventeen Portuguese deaths and twenty-two Indian.

India's action created world-wide diplomatic excitement. The Afro-Asian and communist states extolled the action while the Western governments condemned it with various degrees of indignation. The disproportionate attention given to the Goan affair, the deep analyses of its causes and affects by publicists and statesmen, resulted directly from the characterization of India as a peace loving, even pacifist, nation, an image which had initially been encouraged by Gandhi and was never convincingly challenged in the statements of Nehru and other prime spokesmen. A number of people in the West, even some with official responsibilities, relied to a degree that they might not have admitted on India's adherence to principles of order and law in international affairs, while most of the rest of the world's states violated those ideals. The harsh reality of the Goan invasion, unmitigated by the legal and moral confusion which a lengthy prior political confrontation and perhaps an Indian ultimatum might have engendered, intruded into sensitive minds as a fresh cause for disillusionment and worry. Less sensitivity was evident among those critics who found relief in the descent of India from its allegedly high plane of international behaviour.

India's most appropriate answer to the opponents of its action was the one seldom voiced but always implicit when great policies have been undertaken : The necessity of state demanded the ultimate incorporation of Portuguese territories into India ; a corporate morality superior to law, and based in this case on the axiom that nationalism must prevail over colonialism, governed India's action.

When Portugal brought the Goan issue to the Security Council, on December 18, 1961, its case could be simply stated : India was guilty of a breach of international law ; the nationalist claim that the territory and people of India had to be governed by the Indian Union had no legal basis. The excitement surrounding the Council's sessions on Goa was heightened by the blunt reply of the Indian representative, C. S. Jha, who offered probably the most responsible and encompassing challenge in UN records to those portions of the Charter and international law that upheld European colonialism. In India's view there was "no legal frontier" between India and Goa, because Goa, Daman, and Diu had been "illegally occupied— occupied by right of conquest by the Portuguese. The fact that they have occupied it for 450 years is of no consequence. . . ." India's reoccupation could not be regarded as aggression : ". . . there can be no question of aggression against your own people, whom you want to bring into freedom."[76] It did not require special training to perceive the difficulty in accepting that argument : the boundaries of a good many states had been fixed on the basis of conquest, and that included India's boundaries as well.[77] Closer to the point was the contrary observation which Jha also made, that many states had achieved their freedom and their present territorial boundaries by force and therefore India's conquest of Goa would have to be recognized ultimately as legitimate.

But in a more fundamental exposition of his government's position the Indian representative spelled out the further implications of India's action. International law which supported colonial powers' control over parts of Asia and Africa, he said, "is no longer acceptable." Because of the changes in political relations in this century, and in particular the resolutions against colonialism passed by the General Assembly, international law, never a static body of rules, underwent changes. Anti-colonialism became a "new dictum of international law. That is how international law is made. . . ."

The UN debates on India's spectacular affirmation of the "new" international law explored that aspect of the Goan situation fully and of course inconclusively. The American representative in the Security Council sessions, Adlai Stevenson, refused to be pulled into the legal merits of the dispute, while the US government had not clearly defined its reaction to the concept of a just anti-colonial war. Instead the ambassador denounced India's resort to force as a violation of the UN Charter and did so in words which were uncompromising and bitter. After the defeat, by the Soviet veto, of a Western-sponsored resolution calling on India to withdraw from Goa and seek a peaceful settlement Stevenson dramatically announced that : "Tonight we are witnessing the first act in a drama which could end with the death of the [UN] organization."[78] The opposing resolution offered by Afro-Asian states called on Portugal to "cooperate with India in the liquidation of her colonial possession in India" and received only four votes.

India's facile conquest of the Portuguese possessions in 1961 proclaimed that in international affairs it had unabashedly entered the realm of *réal politique* : no effort was made to conceal the fact that India's tangible interests had become the supreme determinants of policy. The military confrontation vis-a-vis China forced the pace of that development, which had only been delayed by Nehru's sensitivity to India's reputation in the world and his major reliance on intangible power to achieve national objectives.

NOTES AND REFERENCES

[1] Some of the most important publications are noted in the bibliography, although most of them are only peripherally concerned with international relations.

[2] A higher figure, of over eight million, was offered by a news agency in 1966, *Statesman Overseas Weekly*, Dec. 17, 1966. The Indian government kept no full statistics on overseas emigration, much less accounts of Indians returning home for good. The term, Indians (or persons of Indian origin) overseas, includes the children of Indian parents living abroad, who surely made up a large share of the total population.

[3] The nonassimilability of Indians abroad has almost become a sociological maxim. The discovery that the gypsies, one of the least well assimilated groups after centuries of habitation in any country, originally migrated out of India came as no surprise to those who knew modern Indian communities abroad. see Chaman Lal, *Gypsies*: *Forgotten Children of India*, New Delhi 1962.

[4] P. Kodanda Rao, "Indians Abroad," *Indian Year Book of International Affairs*, vol. IV (1955), p. 44.

[5] Robert A. Huttenback, *The British Imperial Experience*, pp. 131-32.

[6] e.g. Dharm Yash Dev, *Our Countrymen Abroad*. Also N. V. Rajkumar, *Indians Outside India*, A. I. C. C., New Delhi.

[7] Nehru, statement in the Lok Sabha, Sept. 2, 1957, *India's Foreign Policy*, p. 130.

[8] From the Lok Sabha debate of Dec. 17, 1957, *ibid*., p. 131. In the same statement Nehru advised overseas Indians : "If you cannot be, and if you are not,

friendly to the people of that country, come back to India and [do] not spoil the fair name of India" by exploiting indigenous people and refusing to identify with local interests.

⁹ The early volumes of *India Quarterly* contain useful notes on overseas Indian communities. Other book-length studies are Dwarka Nath, *A History of Indians in British Guiana*, London 1950 ; Hilda Kuper, *Indian People in Natal*, Natal Univ. Press 1960 ; Burton Benedict, *Indians in a Plural Society : A Report on Mauritius*, London 1961 ; Morton Klass, *East Indians in Trinidad : A Study of Cultural Persistence*, N. Y. 1961 ; Adrian C. Mayer, *Indians in Fiji*, London 1963.

¹⁰ For an intimate study of Gandhi's work read his own *Satyagraha in South Africa*, Ahmedabad 1928, preferably in the context of a fuller study of the period.

¹¹ One of the most famous Congress emissaries was Gopal Krishna Gokhale, who visited South Africa in 1912 to lend support to Gandhi's movement. His speeches on the treatment of South African Indians reflected his moderate nature and his agreement with Gandhi that amelioration of the Indians' position could come about by conceding to the Europeans' demand that Indian immigration cease, in order to avoid an ultimate submersion of Western civilization by waves of non-European settlers. By accepting that much of the European stand, Gokhale and Gandhi aroused bitter attacks on themselves from Indian nationalists. see D. G. Karve and D. V. Ambekar, *Speeches and Writings of Gopal Krishna Gokhale*, vol. : Political, part IV.

¹² Text of the agreement in B. V. Govinda Raj, *India and Disputes in the United Nations*, Bombay 1959, pp. 268-69. The Indian government later contended in debates in the UN that this agreement (and a supplementary joint communique in 1932) should have the force of a treaty which the Union of South Africa had violated. South Africa denied that the agreement had the force of a treaty because it was not registered with the League of Nations. V. S. Srinivasa Sastri, the Liberal representative of India at imperial conferences, was sent as agent to South Africa under the terms of the 1926 agreement. For his work there and an assessment of the Capetown Agreement see P. Kodanda Rao, *The Right Honourable V. S. Srinivasa Sastri*, chapters 24, 25, 26.

¹³ Some will say that because South Africa was then, and is today, more attractive to its Indian citizens than India itself would be, the Union government should not be condemned for its racial policies. Such an argument would place the Indians in the position of petitioners and puppets within their own political system rather than acknowledge that they have as much right to the full benefits of citizenship as anyone else.

¹⁴ See K. N. Raj, "Sanctions and the Indian Experience," in Ronald Segal, ed., *Sanctions and South Africa*, Baltimore 1964. We are indebted in this discussion also to J. Theodore Anagnoson for his unpublished paper, "India and the Indians in the Union of South Africa, 1941-1955," American University, 1966.

¹⁵ C. Kondapi, *Indians Overseas 1838-1949*, p. 527.

¹⁶ Speech at the UN on Nov. 20, 1947 ; extract in S. L. Poplai, *India 1947-50*, vol. II, *External Relations*, London 1959, p. 575.

¹⁷ The discussion of the UN's treatment of the dispute appeared earlier, in chapter IV.

[18] In a parliamentary paper of 1908 confirming the Colonial Office's policy which remained until the end of British rule, the following sentence exposed the compromise with principles that characterized most British official attitudes on racial relations : "With regard to the granting of land to Indians, it is not consonant with the views of His Majesty's Government to impose legal restrictions on any particular section of the community, but as a matter of administrative convenience grants should not be made to Indians in the upland areas." Quoted in Gangulee, *Indians in the Empire Overseas*, p. 92.

[19] Gokhale's post-war reform scheme, published after his death in 1915, ended with this sentence : "German East Africa, if conquered from the Germans, should be reserved for Indian colonization and should be handed over to the Government of India." Karve and Ambekar, *op. cit.*, p. 317.

[20] In Dharm Yash Dev, *Our Countrymen Abroad*, p. 27. (Dev was secretary of the A. I. C. C. Department of Indians Overseas in 1940.) A similarly ambitious proposal to make east Africa an "Indian colony" came from the Aga Khan, whose Khoja Ishmaili followers were, and are, a prosperous settler community more fully committed to the area than most Indians. See H. H. the Aga Khan, *India in Transition : A Study in Political Evolution*, Bombay 1918, chapter XIII, "India's Claim to East Africa."

[21] UK White Paper, *Indians in Kenya*, cmd. 1922, July 1923.

[22] Sastri accused Britain of submitting to the threat of a white settler rebellion, which it could not have suppressed with British troops, while ignoring the Indians, who could not make a similar threat. Kodanda Rao, *op. cit.*, p. 147f. The new British dispensation continued the reservation of the highlands for white settlers but granted Indians five elected members in the legislative council, to eleven for the Europeans.

[23] See the summaries of Asian economic preponderance in Kenya, Tanganyika, and Uganda in Delf, *Asians in East Africa*, pp. 44-58. Apart from owning most of the business firms in the 1950's, the earnings of Asian employed persons in Kenya averaged about £480 per person in the early 1960's, compared with about £75 for each African, per year. Similar disparities existed in Tanganyika and perhaps greater ones in Uganda. Standards of education among Asians were far above those of Africans. In Zanzibar Asians also enjoyed the dominant position in marketing the island's main commercial crop, cloves.

[24] Speech in parliament, March 17, 1950, *Speeches 1949-1953*, p. 150.

[25] See the discussion on the question of racial hostility between Indians and Africans, the former's "spiritual condescension" and their terror at the thought of intermarriage, in the writings of Agehananda Bharati, e.g. "Portrait of a Minority ; Asians in East Africa," Oxford Univ. Press, Nairobi, pamphlet, n.d. ; "Problems of the Asian Minorities in East Africa," *Pakistan Horizon*, Karachi, vol. XVII, 4 (1964) ; "The Indians in East Africa," *Sociologus*, Berlin, vol. 14, 2 (1964) ; "The Unwanted Elite of East Africa," *Trans-Action*, St. Louis, July-Aug. 1966.

[26] Of a total Asian population of 180,000 in Kenya only about 50,000 were Kenyan citizens, despite the government's willingness to grant them citizenship. Many had British passports, an "escape permit" regarded as having high value. See the *Hindu*, Oct. 8, 1967.

[27] Those figures, however, included Arakanese Muslims (about 200,000 in 1931) originally from Bengal, who could be considered a permanent ethnic minority in the country.

[28] See S. Satyamurti, *The Indo-Burmese Immigration* : *A Nation in Revolt,* Indian Overseas Central Assoc., New Delhi 1941. The "nation in revolt" was not Burma, but India, alleged to be incensed by the restrictive terms of the agreement, reached by G. S. Bajpai with the Burmese leader, U Saw. Bajpai conceded that Burma had a right to determine the composition of its own population, but the negotiators agreed that Indians "who have wholly identified themselves with the interests of Burma should enjoy the same rights as members of the permanent population."

[29] The judgment of a knowledgeable Indian ex-Burmese government official, Nalini R. Chakravarti, in his unpublished M. A. thesis, "Indians in Burma," American University, 1967, p. 55.

[30] *ibid.*, p. 84.

[31] See chapter IX.

[32] India's formal claim of compensation for nationalized properties was still outstanding in 1958, when the *Annual Report* of the Ministry of External Affairs explained : "While the government of Burma are responsive to our request in matters concerning Indian nationals, the extent of actual amelioration has been rather limited because of Burma's own serious economic and other internal problems." p. 13

[33] The *Hindu*, June 2, 1964.

[34] There was a third group of persons of Indian origin, the Ceylon Tamils, whose status as a permanent part of the Ceylonese nation never became an international issue because their ancestors had resided in the northern portion of the island for centuries.

[35] See Agent of the Govt. of India in Ceylon, *Reports on the Working of the Indian Emigration Act, 1922 . . .* , Calcutta and Delhi.

[36] Indo-Ceylon Relations Exploratory Conference Dec. 1940, *Report of Proceedings*, p. 4.

[37] *ibid.*, pp. 8-9.

[38] *ibid.*, p. 16.

[39] *ibid.*, pp. 17, 18.

[40] Poplai, *op. cit.*, pp. 91-123.

[41] In reference to naval strategy Panikkar insisted that India should make sure that the Indian Ocean remained free from military establishments or naval forces hostile to India. The Trincomalee base should be integrated into Indian naval planning, because "Trincomalee is the only harbour on the east coast of India [sic] which affords sheltered accommodation for a fleet at all seasons." Panikkar, "The Strategic Problems of the Indian Ocean," Allahabad, pamphlet, 1945, pp. 16-18.

[42] Cited in K. Natesa Aiyar, "The Indo-Ceylon Crisis," p. 4.

[43] For further analysis of these points see Kodikara, *Indo-Ceylon Relations Since Independence*, pp. 35-40.

[44] Text of agreement in *Foreign Policy of India* : *Texts of Documents 1947-64*, pp. 189-91.

⁴⁵ By 1963, when virtually all Ceylonese registrations had been processed, only 134, 187 Indians (and Pakistanis) had been registered as citizens of Ceylon, out of a population of nearly 830,000 which had been covered by applications for citizenship. Urmila Phadnis, "The Indo-Ceylon Pact and the 'Stateless' Indians in Ceylon," *Asian Survey*, vol. VII, 4 (April 1967), p. 227

⁴⁶ Ceylon Tamils also, who represented 11 per cent of the total population and whose citizenship was never questioned, claimed serious grievances against the Bandaranaike government. For a discussion of this problem, see Wriggins, *Ceylon : Dilemmas of a New Nation.*

⁴⁷ According to an official of the Indian high commission in Colombo in 1964.

⁴⁸ See the joint Indo-Ceylonese statement on various global problems issued during Nehru's visit to Ceylon in May 1957, *Foreign Policy of India : Texts of Documents 1947-64*, pp. 285-86.

⁴⁹ An area of potential disagreement was skirted in late 1964, when Ceylon sought India's support for declaring the Indian Ocean a nuclear-free zone. As an insignificant military power Ceylon's interest appeared directed toward restricting the level of naval armament in the ocean surrounding its territory. India recognized then its own need of friendly states' controlling the ocean, possibly with nuclear-equipped naval and air forces. Its reply to Ceylon, announced in the Lok Sabha on Nov. 17, 1964, was vague and inconclusive.

⁵⁰ *Foreign Policy of India, op. cit.,* pp. 196-97.

⁵¹ Joint Indo-French communique of Aug. 26, 1947, in Poplai, *op. cit.,* p. 55.

⁵² Text in *Foreign Policy of India, op. cit.,* pp. 15-20.

⁵³ For the French perspective on these and other developments see Alain Coret, "La Cession de l'Inde Francaise."

⁵⁴ Texts of the 1954 and 1956 accords are in *Foreign Policy of India, op. cit,,* pp. 21-39, 207-15.

⁵⁵ A useful discussion of Portugal's concept of a unitary nation-state and a sober defense of its position on colonialism appears in the Portuguese foreign affairs minister from 1961, Franco Nogueira's *The United Nations and Portugal : A Study of Anti-Colonialism,* London 1963.

⁵⁶ Nehru's expectations of eventual discussions with Portugal on Goa were stated in the Lok Sabha on July 26, 1955, Nehru, *India's Foreign Policy*, p. 115.

⁵⁷ In a speech on July 10, 1953, delivered at the first plenary meeting of the National Union in Lisbon, Salazar said that he was resigned to a course "of serenity and steadfastness, in the hope that the Indian leaders, honouring their declarations of peace, will not try to sacrifice the rights of aliens to their rigidly geometric political conceptions." Salazar, "Portugal and its Overseas Provinces," Agencia Geral Do Ultramer, Lisbon, pamphlet, 1953, p. 15.

⁵⁸ Speech in the Rajya Sabha, Dec. 12, 1957, *India's Foreign Policy*, p. 125. By act of parliament in 1961 an amendment to the Indian constitution integrated the two areas into the Union.

⁵⁹ *Judgment of the International Court of Justice on the Right of Passage over Indian Territory (Merits),* pp. 22-23.

⁶⁰ Portugal's position in Goa would have been much strengthened if it had offered to hold a plebiscite among its people, but such an offer would have embarrassed the Lisbon government in its African territories and probably also in the

22

metropole. Many impartial visitors to Goa and some high ranking Indians in private concluded that the Goan people had no desire to lose their unique economic and perhaps their cultural position by being absorbed into India.

[61] Speech in the Lok Sabha, Sept. 17, 1955, *India's Foreign Policy*, p. 118.

[62] Statement in the Lok Sabha, July 26, 1955, *ibid.*, pp. 115-16.

[63] *idem.* In September 1954 NATO had informed India that Portugal could "ask the North Atlantic treaty powers to consult on a threat to the security of Portuguese territories in India. But Portugal could not, under the treaty, expect the North Atlantic powers to come to the defense of Goa. . . ." *New York Times*, Sept. 5, 1954.

[64] Speech in the Lok Sabha, Sept. 17, 1955, *India's Foreign Policy*, p. 120.

[65] *New York Times*, Dec. 5, 1955. The US-Portuguese communiqe appeared two days earlier ; the State Department's statement of neutrality on Goa appeared in the *New York Times*, Dec. 6, 1955.

[66] *ibid.*, Dec. 7, 1955.

[67] Speech in Bombay on June 4, 1956, to a large gathering of Goans. Embassy of India, Washington, D.C., press release no. 16, June 6, 1956.

[68] Speech in the Lok Sabha, Aug. 16, 1961 ; reprinted in Ministry of External Affairs, "Prime Minister on Goa," New Delhi 1962, p. 3.

[69] Statement in the Lok Sabha, *ibid.*, p. 5. Nehru presented a fuller view of his revised thinking on Goa to a seminar on Portuguese colonies, in New Delhi, Oct. 20, 1961, in which African leaders participated, *ibid.*, pp. 6-10.

[70] Salazar's speech to the National Assembly on Jan. 3, 1962 ; reprinted by the Secretariado Nacional da Informacao, Lisbon 1962.

[71] Full documentation may, in fact, not existi n the records of the Ministry of External Affairs. No white paper on Goa was released, though public interest suggested the desirability of doing so.

[72] Nehru told the Lok Sabha on Dec. 7, 1961, that "in the eyes of the African leaders, and especially those struggling against Portuguese colonialism in Africa, Goa was playing an important part. They attach much importance to Goa and what happens in Goa. . . ." He noted further that "we have been criticized for our restraint, call it lack of a spirit of adventure, lack of this or lack of that. So it became almost inevitable for us to take action. . . .", "Prime Minister on Goa," pp. 11, 15.

[73] Press conference, Dec. 28, 1961, *ibid.*, pp. 22-43.

[74] Such was the consensus among knowledgeable persons in the Indian government. Journalists' accounts frequently supported this undocumentable version of the events ; see, e.g., Welles Hangen, *After Nehru, Who?* ; London 1963, pp. 90-95, an account written after experiencing the Indian "liberation" from inside Goa.

[75] "Prime Minister on Goa," p. 29.

[76] This and subsequent excerpts are from *SCOR*, 987th meeting, pp. 10-11, and *SCOR*, 988th meeting, p. 17.

[77] Quincy Wright's elaboration of that point for the specialists appeared in "The Goa Incident," *Amer. Journ. of Int. Law.*, vol. 56, 3 (July 1962), in which he contrasted Nehru's legal defense of the Himalayan boundaries with his apology for the Goan take-over. An objective discussion of the same issue

is Pritam T. Merani, "The Goa Dispute," *Journ. of Public Law*, vol. 14, 1 (1965).
Defenses of the Indian position on Goa can be found in K. Narayana Rao, "The
Problem of Goa," *Ind. Year Book of Int. Affairs*, vol. V (1956) and in J. S. Bains.
India's International Disputes, Bombay 1962.

[78] *SCOR*, 988th meeting, p. 27.

PART THREE

THE SUCCESSES AND FAILURES
OF NONALIGNMENT

CHAPTER XIII

INDO-AMERICAN RELATIONS: EXAMPLES OF CONFLICT

To ONE READING, or writing, these pages in the late 1960's, the recorded early stages of Indo-American relations may seem an almost fictional introduction to the realities of the present. The attitudes and happenings of two decades and longer ago feature some issues long forgotten and many which have matured much differently than expected. Indian officials' fear of receiving too much US economic aid, American public leaders debating the degree of Nehru's communist leanings, and the experience of the Indian ambassador to the US of discrimination on racial grounds at the Houston, Texas, airport in August 1955 are all incidents of of a bygone era suggesting lines of development in Indo-American relations that were soon blotted out.

The relations between India and America were never planned and have never been predictable, and no general line of development is visible in them, even from hindsight. Very few long-term agreements guide them, even at present. The two states stumbled into each other's presence, so to speak, in the 1940's, unprepared ; spent ten years measuring each other's character and intentions ; and then settled down to the serious task of constructing mutually beneficial ties. By the mid-1960's those ties were in part built and were bearing an increasing load of physical and intellectual interchanges. That relations between the two greatest and most dissimilar democratic republics did not mature into settled patterns earlier, despite some eagerness on both sides, resulted from the unusual degrees of independence in foreign policy-making by both governments and from the fact that not only two governments but the public opinions of two free peoples affected foreign relations on both sides.

Some Indian and American officials and many writers following their lead have opined that the objectives of their two countries in world affairs in the 1950's were the same and only the means of carrying them out differed and caused the illusion of mutual conflict. Those, such as V. K. Krishna Menon and John Foster Dulles, who knew the workings of the relationship never encouraged such an optimistic view in frank conversation, because in immediate objectives the two states were if not on directly opposite sides of many issues at least frequently in disagreement. (In long-term objectives, such as peace and prosperity, of course, most states appear to agree.) Indo-American disagreements were usually limited to verbal exchanges at arms' length, to commentaries on the other state's foreign policies. In the areas of tangible national interests, such as military security and economic advantage, India's contacts with the US were less persistent, usually less well publicized, and probably less important for both states than contacts at the level of ideological disputation. American military aid to Pakistan in the 1950's constituted the most serious US infringement of India's tangible, in this case security, interests. The New Delhi government, however, concentrated its protest against that move at the level of principle, rather than expediency—the "no-war area" had been breached, rather than Indian security threatened. Given this comparatively low level of interconnection between the vital interests of India and the US an intriguing question, underlying the discussion on Indo-American conflicts in the present chapter, is why the involvement between the two countries should have been as intense as it was. In the following chapter, which deals with Indo-American relations in the context of economics, the importance of the connection between the two states is obvious and needs no elaborate explanation.

The major Indo-US involvement in the 1950's resulted from the participation of both states in the global ideological disputations of the post-Second World War period, each as the leading spokesman for its respective ideological grouping. Much of this verbal conflict emanated from the chambers of the UN and UN-sponsored conferences, to a global audience which frequently witnessed Indian and American representatives in vigorous controversy. The two governments were influenced by each other's views and policies, but political relations did not take the form of constructive interchange of information and assessments, much less of continuing collaboration for common international purposes. Indo-American political relations were usually those of contenders in a great global debate. Hence the intensity of the proceedings.

Searching for the rationale which could provide the reasons for the other state's policies Indians and Americans often concluded that personal attitudes had the most influence on official actions ; discussions of national interests formed lesser parts of the explanations. Because much of the Indo-US relationship was made up of the contacts of Indian and American policies in an ideological arena ; and because the two countries were democracies guaranteeing free presses and public platforms ; and finally because the two governments had no traditional mutual relations—for these reasons political opinions, public attitudes, and personal assessments formed an unusually significant part in most Indo-American contacts. Having little more at first on which to base relations than the personalities of the Indians and Americans involved—and finding them sufficiently outspoken on both sides so that a firm impression could be formed—both governments gave undue attention to what Nehru or Krishna Menon, Dulles or Richard Nixon said and what sort of people they were.[1] Indians soon adjusted to the idea that the US was the current embodiment of Western power, progress, and personal agressiveness, while Americans transferred their images of non-Western economic backwardness, social inefficiency, and pathetic but dignified mass humanity from China to India. In addition both informed publics were guided by their respective governments to the view that the other state represented an opposing ideological posture. From this approach to Indo-American relations, conflicts were thought to be due to misunderstandings between the two governments and peoples, and most beneficial relations were thought possible mainly through efforts to comprehend the others' points of view.

As it happened, Indo-American relations improved in the 1960's, but not so much because of clearer understandings of each other's point of view as because of increased collaboration for common concrete objectives and thereby growing recognition on both sides that their national interests were compatible. General reductions in "cold war" ideological conflict caused some of the improvement, but far more important were the adoption of mutually reinforcing policies on China, on certain African problems, on the administration of the UN secretariat, on communist subversion in southeast

Asia, in addition to the increases in US and Western economic aid to India. Under those conditions many of the earlier publicized conflicts were neglected or dismissed. A bilateral relationship affecting tangible interests on both sides began to be acknowledged.

THE UNPRODUCTIVE RELATIONS OF THE 1940's

The slow maturing of Indo-American relations after the Second World War was no surprise to those in both governments who knew how few and how lacking in beneficial influence were the prior political contacts. India's economic connections with the US had been of some significance before the war;[2] bilateral trade led to a balance of payments advantage consistently held by India. In percentages, in the three pre-war decades, about seven per cent of India's imports and ten per cent of its exports resulted from trade with the US. At the same time, Americans were purchasing in India about three per cent of their total foreign purchases and exporting to India an average of about one per cent of total exports. Given the commodities making up that trade, expansion was not likely.

Indian exports to America consisted of jute and jute products, shellac and lac, tea, mica, cashew nuts, hides and skins, wool, pepper, short-staple cotton, manganese, and ilmenite. The American export trade to India was composed mainly of mineral oil and manufactures : kerosene and lubricating oils, machinery, motor cars, iron and steel goods and hardware ; American tobacco also entered the trade. In total values, India shipped goods to the US worth about $47 million in 1901, $47 million in 1911, $78 million in 1921, $58 million in 1931, and $131 million in 1941. The comparable figures for US exports to India were $5 million, $11 million, $56 million, $36 million and $98 million. During the war Indo-US trade increased because of the emergency needs of both countries ; for the first time imports from the US exceeded those from Britain, and the trade balance shifted in favour of the US. American business investment in India before independence was insignificant. The value of all foreign investment in 1948 was about $ 1 billion, the bulk of it British. American holdings amounted to about $ 60 million at that time.

Indo-American political relations before independence pro-

vided a narrower base for post-independence contacts than economic relations. Of course, official India dealt indirectly with the US,
through the British foreign office establishments—until the war,
when the Indian and American governments exchanged missions.
In Washington Girja Shankar Bajpai became the agent-general
for India, attached to the British embassy. (His later elevation
to the secretary-generalship of India's external affairs ministry
did not, unfortunately, introduce an element of experience into
Indian policy towards the US, possibly because the foreign minister, Nehru, regarded Indian Civil Service officers as competent
to carry out, but not to formulate, policies.) On an unofficial
level, the Indian National Congress, Gandhi and Nehru in particular, entered a bid for American support for Indian independence
during the Second World War. Earlier, isolated examples of
American support for Indian nationalism lent substance to the
belief that the US government would be the most helpful foreign
agency in backing Congress objectives.[3]

In the critical year of the war, 1942, Indian leaders negotiated
with the Churchill government, and among themselves, on behalf
of immediate concessions towards self-government and asked for
the intervention of the US, particularly of President Franklin D.
Roosevelt. When Colonel Louis Johnson arrived in Delhi as F. D.
R.'s personal representative and took part in the negotiations of
the Cripps mission Indian expectations of positive US intervention
were naturally raised. Johnson demonstrated his sympathy with
the nationalist cause, as did William Phillips, sent to India in late
1942 on a fact-finding mission for the president. Statements by
American officials, such as the declaration of Under-Secretary
of State Sumner Wells on Memorial Day 1942,[4] proclaimed US
opposition to colonialism and implied American unwillingness
to fight the war in order to protect the British empire. When, however, Winston Churchill demonstrated as much adamancy in facing
opposition in India as he did facing it in any theatre, and the Indian
administration moved swiftly to jail Congress leaders and suppress
the "Quit India" campaign, the US government fell into line with
its major ally's wishes. Phillips' unsuccessful endeavours from Delhi
and in Washington to persuade Roosevelt to intervene in the Indian
crisis created disappointment in India and a suspicion that American
troops in the subcontinent would support the unwavering British

presence there. The British viceroy undermined Phillips' mission by refusing to allow him to visit Gandhi, then under detention. Churchill, in an interview with Phillips, revealed a "complex about India from which he would not and could not be shaken."[5]

President Roosevelt apparently felt that Churchill should not be pressed to grant political concessions in India when his back was against the wall, so to speak, and American newspapers began to view Congress' tactics of offering wartime collaboration in exchange for political reforms as a kind of blackmail. The only significant help that Indian nationalists received from a foreign state during the war came from Chiang Kai-shek's government, which tried to impress the Americans of the urgency of gaining the Indian peoples' support for the struggle. The US response to China's warning that the United Nations' effort in Asia would suffer from Britain's refusal to grant concessions to the Congress was that the greatest menace to the Indian people came from the Japanese and that in order to pursue the war successfully no public support should be given to those opposing British rule. The American government and public opinion were not prepared to embarrass Britain in its time of peril for the sake of the theoretical principle of self-determination and openly criticized what was reported as the Congress leaders' lack of sympathy with the allies.[6]

Mutual distrust between independent India and the US was rooted in the 1942 crisis in India, when Congress leaders' appeal to Americans found no official and little unofficial response. The distress of Gandhi and Nehru was open and severe ; their appreciation of US policy and war aims became less favourable. Nehru showed the greater bitterness, attacking the US in an open session of the All-India Congress Committee for its policies on Asia, for its racial superiority, and for its "machine age culture." [7]

Thus, despite unprecedented physical contacts during the war —vastly increased trade and thousands of American troops in India—no basis was laid for a beneficial relationship when both states could conduct their affairs as equals in sovereign status. But each state began to recognize the importanec of the other and both raised their official missions to embassies during the period of India's Interim Government, in 1946. In that year also the governments signed their first bilateral agreement, a settlement on wartime mutual aid and an air transport accord. Some importance may have been attached in India to the passage by the American Congress of the Indian Immigration and Naturalization bill in June 1946, thereby making eligible for American citizenship some 4,000 Indians already settled in the US and setting a symbolic quota for new Indian immigrants. Until the 1965 amendment of the Immigration and Nationality Act which phased out the quota system by July 1968 Indians, like many other national and racial groups, faced discrimination in gaining permission to settle or obtain citizenship in America ; however, hundreds of Indians in fact took up residence and citizenship in the US because of their special skills, private sponsorship, and family connections.

The end of the war and India's independence did not intensify Indo-American connections : there were few if any areas of overlapping national interests, and scarcely any business, intellectual or cultural contacts between the two countries. Hints of the close economic relations a decade in the future appeared in India's purchase of 650,000 tons of foodgrains in the US to relieve shortages in 1946, and in a World Bank mission's tour of India in early 1949, which led to substantial loans ($ 44 million) for railways and agricultural development. But both governments were so strenuously engaged in affairs closer to home—the aftermath of partition, economic problems, the new republican constitution, and fighting in Kashmir and Burma ; the threats of economic and political collapse in Europe, the development of the bi-polar power struggle, and the communist victory in China—that no close relationship materialized at that time.

Nehru's visit to the US in the autumn of 1949 gauged the depth of possible Indo-US mutual involvement and found it shallow. The visit, of almost one month, including time in Canada, presented many official and unofficial opportunities to publicize India's case on world affairs and to seek American assistance. On the whole the effort was premature and unsuccessful.[8] Nehru's presence in Washington confirmed what American diplomats, including the ambassador in Delhi, had been reporting : that the prime minister was unwilling to take a strong anti-communist position internationally ; that he was sympathetic to the Chinese communist revolution ; that he distrusted capitalism and disliked capitalistic societies ; that he believed that world peace was most seriously menaced by colonialism, racialism, and poverty ; and that he was personally difficult to deal with. Nehru, in turn, was distressed by the lack of response in the US to Indian needs, by the uncultivated opulence of much of America, and by the unsubtle and brash personal approaches of many Americans. Later he added to these distresses his familiar complaints about America's strange obsession with the "communist menace," the US government's overready resort to force in pursuing its national interests, and its neutral attitude towards India's main international objectives.

The supreme Indian and American leadership parted in November 1949 acknowledging that their policies and assessments diverged in fundamental ways. Nehru's request for economic assistance, made to the Congress and on public platforms but apparently not explicitly in direct negotiations with the administration, was not acted upon. There would be no Marshall Plan for Asia or even much economic assistance under the aegis of Point Four. The American government's desire to support or create a bastion of anti-communism in Asia found no response from Nehru, except a very categorical rejection of rigid military blocs and ideological dogmatism. The Indian and the US governments, in fact, had discovered by the time of Nehru's visit, much to their regret and somewhat to their embarrassment, that as the inheritors of the same political tradition and greatly in need of each other's suport for specific objectives they nevertheless had committed themselves respectively to separate postures in the global political arena. As a result, the US could not firmly reinforce India's primary international objective, the eradication of colonialism ; and India was unwilling to support the paramount American goal, the containment of communism.

India's refusal to align itself with the Western grouping of states, of which it had been automatically a member until 1946-1947, had a special meaning for the Indo-American relationship. India's independence in world affairs had to be achieved by disentangling itself from Western foreign policies, which as promulgated through the British empire had long determined India's external relations. But to make this effort convincing to everyone, Nehru and other officials had frequently and dramatically to proclaim their opposition specifically to US positions in world politics, particularly when they were coloured by ideological overtones. No government, least of all the Soviet, expected India to support the international positions of the communist states ; there was no precedent for such an alignment, no established mutual Indo-Soviet interests. Indian nonalignment, initially a declaration of independence in foreign relations to supplement the achievement of self-government domestically, constituted a break-away from Western policies, and the burden of proving nonalignment fell on those who spoke out, in largest measure, against the US, representing the West.

For several years the American government interpreted India's criticisms and its refusal to collaborate in Western collective security efforts as a form of open hostility undermining American foreign policy objectives. (The nonalignment of Yugoslavia, a state having moved away from a Soviet alignment, was acceptable.) As leader of the "free world" and promulgator of a universalist ideological position the US expected non-communist states to follow the lead offered, and if they did not there was a suspicion in Washington that those states overtly or covertly sought to reinforce the objectives of the communist bloc. The simplistic Marxist-Leninist notion that the world's governments could be classified as either one of two main types had gained acceptance in the US, where a pluralistic view of the world's societies had traditionally been proclaimed. The result was the facile, uncritical and very general conviction popularized by American officials and such prominent newspapers as the *New York Times* that India's government betrayed its demo-cratic political heritage, refused to face the challenges of the real world of power, and knowingly increased the prestige of "interna-tional communism" by refusing to align itself with Western policies and by very frequently criticizing the US. In the great struggle of ideologies India refused to commit itself ; in the division of world opinion, the "battle for men's minds," in which every government, ultimately every person could be counted, India appeared to hold back. Such a wavering and indecisive posture could be called "immoral."[9] At the very least it seemed unfriendly, at a time when the world's most powerful state "needed all the friends it could get" and unpopularity seemed the harbinger of defeat.

The Indian government cherished its nonalignment the more whenever spokesmen for a great power brought pressures to bear to sway it. The experience of receiving such pressure served chiefly to strengthen the resolve of Indian officials to retain their indepen-dence of action, which included refusal to adhere to any military alliance system. This characteristic of the nonaligned posture was not tainted by an unpublicized act in March 1951, Ambassador Vijayalakshmi Pandit's signing a mutual defense assistance agreement with the US. The agreement included the standard wording about participation "in arrangements for individual and collective self-defense" in support of the purposes and principles of the UN Charter,[10] but her action had the effect only of clearing the way, under American law, for India's purchase of American weapons, which occurred in limited amounts, and receipt of US economic assistance, which at that time was authorized under the Mutual Security Act. In 1958 India and the US exchanged assurances of India's acceptance of the terms of the 1954 Mutual Security Act, which permitted the American president to extend aid to any country whose increased ability to defend itself was determined to be important to the security of the US. These pro forma agreements overcame administrative barriers to the goals that both governments wished to pursue, and a reading into them of high political meanings would have been misleading.

SPECIFIC CONFLICTS IN THE 1950's : US SECURITY POLICIES IN ASIA

The power of the US and of any other outside state should not, according to the Indian government during the first decade and more after independence, be allowed to penetrate deeply into Asian politics. The first objective of Indian foreign policies in post-war Asia was thought to be the elimination of the Western presence there ; the second the establishment of a grouping of states which could powerfully sponsor Asian objectives in the global arena.

The first part of this programme, sweeping but vague in the details of its operation, thinly veiled by diplomatic language in Nehru's writings and speeches, came into direct opposition to US objectives and traditional policy. For the US had supported and wished to continue to ally itself with one Asian state, China, which it expected would become predominant with American help, and would continue to further American interests. The communist victory in China forced the US away from China and opened up the possibility that India could replace China as the predominant Asian power allied with the US. Instead, even before a decision was reached in Washington to try to replace the Chinese tie by one with India, India announced its opposition to alliances and suggested the lines along which it wanted to see Asian politics develop. For the US only one course remained by which it might retain influence in Asia and at the same time check the power-seeking drives of China. That was to exert its influence through the smaller, peripheral Asian states, many of which had traditional fears of China (and even India) and needed the backing of a foreign power to protect them against an expanding Chinese sphere.

While American policy in Asia was being revised, ironically to inhibit a development—the emergence of China as regionally preponderant—which had earlier been a US objective, India was seeking close ties with the People's Republic of China as a second major objective of its Asian policy. It had, verbally at least, identified itself with certain Chinese objectives, notably the withdrawal of the Western colonial presence in Asia. As described elsewhere, Nehru was fostering an Indo-Chinese collaboration which he hoped would achieve the mutually held goal of an independent and influential Asia. The catalyst which forced an overly-rapid development of the Asian policies of all major powers appeared in June 1950, when the Korean War broke out. Nehru's instinctive horror of open aggression and the sanction of the UN Charter initially overcame his suspicion of the US giving armed protection to an Asian state ; India supported the early Security Council resolutions on Korea. But as the UN's Korean objectives became inextricably mixed with the American policy of containing China, India's efforts to befriend China and its opposition to Western military presence in Asia overcame the earlier stand on UN-US action in Korea.[11] The switch in India's Korean War policy solidified Indo-American disagreements on Asian affairs.

As the far eastern military crisis expanded in the early 1950's India proclaimed its opposition to all American security policies in Asia, from assistance to French and British colonial regimes in southeast Asia and protection of the Nationalist Chinese regime on Formosa to the establishment of defense pacts with peripheral Asian states, such as South Korea and the Philippines. Later, India's opposition to US Asian policies focussed on SEATO and US relations with South Vietnam. Indian spokesmen argued that not only were America's relations with certain smaller Asian states detrimental to the independence of the region but also that American

23

security policies had the unintentional effect of increasing Chinese militarism by surrounding China with hostile bases. Thus, by the early 1950's India and the US had adopted such opposing stands on Asian affairs that only Nehru's determination to avoid military alliances and his openly expressed doubts about China's policies in the Himalayas and southeast Asia kept India from appearing to support all Chinese objectives in Asia. India's refusal to collaborate in the containment of China forced the US into the strategy of the peripheral defense system, and its opposition to US policies, although merely verbal, undermined their effectiveness.

During the Korean War, in 1951, a symbolic episode of the Indo-American conflict of policies in Asia emerged suddenly from the US decision to sign a peace treaty with Japan and thus formalize peace-time relations with that country. A US-UK joint peace treaty draft was circulated in the summer to some fifty states which were still technically at war with Japan, in preparation for a conference in San Francisco in September, at which time the treaty was to be signed. India was presented with the draft treaty and invited to the signing. But New Delhi had two major objections to the draft, reflecting contemporary policy differences with its erstwhile Western allies. One was a failure to recognize full Japanese sovereignty by the terms of the treaty itself : the Ryukyu and Bonin islands remained under US administration, and US-Japanese security arrangements formed part of the document. The other was the treaty's failure to specify the return of Formosa to mainland Chinese authority and thus its obvious unacceptability to the Peking regime. The US showed no willingness to compromise on those issues which had serious implications for American far eastern strategy. The obvious haste of the proceedings and the disinterest of the treaty's manager, John Foster Dulles, in consulting personally with Indian officials promoted further discord. India did not attend the San Francisco conference but made its views on the treaty known through diplomatic correspondence.[12]

Although the US government gained in respect and understanding for India's nonalignment as a result of Korean War diplomacy, the Indian government did not reciprocate with appreciation for American policy. The conflicts in Indian and American policies in Asia spread after the war ended and the US extended its defense alliance system into southern Asia and the middle east, areas of

Indian interests. Nehru was critical of the US determination to maintain a dominant military position in Asia, as a check on growing Chinese power—an American strategy baldly stated by Assistant Secretary of State Walter S. Robertson.[13] Nehru's critique of US policy caught the imagination not only of Indians but of many thoughtful people and formed a part of the international reputation of India's leader. "Some people imagine," Nehru told parliament on September 17, 1953, "that a country's policy should be what they call a 'strong' policy—strong policy apparently meaning that we should go about looking as fierce and ferocious as possible, threatening everybody, telling everybody that we will punish them if they don't behave as we want them to behave. Now, that kind of thing may sound very well at a public meeting and may evoke applause, but the fact is that that represents great immaturity in political thinking or understanding. Mature nations...do not behave in this way."[14]

Late in 1953 the US Defense Department held conversations with Pakistani representatives in Washington with a view to establishing a new American military connection with an Asian state. The area from Turkey to the Philippines along the southern flank of the Soviet and Chinese heartland was unprotected by pro-Western forces, except for the uncertain French and British efforts in Indo-China and Malaya. Apart from South Korea there was no US supported indigenous military establishment on the entire Asian mainland. In the perspective of American military leaders Pakistan's geographic situation qualified it admirably as a possible bastion against Soviet-Chinese expansion. When, after initial hesitation and some individual American opposition to the move, the Eisenhower administration sanctioned a military aid programme for Pakistan, it was adopting a course of open hostility towards India —or so it seemed from New Delhi's point of view.

Nehru's analysis of the American intervention stressed two complaints. First, Pakistan's participation in a great power alliance system fractured the geographic solidity of the nonaligned grouping of states, destroyed the integrity of what Nehru called the "no-war area" in Asia. "We, in our own quiet way," Nehru explained to the upper house of parliament, "worked for and looked forward to this area.... Naturally we hoped that Pakistan ... would belong to that area also. Now, if any military aid comes to Pakistan from the

United States it is obvious that Pakistan drops out of that area. . . .
the cold war, as it is called, comes to Pakistan and, therefore, comes
to India's borders. . . ."[15] Second, the US-Pakistani connection
resembled the initial stages of many Western imperialist ventures
in India, wherein a relatively weak local power to increase its strength
vis-a-vis its neighbour accepted foreign military assistance and thus
gradually lost its independence and acted as a vehicle for introducing
alien influence into the country. The 19th century subsidiary alliance
system of the British in India must have come to his mind when
Nehru thought "of any military aid freely given from a country
of the West, or any country, to a country of the East," as one phase
of "the history of colonial domination gradually creeping in here
and establishing itself. . . ."[16] Unstated was Nehru's further worry
that increased Pakistani strength would adversely affect India's
position in Kashmir.

By any standards of judgment the American build-up of Pakistan's military forces, particularly after the deliveries of sophisticated
weapons such as jet fighters towards the end of the 1950's, impinged
upon India's security interests. The American move in fact had
not only the goal of preparing a local Asian ground force for possible
use against Soviet or Chinese moves into the middle east or southeast
Asia but the purpose also of checking India's power and influence
in the region.[17] The latter purpose was partially achieved, as American arms created an unnatural and explosive alteration of the power
balance in the subcontinent. The former purpose was never achieved
because Pakistan's leaders were unwilling to commit their forces
away from the Indian frontiers ; American officials, however,
maintained that somehow the northern tier and southeast Asian
defense systems were strengthened by American support of Pakistan.
In 1954 SEATO was established, with Pakistan as the anchor
member in the north, and the next year Pakistan was brought into
the middle east defense system, the Baghdad Pact.

The US commitment to Pakistan deepened in 1958 and 1959 ;
an American electronic intelligence gathering system was established
in northern Pakistan to monitor signals from the Soviet Union,
and ultimately air fields were built, one of which accommodated
the U-2 reconnaissance aircraft shot down by the Russians in 1960.[18]
A new bilateral agreement was reached under the format of the
Eisenhower Doctrine for the middle east which Pakistan interpreted

publicly as an American promise to assist in meeting any (i.e. Indian) "aggression" against Pakistan.[19] The US government at that time, as before, assured India that its support of Pakistan was aimed only against aggression from communist states and further gave guarantees in seemingly good faith that it would give India support in case Pakistan attacked with its American-equipped armed forces. President Eisenhower had written to Nehru along these lines in early 1954,[20] and in 1956 in New Delhi, Secretary of State Dulles provided Indians with the following reassurance : "I think there can be every confidence on the part of India that there will be no use of these armaments [supplied to Pakistan] in any aggressive way against India. Certainly Pakistan knows if that should happen there would be a quick end to its good relations with the United States. On the contrary, under the principles of the United Nations Charter, the United States would be supporting India if it became a victim of any armed aggression."[21]

India acquiesced in the decade-long building up of Pakistan and, trusting the US intention and ability to control its ally, did not allow the American alliance structure's penetration of southern Asia to preclude other kinds of cooperation with the US. When American Patton tanks were used by Pakistan in May 1965 against Indian forces in the Rann of Kutch, and when full-scale Pakistani armoured and air attacks struck India in September the US government refused to give support to India, or even publicly express regret for Indian losses from American arms. Unexplainably, Indians placed full responsibility for the three-weeks war on Pakistan, although some officials expressed mild disillusionment at American inaction. But everyone knew that Pakistan felt strong enough to attack solely because of its advanced American equipment.[22]

FURTHER INDO-AMERICAN CONFLICTS OF INTERESTS

India's conflicts with American security policies in Asia had no other violent outcomes than the one just mentioned, but opposing policies of lesser significance provided the subjects for years of steady debate. On the Kashmir question the American political tradition found an appeal in self-determination by the Kashmiris as the appropriate solution to the Indo-Pakistani dispute. The American government and public opinion for many years tended towards the view that India was reluctant to fulfill the pledge to hold a plebiscite. Furthermore, there was some US inclination, and a great deal of pressure from the Pakistani government, towards support of Pakistan's case simply on grounds that Pakistan was a military ally. Nevertheless the US never took a public stand favouring Pakistan's demands on Kashmir ; however, it often supported renewed discussion on Kashmir in the UN or bilaterally, and this alone appeared to Indians as bias. At one time, shortly after the dispute broke out, Sheikh Abdullah discussed his plan for an independent Kashmir with an American ambassador, and the conversation was probably overheard. Although the US is not known to have encouraged the Sheikh or to have ever sought a military base in Kashmir American interest in that area gave Indians some cause to speculate.[23] Adlai Stevenson's visit to the state in 1953 caused even official Indian statements about possible foreign interference. The chief US concern in the Kashmir dispute, however, was always its threat to subcontinental peace and its costly drain on Indian and Pakistani resources. The often misapplied efforts of American officials to mediate the dispute sought *any* settlement of it, rather than a particular outcome that might conceivably favour certain secondary US interests.

Included in a broader range of Indo-US conflicts of policies were the disagreements about southeast Asia. In abrupt contrast to Indian diplomacy, largely limited to proclamations, US policies in the region veered frequently towards the use and threat of force. Neither government's objectives were effectively promoted, partly at least because Indians and Americans worked at cross-purposes, sometimes with the object of undermining each other's interests. From Burma to Indonesia and the Philippines in the post-war years civil disruption, outside attacks, and administrative weakness brought dangers and miseries that neither India nor the US could ignore. But the two states could not agree on common policies, although some of their aims, namely the stability of the region, economic progress, and democratic government, coincided. The Indo-US conflict of policies in southeast Asia, as elsewhere, centred on the proper priorities in supporting nationalism and combatting communist-led movements. India urged recognition of almost any popularly based nationalism as the best ultimate assurance that a people would reject outside control and demand democracy. This almost classic faith in the beneficial results of nationalism, manifested by declarations of support for nationalist causes and admonitions to other states to avoid interfering with the workings out of popular will, confronted American policies aimed at defeating communist leadership first, if necessary by backing colonial regimes. The Indo-American difference of approach to the recurring political crises in southeast Asia centred for many years on Vietnamese affairs. US backing of the French and later Bao Dai's government struck New Delhi as American complicity in what was essentially colonialism, however masqueraded as anti-communism or defense against Chinese expansionism. When India itself recognized the dangers of communist subversiveness and Chinese aggressiveness in southeast Asia, by the early 1960's, it slowly altered its policy on Vietnam, as described in chapter X.

Most prolonged Indo-US conflicts flourished in the context of Asian affairs. But on global issues too, such as disarmament and human rights questions in the UN, the main representatives of the nonaligned and the Western groupings of states carried on debates lasting for many years. Of shorter duration were the disagreements and the verbal disputes arising from crises in Europe, notably in Berlin and Hungary. As a result of the latter episode, in late 1956, the suspicions of many private Americans that Nehru's government was not sincerely committed to human freedom and was instead anxious to cultivate close relations with the communist states appeared to receive alarming confirmation. Those who had sympathized with Nehru's domestic leadership and had tried to justify to other Americans the Indian position of nonalignment vis-a-vis great power disputes could find no voice to defend India's hesitation to condemn Soviet armed intervention in Budapest. Officially, the relations of India and the US scarcely suffered by their profoundly different reactions to the Hungarian crisis, as the successful Nehru-Eisenhower meeting in December 1956 demonstrated. Chapter XVI carries this discussion further and outlines the Indian position on the US-Soviet dispute over Berlin.

As previous chapters have shown, Indian and US foreign policies came into conflict on many colonial issues, often unnecessarily, because the US was in ultimate agreement with India that all nations should be self-governing. But the US placed a lower priority on taking nominally anti-colonial positions than on the require-

ments of providing for administrative stability in dependent territories, of avoiding a communist accession to power there, and of
maintaining the strength and unity of the Western alliance system.
In General Assembly and Trusteeship Council proceedings on
many issues related to colonialism, especially during the first decade
of the UN's existence, India discovered the US and its Western
allies with colonial dependencies voting in opposition to the newly
independent countries in a fairly consistent pattern. In almost all
such cases the US votes reflected a difference in global political
posture from India's rather than conflicts of vital national interests,
which for both countries did not reside in the fate of UN debates
on colonialism.

However, as dependent areas gained their independence and more
numerous and radical voices rose to protest delays in the process
of Western withdrawal, India and the US found some common
objectives in colonial affairs. As discussed elsewhere, India's function in the latter part of the 1950's became one of trying to reconcile
the more extreme opposing positions on colonial questions, and the
US often worked for the same ends. On the questions of Algeria
and Cyprus, and later on sub-Saharan African issues, such as the
Congo, India and the US avoided doctrinaire postures and sought
only the common goal of peace and freedom.

One exception, but not a set-back, to the unpublicized conver-
gence of Indian and American positions on colonial issues arose
from the long postponed and over publicized Indian occupation
of Goa in 1961. America's UN ambassador, Adlai Stevenson, on
that occasion enunciated probably the most telling attack ever
made officially by the US on an Indian action, and it hurt Indian
listeners the more because they respected Stevenson's liberal views.
In the Security Council on December 18, 1961, the American delegate
observed that "what is at stake today is not colonialism;.... It is
a lamentable departure not only from the Charter but from India's
own professions of faith."[24]   On no other public issue was an
Indian position as critically discussed and publicized in the US
as was the forcible end of Portuguese rule in India. From the *New
Republic* to *Time* magazine the press condemned and ridiculed the
action, not for love of Portuguese colonialism but for regret over
Nehru's seeming fall from his self-constructed pedestal of high
purpose. During the 1962 session of the US Congress the Goa

action was cited as reason for urging a cut in appropriations for Indian aid. So vigorous and outraged sounded the American public reaction that one student of the phenomenon[25] concluded that India's resort to the use of force in Goa was taken in the US as a moral vindication for America's more frequent resort to arms ; criticism could at last be uninhibitedly aimed at one who had often condemned US actions.

But the US government, Stevenson apart, took the Goa episode in its stride. Never was there any intention to support Portuguese rule in India ; there had been clear disclaimers from Washington and London that the NATO alliance would or could be activated to protect any overseas Portuguese territory.[26] By 1961 the US was no longer as dependent on the Portuguese Azores islands air refuelling base as it had been in 1955, when it was preparing to renegotiate the Azores treaty. On four occasions in 1961 the US voted with India on anti-colonialist resolutions in the UN, one of which censured Portugal for its "repressive measures" in Angola ; and American representatives made it clear that they regarded Goa as a colony, not a province. After the Goa take-over the Kennedy administration, in May 1962, managed to turn back the Congressional drive to express disapproval of Indian foreign policy by reducing the foreign aid to that country. The Goa issue quickly faded out as an important irritant in Indo-American relations and failed to deflect the growing collaboration of the 1960's.

The Goa episode was an extreme example of many Indo-American conflicts which were not always manifestations of opposing tangible interests but often merely commentaries by one state on the policies of the other. Customarily those conflicts assumed an air of intensity because of their setting in the UN, which stimulated publicity, or because they expressed values seemingly at stake in the arena of ideological combat. The many conflicts in Indo-American relations gave way to agreements when both governments began to base their mutual relations on a growing area of concrete involvements, first economic and then military, which placed in proper perspective disputes and conflicts of policy that flourished mainly at the verbal level.

Despite the intense debate and criticism between the two countries and their failure to reach any beneficial political accords, the decade of the 1950's in Indo-American relations laid a firm, though by no means deep, foundation for future collaboration. Chiefly, this was because the governments and informed publics came to respect each other's interests, to be realistic in their expectations about each other's policies, and to develop some familiarity with each other's domestic life. Because of the rapidly increasing intellectual and cultural exchanges between them the two peoples discovered each other, and thereby foresook the earlier stereotyped mental images of the other's way of life. Thousands of students, teachers, journalists, and government officials on permanent or special assignments travelled in both directions, creating a bridge which could promote the common interests of the two states, once those interests were clearly identified.

NOTES AND REFERENCES

[1] Comparing Krishna Menon's impact on public opinion in Britain, where he was high commissioner from 1947 to 1952, with that in the US suggested that the British made up their minds about India on the basis of much more knowledge about the country and about British interests there than was available in the US, and thus did not react so strongly to a single man's poor public image. Menon did not suit American stereotypes about Indians as calm, somewhat passive, philosophical, and benign people. He was sardonic, vigorous, prone to outbursts of passion, and never lost his fox-like alertness. People and some diplomats were confused. Only those who knew him "off-stage," such as the American UN ambassador, Henry Cabot Lodge, had a more favourable impression of Menon.

Mr. Dulles' early estimates of the Congress regime in New Delhi must have remained in some Indians' memories for many years. Before Indian independence, while Dulles was a member of the US delegation to the UN, he reportedly declared to the National Publishers' Association that "In India, Soviet Communism exercises a strong influence through the interim Hindu government." N. Y. *Herald Tribune*, Jan. 18, 1947. On the assumption of independence he welcomed the new "Hindu" government in New Delhi. Although Dean Acheson, the secretary of state while Dulles carried out special presidential missions, did not offend Indian officials by inappropriate remarks, his understanding of the subcontinent was rudimentary. He once told one of the authors, at Yale, that in the early 1950's the US administration was "blind" to happenings in south Asia, being preoccupied with Europe and the far east. Acheson found Nehru "terribly difficult" to deal with and resented his criticisms of the US.

[2] A discussion of this subject appears in L. K. Rosinger, *India and the United States*, chap. 5.

[3] The American press in the 1920's and 1930's was fairly sympathetic to the Indian nationalist movement, and some journals were consistently critical of British rule, despite the fact that more than one-half of the news from India flowed through the British news agency, Reuters. Occasionally congressional

opinion expressed views favourable to Indian aspirations for independence, e.g. Senator Blaine's resolution in January 1930 offering support for Indian independence, a goal just adopted by the Lahore session of the Congress. See Harnam Singh, *The Indian National Movement and American Opinion*, and S. K. Arora, *American Foreign Policy Towards India* ; of less importance is Sujit Mukherjee, "Early American Images of India," *India Quarterly*, vol. XX, 1 (Jan.-March 1964).

[4] "If this war is in fact a war for the liberation of peoples, it must assure the sovereign equality of peoples throughout the world. . . . Our victory must bring in its train the liberation of all peoples. . . . The age of imperialism is ended." Quoted in L. S. Finkelstein, "American Policy in Southeast Asia," Institute of Pacific Relations, N. Y. 1951, p. 6.

[5] William Phillips, *Ventures in Diplomacy*, Boston 1952, p. 390. For other, similar Indian appeals for American support during the war see Bimla Prasad, *The Origins of Indian Foreign Policy*, Calcutta 1962, pp. 220-22.

[6] Thorough discussions of the points in this paragraph are in M. S. Venkataramani and B. K. Shrivastava, "The United States and the Cripps Mission," *India Quarterly*, vol. XIX, 3 (July-Sept. 1963) ; "The United States and the 'Quit India' Demand," *ibid.*, vol. XX, 2 (Apr.-June 1964); and "America and the Indian Political Crisis, July-August 1942," *International Studies*, vol. VI, 1 (July 1964).

[7] See *International Studies, op. cit.*, pp. 41-42.

[8] See James Reston's critique of the first visit on the occasion of Nehru's second trip to the US ; *New York Times*, Dec. 16, 1956.

[9] This descriptive term was used by Dulles in an address in June 1956 ; Department of State *Bulletin*, vol. XXXIV, 886 (June 18, 1956), pp. 999-1000. But two months earlier President Eisenhower had said in reference to several newly-independent states : "Some of them are concerned to avoid involvements with other nations, as we were for many years. Certainly we Americans should understand and respect these points of view. We must accept the right of each nation to choose its own path to the future." Cited in *ibid.*, vol. XXXIV, 879 (April 30, 1956), p. 700.

[10] The agreement is in Dept. of State publication 4221 of 1951.

[11] Nehru told an American correspondent that "The great influence of the United States in Asia for a long period came from the fact that she stood apart from the European powers. So the United States was separated in people's minds from European colonialism. If the United States should come physically into Asia, she will lose that approach of a disinterested great power." *New York Times*, Nov. 11, 1951.

[12] See Ministry of External Affairs, "Japanese Peace Treaty—Selected Documents," New Delhi, Aug. 1951.

[13] On Jan. 26, 1954, and cited by Nehru in the Lok Sabha, March 1, 1954 ; see *White Paper : Kashmir : Meetings and Correspondence between the Prime Ministers of India and Pakistan* (July 1953—Oct. 1954), p. 77.

[14] *House of the People, Official Report*, vol. VIII, pt. II, col. 3976.

[15] *Council of States, Official Report*, vol. V, Dec. 24, 1953, col. 3549. Directly

answering Nehru's words Deputy Assistant Secretary of State John D. Jernegan asserted that "We in the United States believe the cold war is already on the subcontinent, as it is in every other place in the world." Jernegan's speeches on April 3, which included the above statement, and March 6, 1954, revealed how carefully the State Department weighed India's reaction to American aid to Pakistan. Each of Nehru's objections was answered sympathetically and fully. State Dept. press releases nos. 176 and 114.

[16] *House of the People, Official Report*, vol. X, pt. II, Dec. 23, 1953, col. 2976.

[17] According to a thoroughly reliable witness, Vice-President Nixon explained in 1954 that US military assistance to Pakistan would create a useful counter-force to Nehru's neutralism. See Selig Harrison, "America, India, and Pakistan : A Chance for a Fresh Start," *Harper's Magazine*, July 1966, p. 59.

[18] See Harrison, *ibid.*, for the most complete discussion of these US "special facilities."

[19] India protested to the US about Pakistan's interpretation of the bilateral agreement of March 5, 1959, and was assured by Washington that "the Eisenhower Doctrine restricts the use of United States armed forces to cases of armed aggression from any country controlled by international communism"—in Nehru's words, in parliament, March 13, 1959, *India's Foreign Policy*, p. 475.

[20] Eisenhower's message, of Feb. 24, 1954, is in Dept. of State, *American Foreign Policy 1950-1955 : Basic Documents*, vol. II, Washington 1957, pp. 2192-93.

[21] As reported in the *New York Times*, March 11, 1956.

[22] Including former American ambassador to India, John K. Galbraith, who told the Senate Foreign Relations Committee in 1966 that : "If we had not supplied arms, Pakistan would not have sought a military solution." Reported in the *Washington Post*, April 26, 1966.

[23] Beyond speculation is the outright condemnation of American motives in Kashmir, and in all other areas of Indo-American concern, especially economic, to be found in the well-researched, pro-communist publication, *American Shadow Over India* by L. Natarajan, Bombay, People's Publishing House, 1952.

[24] *SCOR*, 987th meeting, pp. 16-17. To balance his outrage against Indian policy Stevenson wanted to take note of the anachronism of Portuguese colonialism, but the State Department insisted that all allusions to Portuguese colonialism be cut from his speech. Arthur M. Schlesinger, Jr., *A Thousand Days : John F. Kennedy in the White House*, Boston 1965, p. 527.

[25] Deborah Opperman, "The United States Reaction to the Goan Incident," an unpublished paper, American University, 1965.

[26] See *New York Times*, Sept. 3, 1954, p. 3.

CHAPTER XIV

THE AMERICAN TIE AND FOREIGN ECONOMIC RELATIONS

THE ECONOMIC TIES established between India and the US in the 1950's provided a productive contrast to their political dialogue; the two countries tended to carry on their economic and political relations with each other at separate levels of discourse. However, the distinction was not consistently observed ; certain decisions of the US Congress on economic aid were specifically affected by the policies followed by the Indian government, and India's attitudes towards global events in the 1960's to some extent were influenced by its receipt of American assistance. India's economic diplomacy aimed at maximizing the international aid available to it for expanding its domestic productivity and its external trade. The response that it met from the US and other industrial countries of the West forms the substance of this chapter.[1]

At the height of Indo-American policy conflicts over the conduct of the Korean war, in early 1951, the US Congress authorized for India the largest single grain allocation ever to have left American ports ; it enacted Public Law 480 loaning India rupees 90.3 crores ($ 2 billion) for the purchase of 190 million tons of wheat. The bill received painfully slow treatment from the time it was introduced on an emergency basis by a bipartisan group of senators and representatives in February to its final passage on June 15. That was partly because of awkwardness in both governments about how the transfer should be handled—the State Department proposed an outright gift, whereas Nehru wished a loan and then evinced doubts about its terms. The bill passed, despite American resentments about India's apparently pro-Chinese policy in Korea, for two immediately relevant reasons : the humanitarian motive of a "people of plenty" asked to assist others lacking even basic sustenance ; and a political awareness that the US "must counter the false promises of communist imperialism with constructive action for human betterment...

[so that Americans can] make human liberty secure against the forces which threaten it throughout the world today."[2] A longer-range US objective, incorporating these two points, was extended from its initial European context to apply also, at that time and later, to India : the advancement of the non-communist world within an international political framework that the American democracy could support.

The 1951 wheat loan was the first substantial US economic assistance programme for India, but it did not inaugurate a new programme of Marshall Plan-like aid to India. The US, the only country then able to offer economic assistance, regarded the underdeveloped world as incapable of absorbing large amounts of capital inputs. Furthermore, in 1951, India was not seeking a programme of massive economic assistance. Foreign aid was officially regarded as a threat to the independence of the recipient, and India's sterling balances still seemed sufficient to meet its balance of payments deficits. India's wartime credits held in the UK (amounting to £1,299.4 million in April 1946) provided a deep cushion under the balance of payments for a decade after independence ; sterling was made available to India at a normal rate of £ 35 million each year.

Nevertheless, the year 1952 marked the beginning of a modest ($ 53 million) US programme of economic and technical assistance to India, under the Mutual Security Act along lines worked out in New Delhi by the dedicated, popular American ambassador, Chester Bowles. The US effort then was aimed at increasing food production and raising living standards in the rural areas, and those purposes remained central to the American aid programme in India in the years following. In contrast, the reasonings given by the US administration's spokesmen for the Indian aid programme and the responses of the Congress during the ensuing decade reflected uncertainties about purposes and quantities and means of transferring economic assistance, whose result was confusion and complexity in the actual programmes undertaken.[3]

India's first five-year plan statement evidenced no great reliance on foreign economic assistance, though it expected increased levels of foreign investment. The text modestly observed that : "In these early stages of development further external assistance would certainly be useful...,"[4] and the Western economists in an International Monetary Fund mission to the country reinforced this spirit of complacency in February 1954 by ending their report with the following sanguine opinion : "With a proper development programme and sound monetary policies, India should be able to meet these and future foreign obligations it will incur."[5] In fact, however US economic assistance during the first plan had an important function in alleviating some strain on India's balance of payments. India received grants and loans of rupees 113.2 crores (about $237 million). Also, the surplus agricultural commodities programme, under the Agricultural Trade and Development Act of 1954, Public Law 480, granted rupees 26.1 crores (about $54 million) of goods ; and the Ford Foundation contributed rupees 5.6 crores (about $11 million).[6] By the end of the plan period the US had made overwhelmingly the largest foreign contribution to Indian development, although a portion of the allocated aid was not utilized. It had set the precedent of economic assistance to underdeveloped countries and had discovered with India an area in which the two states could collaborate successfully.

Economic aid is in most respects a substitute for trade and investment and often a poor one, which is costly to the recipient both economically, because foreign aid sometimes inhibits domestic initiative, and politically. But in the case of Indo-US relations economic aid was a necessary substitute : a balanced trading relationship was impossible because India could not expand exports to America, while requiring American goods for development, and because American businessmen exhibited extreme caution in investing in India. Nevertheless, Indo-American trade in the early 1950's moved in larger quantities than did aid ; US investment in India continued to be negligible.

In the years before 1951, India's trade with the world at large fluctuated widely. In general, imports rose across the list of major commodities more rapidly than exports, and in the three years from 1948-1949 to 1950-1951 India had to draw rupees 583 crores in foreign exchange from reserves to offset the balance of payments deficit. During that period the US was India's second most important trading partner, following the UK. In 1949 Indo-American negotiations began on a commercial treaty, but they were unsuccessful because India was unprepared to alter its special trading relationship with the UK and agree to the American demand for most-favoured nation treatment. Indo-American trade continued to be governed by the treaty of commerce and navigation between the US and the UK signed in 1815 and by temporary ad hoc arrangements ; there has been no treaty of friendship and commerce up to the present writing.

After the war Indian imports from the US rose markedly, due to emergency shipments of foodgrains and structural increases in the demands for raw cotton, industrial raw materials, and capital and capital maintenance goods. (The consumer goods trade was never prominent.) Although restrictions were placed on imports from America because of shortages of dollars, the Indian government could not reverse a trend which, in contrast to the pre-war situation, gave India an adverse balance of trade with the US. During the Korean war India's exports to the US received a stimulus, but the pattern of overall trade deficit was well established by the 1950's. India had to rely on traditional exports to the US, which faced relatively inelastic demand : jute and jute products (generally accounting for over one-third of the total value), tea, cashew nuts, ores and metals, shellac, oilseeds and mica. Adding to these commodities cotton textiles, raw wool, hides and skins, spices, tobacco, and sugar completed the list of India's main exports to world markets to the mid-1960's. They could not easily balance India's needs for machine tools, generators, oil refineries, heavy equipment, industrial chemicals, and other products of the advanced economies.

With the sterling balance cushion and a tight rein on dollar imports India launched its first five-year plan without giving much attention to how exports should be raised to meet the growing cost of imports. The Indian economy, still comparatively uncontrolled,[7] would somehow struggle through, economists felt. Yearly increases in percentages of total exports made up by manufactures and semi-manufactures produced some optimism that ultimately India could more nearly balance its trade, and in the meantime world demands for India's raw material products would increase. One such demand came from the US, for manganese. During the first five-year plan period India was the major foreign supplier to the US of this ore. India was the second largest producer in the world in those years, following the Soviet Union and followed by Ghana and South Africa ; Russian deliveries to the US had stopped, and therefore Indian manganese made up a critical one-quarter to one-third of American imports. The Indo-American manganese trade was a tangibly advantageous relationship well understood, though not publicized, by both governments during a time of their greatest verbal political disputes.[8] India's manganese exports, almost entirely to the US, rose from rupees 1.8 crores in 1948-1949 to rupees 15.7 crores in 1951-1952 and 24.2 crores in 1953-1954, after which there was a decline as the US began to find substitute sources of the ore in Brazil and African states, then regarded as more controllable—that is, politically more reliable.

In contrast to the Government of India's mild encouragement to increased exports and its desire for assistance, "without strings," from industrial states, the official position on foreign investment appeared hostile at independence. Indians and Western capitalists upheld mutually conflicting positions. Each side misread and exaggerated the other's intentions : Indians exhibited fears of economic domination through the flooding in of Western, chiefly American, businessmen and raised the warning flag of possible nationalization to deter the supposed economic aggressor. Americans adopted the classic posture of defense of free enterprise and advised Indians that development could not take place without foreign investment ; some Americans publicly expressed their views that guarantees of fair treatment of American investors were a prerequisite to US government assistance.[9] Such statements flowed from the meetings of the United Nations Economic Commission for Asia and the Far East (ECAFE) at Ootacamund, June 1948, and the India-America Conference at New Delhi, December 1949.

India's leaders soon recognized the benefits of foreign investment and abjured policies of radical socialism or a nationalization of foreign business on principle. But the government vacillated, and conflicting directives issued from the capital, until on April 6, 1949, Nehru made his famous statement promising equal treatment of Indian and foreign businesses, no restriction on profit remittances or withdrawal of foreign capital, and fair compensation in case of nationalization.[10] He enunciated the principle that major ownership and control of all new businesses should be in Indian hands, but that in exceptional cases foreign control would be allowed. The response of foreign capital to the apparent change of policy in

24

India was poor. Most American investors, facing advantageous investment possibilities elsewhere, could not be persuaded to put funds into India. Some British investors were leaving India, especially those in plantations and mining, where profits were discouraging. Total foreign investment in private enterprise in India could be estimated at rupees 255.8 crores in June 1948, of which 11.2 crores was American and virtually all the rest British.[11] By the end of 1953 foreign assets increased by rupees 140 crores, mostly the result of plough-back of profits ; about 65 crores represented investments in oil refineries. The small amount of new funds suggested the minor part that foreign capitalists were planning to play in India's industrial growth.

The investments made in the early 1950's by Burmah Shell, Standard Vacuum and Caltex with the heaviest American financing ever to enter India, deserve special attention because of the magnitude of the investment and the unusually strained relations between the firms and the government that later emerged. By allowing private foreign investments without a controlling Indian share to enter a field crucial to development and by assuring that the companies would not be subject to nationalization for twenty-five years, the government was making major concessions ; in return the new oil refineries provided training and employment for Indians in all phases of the operations and soon met all domestic needs for gasoline. The plants depended upon imports of crude oil, chiefly from the Persian Gulf. The government's concessionary policy towards the companies, thought necessary to attract the initial investment, caused some rethinking in the mid-1950's and acute disagreements by 1958 on the matter of pricing.[12]

Indians claimed that lower prices for crude oil could be obtained from other sources, namely from Russia, but the companies refused to buy oil elsewhere and maintained artificially high prices in India. With Soviet and Rumanian encouragement and assistance[13] in the late 1950's the Indian government was able to enter the field as a competitor ; it hoped thereby to force some changes in the pricing policy of the Western oil companies. This method did not immediately succeed, and the controversy became in one sense a struggle between Western and Soviet influences on the Indian government. In 1961 the Aid India Consortium and the IBRD pressed New Delhi to relax its oil policy—one of the many examples of the World Bank's predilection in favour of Western and private enterprise in underdeveloped countries,[14] and new agreements were reached benefiting the companies. But the government had demonstrated its ability to use diplomatic nonalignment to try to achieve economic as well as political independence and had also expanded the public sector oil industry. In 1963 it reached an understanding with another American company, Phillips Petroleum, to build and operate a refinery in Cochin with the Indian government as a majority stockholder. This agreement was the basis of further arrangements to expand public sector refining at Madras and Calcutta with other than Soviet assistance.

Indo-US aid, trade, and investment relations by the mid-1950's were not crucial for either country's economy, although they constituted the strongest bond of mutual interests yet established between the two states. But during the course of the second five-year plan, a series of developments produced a profound economic involvement between India and the US. After years of public and specialists' debates on the mechanisms of economic development, general agreement appeared to emerge in India and the US that large-scale government-to-government assistance would be necessary if India was to break out of the circle of poverty. Only the US could afford to make available enough economic assistance for what was termed the "take-off" into self-sustained economic growth.

Studies had multiplied showing that in the case of India, and several other countries as well, the chief obstacle to development was a shortage of capital, not skills ; that exports from such countries could not finance new major industries ; and that absorptive capacity was far greater than the current amount of foreign investment. Population studies presented evidence that even the most concerted steps towards rapid economic development could barely raise living standards, when the rate of population growth was increasing also, and that population expansion could best be checked in urban or modern economic milieux. These basic facts, with their inevitable theoretical elaborations and exaggerated public versions, were immediately translated by both the Indian and American governments into the political potentialities of popular revolt against a democratic but economically ineffective regime in India. The communist party's election victory in Kerala in March 1957 illustrated the possible dangers ahead.

Further developments smoothed the way towards deeper Indo-American economic involvement. In 1955 the Soviet Union initiated its economic assistance effort in India, which stressed major capital goods investments (which the US had avoided, except in electric power).[15] Although India's drawing on these Soviet commitments was slow—by March, 1962, only about one-quarter of total Soviet assistance was utilized[16]—their effects on the US government were soon noticed in increased sympathy for Indian development requirements. There was no hesitancy, by 1956, for American officials to speak about peaceful economic competition with the Russians for influence in India,[17] although where no competition existed, in Pakistan, total US aid was far greater and economic aid relative to population several times larger than in India. Western offers of aid, as for example in steel production, armaments, and an atomic power facility, were stimulated so blatantly by prior Russian offers that Soviet leaders with some humour took partial credit for them. From the Indian standpoint acceptance of a much closer dependence on the US could be tolerated because Indian nonalignment was finally becoming respectable in American circles, and strenuous attempts to dislodge India from that posture had ceased.[18] After surviving many months of verbal thrusts and counterthrusts over the issues of the US security pacts, the Chinese off-shore islands, the crisis in Indo-China, disarmament, Western policy on the Suez Canal and Indian policy on the Hungarian revolution, and in addition the impressive visits to India of high Soviet and Chinese leaders, Indo-American political relations suddenly seemed to improve at the end of 1956.

India's vastly increased need for capital imports in the second five-year plan, which began in 1956, required the support of the US Congress, which had recently cut back aid to India largely because of annoyance over Nehru's foreign policy. The Indian government, its independence of action firmly established, began to seek the necessary congressional goodwill. Former American ambassadors to India, Bowles and John Sherman Cooper, along with the then ambassador, Ellsworth Bunker, were foremost among those who pleaded India's case ably and vigorously in Washington. Nehru's second visit to the US was planned for late in 1956, and it fortuitously coincided with one of the most dramatic US foreign policy decisions of the post-war period, the condemnation of the

British-French-Israeli invasion of Egypt. Nehru was impressed by the American stand : "I imagine that all its riches and power have not increased the reputation of the United States so much as a certain attitude that it has taken up in recent weeks. A certain attitude in regard, let us say, to Egypt. . . . Military power has brought it respect. . ., but the type of respect that [resulted from] the action of the United States in regard to the Egyptian question was something infinitely different, deeper, and something worth having. The United States got these."[19]

The Nehru-Eisenhower lengthy session together at the quiet presidential farm near Gettysburg came as a successful contrast to the disagreeable urban setting of Nehru's 1949 visit. Both leaders had established their bonafides as advocates of a peaceful world, and they had reacted similarly to the Suez crisis. Their meeting in December 1956, viewed a decade later, symbolized the beginning of increasingly beneficial ties between the two countries : a vastly expanded American aid programme and a dropping off of the sharper sort of Indian criticisms of US policies—indeed, occasional support for them. This was not a quid pro quo, but the response of both states to altered international conditions, especially to the tempering of the "cold war" which set in after major conflicts had been twice avoided in 1956. Of great significance was the shift in US economic assistance policy away from efforts to combine it with the military build-ups in allied states to a wider region, which included India.

THE INTERNATIONAL COMMITMENT TO INDIA'S DEVELOPMENT

Nehru invited outside support for the ambitious goals of the second plan, and the US government responded with enlarged commitments, a new aid mechanism, and an unprecedented effort to achieve public support for economic assistance to underdeveloped countries. The largest share of the increased aid allocations represented shipments of surplus commodities, chiefly wheat, under PL 480. The other major source of American assistance was channelled through the Development Loan Fund (DLF), established in 1957 to provide long-term, low-interest loans repayable in rupees—in effect virtually grants—for power projects, railway and transport equipment, manufacturing industries, and the procurement of steel and other essential goods. Most of the DLF aid was tied to purchases in the US, as were more conventional dollar-repayable loans from the Export-Import Bank (whose total of Indian loans to March 1967 was an authorized rupees 313.2 crores).

The US Department of Commerce calculated that by 1960 India was financing 90 per cent of its non-food imports from the US with aid funds.[20] The following table shows US government aid authorizations for the first two plan periods in crores of rupees and millions of dollars.[21]

| Type of aid | To end of 1st plan | | Type of aid | During 2nd plan | |
	Rupees	Dollars		Rupees	Dollars
Wheat loan, 1951	90.3	190.0	DLF loans	196.9	413.5
TCA rupee loans	27.0	56.7	other loans	24.7	51.8
TCA grants	86.2	181.0	TCA grants	44.1	92.6
PL 480 grants	26.1	54.8	PL 480 grants	38.1	80.0
PL 665 loans	16.9	35.5	PL 480 loans	1113.0	2337.3
			PL 665 loans	15.0	31.5
Totals	246.5	518.0		1431.8	3006.7

In further promoting its new concentration on economic development of underdeveloped countries the US government wished to make some of its aid commitments in an international setting and thereby induce other non-communist industrial states to do the same. On US initiative the World Bank convened a meeting of capital exporting countries in August 1958 to form an Aid India Consortium, initially composed of the US, the UK, Germany, Canada, and Japan, along with the Bank itself ; later it included France, the International Development Association (IDA, the soft-loan satellite of the World Bank), and by 1962 Australia, Belgium, Italy, and the Netherlands. The first meeting was called to face an emergency of India's unpredicted and sudden loss of foreign exchange. The decline beginning in 1956-1957 is graphed on page 375.[22]

The unanticipated adversity in India's balance of payments was immediately the effect of increased economic activity—and poor coordination between various ministries sanctioning imports. The cushion of sterling balances was almost gone by 1958, and the limits of International Monetary Fund withdrawals had nearly been reached. For lack of adequate foreign exchange the second plan had to be cut back to its "core projects," and even for the completion of those the Consortium had to take decisive action. Led

by the US the group underwrote the foreign exchange requirements
for the remainder of the second plan, and Indian economic development thereby became an international economic problem of unique
significance. Pledges by the Consortium represented the sum of
individual government's respective aid programmes and were subject
to authorizations from appropriate legislatures.

INDIA'S FOREIGN EXCHANGE RESERVES

Consortium meetings discussed the fact that India's most serious
problem was shortages of foreign exchange to settle current accounts
and that therefore the most useful assistance was allocations untied
to purchases for specific projects or in specified countries. "Tied aid"
often resulted in higher costs for India and almost certainly in slower
utilization of the aid. Nevertheless, by 1962 only three per cent of
total Consortium aid was untied to both currency and projects ;
the US and Germany experimented with a few loans of that kind.
The American Congress held control over aid authorizations

and by the end of the 1950's had developed an unusually keen interest in Indian economic advancement. Incorporated in the mutual security legislation of 1958 was a Senate resolution sponsored by Senators John F. Kennedy and John S. Cooper, expressing the sense of the Congress that "it is in the interests of the United States to join with other nations in providing support . . . adequate to assist India to complete successfully its current programme for economic development." The next year a similar resolution was passed urging the transfer of massive aid on a regular basis, similar to the Marshall Plan for Europe. The World Bank President, Eugene Black, arranged for an international commission to assess south Asian needs ; its three members, Oliver Franks (UK), Hermann Abs (Germany), and Allan Sproul (US), left for India and Pakistan in February 1960. Their report justified the heavy commitments from the Consortium made to the third plan.

No formal machinery was set up in India, as it had been in Europe in 1948, to provide the multi-national collaboration needed for effective aid-giving. Instead the World Bank acted as a clearing-house of assistance needs and commitments, and in New Delhi the personal involvements between planning and executing officials and foreign aid mission personnel grew deeper.

Hoping to match congressional interest in India with public awareness, the Committee for International Economic Growth and several co-sponsors, such as the Massachusetts Institute of Technology and the Asia Foundation, held a conference on India and the United States in Washington in May 1959. Emphasizing trade and investment and stimulating an enthusiastic discussion on aid programmes and sobering projections of population growth, the conference suitably reflected the striking increase in US knowledge about and involvement with India which had taken place in one decade.[23]

Official US activity on behalf of India reached the point of highest drama when, in December 1959, President Eisenhower spent five days in that country. The president's reputation as an opponent of the "cold war," as one who publicly respected India's nonalignment, and as the promoter of the increasing economic aid programme to India provided the background to one of Eisenhower's most success-ful encounters with a foreign public. China's recent aggressiveness in the Himalayas made India's relations with the US an urgent concern in New Delhi. The welcome that the president received in public appearances and his responsiveness to the Indian setting symbolized "a change in the mood of India and in the attitude of the United States."[24] Besides some eloquent statements of American purposes which could elicit Indian support,[25] Eisenhower constantly restated his government's commitment to help India's economic development.

In 1960 US aid to India reached its highest level since the programmes began, a level sustained for the next five years during the transition from the second to the third five-year plans. In addition, the US in 1960 made the largest national commitment to the fund established to facilitate a settlement of the Indus Waters dispute.[26] The largest component of the expanded total of US aid to India by that time had become the transfers of surplus grain under PL 480 (and PL 665).[27] No other Indo-US economic transaction was as mutually binding as that programme, involving millions of Indian consumers, tens of thousands of American producers and transport workers, and fiscal and agricultural policies in both countries. India's yearly deficit of foodgrains, by 1965 amounting to several millions of tons, was being met largely by importing surplus American grain, mostly wheat. By 1964-65 one-fifth of the American wheat crop was being shipped to India.[28] Other products, rice, corn, tobacco, and cotton, also came in under the programme. The following table shows the values of agricultural commodity import authorizations and utilizations, under PL 480 (and PL 665) :[29]

					(in crores of rupees)
Authorizations to end of 2nd plan	Utilizations to end of 2nd plan	Authorizations to end of 3rd plan	Utilizations to end of 3rd plan	Authorizations April 1966 to March 1967	Utilizations April 1966 to March 1967
1144.8	547.4	450.6	852.9	392.6	322.2

India continued to import limited quantities of foodgrains from the world market, but by the 1960's the US supplied the bulk of the country's importations to meet its growing food deficit. It was a programme that once begun was difficult to terminate, and it influenced foreign policies in both countries in undocumentable ways.[30] A great economic value to India of the PL 480 programme resided in its possible uses for price stabilization and disinflation, but perhaps of even more benefit was the relief that it provided from India's using foreign exchange for purchases of consumer goods. Public Law 480 (title I) commodities were purchased on the open market in the US with funds loaned to India ; repayment of those funds was in rupees made to a US account with the Reserve Bank of India. Of the programmed uses through April 1, 1967, of the so-called rupee counterpart funds owned by the American government, 76 per cent was transferred back to the Indian government as loans and grants to be used for projects included in the plans. Most grants were used for health and education projects and most loans for power and water undertakings. Part of the remainder of the funds was used for local expenses of the American mission in India and for so-called Cooley loans to private Indian and American firms ; the rest remained deposited in the US government account in the Reserve Bank.[31] The PL 480 programme benefited both states in obvious ways, while it also raised possibilities of severe administrative problems and even conflicts of policy in the future. Most of the US rupee deposits could not be released without special agreement on their use, but public awareness of the huge foreign holdings of counterpart funds led both governments to consider ways of reducing their importance.[32]

During the third plan most foreign assistance arrived as loans, not grants. With the establishment of the US Agency for International Development (AID) in 1961, newly authorized American development aid had to be repaid in dollars rather than rupees, as under the DLF loans ; but with only nominal interest charges and permission to extend a loan for a period of up to 50 years this procedure was "scarcely distinguishable from grants."[33] By the end of the third plan the American share in the grand total of foreign assistance allocated to India in that plan period was about one-third, as the following enumeration of major contributions indicates :[34]

ALLOCATIONS TO THE THIRD FIVE-YEAR PLAN

	(in crores of rupees)
Total	2943.7
US	1268.9
IBRD and IDA	423.1
West Germany	308.6
UK	254.4
Japan	138.2
Canada	117.3
USSR	104.3

In one respect India and the US tolerated a basic and continuing discrepancy in their requirements for external assistance. India reserved to the public sector the development of key industries, such as steel, heavy machinery, petroleum, and aircraft production, but the US government was reluctant to contribute directly to industrial projects under public control and management. A famous illustration of this circumstance were the Indo-US negotiations on constructing a fourth public sector steel mill at Bokaro in Bihar. The three previously constructed public sector steel mills, at Rourkela, Bhilai, and Durgapur, resulted from private and public investment from West Germany, the USSR, and the UK. The Bokaro negotiations, dragging on for months and years, revealed the disagreements possible between governments with different economic philosophies and experiences. American negotiators stressed the need for some private capital involvements and adequate authority for American engineers to function without unnecessary government interference. Gradually India accepted the major American conditions without, however, retreating from its major requirement for public control of the plant. Although feasibility studies multiplied and raised questions of technical and financial importance, which some American congressmen thought unanswerable, American political opposition to US support of Bokaro became the prime obstacle to an agreement. An official report to the president in March 1963 enunciated the well established American attitude, that US public funds should not aid foreign projects that compete with private business.[35] Congress indicated in August 1963 its strong opposition to investing in the project, and therefore the Kennedy administration was relieved when India itself withdrew the request for assistance, in September.

The failure of the Bokaro negotiations was only temporary for India ; the Soviet government offered to build the plant. The US aid programme, though unwilling to assist public sector heavy industry, made important contributions to electric power generation, and in 1963 India and the US signed a 30-year agreement for cooperation in development of atomic power plants. The first was to be constructed at Tarapur, near Bombay.

To summarize India's position as the recipient of the largest amount of American and international economic aid since the European Recovery Programme, transfers of capital on government account "permitted India to finance three-fifths of her import surplus during the second plan ; all of it and more in recent years. It supplied one-eighth of public investment during the first plan, 28 per cent during the second, and was expected to contribute slightly over half during the third."[36] Because of the spectrum of aiding agencies and states, India obtained a balanced pattern of external assistance, the US being interested in agricultural surplus shipments, infrastructure projects, and rural progress, while Germany, the USSR, and eastern European countries helped in the industrial sector. As the plans increased in size, so did the aid.

TRADE AND INVESTMENT

In historical perspective, aid programmes may be seen a pump-primers for the expansion of international trade, and some so-called aid agreements might better be termed trade promotion schemes, e.g. the American Export-Import Bank loans and some of the German, Japanese, and Soviet loans. But through the second plan increased trade was mainly one-way : India's development and the foreign assistance it received did not promote exports significantly. Following the foreign exchange crisis in the mid-1950's an export promotion programme was organized by the government, but except for some notable successes in developing new markets for sales of light machinery and handicrafts, it could not affect the picture of India's growing trade imbalance. The following tabulation illustrates the point :[37]

THE FOREIGN TRADE OF INDIA

(in crores of rupees)

Year	Imports	Exports	Total value of foreign trade	Balance of trade
1950-51	672.91	601.71	1274.62	− 71.20
1955-56	692.75	599.40	1292.15	− 93.35
1960-61	1122.48	642.07	1764.55	−480.41
1961-62	1093.08	660.34	1753.42	−432.74
1962-63	1133.15	685.49	1818.64	−447.66
1963-64	1223.75	793.25	2017.00	−430.50
1964-65	1262.81	814.56	2077.37	−448.25

The imbalances in trade flows had to be met by foreign loans and grants, drafts from foreign exchange reserves, and drawings from the holdings of the International Monetary Fund.

Of the major exports, tea showed gains through the early 1960's, ores were somewhat higher, while jute products declined in sales, as did vegetable oils. Changes took place in the regional pattern of India's trade : the decreasing importance of sterling area trade was balanced by the increased trade with Russia and eastern Europe and with West Germany. Exports to the US during this period showed no improvement : the total for the second plan period was exactly the same as for the first.

But from 1960 to 1965 India's exports to the US grew by 50 per cent and included new items, such as wool carpets, iron pipes, and sewing machines, hinting at the possibility of an export break-through into developed economies' markets in the future. Simultaneously, the US became India's largest supplier with twice the exports of Britain in the years, 1962 through 1964. This was the result of increases in the PL 480 grain trade and some elevation in aid credits. The Indo-US imbalance in trade favouring the US, incidentally, would have been reversed if grain shipments had been discounted, in these and previous years. India's sales to the US exceeded its purchases by well over $200 million in the period, 1951 to 1961, if grain was ignored.[38]

India's overall export returns rose rapidly in the early 1960's, by over seven per cent per annum, after the stagnant decade of the 1950's but dropped off again in 1965-66, due partly to lower prices and also to the Indo-Pakistani war. India's failure to expand exports resulted in large measure from the domestic market orientation of its business firms, the nature of its economic specializations, and the early complacency of the government in this matter. Some part of India's problem of trade imbalance also could be attributed to the unwillingness of industrialized countries, especially the US, and western Europe, to make a place for Indian manufactured goods.

More encouraging than India's overseas trading relations were the marked increases in American and other foreign private investment in India during the later 1950's and 1960's. Improved Indo-American political relations after 1956 brought a more favourable atmosphere for American private ventures, and the economic expansion of western Europe stimulated some movement of capital from there. In 1959 India and the US entered an agreement providing for guarantees against nonconvertibility into dollars of receipts of American business in India, and an expropriation guarantee was later added. Agreements to preclude double taxation were reached with many Western countries, and foreign investors benefited from the various concessions offered to domestic firms by the government to stimulate investments. In short, the investment climate in India increased its attraction for foreigners—tax holidays and other inducements as well as a superb record of fair dealing on profit and capital repatriations received praise from many foreign capitalists. Total private foreign investment increased from rupees 255.8 in 1948 to rupees 566.4 in 1960, again partly due to ploughed-back profits. Private British investment was the largest part, 65 per cent, of the total—80 per cent of the private holdings—with the World Bank next with 18 per cent followed by the US with 16 per cent. The following presents a simplified statement of major foreign investment in 1955 and 1960, in crores of rupees : [39]

	1955	1960
Great Britain	376.8	446.4
US	39.8	112.7
Switzerland	6.6	8.9
West Germany	2.5	6.8
Others (including World Bank)	30.4	115.7
Totals	456.1	690.5

Investments in light manufacturing and petroleum industries dominated British and American holdings, with British investors maintaining additional interests in tea plantations and mining. Three-quarters of all foreign investment was direct, rather than by purchasing shares in Indian corporations. It was, in part, that earlier tendency for foreigners to obtain control of new ventures, rather than to collaborate with existing Indian enterprises, that had led to Indian criticisms and to restrictions on majority control by foreigners, except in special cases. Almost all new enterprises licensed by the government had to have at least 51 per cent control by Indians and were under obligations to replace foreign technical personnel as soon as possible by Indians.

In contrast to the Bokaro negotiations, noted earlier, private US concerns made the major contributions towards completing in 1958 a one-million ton capacity addition to the Tata Iron and Steel Company's plant at Jamshedpur. It received little publicity ; yet it showed the possibilities of Indo-American collaboration in private industrial investments. The Phillips contract with the Indian government, mentioned above, demonstrated the advantages of private US firms collaborating on a minority share basis with the government ; Phillips was to run the plant, and it went into production in late 1966. The American International Oil Company followed a similar pattern by accepting minority share holding and management rights for a limited period in a major refinery project controlled by the government in Madras ; the company also agreed to collaborate with the government in building a fertilizer complex at the same place.

Expansion of investments of the more conventional type was more common than these special arrangements. Old American Companies in India, such as Firestone Tyre and Union Carbide, were expanding their facilities while many new arrivals began to make their marks : Parke, Davis and Merck pharmaceutical companies, Kaiser Aluminium, Goodyear, Dow Chemical, and others. Indian officials and businessmen welcomed these firms ; but they had to fit into the frame of India's planning and meet other criteria of suitability.

The government's reluctance to throw open the country to foreign investment in all industries and under still more attractive conditions had to be seen in the light of the relatively higher cost to India of foreign private investment over public investment in the same industry. Because India allowed remittance of profits and capital gains, and profits in the short-term were considerable, foreign investors had, in effect, to be paid off in hard currencies at a rate higher and faster than even conventional loans to the government made directly, to say nothing of some exceptionally long-term loans. Whereas a private investment usually brought a yearly return of 10 per cent or more to the investor in his own currency soon after the investment was made, a loan from the investor's government could be paid off at a rate of perhaps two or three per cent annually, after ten years or more.[40]

No one should have been surprised when Indians evidenced

worry, or resentment about the huge share of the modern sector of their economy controlled by foreigners, mainly British. One estimate indicated "that foreign-controlled assets formed slightly more than two-fifths perhaps of the total in the organized or large-scale private sector at the end of 1961, or one-quarter of the modern sector as a whole."[41] According to the Ministry of Finance, "Foreign-associated issues accounted for 41 per cent of all authorized capital (1951-63) and for 59 per cent of authorized capital in the private sector (1957-63)."[42] If nothing else, that information demonstrated that foreign support for Indian private enterprise, in the industrial field at least, was necessary to keep that sector vigorous and expanding.

Conclusions drawn from a glance at India's foreign economic relations and especially Indo-American economic ties might not have been precise, but they were more encouraging than any other aspect of India's dealings with the US. All the world's industrial states, led by the US, had committed themselves to meeting India's external development needs. The procedures worked out for the unprecedented and overwhelmingly one-way flow of goods and services afforded comparatively efficient use of the inputs provided and, above all, permitted the Indian government to retain almost total freedom of action in planning and executing its own development programmes.[43] Economic aid enabled the government to build up infrastructure and improve social services without overt compulsion in mobilizing resources.

However, the internationalization of India's development effort created new difficulties for India. The burden of debt on hard currency loans of the 1950's began to detract from the usefulness of new assistance loans by the 1960's : India had been receiving unsound development finance, because most of the loans had to be repaid over too short a term. Recognizing that fact the US and the World Bank tried to place India's financing on sounder basis ; the IDA began to give loans for 50-year periods with no immediate payments for ten years and low charges thereafter. As of March 1967 IDA had made the equivalent of rupees 667 crores available to India. By its foreign assistance act of 1961, setting up the Agency for International Development, the US government began to make similar loans.

The tying of loans to purchases of goods in the loaning country became the standard practice especially after the US attached that condition as an assist to its own foreign exchange position. Tying loans to country-of-origin increased the cost of imports to India ; in US aid programmes it was in reality a subsidy to American private interests. When the subsidizing effects of foreign aid were coupled with the short-term loan financing of the 1950's the Indians could ask the legitimate question : was aid really an economically unselfish transfer of resources by the donor ?

If one purpose of Western aid programmes was to propel the Indian economy in the direction of self-generating growth and a strong position internationally, then that purpose was being undermined by Western trade policies. As underdeveloped economies raised up fledgling industries, often with the help of foreign capital, they found the markets of the advanced countries partially closed to them. In some cases special tariffs or quotas were set up to hinder the exports from countries, such as India, whose economic well being was allegedly important to the industrial states. India was loaned huge sums for development, which when ultimately translated into industrial products for export were considered threats to the originators of the loans. In no way other than increasing exports of manufactured goods could India hope to repay the loans it had received, given the inelastic demand for its raw materials, but by the mid-1960's no advanced country was offering to cut back its restrictions to allow the purchase of Indian exports sufficient to relieve the indebtedness in the calculable future.

The import barriers set up around the western European economies after the creation of the Common Market adversely affected Indian exports, even of traditional products, such as jute. The Common Market tariffs and quotas seemed to negate the enlightened aid policies of certain members of the Consortium, notably West Germany. The American case was a mixed one, especially in the cotton textile field. Facing a rapid rise in cotton textile imports by the early 1960's, due partly to an earlier liberalization policy, the US government had to defer to domestic producers, who claimed that they were menaced by such exporters as India, Pakistan, Hong Kong, and Japan. The result for India was the establishment of an annual quota in 1962 decided by Indo-US agreement, which effectively placed a ceiling on the most lucrative of the expanding Indian exports to the US, but it was a modestly rising ceiling in accordance with the stipulations of the agreement.[44] An American could con-

25

clude after observing the phenomenon of US policies on tariffs and quotas : "One persistent question intrudes itself at this point : To what extent is the American Government using foreign aid as a substitute for the politically more difficult measures which would in fact contribute far more than foreign aid to the political survival and economic development of the newer countries."[45] John Lewis warned that "If the West cannot overcome its own political inhibitions enough to extend India some solid assistance on the trade front, the rest of the help it is supplying will lose much of its importance."[46]

FURTHER POLITICAL AND MILITARY RELATIONS WITH
THE UNITED STATES

Benefiting from the experience of collaboration in economic affairs Indo-US political relations improved in the 1960's, and limited military collaboration began. In the Congo Indian and American objectives merged in early 1961 when the UN operations there were threatened with failure unless India transferred combat troops to the UN command.[47] In some other areas of UN diplomacy the Indian and American positions in the 1960's converged, notably on issues of Portuguese colonialism and the organization of the office of the secretary-general. India's decision to oppose the Soviet Union's "troika" plan for the secretary-generalship in 1961 reinforced American efforts to defeat that proposal. The gap between Indian and American attitudes towards disarmament narrowed somewhat at the Geneva negotiations. Regarding southeast Asia the US adopted India's policy of neutralizing Laos, and India gained respect for the American position of strength in the region.

Those developments prepared the setting for Nehru's third visit to the US in November 1961, made in order to consolidate with President Kennedy's administration gains already registered during the previous Republican regime. But the Nehru-Kennedy encounter in November 1961 was tainted by the fact that the new administration, despite the pro-Indian reputation of its chief, was showing considerable solicitude for Pakistan's military requirements: a visit to Pakistan by Ambassador Harriman had reassured President Ayub Khan about American intentions to stick to the alliance, a dozen supersonic fighter aircraft had been delivered to Pakistan, and more sophisticated equipment was to follow. Also, sharp American criticisms were being directed against Krishna Menon's and Nehru's failures (the latter at the Belgrade Conference) to single out Russia's responsibility for the resumption of nuclear testing. Possibilities of closer Indo-American contacts in the future had been suggested by Secretary of Defense Robert S. McNamara's request of Congress in June 1961 for authority to send arms to "neutral" states, but at the end of the year Indian leaders publicly denied having any intention of obtaining large quantities of American arms.

In blunt contrast to Kennedy's long-standing admiration for Nehru and the excitement aroused in India by Kennedy's election, the meeting of the two liberal world leaders was, as Kennedy later described it, "a disaster ... the worst head-of-state [sic] visit I have had."[48] The Indian leader had aged markedly since his last trip to America and was a disappointment to the more vigorous new president. "Though Kennedy retained his belief in the necessity of helping India achieve its economic goals, he rather gave up hope, after seeing Nehru, that India would be in the next years a great affirmative force in the world or even in South Asia."[49] The developing crises in southeast Asia, particularly in Vietnam, most worried Kennedy, and he sought Nehru's views and his support on that region's problems. Earlier in that year Vice-President Johnson had made similar overtures in New Delhi, urging Nehru to take a more active interest in southeast Asia ; Nehru at that time had declined with vigour, explaining that his country had an abundance of problems to face nearer home.

But the Nehru-Kennedy talks succeeded in establishing some community of objectives in southeast Asia, never possible before 1961. The bases for it were India's increased attention to Chinese penetration into the region and the US willingness to encourage liberalism and nonalignment of the governments there, provided that they did not adopt pro-Chinese communism.

Almost one year later the two states found sudden cause for an unparalleled deepening of their mutual involvement, when the Chinese forces were pressing into Assam. After the Chinese breakthrough on October 20 Nehru asked for military assistance from the US and all other states, and within twelve hours, at a time when a crisis in Cuba was nearing its climax, the administration in Washington decided to extend aid on a joint basis with the UK. The new foreign assistance act of September 4, 1961, permitted the US to extend military support to nonaligned states, and American aircraft began to fly arms into Calcutta and thence to the northeastern frontier. An earlier reluctance of the State Department to accept Indian border claims in the Himalayas because of likely protests from the Nationalist Chinese government was overruled by the necessity of giving legal sanction to a new version of containment, and the US acknowledged the validity of the McMahon Line. On November 14, 1962, a new Indo-US military agreement supplanted the mutual security accord of 1951, specifying the enemy, China, and on July 22, 1963, the US announced agreement with Britain and India to strengthen the latter's defense against possible air attacks from China. The strong indication that the US would give air support to India remained as the major US contribution to India's Himalayan defense strategy.

Formal negotiations on an Anglo-American long-term military aid programme were followed in December 1962 by a US-UK decision to extend to India emergency military aid worth $120 million, one-half of which, from the US, would equip and support six Indian mountain divisions. In addition, the US furnished transport aircraft while the Commonwealth assumed the task of strengthening India's air combat capability. In 1963 tri-partite discussions continued, over excited objections from Pakistan, and the following year India signed loan agreements with the US for building and modernizing ordinance factories ; the US also offered unspecified military assistance grants, on the approval of Congress. Part of this and the programme for fiscal year 1966 were held up when Pakistan attacked in 1965 and the US cut off military aid to both sides.

On a comparatively small scale, Indo-US military relations in the years after the Chinese attack provided opportunities for tangible collaboration. But, in the absence of specific political understandings, the contacts, mainly through the American military aid mission in New Delhi, assumed an ad hoc quality. The Indian government lacked confidence in US policies in south Asia, which seemed still more heavily committed to Pakistan than to India, and was anxious to retain its close contacts with the USSR. The US, on the other hand, though fully accepting India's nonalignment, was reluctant to solidify a political relationship with India.

Viewed over the two decades since the end of the Second World War, Indian-American relations were marked by an extraordinary number of verbal disputations and mutually conflicting policies towards international problems. But firm collaboration emerged on economic matters, notably on the transfer and use of economic aid. By maintaining the posture of nonalignment, determining its own development needs, and administering its plans successfully India upheld its share of the aid relationship. The US, for its part, fulfilled its commitments (and extended emergency food aid beyond them), respected India's methods of handling the aid, and, perhaps surprisingly, gave no evidence that it resented Indian acceptance of Soviet economic assistance.

NOTES AND REFERENCES

[1] Chapters XV and XVI consider the economic ties established between India and the USSR and the socialist countries.

[2] President Truman's message to Congress on the bill ; H. Doc. 56, 82nd Cong., 1st Sess., Feb. 2, 1951.

[3] For a discussion of the confusion and complexity that matches the subject, see Charles Wolf, Jr., *Foreign Aid : Theory and Practice in South Asia*, Princeton 1960.

[4] *First Five Year Plan*, Peoples' Edn., p. 34.

[5] From a "Summary of the Report of A Mission of the International Monetary Fund to the Government of India," released to the press Feb. 8, 1954.

[6] From Reserve Bank of India, *India's Balance of Payments 1948-49 to 1961-62*. Conversion into dollars done at the rate, 1 rupee equals $.21. Accuracy in many such tabulations depends on what is being measured, and the reader should realize that aid can be granted or loaned, utilized or not utilized, made available in hard or soft currencies or in commodities, and channeled through different agencies. The figures herein generally include all these forms. Yearly tabulations of aid to India from all sources are available in the publication, *External Assistance*, by years, issued by the Ministry of Finance, Govt. of India. Unless otherwise noted, aid figures given in this chapter are taken from this publication. An easily obtainable chart showing US aid is found in Norman Palmer, *South Asia and United States Policy*, pp. 142-43.

[7] "By almost any test, the economy of India is less responsive to public guidance and direction than that of the United States. Indeed it is one of the world's least controlled or 'planned' economies." John K. Galbraith, "Rival Economic Theories in India," *Foreign Affairs*, Vol. 36, 4 (July 1958), p. 589.

[8] See discussion in M. S. Venkataramani, "Manganese as a Factor in Indo-American Relations, " *India Quarterly*, vol. XIV, 2 (April-June 1958).

[9] Those attitudes were expressed by the Indian ambassador to the US and the

American ambassador in New Delhi ; see Rosinger, *India and the United States*, p. 48f.

[10] In *Constituent Assembly Debates*, vol. IV, pt. II, p. 2385.

[11] Reserve Bank, *op. cit.*, p. 58f. The uncertainty about all data on foreign private investment is discussed therein, pp. 56-57, and in Michael Kidron, *Foreign Investments in India*, p. 185f.

[12] On the oil investments see Kidron, *op. cit.*, p. 167f.

[13] See ahead, chapter XVI.

[14] *ibid.*, pp. 172-73 ; p. 153f.

[15] See W. Malenbaum, *East and West in India's Development*, p. 38f, and chap. XV, ahead.

[16] Reserve Bank, *op. cit.*, pp. 53-54.

[17] See Dorsey in *Dept. of State Bulletin*, vol. 34, May 14, 1956, pp. 792-96 ; Dillon in *ibid.*, vol. 37, March 3, 1958, pp. 499-500 ; Dulles in US Cong., House Appropriations hearings, *Mutual Sec. Act for 1959*, 85th Cong., 2nd sess., p. 281.

[18] A thorough discussion of the shift in US attitudes toward nonalignment appears in Cecil V. Crabb, Jr., *The Elephants and the Grass*, N. Y. 1965, chap. VI.

[19] Address to the American Association for the United Nations, Dec. 20, 1956 ; in "Nehru Visits U.S.A.," Info. Service of India, Washington, p. 50.

[20] Dept. of Commerce, *International Commerce*, Jan. 10, 1966, p. 44.

[21] Reserve Bank, *op. cit.*, pp. 140-42. The presentation has been simplified, and figures here exclude US Export-Import Bank loans amounting to rupees 102.6 crores to Air India ; they were conventional loans repayable in dollars and could scarcely be regarded as aid.

[22] Source : Reserve Bank, *op. cit.*, p. 45.

[23] See the compiling of the conference minutes in Selig S. Harrison, *India and the United States*. Vice-President Richard M. Nixon and Indian Ambassador M. C. Chagla spoke at the opening of the conference and were followed by a galaxy of such figures as Senator John F. Kennedy, Lady Barbara Ward Jackson, John D. Rockefeller, 3rd, Ashok Mehta, the then Socialist Party leader, and Averell Harriman.

[24] In the words of Walter Lippmann, who also explained that "The central objective of the President's trip was quite evidently to reach an understanding with India. This new relationship is in no sense a military alliance. It is a moral partnership based on a recognition of the fact that the survival and progress of India is of crucial importance to us and to the peace of the world." *Washington Post*, Dec. 17, 1959.

[25] As in the president's address to a joint session of the Indian parliament on Dec. 10. Text in *New York Times*, Dec. 11, 1956.

[26] See chap. V.

[27] About 42 per cent of utilized aid up to the end of the second plan period was in the form of commodities, the bulk of which was foodgrains from the US, according to V.K.R.V. Rao and Dharm Narain, *Foreign Aid and India's Economic Development*, pp. 41-42.

[28] Two-fifths was shipped to other countries ; from an address by Lester R.

Brown, acting administrator of the International Development Service, US Dept. of Agriculture, Feb. 8, 1966 ; USDA 393-66. A very detailed and politically sensitive study on the Indo-US relationship under PL 480 is Norman K. Nicholson, "Politics and Food Policy in India," unpubl. Ph. D. dissertation, Cornell Univ. 1966.

[29] Source : *External Assistance 1966-67*, appendix II.

[30] During the severe food shortages in 1966 the US increased grain shipments drastically, but at the same time conditioned future aid for the fourth plan on India's undertaking agricultural programmes and policies to lessen its dependence on the US, a dependence which could easily become politically and economically embarrassing.

[31] The US deposits of rupees from PL 480 sales amounted to rupees 630 crores at the end of March 1968, after withdrawals for grants and loans to the Indian government, Cooley loans, and US uses in India. Ministry of Finance, *Explanatory Memorandum on the Budget of the Central Government for 1968-69*, p. 83. The total money supply at that time was rupees 5,350 ; *Reserve Bank of India Bulletin*, June 1968, p. 801.

[32] The US government advised India and other recipients of PL 480 commodities in 1966 that within a few years, a maximum of five, repayment for commodity purchase loans would be in dollars. A sophisticated discussion of the place in the Indian budget and economy of PL 480 food grains and counterpart funds is that of H. Venkatasubbiah, *Hindu Weekly Review*, May 17, 1965.

[33] John P. Lewis, *Quiet Crisis in India*, p. 312.

[34] *External Assistance 1965-66*, appendix II.

[35] *The Scope and Distribution of United States Military and Economic Assistance Programmes*, or the Clay Report, Dept. of State, Washington 1963, p. 5.

[36] Kidron, *op. cit.* (1965), p. 123.

[37] From *India 1966*, p. 325.

[38] US Dept. of Commerce, *Overseas Business Reports*, Jan. 1963, p. 6.

[39] Reserve Bank of India, *op. cit.*, p. 61. The US Commerce Department accepted a higher figure for American investment in India in 1960, approximately $300 million (rupees 142.8 crores), about 70 per cent of which was in the petroleum field. Dept. of Commerce, *Investment in India*, Washington 1961, p. 11.

[40] See Kust, *Foreign Enterprise in India*, pp. 55-56 ; Kidron, *op. cit.*, pp. 305-307. Kidron also notes that foreign investors were large users of foreign currencies : "during the fourteen years for which data exist, in which the foreign investment stake has more than doubled, foreign investors as a whole have taken out of the general currency reserve nearly three times as much as they contributed directly." p. 310.

[41] Kidron, *op. cit.*, p. 186.

[42] Quoted *ibid.*, p. 258.

[43] By the mid-1960's the US government, expressing itself through the president, Congress, and the USAID mission in New Delhi, began to put pressure on India to change its economic developmental policies to make them more nearly conform to US views on the most effective means of reaching self-sustained growth in the industrial sector and self-sufficiency in food production. To som

extent, possibly because of its great dependence on American shipments of grain at that time, India acquiesced to some of the US recommendations. See Nicholson, *op. cit*, pp. 278-79, 330, 350-51.

[44] A thorough study of the agreement and its effects on textile imports into the US market was made by James H. Weaver of the American University and Ira Winakur of Gallaudet College. Conclusions were presented in their paper, "The Impact of United States Cotton Textile Quotas on the Underdeveloped Countries" (1966).

[45] Palmer, *op. cit.*, p. 117.

[46] Lewis, *op. cit.*, p. 247.

[47] See ahead, chap. XIX.

[48] As reported by Arthur M. Schlesinger, Jr., in *A Thousand Days*, Boston 1965, p. 526.

[49] *idem.*

CHAPTER XV

TRANSFORMATIONS IN INDO-SOVIET RELATIONS

DESPITE THE GEOGRAPHICAL proximity of India and Russia historical circumstances had permitted little or no contact between the two countries until recently. British control over India and Anglo-Russian rivalry sealed the subcontinent off from possible Tsarist influence. The intellectual impact of Marx, Lenin, and post-1917 developments in the Soviet Union were felt by relatively few Indians though they formed an important ingredient in the outlook of Jawaharlal Nehru. The Soviet image of India was inadequate, doctrinaire, and contemptuous of the Indian national movement led by Gandhi. Stalin's preoccupation with internal Soviet problems, and with Europe, during his life time and the absorption of most Indian leaders with domestic affairs before and immediately after independence not only perpetuated the mutual ignorance, but also cushioned the two countries from the shocks of seeing a war-time alliance rapidly dissolve into hostility.

Though the previous lack of meaningful contact between India and Russia had its obvious disadvantages it also enabled both governments to formulate their policies towards the other on a rational rather than on an emotional basis. The lack of commonly shared abstractions such as "Asianness," "socialism," or "democracy" precluded misunderstandings about adherence to supposedly common values ; the dissociation of Russia from European colonialism obviated the need of overcoming deeply felt resentments and suspicions ; the absence of a common border or ethnic and religious minorities in each other's territories permitted India to watch the growth of Soviet power without a sense of imminent peril. It was against that background of a clean slate that Nehru's policy on the Soviet Union and his responses to Soviet initiatives in the 1950's could best be understood.

Because of the rationalism underlying Indo-Soviet relations, on two occasions in the post-Second World War period the policies of one government toward the other shifted markedly without crisis or an agony of public reassessment. The Congress government's view of the Soviet role in the world differed radically from that of the British-Indian government, and Nehru's policy toward the USSR was a quiet refutation of the century-old British policy. The Russian government also demonstrated capacity for change and altered its earlier assessment of India in the post-Stalin period. Furthermore, first India and then the Soviet Union sought to keep the relationship on the level of external affairs conducted between two governments, rather than two peoples—the wordings of some proclamations notwithstanding. Considerable emphasis was placed on non-interference in each other's home affairs, one of the articles of the *panchasheel* on which the two governments agreed to conduct their relations after 1955. For this reason the fortunes of the Communist Party of India (CPI) played only a minor role in the relationship, although it was partly from the attitude of Moscow toward Indian communism that one could gauge Soviet policy on India.

The course of Indo-Soviet relations from 1919 to 1962 could be divided into four periods, three of which are discussed in this chapter. Before Indian independence the effect of the world communist movement on Indians was of more importance than the formal and changing relations between the British and Russian governments. Between 1947 and 1952 India's efforts to solve its domestic problems and play an independent role in a bi-polar world won little recognition from the Soviet Union but much criticism for the alleged "bourgeois" or pro-Western character of its efforts. The years 1952 to 1956 were the most eventful for India and for Russia. The death of Stalin opened new doors for Soviet policy. Nehru's international reputation reached an acme and India's importance could no longer be denied by the major powers. Trade was opened between India and the Soviet bloc, cultural and economic delegations were exchanged, and the visits of Nehru to the USSR and of Bulganin and Khrushchev to India created an atmosphere of exuberant friendship summed up in the phrase "Hindi-Russi bhai bhai" (Indians and Russians are brothers). At the same time in the larger world the separately inspired Indian policy of a nonaligned "peace area" based on the *panchasheel* and the Soviet campaign for peaceful coexistence between socialism and capitalism gained an enhanced similarity, in contrast to American containment policy as executed by John Foster Dulles.

The period 1956 to 1962 was one of consolidating the friendship in bilateral cultural, economic and political relations. India won increased Soviet assistance for its development plans and Soviet support for its stands on Kashmir and Goa, without incurring open hostility on the subject of its border dispute with China. India maintained a nonaligned stance on "cold war" issues vitally affecting the Soviet Union and was less critical publicly of Soviet policy in Hungary or on disarmament than were many other Afro-Asian countries. Despite important differences of opinion on such questions as methods of economic development or effective international organization New Delhi regarded good relations with Moscow as a vital part of its foreign policy. After 1962 the relationship was altered by the increasing possibilities of an East-West detente and by the diminished power status of India. China's hostility toward both India and the Soviet Union provided still another area of mutual interest in a friendship carefully built up by the two governments.

In 1918 the Montagu-Chelmsford report on Indian constitutional reform stated that "the revolution in Russia in its beginning was regarded in India as a triumph over despotism ; . . . it has given impetus to Indian political aspirations."[1] The impact of the Bolshevik revolution on Indian nationalist intellectuals[2] was sensitively reflected in the attitudes of Jawaharlal Nehru. In his reactions there were three distinct strains which governed his later policy. First, he was intellectually attracted by the "scientific" outlook of Marxism as an interpretation of history and of socio-political change. In his autobiography he wrote, "Communism and fascism seem to be the major tendencies of the age. . . . As between fascism and communism my sympathies are entirely with communism."[3] With fascism he associated imperialism, against which he believed that the communists and socialists were the most reliable fighters. However, this attraction for Marxism was limited to its broad features rather than to its fine points, and he admitted a dislike for the dogmatism that so frequently characterized the communists of his acquaintance. Nehru himself was "very far from being a communist. My roots are still perhaps in the nineteenth century, and I have been too much influenced by the humanist liberal tradition to get out of it completely."[4] Gandhi's influence reinforced his dislike for violence, and his adherence to democratic values was always very strong. For him the central problem was "how to combine democracy with socialism, how to maintain individual freedom and initiative and yet have centralized control and planning of the economic life of the people, on the national as well as the international plane."[5]

Secondly, because Nehru was a nationalist rather than an ideologue, he was completely out of sympathy with the CPI, which he found "is completely divorced from, and is ignorant of, the national traditions that fill the minds of the [Indian] people."[6] He condemned the party for following policies dictated by Moscow, which were only comprehensible on the basis of what was good for Russia, and not on what was good for Indian nationalism. That view, formulated during the critical years of the nationalist struggle, characterized the Congress government's domestic policies after independence.

Thirdly, and most important, Nehru early conceived an admiration and sympathy for the Soviet Union as a state, which outlasted several disillusioning shocks and reinforced the policy of seeking a Russian friendship for India. Nehru returned from his short visit to the Soviet Union in 1927 with very favourable impressions which he disseminated in articles[7] and talks, and which were reflected in the Congress pronouncements on the international scene from then on.[8] Although Nehru was repelled by much that he saw in the Soviet Union, his further reading, his understanding of Russian resentment of its treatment by the West, and his observing of the Soviet Union as a bulwark against fascism reinforced his conviction that Indians should be constantly alert to developments within Russia, which could have a direct bearing on India's future.

Russia "cannot be ignored by us," wrote Nehru, "because she is our neighbour, a powerful neighbour, which may be friendly to us and cooperate with us, or may be a thorn in our side. ... The bogey of war with Russia is ever with us. ... The old political rivalry between England and Russia continues. ... How far must India inherit this rivalry or be made to suffer from it?"[9] The Indian nationalists, including Gandhi, rejected and mistrusted British fear of Russian designs on India ; they believed that whatever the threat, it was a result of Anglo-Russian rivalry rooted in the past and would vanish with the withdrawal of the British from India. Moreover, it was clear to them that Russia had acted as a counterpoise to British ambitions of controlling all the area between India and Constantinople and could be relied upon to voice strong opposition to Western colonialism in Asia and Africa. Though by 1944 Nehru was able to see that the Soviet Union was already "showing an expansionist tendency and is expanding its territories more or less on the basis of the tsar's empire,"[10] he associated imperialism with capitalism and not with socialism. By the time of his final release from prison Nehru had formulated the premises and objectives of Indian foreign policy, and a friendly approach to the second strongest power emergent from the Second World War was inherent in his analysis.

Nehru's fascination for Russia also arose directly from his constant concern with the question of how the Indian people were to transform themselves into a modern, industrializing nation. Russia's agricultural economy and its social backwardness had been similar to those of India, so that Nehru felt that "if Russia finds a satisfactory solution for these, our work in India is made easier."[11] Although he wrote with sincerity of his dislike for the coercive element in Soviet methods, Nehru admired the stupendous progress made by the Russians in mobilizing their resources and in recovering from the costs of war. In exploring new avenues of thought and new methods to overcome the dead weight of India's past, Nehru was inclined to favour socialism as being more applicable to Indian conditions than undiluted capitalism.

The Russian revolution and its aftermath had a different kind of impact on some other Indians. Active rebels against British rule—many of them emigres—they regarded the new Bolshevik rulers of Russia as a potential source of assistance for overthrowing the existing regime in India. Educated, activist, and alienated from traditional Indian values, they found in the socialist programme of rapid economic and political advancement an attractive alternative to the Gandhi-led non-violent gradualist national movement. Outstanding among them was M. N. Roy, who directed the initial stages of Indian communism and played an important role in the Comintern until he finally broke with it in 1929, in disagreement with its policy on the Indian issue. The manner in which Moscow dealt with the Indian communists demonstrated the initial Russian ignorance and dogmatism about Asia and later the subordination of the needs of the international communist movement to the interests of the Soviet Union.

The articles written by Marx on India described the destructive effect of British colonialism on traditional Indian society but assigned to British rule a progressive role as a historic necessity linking the "oriental despotism" of the past with a future "socialist freedom." Marx and Engels had made little ideological attempt to fit Asia into their predictive analysis, which was predicated on the industrialized countries of western Europe. Lenin, however, amended the doctrine to include imperialism as an inevitable stage of capitalism. He thereby explained the failure of the proletariat to revolt in the developed countries as a result of their being "bribed" by the capitalists with the super-profits from the colonial dependencies. Lenin postulated that the result of internationalizing exploitation would inevitably be national wars against imperialism in Asia. When the Bolshevik hope of widespread revolution in the wake of the First World War in Europe was finally dissipated in 1919 Lenin thought anew about Asia. He argued that just as socialism in Asian countries would be reinforced by victorious workers' movements in Europe, so also revolution in the Western countries would be greatly assisted by the revolts of the dependent Asian peoples against their rulers.

The ultimate victory of socialism was thus linked with successful Asian nationalism. The Soviet Union, operating through the Communist International, became actively interested in undermining its enemy, the UK, by assisting in the revolutionary struggle of Britain's vulnerable jewel, India, and extending its own influence into Turkey, Iran and Afghanistan. The goal of drawing the Asian peoples into alliance with the Russian peoples was no simple one to achieve, nor was there any agreement on what strategy should be used to promote the process, or what attitude should be adopted towards the "national bourgeoisie" in Asia. Tactics were changed periodically as one viewpoint or the other met with favour in the Kremlin.

The question of communist tactics among the colonial and dependent nations was first and most fully discussed at the second congress of the Communist International held in mid-1920 and the Baku Congress of the Peoples of the East in September of the same year. At the first of those congresses Lenin and M. N. Roy presented separate theses, both however proceeding from the same assumption that Asian countries were going through the stage of a bourgeois democratic revolution. Lenin maintained that the communist parties there must "give active support to the revolutionary liberation movements," carry on the struggle against reactionary influences, support the peasants against the landlords, group together the elements "of the future proletarian parties," but also "be ready to establish temporary relationships and even alliances with the bourgeois democracy of the colonies."[12] M. N. Roy, on the other hand, drew a distinction between two movements growing in the dependent areas : "one is the bourgeois-democratic nationalist movement, with a programme of political independence under the bourgeois order. The other is the mass struggle of the poor and ignorant workers and peasants for their liberation from various forms of exploitation."[13] The first task of the communists should be to organize the latter and lead them to revolution.

Unlike Lenin, Roy believed that organized revolutionary parties already existed in most colonies and that the communists should work with them and not cooperate with the nationalist bourgeois organizations. In the case of India, Roy insisted that Gandhi's influence was a reactionary force and he himself directed his efforts towards building a workers and peasants party and organizing an Indian communist party that could either capture the National Congress through some of its influential members, or eventually become the sole leader of the nationalist movement. Lenin's thesis was accepted by the Communist International, and it became the basis of Soviet practice at that time. But Roy's supplementary thesis was never unimportant and underlay the "left" strategy which Moscow on occasions adopted later.

The revolutionary zeal that first motivated Soviet policy toward the countries on its southern borders was soon tempered by the interests of its own security. By 1921 the Soviet government concluded treaties with the nationalist governments of Turkey, Iran, and Afghanistan, which while assuredly protecting Soviet interests against British influence did nothing to further the cause of local communists. Its ambitious plans for the "liberation" of India by cadres from a revolutionary training school set up at Tashkent and supported by men and supplies passing through Afghanistan foundered. The vigilance of the British-Indian authorities both externally in sending warnings or ultimatums to Moscow and internally by surveillance of the mail and the activities of those in contact with M. N. Roy largely frustrated subversive efforts.

The Indian government's arrest and trial of the more important communist leaders in 1924 heralded an even stricter policy of antagonism to the CPI. The Soviet Union was too anxious to gain a position of respect in the councils of Europe and the League of Nations to pay much attention to India. The CPI made little headway. Harassed by the authorities, unable to transfer to itself the allegiance of Congress members, forced to follow Moscow's switches of policy, the communists could not identify themselves with the mainstream of Indian political life. During the Second World War it was instructed to support the British, as Russia's allies, just at the height of the nationalist "Quit India" movement in 1942. By 1944 the CPI was isolated and discredited in India. And internationally the movement gave scant support to Indian nationalism. Despite the overall anti-colonial stand of the Soviet Union, statements on India by Soviet leaders until 1946 were remarkably uncritical of British rule; Stalin made no attempt to persuade Churchill to free India in the interests of the allied war effort.[14]

THE EARLY PERIOD OF INDO-SOVIET RELATIONS

The years 1947 to 1952 form a prelude to the cordial Indo-Soviet relations later established. During those years India enhanced its status from that of a new dominion engulfed in the domestic problems following partition to that of a republic whose independent line commanded the attention, if not the gratitude, of the two major powers. The Soviet Union opened diplomatic relations with India in April 1947 and received as ambassador Mrs. Vijayalakshmi Pandit, whose appointment to this post was one of the first actions of Nehru as de facto premier of the Interim Government. But she was ignored by Stalin. Obviously, India's continued membership in the Commonwealth and Nehru's visit to the US in 1949 reinforced the then current Soviet line that the government of India was merely a tool of the "Anglo-American imperialists." Although Nehru had not altered his earlier assessments of Russia's importance as a potential friend of India, his attitude toward Russia in the early years of independence seemed cautious and even cool. His thinking about

the USSR was probably influenced by the following : his dislike
for the activities of the CPI, his desire to treat the People's Republic
of China as an independent Asian power rather than as an adjunct
of the European communist world, his awareness of the Soviet
share of responsibility for hardening "cold war" tensions and for
prolonging the Korean War, and his fear that Soviet inspired
uprisings in neighbouring southeast Asian countries would increase
the instability of the region.

The CPI's support for the Nehru government immediately before
and after independence was short-lived. In December 1947 the
central committee met and passed a resolution embodying all the
essential elements of a "left" strategy condemning the Indian bourgeoisie as an "ally of imperialism" and declaring the aim of the communist movement to be "such a fundamental reorganization of government both in India and Pakistan as will assure complete independence and progressive democracy as a transition to Socialism."[15]
The second congress of the CPI held in February and March 1948
ratified this thesis. Under the leadership of B. T. Ranadive the
party launched a programme of violence, strikes, and insurrections
planned to culminate in a nation-wide railway strike on March 9,
1949, in the mistaken belief that revolution was imminent in India.[16]
Spectacular because of its relative success was the Telengana uprising
in Hyderabad.

Ranadive reinforced his own inclinations with the argument
that his "left" strategy met with Moscow's approval. In June 1947
the USSR Academy of Sciences held a session on Indian studies,
where specialists on India advocated an abandonment of the "right"
strategy of cooperation between the communists and the Congress.
More publicized, and of greater import, was the report presented by
Andrei Zhdanov at the founding meeting of the Communist Information Bureau (Cominform) in September 1947 setting forth the
doctrine that the world was divided into two definable and hostile
camps. Its brief paragraph on the colonial areas could be read so
as to qualify only movements of "national liberation," i.e., communist-led, for Soviet support and to envisage the use of armed force
in the process of revolt. On the other hand, Soviet commentaries
appearing in 1948 warned against the premature use of violence :
Moscow was clearly undecided on the strategy to be adopted in
India. But it did not then denounce Ranadive for his radical

approach. And the Southeast Asian Youth Conference in Calcutta in February 1948, at which Soviet delegates were influential, also advocated communist-led civil war and violence in the countries of south and southeast Asia.

The question of precisely the kind of influence that Moscow exerted over Indian communism was less important than the current Indian belief that the CPI was controlled by the Communist Party of the Soviet Union (CPSU). Thus, the burden of communist inspired riots and strikes adding to an already unstable scene in newly independent India was not likely to endear the Soviet Union to the Government of India. Nor did New Delhi's measures to counteract such threats to law and order invoke approval in Moscow. In February 1950 the provisional Indian parliament passed the Preventive Detention Act—it has been periodically extended—aimed primarily against the communists.[17] The CPI's attempt at revolution failed, partly at least because the larger part of its organization was rendered impotent by the authorities.

Nehru's reactions to the violent and disruptive tactics of the Indian communists could have been expected. "I think the Communist Party in India is the stupidest party there has ever been anywhere," he said at a press conference in London in November 1950 and continued : "It has done more damage to communist ideals than any opponents of Communism, because it has set itself out to fight every natural nationalist urge of the Indian people."[18] Nehru's dislike for the anti-nationalist character of communist parties and their methods—as distinct from Marxist theory— applied particularly to southeast Asia.[19] On numerous occasions Nehru referred with approbrium to the expansionist nature of world communism, and of the extra-territorial conditioning of communist policy in India.

Nehru looked on the world as a collection of states with which India could seek the friendship necessary to her national interest with little concern for the ideologies that they professed. With regard to "the conflict which divides the world today," Nehru said, "I don't agree that it is essentially ideological. I regard it rather as a power conflict in which communism is used as a tool by one side and a target by the other."[20] Similarly, he always made a distinction between Russia and China instead of classifying them together as a monolithic ideological bloc. It was in India's interest to have good relations with both giant neighbours to the north, and that interest could still be served by adopting an attitude of rigid ideological hostility towards their communist governments. The Soviet Union had not yet chosen to cultivate the friendship of India, and Nehru turned to China for closer ties.

India's diplomacy during the Korean War had a profound effect on the thinking of the communist governments. The Soviet Union and certain of its allies came to recognize and accept India's posture of nonalignment as a respectable and even valuable stance in world politics as a result of India's skillful manoeuvring between the two power blocs. While Indian diplomats and Nehru treated the West as a unit during Korean war negotiations, they assumed that Chinese and Russian interests in the conflict diverged. Whereas the USSR may have provoked the attack by North Korea, China entered the conflict, Indians argued, as a defensive measure. India expected China to respond more favourably to peace efforts than the Soviet Union. As it happened, India was unable to break apart the unified Russian-Chinese diplomatic front on Korean problems, and peace finally came apparently when the Soviet Union agreed to it. At the conclusion of India's custodianship of the prisoners of war both Russian and Chinese governments gave public appreciation of India's role. Whatever may have been Peking's motive in so recognizing India's efforts, Moscow's statements by that time were genuine openings for improved Indo-Soviet relations.

THE BEGINNINGS OF INDO-SOVIET FRIENDSHIP

The Korean conflict bridged the years of change in Soviet policy on India. After 1952 relations between the two states developed into a friendship important to both. But even before the post-Stalin leadership began actively to woo the uncommitted nations there were manifestations of a less hostile attitude to the government of India emanating from Moscow. The earliest indication was the directive issued to the CPI in 1950 to abandon its "left" strategy calling for armed struggle and establish a broad front with other leftist parties in order better to contest the first Indian general elections of 1952 ; also, to take note of and support the "progressive" elements of Nehru's foreign policy.

The new Soviet view was influenced by Chinese experience and "neo-Maoist" strategy as articulated by Liu Shao-chi in November 1949. That strategy stipulated the formation of an anti-imperialist front, with the working class uniting with other classes including some parts of the bourgeoisie, and "the employment of armed violence only in countries where appropriate, India apparently not being among these countries."[21] Moscow issued its instructions to Asian communists in an editorial of the Cominform journal, *For a Lasting Peace, For a Peoples Democracy,* on January 27, 1950, quoting Liu's statement that "the path taken by the Chinese people . . . is the path that should be taken by the people of many colonial and dependent countries in their struggle for national independence and people's democracy."[22] The instructions took effect with the meeting of the central committee of the CPI in December 1950.

In early 1951 the party's weekly, *Crossroads,* began to write appreciatively of Nehru's "peace role" in Korea and on the subject of his opposition to nuclear weapons. In April 1951 the CPI published a new programme and a statement of policy adopting a "neo-Maoist" approach and rejecting the immediate use of violent methods to achieve power. In September it challenged the government of India to stop following a repressive policy towards party members and in return promised to abjure terrorism and function as a legal party employing constitutional means to contest for power. The Indian communists stood in the 1952 elections on a platform of a popular front, land reform, linguistic states, and a foreign policy of friendship for the "camp of peace," i.e., the Soviet Union and China. Following closely the gradually softening Soviet attitude towards Nehru's government the CPI first acknowledged certain benefits in India's generally unacceptable foreign policies, then decided that Indian foreign policies were tolerable but that domestic policies were not, and finally came to accept not only Nehru's foreign policies but some of his domestic programmes as well.[23]

The Soviet Union itself initiated friendly advances to India at a slow pace. The tentative moves before the grand visitations of 1955 acquired significance because they contrasted sharply with the infertility of the earlier relationship. In 1951 the Indo-Soviet Cultural Society was formed, initiating a Russian cultural drive which grew in popular appeal as cultural missions, dance troupes, films, books and intellectual visitors were exchanged between the two countries. The distribution of well printed, inexpensive books in India, the translation and publication of Indian fiction as well as Nehru's writings in the Soviet Union, and the import of Indian music in staff notation for use in Moscow and east European capitals all added up to an impressive effort that has been called "the Soviet cultural offensive." If in terms of actual exchanges Soviet cultural contacts with India were not as large as those with Europe and America, the space devoted to them by the Soviet press was greater. "For example," by a reliable calculation, "during the years, 1954-1957, 196 Indian delegations visited the Soviet Union, compared to 348 from France and 368 from Great Britain ; *Pravda's* reporting on exchanges with India, however, gave them twice as much space as those with France and considerably more than to those with Great Britain." At the same time, "Soviet cultural propaganda ... was perhaps more successful in India than in any other non-communist country."[24]

But domestic politics and cultural exchanges were on the fringes of Indo-Soviet diplomacy. On January 10, 1952, the Soviet delegate to the UN broke his country's prolonged silence on a subject of acute concern to the Indian government, Kashmir. He made an elaborate statement of the Soviet view of the problem, which included allegations of "imperialist" interference in Kashmir aimed at obtaining a military base to be used by the West. Russian diplomatic intervention in the Kashmir dispute appeared to have been motivated not only by a desire to record Soviet support of India but also by an interest in limiting the UN's role in the state, which nearly adjoined Russian frontiers. The Soviet delegate therefore supported India's stand that the Kashmiri people themselves through their constituent assembly had already exercised the right to decide their future.

In April 1952 Stalin ended his apparent indifference to the presence of an ambassador from India in Moscow and received Dr. Sarvepalli Radhakrishnan, who had succeeded Mrs. Pandit in that post. The following year, barely two weeks before his death, he met with the last foreign diplomat to see him alive, the new Indian ambassador, K. P. S. Menon. Stalin listened without comment to Menon's explanations of India's foreign policy objectives and methods, illustrated specially with the then current diplomacy on the Korean conflict, but voiced questions about the capability of the Indian defense forces, India's relations with Japan, and whether the possibility of a federation between India and Pakistan had been considered. The Russian leader gave the impression that "his government has not yet decided its policy towards Pakistan."[25] Menon's most vivid impressions of Stalin were of his simplicity, his shrewdness, and of his ruthlessness, which would make him impervious to a Gandhian approach of bringing about a "change of heart". After Menon's close exposure to the Soviet dictator, who presumably reflected the attitudes of the government that he controlled, it was hardly surprising that New Delhi referred much less to moral considerations and human conscience when addressing the USSR than when addressing the Western democracies.

The news of Stalin's death was received in official India not with jubilation, but with an adjournment of parliament following a speech by the prime minister remarkable for its emphasis on the greatness of Stalin. In view of the fact that the USSR had sent no message of condolence on the assassination of Mahatma Gandhi, and that Stalin was responsible for formulating the Soviet line that Gandhi was an "agent and tool of British imperialism," Nehru's tribute to the communist leader could be regarded as a gratuitously friendly gesture toward Russia. He spoke of Stalin's will, his courage, his tremendous achievements in building up his country, and of "this man who created in his life-time this bond of affection and admiration among vast numbers of human beings. . . ." At a time when Stalin's contributions to the "cold war" were by no means small Nehru could express the belief "that his influence was exercised generally in favour of peace. When war came he proved himself a very great warrior, but from all the information that we have had, his influence has been in favour of peace. . . . when our Ambassador saw Marshall Stalin . . . he [Stalin] expressed himself to him in favour of peace and his desire that peace might not be broken in the world."[26]

It was later understood that the "new look" of Khrushchev's Russia had been germinating in the last year of Stalin's life. The political and economic causative factors were already present, though new leadership and time were needed for their maturing. The most important feature of the "new look" from the point of view of international relations was Moscow's revision of two basic Leninist doctrines : the inevitability of war between capitalism and socialism, and the necessity of violent revolution as a "mid-wife" of socialism. From that revision flowed two important policies, one of acceptance of the status quo in Europe and the tactic of coexistence with the West, and the other of choosing the economically underdeveloped and diplomatically uncommitted nations as the principal battle-field for peaceful competition with the West. The latter policy involved coming to terms with the "national bourgeoisie" leadership in those countries both theoretically and politically. The Soviet leaders did so by acknowledging both the importance and the independence of the nonaligned and many other Afro-Asian coun-tries[27] and by adopting an attitude of "those who are not against us are for us". In August 1953 Prime Minister Malenkov made the first truly friendly reference to a non-communist state, India. "India has made her own significant contribution to the efforts of the peace-loving countries directed to the ending of the war in Korea," he told the Supreme Soviet. "Our relations with India are growing stronger and cultural and economic ties are developing. We hope that relations between India and the Soviet Union will continue to develop and strengthen with friendly cooperation as their key-note."[28]

The most decisive cause for an ideological rethinking on the inevitability of war was undoubtedly the development of a nuclear stalemate between the USSR and the US, which would have made any war between them catastrophic for both. Soviet policy makers rapidly came to terms with reality. Stalin at the 19th party congress held in October 1952 aired the view that it might be possible for the Soviet Union to keep out of the wars that were bound to ensue as long as capitalism existed ; Malenkov said in 1953 that a nuclear war might destroy both communism and capitalism ; finally Khrush-chev stated at the 20th party congress in 1956 that war must no longer be regarded as inevitable, and that it was conceivable that socialism would be achieved in certain countries by natural evolu-tion, even through parliamentary means. Such a withdrawal from dependence on war as an instrument of policy facilitated under-standing with India, whose prime minister spoke frequently and passionately about the need to develop in the world a "climate of peace" rather than an atmosphere of war if civilization was to be preserved.

The principle of peaceful coexistence had its greatest significance when applied between states following different social systems, such as India and the USSR. For India, the acceptance by the Soviet Union of the *panchasheel*, India's concretely defined version of coexistence, in the Nehru-Bulganin joint declaration of June 23, 1955,[29] provided public witness to the fact that Moscow preferred good relations with the Indian government to support of the CPI. Nehru's reservations about the international communist movement, however, remained. On July 19, 1955, after his return from a visit to the USSR, Nehru observed that "a logical application of the Five Principles embodied in the Nehru-Bulganin declaration would result in the liquidation of the Cominform, the fading out of it."[30] The Cominform was not in fact abolished until April 1956, after the 20th party congress had formalized the shift in Soviet policies.

The similar Soviet and Indian pronouncements on conducting foreign relations so as to create and widen a "peace area"[31] acquired a heightened significance because of current US policies. The Republican administration had begun actively setting up military alliances with countries in south and southeast Asia to complete the containment of the communist bloc. That policy was viewed in Moscow as creating a dangerous encirclement. An important Soviet objective, therefore, from the mid-1950's was to break out of the so-called containment wall by establishing ties with countries outside the Western alliance system in Asia. Despite the different origins and different degrees of their opposition to American security policy at the time,[32] the positions taken by India and the Soviet Union appeared identical. The Indo-Soviet joint communique of December 13, 1955, stated that "The statesmen of the USSR and the Prime Minister of India have agreed that the establishment of military alliances or... regional blocs is not a means of safeguarding peace and security. Such alliances have extended the bounds of the "cold war" and have introduced the element of instability in the respective areas, have increased fear and tension and created additional obstacles in the way to the peaceful development of the respective countries."[33]

The most consistently reiterated common interest of India and the USSR in the 1950's was anti-colonialism. So far as Asia was concerned, such reiteration was more than a rhetorical play, for both countries had similar objectives in that vast area. They wanted Asia, particularly southeast Asia, to become an "area of peace," free of American and perhaps also Chinese overarching presence. In Indian as well as in Soviet interest, there should have been a diversity of states in Asia with a plurality of power centres—and for the same reason : India realized that it lacked the power and influence, and even the ambition, to dominate Asia ; the Soviet Union knew that its geographical position prevented it from playing a dominant role.[34] Therefore, both sought, instead, friendly cooperation with the nonaligned countries of the region.

An overly aggressive Russian identification of its aims with those of India sometimes produced Indian embarrassment, and strong domestic pressures helped to preclude any confusion of nonalignment with a pro-Soviet foreign policy. Some Indians resented being exposed to the rhetoric of Marshal Bulganin and Nikita Khrushchev during their tour of India in 1955, when it implied that the Russians and their hosts were "allies" against American "imperialism." Already in 1954 there had been a parliamentary and public debate in India on the advisability of developing friendly relations with the Soviet Union, which might militate against good relations with the West, and in December 1953 the government had found it necessary to issue a public denial of any defense pact, secret or otherwise, with the USSR, China, or any other country.[35] The Russian leaders failed to push Indian anti-colonialism into an anti-American stance. And, as was noted in chapter IV, the Indian and Soviet ideas on the implementation of the principle of self-determination and freedom of dependent peoples were by no means identical.

Whatever may have been the degree of similarity in Indian and Soviet political interests, the most tangible bond that developed between them was economic. Along with the Soviet revision of doctrine on the inevitability of war and its new tolerant, even friendly, attitude towards the non-communist governments in the underdeveloped countries went an extension of economic diplomacy into those areas. The Russians in the mid-1950's were prepared to increase trade and offer material assistance to states outside their ideological and economic bloc in order to open up markets and sources of supply for their own expanding economy. The post-war plan for national reconstruction had been successful materially ; by 1951 the Soviet Union was able to send a gift of food and money to India for flood and famine relief.[36]

The theory behind the new economic policy was enunciated

in 1957 by the Soviet economist, V. Avarin : "It is self-evident that the industrial development of such big countries as India, Indonesia, and others, will require for a long time to come an immense quantity of all sorts of equipment, machinery, workshops, half-finished products, transportation equipment, and other means. ... Experience has proved that the more a country is industrially developed, the more it needs goods, including those which are imported from abroad. ... Hence, it is obvious that the greater the industrialization of India and other Asian countries, greater also will be the opportunity ... for mutually beneficial trade and economic cooperation."[37] The political objective of reducing the dependence of such countries as India on the former metropoles and the Western markets was not lacking. The Soviet policy-makers probably believed that the industrialization of India would hasten the process of history in the direction of socialism.

On the Indian side, the need for rapid industrialization called for increasing state control over the economy and larger amounts of foreign capital imports than were available in the West alone. Given, in addition, the prevailing prejudice against state control of heavy industry on the part of the US government, India's interest was to cultivate government-to-government economic assistance and commercial relations with the socialist states. In December 1953 the first five-year trading agreement was concluded between India and the USSR, and in June and November 1954, respectively, India signed trade agreements with Hungary and East Germany. At about the same time, at the ECAFE meeting in Kandy in February 1954 the Soviet government first opened the prospects of economic and technological aid to Asia ; in November 1954 an Indian cabinet minister formally welcomed Soviet assistance under the UN technical assistance programme ; on February 2, 1955, an Indo-Soviet agreement was signed for the setting up of a modern integrated iron and steel plant in India, in the public sector, with a production capacity of one million tons of steel ingots. The steel mill under that contract, at Bhilai in Madhya Pradesh, was ultimately rated as the most successful public steel project in the country by many Indian and foreign observers.[38] In November 1955 Russian and east European experts arrived to discuss oil prospecting and drilling in India, and in the remainder of the decade substance was given to the Soviet offer to assist in India's task of converting itself into a modern economy. No specific political strings were attached to Russian aid, nor any assumptions publicly made that India would become a socialist state, Soviet style.

However, at about the time when Russian economic aid began to appear, the Congress party's commitment (in theory) to a "socialist pattern of society" received a great deal of domestic attention. Nehru, especially, spoke frequently, feelingly, and yet vaguely about such a society, "in which there is equality of opportunity and the possibility of everyone to live a good life."[39] But despite Nehru's talk of socialism ; despite his admiration for the achievements of the Soviet Union ; and despite the fact that the drafting of the second five-year plan was much influenced by the experience of the centrally controlled economies through Professor Mahalanobis' model of balanced growth and the Polish advisor to the Planning Commission, Oscar Lange, India made no effort to emulute the Soviet methods of achieving their type of socialism.

Nehru scorned a reliance on Marxist dogma as a practical guide to economics in the mid-20th century and abhorred the idea of inflicting the type of regime on the Indian people that Stalin had inflicted on the Russians. At a time when good relations were developing between India and Russia and while the second plan was being spelled out, Nehru referred several times to the difference of approach in the two countries. "Russia does not have a democratic system of Government," he said. "People there had to pay a heavy price and undergo great suffering in order to achieve what they have done. Many of the freedoms which the people enjoyed in India are lacking there. We are trying to achieve our goal by democratic methods."[40] And again : "the price paid for rapid industrialization has been terrific in some socialistic countries. I am certain that no country with any kind of parliamentary democracy can possibly pay it."[41]

THE CLIMAX

The flow of cultural delegations, technicians, and scientists between the two countries that began in 1954 was inconspicious in comparison to the grandstand exchange of visits in 1955. The journey of Prime Minister Nehru to the Soviet Union for two weeks in June 1955 and the return visit of Soviet leaders, Bulganin and Khrushchev, to India for three weeks in November and December 1955 climaxed the new relationship between the two countries.[42] On both occasions the preparations made by the host countries were elaborate, the tours of the guests prolonged, the crowds enormous and enthusiastically welcoming, and the press coverage international. No future visits by the dignitaries of either country—and there were many— were as glamorous or perhaps as significant as these first ones were.

Through recognition and endorsement by the USSR India's posture of nonalignment gained viability. In Moscow Nehru "left the Soviet Government in no doubt as to where India stood in her foreign policy" and made it clear that "he would not budge an inch from the independent policy which he had chalked out for India."[43] In India the Soviet leaders allayed apprehensions about "the possibility of the USSR making . . . its friendship with India conditional on . . . India's refusal of business like cooperation with the United States and other Western countries."[44] As Ambassador Menon said on Moscow Radio, "Ours is not a jealous friendship. It does not exclude friendship with other countries. . . . And we are happy that this basic attitude of ours has met with the full understanding, sympathy and appreciation of the Soviet Government."[45] The marked improvement in Indo-American relations after 1956 gave the final seal of respectability to nonalignment.

India's prestige was enhanced in the international community by the attention paid to it by the Soviet leaders and by their frequent allusion to India's potentiality as a "great power." More tangibly, Soviet insistence that India be included in conferences on Asian problems and in negotiations on disarmament added weight to India's views on such matters, even when it did not become a participant in the negotiations. Within India, the public demonstration of Soviet approval for the Congress government (including Bulganin's and Khrushchev's donning Gandhi caps while in Bombay and ignoring the leaders of the CPI) enhanced its prestige vis-a-vis the communists.

As a further benefit from the Russian leaders' tour, India received explicit support for its stand on two problems threatening its territorial integrity, Kashmir and Goa. According to the Russians, "the Kashmir question has already been settled by the people of Kashmir themselves. They consider themselves an integral part of the Republic of India. . . . The Soviet Government supports India's policy on the Kashmir question. . . ."[46] The issue of Portugese rule in Goa greatly excited Indians in 1955, and it must have been with mixed feelings that the Indian government—then trying to deflate public demands for a take-over—received the enthusiastic endorsement of the Soviet leaders for the "liberation" of Goa. In his report to the Supreme Soviet Bulganin said that "the Soviet Government supports this just demand of India and holds that the preservation of a Portuguese colony on Indian territory . . . is a disgrace for the civilized nations."[47]

The Russian economic assistance that increased rapidly after the Bulganin and Khrushchev visit was doubly beneficial to India because it stimulated increased American aid. Khrushchev was already aware of that phenomenon of "competitive coexistence" when he reported to the Supreme Soviet : "Some of the more sensible bourgeois leaders say now that the capitalist countries have to increase economic help to underdeveloped countries. This is not a bad idea. Let the capitalist countries render such help. This is much better than to involve these countries in military blocs and alliances. This help . . . cannot but be regarded as some kind of help by the Soviet Union to these countries. If there would be no Soviet Union would the monopolist circles and the imperialist states render help to the underdeveloped countries? Of course not."[48]

As a result of the rapprochement between India and the Soviet Union the latter revised its doctrinal assessment of Mahatma Gandhi from one of scorn and denunciation to one of praise, as a tribute to Indian nationalist sentiment. The communist view of Gandhi from the 1917 revolution until 1956 reflected its fluctuating attitude toward India and the colonial bourgeoisie : he was regarded more as a symbol, as a representative of a class, than as a man.[49] At first the communists saw Gandhi's policies as practical and laudable despite their incompatibility with modern technology ; later they regarded him as a spent force. And in 1928 the Sixth Congress of the Comintern adopted a resolution stating that "trends such as Gandhism in India . . . idealize the most backward and economically reactionary forms of existence. . . . Gandhism increasingly becomes an ideology directed against the revolution of popular masses. It should be the object of a resolute struggle on the part of Communists."[50] The concepts of civil disobedience and non-violence struck the Soviets as ludicrous ; in 1947 Gandhi was called a betrayer of the working class and Gandhism "an ideal system for covering up a deal between the imperialists and the feudalists."[51]

By 1952 Soviet orientalists were not even allowed to concede any positive role to Gandhi, as they did to China's Sun Yat-sen. It was a caricature of Gandhi that appeared in the 1954 edition of the *Great Soviet Encyclopedia*, translations of which reached India at the time Russia was courting favour and confidence. The Indian press deplored the perverted account of India's late leader current in the Soviet Union ; the Indian government formally protested the item ; and in December 1954 the Soviet constitutional historian, Kozhevnikov, promised to see that a correction was made. The offending page was removed. During their visit to India Bulganin and Khrushchev paid tribute to Mahatma Gandhi by performing the usual ceremony of laying flowers at his memorial stone. In 1956 the Soviet scholars produced a complete rehabilitation of Gandhi ; the 20th Party Congress had already paid many tributes to India and had congratulated Bulganin and Khrushchev for "justly acknowledging the prominent role played by Mahatma Gandhi in the history of the Indian people."[52] The main points of the reassessment as written by Dyakov and Reisner in November 1956 were to correct the definition of *satyagraha*, to depict Gandhi as fighting genuinely for Indian freedom, and to praise his personal habits, his opposition to Hindu-Muslim antagonism and to the caste system, and to show that Gandhi's was a positive role in the development of the national liberation movement.

NOTES AND REFERENCES

[1] *Report on Indian Constitutional Reforms*, Calcutta 1918, p. 14.

[2] See Zafar Imam, "The Effects of the Russian Revolution on India, 1917-1920," in S. N. Mukherji, ed., *The Movement for National Freedom in India*, St. Anthony's Papers no. 18, London 1966.

[3] Nehru, *Toward Freedom*, N. Y. 1941, p. 348.

[4] *idem.*

[5] Nehru, *Discovery of India*, N. Y. 1946, p. 560.

[6] *ibid.*, p. 528.

[7] Those articles were later published under the title, *Soviet Russia : Some Random Sketches and Impressions*, 1929 ; and Bombay 1949.

[8] See Bimla Prasad, *The Origins of Indian Foreign Policy*, for Congress Party stands on the Soviet Union prior to independence. Pages 190-92 describe Nehru's dual reaction to the Russian invasion of Finland which was similar to his posi-

tion on the Hungarian question in 1956. In both cases Nehru's attempt to understand or justify the Soviet actions in the light of external pressures gave way to his natural sympathy for a small country fighting for its freedom.

[9] *Soviet Russia, op. cit.*, p. 3.

[10] *Discovery of India, op. cit.*, p. 553.

[11] *Soviet Russia, op. cit.*, p. 4.

[12] Lenin's Thesis on the National and Colonial Questions, in Eudin and North, *Soviet Russia and the East*, pp. 63-65.

[13] Supplementary Thesis on the National and Colonial Questions presented to the Second Congress of the Communist International by M. N. Roy, *ibid.*, pp. 65-67.

[14] See D. N. Druhe, *Soviet Russia and Indian Communism*, p. 241. Both the US and China had sent unofficial envoys to meet nationalist leaders in India, but not the Soviet Union. Pattabhi Sitaramayya wrote, "It was as if the Russians decided to gaze at India through British eyes. . . ." *History of the Indian National Congress*, vol. II, Bombay 1947, p.7 47. See also Bimla Prasad, *The Origins of Indian Foreign Policy*, for the view that Britain could not have banked on Soviet sympathy for or silence on its rule in India indefinitely ; pp. 233-34.

[15] Quoted in John H. Kautsky, *Moscow and the Communist Party of India*, p. 38. See chapter 1, "The Three Strategies of Communism," for the definition and explanation of the "left," "right," and "neo-Maoist" strategies as used in this chapter.

[16] Details are given statewise in the Government of India, Ministry of Home Affairs publication of 1949, *Communist Violence in India*, cited and summarized by Overstreet and Windmiller in *Communism in India*, p. 278f.

[17] By August 1949 over 2,000 communists were under detention ; and at the end of 1951 1,160 of the 1,641 persons detained under the Preventive Detention Act were communists ; cited by Overstreet and Windmiller, *op. cit.*, p. 478.

[18] Quoted in Dorothy Norman, *Nehru, the First Sixty Years*, vol. I, N. Y. 1965, p. 517.

[19] "If Communism—or any other ism—becomes violent, then any state has to supress it. Communists in Southeast Asia have, firstly, by their extreme violence and terrorist methods, and secondly, by going against one of the dominant urges of these countries—that is, nationalism—performed a counter-revolutionary act." Nehru's press conference, July 7, 1950 ; *India News Bulletin*, Washington, July 12, 1950.

[20] As quoted in *Look* magazine, vol. 18, 22 (November 2, 1954), p. 32.

[21] Kautsky, *Moscow and the Communist Party of India*, p. 99.

[22] Quoted in *ibid.*, p. 103.

[23] See Harry Gelman, "The CPI : Sino-Soviet Battleground," in Barnett, *Communist Strategies in Asia*, p. 104.

[24] F. Barghoorn, *The Soviet Cultural Offensive*, pp. 188, 197.

[25] K. P. S. Menon, *The Flying Troika*, London 1963, p. 31.

[26] *LSD* vol. I, pt. II, March 6, 1953, cols. 1568-70.

[27] As Khrushchev said to the 20th congress of the CPSU, Feb. 14, 1956, "The peoples of the East are playing an active part in deciding the destinies of

the whole world, are becoming a mighty new factor in international relations. In contrast to the pre-war period most Asian countries now act in the world arena as sovereign states or states which are resolutely upholding their right to an independent policy." Quoted in Ton That Thien, *India and Southeast Asia*, Geneva 1963, pp. 282-83.

[28] Quoted in Menon, *op. cit.*, pp. 57-58.

[29] *Foreign Policy of India : Texts of Documents 1947-59*, p. 185.

[30] *Indiagram*, No. 745, Embassy of India, Washington, July 21, 1955.

[31] The Indian government's advocacy of peace was distinct from the worldwide communit front peace movement, which originated in Breslau and Paris in 1948 and 1949. See Overstreet and Windmiller, *op. cit.*, pp. 411-29, for an account of the Indian branch of that movement, its important members, its congresses, its appeal for some non-communists, and the encouragement that it received from the Nehru-Chou En-lai communique on *panchasheel* in June 1954.

[32] K. P. S. Menon wrote that, when drafting the joint communique at the end of Nehru's visit to the Soviet Union in June 1955 the Russian government suggested an addition "to the effect that both governments condemned that policy of creating military blocs and that neither would participate in any coalitions or actions directed against the other. Such a guarantee would have amounted to a negative military alliance. When our position was explained to Kusnetsov he immediately agreed to drop the Soviet amendment." Menon, *op. cit.*, p. 119.

[33] From Bulganin and Khrushchev, *Visit to India*, p. 35.

[34] cf. Sisir Gupta : "In this sense there is a similarity between the Chinese and the Western role in Asia and a similarity between the roles of India and the Soviet Union. In the case of China and America, the basic assumption is that they can and will play a dominant power role in Asia ; in the case of India and the Soviet Union, the asumption is that they cannot do so, even if they had the necessary desire or ambition." Gupta, "Bases of Friendship," *Seminar*, no. 73 (Sept. 1965), p. 30.

[35] As reported in the *Hindu*, Dec. 30, 1953.

[36] In a previous year of acute food shortage in India, 1946, the USSR made no attempt to relieve the Indian distress, either directly or through international agencies. See M. S. Venkataramani, "The Soviet Union and the Indian Food Crisis of 1946," *International Studies*, vol. IV, 4 (April 1963), pp. 395-403, for an account of how Stalin turned a deaf ear to all Indian appeals for assistance.

[37] Quoted in W. W. Kulsky, *Peaceful Co-existence*, pp. 276-77.

[38] See John P. Lewis, *Quiet Crisis in India*, Washington 1962, pp. 295-99, for a comparison of the three steel mills built in the public sector during the second-plan period. He attributed the "extraordinarily high morale of the Indian participants in the [Bhilai] project" and its relative success partly to the astutely drawn contract, which "forced detailed partnership, explicit binational cooperation and agreement at every stage of the project."

[39] Nehru's speech in the Lok Sabha, May 23, 1956 ; *Speeches, 1953-57*, p. 96.

[40] Quoted in Cecil Crabb, *The Elephants and the Grass, A Study of Nonalignment*, N. Y. 1965, p. 140.

[41] Nehru, speech in the Lok Sabha, Dec. 21, 1954 ; *Speeches, 1953-57*, p. 11.

[42] See M. S. Rajan, *India in World Affairs 1954-56*, Bombay 1964, pp. 310-31, for a full account and assessment of the visits. Never before had a non-communist leader been asked to address the Soviet people, as Nehru did at the Dynamo Stadium, or been conducted through an atomic power station.

[43] Menon, *op. cit.*, p. 118.

[44] Bulganin and Khrushchev, press conference, New Delhi, December 14, 1955 ; *Visit to India*, p. 44.

[45] Menon's broadcast from Moscow, June 22, 1956; *FAR*, vol. II, 6 (June 1956), p. 93.

[46] Bulganin and Khrushchev, *Report to the Supreme Soviet on the Visit to India . . .*, pp. 17-18.

[47] *ibid.*, p. 17.

[48] *ibid.*, pp. 42-43.

[49] See Kyril Tidmarsh, "The Soviet Re-assessment of Mahatma Gandhi," in Iyer, *South Asian Affairs*, St. Anthony's Papers, no. 8.

[50] Quoted in Kulski, *op. cit.*, p. 214.

[51] Quoted in Tidmarsh, *op. cit.*, p. 103.

[52] Quoted in Menon, *op. cit.*, p. 138.

CHAPTER XVI

THE FULFILMENT OF INDO-SOVIET RELATIONS

THE CONSOLIDATION OF friendship between India and the Soviet Union vindicated Nehru's policy of nonalignment. First in economic and later in military relations the Indo-Soviet tie gave meaning to the rupture of the colonial bond by providing an acceptable alternative to complete dependence on, or futile defiance of, the Western powers. On the other hand, India's neutrality in the "cold war" episodes which verged on open conflict between the great powers was justly regarded in Moscow as a success for its policy of cultivating India. India and the Soviet Union each had a place in the global strategy of the other. They were natural, though only partially realized, collaborators in an attempt to create centres of power independent of Western dominance. In addition, as two great land powers in Asia they became informally allied by the fact of their common hostility towards the other great land power, China. But the interests of India and the Soviet Union were less than identical ; the exigencies of their respective ideologies and foreign policies precluded any explicit alliance between them.

With the beginnings of a Soviet-American rapprochement India's mediatory services became less essential, and its nonaligned posture was taken for granted by the great powers. But simultaneously Soviet support for India, which was faced with a hostile Chinese-Pakistani combination on the subcontinent and in Afro-Asia generally, increased. For reasons discussed in chapters XIII and XIV, India could not call upon the US to help to balance this combination, which the USSR was partly able to do. As the scope of contacts between India and Russia broadened, minor irritations and disappointments increased in number. But a decade of good relations with the USSR and its allies benefited India both diplomatically and economically. Partly because of these gains the Congress government tolerated Soviet criticisms of its politics in the mid-

1960's—as indeed it tolerated criticism from other sources. New Delhi feared the potential power of the Indian communists, but those among them who were guided by Moscow were found to be much less dangerous to the established order in India than those who turned for inspiration to Peking. For these reasons, in addition to those discussed in the previous chapter, Prime Minister Nehru and Chairman Khrushchev cemented a formerly nonexistent link between their countries. They and their successors built upon it solidly, perhaps to forestall any sudden and swift dismantlement in either capital.

ECONOMIC COOPERATION

The pillar of Indo-Soviet friendship was the economic cooperation ushered in by the first Indo-Soviet trade agreement of 1953 and the 1955 agreement on setting up the Bhilai steel mill. But still earlier, by putting into practice the idea of state planning of the national economy, the early Soviet leaders made a permanent contribution to the thinking that lay behind the Indian development plans. The chief characteristics of India's second five-year plan showed a similarity to the Soviet model of the 1920's,[1] and the resolutions on industrial policy[2] and on a socialistic pattern of society passed by the Indian parliament during the 1950's heightened the impression of a socialist bias in Indian planning. The "socialism" of Nehru and the planning commission, however, was more strongly tinged with Gandhism and Fabianism than with Bolshevism, and the practical impact of the Soviet model was small. The Indian government upheld the constitutional provisions guaranteeing the individual rights to property, refrained from enhancing its own role by nationalizing existing industry even when foreign-owned, forewent agricultural land reform, and gave a much higher priority to village and small industries than did the Soviet plans. Moreover, it cannot be emphasized enough, that by refusing to galvanize the economy by force, or coercively to collect the savings of the population ; by maintaining a democratic political system dominated by a class whose commitment to socialism was, at best, verbal ; and by continuing to rely on Western capitalist-oriented assistance, India diluted the initially strong Soviet influence on its economic thinking.

Soviet assistance in the implementation of India's plans for industrialization was, in contrast, of undiluted importance in building the framework for India to become a great industrial nation. Steel was frequently used as a symbol of Indo-Soviet friendship, and Bhilai as the portent of the future. Bhilai was also an example of speedy and efficient collaboration between two markedly different economies. The agreement was reached in February 1955; in March a site was chosen close to a source of high grade iron ore, a detailed project report was submitted, modified, and accepted within one year, and work started in May 1956. The first open-hearth furnace was inaugurated in October 1959, and by January 1962 the factory attained its full-rated capacity of one million tons of steel ingots a year which were then processed into marketable products at Bhilai's rolling mill. In February 1962 a new contract was signed for the expansion of the Bhilai works and up to 1965 the production curve showed a steady upward trend. The initial Soviet credits amounted to rupees 64.74 crores. India also reaped indirect advantages from Bhilai in that its improved bargaining position enabled it to set up two other steel factories in the public sector with British and German aid, offered at acceptable terms.

American assistance was expected for another steel plant, at Bokaro, but was not forthcoming. Shortly after withdrawing its request to the US government early in 1964 India announced Soviet willingness to aid the project—thus creating newspaper headlines reminiscent of the Aswan Dam sensation. The negotiations over Bokaro proved to be more prolonged, difficult, and closely bargained than for Bhilai, but India and the USSR eventually signed an agreement on January 25, 1965, for the construction of an integrated steel plant with a 1.5 to two million ton capacity expandable to four million tons. The Soviet credits amounted to rupees 100.5 crores.

Between 1957 and 1964 agreements were reached with the USSR (and certain eastern European states) on the setting up of many projects designed to relieve India's costly dependence on the import of capital goods.[3] Chief among them were the heavy machine building plant at Ranchi, a coal mining machinery plant at Durgapur, a foundry forge plant at Ranchi with Czechoslovakian aid, and a heavy electricals equipment plant at Hardwar. Smaller machines, precision instruments, and machine tools were to become important new items in India's export list, and some of these were produced at the surgical instrument plant at Madras, the two complementary precison instrument-making plants at Kotah (Rajasthan) and Palghat (Kerala), the opthalmic glass project at Durgapur, and at a pump and pressures project near Hardwar. Supplementing the steel plant at Bhilai were the Korba coal mining project and the Kathara coal washery project nearby. Asia's largest antibiotics plant was erected at Rishikesh and a synthetic drugs plant in Hyderabad. The augmentation of power resources was a major objective of all Indian development plans, and assistance was received for this from several countries. Soviet funds and equipment were directed to the Neyveli thermal power station near Madras—unique in its use of the locally available lignite ; the Bhakra right-bank hydropower station—the largest in Asia ; and two smaller thermal power stations at Korba and Obra—expected to speed up the industrialization of the region around Bhilai.

Still more spectacular was the impact of the Soviet Union on India's petroleum market. A group of top Soviet oil experts was invited to make a study tour of India in 1955. The Russians assessed that India had reserves of oil worth commercial exploitation, because it lay on the great oil belt extending from Burma to the Persian Gulf. The Indian government was sceptical of their advice, relying then on the Anglo-American oil companies' opinions ; Standard Vacuum Oil Company had reported failure in its prospecting attempts, and the prevailing consensus among the oil companies was that Indian oil, if it existed at all, would not be a substitute for imported middle eastern oil. Nevertheless, the Indian oil and natural gas commission was set up in 1956 and started its operations with Russian and Rumanian advice and assistance. Rapid success in finding oil at Jwalamukhi in May 1958, Cambay in September 1958, Ankleshwar in May 1960, and Rudrasagar in January 1961 transformed the Indian mood from pessimism to excitement at the birth of an indigenous oil industry. The establishment of the Indian Oil Company as a public sector distributing agent in 1959, purchasing crude oil from the USSR after 1960 with rupees, provided competition for the foreign oil companies and enabled the government to obtain a lowering of petroleum prices. A Soviet aided oil refinery went into operation in 1964.

Of less immediate significance was the "gift" made by the Soviet leaders of equipment for a 30,000 acre government mechanized farm set up at Suratgarh (Rajasthan) in 1956. A further grant of workshop machinery followed in 1960, and in 1964 the two countries agreed on the establishment of a similar farm at Jetsar nearby. Supplies for the latter were procured against Soviet credits and heralded the entry of Soviet made agricultural machinery, especially low-priced tractors, onto the Indian market.

By 1965 the Soviet Union had become the second largest national contributor to Indian development with an investment of rupees 488.3 crores up to 1966 ;[4] the bulk of that assistance had been allocated to the second five-year plan. The east European countries played a complementary and relatively minor role in these arrangements with Rumania heading the list of aid givers, followed by Hungary, Yugoslavia, East Germany, Poland, Czechoslovakia and Bulgaria.[5] India and Afghanistan together received three-quarters of the total Soviet aid to Asia, excluding the middle east.

There were certain characteristics of Soviet assistance which increased its acceptability to India ; Soviet public relations capitalized on the favourable comparison that these features made with conditions of Western aid and investment. First, it was a government-to-government programme for expansion of public sector industry, a field which Western concerns were reluctant to enter. Despite efforts made by the Indian government to heed the insistent Western advice to attract private foreign investment, it could not fail to see the contrast between a foreign owned and operated concern repatriating dividends in foreign exchange, and an enterprise owned and operated by Indians, albeit with foreign assistance. Second, the USSR appeared to offer "aid without strings"[6] by refraining from criticism of overall Indian foreign and economic policy. It accepted the fact of a mixed economy, though it helped only one sector, and it had no quarrel with nonalignment ; its help was a buttress to already formulated Indian policy. While the danger of Moscow's attempts to influence policy by withholding economic assistance could not be ignored, in the case of India such a threat was not used as a public weapon of diplomacy to the same extent that it was by Washington and London. The Russians also created the impression that they did not quibble with India's assessment of the feasibility or desirability of a particular project, as did the World

Bank. However, continued differences over the Bokaro project indicated that the Soviet Union considered its investment as carefully as did any other country.

A third characteristic of Soviet aid was the emphasis on programme aid instead of project aid. As the above enumeration of projects indicated, an effort was made to build mutually supporting industries which could generate further development in a given area. Bhilai formed one such nucleus, Ranchi another, and the basis of a petro-chemical industry was laid in Gujarat. Fourth, the comprehensive agreements made, covering designing, supply of raw materials and equipment, and the training of Indian personnel,[7] reflected a sensitivity to India's requirements of using progressively more and more of its own materials and men. The sense of self-reliance was enhanced when, for example, the Koyali oil refinery used the designs of the Central Design Institute at Baroda rather than the Soviet-made designs applied to the earlier refinery at Barauni ; the heavy machine building plant at Ranchi produced equipment for the heavy electricals plant at Hardwar and took orders for the expansion of the steel plants at Bhilai and Durgapur ; and while the Bhilai plant used only 13.4 per cent of Indian materials, the Bokaro plant was scheduled to use 63.7 per cent.[8] A fifth advantage to India accrued from the closed nature of the Soviet social and political systems. It enabled the USSR to send high calibre technicians to India with greater ease and fewer emoluments than their Western counterparts in private industry ; the relatively modest and isolated living of Russian and east European personnel and their ostensible confinement of interest to their immediate jobs made them less obtrusive on Indian society than the ubiquitous and mobile Americans, and therefore generally less resented. Moreover, Indians trained in the Soviet Union were not considered part of the "brain drain" of skilled Indians migrating abroad, because they tended to return to India.

As a sixth advantage Soviet aid was clearly based on a long-term commitment, which was one of the most insistent demands of India for external aid. In 1965 the USSR and India took an initial step in dovetailing their economic plans—one of the recommendations of the United Nations Conference on Trade and Development —which could have great significance if continued. Finally, though Soviet and east European loans to India were "tied" to purchases from those countries, unlike the IBRD global tender credits their terms were comparatively easy. Typically, they carried a $2\frac{1}{2}$ per cent interest rate over a 12-year repayment period beginning one year after delivery, and, most important, were repayable in rupees to be used for imports of Indian goods. The gold clauses included as possible safeguards against nonpayment had not been invoked up to 1968 ; and despite its growing burden of debt servicing the Indian government had not asked for deferments from the USSR and eastern Europe up to 1968.

By specifying repayment of loans in goods to be bought with rupees centrally held in India[9] the aid programmes of Russia and eastern Europe were inextricably bound into their trade with India ; a five-year India-USSR trade and payment agreement which came into force on January 1, 1959,[10] set a new pattern of genuine bilateralism in India's foreign economic relations. Rupee balances were no longer to be convertible into sterling, as stipulated in earlier agreements, but were to be used for the purchase of goods agreed upon by both parties. Schedules of traded commodities were to be drawn up at the beginning of each year setting quantitative targets. This provision obviated some of the risks in free market trade but were designed to allow for flexibility in supply, demand, and price setting.

The turn-over of trade between India and all the countries of eastern Europe, including the USSR, increased by 750 per cent in the decade ending 1966.[11] The volume of Indo-Soviet trade alone rose from rupees one crore in 1953 to rupees 88 crores in 1958 to rupees 176 crores in 1965, with a declared intention of raising it to rupees 300 crores by 1970.[12] The Soviet Union became the third largest buyer of Indian products and the fourth largest supplier, and India was one of its most important trading partners among the developing countries.[13] This expansion in trade was accompanied by a diversification in the products exchanged which was of equal value to India. Soviet supplies were initially industrial raw materials and wood pulp but soon rose to include petroleum, capital goods, agricultural machinery, and newsprint. Soviet imports also grew beyond India's staple cash earners of tea, spices, jute and jute products, and textiles.[14] Ready-made leather shoes, medicines, and cotton piece-goods were early items of a non-traditional type, with cashew nuts, resin, electrical and engineering goods added later. India's capacity to produce consumer goods was growing at a time when Soviet demand for such items was increasing.

Under the provisions of the third Indo-Soviet trade agreement of 1965 the proportion of manufactured or processed goods in India's exports to Russia was to be 45 per cent. After a two-year lag, 1968 brought a dramatic development in the shape of visiting Premier Kosygin's offer to provide a market in the USSR for the railway wagons and other types of machinery produced in India's recession-hit public sector heavy industries. Despite these new developments, however, the pattern of trade between India and industrialized eastern Europe, including the USSR, tended to be similar to that between India and the industrial countries of the West. India's capacity to utilize the new openings for its manufactured goods would later depend on its ability to increase production and speed of delivery so as to counteract possible competition from western European sellers, whose contacts with eastern Europe and Russia were gradually increasing.

India's contacts with the Soviet Union and eastern Europe were greatly facilitated by agreements setting up a regular steamship line in 1956 and a direct air contact in 1958.[15] Combined with the telecommunications links established between New Delhi and eastern European capitals after 1956, these agreements broke the age-old isolation between the peoples of India, and Russia and eastern Europe.

Features of trade with eastern Europe most attractive to India were the assured market there for Indian manufactured and processed goods not easily sold in hard currency areas, the possibility of obtaining capital goods on a barter basis, and the determined effort by both sides to balance the trade. But this type of bilateralism, frowned upon by GATT, posed dangers of diverting Indian exports away from their traditional and hard currency markets and of bulk purchases made from India being dumped on the world market by an eastern European country. The annually agreed upon schedules of commodities with their quantitative targets and price limits provided important safeguards against both dangers by enabling the Indian government to decline a sale when faced with a genuine problem of diversion or a fear of dumping. For the most part, however, India's trade with the USSR and eastern Europe after 1954 represented new trade and was closely supervised by the State Trading Corporation, set up in 1956 to coordinate with similar organizations in the centrally controlled economies.

The value of bilateral trade conducted with non-convertible rupees was reduced for India by the lack of any multilateral payments system within the eastern grouping which could have compensated for the differences in tastes and purchasing power of the individual countries, and whose existence would have made the rupee a partially convertible currency. Many Indians also feared that an increase in exports to the Soviet Union and eastern Europe unaccompanied by an increase in foreign exchange earnings would reduce the force of India's appeals to the West for clemency in debt repayment terms. Thus, controversy surrounded the growing economic cooperation between India and the socialist states.[16]

The extent of Indo-Soviet economic cooperation indicated the powerful motives that lay behind it. In addition to those economic and political reasons specified in the previous chapter, other considerations helped to stimulate continued Soviet assistance to India. To the extent that the USSR stepped into aid projects for which India had unsuccessfully looked for help from the US, it gained a certain leverage in New Delhi. Also, Soviet observers concerned with the ultimate victory of socialism in India found it difficult to assess the actual or potential strength of an Indian proletarian class, but they could assert confidently that "the growth of state capitalism accelerates the creation of material prerequisites for the struggle of national democracy and socialism."[17] Finally, Soviet leaders could not fail to be impressed by the size of India's population and the necessity of ensuring that its future lay away from a combination with the still larger population of China, in hostility to the relatively small numbers of Russians.

DILEMMAS OF THE HUNGARIAN CRISIS

India and the Soviet Union sought each other's support for immediate political objectives as well as for their longer-range policy goals. India's three territorial concerns were Kashmir, Goa, and the areas occupied by China after 1958. As already pointed out, the USSR gave open support to the idea of integrating Kashmir and the Portuguese enclaves into the Indian Union ; it used its veto power in the Security Council to prevent passage against India's wishes of any Western sponsored resolution on either subject. Russia's attitude on the Sino-Indian territorial conflict is dealt with later in this chapter. On the other side, Soviet security interests were primarily bound into its confrontation with the Western alliance. Chapter III explained that India gave the USSR a kind of negative support in this struggle by withdrawing itself from the Western sphere of political and military influence. In the Hungarian crisis India's nonalignment and its relations with the Soviet Union were both subjected to strains ; the outcome may have added some strength to the foundation of Indo-Soviet friendship.

During November 1956 the Indian government performed a delicate balancing feat by expressing its feelings of admiration and sympathy for the revolting Hungarian people, on the one hand, and, on the other, by publicly giving credence to Soviet explanations of the crisis and opposing condemnatory or punitive moves against the USSR in the General Assembly.[18]

Sections of Indian as well as Western public opinion were outraged by Nehru's calm viewing and cool handling of Soviet troop movement into Hungary, which was as poignant as the concurrent invasion of Egypt, about which the government's statements were unambiguously condemnatory. The difference in approach lay partly in international alignments over the two issues.[19] Nehru, who at the outset had no assurance that the Western response to the Hungarian revolutionaries' call for assistance would be limited to diplomacy, regarded that explosion in Europe as posing a greater threat of world war than the Suez crisis. Over Suez the US and the USSR were not in hostile confrontation ; in central Europe they were. Nehru acted in such a way as to lessen the chances of a great power clash. As he told the Indian parliament, "If war is there, there is no democracy left, there is no freedom left, there is nothing worthwhile left. That is the main thing."[20] His sympathy for the Hungarian revolutionaries gave way to his fears of an open conflict which were reinforced by the reports he received from the Indian emissary in Prague that the common people there were preparing for war.

The other reason that the Indian government could view events in Hungary dispassionately was because it had no sense of involvement with the people of eastern Europe and but slight official contact with them in 1956. A resident mission was opened in

Budapest in October 1956 (the Indian ambassador to the USSR having been concurrently accredited to Hungary), but the arriving chargé d'affaires had not witnessed the build-up of events and feelings into an anti-government tide. The Hungarian revolution took India by surprise.

Nehru made his first public comment on the evening of October 25 at his press conference. He spoke about the "national uprising" taking place in Hungary and voiced his expectation that it would take a turn similar to the movement that he had welcomed in Poland for greater national identity and democratization. Briefly, it appeared that such an expectation was justified, when the USSR recalled its troops from Budapest, offered to negotiate fresh relations with Hungary, and announced its willingness to discuss the grievances of the Hungarian people, including the question of Soviet troops stationed in the country.[21] But on November 1 the government of newly appointed Imre Nagy repudiated the Warsaw Pact and tried to gain external guarantees for Hungarian neutrality. The USSR was not prepared for a neutral Hungary or for a break-up of the year-old Warsaw Pact with which it confronted NATO. When the revolution swept beyond Nagy's control into chaos, Soviet troops were reintroduced into Budapest and began their repression of the revolt on November 4. On November 11 Janos Kadar was installed with a new government, signifying the failure of the revolution. A heroic moment of success had been lost, not for lack of courage or endeavour, but, as Nehru later pointed out, because "small nations are being dragged hither and thither, pushed about and made to suffer because of the rivalries of great Powers."[22]

On November 5 the Indian ambassador in Moscow conveyed India's deep concern with and regret over the events in Hungary.[23] Nehru had refrained from commenting on Soviet repressive measures probably because a breakdown of direct communications between New Delhi and Budapest led him to doubt the authenticity of newspaper reports mainly from Western sources. But at the inauguration of a UNESCO conference in New Delhi on November 5 he dwelt sadly on the contrast between the noble declarations of states in the preamble to the UNESCO constitution and their ignoble deeds—using armed force in Egypt and in Hungary to "commit outrages on human dignity and freedom." In the weeks following he expressed stronger repugnance at the Soviet intervention. However, Nehru also asked the Soviet government for its narration of events in Hungary and presented the reply received to the AICC meeting on November 9 as a "partial account."[24] Despite this qualification, reports of Nehru's speech spread the impression in the Western press that the Indian prime minister had accepted the Soviet explanation of the "civil conflict," "confusion," and "counter revolution" in Hungary which the USSR was suppressing in the interests of law and order.

The Hungarian revolution did not result in war but in highly charged debates in the General Assembly. There Nehru's policy was acted out by Krishna Menon.[25] Menon asserted that the crisis could not be overcome peacefully without the cooperation of the Soviet and Hungarian governments, which in turn could not be secured by antagonizing them but, hopefully, by a united UN appeal, particularly from the nonaligned countries. He failed to persuade the Western delegations to accept this point of view. The near unanimity of the Assembly in the concurrent debates on the Suez crisis contrasted with the voting on the Hungarian question. The General Assembly was divided into three groups : the US-led majority, including some Afro-Asian states ; the Soviet-led minority of socialist states ; and a group of fifteen nonaligned states which tried to dilute the "cold war" flavour of the debate. Of the eleven resolutions passed on the situation in Hungary during the second emergency session and eleventh plenary session of the General Assembly India abstained on seven of them, voted for three, and against one.

The Assembly's first resolution on Hungary (1004 [ES-II] of November 4, 1956) established the pattern of voting. Sponsored by the US, the resolution was strongly condemnatory of Soviet intervention in Hungary, asserted the right of the Hungarians to choose their own government, and called for free entry of the secretary-general and his nominees to report on the situation to the UN. India abstained because it opposed certain paragraphs of the resolution and not, Menon explained, because there had been no time given for the delegation to receive instructions from its governments—the Burmese complaint—before voting. India's objections remained consistent : it abstained from voting on those resolutions which used language inimical to conciliation, those which were ideologically motivated, those which assumed conditions in Hungary not yet proven as facts, those which implied a non-independent status for Hungary, and those which tried to introduce UN personnel into Hungary without the explicit consent of the Hungarian government.

The single resolution against which India voted (1005 [ES-II] of November 9, 1956) included, inter alia, a proposal to hold elections in Hungary under the auspices of the UN. India opposed such a "dangerous precedent," which could have been used in the Kashmir dispute, and which offended against UN respect for the sovereignty of member states. In the joint Indian-Ceylonese-Indonesian sponsored resolution (1128 [XI] of November 21) Hungary was urged to permit the entry of the secretary-general's nominees, but "without prejudice to its sovereignty"—a phrase Menon specified as crucial. The two resolutions, besides its own, which India supported (1007 [ES-II] of November 9, 1956 and 1129 [XI] of November 21) called for resettlement of refugees and large-scale immediate relief to the Hungarian people by contributions from governments and private organizations. India itself contributed to the International Red Cross and pleaded that its work in Hungary be carried on free from political pressure. Furthermore, Nehru's government was the first to reveal casualty figures for the Hungarian revolution.[26]

On the political aspects of the Hungarian crisis India believed that the best solution lay in a general disengagement in Europe. However, it had no specific proposal on how the Warsaw Pact and NATO countries could achieve this at a time when passions were running high on both sides. India consistently advocated a withdrawal of Soviet troops from Hungary, and Nehru spoke about their presence there as a "continuing intervention" or semi-permanent aggression, which was implicit in the stationing of foreign troops under the provisions of any military alliance.[27]

India's most immediate and pressing concern was to secure the entry of the secretary-general into Hungary, and it turned its best efforts at every point of contact with the Soviet and Hungarian governments to this end. Having offended the Western powers India was not in a position itself to mediate but hoped that Hammarskjöld would be acceptable to the socialist countries. Nehru urged a tour by the secretary-general and his submission of an objective report as a corrective to the rumours circulated about conditions within Hungary. Official Soviet and Hungarian denials of large-scale deportations and reprisals were belied by their refusal to permit entry to UN representatives, and the point was not ignored by India. Menon almost entreated the Soviet Union to accede to a request backed by the UN as a whole, and thus to perform the "moral duty" that each member state had, "to accept the presence of the Secretary General within their country at any time." Failure to so persuade the USSR was galling, and Indian disappointment was understated by Menon when he said, "we feel that it is a lack of courtesy to the United Nations and a violation of the spirit of the Charter, . . . that the two governments concerned should have protracted this matter for so long, so that the Secretary General has not been able to visit the area."[28]

Not all informed Indians supported their government's careful and somewhat biased diplomacy during the Hungarian crisis. Several major newspapers published an open letter of outspoken criticism by Jayaprakash Narayan on November 18 and otherwise contributed to a public debate on the issue. During parliamentary debates in November and December Nehru had to defend his policy at length. He spoke about the course of events in eastern Europe in an historical vein but also gave an account of more recent happenings in Hungary. He based his information not only on special reports received from Ambassadors K. P. S. Menon and J. N. Khosla in Moscow and Prague, but also on communications from President Tito. India and Yugoslavia followed similar lines during the Suez and Hungarian crises ; Tito was particularly well abreast of liberal developments in eastern Europe and the Soviet Union in 1956. Nehru admitted that "Yugoslavia is a country with which we exchange our appraisals on the world situation more frequently than with any other country. . . . I am free to confess that we have, to some extent, been guided by their appraisals of the European situation."[29]

In Nehru's ultimate assessment of the Hungarian crisis two points stood out. He stressed the nationalistic element in the revolution, saying, "the major fact is that the people of Hungary, a very large part of them, claimed freedom from outside control and interference, objected to the Soviet forces coming, wanted them to withdraw and wanted some internal changes in their Government."[30] He emphasized too, his objection to the stationing of foreign forces anywhere, and their use, such as in the case of Hungary, to suppress a national uprising. The legality of the presence of the Soviet forces under the provisions of the Warsaw Pact notwithstanding, "the fact is," said Nehru, "the Soviet armies were there against the wishes of the Hungarian people."[31] Above all, Nehru tried to halt the drift towards war in central Europe. Once that danger had receded, once he had been forced to recognize the depth of sympathy within India for the Hungarian revolutionaries, and once he had received more direct information, Nehru grew more critical of Soviet actions. On November 14 he met the prime ministers of Ceylon and Indonesia to discuss the international situation, and they expressed their "deep distress" over the tragic turn that events had taken in Hungary.[32] Nehru's speeches in parliament contrasted with his brief remarks at the beginning of the revolution and his speech to the AICC of November 9. And when Nagy and others were executed by the Soviet government in June 1958 Nehru did not hesitate to express publicly his shock and to convey his concern to the Soviet leaders.[33]

INDIA AND THE GERMAN QUESTION

The hub of the "cold war" in Europe was the German question ; no other issue so frequently threatened to erupt into conflict between the two great powers. Nehru's declamations against the "climate of war" and his appeals to the leaders of the great powers to resolve their differences peacefully were as responsive to the crises in central Europe as they were to the arms race, although Nehru refrained from proffering mediatory solutions to the former as he did for the latter. India's general predilection on the German question was in favour of any step which would create a "climate of peace," a move away from prevailing hostility. Its support could be assumed for any of the proposals made from time to time which envisaged a general disengagement in Europe, whether through a nonaggression pact between the Warsaw Pact and NATO countries, a creation of an atom-free zone in central Europe, a withdrawal of all foreign armies, or through the development of peaceful contacts between east and west Europe.

The Indian government held that the tension in central Europe was greatly increased by the incorporation of West Germany (the Federal Republic) into NATO in 1954 and of East Germany (the

German Democratic Republic or GDR) into the Warsaw Pact created in 1955. "The major problems of Europe such as the very important problem of Germany," said Nehru, "would be much nearer solution if foreign forces of both sides were removed."[34] Nevertheless, he did not seriously urge a dissolution of NATO or the Warsaw Pact—anticipating, no doubt, the futility of such a suggestion—and his criticism of those two alliances was much less bitter than that of SEATO or CENTO.[35] Instead, India's self-appointed task during the 1950's was to persuade the leaders of the US and the USSR of the nonaggressive intentions of the other. It is only by looking back over the Soviet acceptance of a stalemate in Berlin in 1949 and 1961 and Western acquiescence in continued communist control in eastern Europe that the intentions of both Moscow and Washington to avoid an actual conflict becomes obvious ; for most of the period under review the risk of another war beginning in Germany was a real one. The German problem was a legacy of the breakdown of the war-time alliance against that country and, briefly, had three aspects : the question of reunification, the definition of Germany's eastern and southeastern frontiers ; and the continued existence of West Berlin as a freely accessibly island of the Federal Republic surrounded by East German territory.

India, whose security was unaffected by the size or strength of Germany, was willing to subscribe to the idea of German reunification. In communiques issued with leaders of the Federal Republic India expressed the hope that "the parties concerned will reach an early agreement about the peaceful unification of the two parts of Germany in accordance with the wishes of the German people" and with "due regard to the security requirements of Germany and other countries in Europe."[36] However, Nehru saw that in the absence of conditions conducive to a general settlement and with the crystallization of different systems in the two parts of Germany it seemed unlikely that reunification could take place on terms acceptable to both sides. In 1960 and 1961 he expressed his opinion that while German unification seemed to be the normal and desirable development, "at the present moment there are two countries, and two Governments [in Germany] . . . they are a fact of geography. . . . and to ignore the existence of one of them or either of them is just to shut your eyes to facts."[37]

28

Yet, contrary to the implications of this pronouncement India did not consummate its acceptance of the division of Germany by formal recognition of the GDR. Instead, and as an exception to its general practice of equal legal treatment to the two halves of countries dismembered by "cold war" exigencies, India established diplomatic relations with the Federal Republic as early as December 1949, but had not opened even consular relations with the GDR up to 1968. Frequently criticized by Indian communists for such discrimination against East Germany, Nehru explained that he was reluctant to take any step that would finalize the partition of Germany or come in the way of eventual reunification. He reasoned that it had been easy to convert India's military mission in West Germany, which had been closely associated with the military missions of the Western allies, into a diplomatic mission at Bonn, whereas there was no such continuity of relationship with East Germany. There was, thus, an implied recognition of the Federal Republic as the "successor" German state.

The unspoken reasons for India's decision were more powerful. In 1955 Bonn had expounded what came to be known as the "Hallstein Doctrine" : it refused to have relations with (or give economic aid to) any state (excluding the Soviet Union) which recognized the GDR, and it made strenuous efforts to keep East Germany isolated from the non-communist world. By the time India had developed important economic relations with West Germany it would have needed a strong incentive to test Bonn's resolve. Moreover, India did not suffer from its refusal to offer formal recognition to the East German state as long as New Delhi's relations with Moscow were good.

Nevertheless, India participated annually in the Leipzig industrial fair, signed periodic trading agreements with the GDR, and accepted a resident trade representative from that country—though the gesture was not reciprocated. East German financial and technical assistance was used in setting up chemical and raw film industries in India, and by the mid-1960's the two countries were important trading partners. In 1959 Premier Grotewohl visited New Delhi, briefly ; the ceremonies usually connected with the visit of a head of government were vastly scaled down, and no joint statement was issued by the two prime ministers. Nehru tried to give the impression that these contacts were of greater significance than the decision not to treat the GDR as an independent country. He told parliament that "we have trade relations with the East German Government. De facto we recognize it."[38] But the sense of this and other similar statements made by him was factual rather than legal ;[39] by virtue of the ambiguity India contrived to benefit from good relations with both parts of Germany.

There was no such ambiguity in the Indian view that the eastern and southeastern borders of Germany should be defined along the lines of the post-war settlement and the Oder-Neisse line be universally endorsed. Standing outside the Western alliance, India was not obliged to support the Federal Republic's claim that the legal boundaries of Germany were those of 1937. As India saw it, while West Germany was pledged to a revision of frontiers between East Germany and Poland and Czechoslovakia, Bonn's assurances not to seek modification of its own borders, or reunification of Germany, by force, were open to question. East European fears of a revanchist West Germany, rearmed, was a major stumbling block to any general settlement in Europe, and the whole atmosphere, as Nehru put it, was "vitiated by the uncertainty in regard to frontiers." He added, "if anything is certain, it is this, that any attempt to change that [German] frontier will lead to war. I am surprised, therefore, that this matter should be left vague and in the air."[40]

Of all the aspects of the German question Berlin was the most likely to cause war. At no time did the Indian government lend support to the Soviet objective of eliminating the Western presence in Berlin, but neither did it subscribe fully to the Western position. The 1958-1959 Soviet proposals for a peace treaty with Germany, which included the idea of Berlin as a "free city," were circulated to all countries formerly at war with Germany, and they sounded superficially attractive to Indian ears. The suggested demilitarization of Germany was bound to be welcomed, and the government was prepared to lend credence to the proffered Soviet guarantees for free international access to Berlin and maintenance of West Berlin's special social and economic system. However, New Delhi was equally ready to give moral support to the mayor of West Berlin, Willy Brandt, when he made a brief visit in early 1959 to explain the implications of the Soviet proposal. The Western powers predictably rejected the Soviet draft treaty, but the Khrushchev-Eisenhower talks of 1959 held out promise of more comprehensive

East-West negotiations and were accordingly praised by India.

After the Berlin blockade of 1948-1949 the most serious crisis occurred in the summer of 1961, when Khrushchev announced a deadline for negotiating a German peace treaty. Because the vital interests of both alliances were involved and military preparations accompanied diplomatic moves, and because there was a personal confrontation of wills between Khrushchev and Kennedy, the 1961 crisis teetered at the edge of war. This danger evoked from Nehru, for the first time, in August, long statements in parliament on the German question as a whole and the then current Berlin crisis.

Nehru's statements contained no mention of the recently constructed Berlin wall or any sympathetic reference to the flow of refugees from East Germany, indicating the care he took to avoid criticising the GDR and Soviet governments for their handling of territory and populations under their control.[41] Instead, he spoke about the changed circumstances since the arrangements had been made for allied occupation of Germany and Berlin in 1944-1945 and said that in view of those changes, "the Soviet and East German authorities could very well argue that they have the right to regulate and control the movement from the East Berlin area to the West Berlin area."[42]

On the issue of Western claimed transit rights to West Berlin, a vital question in the 1961 crisis, Nehru was equivocal. At first he refrained from expressing any opinion about the legal issues involved but offered as his view "that the fullest facilities for access to West Berlin should be given." Since any interference with access created an escalation of fears on both sides, Nehru believed that it "could be made clear, that whatever else happens this access to West Berlin will remain."[43] But later, on August 23, in response to a question in the Rajya Sabha, he dealt more fully with the arrangements that had been made in Berlin since 1944. Nehru remarked that the four-power communique of January 20, 1949, "did not invoke any right of access but merely mentioned 'obligation' on the part of the occupation authorities to take the necessary measures 'each in its own zone'."[44] Basing his remarks on a brief prepared by the External Affairs Ministry, he asserted that the Western powers' access to Berlin was derived from verbal agreements and had developed "not as a right but as a concession from the Soviet authorities."[45] Nehru backed up this interpretation—in direct contradiction of the Western claims—by referring to the decision of the International Court of Justice in the Dadra and Nagar Haveli case ; according to the ICJ, the right of transit was not inherent in the right of occupation but separately based on agreement with the authority controlling the transit routes.

As the crisis cooled down, with Berlin then physically divided by a wall, Nehru's views remained ambiguous, but his government tried to re-establish its neutrality in the East-West debate on Germany. From the joint communique issued at the end of Nehru's visit to the USSR in September 1961 it is clear that the Indian and Soviet views did not coincide on Germany, beyond expressing the desirability of a peaceful solution agreeable to all the parties concerned ; Nehru only "noted the views expressed by Chairman Khrushchev"[46] but was not persuaded by them. After vacillating on the main points of an old Western-Soviet dispute and thus virtually inviting renewed pressures from both sides, the Indian government resumed its more accustomed nonaligned position on Germany. In September 1964 President Radhakrishnan in Moscow reiterated Nehru's stand of September 1961 ;[47] until 1968 it had not been altered.

India's interest in central Europe lay not in any specific solution to its problems but in the preservation of peace. The one solution that India would have favoured at any time, of a non-military, neutral, Germany, was an impossibility after the mid-1950's. Short of that, India was prepared to back the status quo as long as it kept at bay the threat of war.

THE RUSSIAN-INDIAN-CHINESE IMBROGLIO

Friendship between India and the Soviet Union was erected on a platform of the *panchasheel*, and every important joint communication reaffirmed it as something more than a slogan. As explained in the previous chapter, Soviet adoption of peaceful coexistence as a policy was the result of a drastic amendment to the Stalinist view of the world. The 20th Congress of the CPSU in 1956 formalized the new doctrine and became the reference point of significant improvements in Russia's relations with India ; China later referred to the same point as the start of its ideological dispute with the Soviet Union.

The deductions drawn by Moscow from its fresh assessment of world trends in the nuclear epoch were pleasing to New Delhi. Those deductions included the rejection of general war as inevitable and a discouragement of local wars ; an approach to negotiation with the West especially on the subject of disarmament ; postulation of the possibility of peaceful, parliamentary transition to socialism instead of through violent revolution ; engagement in economic cooperation, which involved giving economic assistance to countries such as India ; and an acceptance of "national bourgeois" governments as worthy of friendship and cooperation. But it was to these very amendments of Soviet policy that China most strenuously objected, on grounds that since Soviet advances in military technology made in 1957 (when the Sputniks were orbited), the "east wind" was "prevailing over the west wind,"[48] and the struggle against the "imperialists" in the West and the "reactionaries" and "neutrals" in countries like India must be intensified. In the Chinese throwback to the M. N. Roy thesis on national liberation movements, presented in 1922, the Nehru government was considered not "progressive" but one that must be overthrown by Indian communists.[49]

By September 1959 the Indian-Chinese territorial dispute could no longer be glossed over. On September 9 *Tass* issued a statement on the Himalayan frontier incidents which reflected the cautious neutrality of the Soviet position. This editorial made four points which were to be repeated in future Soviet pronouncements : the incidents would be used in the West, *Tass* said, as part of a campaign to drive apart the two largest states in Asia and to discredit peaceful coexistence ; it was a matter of great regret that the frontier incidents had taken place at all ; the Soviet Union had friendly relations with both China and India, built respectively on "fraternal" ties of international socialism and "friendly collaboration" in accordance with the ideas of peaceful coexistence ; and the Soviet government hoped that India and China would adjust their misunderstandings and work together for peace.[50] On October 30 Khrushchev reiterated this position before the Supreme Soviet, while also expressing grief for the kin of all military casualties and his hopes that friendly negotiations between India and China would eliminate repetitions of the hostilities.[51] Coming after Khrushchev's futile discussions in Peking, Soviet neutrality on the Indian-Chinese frontier clash must have been particularly galling to the Chinese. It was the first time that the USSR had refused to side with its ally in a dispute between a socialist state and a non-socialist state ; the Indian government was correspondingly pleased.

Clearly, the Soviet Union did not relish the embarrassment of making a choice between supporting India or China should they push their differences to a point of military conflict. The Russian leaders lectured to both Indians and Chinese on the importance of peace and friendship between them and cited the USSR's settlement of a frontier dispute with Iran as an example of what could be accomplished if the issue of national prestige were not entangled with a border question. India joined the Soviet Union in stressing the need of solving national differences by peaceful negotiation, for example, in the joint communique issued on the occasion of President Voroshilov's first visit to India, in early 1960.[52]

Between February 11 and 16, 1960, Khrushchev visited India again, and at that time the Indian public was told that the government had despatched a note to Peking, which, inter alia, invited Premier Chou En-lai to talks in New Delhi on the border question. In parliament Nehru went to some pains to disavow the public speculation that his talks with Khrushchev were directly related to the sending of the note—dated February 12, but prepared earlier, he said. Nehru denied that he had asked the Soviet premier "to do this or that for us" or to bring pressure to bear in Peking. However, he did admit to discussing the China problem and was optimistic that Moscow would exercise a beneficial influence on Chinese policy. The prime minister told the house that both Eisenhower and Khrushchev were "exceedingly friendly" to India ; "that is all I wanted and it would have been embarrassing for me—and for the other party—to try and push questions to either of them and demand an answer." Instead, "it is for them to consider what they are going to do and how they are going to do it."[53]

Nehru's confidence in the Soviet interest in India was not misplaced. The Nehru-Khrushchev communique stated : "As between India and the Soviet Union, at no time have their mutual relations rested on a firmer basis of friendship and understanding than now."[54] And, indeed, the year, 1960, witnessed an enhanced level of Indo-

Soviet cooperation ; new agreements were signed to extend trade, technical assistance, and cultural relations ; fresh Soviet credits, for the expansion of existing projects and the setting up of new ones were made available ; contacts between India and Russia and other eastern European countries increased.

That year was also one of increasing vituperation in Soviet-Chinese disagreements and of severe diminution in their economic cooperation. The Russians appeared to threaten economic sanctions against China or its expulsion from the socialist camp in an effort to bring Peking into line with Moscow. The Soviet Union refused to share nuclear technology with the Chinese and in August 1960 withdrew its technical advisers and specialists assisting China's development programme.[55] China attacked the main planks of Khrushchev's policy in high ideological terms in an article, "Long Live Leninism," published in *Red Flag* in April 1960. At the Bucharest conference of communist parties held in June of that year Khrushchev replied in detail. He attacked not only China's arguments but also its international behaviour. He had much to say about India, rejected Chinese charges of being let down by lack of Soviet support, and claimed that it was China which, by quarelling with India on a purely national issue, was harming the cause of socialism.[56] Argument between the Soviet and Chinese positions was carried on in confidential letters and newspaper articles and came to an open head at the Moscow conference of 81 communist parties (including the CPI), held in November and December 1960. Though the final communique glossed over the differences, and though it was not until 1963 that the USSR and China attacked each other by name publicly, no person present at the Moscow conference could have retained any illusions about the homogeneity of the communist movement.[57] "Fractionalism" existed for a fact, and was echoed in communist parties all over the world.

The issues in the ideological dispute between Moscow and Peking were not new to the CPI, which, since its inception, had been arguing along the same lines while deciding on the correct policy to follow in India. The Indian communists were divided, in essence, between those who believed in forging a broad front of many classes, including portions of the bourgeoisie, in order to fight foreign imperialism and internal reaction within the framework of the Indian constitution and parliamentary democracy, on the one hand ; and, on the other, those who encouraged mass struggle against the legal, political, and social order in India and condemned collaboration with its ruling classes. The CPI finally split formally in April 1964 when the latter, more leftist group formed the Communist Party Marxist (CPM). The influence of both parties was particularly dangerous in eastern India, where, after 1960, the Chinese actively tried to alienate the population from the Indian government. The government charged some members of the CPM with having extra-national loyalties and arrested them under the Defence of India Rules in 1964-1965.[58] Needless to say the Chinese government castigated both the Indian government and the right-wing group of the CPI. The two parties contested the 1967 elections separately but joined to form coalition governments in West Bengal and Kerala. Their differences continued, however, and even more leftist splinter groups were spawned, reflecting the increasing disharmony in the communist world during the 1960's.

The Chinese invasion of India in the autumn of 1962 was partly an attempt to challenge the Soviet thesis that India was genuinely nonaligned and that peaceful coexistence with it was possible, and to put Soviet neutrality in the Sino-Indian dispute to a severe test. At that time the USSR was preoccupied with a grim confrontation with the US over Cuba ; solidarity within the socialist camp must have appeared particularly desirable ; Soviet newspapers at first ignored hostilities on the Indo-China border. On October 25 *Pravda* broke the silence to comment on the conflict between India and China which by then had brought Western assistance as well as sympathy to India ; the Chinese had proposed a cease-fire, which India had rejected. The *Pravda* editorial, reflecting the official Soviet position, was not well received in India. It praised the Chinese cease-fire proposals and urged India to accept them appreciatively, advised the CPI not to be chauvinistic, criticized Western aid to India, and denounced the McMahon Line. In the UN as well as by letter, the Soviet government urged India to yield to Chinese terms.

The Russian government did not, however, condemn India. It found itself in a position of failing to placate China while risking the loss of Indian friendship, Nehru's confidence, and a reversion in New Delhi from nonalignment to complete dependence on the West.[59] This would have involved a sacrifice of "many years of difficult negotiations and patience," and "years of hard striving for Indian friendship and Indian neutrality."[60] On November 5 *Pravda* demonstrated a shift back to neutrality by calling for a cease-fire without endorsing the Chinese proposals and by praising India as "peaceful." More significantly, Soviet newspapers started printing important Chinese and Indian communications or speeches side by side, without comment.[61] On December 12, Khrushchev made a lengthy speech on foreign policy before the Supreme Soviet, in which he reiterated the Soviet stand of September 1959 and indirectly charged the Chinese of "adventurism," which could endanger the whole socialist movement. He questioned the Chinese justifications for their military advance into India and added that, "we also absolutely disavow the thought that India wanted to start a war with China."[62]

The Chinese responded quickly with an editorial in the *People's Daily* on December 15 and a long, confidential memorandum circulated to all socialist countries in late December, containing 21 pages on India. Besides explaining their attack on India, the Chinese accused the Soviet Union of wrongly interpreting the disposition of the Nehru government as neutral, when in fact it was already in league with "Indian reactionaries" and "Western imperialists." The Soviet reply to the Chinese accusations contained an almost pathetic description of the dilemma into which the Kremlin had been placed. It described India as willing to negotiate, trying to maintain neutrality and independence, and willing to accept Soviet mediation with China even though "the USSR supported China in all the preceding negotiations." It described the Soviet embarrassment when, without any consultation, its ally invaded a country to which the USSR was bound by well known treaties, and it pleaded that China knew that Russia was "supplying India with the means of self defence, which represented a tremendous victory over the United States and England." Then it added, "that same China requested from the USSR aid in the invasion which it had itself provoked." The note explained that Moscow had acted first to cut off military supplies to India, but that after deciding that "there were no grounds for not fulfilling its commitments to friendly India, it informed the Indian government that it would carry out all its treaty obligations, both civilian construction investment and military."[63]

Throughout 1963 the polemical battle between Russia and China raged, and the masks were dropped. On March 9 the *People's Daily* ushered in the first scene of the Sino-Soviet border dispute by denouncing all "unequal treaties," including those signed with Tsarist Russia. After this, the Soviet Union's interest in maintaining the friendship of India was reinforced by strategic considerations. At the end of 1964 the fall of Khrushchev—at least partly due to the rupture in relations with China—and the explosion of China's nuclear device encouraged Peking to demand the cessation of all Soviet support to the Indian government.[64] But the "revisionism" of which Khrushchev had been accused did not come to an end in Russia, nor did its basic national interest of maintaining a presence on the Indian subcontinent. The post-Khrushchev leadership continued the main lines of his foreign policy, including close relations with India.

SOVIET MILITARY SALES TO INDIA

The year, 1960, added a new dimension to the Indo-Soviet link, when New Delhi turned to Moscow for purchases of military equipment. India's effort to improve the security of its Himalayan border after 1959 led, among other things, to a search for transport aircraft and helicopters capable of operating efficiently at high altitudes. In the summer of 1960 an Indian technical delegation toured the US to supplement the procurements of transports and helicopters obtained in 1953 and 1954. But in October a mission also visited Moscow. The Indians negotiated the purchase of what was to become the bulk of India's military air transport, Ilyushin-14s and Antonov An-12 heavy air freighters, and Mi-4 Hound helicopters. Further orders in early 1962 augmented the supply.[65] From that point it was but a short step to enlist Russian assistance in the task of modernizing the Indian combat air force and navy.

The government defended this step away from India's traditional sources of military supplies by asserting its right to buy military goods anywhere it pleased in order to demonstrate its independence. However, the move to Moscow was less of a symbolic gesture than a conscious attempt to obtain Soviet underwriting for Indian defense against China. By inaugurating military shipments to India the Soviet Union seemed committed, in 1960, at least to a policy of neutrality in the Sino-Indian dispute, and events bore this out. Comments by Nehru and Krishna Menon in 1961 and 1962 revealed the political reliance that they placed on Russia's agreement to furnish equipment that would surely be used on the borders of Tibet.[66] It was significant that India decided on Soviet purchases in 1960, after its brush with China. Russian or Czechoslovakian military equipment would probably have been available in earlier years for India as it was for Egypt and Indonesia. Soviet leaders had presented Nehru with two Ilyushin II-14 commercial aircraft on his visit to Russia in 1955 and reportedly offered the 11-28 bomber at less than one-half the market price of the British Canberra, which India ultimately decided to buy in 1956.[67] In the summer of 1956 rumours started that India had received an attractive offer of the MIG fighter, and Marshal Zhukov's presence at the Republic Day celebrations in 1957 intensified public speculation on the possible transfer of Russian arms to India. However, the government denied such reports and continued to make the bulk of its military purchases in the UK ; in 1956 it negotiated for the production of the British Folland Gnat fighter plane in India under license.

India had good reasons for following the pattern of military purchases in the West. One, frequently given by Nehru, was to maintain consistency of equipment, especially in the more sophisticated items such as aircraft. Another was to avoid giving offense to London and Washington. But, on the other hand, India saw the disadvantages in excessive reliance on the UK or any single source of supply and was alert to the questions of price and of the ultimate transfer of major arms production from foreign to domestic locations. All those considerations existed in the mid-1950's, but not until 1960 did New Delhi turn towards Russia for military supplies : the new element in the equation of political concerns was of course the recently announced hostility of China.

The political controversy surrounding the Indo-Russian MIG deal lasted for many years in India and abroad. In 1956 India had embarked on the production of the HF-24 jet fighter plane at Bangalore, but in 1962 a suitable engine for it, capable of producing mach 2 speed, had not yet been found. The British engine originally planned had proved undesirable, and a switch was made to the Russian MIG-19 type engine ; in mid-1962 an agreement was reached on the production of the engine at Bangalore, modified to fit the Indian aircraft body. But reliance on the HF-24 to re-equip the air force was regarded as unwise, and New Delhi therefore aimed to purchase and then produce some world class front line aircraft. Its acquisition became more urgent when Pakistan received 12 supersonic American F-104 Starfighters in 1962 to augment its already modernized air force. The government decided to match those planes, if possible, and also to out-class Chinese MIG-19s. Ultimately, India wanted to produce a world class plane in India at a price and on terms feasible for a country short of foreign exchange.

Its preference was for the F-104, but the American government did not then, or later, consider it possible to respond favourably to India's probing in that direction, because of expected objections from Pakistan. India therefore turned to the MIG. The Soviet Union not only agreed to supply it but offered to arrange for its production in India—a step toward military self-sufficiency which New Delhi found very tempting. On June 13, 1962, Nehru told the press about the more attractive features of the MIG, mentioning the possibility of manufacturing it in India, but said that no formal negotiations had taken place.[68] The Indian air force was still in the stage of evaluating performances of various aircraft and had sent missions to the US, France, and the UK. The British and American governments were anxious to forestall Indian purchases of Russian jets and made attempts to persuade New Delhi to buy British Lightnings instead. India's vacillation before deciding finally on the MIG may have been partly due to the sincerity with which it examined other possibilities, and partly to a hope that the US and the UK would make an attractive enough offer to meet India's terms, and thus outbid the Russian offer. Efforts to obtain an Anglo-American counter-offer may have precluded India's pursuing more seriously the purchase of aircraft from France.

In August 1962 Menon finally told parliament that an agreement in principle had been reached with the Soviet Union to purchase two squadrons of MIG-21s. In October India and the USSR signed an agreement on the purchase and subsequent manufacture of that aircraft in India. The Chinese invasion delayed the arrival of the MIGs, but plans for their production proceeded in 1963, when Nasik was chosen as the site for the air-frame factory and Koraput, Orissa, as the engine plant. In October 1963 the new defense minister, Chavan, announced that air-to-air missiles and radar equipment complementary to the MIGs would be manufactured at Hyderabad. In the spring of 1964 six MIGs arrived in

India, and a detailed agreement on the establishment of the factories to produce them in India was reached on the eve of President Radhakrishnan's visit to the Soviet Union in September. After delays of a political and technical nature lasting for several years India announced in the spring of 1968 that MIG assembly from imported components had begun at Nasik.[69] At the Republic Day parade of that year Premier Kosygin and President Tito witnessed the fly-past of MIG-21s and the display for the first time of a surface-to-air missile also procured from the Soviet Union. The parade also featured a Soviet light tank purchased for the army under an agreement of September 1964.

India did not devote the same attention to its navy as to the army and air force. Modest attempts were made to broaden the capabilities of the navy by adding new types of vessels while continuing to replace obsolete units. India turned to the UK and the US for assistance, but Western assessments of India's naval needs fell short of Indian demands, particularly on the matter of new types of vessels. Not for the first time, the Soviet Union moved to fill the gap. In 1965 India accepted a Soviet offer of frigates and concluded an agreement on the provision of submarines.[70] Early in 1968 the first of three Russian conventional submarines was reported enroute to India manned by an Indian crew trained in the Soviet Union. With the expected withdrawal of Britain from the Indian Ocean by 1971, India could look forward to an interest in that sea by Russia that would be unprecedented in modern history. In February 1968 Indo-Russian discussions on a possible joint survey of the Indian Ocean took place in New Delhi ; in March a Soviet cruiser accompanied by two destroyers paid a visit to Madras.

The importance of India's military purchases from the Soviet Union could not be gauged solely by quantity—although Russian equipment made up a significant share of imported military goods by the later 1960's—but by their nature and timing. Soviet military sales were made against deferred payments in rupees, which amounted to a substantial kind of Russian military assistance. India found it possible to accept such aid not only because wars with China and Pakistan gave defense a higher priority than it had hitherto enjoyed, but also because Russia did not demand a military alliance with India or formal assurances from New Delhi restricting the deployment of the transferred equipment. (This was in contrast

to US strictures on the use of its military aid provided after 1962.)
The bulk of Soviet military supply flowed into India after the Sino-
Indian conflict of 1962. While a cause of severe displeasure in
Peking, it was naturally a source of satisfaction in New Delhi,
because of the Russian political commitment that it signified.

THE DEEPENING RUSSIAN INVOLVEMENT
IN SOUTHERN ASIA

One of the most conspicuous results of Soviet policy after 1954
was that, for the first time in history, Russian presence was felt
in south and southeast Asia. India was the keystone in Russia's
policy of extending its influence into non-communist Asia, and New
Delhi regarded the novel Russian moves as beneficial rather than
malign. Particularly after the Cominform was disbanded in 1956
India was anxious to draw the Soviet Union into the broad grouping
of Asian and African states because of the anticipated value of
Russian support. It put forward that idea before the Bandung
conference in 1955 but abandoned it in the face of opposition. A
more determined effort was made to invite the Soviet Union to the
second Afro-Asian conference projected for 1965 in Algiers. At the
preparatory meeting in Jakarta in April 1964 Foreign Minister
Swaran Singh reasoned in favour of Soviet participation as a full
member— along with Mongolia and the two Koreas, other "errors
of omission" made in 1955—citing, first, Russia's geographic location and, second, "its interest and concern in the problems and
tribulations of Afro-Asian countries . . . [and its] notable role in
assisting the freedom movements in Asia and Africa."[71]

The foreign minister pressed the point of recognizing the USSR's
constant support for Afro-Asian causes, in and outside the UN,
during his tour of African states in June 1965, and he and other
Indian officials held that the majority of Afro-Asian states favoured
Soviet presence at the proposed Algiers meeting. But those opposing
Soviet participation also had a strong following, and the controversy partly explained the collapse of the conference. India's most
important reason for urging an invitation for Russia may well
have been to obtain its balancing weight to counter the anti-Indian
line-up of China, Pakistan, and Indonesia. It was doubtful that the
full implications of including a great power as an intimate member

of the Afro-Asian grouping, where the accent on nonalignment was almost as strong as on anti-colonialism, had been fully worked out in New Delhi.

In 1965 India discovered that its policy of encouraging the Soviet presence in Asia did not always rebound to its own short-term advantage. Since 1958-1959 important changes had occurred in the alignment of that quadrilateral of powers, the USSR, China, India and Pakistan ; the simple equations valid earlier no longer applied once China's apparent friendship for India had disappeared. Pakistan's new diplomatic manoeuvrability was synchronized with the changing temperature of Sino-Indian relations, and by the end of 1962 a Pakistani-Chinese rapprochement was progressing rapidly. It soon took the form of major Chinese arms deliveries to Pakistan, which troubled Moscow almost as much as they did New Delhi. The Soviet response was to assume a friendlier stance towards Pakistan so as to prevent too close a relationship with China. This approach was facilitated by the increasing criticism of the US emanating from Rawalpindi ; the Soviet quarrel with Pakistan was based on the latter's alliance with the US, and as early as 1955 Bulganin and Khrushchev had indicated Russia's desire to have a similar relationship with Pakistan as with Afghanistan and India.[72] During the 1960's the USSR succeeded in improving its relations with three states on its southern border, all allies of the US—Turkey, Iran, and Pakistan. In April 1965 President Ayub visited Moscow for the first time and was favourably received, and in April 1968 Premier Kosygin made his first visit to Pakistan, as a climax to many years of cautious approaches.

The Soviet stake in India was too great to be jeopardized by indiscreet gestures towards Pakistan. Soviet leaders assured India that "when, the Soviet Union is trying to improve its relations with a third country, this doesn't have to be at the cost of Soviet Indian friendship."[73] The Indian government also kept telling the public that no loss was incurred by India through Soviet interest in Pakistan. Nevertheless, Indian anxiety grew when the Soviet Union seemed to lose interest in reiterating its earlier ringing statements on Kashmir being a part of India, and when it started supplying military equipment, as well as economic assistance, to Pakistan. Moscow tried to combine a sensitivity for Pakistani susceptibilities in public communiques with a private re-endorsement of support for the

Indian case on Kashmir ; it did so by blaming the aggravation of that problem on the West. Pakistan's hope of reversing the Soviet stand on Kashmir was unfulfilled in 1968, however, Ayub did succeed in obtaining Soviet neutrality during the Kutch episode in the summer of 1965.

Shortly thereafter, Pakistan's attempted *tour de force* in Kashmir resulted in a war towards which both the USSR and the US adopted a neutral position. Soviet diplomacy during and after the second Kashmir war revealed new facets of its policy in southern Asia. Russia joined with the US in efforts to bring about a cease-fire through the Security Council and in direct diplomacy in New Delhi and Rawalpindi. This was in keeping with the general Soviet line of discouraging local wars. More directly, however, it was the result of Soviet apprehension about the influence that China might gain on the subcontinent by prolongation of the hostilities. The Soviet government expressed its condemnation of "certain forces seeking to profit by the worsened Indo-Pakistani relations and trying to push the two countries towards the further aggravation of the military conflict. . . . by their incendiary statements." And again, "No government has the right to add fuel to the flames."[74]

Secondly, Soviet leaders tried to bring about a detente between India and Pakistan so that the subcontinent could be a stable entity and both sides could concentrate on economic development. As *Pravda* expressed it, "the strengthening of ties between the USSR and Pakistan should be viewed as a part of a general policy which is directed towards securing peace in Asia and the whole world. We would like Soviet-Pakistan relations, like our traditional friendship with India, to become a stabilizing factor for the situation in Asia and facilitate the normalization of relations between India and Pakistan."[75] Soviet diplomacy was sufficiently persuasive for the Indian prime minister to respond favourably to Kosygin's offer of good offices and the site of Tashkhent to facilitate direct talks between the two warring countries.

In any ultimate analysis, Soviet policy appeared to aim at enhancing its own influence on the subcontinent. In this it was successful. Though the US and the USSR held similar views, publicly, on the disastrous effects of conflict between India and Pakistan, and though both brought pressure to bear for a cease-fire, the prestige of the US was badly damaged in both New Delhi and Rawalpindi

29

by its stand on the war, whereas that of the USSR improved. The Tashkhent Declaration marked a triumph of Soviet diplomacy. Though unpopular in many Indian circles, the signing of the Declaration further testified to the influence that Russia had by that time acquired in New Delhi.

The central core of the Indo-Soviet link was the coincidence of some of their national interests ; at no point did the vital interests of India and the Soviet Union clash. Above all other binding ties were their trade relations, and Soviet economic and military aid to India. The cooperation between the two countries in the industrial field was impressive, and India's economic success or failure would also affect the USSR. And at the end, as it had been in the beginning of the friendship, there remained Soviet support for Indian nonalignment. That posture seemed to have lost its perquisites when the global confrontation appeared to become one of the "have" and "have-not" countries rather than of the West and the socialist states ; and India was ranged against both great powers on issues of international economic arrangements or a nuclear non-proliferation treaty. But the Russians kept praising India's nonalignment as an expression of its commitment to peace, and India clung verbally to that creation of Nehru. As Prime Minister Sastri said in Moscow, epitomizing the case, "we are firmly convinced that the policy of nonalignment and peaceful coexistence is the best means of preserving our independence and sovereignty. . . . It is no exaggeration for me to say that our ability to pursue this policy has to a large extent been due to the understanding and support which your Government has extended to this policy."[76] Mrs. Gandhi publicly repeated this sentiment and maintained close contacts with Soviet leaders.

NOTES AND REFERENCES

[1] Notably, direct state investment in the means of production, preference for heavy industry over light and consumer-goods industries, increased scope for the public sector, a preference for capital-intensive processes over labour-intensive ones in new industries, a large total outlay as compared with the first plan, all encompassed within the belief that the government could most effectively mobilize the untapped resources of the country.

[2] The Industrial Policy Resolution of 1956 declared the expansion of the public sector, both absolutely and relatively to the private sector, essential and enumera-

ted categories of industries with the intention that "all industries of basic and strategic importance, or in the nature of public utility services, should be in the public sector."

[3] See "Ten Years of Soviet Indian Economic Cooperation," *News and Views from the Soviet Union* (USSR Embassy, New Delhi), vol. XXIV, no. 8 (Feb. 2, 1965).

[4] *External Assistance, 1965-66*, appendix II.

[5] Reserve Bank of India, *India's Balance of Payments, 1948-49 to 1961-62*, Bombay 1963, p. 43.

[6] See Joseph Berliner, *Soviet Economic Aid*, New York 1958, pp. 152-57, for a discussion on "aid with no questions asked."

[7] See Sudhir Ghose, *Gandhi's Emissary*, London 1967, pp. 284-87, for a private assessment based on observation of the differences between the American and Soviet methods of training Indian steel engineers, the latter being judged more effective for Indian needs.

[8] "Ten Years of Soviet Indian Economic Cooperation," *op. cit.*

[9] See Mathew Kust, *Foreign Enterprise in India, Laws and Policies*, Chapel Hill 1964, p. 50, for a discussion of the advantages and disadvantages of such an arrangement.

[10] *FAR*, vol. IV, 11 (Nov. 1958) : texts of trading agreements between India and the USSR, Poland, and the German Democratic Republic.

[11] See statement of India's deputy minister for commerce in the *Indian Express*, April 5, 1968. Also see Manmohan Singh, *India's Export Trends*, Oxford 1964, p. 254, table XI.I, "India's Exports to Eastern Europe 1955-60."

[12] *Indian Express, ibid.* ; India's exports to eastern Europe in 1966 amounted to rupees 157 crores out of a total of rupees 810 crores.

[13] See Milton Kovner, "Soviet Aid and Trade," *Current History*, Oct. 1967, for a discussion of the USSR's expanding trade with the underdeveloped countries as a group.

[14] See "Ten Years of Soviet Indian Economic Cooperation," *op. cit.*, p. 27, for a list of Soviet imports from India between 1959 and 1964.

[15] See text of agreement between Air India International and Aeroflot in *FAR*, vol. IV, 6 (June 1958).

[16] See D. K. Rangnekar, "Economic Cooperation," in *Seminar*, no. 73 (Sept. 1965). The author alleged : "The impression seems to have been created that we approach the Soviet Union only when our western friends rebuff us," thus leading to the "unfortunate tendency in certain quarters in Delhi to treat the Soviet Union as the 'rescuer of the last resort'." (p. 35).

[17] See L. A. Gordon and L. A. Friedman, "Peculiarities in the Composition and Structure of the Working Class in the Economically Underdeveloped Countries of Asia and Africa," in T. P. Thornton, ed., *The Third World in Soviet Perspective*, Princeton 1964, p. 187.

[18] See Surjit Mansingh, "India and the Hungarian Revolution," *India Quarterly* vol. XXI, 2 (April-June 1965).

[19] The difference in approach lay also in Nehru's understanding of colonialism, which he regarded as mainly a phenomenon of European political expansion into

Asia and Africa. Speaking at the Bandung conference on a proposal to condemn "other forms of colonialism," namely Soviet, he said, "Speaking technically, however much we may oppose what has happened to countries in Eastern Europe and elsewhere, it is not colonialism. . . . the use of the word is incorrect. . . . the United Nations recognizes these countries as sovereign, independent countries. . . ." *Asian African Conference : Speeches of the Prime Minister of India in the Closed Sessions*, New Delhi 1955, pp. 2-3.

20 *LSD*, vol. IX, Nov. 20, 1956, col. 572.

21 *Pravda*, Oct. 31, 1956 ; quoted in Melvin J. Laski, ed., *The Hungarian Revolution*, London 1957, p. 146.

22 Quoted in the *Congress Bulletin*, no. 11 Nov. 1956, p. 561.

23 K. P. S. Menon, *The Flying Troika*, London 1963, p. 171f.

24 Nehru, speech to the AICC, Nov. 9, 1956 ; see *Hindustan Times*, Nov. 10, 1956.

25 During the Lok Sabha debates on Nov. 19 and 20 Menon was attacked as not correctly representing India on the Hungarian question. Nehru replied, "I should like to make it perfectly clear that there is complete unison of thinking and action in the Government of India and our representatives." *LSD*, vol. IX, Nov. 20, 1956, col. 589.

26 Nehru, speech in Rajya Sabha, Dec. 13, 1956, *Speeches, 1953-57*, p. 336 : 25,000 Hungarian and 7,000 Russians, he said, were killed in the uprising.

27 *LSD*, vol. IX, Nov. 19, 1956, col. 384.

28 *GAOR*, 608th Plenary Meeting, Dec. 4, 1956, p. 522. Secretary-General U Thant visited Budapest in 1963 after the Hungarian question had been removed from the agenda of the General Assembly.

29 Lok Sabha, Nov. 20, 1956, *India's Foreign Policy*, pp. 581-82.

30 Lok Sabha, Nov. 19, 1956, *Speeches, 1953-57*, pp. 325-26.

31 *ibid.*, p. 330.

32 See *Foreign Policy of India : Texts of Documents, 1947-64*, pp. 276-77.

33 See Nehru's statement at a press conference, New Delhi, July 3, 1958, *India's Foreign Policy*, p. 563.

34 Rajya Sabha statement Dec. 13, 1956, *Speeches, 1953-57*, p. 338.

35 India's severest criticism of NATO was for its indirect involvement in the anti-nationalist actions of France and Portugal in Algeria, Goa, and Portuguese Africa, and of the Warsaw Pact at the time of Hungarian revolution in 1956.

36 From the first and third India-Germany joint communiques, *Foreign Policy of India : Texts of Documents, 1947-1964*, pp. 306, 310.

37 *RSD*, vol. XXXV, Aug. 23, 1961, col. 1140.

38 *LSD*, vol. LVI, Aug. 17, 1961, col. 2784.

39 See K. P. Misra, *India's Policy of Recognition of States and Governments*, Bombay 1966, p. 89.

40 *RSD, op. cit.*, col. 1374.

41 See Arthur Schlesinger, Jr., *A Thousand Days*, London 1965, pp. 356-62, for an account of the careful response made by the US administration to the closing of the East German border on and after Aug. 13, 1961, in contrast to the reaction of the American press.

[42] *RSD*, *op. cit.*, col. 1378.

[43] *LSD*, vol. LVI, Aug. 16, 1961, cols. 2407-08.

[44] *RSD*, *op. cit.*, col. 1379.

[45] *ibid.*, col. 1381.

[46] Sixth India-USSR joint communique, Moscow, Sept. 11, 1961, *Foreign Policy of India, op. cit.*, p. 506.

[47] Seventh India-USSR joint communique, Moscow, Sept. 19, 1964, *ibid.*, p. 513.

[48] Mao Tse-tung's speech in Moscow, Nov. 18, 1957. Quoted in Donald S. Zagoria, *The Sino-Soviet Conflict, 1956-61*, Princeton 1962, p. 160.

[49] See account of Teng Hsaio-ping's speech, in Edward Crankshaw, *The New Cold War : Moscow vs. Peking*, Baltimore 1963, p. 127.

[50] *Tass*, Sept. 9, 1959 ; quoted in David Floyd, *Mao Against Khrushchev*, London 1964, part II, "A Chronology of Documents and Significant Events," pp. 261-62.

[51] See Crankshaw, *op. cit.*, pp. 90-91.

[52] Fourth India-USSR joint communique, New Delhi, Feb. 6, 1960, *Foreign Policy of India, op. cit.*, p. 498.

[53] Lok Sabha, Feb. 22, 1960, *FAR*, vol. VI, 2 (Feb. 1960), p. 42.

[54] Fifth India-USSR joint communique, New Delhi, Feb. 16, 1960, *Foreign Policy of India, op. cit.*, p. 503.

[55] See Zagoria, *op. cit.*, pp. 335, 344.

[56] See Crankshaw, *op. cit.*, p. 108.

[57] See *ibid.*, pp. 122-35, for an account of the Moscow conference.

[58] See India, Home Ministry, "Anti-National Activities of Pro-Peking Communists."

[59] A Soviet official in Calcutta, speaking to the crew of a Russian tanker on Nov. 24, 1962, reportedly "stated that due to the Sino-Indian war the Indian Government . . . was at the beck and call of the Americans." Hearing this, seaman V. S. Tarasov sought asylum on board a nearby American ship and achieved wide publicity. Subsequently he stood trial on fabricated charges of theft, of which a New Delhi court pronounced him innocent. No cause being found for his extradition to the USSR he left India a free man. See C. L. Sareen, *USSR vs Tarasov : A Test of Indian Justice*, New Delhi 1964, p. 151.

[60] Confidential letter from the CPSU to all socialist countries, late Jan. 1963 ; quoted in Floyd, *op. cit.*, p. 366.

[61] See R. Vaidyanath, "The Reactions of the Soviet Union and other Communist States," *International Studies*, vol. V, I & 2 (July-Oct. 1963), pp. 70-74.

[62] Quoted in Floyd, *op. cit.*, p. 331.

[63] Confidential letter of the CPSU, *op. cit.*, pp. 366-67.

[64] See Harry Hanak, "Soviet Foreign Policy Since Khrushchev," *The Year Book of World Affairs, 1966*, London 1966, p. 51.

[65] Lorne J. Kavic, *India's Quest for Security : Defense Policies, 1947-1965*, Berkeley 1967, p. 105.

[66] Menon was reported to have said that the Soviet Union had indicated its

unwillingness to support China by providing defense equipment to be used against China ; had it been the Soviet intention, he said, to "support China or ... weaken us in this dispute it could have refused to sell the equipment to us," *Asian Recorder*, 1961, p. 3865.

[67] See Kavic, *op. cit.*, p. 104.

[68] Nehru, *Press Conferences, 1962*, pp. 29-34.

[69] The *Hindu*, April 28, 1968.

[70] See Kavic, *op. cit.*, p. 201 ; and Chavan's statement, in *LSD*, vol. XLV, Sept. 6, 1965, col. 3877.

[71] *FAR*, vol. X, 4 (April 1964), p. 123.

[72] Bulganin reported to the Supreme Soviet on Dec. 29, 1955 that "the Soviet Union would like to have no less friendly relations with Pakistan than it has with India, Burma and Afghanistan, and it is not our fault that this is so far not the case. However, the Soviet government has endeavoured, and will continue to do so, to improve our relations with Pakistan." Bulganin and Khrushchev, *Visit of Friendship to India, Burma and Afghanistan*, Moscow 1956, p. 249.

[73] Kosygin's speech during Sastri's visit to the USSR, May 1965 ; quoted by R. Vaidyanath, "Some Recent Trends in Soviet Policies Towards India and Pakistan," *International Studies, vol. VII*, 3 (Jan. 1966), p. 438.

[74] *Tass*, statements of September 8 and 13, 1965 ; quoted *ibid.*, p. 440.

[75] *Pravda*, Aug. 24, 1965 ; quoted *ibid.*, p. 434.

[76] On March 12, 1965, *Speeches of Lal Bahadur Sastri*, p. 119.

CHAPTER XVII

THE CONFRONTATION WITH CHINA

THE ULTIMATE ADVANTAGE for India in its growing collaboration with the Soviet Union by the 1960's was the support it received from Russia in its efforts to contain Chinese power. The coincidence of strategic interests between India and the Soviet Union, once the ideological barriers were overcome, seemed in New Delhi to constitute a major foundation of its foreign policies, comparable to the economic aid relationships established with foreign states. Of course, Indian and American interests also coincided with respect to the containment of China. But so long as the US was tied to its military and political commitment to Pakistan and was pursuing policies in other parts of Asia which India could not accept, a joining of Indian and Russian strategic interests appeared to be a more fructuous relationship than one which theoretically might have been established with the US.

The year 1959 marks the beginning of the Indo-Chinese confrontation. It forced the New Delhi government into closer collaboration with foreign states than was thought possible or necessary in earlier years, when nonalignment had been premised, in part, on a high degree of military security for the country. The earliest serious Indo-Chinese conflict, as noted in chapter VII, did not concern the alignment of the frontiers, but centred on Tibet, where Indian and Chinese interests had been in opposition for at least one-half century. In 1959 as well, the conflict emerged as the result of internal Tibetan events over which neither India nor China had great control.

In March of that year the localized fighting between Tibetans (chiefly Khampas) and Chinese spread to the Tibetan capital and rapidly into the regions between Lhasa and the Indian and Nepalese borders. The fiction of the Tibetan government's cooperation with the Chinese in suppressing provincial disturbances could no longer hold, as the people of Lhasa, reinforced by refugee Khampas, demonstrated against the occupying Chinese officials and troops, and the Dalai Lama fled his capital. Prime Minister Nehru, with almost an identical caution to that displayed during the early stages of the Hungarian uprising, at first refused to acknowledge that the Tibetan fighting was large-scale and faced a very critical Lok Sabha on March 23 with the remark that India had no intention of inter-fering in the internal affairs of China "with whom we have friendly relations." One week later, however, on the eve of the Dalai Lama's entry into India, through Towang in the North East Frontier Agency (NEFA), Nehru altered his views and told the legislature that his government would not limit discussion on Tibet and that although he wished to retain "friendly" relations with China "our sympathies go out very much to the Tibetans."[1] The next month in a major speech on the Tibetan fighting Nehru called it the result of a "nation-alist upsurge."[2] The Dalai Lama was welcomed to India, although he was not allowed to establish a government in exile there. His entourage and subsequently 20,000 refugees (in 1959 alone ; by 1962, about 30,000) were also given sanctuary, and thereby the terms of political confrontation between two opposing systems across the Himalayas were fully defined.

China explained the hostile confrontation by stating that the "reactionary" upsurge in Tibet had its "base" in India, at Kalimpong, where "American and Chiang Kai-Shek clique special agents, Tibetan reactionaries and local special agents" were operating to "attain the traitorous aim of separating the Tibetan region from the People's Republic of China."[3] Indian denials about Kalimpong's role in the rebellion were issued, as expected ; Nehru's chagrin when dealing with Chinese charges in parliament was patently sincere.[4] The Chinese, however, had launched a major propaganda campaign, during which official statements had minor value. New Delhi found itself having to face an increasingly elaborate exposition of Indian "expansionism" backed by Western "imperialism" which accounted not only for Chinese troubles in Tibet but also for the Himalayan border dispute. The Chinese and Tibetan presses described the "plot" to "abduct" the Dalai Lama, instigated by enemies of China in India and elsewhere. (India's offer to allow the Dalai Lama to be interviewed by the Chinese ambassador, or anyone else appointed by Peking, in order to judge whether or not the Tibetan leader was

THE CONFRONTATION WITH CHINA 457

"under duress" was unavailing.) By permitting "anti-Chinese" forces to operate in India Nehru's government had allegedly violated the spirit of the *panchasheel* accord.

The deprecating analysis of Indian political leadership current in the Soviet and Chinese communist writings in the early 1950's again appeared, describing the Indian government as a "bourgeois" regime which maintained links with "imperialist Western circles" seeking to control the Indian economy and political system under the fabricated guise of aiding an independent national state.[5] According to this analysis, there was a fundamental conflict between the "progressive" forces on the ascendancy in China and Tibet and the "reactionary" system in India, which would ultimately be resolved only by the revolutionary installation of a "socialist" government, led by the proletariat, in India. The fighting in Tibet was a phase of that conflict.

THE INTERLOCKING BORDER DISPUTE

Interlocked with the Chinese explanations of the political and military situation in the Himalayan region was the Peking government's exposition of the Indo-Chinese border dispute. The Indian government's attention from 1954 had been directed to the so-called middle sector of the Indo-Tibetan frontier, but by 1957 a far more spectacular event was taking place in the far reaches of Ladakh, a province of Kashmir between Sinkiang and Tibet. It was an area which Indian patrols seldom visited and only a handful of explorers had tried to map. In 1957 the Chinese successfully completed a road linking Yarkand in Sinkiang with Gartok in Tibet. Indicative of India's administrative ineffectiveness in this area was the fact that an Indian reconnaissance party apparently first discovered the road's location in the autumn of 1958, although work on it must have been going on for several years prior to September 1957, when the Chinese announced its completion. The road, which followed an old caravan track, became China's most secure route into Tibet, because it circumvented the hostile tribal areas ; possession of it was of crucial importance to Peking. New Delhi sent a mildly worded "Informal Note" to the Chinese ambassador which mentioned, among other things, that no visas had been obtained by Chinese workers engaged in road building—a petty complaint in view of the magnitude of the Chinese movement into Indian-claimed Ladakh.

In the summer of 1959 an Indian police party was captured by "a Chinese armed detachment" in eastern Ladakh and later released after having discovered a Chinese camp at Spanggur. Nehru in a comprehensive letter to Chou En-lai of September 26, 1959, stated that the Chinese intrusions in the Spanggur area were "particularly marked. . . . Chinese forces have been pushing forward in an aggressive manner during the last year or two in disregard of the traditional frontier. The Chinese have only recently established a new camp near the western extremity of the Spanggur lake at a point which even according to some official Chinese maps is in Indian territory."[6] About one hundred miles north of this Chinese camp, near the Kongka pass, a military engagement on October 21 resulted in the loss of nine or ten Indian lives and capture by the Chinese of ten other Indians, all part of a border patrol well within Indian-claimed territory. That clash, by far the most serious reported to date, appeared likely to compel New Delhi to take the forceful defensive measures that had been considered but then postponed to allow for a political settlement.

For several months preceding the Kongka incident serious Indian-Chinese clashes were also taking place at the other extremity of the international boundary, in NEFA, where Indian administration had only begun to penetrate in the 1950's.[7] In 1957 and 1958 Chinese parties were spotted passing through NEFA, but those violations were not considered critical. After the Tibetan revolt in the spring of 1959 Chinese troops rushed into southwestern Tibet and by the summer of 1959 appeared for the first time in large numbers along the McMahon Line, defining the NEFA-Tibet boundary. They were probably endeavouring to seal off the escape routes into India, and clashes with Indian outposts followed. The Indian ambassador in Peking protested on August 28, 1959, against a successful Chinese attack on Longju, a checkpoint four miles inside the Subansiri frontier division of NEFA, which India had established to handle refugees from Tibet. The ambassador termed the attack, in which three or four Indian troops were reported missing, "a case of deliberate aggression on Indian territory."[8] Nehru on the same day related the Longju attack to an angry Indian parliament and announced that the entire border area of NEFA would be guarded henceforth by the regular Indian Army, in place of the Assam Rifles. "There is no alternative for us but to defend our country's borders and integrity," he said.[9] At the same time he revealed that another Chinese attack had occurred earlier in August in the Kameng Frontier Division of NEFA, in which about 200 Chinese literally pushed a dozen or so Indian policemen back from the frontier at Khinzemane. The Indians later returned to the border and stood fast even when the Chinese ordered them to lower the Indian flag.

In 1959 the limited border issues and related military clashes between the two countries were finally revealed as parts of the broader framework of the political conflict between China and India, ideologically based and extending geographically beyond the Himalayas. The Tibetan revolt had precipitated the Chinese government's acknowledgement of its basic hostility towards India and its interpretation of the frontier problem in terms of that hostility. The Chinese-Indian frontier zone, according to Peking's view, marked an area where Chinese security interests clashed with the aims of Indian "expansionism" backed by Western "imperialism." The Indian government began slowly to readjust itself to those newly-defined terms of reference—despite occasional hints of disbelief by the prime minister that the Chinese intemperance was anything more than a negotiating posture.

Apart from justifying the immediate steps taken to gain control over Tibet the Chinese government's analysis of the frontier problem also explained its claims below the Himalayan watershed in NEFA and in Ladakh. According to that argument, imperialists, working through Indian expansionist circles, not only presented a current threat to Chinese integrity but also had encroached on Chinese territory in the past ; India now upheld the historic imperialist claim to NEFA and Ladakh, as well as to a sphere of influence in Sikkim, Bhutan, and Nepal. Almost the entire Indo-Chinese border therefore, required rectification in order to offset the effects of "prolonged imperialist aggression."[10] The first complete statement of the Chinese claims on the frontier appeared in Chou En-lai's letter to Nehru of September 8, 1959, although a fair warning of the Chinese stand was delivered in an earlier letter, of January 23, 1959, in which Chou explained that he had not made clear the complete Chinese claims any sooner because "conditions were not ripe for settlement." The September letter reviewed the history of British expansion into the Himalayas and explained that "this constitutes the fundamental reason for the long term disputes over and non-settlement of the Sino-Indian boundary question."[11] The claim then amounted to about 40,000 square miles of territory over which India's recent maps showed clear sovereignty; later Chinese claims totalled over 45,000 square miles.

It was difficult for the Indian government, and agonizing for the prime minister, to try to reformulate the border dispute on the postulate of China's fundamental hostility toward India and its announced ambitions of reincorporating territories allegedly taken from China by "imperialists." Had the Chinese attempts at forceful settlement been foreseen by those in positions of high authority in New Delhi, some compromises by India might have been proposed before 1959 in order to obtain Chinese agreement on a border delineation. After tensions grew and force had been used against India, a compromise solution might still have been desirable, but for any Indian government was politically less feasible than before. Indeed, there had been earlier hints of the ultimately militant Chinese stand, but Nehru could legitimately argue, up to 1959, that China would probably settle the border disputes without resorting to large-scale military force and on the basis of negotiation and possible compromises. After 1959 the hope that China would refrain from using force to obtain its objectives was often expressed by government spokesmen, but that hope was not realistically based, as a growing number of Indian politicians, publicists, and certain officials in the External Affairs Ministry were asserting. India's objective of containing Chinese power within Tibet could no longer be pursued by the non-military methods followed earlier.

Nevertheless, from 1959 to 1962 the Indian government assumed the classic position of the militarily unprepared democratic state which looks upon its own military build up as possibly disruptive of the peace and capable of being misconstrued by others, while it regards military preparations and propaganda by other states as capable of being appeased.

Although the Indian government did not publicize its anxiety about the border until August 1959, when Nehru could no longer conceal the growing conflict from Parliament,[12] there had been some concern in the External Affairs Ministry as early as 1950, when the Chinese moved into Tibet. K. M. Panikkar, the ambassador to

China, had raised the issue with Peking in September 1951 ; and on other occasions, such as during the negotiations on the 1954 agreement, Indian diplomats had provided openings for the Chinese to raise the question of the border alignment. Peking had given assurances that no border problems existed between the two countries.[13] The Indian government had decided that it should not press the issue or invite discussion with the Chinese on boundary delineation, but rather publicize the Indian position on the boundary and trust that the "lapse of time and events will confirm it, and by the time perhaps, when the challenge to it came, we would be in a much stronger position to face it."[14] Indian anxiety about the border increased after the signing of the 1954 agreement because of the recurrence of border incidents involving small Indian and Chinese patrols and because the Peking government persisted in circulating maps which showed nearly all of NEFA, small pockets on the Indo-Chinese boundary between Nepal and Kashmir, and the entire eastern bulge of Ladakh as parts of China.

In the autumn of 1959, following the efforts to suppress the Tibetan revolt, the Indo-Chinese border clashes rapidly became a succession of major incidents, in which Indians were fired on and killed while attempting to challenge Chinese control over strategic points along the entire frontier. The Chinese resort to force against the Indians could not be explained entirely as an aspect of subduing the rebels and, in view of the manifest desire of India to settle the border controversy peacefully, must have followed a decision by Peking to achieve its aims through force. Nehru believed that the Chinese moves were the result of a gradual shift in Chinese policy finally culminating in clear-cut aggression. When the Indian government revealed the full extent of the growing controversy with Peking, by publishing its first White Paper in September 1959, Nehru's leadership in foreign affairs was being challenged, and confidence in his China policy declined steadily for the next five years. The Indian public's outrage over the Chinese moves on the frontier and in Tibet stiffened Nehru's stand on all aspects of the border dispute, as the Chinese government might have anticipated. But despite its preparations for frontier defense it was chiefly with words and diplomatic manoeuvres, rather than with military preparations, that the government sought to contain Chinese advances.

India's verbal defense of its border advanced at a faster pace than the course of events on the frontier. No further shooting incidents were reported until 1962. However, the number of communications exchanged between the two governments swelled to a point at which even a contemporary historian starved for valid material suspects that he has too much of it. India's diplomatic strategy supplemented its verbal defense against China. For the first time, in 1959, the Indian government became consciously aware of the advantages of great power support for its defense policy. India could rely on the American government in a struggle with China : President Eisenhower's visit to India in December 1959 demonstrated the high degree of confidence that the US had developed toward India during the latter years of the Republican administration.[15] The British government, too, in an ultimate choice could be counted on to support India in a conflict with China, but the government in London could not be expected to support India's border delineation at the cost of economic advantages in China and a secure Hong Kong. Of possibly greater immediate value to India than support from the Western powers was the assistance that the Soviet Union could provide, and despite its military alliance with China Russia offered evidence that it would lend its weight towards a negotiated settlement of the Sino-Indian conflict.

THE 1960 TALKS : THE INTENSIFIED CONFRONTATION

The recognition of India's need for foreign support in the emerging crisis with China as well as his desire to have Chinese intentions clarified led Nehru to agree to hold talks on the frontier problem with Chou En-lai in 1960. The Chinese foreign minister had proposed discussions in November 1959, shortly after the Kongka clash, the most serious to date. During the following months of December and January Nehru declined Chou's request for a meeting, on grounds that diplomatic discussions on the disputed facts about the frontier should first be held ; his government was particularly reluctant to enter discussions while the Chinese regarded delimitation of the entire[16] border as a proper subject for negotiations. In his reluctance to hold a meeting with Chou En-lai the Indian prime minister faced a testing of the principle which he had often urged other governments to accept, that even at the depth of a crisis contending parties should be willing to hold discussions. The initial refusal to negotiate was accompanied by a thoughtful probing by Nehru of the basic postulates of his foreign policy, and uncertainty was the immediate result.[17] In the winter of 1959-1960 India's negotiating position was weak, and Nehru could not escape repeating the lesson of politics often cited by John Foster Dulles. "Negotiation," Nehru told the Lok Sabha, "always carries weight if there is strength behind it. A weak country or a weak person cannot negotiate at all."[18]

But refusal to hold talks with Chou En-lai not only reflected India's relative military and administrative weaknesses in the frontier areas but also gave an impression that the government had doubts about the validity of its own claims. Leaders and representatives of foreign governments suggested to New Delhi that its position would elicit more international support if it responded favourably to the Chinese offer and demonstrated through negotiations the superiority of its case.[19] Therefore, in order to gain outside support as well as to adhere to his own formula for seeking political settlements, Nehru invited Chou on February 5, 1960, to come to New Delhi, not for "negotiations," but for "talks."

The government's decision to invite Chou En-lai was unpopular, although the prime minister tried to alter the appearance of having changed his mind by explaining that he would "meet" the Chinese premier, not try to negotiate a final settlement. Accompanying the invitation was a lengthy note setting forth India's case, and Nehru advised Chou that he did "not see any common ground between our respective viewpoints."[20] But in any case the Indian government would have a better estimate of Chinese intentions after a meeting. "Discussions may not be fruitful and yet they may be advisable," Nehru told the press on February 24. Chou En-lai accepted Nehru's invitation at once, and the meeting took place in April 1960.

It was possible that both governments desired a peaceful settlement of the border dispute at that time. The Chinese government possibly saw no value in allowing an explosive dispute with India to continue, which could deny to China India's political support on certain issues and, moreover, might arouse the Indian people into an anti-Chinese and anti-communist crusade if it were to erupt into a major conflict. An advantage to China lay in reaching a border agreement with India, just as it had recently done with Burma and Nepal—the disputed territories involved, however, being small compared to those on the Indo-Chinese frontier.[21] Such a settlement would not inhibit Chinese political aims in the Himalayas and might in fact advance them. It was obvious that China would never willingly give up control of the Aksai Chin roads. The general Chinese proposal to India, never made public, was to exchange China's relinquishment of its claim to most of NEFA for India's abandonment of its claim to the Aksai Chin part of Ladakh.[22] As the Indian government interpreted it, this meant that China was prepared to give up a claim to one part of Indian territory, if India turned over to China another part of Indian territory already under Chinese occupation.

The Chinese offer of a trade of India's Aksai Chin claim for China's NEFA claim was rejected ; such a settlement would be regarded as appeasement by non-communist Indians, and it would have implied a weak Indian posture which China would have been likely to challenge again. Other approaches to a settlement were mooted by some Indians, for example, a trade of Indian claims in Aksai Chin for the Chumbi Valley, but the Chinese conveyed no interest in arrangements requiring their loss of territory. The only evident results from the talks between the Indian and Chinese prime ministers came in the form of an agreement for official teams to meet and examine the documents supporting the territorial claims of each side.

The boundary officials met in a series of sessions lasting from June to December 1960 and produced a large mass of documents, historical, cartographical, and administrative, selected to support one position or the other.[23] The Chinese presented their case incompletely and with a lack of skill and care that could only suggest that Peking placed very little reliance on any objective assessment of the border alignment as determined by treaties, custom, and administrative traditions.[24] Peking was apparently determined to retain or obtain control over a part of Ladakh and perhaps other areas as well regardless of its legal rights as prescribed by international law. The Indian case, on the contrary, was well documented, having been prepared by scholars of high abilities, and presented in an academically appealing manner. The essential problem faced by both the Chinese and the Indian teams was to establish that their respective sovereignties existed over territories (the Aksai Chin part of Ladakh and NEFA) which had never been under any continuous administrative control by either side until the 1950's. Neither team offered conclusive proof of its claims in all sectors of the border. But the Indian case overall was weightier and more convincing than the Chinese.[25]

The boundary teams' meetings and their reports had the effect of reinforcing India's conviction that settlement based on political compromise was by then out of the question. For a decade Nehru and other Indian leaders had endeavoured to show their support for the Chinese communist revolution and for China's interests internationally. They assumed that any dispute between the two states could only be settled by peaceful negotiation, in view of the publicized identities of interests established over many years. China's response to Indian overtures of support and sympathy rapidly disillusioned non-communist Indians, including Nehru. It was the harsh style of Chinese diplomacy toward India, the often unprovoked aggressive Chinese acts, the crude anti-Indian propaganda, and the unnecessarily rough treatment given to captured Indian patrols which struck at the pride of Indians and irritated them to the point that by 1960 they could not have approved any settlement involving an uncompensated for loss of territory.[26] The Indian public's emotional reaction against China thus placed limitations on New Delhi's diplomacy.

Nehru was aware that no settlement would come while India was weak. "In the final analysis," he told the Lok Sabha, "it comes to this, that we must build up our strength and, as I have said previously . . . this [border dispute] is not a matter which we can dispose of by a discussion." He had India's long-term objective clearly in his mind : "The basic thing is that we become a modern state, not remain in a backward condition economically and socially."[27] Nehru understood then that India's security and the peace of Asia depended upon the creation of a relationship of power between India and China such that China could not bring further areas of southern Asia under its influence. If any settlement with China in the Himalayas was possible it would come only when a more equitable balance of power was established in that region. However, for the next two years Chinese power increased more rapidly than Indian on all sectors of the frontier ; Nehru's realistic assessment that a settlement by exclusively political means was no longer

30

possible was not translated into military and administrative measures sufficient to check the Chinese moves.

In 1961 the Indian government's publication of both boundary teams' reports crystallized its legal stand and exposed the Chinese aims to the extent that no Indian concessions were henceforth likely.[28] The Indian team's report persuaded Nehru for the first time that his government had a superior claim to both NEFA and Ladakh— he had previously expressed his doubts about Ladakh—and it justified the no-compromise attitude of some External Affairs Ministry officials toward China. Issuance of the reports increased respect for India's position among friendly governments, some of which had been urging concessions to China because they were unconvinced of the strength of India's case. Nevertheless the diplomatic and legal advantages resulting from India's report could not compensate for its real military and administrative weaknesses. Given the nature of Chinese aims and methods, diplomacy and legal briefs could only postpone an ultimate confrontation of power ; certain External Affairs Ministry China specialists understood this and urged a rapid build-up of physical power to support India's legal claims and undergird its uncompromising political posture. But the tripod of diplomatic, military, and administrative supports for India's China policy had two weak legs ; in 1962 it collapsed.[29]

After the Chinese government had made clear its intentions of advancing its claims and relying on force to support them, the Indian government had no reasonable choice other than to postpone substantive negotiations while trying to improve its physical position on the frontier. Diplomatic contacts on the border issue declined over Chinese protests that India was unwilling to negotiate. The Indian frontier forces, the army and local military units, were not strengthened to a level commensurate with Chinese forces because of inadequate communications and because of unwillingness to withdraw troops from the Pakistani front. Still considerable improvements in levels of Indian military strength along the entire frontier were apparent to the Chinese. In NEFA the Indian army developed several strong points for defense at passes in the rear of the McMahon Line border and along the border itself[30] and sped up the long-overdue road building projects without which supplying of forward posts in the NEFA terrain was almost impossible.

Indian preparations in Ladakh concentrated on establishing new military posts, forty-three of which were set up by the middle of 1962. The Indians employed a new tactic of placing posts behind and between Chinese posts in Ladakh, to the great annoyance of the Peking government. Despite its comparative weakness militarily during these years, India was in fact engaged on a "forward policy" on the frontier which was intended to check Chinese advances everywhere and, if possible, force Chinese withdrawals in Ladakh. That policy was apparent to the Chinese during an incident near the Galwan river in Ladakh in July 1962. There the Indians had established a post to cut the communications of a forward Chinese garrison and were supplying it by helicopters. The post was surrounded by Chinese troops in superior numbers who, however, left a passage free hoping that the Indians would retreat. The Indians held their ground, and the Chinese finally withdrew. Peking could calculate, after the Galwan confrontation, that a major military show-down was the only means of convincing India that tactical moves or even skirmishes alone would not decide the frontier issue.

A stronger Indian diplomatic line accompanied the "forward policy" on the frontier. New Delhi refused to negotiate a renewal of the 1954 agreement with China on Indo-Tibetan trade and intercourse, and it expired in June 1962. Thus the remaining economic links between India and Tibet and the movements of persons across the border virtually came to an end. Indian trade agencies in Gyantse, Yatung, and Gartok terminated their work after years of harassment by the authorities in Tibet.

In notes to the Chinese government in the spring and summer of 1962 India made clear its determination to undermine the Chinese position in the areas of confrontation in Ladakh at the possible cost of armed clashes. Nehru explained in the Lok Sabha on August 6 that "it is very difficult for Chinese forces to advance now because of the establishment of Indian posts at various points without an actual conflict between the two."[31] In the same month he indicated in parliament that India was trying to strengthen its frontier forces so that an ultimate settlement by peaceful negotiations would be considered desirable by China. But at any time India was prepared to enter "talks" to reduce border tension and to arrange for a mutual withdrawal of forces, and such talks on reducing tensions in Ladakh were set for October 15, 1962.

THE CHINESE ATTACK AND ITS RESULTS

The increasingly vigorous political statements from New Delhi, the government's assurance that it could face Chinese military pressure without resorting to negotiations, the improvements in the capabilities of Indian frontier troops and their probing manoeuvres provided the immediate Indian setting for Chinese attacks in September and October 1962. The Chinese insisted on maintaining the military initiative in the frontier regions, proving their military superiority, and, if possible, forcing the Indians to negotiate a boundary settlement favourable to Peking. Preparations for the Chinese offensives in Ladakh and NEFA had been undertaken for several months, judging from the sustained character of the advances in October. The attacks came at the end of the Himalayan fighting season, after which no major Indian counterattacks would have been feasible.

The broader motivations of the Peking government in undertaking a risky venture hundreds of miles from the main centres of its power will remain unknown for sometime. Undoubtedly, China's deteriorating relations with the USSR was an aspect of its political calculations. A Chinese-Indian conflict would force Russia to choose whether to continue aiding nonaligned India and thus further undermine the unity of the communist states or to support China and thus give up its political aims in the subcontinent. Peking's hopes of shaking Nehru's domestic support by creating disillusionment with the effectiveness of nonalignment and forcing the Congress government to acknowledge its reliance on Western backing may have been an added benefit that it expected from precipitating a new crisis. The Russo-American confrontation over Cuba attendant upon the placement of Soviet rockets on the island may have increased Chinese confidence that the great powers could not act effectively to help India, at least for the short duration of the Chinese offensive. Assuming that Peking could anticipate the extent of its forthcoming military successes—which is doubtful—it may have wished to undermine India's prestige in Asia and Africa and lend some credence to the otherwise unsubstantiated Chinese claim that its industrial advancement was proceeding more successfully than India's.

The Chinese moves to regain the military initiative and force

India to give up its territorial claims in Ladakh began not in Ladakh, but in NEFA, where on September 8, 1962, Chinese troops moved across the Thagla Ridge and established themselves at Dhola (Che Dong), two and one-half miles south of it.[32] The Indian government issued a mild protest over the Chinese presence at Dhola, and when that had no effect moved up troops from Towang. Skirmishes followed through the middle of October, during which Indian leaders, including Prime Minister Nehru, announced that the invading troops would have to be thrown out.[33] After a month's build-up in the Thagla Ridge-Khinzemane region the Chinese invasion of NEFA began on October 20, following an initial Indian attack on the Ridge. Khinzemane and Dhola fell at once, and within a week Indian units spread out over the Kameng Frontier Division were swamped by forces superior in numbers and fire power. The Chinese also launched attacks near Longju and Walong, critical points further east in NEFA, and in Ladakh.

In contrast to all earlier fighting on the NEFA frontier, the Chinese attacks continued to press forward upon Indian defenses, which gave way more easily than the Chinese could have anticipated. The geographical span of the operations kept the Indian military off balance, but poor leadership in the Indian top ranks in NEFA appeared to turn a series of tactical setbacks into a strategic rout. Within one month Chinese forces caused the retreat of Indian troops from Towang and from the strategic Se La and Bomdi La, passes in western NEFA ; from Walong in the east ; and had eliminated the new Indian posts in Ladakh. In NEFA the Chinese were poised in the foothills overlooking the Assam valley, 150 miles from the McMahon Line.

When the Chinese capture of Towang, the important Buddhist centre, appeared imminent, Chou En-lai, on October 24, proposed a cease-fire and mutual withdrawal of forces from the current line of contact, followed by talks to settle the dispute. Acceptance of the proposal would have left India in the weak position of acknowledging the Chinese occupation of Ladakh as a basis for negotiations, and therefore Nehru refused the offer on October 27. Later he explained that the Chinese attack had "shattered any hope . . . about settling India-China differences peacefully. . . ." Their "demand" for a cease-fire, Nehru wrote to Chou, is one "to which India will never submit whatever the consequences and however long and hard the struggle may be." To submit to Chinese terms then "would mean mere existence at the mercy of an aggressive, arrogant and expansionist neighbour."[34] On October 26 the Indian government proclaimed a state of emergency and immediately sought foreign "sympathy and support" (as Nehru's letter to heads of governments on October 27 expressed it) for what might have been the beginning of a continuing war on both extensions of the frontier.

At the critical point when the Indian defenses in Assam had collapsed and China held the initiative in Ladakh, the Peking government announced, on November 20, a unilateral cease-fire and withdrawal of its forces. This clever political move marked the end of an episode in NEFA that Indian military officers called a debacle. When the facts were known, demoralization resulted within many informed circles in the country. Congress leaders had forced the defense minister, V. K. Krishna Menon, to resign on November 7, and the government later transferred senior military officers responsible for the NEFA defeat to inactive posts. One year after the invasion the new defense minister, Y. B. Chavan, informed parliament of the results of an inquiry into the Indian reverses. He exposed certain inadequacies in the training of Indian troops for mountain warfare against the Chinese and in intelligence work ; more significantly he cited poor leadership as a major cause of the disaster. The "general standard amongst the junior officers was fair," the report stated. At levels higher than the brigade "shortcomings became more apparent."[35]

Close associates of the prime minister said that he never recovered from the shock of the Chinese attack and from the unexpected weakness of Indian defenses. More important, perhaps, than the prime minister's discouragement was the loss of self-assurance among Ministry of External Affairs officials, who several years later continued to act on the belief that India's influence in world affairs had been shattered almost beyond repair because of its inability to face successfully the threat of China.[36] Whether by intention or as an unforeseen by-product of their success, the Chinese military operations undermined the prestige of India, especially in the governments of smaller Afro-Asian states, and corroded the confidence of Indians in their government and its foreign policy.

The crisis with China provided the Indian government with a

test for judging the extent of support it had from foreign powers more accurate than the issues of Goa or even Kashmir. When Nehru called upon foreign powers for support the response was disappointing among those states which had followed and benefited from the policy of nonalignment. The Indian government discovered to its dismay that nonalignment could become an instinctive reaction to any international conflict, not just one between the great powers : many nonaligned states chose to regard the Indo-Chinese struggle impartially and refrained from official comments other than the hope that both sides would work for a peaceful settlement. In southern Asia only those countries having military relations with Western powers, except for Pakistan, announced support of India. For the others, China's military power in their vicinity and India's apparent weakness must have suggested long-range dangers involved in supporting India. In addition, the Chinese case on the merits of the border dispute, which was expounded in Chou En-lai's letter of November 15 to Afro-Asian governments and by intensive Chinese diplomatic activity in Asian and African capitals, raised doubts about India's stand and in some cases produced informal support for China's position.

For aid in meeting Chinese aggression the Indian government found that the only automatically favourable response came from Western governments, particularly the US. United States aircraft flew in emergency small-arms and supplies to Calcutta, and the American and British governments announced that they would provide the Indian army and air force with necessary aid—without insisting on any political conditions from India. During the last week in November American and British delegations met Nehru and leaders of India's defense establishment to arrange further short-term military support. Longer-term support, notably for air defense in case of another Chinese attack, became the subject of continuing discussions between India and Western governments. Apart from the question of strengthening Indian armed forces the new military relationship with the West gave India the assurance that in a war with China it could depend on specific kinds of help from outside.

The self-imposed Chinese cease-fire from November 22, followed by their withdrawal in December behind what Peking termed "the line of actual control of November 7, 1959," formed part of Peking's effort to obtain a favourable response to its case from Afro-Asian states and to force the Indian government to negotiate a settlement. India could not fail to comply with the conditions of the cease-fire ; that is, it could not risk re-occupying militarily all of the areas recently under Chinese control. But the government did not agree to negotiate a border settlement by first accepting the Chinese proposal of a demilitarized zone along the 1959 "line of actual control" as defined by China, because such an acceptance would have severely undermined India's defense positions.[37] China's official statements continued to stress, as before the invasion, its desire for discussions with New Delhi. India found it necessary and possible to avoid unconditional negotiations with a militarily superior state for several years following its military reverses, and it was assisted in maintaining that stand by certain of the Afro-Asian governments which became involved in the dispute.

In December 1962 representatives of Ceylon, Egypt, Ghana, Burma, Indonesia, and Cambodia met in Colombo and framed proposals to assist an Indo-Chinese settlement. Mrs. Bandaranaike, prime minister of Ceylon, visited Peking (accompanied by Foreign Minister Subandrio of Indonesia) and Delhi (with Prime Minister Aly Sabry of the UAR and Kofi-Azante Afori-Atta of Ghana) in December and January to obtain agreement on the proposals. Peking gave "acceptance in principle" but plainly disliked the intervention by third states. A major debate ensued in India, centring in parliament and concentrating on two features of the so-called Colombo proposals : one, their failure to cite China as an aggressor and thus their treatment of both sides as equals— a mediating technique often employed by India ; and, two, their definition of the Chinese withdrawal line in Ladakh as the Chinese "line of actual control" of November 1959. Since the invasion began Nehru had frequently stated that the Chinese should withdraw to the positions prior to September 8, 1962, as a pre-condition for negotiations.[38]

The considerable opposition in India to acceptance of the Colombo proposals was overcome, in parliament at least, by the massive Congress party majority, and the government announced its agreement, after the Colombo states had issued certain "clarifications" of the proposals' terms. In fact, when maps were published which plotted the proposals' expected effects on India's military position the government could ascertain that those effects would not be great, and it recognized that there would be a definite advantage from the stabilization of a twenty kilometre demilitarized zone. India's acceptance of the Colombo proposals was followed in March 1963 by China's establishment of new checkposts in Ladakh, six (later seven) of which were in the de facto demilitarized zone. Because the Colombo proposals provided for checkposts in that zone only by mutual Indo-Chinese agreement, India maintained that China was disregarding the proposals; thus no negotiations on a more nearly permanent cease-fire or on a border settlement took place at that time. India's suggestion in April 1963 that in case bilateral negotiations should fail, the border dispute might be submitted to the International Court of Justice or to an impartial arbitration tribunal was rejected by China.

The Indo-Chinese dispute over the control of some 45,000 square miles in regions desolate or remote from the centres of modern political life developed, in the four years, 1959 to 1963, into a political conflict as critical as any in Asia since the Second World War. Because the US, the USSR, and the UK were not directly involved militarily in the Himalayas and because their political concerns with the outcome of the conflict were only periodically aroused and never specifically defined (as they were, for example, in Vietnam), the Indo-Chinese dispute did not elicit the thoughtful attention by statesmen and political leaders that it deserved. Even in India, public and governmental attention to the far-reaching significance of the Himalayan struggle was spasmodic,[39] and the state of emergency did not include the adoption of a national programme for long-term conflict with China.

The relatively little international preoccupation with the occasional military eruptions and the continuing political struggle in the Himalayas reflected the view of most governments that China had no intention of launching a major attack on India and that India's own defense preparations, supported by its industrial growth, could cope with any limited military threats in the Himalayas. The absence of a crisis atmosphere inside India might in the future be judged as evidence of complacency; from without it provided a reasonable excuse for sympathetic foreign governments to avoid deep entanglements in yet another problem—one which India regarded as uniquely its own. The New Delhi government did not raise the frontier dispute or the 1962 Chinese invasion in the UN partly because it did not wish to invite greater outside involvement in its military establishment than the limited Western aid programmes already signified, nor wish to risk giving the appearance of modifying its nonalignment posture by seeking commitments from UN members to support the Indian position. Furthermore, India did not find it necessary to press other governments, in this case primarily the Soviet Union, to a firm position of commitment to India's case against China when India was receiving most of the material and political assistance that it wanted. Finally, India's experience in the UN with the Kashmir dispute militated against its taking any future dispute to the international organization.

What made the conflict in the Himalayas critical was the political threat that it raised to India's power in southern Asia. India's territorial losses suffered in Ladakh, the increased concentration of Chinese power in Tibet, and even the demonstrated weakness of the NEFA frontier were not so much military as political dangers. The Chinese government had correctly identified the confrontation with India as a political one in its ideological propaganda associated with the frontier dispute and Tibet. Having achieved its territorial ambitions in Ladakh in a de facto manner and proven at one time its military superiority along the entire frontier, China could pursue its apparently major aim of eliminating India as a serious political rival in southern Asia.

The Chinese military successes cleared the way for further attempts at political and economic penetration into the Himalayan border states. Publication of Chinese maps showing Nepal, Sikkim, and Bhutan as well as NEFA as territories seized by "imperialism"[40] and Chinese propagation of the idea of a Himalayan federation with China's backing suggested different lines of policy which would further the same objective, domination of all the frontier territories. The Himalayan federation was to include not only NEFA but Nagaland, where the Indian government's heavy-handed efforts to incorporate the Naga tribes into the Union after 1947 led Naga guerilla forces to seek and obtain arms from foreign states.[41] In the absence of an Indian settlement with the Nagas, Chinese support for the tribal independence movement could undermine the security of Assam as seriously as a Chinese military force on the McMahon Line border.

The Indian government had recognized the Chinese threat to India's power in the southern Asian region for many years before the 1962 invasion and had sought to limit or reduce that threat by diplomatic means. China's military successes in the Himalayas, however, demonstrated to India as well as to other nonaligned states, that *panchasheel* accords and other political manoeuvres were of little use in meeting threats or uses of force. The only gain for Indian security that nonalignment itself provided came from the opportunity that that posture offered to receive military backing from both the US and the USSR. In that unique advantage lay India's best defense against an all-out conventional Chinese attack in the years to come. The possible reaction of the great powers, and of India itself, however, to a Chinese nuclear threat to the subcontinent could scarcely be predicted.

NOTES AND REFERENCES

[1] *LSD*, vol. XXVIII, March 30, 1959, cols. 8520-21.

[2] Speech in the Lok Sabha, April 27, 1959, *Speeches, 1957-1963*, p. 190.

[3] *Notes, Memoranda and Letters Exchanged between the Governments of India and China (White Paper)*, no. I, pp. 60-62. Future historians will find interest in solving the problem of whether or not the Chinese allowed the Dalai Lama to escape to India. They may inquire why, during two weeks of slow trek from Lhasa to Towang, the Dalai Lama was not stopped by Chinese troops, which were in the region. The Chinese could no longer control the Dalai Lama, nor could they dispose of him by themselves ; his presence in India provided a useful argument in support of the Chinese charges that India was interfering in Tibetan affairs. It was the Chinese press which first announced that the Dalai Lama had crossed into Indian territory.

[4] So sincere were Nehru's reactions to the Chinese charges that on April 2, 1959, he told parliament that Kalimpong was indeed a spy and espionage centre harbouring people of many nationalities, thus seeming to dilute the firm denials about Kalimpong's role offered the day before by Home Minister G. B. Pant and Mrs. Lakshmi Menon. See *LSD*, vol. XXVIII, cols. 9272-73.

[5] See, e.g. the article in the Peking *People's Daily* of May 6, 1959, entitled "The Revolution in Tibet and Nehru's Philosophy." Three years later, on October 27, 1962, the same newspaper brought out "More on Nehru's Philosophy in the Light of the Sino-Indian Boundary Question," which continued the theme of India's collaboration with Western imperialists in order to explain the current international conflict. Both articles are in *The Sino-Indian Boundary Question,* Peking 1962. The full flavour of Chinese accusations against India and explanations for the Tibetan rebellion can be gained from the New China News Agency (Peking) reports of the uprising, March 23-30, 1959 ; also Chou En-lai's address

to the preparatory meeting of the Second National People's Congress, April 18, 1959 ; both in monitored foreign radio broadcasts.

[6] *White Paper*, no. II, pp. 42-43.

[7] See Nehru's press conference, Nov. 15, 1953, when he acknowledged that "there are large parts" of NEFA "where there is no administration at all." Nehru, *Press Conferences, 1953*, p. 83. See also Alastair Lamb, *The China-India Border*, p. 167, which explains that Indian administration was replacing Tibetan control only in the 1950's in sectors near the McMahon Line.

[8] *White Paper*, no. I, p. 44.

[9] *LSD*, vol. XXXIII, 1959, cols. 4866, 4869.

[10] Nehru pointed out that the boundaries of most great states, including China and Russia, emerged from expansionist, or imperialist, periods of history and could not for that reason alone be arbitrarily revised at a later period. Speech in the Rajya Sabha, Sept. 10, 1959, *Speeches, 1957-1963*, p. 210.

[11] *White Paper*, no. I, p. 53, and no. II, p. 27.

[12] He had not given publicity to the four-year-old diplomatic correspondence on the border issues "in the hope that peaceful solution of the dispute could be found by agreement by the two countries without public excitement on both sides." Letter to Chou En-lai, Sept. 26, 1959, *White Paper*, no. II, p. 34.

[13] See Nehru's speech in the Lok Sabha, Nov. 25, 1959, Nehru, *India's Foreign Policy*, p. 359f.

[14] Speech in the Rajya Sabha, Dec. 9, 1959, *ibid.*, p. 377. Nehru acknowledged that "a lingering doubt remained in my mind and in my Ministry's mind as to what might happen in the future."

[15] The American government gave no official opinion on the merits of Indian boundary claims, for several reasons : it judged that Western backing on that issue would be regarded as evidence of a collaboration which would embarrass India ; the US did not wish to arouse criticism and opposition from the Formosa government, which generally supported Peking's claims ; and the State Department was apparently not convinced at that time of the superior merits of the Indian claims.

[16] Minus the short border between Sikkim and Tibet, which China acknowledged had "long been formally delimited and there is neither any discrepancy between the maps nor any dispute in practice," *White Paper*, no. III, p. 79.

[17] He told the Lok Sabha on Nov. 25,1959, that he wished the House to shoulder part of the "grave responsibility" of decisions then facing his government "and tell us what we should do about it." Such a willingness to admit doubt and such an offer, sincere or not, to seek guidance from the legislature suggests the impact of the crisis with China on Nehru's mind, *India's Foreign Policy*, p. 359.

[18] *LSD*, vol. XXXVII, Dec. 22, 1959, col. 6720.

[19] cf. Nehru's statement in the Lok Sabha, *ibid.*, cols. 6720, 6725 : "For us to say, as some Hon. Members hinted at, that 'Do not talk to them ; do not negotiate' is a thing which ... will not be understood by any country in the wide world. .... The moment you refuse to [negotiate] ..., you are wrong before the world, and the world will think you are afraid of negotiation."

[20] *White Paper*, no. III, p. 83.

21 On Jan. 29, 1960, China and Burma agreed on a boundary between them which largely followed the watershed principle of the McMahon Line. With Nepal China signed an agreement on March 21, 1960, which specified principles of topography and actual jurisdiction, on which the Nepal-Tibet boundary was to be demarcated.

22 See K. P. S. Menon, *Flying Troika*, London 1963, p. 320.

23 No attempt will be made here to summarize or evaluate the legal aspects of the border conflict. See Bibliography for citations of works dealing with this complicated and controversial problem.

24 See Margaret Fisher, Leo Rose, Robert Huttenback, *Himalayan Battleground : Sino-Indian Rivalry in Ladakh*, p. 129f.

25 cf. Alastair Lamb : the Chinese had a good claim to "a few small tracts of territory south of the McMahon Line and, perhaps (if there are such things as legitimate claims over desert country), to the northern part of Aksai Chin through which runs their road. All this amounts to about 7,000 square miles of territory out of a total Chinese claim of more than 45,000 square miles. For the remaining 38,000 or so square miles the Chinese case, on grounds of history, tradition, treaty, and administration is nowhere particularly good or worthy of the attention of a Great Power. In the Assam Himalaya, with the exception of the border tracts already noted, the Chinese claim can only be described as absurd ; and there are reasons to suppose that the present Chinese Government regards it as no more than a bargaining device." *The China-India Border*, p. 175.

26 viz. Nehru's statement in the Lok Sabha, Sept. 12, 1959 : ". . . it is not a yard of territory that counts but the coercion. Because, it makes no difference to China or India whether a few yards of territory in the mountain [sic] are on this side or on that side. But it makes a great deal of difference if that is done in an insulting, aggressive, offensive, violent manner, by us or by them. All that counts." *India's Foreign Policy*, p. 354.

27 *LSD*, vol. XXXVII, Dec. 22, 1959, cols. 6725-26. Nehru spoke much about the industrial basis of military power during this period. On Dec. 8, 1959, in the Rajya Sabha he said that "the strength of a nation comes from technological developments of that nation; everything else is not real strength . . . all the courage in the world does not ultimately take the place of technological progress in the modern world." *RSD*, vol. XXVII, col. 1713.

28 Nehru and the External Affairs Ministry carefully considered the results of publishing the reports, knowing that publication would make any future political compromises virtually impossible to justify satisfactorily to the Indian public. It may have been that with the decision to issue the reports went also the decision not to bend under Chinese pressure or make a settlement that would be unpopular in the country. The Chinese delayed publicizing their report until 1962, when a partial version was released.

29 Responsibility for the continuing weakness of Indian military posture towards China after 1959 was often attributed to V. K. Krishna Menon because of his capacity as defense minister and closest advisor to Nehru. Additional responsibility rested on Menon because, being in close touch with the External Affairs Ministry, he was the only person, other than Nehru, in a position to co-

ordinate diplomatic and military policies. Menon apparently thought that diplomacy could substitute for military preparedness ; others knew that the Chinese were not impressed by words alone.

[30] According to Lt. General B. M. Kaul, corps commander in NEFA in 1962, "In NEFA . . . we went near the McMahon Line in right earnest for the first time in 1962 and hardly established a few small posts along the border before the Chinese launched their attack." Kaul, *The Untold Story*, p. 433.

[31] *LSD*, vol. VI, col. 121.

[32] This place, near the tri-junction of India, Tibet, and Bhutan, and the much-disputed Khinzemane, has the unusual status of being between the true Himalayan watershed, to the north, and the mapdrawn McMahon Line, to the south. India claimed and occupied territory up to the true watershed, which was incorrectly drawn by McMahon at the time of the Simla conference in 1913-1914. Following the watershed principle India did not claim or occupy the much larger area north of Longju, which the McMahon Line shows as part of India but which is north of the watershed.

[33] Cited in the *Hindu* and the *Times of India*, Oct. 13, 1962 ; see also Kaul, *op. cit.*, p. 387.

[34] *White Paper*, no. VIII, pp. 11-12.

[35] *RSD*, vol. XLIV, Sept. 2, 1963, col. 2370.

[36] After arguing for years the case for moral or political influence as the basis for India's power, many Indians appeared to adopt a *réal-politique* view of India's foreign relations after 1962 and judged that its influence depended chiefly on its military capabilities.

[37] It would have required withdrawal of Indian troops from positions in NEFA and in the frontier sector between Nepal and Kashmir which they were occupying in September 1962.

[38] Such a condition was a considerable modification of the pre-September 1962 stand that Chinese troops withdraw entirely from Ladakh (the Indians also withdrawing from forward posts) before negotiations could take place. The Indian government's insistence on the September 1962 military positions instead of the November 1959 "line of control" proposed by China was explained by the fact that by September 1962 Indian border forces had improved their positions in Ladakh by the establishment of the 43 new posts.

[39] Except in the limited circles of military and civilian officials whose experience and duties brought continuous awareness of the China problem.

[40] In *A Brief History of Modern China*, Peking 1954, by Lui Pei-hua, cited in *International Studies*, vol. V, nos. 1-2 (1963), p. 16n.

[41] See statement by Michael Scott, *Statesman* (Calcutta), Sept. 10, 1964. Foreign Minister Chagla made the formal charge of Chinese support of the Nagas in parliament on April 11, 1967 ; see *Hindustan Times*, April 12, 1967.

CHAPTER XVIII

SOME LESS PUBLICIZED RELATION-SHIPS: WITH CANADA, WEST GERMANY, AND JAPAN

LIKE ALL NEW STATES India began its independent career in world affairs by cultivating relations with the major world powers. Pre-independence ties with certain lesser powers in Asia and Africa were maintained, but New Delhi did not energetically nurture them, until events of the 1960's demonstrated that a cluster of minor sympathizers could be almost as valuable as a major supporter. With most of the world's states India had few and infrequent connections in the early years of independence. Europe, outside the UK, was alien to most of India's Westernized leaders ; the far east was exotic and unexplored ; and the western hemisphere, apart from the US and perhaps Canada, was an unknown wilderness. As the scope of Indian diplomacy and trade relations gradually widened during the 1950's, governments and peoples new to Indian experience began to occupy significant places in Indian foreign relations, and by the 1960's New Delhi had begun to consolidate links with certain middle-ranking states and showed an openness of mind toward any potentially new, beneficial contacts.

A recital of the details of India's relations with all states not previously dealt with would make confusing reading, particularly inappropriate to the latter sections of this survey. Descriptions of the diplomatic dealings with Mongolia and Australia in the east, of close cooperation in the UN and economic assistance from Scandinavian countries, of various contacts with France, and of the discoveries of mutual interests between India and Latin American nations should tantalize scholars, especially in the future, as the public records grow in size and reveal the direction in which events have been moving. But this chapter will, we hope, be considered adequate if it treats of India's relations with three states of greater than average importance to New Delhi, all of which fell into the

479

category of middle-ranking powers not within India's traditional sphere of close contacts—Canada, West Germany, and Japan.

LINKS WITH CANADA[1]

Of the three countries just mentioned Canada, despite—or perhaps because of—its intimate association with the US, experienced the greatest ease in building cordial and collaborative relations with India. The initiative for that relationship came from Canada, searching for a role in international affairs that would suit its status as a middle-ranking state and would make possible a degree of independence from American and British policy guidance. Membership in the Commonwealth opened up the possibilities for Indo-Canadian contacts, but that formal connection alone could bring no striking advantages—witness the comparatively unproductive relations that existed between India and Australia,[2] or New Zealand. The entente that developed between India and Canada was founded on similarities of thought and approach, or style, in international affairs—very little more than that to begin with. Because of the closeness of the tie, economic relations achieved major importance by the mid-1950's.

The auspicious beginnings of Canadian gestures towards India took place during the Second World War, in 1942, when Prime Minister Mackenzie King gave support to India's nationalist demand for equality of status with the dominions within the Commonwealth.[3] After Indian independence Canada proved to be, apart from the UK, the most helpful and sympathetic member of the Commonwealth in devising the means by which India could remain in the organization without sacrificing its nationalist ideals. Nehru expressed appreciation for that Canadian contribution on his first visit to Canada, in 1949.[4] Canada's conception of the Commonwealth, as a multi-racial, loosely organized club, with no authority to interfere in a member's domestic affairs or to recommend foreign policies, coincided nicely with India's.

During the first conflict of Indian and Western interests in global politics, the diplomacy of the Korean War, New Delhi discovered, possibly unexpectedly, that Canada shared many of its views on the conduct of the UN operation and on the settlement of the conflict. Like India, Canada opposed crossing of the 38th parallel and assisted the efforts in the UN (guided by Benegal Rau) to achieve a truce after the Chinese had intervened ; it voted for the Indian resolution on prisoners of war and urged India's inclusion in a post-war political conference.[5] Canada followed the US lead in refusing to recognize the communist regime in China, but it did not join SEATO and thereby registered its dissociation from some aspects of American strategy in Asia.

Very early in the post-war era Ottawa expressed a consistent support for the nationalist mode of thought in Asia, which was unique among states of the Western alliance. Canadian sentiments sympathizing with Asian countries' desire to achieve meaningful independence, which often meant escaping from excessive Western influence, derived from the historical experience of north America's quest for an identity separate from Europe—shared, it might be mentioned, by the US, whose central position in the anti-communist alliance, however, often seemed to require illiberal stands on colonialism. Canada did not normally side with India in UN debates on colonial issues, but neither did it predictably support Western governments, and its neutrality in those cases could be taken as a gain by Afro-Asian states. Canada's views on Asia found acceptance in India partly because, as Lester Pearson put it, "the main avenue of approach for Canada to the problems of Asia has been by way of the Indian subcontinent."[6] Nehru acknowledged, on his second Canadian visit in 1956, the value of the "link" between the West and the newly independent Asian countries that Canada's diplomacy embodied.[7] Postwar Canadian governments found nothing reprehensible in Nehru's posture and doctrine of nonalignment, which was correctly understood as an expression of India's search for international independence. When the Canadian prime minister visited India in February 1954 he announced that "we fully understand the historical and other factors which underlie your policy," although Canada's interests at the time called for a different posture. "If India," he said, in seeking ways to lessen "cold war" antagonisms, "considers it best to refrain from commitments which others find advisable, we certainly do not question this. The world already has reason to be grateful to India for her achievements in the field of international conciliation. . . ."[8]

Canada, too, was prepared to engage in peace-making endeavours, although its membership in the Atlantic alliance lessened its effec-

31

tiveness. In 1954 Canada joined India (and Poland) in the international control commissions in former French Indo-China to try to enforce the Geneva agreements. The Suez crisis again brought out the similarity of Indian and Canadian interests and diplomatic style. In the UN, Afro-Asian and Canadian resolutions on the crisis supplemented each other, and Indian and Canadian diplomats helped to frame the plans for the UN Emergency Force in Gaza ; both of their governments later supplied troops for the UNEF.[9] To a lesser extent in the Congo crisis India and Canada collaborated in providing troops, logistic support, and financial contributions for a controversial UN operation. Canadian statesmen in the UN and elsewhere could not be counted on to adopt the uncompromisingly anti-communist line that characterized most Western diplomacy in the 1950's, and thus on occasions Canada itself appeared to have adopted an almost Indian-like nonaligned position.[10] The major architect of post-war Canadian foreign policy, Lester Pearson, expressed as early as 1950 the view that, "The tendency to see our main international problem as essentially one of dealing with communism, and to view the world safely in bi-polar terms of cold war ... is dangerously over simplified."[11] Such a style of thought, supported as it was by diplomatic action, placed Canada close to India, somewhere on a political bridge (though not as close to the centre of it) between the "cold war" antagonists. Collaboration in peace-making and peace-keeping enterprises was therefore one of the most successful types of Indo-Canadian relations.

But into this setting of political accord, initiated by Canada and enthusiastically reinforced by India, intruded an element which could have tainted the relationship if both states had not endeavoured to overcome the difficulty. It was the problem of Canada's racial policy as it affected immigration of Indians. After a small group of Sikhs had migrated to British Columbia in the early 20th century Canada imposed restrictions on the further entry of Indians by requiring of all immigrants substantial funds on arrival and prohibiting the entry of anyone who had not made a continuous voyage to Canada, which was impossible from India. British Columbia, meanwhile, restricted the voting rights of resident Indians. In the 1920's and 1930's the nationalist protests in India against the racially motivated Canadian policies grew predictably vigorous ; the new Indian government in December 1946 requested Ottawa to persuade British

Columbia to confer the franchise on Indians and thus "rectify the present anomalous position which is a source of humiliation to Indians."[12] Gradually Canada responded. British Columbia gave voting rights to its Indian settlers, numbering less than 2,000, and in 1947 the Ottawa government revoked the continuous voyage regulation.

In 1951 India, along with Pakistan and Ceylon, obtained a low quota for emigrants to Canada, but Indians who already had citizenship could not secure admission of as many relatives as other Canadians were allowed.[13] Following a protest by Indo-Canadians to the Commonwealth Prime Ministers' Conference in 1956 Canada loosened slightly its rules on Indian immigration.[14] During the 1950's the Indian government made no official protest on the immigration question because by then Indians resident in Canada had been granted legal equality, and India respected the right of any state to establish whatever limits it chose on immigration. Finally in 1962 Canada, anticipating a similar US move by three years, abolished the racial or national criterion for issuance of immigration visas. Immigrants would henceforth be admitted on the basis of skills and other individual qualifications.

Canada's views on racial relations externally showed a liberal awareness earlier than did its domestic policies. The Ottawa government had taken a moderate stand on apartheid and other racial policies in South Africa, until the issue threatened to break up the Commonwealth in 1960 and 1961. When the Canadian prime minister, John G. Diefenbaker, discovered that the 1961 Commonwealth Prime Ministers' Conference was in danger of dividing along racial lines on South Africa he "decided that it would be intolerable if colour were made to seem the deciding factor on so fundamental an issue, and he was very much aware of the prestige that would attach to Canada in Afro-Asian eyes if the senior Member of the 'White Dominions' sided with those whose people were of different pigmentation. He accordingly took the lead in demanding that the Prime Ministers declare that racial equality was a root principle of the modern Commonwealth of Nations."[15] But before the issue was forced to a show-down decision South Africa withdrew from Commonwealth membership. Canada's decision to preserve the integrity of the new Commonwealth, at the expense of an old member, was a predictable extension of its efforts to bridge the gap between the West and the non-West.

The various Canadian overtures towards India, and thence towards the Afro-Asian world, could be explained in part as an enlightened policy for the benefit of the West as a whole carried forward by a state with virtually no encumbrances or commitments that could inhibit a principled approach to political relations. In addition, the special status that Canada thereby achieved among Afro-Asian states added significance to the independent role that it wished to play in world affairs. From India's point of view, the greatest value that resulted from the entente with Canada lay in the economic benefits that its prosperous north American supporter could provide. From early in the 1950's Canada supplied those benefits in greater abundance relative to its size than the US was doing. Most of Canada's assistance to India was counted as Colombo Plan aid, but it resulted from bilateral agreements, nearly all of which authorized grants, not loans, as the method of financing the transfers of materials, equipment, and technical services. The bulk of the loans represented transfers of surplus Canadian wheat by a scheme similar to the US PL 480 arrangement. From 1950 through 1964 Canada authorized C$388.7 million (rupees 179.3 crores) in grants and loans for India, of which C$283.35 million (rupees 131.7 crores) was in grants[16]—the largest proportion of grants from any aid giving country. India was the heaviest recipient of Canadian external assistance during that period.

Canada's aid programme began during the first five-year plan with rupees 32.3 crores of authorized assistance which was increased during the second plan to rupees 58.3 crores—all in grants. During the second plan the wheat loans began, with a rupees 15.7 crores authorization. Canada concentrated on assisting major development projects in the first two plan periods and was credited with three major dam building projects, Kundra, Mayurakshi, and Umtru. In addition, Canadians helped India build its first nuclear reactor, at Trombay in Bombay. During the third plan Canada increased its assistance along with the other members of the Aid India Consortium and introduced export credit and development loan schemes to supplement the general assistance. Another major dam project, at Idikki, was later added to Canadian and Indian undertakings. And further help was promised for another nuclear power station, at Rana Pratap Sagar in Rajasthan ; an unusual feature of the agreement for that project provided for continuing exchanges of information between scientists at the Rajasthan reactor and those at the Douglas Point nuclear generating station in Canada, after which the Indian plant was modeled.

Indo-Canadian trade figures naturally recorded the increases in Canadian assistance, as well as the growth of purely commercial relations. Indian exports fell almost entirely into the traditional categories and were holding at approximately rupees 20 crores annually in the early 1960's. Canada's exports to India of processed raw materials, such as wood pulp and fertilizers, as well as wheat, were not creating for India an intolerably unfavourable balance of payments in the 1960's.

In Canadian statements on economic aid an enlightened note was often struck, emphasizing Canadians' willingness to share economic burdens that were the responsibilities of the world, not merely of the underdeveloped countries.[17] The Canadian electorate did not manifest the hostility towards aid programmes that the American electorate did, and therefore Ottawa officials were not forced to spell out the political (and military) rewards and expectations that foreign aid implied, with the controversial "strings" that such enunciations would have postulated.

Economically as well, the Canadian aid programmes seemed uniquely far-sighted in not creating an Indian indebtedness that would produce financial and possibly political difficulties later. In April 1966 the Ottawa government may have set a precedent that other aid giving states would eventually decide to follow, when it cancelled the remaining payments on a wheat loan extended to India in 1958.

THE SLOWLY DEVELOPED RELATIONS WITH WEST GERMANY

In contrast to its links with Canada, which could easily be traced to the pre-independence period of Commonwealth ties and some Indian emigration, India's relations with both West and East Germany developed only after the Second World War. (The work of 19th century German Sanskritists was of no benefit to international relations.) Early in the 1950's Prime Minister Nehru showed concern with the problems of post-war Germany, several years before the two countries had established the economic connections that became their main link. His government identified the artificial border of West and East Germany and the division of Berlin as potential sources of great power friction and exerted the slim influence that India possessed on European affairs always in behalf of a European detente based on a German peace treaty acceptable to all sides. When crises centred on Germany or specifically Berlin Nehru was usually reluctant to offer advice on possible terms for a settlement. But officially and in principle he supported the idea of German reunification by peaceful means, as several joint communiques showed.[18] India extended full diplomatic recognition only to the Federal Republic of Germany, referred to as Germany in this chapter.

The Indo-German exchange of state visits in 1956, Deputy Prime Minister Franz Bluecher travelling to India, and Nehru touring in Germany, signalled the beginning of a formidable array of economic assistance and investment ventures emanating from the recently recovered German industrial structure. The decision of the Bonn government to undertake major aid projects in India marked Germany's assumption of responsibility in world economic affairs and demonstrated its recognition of India's economic future as important to the interests of non-communist countries. In a more short-term calculation German economic aid stood as an inducement to preclude a de jure recognition by any underdeveloped country of the East German government : no external assistance was granted to a country having diplomatic relations with the German Democratic Republic. In addition, American pressure on Bonn to increase its assistance to underdeveloped countries was continuous in the latter 1950's and early 1960's, and the results showed up in Germany's contribution under the Aid India Consortium, of which it was a charter member. German industrialists, simultaneously, were extending into foreign areas the investment surge by which the Federal Republic had reached new heights of prosperity, and they concentrated in India an important share of their total involvement in the underdeveloped countries. Partly as a result, Indo-German trade increased rapidly, until by the 1960's imports from Germany ranked third among India's foreign sources of supply, after the US and the UK ; exports to Germany occupied a much lower position in the total of Indian goods sold abroad.

The most dramatic example of Germany's early economic connections with India was the one million ton steel factory built at Rourkela, with an initial loan of rupees 77.8 crores authorized during the second five-year plan, 1956-1961. (There was no German economic aid during the first plan period.) The Rourkela plant, which became the most embarrassing element in Indo-German relations, began as private business for some forty German contractors engaged by the newly formed public enterprise, Hindustan Steel Company. During India's foreign exchange crisis beginning in 1957 New Delhi approached the Bonn government for financial credits with which to pay its German contractors, and Bonn responded in 1958 by extending an initial three-year credit at six per cent interest. Such a short-term advance failed to meet India's financial needs, and Germany extended the credit for fifteen years at an interest rate of 5.25 per cent. Germany's involvement expanded with the growth of the plant, and in 1962 it agreed to finance an expansion to a capacity of 1.8 million tons per year.

Most of Rourkela's problems, which found publicity in Germany as widely as they did in India and caused some public disillusionment over foreign aid in general, stemmed from the high degree of sophistication of the flat steel process which the Germans introduced in India and from the frequently acerbic personal relations between German and Indian workmen and engineers. Unlike "the simpler and more robust systems"[19] installed by the Russians at Bhilai, Rourkela's operation suffered frequent disruptions, and in 1961 two hundred Germans had to be sent over to run the complex system. By the end of 1964 the Federal Government's direct and indirect contributions to Rourkela amounted to approximately rupees 170 crores.

The major German economic assistance to India began only in the late 1950's, when aid commitments rose sharply from all prominent Western donors. Earlier German bilateral aid had taken the form mainly of export credits and technical training schemes, which began in 1953. Once Bonn had decided to finance overseas aid at a level commensurate with its own resources Germany swiftly became the second largest foreign contributor to Indian development ; India, in turn, was by far the largest recipient of West German assistance. But German aid was disbursed almost exclusively as loans, carrying almost commercial rates of interest, usually about 5.5 per cent. Repayment became a serious burden on Indian financing, despite German willingness in the mid-1960's to refinance the obligations. In the second plan period Germany authorized rupees

2.1 crores in grants and 133.9 crores in loans ; during the third plan, through 1965, total aid authorizations increased, to rupees 265.8 crores.[20] With the exception of the Rourkela project, German loans were not tied to purchases in Germany.

Of the states giving large-scale aid to India Germany stood foremost in justifying the expenditures as encouragement to free enterprise in the developing countries.[21] The Germans reasoned that foreign assistance could stimulate capitalism abroad, tiding over the underdeveloped economies until private entrepreneurship got firmly established. By a system of guarantees introduced in 1955 to cover political risks of investment in underdeveloped countries the government hoped to stimulate German private involvement abroad which would supplement the public efforts and eventually supplant them. Accurate statistics on flows of foreign capital to India's private sector were rare, but the Reserve Bank of India calculated that German investments rose from rupees 2.5 crores in 1955 to rupees 6.8 crores in 1960 and ranked fourth among investing countries, closely following Switzerland but still far behind the US and the UK.[22] That total rose rapidly in the early 1960's and reached a privately estimated rupees 12 crores by 1965.[23]

Collaboration between Indian and German firms spread to all important areas of Indian industry and included over 300 schemes in 1967 ; the Tata Mercedes Benz trucks to be seen on all Indian roads became a reminder of the new German industrial presence. Indo-German collaboration agreements supported about 4,000 Indian trainees in Germany in the mid-1960's, and an official German sponsored technological institute in Madras increased the opportunities for Indians to benefit from German knowledge and skills. One benefit of German technological collaboration accruing to the Indian government in the 1950's was the development of India's first jet fighter, the HF-24, by a team of German engineers.

India's trade with Germany increased rapidly in the 1960's, but in the lop-sided relationship that typically accompanied aid programmes. India's imports from Germany in 1961-1962 were worth rupees 123 crores and in 1964-1965 rupees 109 crores ; for the same years its exports to Germany were only rupees 21 and rupees 18 crores, respectively. As was the case with the European Economic Community as a whole, Indian exports fell mostly into the traditional lines of tea, jute goods, and coffee. Indian manufactures of a

modern variety and even traditional items entered the German
(as the EEC) market subject to quotas and high tariffs. With the
largest trade imbalance with India among EEC countries Germany
began to show interest in the mid-1960's in adopting more liberal
import policies, without which its goal of popularizing and spreading
the free enterprise system could not be realized.

BRIDGING THE GAP BETWEEN INDIA AND JAPAN

Perhaps the most tantalizing diplomatic potentiality in post-Second
World War Asia was that of an Indo-Japanese accord. The great
differences between the two countries, in size, economy, culture,
and recent historical experience, themselves suggested the innova-
tive possibilities of a rapprochement by which the two states might
complement each other in a new Asia.

Japan's spectacular military and economic progress in the early
20th century had been an inspiration for Indian nationalists. During
the Second World War a charismatic ex-Congress leader, Subhas
Chandra Bose, had sought to collaborate with the Japanese and to
convert Indians in southeast Asia to his view that Indian independence could be won by forming an Indian national army to fight
against the British. His enterprises, backed by Japan, were of only
passing significance. After the war and the successful communist
revolution in China the similarity of political and economic goals
within India and Japan became obvious—the development of democratic and industrialized states. Close economic cooperation between the two countries could have proved profitable to both ;
furthermore, any defense arrangement against China which would
be independent of Western underpinning would have to incorporate
India as well as Japan, in order to be effective.

For reasons based in recent history, however, during the 1950's
and for most of the succeeding decade, notions of an effective Indo-
Japanese collaboration in international affairs remained the property
of writers and diplomats possessing more than average imagination.
Neither state was ready to embark on the historically unprecedented
course of joint action in any field affecting vital national interests.
Japan's reliance on and commitment to the US and India's well
defined nonalignment and its own economic ties elsewhere directed
the two states along different and occasionally opposing courses,

at least until the mid-1960's. An intangible factor that stood in the way of an intimate linking of policies was the feelings of mutual alienness among Indian and Japanese people and their representatives. No two major cultures were more unlike each other than the Indian and the Japanese, as Arthur Koestler's *The Lotus and the Robot*[24] illustrated ; most Indians and Japanese seemed to communicate more readily with persons of any third cultural group than they did with each other.

Yet India and Japan had established contacts of importance to both sides in the inter-war period. These were entirely economic in character. For Japanese exporters— primarily the textile groups— India in the 1920's and 1930's had become a major target for trade promotion. Despite discriminatory tariffs, aimed directly against Japanese goods, and the system of imperial preferences introduced in 1932, the Indian economy continued to absorb an increasing amount of Japanese manufactured goods. By 1938 Japan ranked second among the countries trading with India, and India ranked third among Japan's trading partners.[25]

The Japanese share of India's trade in 1938—about ten per cent of its total imports and about nine per cent of its exports—could not be matched after two decades of post-war business dealings, supported by the modest Japanese aid programme. Indian industries had become much stronger by that time in their home markets, and the government's tariff structure helped to price Japanese textiles, the major pre-war import, out of the domestic market. By the mid-1950's, when Indo-Japanese exchanges again became important following the war-time break, the main commodities traded were no longer those of the pre-war period. The textile trade had declined markedly, although for a few post-war years Japanese rayon had been heavily purchased in India. India and Japan in fact were becoming competitors for textile markets. In place of textiles, Indian purchases from Japan after 1952 consisted of steel products, machinery, rolling stock, and chemicals ; Japanese importers bought from India raw cotton and leather, as before the war, and newer Indian exports of iron ore, manganese, scrap metal, and mica.

As Indo-Japanese trade grew in the 1950's it became imbalanced in favour of Japan, but to a notable degree less so than Indo-German trade. Largely assisted by iron ore exports, of which Japan took nearly 70 per cent in 1960 (about 16 per cent of all Japanese imports of iron ore), India's sales to Japan ranked third among its sales abroad from the early 1950's until 1964, when Russia took over that position. In 1961-1962 India exported rupees 41 crores worth of goods to Japan, while purchasing goods valued at rupees 59 crores ; in 1964-1965 the comparable figures were rupees 60 and 77 crores. Japan, thus, proved to be a profitable trading partner for India, but predominantly in the classic pattern of raw materials being exchanged for manufactured goods. Japan's tariffs favoured the imports of products that could be fully processed in Japan ; semi-manufactured goods, such as tanned skins, and processed raw materials, such as shellac, accumulated higher tariffs than the same base products, or were struck by quotas. Japanese investment in India was negligible.

Non-economic relations between India and Japan showed much slower development than did economic ties, due to inhibitions on both sides. Under American occupation and subsequently in accordance with the terms of the 1951 peace treaty and US bases agreements Japan linked its defense and foreign policies with those of the US in Asia. Although its historic tendency lay in the direction of close connections with Asian countries, its American orientation and also its recent reputation for imperialistic ambitions precluded its energetically seeking collaborative arrangements in Asia during the 1950's, except in limited ways with states similarly linked to US interests. Nehru's most significant gestures on behalf of Asian unity were made while Japan was still under American occupation. Thereafter he directed his efforts to forming an axis of Asian cooperation with China, rather than Japan, although he was ready to express sentiments of sympathy with the Japanese people.[26] India's refusal to sign the multilateral Japanese peace treaty at San Francisco,[27] partly on grounds that its terms failed to concede appropriate independence and equality to Japan, probably resulted from opposition to US policies rather than from a calculation that the move would appeal to the Japanese. The separate Indo-Japanese peace treaty of June 9, 1952, however, showed careful framing in its anticipation of possible future cordiality.[28] India renounced all reparation claims against Japan and agreed to return any Japanese properties in India seized by the government during the war. The treaty incorporated explicit terms for the restoration of all Indo-

Japanese commercial relations on the basis of most-favoured-nation treatment, thereby signifying both sides' desire to encourage trade and other contacts.[29]

Five years after the signing of the treaty the Japanese prime minister, Nobusuke Kishi, visited New Delhi, and a few months later, in October 1957, Nehru went to Japan. Their joint statements on those occasions indicated that Japan was prepared to confirm several of India's diplomatic proclamations on the state of the world, including the main principles of the Bandung conference declaration. Japan had no difficulty in agreeing that nuclear disarmament and an end to nuclear testing was a vital global necessity; the two governments found in their similar reactions to the latter issue the firmest basis for any political agreement.[30]

Japanese interests in Indian economic development began on a tentative scale in the mid-1950's with a few technical assistance schemes for agriculture and small industries. In 1958 a trade agreement was reached along with the first of many yen credit arrangements to facilitate Indian imports of capital equipment from Japan. The periodic extensions of credits to India from Japan's Export-Import Bank carried higher rates of interest than those available from Western countries, 7.5 per cent to 5.75 per cent, which India could justify undertaking only if a product offered by Japan was unavailable elsewhere on better terms. Japan authorized the equivalent of rupees 23.8 crores in credits during the second plan; in the 1960's its assistance rose sharply so that in the first four years of the third plan its commitment totalled rupees 104.7 crores.[31] There were no Japanese grants, except for minor technical aid. As a member of the Aid India Consortium Japan appeared committed to Indian development, but its share in financing the undertaking, under the quasi-commercial credits programme, remained less in proportion to its resources than that of most other contributors.[32]

At a gradual pace in the 1960's Indian and Japanese views on Asian politics began to converge. The shifts in Indian policy could be more clearly recorded, as a result of the Chinese threat in the Himalayas, but Japan, too, demonstrated greater caution in adhering to the American line and quietly cultivated closer economic ties with a China that it did not formally recognize. Prime Minister Hayato Ikeda's visit to India in November 1961 signified at least that the desire for more beneficial ties was recognized on both sides.

Nothing substantial emerged, however, beyond the predictably mutual views on nuclear arms control.[33] Again a gap of years followed with only routine Indo-Japanese business going forward. Then, in 1966, the two states began periodic official discussions of an unpublicized sort but certainly with political content. By that time Indian and Japanese political interests seemed enough alike to provide further clarity to the vision of an Asian entente polarized around New Delhi and Tokyo.

NOTES AND REFERENCES

[1] Greater reliance than has usually been the case has been placed in preparing this section on an unpublished paper of a student at American University, Donald F. Mayer's "Indo-Canadian Relations," 1966.

[2] See R. G. Neale, "Australia and India," *Foreign Affairs Reports* (Indian Council of World Affairs), New Delhi, vol. VII, 6 (June 1958), esp. pp. 65, 69.

[3] Cited in James Eayrs, *Northern Approaches*, pp. 87-88; from the unpublished King papers.

[4] Nehru, speech to the Canadian parliament, Oct. 24, 1949, *India's Foreign Policy*, p. 583.

[5] Soward and McInnis, *Canada and the United Nations*, p. 132f.

[6] Pearson, "The Development of Canadian Foreign Policy," *Foreign Affairs*, vol. XXX, 1 (Oct. 1951), p. 21.

[7] News conference in Ottawa, Dec. 22, 1956, *Asian Recorder*, 1956, p. 1226. The Canadian public's support for the government's efforts to establish beneficial ties with India was described by Edgar McInnis in *The Growth of Canadian Policies in External Affairs*, chap. 8, "A Middle Power in the Cold War," pp. 154-55.

[8] Quoted in Warwick Chipman, "India's Foreign Policy," Canadian Institute of International Affairs, *Behind the Headlines*, vol. XIV, 4 (Oct. 1954), pp. 11-12.

[9] James Eayrs, *Canada in World Affairs, October 1955 to June 1957*, pp. 258-71.

[10] Criticism, and hence recognition, of the Canadian tendencies towards non-alignment appeared in Eayrs, *Northern Approaches*, chap. 7, "The Nostrum of Neutralism."

[11] Pearson, *Democracy in World Politics*, Toronto 1955, p. 28.

[12] Canada, *Official Report of Debates, House of Commons*, vol. I, Feb. 5, 1947, pp. 157-58.

[13] See David C. Corbett, *Canada's Immigration Policy*, Toronto 1957. The Indian quota was 150 persons per year, but a Canadian office with twelve persons on the staff had to be set up in New Delhi to deal with the 20,000 applications in process and more thousands that immediately followed the quota allocation.

[14] See revised Indo-Canadian immigration agreement of May 3, 1957, as well as the 1951 agreement, in *Foreign Policy of India: Texts of Documents, 1947-64*, pp. 187-88.

[15] Eayrs, *Northern Approaches*, pp. 97-98.

[16] India, Ministry of Finance, *External Assistance, 1964*, p. 17.

[17] See, e.g. Prime Minister John Diefenbaker's statement on June 29, 1958 ; Canadian Dept. of External Affairs, "Canada and the Colombo Plan," Reference Paper no. 103, Sept. 24, 1959.

[18] Texts of three communiques in *Foreign Policy of India, op. cit.*, pp. 306-10. Nehru's statements at the time of the Berlin crisis in 1961 were considered earlier, in chap. XVI.

[19] White, *German Aid*, p. 104.

[20] *External Assistance, 1964*, pp. 30-31.

[21] White, *op. cit.*, p. 64.

[22] Reserve Bank of India, *India's Balance of Payments, 1948-49 to 1961-62*, Bombay 1963, p. 62. Michael Kidron's estimates of new investments in the period, 1956 to 1964, show German businesses far ahead of Swiss ; consents for new capital issues included German participation valued at rupees 7.3 crores, while new Swiss participation amounted to rupees 4.1 crores in the same period. Kidron, *Foreign Investments in India*, London 1965, p. 242.

[23] See *The Hindu Weekly Review*, June 28, 1965, p. 5.

[24] New York 1960.

[25] Rokuko Sase, "Recent Developments in India's Economic Relations with Japan," *Foreign Affairs Reports* (Indian Council of World Affairs), New Delhi, vol. VIII, no. 11 (Nov. 1958).

[26] For example, Nehru voiced concern about the Japanese fishermen who had been injured by the nuclear tests conducted by the US in the Pacific Ocean in April 1954. Lok Sabha, April 2, 1954, *India's Foreign Policy*, p. 190.

[27] See chapter XIII.

[28] Earlier, in 1946, the Indian jurist, R. B. Pal, had recorded the sole dissentient opinion at the trial of 25 Japanese persons for alleged war crimes by the military tribunal of the 11 allied powers. His lengthy, closely reasoned recommendation for the acquittal of the accused was based on traditional international law, but also reflected his sympathy for a vanquished Asian state, whose right to justice he upheld. See *International Military Tribunal for the Far East : Dissentient Judgment of Justice R. B. Pal*, Calcutta 1953.

[29] Text of the treaty is in *Foreign Policy of India, op. cit.*, pp. 46-51.

[30] Texts of the joint statements in *ibid.*, pp. 322-26.

[31] *External Assistance, 1964*, p. 47.

[32] See Robert S. Ozaki, "Japan's Role in Asian Economic Development," *Asian Survey*, vol. VII, 4 (April 1967), p. 241.

[33] See Indo-Japanese joint communique of Nov. 23, 1961, *FAR*, vol. VII, 11 (Nov. 1961), p. 426. In Nehru's banquet toast to Ikeda he noted that in trade and economic development there was "room for close cooperation," and that Indo-Japanese cooperation could exist on matters of nuclear weapons. Beyond that, Nehru failed to identify areas of collaboration, whereas Ikeda announced that India and Japan had "a common destiny to fulfil in Asia," *ibid.*, pp. 424-25.

CHAPTER XIX

THE EVOLUTION OF INDIAN POLICY
IN THE UNITED NATIONS

WORLD POLITICS OF the 1960's looked different from those of the 1950's whether viewed from New Delhi or from any other capital. Wars were more common, and the UN's ability to avoid their outbreak or create peace between the contestants was rarely in evidence. The great power coalitions, however, had reached a tacit detente, and the tensions specific to the "cold war" gradually weakened. The great coalitions lost much of their cohesiveness as the fear of war between them diminished. The two leaders of the coalitions experienced similar problems with their respective allies and sometimes held common views on nonaligned and underdeveloped countries ; nonalignment accordingly lost its peculiar *raison d'etre*. China's isolation from the world political system increased, as the split between Moscow and Peking hardened, but simultaneously the preoccupation with China on the part of both major powers as well as India grew, until China became one of the most influential factors in world political and military affairs. The number of new independent states increased rapidly because of decolonialization in Africa, and the Afro-Asian members in the UN thereby became the dominant voting group in the General Assembly. Economic development gained long postponed recognition as a prime concern of the entire international community, not merely of a few donor and a few developing countries.

In accord with the changed circumstances of the 1960's India's external relationships shifted, and its role in the UN reflected most of those shifts. Apart from defending their own national interests Indian representatives at the UN in the 1950's had devoted most of their skills and energies to mediation among parties to major disputes and to the diplomatic struggle against colonialism. In the 1960's the tranquillizing effect of Indian intervention in UN disputes was sometimes felt, but the "climate of peace" theme did not carry

495

the meaning that it had when almost all disputes had been permeated with the fears and suspicions of the "cold war." As the two great powers increased the contacts between themselves, Indian mediating ability lost its relevance. As for anti-colonialism, the burden fell into the hands of the African states in the 1960's, because the only significant remnants of colonialism were in Africa. Indians still mustered enthusiasm when called upon to attack the vestiges of an outworn era, and they stood especially strongly against racial injustices. Their work in these respects receives minor attention in this chapter, however, because India's major preoccupations in UN bodies in the 1960's lay in other areas.

Three such areas deserve most attention in these final pages, which seek to characterize India's contemporary position in world politics while concentrating on UN affairs. They are : peace-keeping operations, arms control negotiations, and what could be called the diplomacy of economic equalization. Although India participated influentially in these areas, its impact on global affairs in the decade of the 1960's was weaker than it had been in the preceding decade. Nehru's voice in the last years of his life failed to carry the conviction in India or in the world that it had before his China policy lost its effectiveness. After his death, on May 27, 1964, no Indian leader had the inclination, much less the talent, to assume Nehru's status as a moulder of opinion throughout the world and as a political innovator in his handling of great diplomatic situations. The Indian government and people, sensing that their internal and external ambitions extended beyond their power to alter men and nations, withdrew a bit from exposed, risky positions. Two wars, two years of acute food storages (1965 and 1966), the weakening of the Congress, and the increased threats to unity focused the attention of all except the professionals in the field away from foreign affairs for several years. India, questioning its hopes and reassessing its resources, passed into a period of mild isolationism.

COLLABORATION IN PEACE-KEEPING OPERATIONS

In the absence of international political conditions envisioned by chapter VII of the Charter, the peace-keeping responsibilities actually undertaken by the UN depended on the willingness and ability of such medium powers as India, whose interests in a particular con-

flict were identified with the world body rather than with one or
another disputing party, to supply the necessary personnel. Because
of its reputation for impartiality, its noninvolvement in military
groupings, its commitment to the UN's peace-keeping function, and
the high standards of performance by its military and civilian personnel, India's services for UN operations to maintain or bring
about peace in troubled areas were frequently called upon.

India's successful direction of the Neutral Nations Repatriation
Commission in Korea, discussed in chapter III, set an example of
effectiveness which could not be maintained in the volatile atmos-
pheres of the two Vietnams, Laos, and Cambodia, where India
headed the International Commissions for Supervision and Control
(not under UN aegis). But another peace-keeping operation, begun
in the 1950's with Indian participation, the United Nations Emergency Force (UNEF), functioned along the Israeli-Egyptian border
and provided the finest illustration to date of an international
presence inhibiting the outbreak of hostilities. The termination of
the UNEF on Egypt's demand and the start of Israeli-Arab fighting
in 1967 could not detract from the record of peace that it provided
for one decade.

The General Assembly on November 4, 1956, directed that a UN
military force should take up positions between the Israeli and
Egyptian armies to secure cessation of the hostilities which had
broken out a week earlier. The officers and men of India and nine
other small and middle-ranking countries were chosen to compose
the emergency force, which was to be stationed mainly in Egypt's
Gaza strip. Because there were no precedents for such an operation
under the secretary-general's direction, Indian officials carefully
spelled out their understanding of the UNEF's purposes : The
UNEF was not, Nehru stressed, a continuation of or a substitute
for the Anglo-French occupation force in the area ; its coming into
being depended on the withdrawal of foreign troops from Egypt ;
it existed with the invitation and consent of the Cairo government
and would function only on Egyptian territory—Israel would not
agree to its presence on its land ; the UNEF would protect the 1949
armistice line between Egypt and Israel from violation and would
be only "a temporary affair."[1]

These Indian stipulations, accepted by the secretary-general,
suggested that for New Delhi the UN's function of keeping the

32

peace, in any part of the world, would have to depend first on the
willingness of the contending states to stop fighting and then on the
agreement of at least one of them to the stationing of UN forces
in its territory. Without openly repudiating those portions of the
Charter which sanctioned the use of force collectively by member
states, India at that time would not approve of UN military operations against any state or states. Nor, furthermore, would it sanction
the use of UN forces to impose any specific political settlement.
Its experience in the Kashmir dispute had demonstrated the possible
dangers of allowing the UN to enforce its decisions in the guise of
maintaining or creating peace. (India's agreement in June 1950
to collective UN action in Korea had been effectively repudiated
by its subsequent opposition to the UN's Korean War policies and
the General Assembly's "uniting for peace" resolution.) In short,
India wanted to avoid the establishment of any UN military force
with general capabilities for taking action against sovereign states.
Therefore, New Delhi insisted upon the ad hoc character of the
UNEF and its functioning with the compliance of Egypt. It was
a fine line for India to draw, between participating in UN peace-
keeping operations of a military character and simultaneously
defending its own or any other state's right to oppose UN intervention in its territory. The critical condition, in India's view, under
which UN peace-keeping might take place, was the consent of a
state to the presence of UN forces.

India committed its men and equipment generously to the UNEF;
the Canadians and the Indians formed the largest contingents of
the force of between 5,000 and 6,000 officers and troops. In 1957,
957 Indians held UNEF assignments; in 1962, 1,249; and in 1964,
about 1,900.[2] Developing its methods to suit the local conditions
the UNEF functioned under close supervision of the secretary-
general. The clarity in the line of authority to the UN Command,
the effective coordination of its logistics, the comparatively smooth
integration of its national contingents, and the absence of meddling
by non-participating states in its working made the operation a
model for possible future UN peace-keeping endeavours. As long
as it continued, the UNEF served India's interests by preserving
peace in an area where conflicts had frequently involved intervention by outside powers. India shared fully Secretary-General Dag
Hammarskjöld's principle of preventive diplomacy—keeping a

local conflict from spreading and thus precluding involvement by the great powers. The secretary-general applied that principle in setting up the UN observation group for the Lebanon in 1958, which India also supported by contributing military personnel to the group, as well as a prominent civilian member, Rajeshwar Dayal.

The objective of eliminating outside intervention stood primary among the aims of the UN's most elaborate peace-keeping venture to date, the Congo operation. Though its organization was modelled on the UNEF, the United Nations Operations in the Congo (UNOC) faced much more taxing local challenges and had to carry out political and military directives that made the UNEF resemble, in comparison, the field work of a specialized agency. The Congo operation in its initiation was the creation of Dag Hammarskjöld. In his presentation of the Congo crisis to the Security Council he managed to circumvent the Congo government's charge of Belgian aggression, made in a telegram of July 12, 1960, and persuaded the Council to deal with the rebellion in the Congo under article 99, which empowers the secretary-general to bring matters threatening international peace to the Council's attention. Hammarskjöld's recommendation for meeting the crisis was to send a UN force to that country, and on July 14 the Security Council authorized him to do so, in order to facilitate the withdrawal of Belgian troops and provide military assistance to the Leopoldville government until its own security forces could meet their tasks. Within a week after the arrival of the first UN contingents, assembled from African states, the Council unanimously passed its second resolution on the Congo (July 22), which reaffirmed the earlier purpose of the UN action. A third resolution of August 9 added to the UN's objectives the extending of operations to the province of Katanga, where Belgian forces (and civilians) were centred, and whose president, Moise Tshombe, had declared secession from the republic. The secretary-general's diplomatic initiatives in New York and his swift deployment of UN troops in this initial stage amounted to preventive diplomacy of the same sort that he had undertaken through the UNEF. Without an active UN presence, the Congo might easily have become an arena of military intervention by great powers.

Although India held no seat in the Security Council in 1960 it publicly approved of the actions of that body and became one of the staunchest defenders of Hammarskjöld's Congo policies. The government approved of the appointment of Brigadier Indar Jit Rikhye as military adviser to the secretary-general in July. Another Indian, Rajeshwar Dayal, followed Ralph Bunche as Hammarskjöld's representative in the Congo in September. Criticized by Americans, Britishers and some Congolese leaders for his frank reporting of chaotic conditions and outside interference in the Congo, Dayal resigned, "at his own request," on May 25, 1961.

The restrictive terms under which the UNOC began its operations, calling for law and order functions but prohibiting military initiatives and involvements in domestic political affairs, made it impotent to cope with the rapid disintegration of the Congolese government, marked by the feud between President Kasavubu and Prime Minister Lumumba, their unconstitutional dismissals of each other, and the seizure of what authority remained by Joseph Mobutu. As the permanent members of the Security Council rapidly lined up behind contending Congolese factions and Belgian troops and advisors increased their influence in Katanga and elsewhere, the General Assembly took over consideration of the crisis under the "uniting for peace" resolution. But clearer and more forceful directives failed to appear in the resolutions passed by the larger body. The disruption in the new state reached its climax when Lumumba was assassinated on February 13, 1961.

In these choatic circumstances India as well as the US and a majority of the Assembly members urged a more powerful role for the UNOC. India in particular came strongly to the support of the secretary-general, whose office and person and the operation he was conducting came under attacks from the Soviet Union, a supporter of Lumumba. Like many others, Indian leaders regarded the Congo operation as a test of the UN's capacity to act in the interests of peace in Africa as well as in the world. "It is now necessary," India's delegate Krishna Menon told the General Assembly on December 15, "for the United Nations to govern or get out" of the Congo.[3] Without specifying the details of a desirable Congolese settlement the Indian government through the years of uncertainty that followed urged the general proposition that foreign troops, i.e. Belgian, not UN, should leave the country and foreign states cease trying to influence the Congolese government ; that Katanga, the economic heart of the country, should be reunified with the centre ; that law and order should be restored so that a legally constituted government could have a fair chance of functioning— under Lumumba, as long as he was alive, because he had the support of parliament.[4] Above all, India believed, in the words of its UN representative, "that the Congo should be kept out of the cold war. None of us wishes to see the development in the Congo of a Korean situation. It is imperative that the Congo should be insulated from the supply of arms and military assistance of all kinds to the various factions contending for power."[5]

In view of the mounting support by west European states on the one hand and by the Soviet Union and China on the other for their respectively favoured Congolese factions, India's political preferences marked a moderate, middle position, from which the secretary- general derived his main support. In early 1961 the new American administration moved closer to the position that a satisfactory solution to the Congo crisis would require the isolation of that state from great power struggles and competition elsewhere. Thus, Indian and American interests in the Congo began to converge. At the same time the main African contributors to the UNOC and Yugoslavia withdrew their troops, criticizing the UN's failure to protect Lumumba from his enemies.

The sudden reduction in the UNOC's military force—from about 19,000 to about 8,000 men—at a time when its effectiveness was already at a very low point, presented Hammarskjöld with an admi- nistrative crisis, and he turned to New Delhi for its solution. He asked for Indian troops to fill the gap opened by the removal of the African forces. His request was reinforced by a similar appeal from the US government. According to Nehru, India's reply to the UN's request "recognized the necessity of the United Nations functioning there but the way it had been functioning was not to our liking nor was it effective, and if they could take up a positive line . . . we would send them help in the shape of Armed Forces but not till we are satisfied that it could be used in the right way."[6] India's conditions for despatching troops included the assurance that they would not be used against forces of another UN member, but only against the Congolese and white mercenaries ; that they would not oppose popular government in the Congo ; that the Indians would operate as a unit under their own commanders ; and that the UNOC would work for early withdrawal of the Belgian forces and an end to

Katanga's secession. On February 21 the Security Council, again taking up the problem, passed a crucial resolution, which authorized the UNOC's "use of force, if necessary, in the last resort" and affirmed that measures should be taken "for the immediate withdrawal and evacuation . . . of all Belgian and other foreign military and para-military personnel and political advisors. . . ."[7]

Because of this mandate for a more vigorous prosecution of the UN's purposes in the Congo, and agreements reached in private between the secretary-general and the major supporters of the operation, India offered 4,700 combat troops on March 3, supplementing 373 Indian medical and technical personnel already in the Congo. The first elements arrived on March 16 in US planes, thus symbolizing the joint Indo-American purpose, which continued until the end of the Congo operation. The US provided air supply for the UNOC in Katanga, and on an operational level—no higher than that— there was coordination between the Indian and American missions in Leopoldville (Kinshasa). When Nehru and Kennedy met in November 1961, in the words of the communique, they "reviewed the United States and Indian contributions to United Nations operations in the Congo, which they regard as an illustration of how that body . . . can help bring about conditions for the peaceful resolution of conflict. . . . The President expressed his special appreciation of the role played by the Indian soldiers in the Congo, who comprise more than one-third of the United Nations force there."[8]

During 1961 the political structure of the Congo began to be rebuilt ; except for Tshombe, in Katanga, the major leaders patched together an accord, and parliament was reconvened, under the protection of the UNOC. UN members, however, could not agree on how to end the secession of Katanga province within the doctrines of "force . . . in the last resort" and political noninvolvement that guided the UNOC's operations. In August 1961 Indian, Swedish, and Irish troops captured over 300 mercenaries in Elizabethville, capital of Katanga, and prepared for a push to expel all mercenaries and thus undermine Tshombe's strength. In September the campaign to end Katangan secession,[9] headed by Indian Brigadier K.A.S. Raja, began on a decisive note, only to be undercut by British and French warnings to Hammarskjöld that the UNOC had exceeded its mandate by intervening actively in behalf of the central government. Hammarskjöld's death in an air crash in the Congo in September and a cease-fire between the UNOC and Tshombe on the 20th added confusion to the UN's purposes; fighting ended, but Tshombe still held power in Katanga.

Heated diplomatic activity in New York and world capitals by states favouring an increased UN role in Congolese affairs resulted in a Security Council resolution on November 24 that changed the course of the fighting. The Council authorized the new secretary-general, U Thant, "to take vigorous action, including the use of a requisite measure of force, if necessary" to eliminate the foreign mercenaries and declared its opposition to Katangan secession and its "full and firm support for the Central Government of the Congo."[10] The UNOC was no longer inhibited in what it regarded as its main mission, to defeat by any means necessary Katangan opposition to the central government.

Vested with clear authority to take the military initiative UNOC troops engaged in the hardest fighting of the operation during December and January, with Indian Gurkha and Dogra units frequently in the forefront. Brigadier Raja's multinational force gained control of Elizabethville by December 18th, with the help of the UN air arm, which included five Indian jet planes. But that phase of the fighting was brought to a halt so that diplomacy could take over the task of ending Katanga's secession. On December 21, 1961, Tshombe nominally accepted the authority of Leopoldville.

During most of 1962 weary political manoeuvrings failed to bring Katanga under effective central control. India held silence, officially, but resented the relatively stationary—and exposed, in view of increasing Katangan air power—position of its forces under UNOC command. By October both India and the US were encouraging the secretary-general to make greater use of the UNOC against Katanga. New Delhi wanted rapid action so that its troops could return to India, then faced by Chinese attacks. Incidents in December touched off the fighting for which both sides had been preparing. Under a new Indian commander, Major General D. Prem Chand, the UNOC launched offensive actions, one of which, the attack on Jadotville, under an Indian Brigadier, had not been sanctioned by UN headquarters. Jadotville was occupied, as were other important Katangan towns in January, while the UN air force was destroying the opposition's air arm, mostly on the ground. At the end of the month U Thant announced that the military phase of the UNOC was completed. Indian troops withdrew shortly thereafter. Their casualties of 24 dead had been surprisingly light in view of the large part that they had taken in all of the critical Katangan operations. India's military role in the Congo, in fact, turned out to have been essential to the success of the UN mission.[11]

The UN operation in the Congo, characterized by the highest level of international collaboration of any UN emergency under-taking, brought an alien interference into a country's internal affairs that New Delhi would have opposed under most circums-tances. But apart from the fact that the legitimate government of the Congo had invited UN intervention and that the secretary-general's direction of the UNOC always had the support of the majority of UN members, the UN's presence in the Congo was speci-ally distinguished because it prevented open intervention there by one or both of the great powers. Congolese politics was rife with alien interests, political and financial, and according to New Delhi's assessment the UN was the least self-seeking of possible interveners. The UN civilian operations, which maintained essential services within the Congo and trained the Congolese in many aspects of modern administration, excelled any similar performance by a single power because they were untainted by a motive of national interest.

The fact that the UNOC aimed its major military actions against the active remnants of European colonialism made involvement in the operation more agreeable to Indians. But New Delhi carried on that involvement at the cost, at least temporarily, of improving its relations with African governments ; it suffered a loss of prestige among the more radical African states. Its moderation on anti-colonial issues, uncompromisingly proclaimed at the Belgrade conference in September 1961 and demonstrated in the Congo as well, tended to isolate New Delhi even from nonaligned Egypt and Yugoslavia.

A major premise of the policy of India and many states toward the Congo crisis was that the prestige of the UN itself was at stake in the Congo ; that once the UN had intervened there it should persist until its tasks had been fulfilled. Support of the UN meant, in this case, support for the secretary-general's office, to which had passed some of the peace-keeping responsibilities that the Charter had envisioned for the Security Council.

The Soviet Union and the socialist states initiated a blunt attack on Secretary-General Hammarskjöld and his newly assumed powers when the conduct of the UNOC ran counter to their interests. Premier Khrushchev set the tone of the attack in a speech to the General Assembly in September 1960. Charging Hammarskjöld with aiding the "colonialists" and the anti-Lumumba factions in the Congo, Khrushchev went on to propose his "troika" scheme for the office of the secretary-general. "In the place of a Secretary-General who is at present the interpreter and executor of the decisions of the General Assembly and the Security Council," he said, "we consider it advisable to set up, in the place of a Secretary-General . . . a collective executive organ . . . consisting of three persons each of whom would represent a certain group of States"[12] — Western, socialist, and nonaligned. The three men would, furthermore, be able to act only in unison, thus affording any "group of states" a veto on the policies of the secretary-general's office. The Afro-Asian states, whose supporting votes would have been required to introduce such an emasculation of the UN, joined in near unanimity to criticise Khrushchev's proposal ; it therefore never had a chance of being adopted. Krishna Menon plainly stated, "We don't believe in an executive which provides for the functioning of three heads that would cancel out each other. . . . We are also against . . . an arrangement which contains a built in veto. We are against any kind of arrangement whereby forward movement would become impossible."[13]

The USSR's disenchantment with the Congo operation—after having initially approved of UN intervention—led logically to its refusal to help to pay for it, and thence to a new crisis over the internal cohesion of the organization. The Soviet Union, joined by France among the permanent members of the Security Council, argued that it was not obligated to pay for UN military operations undertaken against its wishes and allegedly outside the provisions of the Charter. By mid-1963 the total cost to the UN of its involvement in the Congo was just over $400 million. The failure of the USSR, France, and a number of smaller states to pay their alloted share of the budgets for the various peace-keeping operations—although France agreed to contribute funds for the UNEF—brought about a crisis in financing, which the sale of UN bonds beginning in 1962 could not alleviate.

The financial crisis in turn threatened to break up the organization, because the US began to insist, during the 19th General Assembly session, on the enforcement of article 19 of the Charter. That article provided that a member state "which is in arrears in the payment of its financial contributions to the Organisation shall have no vote in the General Assembly if the amount of its arrears equals or exceeds the amount of the contributions due from it for the preceding two years." No persuasion from any source—including a world court decision of July 20, 1962—could alter the Russian and French decisions not to pay for the military operations, and as long as the American threat to try to invoke article 19 remained the Assembly could conduct no important business.

Despite its participation in both the UNOC and the UNEF India as well as many Afro-Asian states were reluctant to apply the sanctions spelled out in article 19. Far more critical than peace-keeping operations or their financing was the continued functioning of the organization's regular activities, according to those states. Perhaps ironically, it had been the Indian delegation at San Francisco in 1945 which had introduced an amendment[14] to the draft charter that ultimately became article 19 ; as a carry-over from its League experience on budgetary matters India wanted to ensure the solvency of the new organization. But India and other states found a way to avoid applying article 19 against members who refused to share the expenses of peace-keeping operations, namely, by distinguishing those operations from the "normal" functions of the UN, although the Charter makes no such distinction explicitly.

Explaining his government's position in the context of financing any future UN peace-keeping endeavour B.N. Chakravarty stressed the ad hoc nature of each such undertaking, whether carried out under Security Council or Assembly authorization. Neither the Charter (article 43) nor the "uniting for peace" resolution, he said, contemplated "forcing Member States to bear a share of peacekeeping costs against their will."[15] Only those states which favoured an operation should be asked to pay for it. In the budgetary crisis of 1964 and 1965 the position of India and a great many other members may have forestalled a US-USSR confrontation over voting rights under article 19. The US, after months of apparent indecision, withdrew the threat to invoke article 19, probably on grounds of broader considerations of its relations with Russia.[16]

Whatever the future of peace-keeping actions by the UN, the result of the crisis over financing appeared to reestablish the relationship between the Council and the Assembly that the Charter intended. The executive powers that had been vested in the secretary-general for carrying out his preventive diplomacy may have been thereby withdrawn and certainly were weakened. India did not oppose that development. As a member of the Special Political Committee on Peacekeeping Operations India affirmed its judgment that the General Assembly should not, even with the assent of large majorities, usurp the functions of the Security Council in despatching troops. India's delegate on the committee proposed, as a practical measure, that when the "parties primarily concerned concur, the great powers may agree, save in exceptional circumstances and for special reasons, not to vote against a proposal involving the despatch of armed personnel even if they are not entirely satisfied about the expediency of such action." But, he continued, the Council did not have the authority to tax the entire UN membership for financing peace-keeping without the concurrence of the General Assembly.[17]

The enlargement of the Assembly to well over 100 members inevitably reduced the efficiency of that body, and the majority of votes having passed into the hands of small and comparatively new states the longer established powers favoured a decline in the Assembly's influence over peace and security matters. But the newer states were anxious that their own improved political status be reflected also in the more exclusive organs of the UN. Accordingly, the Assembly decided, at its 18th session, to increase the memberships of the Security Council from 11 to 15 and ECOSOC from 18 to 27. The enlargement gave greater prominence than before to Afro-Asian representation on those bodies. The permanent membership of both Councils remained the same, despite vague suggestions heard from time to time that it should be increased, with India as a new permanent member on both Councils. India was elected to a seat on ECOSOC in December 1965 and in 1966 for the second time became a member of the Security Council.

THE CONTINUING ARMS DEBATES

The futility of disarmament and arms control negotiations in the

1950's and the breakdown of the moratorium on nuclear weapons testing in September 1961 were particularly disheartening to those states, such as India, which from the sidelines of the arms debate had kept urging the great powers to reach some agreement. When Russia resumed testing, Nehru, then at the Belgrade conference, warned that the danger of war "has been enhanced . . . by the recent decision of the Soviet Government to start nuclear tests."[18] A 10-nation committee meeting in Geneva with membership evenly balanced between the two great coalitions had succumbed to the stalemate in the "cold war" debate, which was dramatically demonstrated at the General Assembly session of late 1960. One year later, however, in December 1961, new hope emerged from a joint US-USSR proposal to set up an enlarged negotiating body, the Eighteen Nation Disarmament Committee (ENDC), whose designated proceddures absorbed all of the main points of India's case on how negotiations should be conducted. (France refused to attend, so the ENDC had only 17 active members.) Recognizing the insistent demands of nonaligned states for a voice in arms discussions the great powers agreed to the participation of eight of them, including India, in the new body.

One of India's functions at the Geneva meetings was to encourage discussions between the major negotiators in a private atmosphere that Indian delegates preferred and sought to create.[19] The more demanding work of Indian and other nonaligned delegations lay in proposing compromise measures that might find favour with the two major nuclear powers, or be difficult for both to turn down. One such effort in 1962 and 1963 sought to resolve the lengthy deadlock over the number of inspections needed to guarantee a proposed nuclear test ban. The *pièce de résistance* of the nonaligned members was their proposal to accept a scientific judgment on the number of inspections required over a period of five or seven years instead of one year ; to make public such a plan "would create a situation in which continued disagreement between the two sides would be nothing short of ridiculous. . . ."[20] The US, UK, and USSR, however, were then in the final stages of productive talks on a test ban treaty and requested the nonaligned states not to intervene with any novel ideas. Without assistance from non-nuclear states the three powers reached a test ban agreement on August 5, 1963, to which India was the first state to adhere.

The conclusion of the first great arms control treaty outside the UN and the UN sponsored ENDC revealed the difficulties of conducting arms control negotiations in a semi-public forum. Over the next five years no agreements to reduce armaments could be reached. The major topic of discussion, nonproliferation of nuclear weapons, was of vital interest to India because it placed central importance on the arms policies of the non-nuclear and the nonaligned states.

New Delhi's reactions to the problem of the spread of nuclear arms and its own policies on the development of those weapons lacked the decisiveness that the importance of such matters might have recommended. The main issues were frequently mentioned but did not receive thorough airing, either in government or in private forums; the Indian democracy may have thereby lost the opportunity for a great debate of the sort that could have strengthened national resolve on security and foreign policy questions. Nehru's death five months before the explosion of the first Chinese nuclear device deprived the nation of its clearest guidance on all foreign policies. In the years following, India's positions on nuclear weapons gradually assumed shape, but a sophisticated public awareness of where the government's decisions might ultimately lead the country was lacking.

The most consistent stand that India adopted on nuclear proliferation was to oppose it, and to oppose it with particular vehemence when states achieving nuclear capabilities refused to enter arms control negotiations or to adhere to the test ban treaty—to wit, France and the Peoples Republic of China. For many years India's representatives in the UN urged nuclear powers not to transfer nuclear weapons to countries which did not possess them and in the early 1960's called for guarantees from non-nuclear states that they would not encourage the spread of nuclear weapons. The government, meanwhile, had been issuing periodic assurances that it had no intention of itself producing nuclear weapons. At a time when the country faced no practical choice in the matter Nehru had said that he "rejoiced in not having the atom bomb."[21] Much later, when India's atomic energy capability was established and well recognized[22] the government still maintained a principled abjuration from nuclear weaponry.

After China gained the capability of exploding nuclear devices the real test appeared of the Indian government's will to remain militarily non-nuclear, and the results were inconclusive. In initial reaction to the news that China was about to explode its first nuclear device Prime Minister Sastri, then at the Cairo conference of nonaligned states, proposed that a mission be sent to Peking to try to alter Chinese intentions. Sastri went on to state that : "We in India stand committed to the use of nuclear power only for peaceful purposes and, even though . . . we are capable of developing nuclear weapons, our scientists and technicians are under firm orders not to make a single experiment, not to perfect a single device which is not needed for peaceful uses of atomic energy."[23] But Indian public criticism against Sastri's self-denying policy led the prime minister to more flexible attitudes in the months following.[24] Mrs. Gandhi similarly refused consistently to deny that India might consider nuclear weapons necessary for its defense.

The great uncertainty about India's ultimate intentions became a major stimulus to the efforts of the US, UK, and USSR to achieve a nonproliferation pact that India might be induced to sign. India was the only state in the mid-1960's which had to face alone the open hostility of an enemy with imminent nuclear arms capabilities, and other governments accordingly speculated over how long India would remain non-nuclear. If India obtained unconventional weapons, Pakistan would follow the lead as soon as it could, and the momentum of nuclear proliferation among middle-ranking states might be difficult to resist.

As the three nuclear powers represented at the ENDC began defining their bargaining positions on a nonproliferation treaty, in 1964 and 1965, India refined its original willingness to accept any great power agreement covering the spread of nuclear weapons. Foreign Minister Swaran Singh's simple plea in December 1964 that non-nuclear states "should declare their readiness not to produce, acquire or test any nuclear weapons"[25] evolved into the conditional acceptance of a nonproliferation agreement articulated by V. C. Trivedi, representative at the ENDC meetings and the General Assembly's 20th session in 1965-1966. India's revised policy, reflecting more exacting formulation than New Delhi had previously brought to bear on the question, began with the proposition that nonproliferation should be regarded as a means to the end of disarmament and therefore should "be coupled with or followed by tangible steps to halt the nuclear arms race and to limit, reduce and eliminate the stocks of nuclear weapons and the means of their delivery."[26] The General Assembly incorporated this view into its resolution 2028 (XX), but the three nuclear powers could not agree on what, if any, disarmament measures should become part of a nonproliferation treaty acceptable to themselves. The nonaligned and some other non-nuclear states were trying, unsuccessfully, to persuade the US and USSR to cut back their own, "vertical," expansion of nuclear arms capability in order to balance a halt in the "horizontal" spread of those weapons.

From time to time Indian officials grappled with the problem of how non-nuclear states could defend themselves against the threat or use of nuclear weapons. Although central to India's policy on nonproliferation, this problem raised dilemmas which seemed insoluble. For several months in late 1964 and in 1965 India appeared to be exploring the idea of a "nuclear umbrella" or "joint nuclear shield" to protect itself. Sastri explained to the Lok Sabha in December 1964 that he had discussed the matter on his recent visit to London.[27] However, the Soviet Union offered no support to a "umbrella" scheme, and Sastri stated that "he would not accept a nuclear shield unless both the USA and the Soviet Union were partners to the guarantee."[28] President Johnson declared on October 18, 1964, just after the first Chinese nuclear test, that "nations that do not seek national nuclear weapons can be sure that, if they need our strong support against some threat of nuclear blackmail, they will have it."[29] But if India accepted a Western guarantee to provide the deterrent in case of a threatened nuclear attack, formal nonalignment and possibly collaboration in other areas with the Soviet Union would be sacrificed. Furthermore, even if an acceptable guarantee could be drafted, Indians expressed doubts that it would have much credibility : even close allies of the US were sceptical of its willingness to use nuclear weapons other than for the defense of its own territory. Finally, if India had to depend entirely on foreign nuclear deterrents Indian defenses would be frozen into a state of permanent inferiority to China's. Faced with these and other theoretical contingencies, important Indian politicians, Congressmen as well as non-Congress spokesmen, demanded that the government give more favourable consideration to obtaining nuclear arms.

The debate in India, partly because of its inconclusiveness, failed to influence the course of negotiations on a nonproliferation treaty.

Furthermore, India's delegates at the ENDC submerged the problems of their own country's defense against a nuclear threat within an increasingly large package of demands made on the great powers. As a step towards nuclear arms limitation, the nonaligned countries urged an extension of the test ban treaty to include underground tests ; they suggested some cut-backs on capabilities of delivering nuclear weapons ; all non-nuclear states sought agreement from the great powers that acquiring nuclear arms would not by itself convey "prestige," that there be in fact a "progressive denial of prestige to the possession of nuclear weapons."[30] Linked to those demands came the General Assembly resolution 2163 (XXI) in December 1966 calling for a conference to draft a convention for the outlawing of the use of nuclear weapons.

As the US, the UK, and the USSR approached agreement on a draft nonproliferation treaty a non-military feature of their position elicited increased Indian caution about signing such a pledge. India suspected that provisions for inspections to ensure that developments in nuclear technology were for peaceful purposes only might hinder its own atomic energy programme. New Delhi had always been wary of accepting international control over any facet of domestic nuclear development, which it judged was the only effective solution to India's shortage of conventional power. Although welcoming the establishment of the International Atomic Energy Agency (IAEA) in 1957, it had opposed any system under its aegis for extensive international control and inspection of nuclear energy production. India insisted on working out bilateral agreements with the US and Canada for assistance in nuclear technology rather than permitting an international agency to supervise the arrangements.[31] Nehru believed that if the IAEA or any such body, semi-independent of the General Assembly, gained a determining role in India's nuclear energy development, his country might be placed in a permanently inferior position vis-a-vis the established nuclear powers, which would assumedly control the international body. The extremity of his concern found expression in his warning to the Lok Sabha "that atomic energy for peaceful purposes is far more important to the underdeveloped countries of the world than to the developed ones. And if the developed countries have all the powers they may stop the use of atomic energy everywhere, including in their own countries, because they do not need it so much, and in consequence we might suffer."[32] Over a decade later India's position on a nonproliferation agreement reflected the same general fear that placing international checks on non-military nuclear development, however laudable in principle, could leave countries such as India perpetually in the rear of peaceful nuclear advances and thus technologically dependent on other countries. This would be certain to happen if no corresponding checks were imposed on the advances in the military uses of nuclear power.

In short, looking into the future of a nuclear age, Indian planners insisted that conditions of equal treatment be written into any international agreements about nuclear energy, that any restrictions on military or non-military nuclear development have a balanced effect on the advanced and the underdeveloped countries, so that the gap between them might not expand more rapidly than was already the case.

In the final stages of drafting a nonproliferation treaty in late 1967 some of India's objections to earlier positions of the great powers were overcome. But after a joint US-USSR final draft was presented to the ENDC on January 18, 1968, India decided not to adhere to it as it then stood. The gap in the treaty which most obviously discriminated against militarily non-nuclear states was the absence of a guarantee against threatened nuclear attacks on them. But India's policy on nonproliferation was in fact no longer contingent on any offer of a "nuclear umbrella" or "shield." India's security could not be allowed to rest on such a commitment from abroad, even if it were forthcoming. Mrs. Gandhi's government, it seemed, did not wish to deny itself the possibility of acquiring nuclear weaponry and thereby establish its own deterrent against any future Chinese nuclear threat.

ANTI-COLONIALISM AND THE COMMITTEE OF 24

One year after the General Assembly had adopted resolution 1514 (XV), on granting of independence to all colonial countries and peoples it debated the issue again, decided that little progress had been made in fulfilling the hopes expressed in the declaration, and established a 17-member committee to try to implement the Assembly's wishes. At the end of 1962 the Assembly increased the membership of the committee to 24 and invited it to consider not

33

only non-self-governing territories but "all territories which have not yet achieved independence," i.e. countries such as Southern Rhodesia. The mandate of the Committee of 24 was soon extended to include the work of the Committee on Information from Non-Self-Governing Territories, the Special Committee for South West Africa, and the Special Committee on Territories under Portuguese Administration. India held a seat on both new committees, which apart from the Trusteeship Council became the only UN bodies responsible for international accountability and supervision over dependent territories. The great questions of Southern Rhodesia, Portuguese territories, and Aden occupied most of the committee's time, but even insignificant remnants of empire, such as Pitcairn Island, merited at least passing attention.

Earlier sections of this book described India's gradual withdrawal from the leadership of the anti-colonialist movement, the higher priority that it gave to other international crusades, arms control in particular, and its moderating influence in the forums where the abolition of imperialism continued to be discussed. There was no reversal of these tendencies. But by the mid-1960's it was clear that they did not signify any diminution in Indian endeavours to undermine colonialism or a weakened conviction that continued domination by Europeans over alien peoples presented a serious threat to peace and a denial of obligations on all UN members. With the Afro-Asian countries dominating the General Assembly and with African members out-numbering Asian by about two to one, the UN intensified its involvement in non-self-governing territories, particularly in Africa, where the hard core cases remained. The establishment of the Committee of 24 with more sweeping authority than that given to the Trusteeship Council or any previous ad hoc bodies,[33] and the prompt and decisive manner in which the Assembly reinforced the actions of the committee, propelled the important remaining cases of imperial control into the centre of international political concern. The force behind that propulsion was the crusading zeal and the frustration of African states, united after the Addis Ababa conference of May 1963 into the Organization of African Unity and thereafter creating for itself a formal caucusing body at the UN. India supported that leadership—steadied was sometimes the better word—because of shared objectives, and also because of New Delhi's policy of friendship with the new African states.

The Committee of 24 took early recognition of the threat to the freedom of African people posed by the White controlled government of Southern Rhodesia. The committee's position was that Britain should not transfer sovereignty to Salisbury until there was a government there which represented African as well as White interests and that meanwhile it should intervene to preclude the emergence in that country of a regime based on the South African model. The UK initially denied the competence of the committee to investigate Southern Rhodesian affairs on grounds that the territory was self-governing and for the same reason declined to take charge itself of Rhodesia's constitutional arrangements. But the committee continued to press for action, the General Assembly passed resolutions to the same effect, and finally Britain began the fruitless task of trying to meet some of the Afro-Asian demands by purely persuasive means.

The government in Salisbury declared, unilaterally, its independence on November 11, 1965 ; the General Assembly and then the Security Council resolved that economic sanctions should be employed by all UN members against the "illegal" regime. By that time the UK, faced by a situation unprecedented in its recent imperial experience, was relying on UN resolutions to support its own action against one of its colonial territories. India and the Afro-Asian states condemned, in the words of India's spokesman, "the handful of men [who] are defying with impunity the urge for freedom of four million people of Southern Rhodesia who rightly demand independence on the basis of majority rule and one man one vote."[34] But their criticism was aimed against Britain, on whom they laid the responsibility for the continued rebelliousness of the white Rhodesians.

The objective of political equality for all people living in Africa, in support of which India claimed a notable record, met its most concerted opposition, physical and philosophical, from the Union of South Africa. Added to its other conflicts with the UN was its refusal to place the mandated territory of South West Africa under a trusteeship, as the other mandate holders had voluntarily done. The issue was the subject of three advisory opinions by the International Court of Justice in the 1950's and then a climaxing, controversial decision in 1966 by which the Court, in denying the right of Ethiopia and Liberia to bring suit, refused to instruct the Union government to alter its administrative arrangements in South West Africa. The General Assembly thereupon, on October 27, 1966, declared that the League mandate was at an end, and the UN took upon itself "direct responsibility" for administration of the territory. South Africa, whose intention was to annex South West Africa, responded by asserting that it would resist any UN move to assume administration. India took a predictable stand against its oldest international antagonist and urged that the UN take whatever action it could, not specifying, however, military action.

Portugal had been deprived of its Indian "province" in 1961 but clung vigorously to Angola and Mozambique in Africa. To the Committee of 24 Lisbon repeated what it had said to India, that its overseas territories were parts of Portugal and therefore could not be dealt with as non-self-governing. The UN debate continued much as it had in the 1950's, except that some African states were stepping up their military assistance to guerilla forces within the Portuguese territories. And if nothing else was achieved thereby, some African states hoped that minor military action might lead to international intervention and a subsequent overthrow of Portugal's rule.

Most of the remaining smaller colonial areas considered by the committee flew British flags, and the UK was distressed to find itself in the dock because of British Guiana, Gibraltar, and Aden, among others, after it had just surrendered its African empire and held nothing but a few enclaves elsewhere. The Indian government tended to sympathize with the British position in the smaller territories, as it had in earlier situations, and found reasons to try to moderate anti-colonialist demands in the Committee of 24. But once resolutions on colonial territories were before the General Assembly India almost always voted with the Afro-Asian majority. By that time Indian delegates had often managed to introduce into resolutions modes of conciliatory thinking and language which they expected would have a beneficial effect on both the colonial powers and their critics. An Indian for many years filled the influential post of rapporteur for the Committee of 24.

THE DIPLOMACY OF ECONOMIC EQUALIZATION

The prospects of India's meeting its increasing foreign exchange needs for economic development through bilateral assistance programmes appeared bleak by the mid-1960's. "Cold war" competitiveness had underlain the effectiveness of the bilateral assistance programmes, and that advantage to India nearly disappeared with the US-Soviet detente. Annual contributions by the Aid India Consortium had levelled off, as the main source of funds, the US Congress, adopted measures to reduce non-military budgets and showed its growing disenchantment with all aid programmes. Other governments, with the possible exception of the Soviet Union, indicated no inclination to expand their aid outlays in substantial measure and over a long period. At the same time, servicing debts from earlier assistance was taking an increasing share of Indian foreign exchange earnings. India therefore tried to induce greater external assistance in its balance of payments difficulties through the UN. This new emphasis on multilateral economic endeavours brought India into closer diplomatic collaboration with other underdeveloped countries and produced a unity of purpose similar to that achieved on anti-colonialism, but not as effective immediately in gaining concessions from the traditional holders of power.

In December 1961 the General Assembly declared the 1960's a "development decade" and recommended that economic policies be aimed at achieving a minimum of five per cent annual growth rate for developing countries by 1970. (India's growth was reaching close to that rate during the 1950's, but the third five-year plan did not maintain the previously established momentum, and the fourth plan was still-born.) Recognizing the need for new machinery to stimulate assistance and development the Assembly one year later called for the convening of a conference on trade and development (UNCTAD) in 1964.

Meanwhile, the attack by developing nations on the unbalanced division of the world's productive wealth was expanding beyond agitation for more ad hoc transfers through the various aid programmes to the demand for a revised system of international trade. Discussions carried on among members of GATT and the findings of the Haberler report on trends in international trade led to the conclusion that the position of the developing countries as exporters in world trade was deteriorating—at just the time when their demands for imports were rising as a by-product of economic advancement. For example, the share of the developing countries in world trade declined from nearly one-third in 1950 to just over one-fifth in 1962. India's share of world exports declined from slightly less than two per cent in 1951 to about one per cent in 1960. Building on earlier statements of purpose in GATT declarations the developing countries, including India, in May 1963 proposed an "action programme" which asked for reduction or elimination of quantitative restrictions, tariffs, and other taxes on exports of developing countries entering the markets of developed countries. For the supporters of that programme, aid could never provide a substitute for increased trade.

The complaint of the developing countries that they faced an unfair, even immoral disadvantage in having to compete with highly advanced countries when they wished to expand their export earnings struck a political note, at base. National deprivation and discrimination, they alleged, was in some measure the result of colonialism and the unwillingness of advanced nations in the post-colonial period to permit an alteration of the international economic system from which they benefited. The division of the world into "haves" and "have-nots" could result in conflicts even more severe than those which resulted from colonialism, even though the military power of the advanced countries presently protected their monopolies of wealth.

Spokesmen for India eschewed the language of threat and hesitated to predict future violence stemming from global inequalities of wealth. But one Indian representative on ECOSOC warned that the demand of newly independent and underdeveloped nations for "an end to poverty, and for rapid economic and social betterment. . . . must be met ; if there was no other way, governments and peoples would use the most drastic measures to raise themselves by their own efforts. A better way, however. . . . was the way of international cooperation."[35] Others argued that no modern, liberal state could tolerate within its boundaries the monopolies of wealth and the discrepancies in living standards that blighted the global community, and that the protestations of both democratic and communist governments about their international purposes rang hollow as long as they failed to check the widening gap between the developed one-third and the underdeveloped two-thirds of the world's population.

The economic case for radical changes in policies on development appeared in its most authoritative form in the documents and discussions of UNCTAD, held in Geneva in the spring of 1964.[36]

There was no disagreement about the fact that economic development in any country stimulated the demand for imports. Imports
had to be paid for by exports or by credits, but reliance on the latter,
i.e. aid, could not be tolerated permanently by the developed or
the developing countries. The main source of export earnings for
the non-industrial countries was, of course, primary and semi-
processed raw materials. With few exceptions, such as oil, the international demand for primary products was inelastic as compared
with the demand for manufactures. Partly for that reason and
partly because of increased wages and profits in industrial countries,
while the prices of raw materials and semi-manufactured goods
tended to remain constant or unpredictably fluctuating the prices
of manufactured goods tended to rise in world markets.

The terms of trade, in other words, were deteriorating for the
developing countries—by about 17 per cent between 1950 and 1961,
again excluding petroleum. Furthermore, the developing countries'
total share even in the world's export of raw materials, other than
oil, had declined—from 41 per cent in 1950 to 29 per cent in 1961 ;
several of the greatest manufacturing countries, such as the US,
were major exporters of primary products, sometimes at prices
below those offered by underdeveloped countries for the same items.
The result of all this was a so-called trade gap between the developing
and developed countries, which partly helped to explain why,
during the "development decade," as before, the economic disparity
between rich and poor countries continued to grow.

Because about 90 per cent of the exports from underdeveloped
or developing countries as a whole consisted of primary commodities, the obstacles to increased earnings from them received prime
emphasis at UNCTAD meetings. For India and certain other less
underdeveloped countries, however, future prospects for export
expansion rested heavily on sales of manufactured and semi-
manufactured goods. For those countries, any meaningful trade
reforms had to include greater opportunities to sell machine-made
items, for which the tariffs and quotas set by the advanced countries
were invariably more restrictive than on raw materials.

The purposes and the functioning of GATT aimed at the expansion
of world trade and equality of treatment among the GATT contrac-
ting parties, which, incidentally, included India. As an instrument
for expanding exports of manufactures from the developing coun-

tries, however, GATT proved itself a failure, as would any arrangements for reciprocal tariff reductions premised on the equality of trading partners. As the secretary-general of UNCTAD pointed out, the economic structures of the developed and the developing countries were altogether different. For example, conventional trade reciprocity demanded that tariff reductions to increase the exports of a developing country to an advanced industrial economy be matched by equivalent tariff concessions by the developing country, a procedure which would be likely to retard the latter's industrialization, usually taking place behind protective tariff walls. Furthermore, because of the stronger position of the established industrial states in world trade, reciprocal tariff reductions would tend to benefit them more than they would the developing countries.

At the UNCTAD meetings in 1964, India and the 76 other developing countries managed to overcome the differing and sometimes conflicting economic interests among themselves ; they pressed for a new approach to world trade not based on reciprocal trading agreements but on the use of trade as an instrument for development of the poorer countries and for the creation of a more equitable distribution of the world's resources. The conference's major decisions had not been implemented by the time of the second UNCTAD in 1968, but they nevertheless committed the developed countries, on paper, to some of the new trade concepts suggested by the developing states and to certain principles of economic aid. Unanimous agreement was reached that limited preferential arrangements, such as between the European Economic Community and certain African countries, should be abolished simultaneously with the application of measures of general scope which could provide the same advantages to all developing countries. Commodity arrangements aimed at securing "remunerative, equitable and stable" prices to producers of primary products was another recommendation of the conference. A guideline for determining the desirable size of aid disbursements by developed countries was featured in the UNCTAD recommendations : each developed country should supply financial resources approaching as nearly as possible to one per cent of its national income. A further generally accepted proposal was to enlarge the functions of the UN Special Fund to include direct assistance for development projects.

On the other hand, the scheme favoured by India for expanding exports to developed countries, namely, nondiscriminatory preferences, was not accepted at the 1964 UNCTAD. That system would require preferential treatment of the exports of developing countries by developed countries (as was already in effect in the Commonwealth and among countries of the French Community) on a generally applicable basis and, of course, not to be reciprocated by the developing countries. As applied to manufactures, the preferences might extend for a ten-year period to each product from each developing country as it entered the international market. New manufacturing industries would thus be able to overcome tariff barriers in advanced countries for long enough to permit them to get a footing, after which they would have to compete on traditional GATT terms of most-favoured-nation treatment.

Such a system would benefit "infant industries" on a global scale with much the same effect as a single country's protection of its new industries before they could survive in a highly competitive environment. The export earnings to developing countries accruing from the introduction of nondiscriminatory preferences would be remarkably different from foreign exchange received as aid because they would not be tied to purchases in any donor country and would probably increase self-reliance in the recipient countries. The developed countries should also benefit from receiving diversified products in exchange for their indirect assistance, instead of merely accumulating indebtednesses.

Concessions to developing countries on the matter of tariffs could not be sought from the centrally controlled, socialist states, which did not rely on market mechanisms to establish prices of goods or demands for imports. Therefore the developing countries, through UNCTAD, requested the socialist states to take account of the export potential of the developing countries in formulating their national plans and increase their imports from the latter—India suggested at double the current rate—on a state trading basis. India was already receiving the benefits of increased exports to the Soviet Union, whose purchases from India grew more rapidly than those of any other major trading partner in the first half of the 1960's.

The first UNCTAD failed to reach concrete agreements that would immediately affect trade relations between the two categories of countries represented at the conference. But it implanted the new concept of linking trade and economic development, and, firmly rooted, that idea showed signs of steady growth in its acceptance by governments. The main institutional mechanism for promoting UNCTAD ideas was the Trade and Development Board, which the conference set up to study and if possible give effect to its recommendations. Parallel interest in UNCTAD formulae for development appeared in the deliberations of the Organization for Economic Cooperation and Development (OECD), composed of the major Western aid-giving countries.

At the 1964 UNCTAD and for several years in the OECD the US opposed the principle of nondiscriminatory preferences, emphasizing instead more traditional measures to increase trade, as lay behind the so-called Kennedy round of tariff negotiations, held under GATT auspices. But by 1967 it had shifted its stand. President Johnson announced the shift at Punta del Este in April : the US would consider proposals for preferential entry of imports from developing countries, provided that the preferences would be temporary, that they be granted to all developing countries, and that other industrial nations also accepted the scheme. The OECD ministerial meetings in December 1967 gave approval to enter negotiations with the developing countries on nondiscriminatory preferences.

Almost simultaneously with the OECD meetings 77 developing countries held a special conclave in Algiers. India's commerce minister had proposed such a meeting in March 1966 to prepare a unified position to present to the second UNCTAD, scheduled for 1968. At Algiers a "charter" was adopted on October 24 which redefined, in greater detail than ever before, the trade reforms that developing countries insisted upon. Beyond recommendations for price protection of primary commodities, for nondiscriminatory preferences applied to manufactures, semi-manufactures, processed and semi-processed goods, and for increased flows of development aid, the "charter" spelled out desired reforms in freight rates and insurance, specified the need to expand the merchant marines of developing countries, urged international aid to develop tourism, and outlined ways of increasing trade among developing countries.[37]

The chief Indian delegate at Algiers spoke realistically of the need, above all, to present a unified front at the forthcoming confrontation with the advanced nations. Recognizing, he said, their condition of "common adversity," the developing countries should promote unity "based on the realization that there is no fundamental divergence in our economic interests and that all the countries represented here . . . have a common stake in the re-structuring of the world economic order."[38]

At the second UNCTAD meetings in New Delhi, however, unity among the 77 was not easily maintained, notably on questions of the priorities for different trade reform proposals, which partly explained the immediately unproductive outcome of the conference. Another part of the explanation for the conference's meagre results lay in the Western states' hesitation to introduce novel trade practices at a time of great instability in the world's monetary system—the US dollar and the British pound and in fact the international monetary system were suffering heavy pressures. UNCTAD's value to India was left in doubt at the close of the 1968 session.

But New Delhi continued its efforts to internationalize external support for development. Apart from UNCTAD, it expected to benefit from other UN related institutions : for example, the new special drawing rights of the International Monetary Fund provided emergency financial help when a major export commodity failed to bring in expected foreign exchange ; the Asian Development Bank, inaugurated in Manila in December 1965, might ultimately supplement in a minor way the activities in India of the World Bank and the International Development Association.

Having reached the probable limits of bilateral aid receipts India joined forces with the other developing countries to extract development assistance on a multilateral basis, which, if successful, would have the advantage of bringing in "untied" foreign exchange, if not of increasing total aid receipts. In direct diplomatic dealings with countries other than its major trading partners India began to stress beneficial economic relations above all other concerns. Its strategy for export expansion called especially for greater efforts in west Asia and Africa, with Latin America a longer term prospect. An illustration of the working of the new strategy was a tripartite agreement to exchange tariff preferences reached in December 1966 by India, Egypt, and Yugoslavia. It was the first agreement for exchange of preferences among developing countries and thus helped to fulfill UNCTAD declarations, while also giving economic substance to the decade-old political links of the three mainstays of nonalignment.

CONCLUSION

In the first half of the 1960's the Nehru era faded away by degrees. The characteristics of the post-Nehru era will be described by future historians. But certain trends could be marked in foreign relations, and, again, they appeared through Indian actions and statements of purpose in the various organs of the UN. Recovering its self-confidence gradually after the 1962 military set-back and Nehru's death about 18 months later, the New Delhi government resumed and indeed increased its diplomatic involvements by the mid-1060's, in the UN and elsewhere. Its foreign policies lacked that single-minded direction, and certainly the olympian exposition, that Nehru had provided. But its external contacts were more diversified and more closely linked to tangible national interests than before, both in regional and in global contexts. The Indian public, too, achieved greater awareness of alternatives in foreign relations after Nehru's strong leadership disappeared, if parliamentary debates and printed public words were valid indicators. A change had occurred, however, in that India no longer stood so exposed as before in international politics, challenging and defending, pronouncing and commenting, seeking to establish its identity and its uniqueness. In the mid-1960's India gave the appearance of a well established firm no longer dependent on shock advertising but conducting substantial orders of business, according to rules that largely suited its interests. By then, in comparison to other Afro-Asian states, it was a status quo power, no longer criticizing the international system in as many ways as it was defending it.

Anti-colonialism and peaceful coexistence were the two major global objectives of Indian UN diplomacy in the 1950's. Throughout most of the 1960's the emphasis lay on creating international arms controls and inducing a more balanced distribution of the world's wealth among all peoples. Policies in pursuit of these latter aims had been simpler to formulate in Nehru's era than they were later. Nonalignment had substituted for an Indian security policy and simultaneously had stimulated the inflow of foreign economic aid. But as nonalignment lost most of its meaning and influence with the great powers India's objectives, in the UN and elsewhere, demanded shifts in policy and in diplomatic style. India had to promote actively and through a great variety of channels its tangible advantages and its continued independence of action. Instead of witnessing the two great coalitions competing with each other for the support of India, New Delhi found itself increasingly in the position of justifying to the US and the USSR in similar terms and at the same time its stands on a nonproliferation treaty, on the need for economic assistance, and for that matter on its relations with Pakistan. It was on the latter issue that India began to feel most strongly the conjoint pressure of the two great powers, in behalf of their newly defined similar interests in the subcontinent.

India's preoccupation with the great powers during Nehru's time, which was a by-product of nonalignment, required comparatively less diplomatic field work than the often unexciting undertakings of the post-Nehru era in minor capitals and in scores of international committees, many of them sponsored by the UN. India was no longer the chief apostle of nonalignment. It was one of many non-nuclear and economically underdeveloped countries, and its influence had to spread widely through those groupings in order to make itself felt at all. Success for Indian objectives in the UN, therefore, lay not in dramatic confrontations with one or the other of the great powers or even in confident leadership of an international grouping of states in the General Assembly or at an ad hoc conference. The effectiveness of Indian diplomacy increasingly depended on the tactful persuasion that it could bring to bear from within a large body of "have-not" countries on both of the great powers.

In the disarmament debates and in UNCTAD the transformations of India's UN role were demonstrated as clearly as its new security needs. Along with other non-nuclear states India tried to impress the great powers of the need for a nonproliferation treaty that would protect the interests of non-nuclear as well as nuclear states. But the US and the Soviet Union were more concerned with their own mutual relations than with satisfying any states in the "third world," and they joined to urge India to sign the draft treaty in 1968. As a developing country India became one of 77 states that tried to extract concessions on trade and aid from the economically advanced nations. But both communist and Western industrialized states showed reluctance to meet the major demands of the 77 as expressed through UNCTAD. If the policies of the great powers should change in order to ensure more rapid economic advancement of the poor countries, it would probably be the result of their conjoined recognition of the dangers inherent in an economically divided world.

The economic advancement of India and its military security, however, would depend more on what happened inside the country than outside of it. One of the greatest legacies of Nehru was the opening up of India to the global environment ; the direction that he gave to Indian society expanded its links with the UK into involvement with all the major centres of power and culture. In so doing Nehru followed the advice of Gandhi, who had conceived of a new India with its windows open to the world, freely exchanging ideas and innovations with all peoples. And the new India is, indeed, a free society, within which all the currents of modern life revolve and enrich the experience of its people. The future of India, therefore, while resting in the hands of its own people and government, is enwrapped in the evolution of modern civilization. Its external relations extend far beyond the diplomatic record that this book has tried to interpret.

NOTES AND REFERENCES

[1] Nehru's speech in the Lok Sabha, Nov. 19, 1956, *Speeches, 1953-1957*, p. 323.

[2] Gabriella Rosner, *The United Nations Emergency Force*, pp. 122-23 ; David Wainhouse, *International Peace Observation*, p. 282.

[3] Cited in *FAR*, vol. VI, 12 (Dec. 1960), p. 403.

[4] See Nehru's statement in the Lok Sabha, Nov. 22, 1960, *FAR*, vol. VI, 11 (Nov. 1960).

[5] C. S. Jha, *SCOR*, 929th meet., Feb. 2, 1961, p. 25.

[6] Statement in the Rajya Sabha, Feb. 15, 1961, *FAR*, vol. VII, 2(Feb. 1961), p. 17.

[7] UN Doc. S/4741.

[8] *Foreign Policy of India : Texts of Documents, 1947-64*, p. 480.

[9] This purpose failed to appear in the secretary-general's annual report for June 1961-June 1962 but was acknowledged by the UN representative in Katanga, Conor Cruise O'Brien in his *To Katanga and Back*, p. 249.

[10] UN Doc. S/5002.

[11] The following observation points to one of the vital Indian contributions to the UNOC : "India was the only contributor that . . . could supply staff officers and troops who had been through big enough wars to give them any useful training." Burns and Heathcote, *Peace-Keeping by U. N. Forces*, p. 185.

[12] *GAOR*, 869th meeting, Sept. 23, 1960, p. 83.

[13] *GAOR*, 1025th meeting, 1961, p. 246.

[14] On May 4 ; *Documents of the UN Conference on International Organization, San Francisco 1945*, vol. III : *Dumbarton Oaks Proposals, Comments and Proposed Amendments.*

[15] Statement of Oct. 6, 1964 : UN Doc. A/AC 113/45.

[16] See Norman J. Padelford, "Financing Peacekeeping : Politics and Crisis," in Padelford and Leland M. Goodrich, *The United Nations in the Balance,* N. Y. 1965.

[17] G. Parthasarathi's statement, Nov. 25, 1966, *FAR*, vol. XII, 11 (Nov. 1966), p. 288.

[18] *The Conference of Heads of State or Governments of Non-Aligned Countries,* Belgrade 1961, p. 113.

[19] See the first Indian representative on the ENDC, Arthur Lall's *Negotiating Disarmament*, pp. 12-17.

[20] *ibid.*, p. 25.

[21] In an address to the US Congress in 1949, *Speeches, 1949-53*, p. 111.

[22] From 1955 the Indian government gave high priority to nuclear development, with the goal of supplementing its power resources. By the mid-1960's it had achieved self-sufficiency in many phases of the creation of nuclear energy. Its deposits of uranium and thorium partially supplied the three reactors at Trombay, which theoretically could produce plutonium for weapons. The Tarapur and the Rana Pratap Sagar power stations could, again theoretically, divert some of their fuel to military purposes, thereby however violating agreements with the US and Canada, respectively. See the chairman of India's atomic energy commission, H. J. Bhabha's "Ten Years of Atomic Energy in India," in *Nuclear India*, vol. 2, 12 (Aug. 1964) ; and his talk over All-India Radio, Oct. 24, 1964, *ibid.*, vol. 3, 3 (Nov. 1964), in which he commented on the long-term inexpensiveness of producing nuclear as compared to conventional explosives.

[23] Speech of Oct. 7, 1964, *Speeches of Prime Minister Lal Bahadur Sastri*, p. 101.

[24] See, e.g. his statement in *LSD*, vol. XXXV, Nov. 24, 1964, cols. 1570-71 (in Hindi). At the All-India Congress session in Durgapur on Jan. 8, 1965, Sastri said that, "Our policy is not to manufacture the atom bomb at present." *Asian Recorder*, 1965, p. 6257.

[25] *GAOR*, 1301st meeting, Dec. 14, 1964, p. 10.

[26] From the memorandum of the eight nonaligned states submitted to the ENDC, Sept. 1965 ; cited in *FAR*, vol. XII, 11(Nov. 1966).

[27] *LSD*, vol. XXXVI, Dec. 9, 1964, cols. 4060-65.

[28] *Statesman* (New Delhi), Dec. 14, 1964.

[29] *State Department Bulletin*, Nov. 2, 1964, p. 613.

[30] Trivedi's statement in the UN Political Committee, Nov. 7, 1966, *FAR, op. cit.*, p. 293.

[31] Examination of the Indo-US Agreement on Civil Uses of Atomic Energy, issued on July 24, 1963, reveals why India could not accept IAEA supervision of the agreement, for which the US had asked : India did not wish to commit itself to general terms for international control over its nuclear industry. The

agreement was unique to the Tarapur project and gave India as much latitude for later reinterpretation of its terms as it was possible to extract from American negotiators. Article VI embodies an unusual formal statement of a difference in US and Indian interpretations of the terms, India insisting that its promise to use any American "material, equipment or device" solely for peaceful purposes derived from the safeguards in the agreement on the use of nuclear fuel.   Text in *Foreign Policy of India : Texts of Documents, 1947-64*, pp. 229-240.

[32] Speech on May 10, 1954, *India's Foreign Policy*, p. 193.

[33] Paragraph 5 of Gen. Ass. resolution 1654 (XVI) directed the committee "to carry out its task by employment of all means which it will have at its disposal within the framework of the procedures and modalities which it shall adopt for the proper discharge of its functions."

[34] Foreign Minister Swaran Singh's statement to the Gen. Ass. on Oct. 7, 1966, *FAR*, vol. XII, 10 (Oct. 1966), p. 246.

[35] R. K. Nehru's statement, July 10, 1963 ; *ECOSOC Off. Rec.*, 36th Sess., 1275 meeting, p. 87.

[36] See in particular the report of the secretary-general of UNCTAD, Raúl Prebisch, *Towards a New Trade Policy for Development*, N. Y. (UN publ.) 1964.

[37] See the "Charter of Algiers," publ. by the Indian Ministry of Commerce, New Delhi 1967. The percentage share of the imports of the developing countries supplied by other developing countries fell from eight in 1950 to four in 1965 ; Manubhai Shah, *Developing Countries and UNCTAD*, p. 29.

[38] From Manubhai Shah's speech, Oct. 14, 1967 ; reprinted in "Charter of Algiers," pp. 32-33.

BIBLIOGRAPHY

A Bibliography of Major References Consulted in the Preparation of This Study and Useful for Further Reading arranged according to the chapters in this book and concluding with a general list.

CHAPTER I
(Inter-War)

ANSTEY, VERA, *The Economic Development of India*, London, 3rd edn., 1942

COYAJEE, J. C., *India and the League of Nations*, Waltair 1932

CHOWDHURI, R. N., *International Mandates and Trusteeship Systems : A Comparative Study*, The Hague 1955

DAS, TARAKNATH, *India in World Politics*, New York 1923

Final Reports of the Delegates of India to the First Session of the Assembly of the League of Nations and subsequent *Reports*, first few with no dates or places of publication ; from 1927 at Delhi, Simla, or Calcutta

GOVERNMENT OF INDIA, *Memorandum Submitted to the Indian Statutory Commission*, vol. 2, Calcutta 1930

HANCOCK, W. K., *Survey of British Commonwealth Affairs*, vol. 1 : *Problems of Nationality*, London 1937

———, Do, vol. 2 : *Problems of Economic Policy, 1918-1939*, London 1940

HARVEY, HEATHER, J., *Consultation and Co-operation in the British Commonwealth*, parts 1 & 2, R.I.I.A. pamphlets, 1949

HOWARD-ELLIS, C., *The Origin, Structure and Working of the League of Nations*, London 1928

IMPERIAL ECONOMIC CONFERENCE 1923, *Record of Proceedings and Documents*, London 1924

IMPERIAL ECONOMIC CONFERENCE, OTTAWA 1932, *Summaries of Proceedings and Copies of Trade Agreements*, London 1932

IMPERIAL WAR CONFERENCES, 1917, 1918, 1921, 1923, 1926, 1930, *Extracts from Summary of Proceedings for various years, and Appendices*, London, various years

KAUL, N.N., *India and the International Labour Organization*, Delhi 1956

KEITH, A.B., *The Constitution, Administration and Laws of the Empire*, London 1924

———, *Imperial Unity and the Dominions*, Oxford 1916

———, *Sovereignty of British Dominions*, London 1929

MANSERGH, NICHOLAS, *Survey of British Commonwealth Affairs : Problems of External Policy 1931-1939*, London 1952

MEHROTRA, S.R., *India and the Commonwealth 1885-1929*, London 1965

PALMER, GERALD E.H., *Consultation and Co-operation in the British Commonwealth*, London 1934

34

PANIKKAR, K.M., *India and the Indian Ocean*, 3rd rev. edn., London 1962

——, *Problems of Indian Defense*, Bombay 1960

PATIALA, MAJOR-GENERAL HIS HIGHNESS THE MAHARAJA DHIRAJ, *Report on the League of Nations Assembly, 1925*, London 1925

PILAI, P. P., *India and the International Labour Organization*, Patna 1931

PRASAD, BISHESHWAR, ED., *Official History of the Indian Armed Forces in the Second World War 1939-1945, Defense of India : Policy and Plans*, Calcutta 1963

PURI, MADAN MOHAN, *India in the International Labour Organization 1919-1956*, Institute of Social Studies, The Hague 1958, mimeo.

RAM, V. SHIVA AND BRIJ. MOHAN SHARMA, *India and the League of Nations*, Lucknow 1932

RAO, P. KODANDA, *The Right Honourable V.S. Srinivasa Sastri : A Political Biography*, Bombay 1963

SASTRI, V.S.S., *Speeches and Writings of the Right Honourable V.S. Srinivasa Sastri*, Madras, Natesan, n.d.

——, *Latters of the Right Honourable V.S. Srinivasa Sastri*, ed. by T. N. Jagadisan, Bombay, 2nd edn., 1963

SARKAR, BENOY KUMAR, *Imperial Preference vis-a-vis World Economy*, Calcutta 1934

SETON, MALCOLM C.C., *The India Office*, London 1926

SUNDARAM, LANKA, *India in World Politics*, Delhi 1944

CHAPTER II
(Commonwealth)

COWEN, ZELMAN, *The British Commonwealth of Nations in a Changing World*, Evanston 1965

JENNINGS, IVOR. *Problems of the New Commonwealth*, Durham 1958

KUMAR, DHARMA, *India and the European Economic Community*, Bombay 1966

MANSERGH, NICHOLAS, *The Commonwealth and the Nations*, London 1948

——, *Documents and Speeches on British Commonwealth Affairs 1931-1952*, vol. II, London 1953

——, *Documents and Speeches on British Commonwealth Affairs 1952-1962*, London 1963

——, *The Multi-Racial Commonwealth : Proceedings of the Fifth Unofficial Commonwealth Relations Conference*, Lahore, March 1954, London 1955

——, *Survey of British Commonwealth Affairs : Problems of War-Time Co-operation and Post-War Change*, London 1958

RAJAN, M.S., *The Post-War Transformation of the Commonwealth*, Bombay 1963

RANGNEKAR, D.K., *India, Britain and European Common Market*, New Delhi 1963

WALKER, PATRICK GORDON, *The Commonwealth*, London 1962

WHEARE, K.C., *The Constitutional Structure of the Commonwealth*, Oxford 1960

ZINKIN, MAURICE AND TAYA, *Britain and India : Requiem for Empire*, London 1964

CHAPTER III
(Nonalignment)

AMERICAN ACADEMY OF POLITICAL AND SOCIAL SCIENCE, *The Annals*, November 1965 : "Nonalignment in Foreign Affairs"
——, *Arab Observer ; The Nonaligned Weekly*, Cairo, no. 225, October 12, 1964, issue on the Cairo conference
Conference of Heads of State or Government of Non-Aligned Countries, Belgrade, September 1-6, 1961 ; publ. by Publicisticko-Izdavacki Zavod 'Yugoslavia', Belgrade 1961
"The Cairo Conference of Non-Aligned Nations" (October 5-10, 1964) ; Information Service of India, New Delhi 1964
CRABB, CECIL V., JR., *The Elephants and the Grass: A Study of Nonalignment*, N. Y. 1965
DAYAL, SHIV, *India's Role in the Korean Question*, Delhi 1959
"INDIA, U.A.R., YUGOSLAVIA CONFERENCE, NEW DELHI, October 21-24, 1966," Ministry of External Affairs, New Delhi 1966
JANSEN, G.H., *Nonalignment and the Afro-Asian States*, N.Y. 1966
LYON, PETER, *Neutralism*, Bombay 1964
MARTIN, LAURENCE W., ED., *Neutralism and Nonalignment*, N.Y. 1963
MILLER, J.D.B., *The Politics of the Third World*, London 1967
RANGE, WILLARD, *Jawaharlal Nehru's World View*, Athens, Ga., 1961

CHAPTERS IV AND XIX
(United Nations)

BALASSA, BELA, *Trade Prospects for Developing Countries*, Homewood, III, 1964
BERKES, ROSS N., AND MOHINDER S. BEDI, *The Diplomacy of India : Indian Foreign Policy in the United Nations*, Stanford 1958
BAINS, J. S., *India's International Disputes*, Bombay 1962
BOLAND, GERTRUDE C., "Solidarity in the General Assembly : The Indian Role 1946-1957," Claremont Asian Studies, no. 10, Claremont, Calif., 1962
BOWETT, D.W., *United Nations Forces*, London 1964
BURNS, ARTHUR LEE, AND NINA HEATHCOTE, *Peace-Keeping by U.N. Forces*, London 1963
CHOWDHURI, R.N., *International Mandates and Trusteeship Systems: A Comparative Study*, The Hague 1955
FRIEDMANN, WOLFGANG, *The Changing Structure of Inernational Law*, N.Y. 1964
GORDENKER, LEON, *The UN Secretary-General and the Maintenance of Peace*, N.Y. 1967
GOVINDA RAJ, B.V., *India and Disputes in the United Nations 1946-54*, Bombay 1959
HIDAYATULLAH, M., *The South-West Africa Case*, Bombay 1967
HOVET, THOMAS JR., *Bloc Politics in the United Nations*, Cambridge, Mass., 1960
INDIAN COUNCIL OF WORLD AFFAIRS, *India and the United Nations*, N. Y. 1957
LALL, ARTHUR, *Negotiating Disarmament*, Ithaca 1964

MYRDAL, GUNNAR, *Rich Lands and Poor*, N. Y. 1957

O'BRIEN, CONOR CRUISE, *To Katanga and Back*, N. Y. 1962

PREBISCH, RAUL, *Towards a New Trade Policy for Development*, UN publ., N.Y. 1964

RAJAN, M.S., *United Nations and Domestic Jurisdiction*, Bombay, 2nd edn., 1961

ROSNER, GABRIELLA, *The United Nations Emergency Force*, N. Y. 1963

SHAH, MANUBHAI, *Developing Countries and UNCTAD*, Bombay 1968

SPANIER, JOHN W. AND JOSEPH L. NOGEE, *The Politics of Disarmament*, N. Y. 1962

SUD, USHA, *United Nations and the Non-Self-Governing Territories*, Jullundur 1965

United Nations Peacekeeping in the Congo : 1960-1964, Brookings Institution, 4 vols., Washington 1966

WAINHOUSE, DAVID W., *International Peace Observation*, Baltimore 1966

CHAPTERS V AND VI
(Pakistan)

ALI, CHAUDHRI MUHAMMAD, *The Emergence of Pakistan*, N.Y. 1967

BERBER, FRIEDRICH J., *Rivers in International Law*, London 1959

BIRDWOOD, LORD, *India and Pakistan : A Continent Decides*, N. Y. 1954

——, *Two Nations and Kashmir*, London 1956

BRECHER, MICHAEL, *The Struggle for Kashmir*, Toronto 1953

BRINES, RUSSELL, *The Indo-Pakistani Conflict*, London 1968

CAMPBELL-JOHNSON, ALAN, *Mission with Mountbatten*, N.Y. 1953

DAS GUPTA, J.B., *Indo-Pakistan Relations, 1947-1955*, Amsterdam 1958

GUPTA, SISIR, *Kashmir : A Study in India-Pakistan Relations*, London 1966

HASAN, K. SARWAR AND ZUBEIDA HASAN, EDS., *Documents on the Foreign Relations of Pakistan : The Kashmir Question*, Pakistan Institute of International Affairs, Karachi 1966

HASAN, K. SARWAR AND KHALIDA QURESHI, EDS., *Documents ... China, India, and Pakistan*, Pakistan Inst. of Int. Aff., Karachi 1966

INDIA, MINISTRY OF EXTERNAL AFFAIRS, *White Paper : Indo-Pakistan Relations : Correspondence between the Prime Ministers of India and Pakistan* (*From July 15, 1951 to August 9, 1951*), New Delhi 1951

——, *White Paper : Kashmir : Meetings and Correspondence between the Prime Ministers of India and Pakistan* (*July 1953-October 1954*), New Delhi 1954

——, Ministry of Information and Broadcasting, *Pakistan's Aggression in Kutch* (with maps), New Delhi 1965

——, Ministry of States, *White Paper on Jammu and Kashmir* (to Jan. 1948), New Delhi 1948

INDIAN SOCIETY OF INTERNATIONAL LAW, *The Kutch-Sind Border Question*, New Delhi 1965

INTERNATIONAL BANK FOR RECONSTRUCTION AND DEVELOPMENT, *The Indus Basin Development Fund Agreement*, Washington 1960

International Studies, New Delhi, vol. 8, nos. 1 and 2 (July-October 1966) : special double issue on India's relations with Pakistan

KHAN, MOHAMMAD AYUB, *Friends Not Masters : A Political Autobiography*, London 1967

KORBEL, JOSEF, *Danger in Kashmir*, Princeton, 2nd edn., 1966

LAMB, ALASTAIR, *Crisis in Kashmir, 1947-1966*, London 1966

PAKISTAN, EMBASSY, WASHINGTON, D. C., *Memorandum on the Indus Waters Dispute*, July 10, 1958

CHAPTERS VII AND XVII
(China)

BHARGAVE, G. S., *The Battle of NEFA : The Undeclared War*, Bombay 1964

BHAT, SUDHAKAR, *India and China*, New Delhi 1967

BUCHAN, ALASTAIR, *China and the Peace of Asia*, N.Y. 1965

BUREAU OF HIS HOLINESS THE DALAI LAMA, New Delhi, *Tibet in the United Nations 1950-1961* (documentary)

CHAKRAVARTI, P.C., *India's China Policy*, Bloomington 1962

CHOPRA, PRAN, *On An Indian Border*, Bombay 1964

Concerning the Question of Tibet, Foreign Languages Press, Peking 1959 (documents)

DALAI LAMA, *My Land and My People : The Autobiography of His Holiness the Dalai Lama*, ed. by David Howarth, Bombay 1964

DUTT, VIDYA PRAKASH, *China's Foreign Policy*, Bombay 1964

FISHER, MARGARET W., LEO ROSE AND ROBERT A. HUTTENBACK, *Himalayan Battleground : Sino-Indian Rivalry in Ladakh*, N.Y. 1963

INDIA, MINISTRY OF EXTERNAL AFFAIRS, *Notes, Memoranda and Letters Exchanged and Agreements Signed Between the Governments of India and China* (White Papers), New Delhi 1959

——, *Report of the Officials of the Government of India and the People's Republic of China on the Boundary Question*, New Delhi 1961

——, Ministry of Home Affairs, "Anti-National Activities of Pro-Peking Communists and their Preparations for Subversion and Violence," New Delhi 1965

——, Ministry of Information and Broadcasting, "The Chinese Threat," Delhi 1963 (chiefly maps)

Indian Press Digests, Monograph Series, no. 1, "Indian Views of Sino-Indian Relations," Univ. of Calif., Berkeley, Feb. 1956

Indian Society of International Law, "The Sino-Indian Boundary : texts of treaties, agreements and certain exchanges of notes. . . . " New Delhi 1962

INTERNATIONAL COMMISSION OF JURISTS, *The Question of Tibet and the Rule of Law*, Geneva 1959

——, *Tibet and the Chinese People's Republic : A report to the Commission by its Legal Inquiry Committee on Tibet*, Geneva 1960

International Studies, Bombay, vol. V, nos. 1 and 2 (July-Oct. 1963), "Chinese Aggression and India"

JAIN, GIRILAL, *Panchsheela and After*, Bombay 1960

KARNIK, V. B., *China Invades India*, Bombay 1963

KAUL, B.M., *The Untold Story*, Bombay 1967

LAMB, ALASTAIR, *The China-India Border : The Origins of the Disputed Boundaries*, London 1964

——, *The McMahon Line : A Study in the Relations Between India, China, and Tibet, 1904-1914*, 2 vols., London 1966

MANKEKAR, D.R., *The Guilty Men of 1962*, Bombay 1968

NEHRU, JAWAHARLAL, *Prime Minister on Sino-Indian Relations*, vol. I : in Parliament ; vol. II : Press Conferences ; from March to Sept. 1959

——, *Prime Minister on Sino-Indian Relations*, vol. I : in Parliament ; vol. II : Press Conferences ; from 1959 to April 1961

PANIKKAR, K.M., *In Two Chinas : Memoirs of a Diplomat*, London 1955

PATTERSON, GEORGE N., *Peking Versus Delhi*, N.Y. 1964

——, *Tragic Destiny*, London 1959

RAO, K. KRISHNA, "The Sino-Indian Boundary and International Law," Information Service of India, Feb. 1963

RAO, GONDKER NARAYANA, *The India-China Border : A Reappraisal*, Bombay 1968

ROWLAND, JOHN, *A History of Sino-Indian Relations : Hostile Coexistence*, Princeton 1967

SATYAPALAN, C. N., "India's China Policy : The First Decade ; An Analytical Interpretation," unpubl. Ph. D. dissertation, Univ. of Penn. 1964

SEN, CHANAKYA, *Tibet Disappears*, Bombay 1960

The Sino-Indian Boundary Question, Foreign Languages Press, Peking 1962 (documents)

SOONG CHING LING, "Good Neighbours Meet ; Speeches in India, Burma and Pakistan (1955-1956)," Foreign Languages Press, Peking 1956

VAN EEKELEN, W.F., *Indian Foreign Policy and the Border Dispute with China*, The Hague 1964

VARMA, SHANTI PRASAD, *Struggle for the Himalayas*, Jullundur 1965

CHAPTER VIII
(Border States)

CHINESE PEOPLE'S INSTITUTE OF FOREIGN AFFAIRS, *New Development in Friendly Relations Between China and Nepal*, Foreign Languages Press, Peking 1960 (documents, 1956-1960)

COELHO, V.A., *Sikkim and Bhutan* (forthcoming)

GUPTA, ANIRUDHA, *Politics in Nepal : A Study of Post-Rana Political Developments and Party Politics*, Bombay 1964

JAIN, GIRILAL, *India Meets China in Nepal*, New York 1959

JOSHI, BHUWAN LAL AND LEO E. ROSE, *Democratic Innovations in Nepal*, Berkeley 1966

KARAN, PRADYUMNA P. AND WILLIAM M. JENKINS, *The Himalayan Kingdoms : Bhutan, Sikkim, and Nepal*, Princeton 1963

KHANAL, YADUNATH, *Reflections on Nepal-India Relations*, Delhi 1964

KREISBERG, PAUL H., "Bhutan's Role in the Himalayan Power Struggle," unpubl. paper, Univ. of Penn., 1963

MIHALY, EUGENE BRAMER, *Foreign Aid and Politics in Nepal*, London 1965

PANT, YADAV PRASAD, *Economic Development of Nepal*, Allahabad 1965

SHAH, RISHIKESH, *Nepal and the World*, Kathmandu 1955

UNITED STATES ARMY, *Area Handbook for Nepal (with Sikkim and Bhutan)*, Washington, D. C. 1964

CHAPTERS IX AND X
(Southeast Asia)

Asian Relations, being the Report of the Proceedings and Documents of the First Asian Relations Conference, New Delhi, March-April, 1947, New Delhi 1948

BHANSALI, K. G., "India's Role in the Settlement of the Indo-Chinese Conflict," unpubl. Ph. D. dissertation, American University, 1962

DOMMEN, J., *Conflict in Laos : The Politics of Neutralization*, N.Y . 1964

DUTT, V.P., "India's Foreign Policy with Special Reference to Asia and the Pacific," 11th Conf., Inst. of Pacific Relations, Lucknow 1950

FIFIELD, RUSSELL H., *The Diplomacy of Southeast Asia : 1954-1958*, N.Y. 1958

GORDON, BERNARD K., *The Dimensions of Conflict in Southeast Asia*, Englewood Cliffs, N. J., 1966

GUPTA, SISIR, *India and Regional Integration in Asia*, Bombay 1964

JANSEN, G. H., *Nonalignment and the Afro-Asian States*, N.Y. 1966

KAHIN, GEORGE MCTURNAN, *The Asian-African Conference*, Ithaca 1956

KOZICKI, RICHARD J., "India and Burma, 1937-1957 : A Study in International Relations," unpubl. Ph.D. dissertation, University of Penn. 1959

LEVI, WERNER, *Free India in Asia*, Minneapolis 1952

MODELSKI, GEORGE, "International Conference on the Settlement of the Laotian Question 1961-62," working paper no. 2 in the Dept. of International Relations Research School of Pacific Studies, Australian National Univ., Canberra 1962

——, *SEATO : Six Studies*, Canberrra 1962

NEHRU, J., *Talks with Nehru : A Discussion Between Jawaharlal Nehru and Norman Cousins*, N. Y. 1951

——, *Asian African Conference : Speeches of the Prime Minister of India in the Closed Sessions*, New Delhi (Ministry of External Affairs) 1955

PANIKKAR, K. M., *The Future of South East Asia*, N.Y. 1944

——, *India and the Indian Ocean : An Essay on the Influence of Sea Power on Indian History*, London 1945

ROMULO, CARLOS P., *The Meaning of Bandung*, Chapel Hill 1956

SAR DESAI, DAMODAR RAMJI, "India's Relations with Vietnam, Laos, and Cambodia : 1954-1961," unpubl. Ph.D. dissertation, Univ. of Calif., Los Angeles 1965

TON THAT THIEN, *India and South East Asia 1947-1960*, Geneva 1963

TRAGER, FRANK, *Burma : From Kingdom to Republic*, N. Y. 1966

CHAPTER XI
(West Asia, Africa)

BENNETT, GEORGE, *Kenya : A Political History—The Colonial Period*, London 1963
FEDERATION OF INDIAN CHAMBERS OF COMMERCE AND INDUSTRY, *India-Africa Trade Series*, New Delhi 1964, 1965, 1966
——, "Report of Indian Industrialists Goodwill Delegation to some African Countries" (Sept.-Oct. 1964)
The Eastern Economist Annual Number 1958, "India and the Middle East"
FISHER, CAROL A. AND FRED KRINSKY, *Middle East in Crisis : A Historical and Documentary Review*, Syracuse 1959
HOSKINS, HALFORD, *British Routes to India*, New York 1928
INDIA, INFORMATION SERVICE, "The Suez Crisis and India," New Delhi 1956
——, Lok Sabha Secretariat, "Suez Canal : A Documentary Study," New Delhi 1956
——, "Suez Canal—Nationalization and After," New Delhi 1956
——, Ministry of External Affairs, "India and Palestine—The Evolution of a Policy," New Delhi 1967
——, Ministry of Commerce, *Foreign Trade of India*, 16 (Sept. 1964) : "Trade Relations with Africa"
INDIAN COUNCIL FOR AFRICA, *Nehru and Africa : Extracts of Speeches 1946-63*, New Delhi 1964
LAQUEUR, WALTER Z., *The Soviet Union and the Middle East*, London 1959
LEGUM, COLIN, *Congo Disaster*, Baltimore 1961
LENCZOWSKI, GEORGE, *The Middle East in World Affairs*, 2nd edn., Ithaca 1956
MISRA, K. P., *India's Policy of Recognition of States and Governments*, Bombay 1966
MUTHANNA, I.M., *Indo-Ethiopian Relations for Centuries*, Addis Ababa 1961
SINGHAL, D.P., *India and Afghanistan : A Study in Diplomatic Relations 1876-1907*, Queensland 1963
SYED, AYUB, *India and the Arab World*, New Delhi 1965

CHAPTER XII
(Minor Problems)

AIYAR, K. NATESA, "The Indo-Ceylon Crisis," Hatton (Ceylon), mimeo, 1941
BENNETT, GEORGE, *Kenya : A Political History : The Colonial Period*, London 1963
CARTER, GWENDOLEN M., *The Politics of Inequality ; South Africa Since 1948*, 3rd edn., London 1962
CHAKRAVARTI, NALINI R., "Indians in Burma," unpubl. M.A. thesis, American University 1967
CORET, ALAIN, "La Cession de l'Inde Francaise," Librarie General de Droit et de Jurisprudence, Paris 1955 ; reprinted from *La Revue Juridique et Politique de l'Union Francaise*, 1955, nos. 3 and 4

DELF, GEORGE, *Asians in East Africa*, London 1963
DEV, DHARM YASH, *Our Countrymen Abroad*, Allahabad 1940
GANGULEE, N., *Indians in the Empire Overseas*, London 1947
GUPTA, B.L., *Political and Civic Status of Indians in Ceylon*, Agra 1963
HOLLINGSWORTH, L.W., *The Asians of East Africa*, N.Y. 1960
HUTTENBACK, ROBERT A., *The British Imperial Experience*, N.Y. 1966
INDIA, AGENT OF THE GOVERNMENT OF INDIA IN CEYLON, *Annual Reports* (from 1934 through 1948), New Delhi
——, Department of Commonwealth Relations, *Question of Treatment of Indians in the Union of South Africa before the United Nations*, New Delhi 1947, 1948
——, Department of Education, Health, and Lands, *Selection of Papers regarding South Africa for Use of Members of the Government of India Deputation to that Dominion*, Delhi 1925
——, Indo-Ceylon Relations Exploratory Conference December 1940, *Report of Proceedings*, New Delhi 1941
——, *Memorandum to the United Nations General Assembly on the Position of Indians in the Union of South Africa* (UN Doc. A/68, Aug. 26, 1946)
——, *Report(s) on the working of the Indian Emigration Act, 1922 (VII of 1922), the rules issued thereunder and of the Labour Ordinances of Ceylon during the year(s)* (1925-1933), Calcutta and Delhi
INTERNATIONAL COURT OF JUSTICE, *Case Concerning Right of Passage over Indian Territory (Merits). Judgement of 12 April 1960.* I.C.J. Reports 1960, reprinted by the Indian Ministry of External Affairs
KARVE, D.G. AND AMBEKAR, D.V., EDS., *Speeches and Writings of Gopal Krishna Gokhale*, vol. two ; Political, London 1966
KODIKARA, S.U., *Indo-Ceylon Relations Since Independence*, Colombo 1965
KONDAPI, C., *Indians Overseas, 1838-1949*, Bombay 1951
KOTELAWALA, JOHN, *An Asian Prime Minister's Story*, London 1956
MAHAJANI, USHA, *The Role of Indian Minorities in Burma and Malaya*, Bombay 1960
NATH, DWARKA, *A History of Indians in British Guiana*, London 1950
NARAIN, IQBAL, *The Politics of Racialism : A Study of the Indian Minority in South Africa Down to the Gandhi-Smuts Agreement*, Delhi 1962
NOGUEIRA, FRANCO, *The United Nations and Portugal : A Study of Anti-Colonialism*, London 1963
RAJKUMAR, N.V., *Indians Outside India*, New Delhi (A.I.C.C.) 1951
RAO, P. KODANDA, *The Right Honourable V. S. Srinivasa Sastri : A Political Biography*, Bombay 1963
RAO, P. R. RAMACHANDRA, *India and Ceylon : A Study*, Bombay 1954
RAO, R. P., *Portuguese Rule in Goa*, Bombay 1963
THOMAS, T.O., *The Right of Passage Over Indian Territory : A Study of Preliminary Objections Before the World Court*, Leyden 1959
THOMPSON, VIRGINIA AND RICHARD ADLOFF, *Minority Problems in Southeast Asia*, Stanford 1955
UNITED KINGDOM, COLONIAL OFFICE, *Indians in Kenya*, cmd. 1922, London 1923
WRIGGINS, W. HOWARD, *Ceylon : Dilemmas of a New Nation*, Princeton 1960

CHAPTERS XIII AND XIV
(US)

ARORA, SATISH K., *American Policy Towards India*, New Delhi 1953
BAUER, P.T., *United States Aid and Indian Economic Development*, Washington 1959
CHAKRAVARTY, B.N., *India Speaks to America*, N.Y. 1966
CHANDRASEKHAR, S., *American Aid and India's Economic Development*, N.Y. 1965
HARRISON, SELIG, *India and the United States*, N. Y. 1961
INDIAN COUNCIL OF WORLD AFFAIRS, *Indian-American Relations : Proceedings of the India-America Conference held in New Delhi, Dec., 1949*, New Delhi 1950
KIDRON, MICHAEL, *Foreign Investments in India*, London 1965
KIELL, NORMAN, *Indian-American Cultural Relations*, N. Y. (I.P.R.) 1949
KUST, MATTHEW J., *Foreign Enterprise in India : Laws and Policies*, Chapel Hill 1964
LATIFI, DANIEL, *India and U.S. Aid*, Bombay 1960
LEWIS, JOHN P., *Quiet Crisis in India: Economic Development and American Policy*, Washington 1962
MALENBAUM, WILFRED, *East and West in India's Development*, Washington 1959
NEHRU, J., "Nehru Visits U.S.A.," Indian Infor. Service, Washington 1956
———, "Prime Minister Nehru's Visit to U.S.A., November 1961," New Delhi 1962
———, *Visit to America*, N. Y. 1950
PALMER, NORMAN D., *South Asia and United States Policy*, N. Y. 1966
RAO, V.K.R.V., and DHARM NARAIN, *Foreign Aid and India's Economic Development*, Bombay 1963
RESERVE BANK OF INDIA, *India's Balance of Payments 1948-49 to 1961-62*, Bombay 1963
ROSINGER, LAWRENCE K., *India and the United States*, N. Y. 1950
SALVI, P.G., *New Directions in India's Trade Policy*, Bombay 1964
SINGH, HARMAN, *The Indian National Movement and American Opinion*, New Delhi 1962
SINGH, MANMOHAN, *India's Export Trends and the Prospects for Self-Sustained Growth*, Oxford 1964
TALBOT, PHILLIPS, AND S. L. POPLAI, *India and America*, N.Y. 1958

CHAPTERS XV AND XVI
(The USSR)

BARGHOORN, FREDERICK C., *The Soviet Cultural Offensive : The Role of Cultural Diplomacy in Soviet Foreign Policy*, Princeton 1960
BARNETT, A. DOAK, ED., *Communist Strategies in Asia*, N. Y. 1963
BERLINER, JOSEPH S., *Soviet Economic Aid : The New Aid and Trade Policy in Underdeveloped Countries*, N. Y. 1958

BRZEZINSKI, ZBIGNIEW, *Alternative to Partition*, N. Y. 1965

BULGANIN, N.A., AND N. KHRUSHCHEV, *Report to the Supreme Soviet on the Visit to India, Burma, and Afghanistan*, N. Y. 1956

——, *Visit to India : Speeches and Interviews by* ——, N. Y. 1956

CRANKSHAW, EDWARD, *The New Cold War, Moscow vs Peking*, Baltimore 1963

——, *Khrushchev's Russia*, Baltimore 1959

DRUHE, DAVID N., *Soviet Russia and Indian Communism*, N. Y. 1959

EUDIN, XENIA JOUKOFF, AND ROBERT C. NORTH, *Soviet Russia and the East 1920-1927 : A Documentary Survey*, Stanford 1957

GEHLEN, MICHAEL P., *The Politics of Co-existence*, Bloomington 1967

IYER, RAGHAVAN, ED., *South Asian Affairs*, St. Anthony's Papers, no. 8., London 1960

KAPUR, HARISH, *Soviet Russia and Asia 1917-27*, Geneva 1966

KAUTSKY, JOHN H., *Moscow and the Communist Party of India*, N. Y. 1956

KULSKI, WLADYSLAW W., *Peaceful Co-existence : An Analysis of Soviet Foreign Policy*, Chicago 1959

MASANI, M.R., *The Communist Party of India*, N. Y. 1954

MENON, K.P.S., *The Flying Troika*, London 1963

NEHRU, JAWAHARLAL, *Soviet Russia*, Bombay 1929, 1949

OVERSTREET, GENE D., AND MARSHALL WINDMILLER, *Communism in India*, Berkeley 1959

ROYAL INSTITUTE OF INTERNATIONAL AFFAIRS, *The Impact of the Russian Revolution 1917-1967*, London 1967

SAGER, PETER, *Moscow's Hand in India : An Analysis of Soviet Propaganda*, Bombay 1966

STEIN, ARTHUR BENJAMIN, "India's Policy Toward the Soviet Union 1953-62," unpubl. Ph.D. dissertation, Univ. of Penn. 1965

THORNTON, THOMAS PERRY, *The Third World in Soviet perspective*, Princeton 1964

USSR, EMBASSY, NEW DELHI, "Ten Years of Soviet-Indian Economic Collaboration," *News and Views From the Soviet Union*, vol. XXIV, 8 (Feb. 2, 1965)

US HOUSE OF REPRESENTATIVES, COMMITTEE ON FOREIGN AFFAIRS, *Report on Sino-Soviet Conflict and Its Implications*, March 1965

ZAGORIA, DONALD S., *The Sino-Soviet Conflict*, Princeton 1962

CHAPTER XVIII
(Canada, West Germany, and Japan)

EAYRS, JAMES, *Canada in World Affairs, October 1955 to June 1957*, Toronto 1959

——, *Northern Approaches : Canada and the Search for Peace*, Toronto 1961

GANGULI, B.N., *India's Economic Relations with the Far Eastern and Pacific Countries in the Present Century*, Bombay 1956

KEENLEYSIDE, HUGH L. ET AL., *The Growth of Canadian Policies in External Affairs*, Durham, N.C., 1960

SOWARD, F.H. AND EDGAR MCINNIS, *Cannada and the United Nations*, N. Y. 1956

WHITE, JOHN, *German Aid : A Survey of the Sources, Policy, and Structure of German Aid*, Overseas Development Institute, London 1965

GENERAL BIBLIOGRAPHY

ALL INDIA CONGRESS COMMITTEE, *Resolutions on Foreign Policy 1947-1966*, New Delhi 1966

BRECHER, MICHAEL, *Nehru : A Political Biography*, London 1959

CROCKER, WALTER, *Nehru : A Contemporary Estimate*, London 1966

KUNDRA, J.C., *India's Foreign Policy, 1947-54 : A Study of Relations with the Western Bloc*, Groningen (Netherlands) 1955

MENDE, TIBOR, *Conversations with Nehru*, London 1956

NORMAN, DOROTHY, ED., *Nehru : The First Sixty Years*, 2 vols., N. Y. 1965

NEHRU, JAWAHARLAL, *Independence and After*, N .Y. 1950 ; later published as *Speeches 1946-1949*, New Delhi 1958

——, *Jawaharlal Nehru's Speeches 1949-53*, New Delhi 1954

——, *Jawaharlal Nehru's Speeches 1953-57*, New Delhi 1958

——, *Jawaharlal Nehru's Speeches 1957-1963*, New Delhi 1964

——, *Press Conferences, 1950* (-annually), Ministry of External Affairs, New Delhi

POPLAI, S. L., *India 1947-50*, vol. II : *External Affairs*, London 1959

SASTRI, LAL BAHADUR, *Speeches of Prime Minister Lal Bahadur Sastri*, New Delhi 1965

LOK SABHA SECRETARIAT, *Foreign Policy of India : Texts of Documents, 1947-58*, New Delhi 1958 ; later edition, ... *1947-64*, New Delhi 1966

SERIALS

The Asian Recorder (New Delhi)

Foreign Affairs Record (abbr. *FAR*) publ. by the Ministry of External Affairs, New Delhi, 1955-

India 19- , pub. by the Ministry of Information and Broadcasting

India Quarterly (Bombay), vol. I, 1944, etc.

Indian Year Book of International Affairs (Madras), vol. I, 1955, etc.

International Studies (Bombay), vol. I, 1959, etc.

INDEX

INDEX

Abbas, Ferhat, 280
Abboud, Ibrahim, 291
Abdullah, Mohammad, 146, 150, 155, 156, 158, 159, 167, 176, 358
Abs, Hermann, 376
Abyssinia, *see* Ethiopia
Acharya, Tanka Prasad, 207
Acheson, Dean, 67, 362
Aden, 25, 49, 293, 514-16
Adoula, Cyrille, 290
Afghanistan, 25, 26, 76, 212, 273, 275, 298, 398, 399, 422, 448, 454 ; India's relations with, 293-94
Afori-Atta, Kofi-Azante, 472
Africa, Africans, 35, 43, 44, 183, 287f., 307, 309f., 330, 360, 496, 499f., 514f, 520, 523 ; India's relations with, 272f. (chap. XI), 504
Africa, east, 19, 22, 288-89, 298, 299, 300, 301, 303 ; Indians in, 307-11
Africa, north, 106, 107, 278, 293
Afro-Asian states, 90, 96, 102, 108, 225, 234f., 251, 262, 274f., 279, 284, 288, 296, 318, 330, 331, 333, 395, 407, 429, 447, 448, 470, 472, 481f., 514f., 524 ; *see also* under UN
Afro-Asian conference 1965, 238, 275, 447
Afro-Asian Solidarity Committee, 274
Aga Khan, 23, 335
Agwani, M.S., 298
Ahmed, Aftab, 144
Aid-India Consortium, 112, 370, 374-75, 376, 484, 486, 492, 517
Aiyar, K. Natesa, 336
Aiyer, P. S. Sivaswamy, 19
Akhnur, 177
Aksai Chin, 464, 477
Aldabra islands, 50
Algeria, 76, 96, 106, 176, 177, 360, 452 ; India's relations with, 278f.

Algerian Provisional Government (GPRA), 278, 280
Ali, Chaudhri Muhammad, 144, 162, 180
Ali, Liaquat, *see* Khan, Liaquat Ali
Ali, Mohammed, 159, 160, 161, 162, 169
All-India Congress Committee, (AICC), 429, 432
All-India Trade Union Congress (AITUC), 20
Alsace-Lorraine, 175
Ambedkar, D. V., 334, 335
Anand, R. P., 115, 116
Andaman islands, 239
Anglo-Iranian oil company, 281
Angola, 289, 361, 516
Andrews, C. F., 301
Anstey, Vera, 29
anti-colonialism, *see* colonialism
apartheid, *see* under race relations, racialism, South Africa
Arab League, 274, 276, 278
Arabian Sea, 22, 272, 308, 311
Arabs, Arab states, 107, 123, 240, 273, 276, 282, 285, 297, 497 ; India's relations with, 273f., 291
Argentina, 212
arms control, *see* under disarmament
Arora, S. K., 363
Asher, Robert E., 117
Asia, resurgence of, 56, 61, 226, 227, 234
Asia Foundation, 376
Asian-African conference 1955, *see* Bandung Conference
Asian Development Bank, 523
Asian Games Federation, 237
Asian Relations Conference 1947, 58, 185, 225, 229, 231, 239, 287

543

35

179, 462 ; membership in European
Economic Community, 47; military
assistance to India, 298, 388, 446,
471 ; on Kashmir, 154 ; private
investment in India, 47, 370, 382,
384, 488 ; policy towards Pakistan,
47 ; *see also* Britain
United Nations (UN), 35, 36, 39, 57,
74, 75, 233, 238, 253, 281, 288,
292, 293, 296, 311, 344, 362, 386,
441, 447, 452, 479, 482 ; Asian-
Arab, Afro-Asian grouping in, 69,
84, 99, 108, 225, 263, 495, 505f.,
514f. ; bodies and agencies : Collective Measures Committee, 87 ;
Committee of, 24, 109, 513f.; Committee on Information from Non-
Self-Governing Territories, 108-10,
514 ; Commission for India and
Pakistan (UNCIP), *see* under
Kashmir ; Conference on Trade
and Development (UNCTAD), 296
423, 517f., 525 ; Disarmament
Commission, 92f. ; Economic and
Social Council (ECOSOC), 112,
507, 518 ; Economic Commission
for Asia and the Far East (ECAFE)
229, 267, 369, 410 ; Educational,
Scientific, and Cultural Organization (UNESCO), 111,428; Eighteen
Nation Disarmament Committee
(ENDC), 508f. ; Emergency Force
(UNEF, Gaza), 87, 285, 482, 497f.,
505 ; Food and Agriculture Organization (FAO), 111; General Assembly, 44, 68, 71, 78, (chap. IV), 198,
276, 279, 285, 287, 306, 307, 329,
332, 360, 427, 429f., 495, 497, 498,
500, 505f., 510f., 525 ; Relief and
Rehabilitation Administration
(UNRRA), 276; Security Council,
66, 74, 146, chaps. V,VI, 232, 284,
285, 287, 331-33, 353, 360, 426, 449,
499f., 503f., 515, veto in, 87,
Special Fund (SUNFED), 112f.,
117, 520 ; Technical Assistance
Board (UNTAB), 267 ; Trusteeship

Council, 108-09, 514 ; Universal
Postal Union, 221 ; World Health
Organization (WHO), 111, 268 ;
see also under name of agency ;
Charter. 84, 85, 98f., 103, 108f., 115,
151, 158, 194, 227, 332, 352, 353,
357, 360, 431, 496, 498f., 504f. ;
Congo operation (UNOC), 87,
290, 292, 499f. ; debates on and
operations affecting : colonial issues, 96, 102f., 229, 232, 278f.,
289, 326, 360, 361, 513f. ; disarmament and arms control, 92f., 292,
359, 507f. ; economic matters,
including assistance, 110f., 516f. ;
Goa, *see* Goa ; human rights, 86,
97f., 359 ; Hungary, *see* Hungarian
crisis ; Kashmir, *see* Kashmir ;
Korean War, 66-74, and *see* Korean
War ; South African racial questions, 98f., 305, 307, 483, 515f. ;
Suez crisis, *see* Suez crisis ; Tibet,
see Tibet ; Indian mediation in.
67f., 495-96 ; international police
force, 87, 497f. ; peace-keeping, 39,
66f., 85, 86, 107, 289-90, 481, 496f.;
secretariat, 115 ; secretary-general,
96, 108, 114, 115, 142, 183, 284,
289, 331, 386, 429f., 497f., 502,
505 ; "troika" scheme, 505 ; "uniting for peace resolution," 69, 87,
498, 500, 506 ; universal membership of, 85, 87, 194
United States of America (US), 10,
20, 33, 37, 39, 41, 46, 60f., 78,
80, 91, 92, 97, 100f., 109, 110,
115, 117, 157, 159, 172, 178, 179,
185, 194, 200f., 206, 208, 231,
232, 234, 236, 240, 242, 243, 252f.,
255f., 265, 266, 268, 271, 282, 283,
285f., 292, 296, 328, 332-33, 395,
407f., 416, 418, 427, 429, 433, 443,
444, 448, 452, 468, 473, 479f., 486,
492, 494, 495, 508, 510f., 517, 519,
522, 523, 525 ; Agency for International Development (AID), 378f.,
391 ; and Congo operation, 500f. ;